NEWSWEEK CONDENSED BOOKS

JACK and MARY WILLIS

_____

LUDOVIC KENNEDY

_____

GARSON KANIN

_____

STUDS TERKEL

_____

"... BUT THERE ARE ALWAYS MIRACLES."

PURSUIT
THE CHASE AND SINKING
OF THE BATTLESHIP BISMARCK

HOLLYWOOD

WORKING
PEOPLE TALK ABOUT WHAT THEY DO ALL DAY
AND HOW THEY FEEL ABOUT WHAT THEY DO

NEWSWEEK BOOKS, New York

NEWSWEEK BOOKS

Joseph L. Gardner, Editor
Janet Czarnetzki, Art Director

S. Arthur Dembner, President

NEWSWEEK CONDENSED BOOKS

James W. Ellison, Consulting Editor
Barbara Graustark, Copy Editor
Susan S. Gombocz, Picture Researcher
Mary Ann Joulwan, Designer

The condensations in this volume have been created
by Newsweek, Inc., and are used by permission of
and special arrangement with the publishers
and the holders of the respective copyrights.

The original editions of the books in
this volume are published and copyrighted
as follows:

". . . *But There Are Always Miracles.*"
Published by The Viking Press, Inc.
Copyright © 1974 by Jack Willis Productions

Pursuit: The Chase and Sinking of the Battleship Bismarck
Published by The Viking Press, Inc.
Copyright © 1974 by Ludovic Kennedy

*Hollywood: Stars and Starlets, Tycoons and Flesh-Peddlers,
Moviemakers and Moneymakers, Frauds and Geniuses,
Hopefuls and Has-Beens, Great Lovers and Sex Symbols*
Published by The Viking Press, Inc.
Copyright © 1967, 1974 by T.F.T. Corporation

*Working: People Talk About What They Do All
Day and How They Feel About What They Do*
Published by Pantheon Books
Copyright © 1972, 1974 by Studs Terkel

CONTENTS

". . . BUT THERE ARE ALWAYS MIRACLES."

A condensation of the book by
JACK AND MARY WILLIS

CHAPTER 1

JACK

I realized I might die, but I wasn't afraid. It seemed painless, even tolerable. I tried to get my legs underneath me, but they wouldn't go. I fought slipping off into unconsciousness. Which way was up? I rolled over and over in the surf, looking for the sunlight through the water. But I couldn't find it, and I was running out of breath. I tried again to get my legs underneath me. They still wouldn't go. I kept rolling and rolling. looking for the light. How long had I been under? It seemed like hours, and I knew I couldn't hold out much longer. What a dumb way to die! I thought, and suddenly my head came free and I yelled for help as loudly as I could.

I felt arms grab me, drag me out of the water along the sandy bottom. I screamed at them to be careful, that I thought I had broken my neck or back. I had no feeling in my body. I was paralyzed from my chest down. They put me on the sand near the edge of the water. Someone brought a piece of driftwood and tucked it under my head. Someone else went to call for help. While we were waiting for the ambulance, the police arrived. They took the log out from under my head and laid me flat on the beach. They asked my name and questioned me about the accident and the lack of feeling and movement in my body. Then, while one went to report in, the other scratched the soles of my feet with a pencil. I could feel it, but it was numb and dull. I felt as if I'd been given a massive dose of Novocain.

I tried moving my arms. They seemed all right, although the left one was weak. Mary was kneeling in the sand next to me.

"Move your fingers," she said.

"I can't move them."

"Here. Squeeze my hand," she said, placing her hand in mine.

"I can't," I said. "My fingers are numb. I can't move them."

"Try your legs."

"I can't. They won't move."

She looked at me almost in disbelief. Then she reached down, grabbed my legs, and tried to prop them up. They flopped down on the sand.

She looked around as though she expected an answer from the crowd of people that had started to gather. They just stared back. Two ambulance drivers arrived. They also questioned me and tested my feet for feeling. They didn't want to move me until a doctor arrived.

Thoughts came rushing in, confused and uncontrolled. I was happy to be alive. I had fought a terrific battle in the water and had won. But that was over, and now I wanted to go home. Now. But I couldn't. I couldn't move. This couldn't be happening to me. I wanted to go back in time. I wanted another chance. I wanted to undo the moment or redo it differently. TAKE A DIFFERENT WAVE !

I had been body-surfing since I was a kid. I should have known better. I shouldn't have taken that wave. I should have waited for another one, one less dangerous. At least I should have gotten my arms out in front of me. I should have protected my head.

All I could see was faces staring at me. I felt like some strange fish that had washed up on the beach, a subject of concern but also of wonderment. I looked at those faces, and tears welled up in my eyes. I may have been touched by their concern, but I may have been crying for myself.

Mary got up to talk with the police, and a little blond man with soft hands shielded my eyes from the late-afternoon sun and wiped the sand off my face. He told me not to worry, that I'd be okay. His voice was kind, his hands tender and loving, like a girl's. More tears. I couldn't control them.

I again tried to move my right arm and found that I could. I tried my left. It was weaker than the right, but I could move it. I tried my fingers and the rest of my body. I still couldn't make them move. I saw all those people looking at me in a way that I had never been looked at before—as an object of pity.

I saw all the concerned faces wanting to help. I could tell they wanted me to move, to jump up and run down the beach as though I'd only had the wind knocked out of me. I could see it in their eyes. I'd never really been seriously hurt, even seriously ill. And I hardly knew anyone who had even been in a bad accident, certainly no one who had been paralyzed. I remembered reading about Roy Campanella, who ran his car into a tree and was paralyzed from the neck down. He has to spend the rest of his life in a wheelchair. I was seized with fear . . . a freaky accident, one in a million, and it was happening to me. I didn't want to panic. I didn't want to scare Mary. I tried to tell myself that maybe it wasn't serious. But I knew better.

The doctor arrived about fifteen minutes after the ambulance. He was wearing horn-rimmed glasses, and he looked to be in his mid-thirties, about my age. If he'd had a putter in his hand, I wouldn't have been surprised. He was wearing black-and-white cotton checked pants and an open-necked polo shirt. He fit right in with the scene. I thought at first that he was a city doctor whom the hospital had called away from a cocktail party, but I heard an ambulance driver say hello to him, and he told me he was from Southampton and had been called while on late rounds at the hospital.

He walked toward my feet. "Can you feel this?" he said as he scratched my feet just as the ambulance drivers and police had done. He then bent my big toe and asked me what I felt. I told him that he'd bent the toe "up." He then bent it down, and I said, "Down." Then he did the same with my other foot, and I responded correctly. He said that was good, "a very good sign." I didn't ask him why that was a good sign. I just let him work and waited for his diagnosis. Then he asked me to move my arms, which I did, but I couldn't move anything else.

The doctor told me his name was Dr. Spinzia. For some inexplicable reason I couldn't call him Doctor. He was my age, and somehow, in this situation, formality seemed ridiculous. I asked him his first name, and he answered Joe. From then on I called him by his first name.

He cradled my head in his hands while four men lifted me gingerly up onto a board to carry me off the beach to the ambulance. When we got to the sand dunes, Joe lifted my head just a little, and I felt bullets shoot down from my shoulders through my arms into my hands. I felt as though I were being electrocuted. I screamed in pain. Raw nerves were being violated by bone. It was the most intense pain I'd ever felt. I wondered how people withstand torture. I felt the blood go out of my head and thought I might vomit. But as Joe lowered my head a little, the pain ceased. They gently placed me in the ambulance, and then Joe and Mary got in with me. On the way to the hospital Joe kept telling me that he'd seen worse accidents than mine, accidents men had walked away from. Mary asked him what he thought it was. He said it looked like a broken neck and that the vertebrae were pressing against my spine, causing prolonged paralysis.

When we arrived at the hospital they pushed me right into the X-ray room.

The first X-rays were of my lower back.

"Looks fine so far," Joe said. "Just terrific—no damage, no dislocation, nothing broken."

A few minutes later after more X-rays he said they could find nothing wrong with my neck either. The news seemed good, I thought, but Joe looked troubled.

"What is it?" I said.

"I don't know. I don't know why you're paralyzed if there is no fracture or dislocation. Maybe your spine snapped out of place and back in again, causing serious abrasions. We're just going to have to wait to see what happens. In the meantime," he said, "we're going to put you in traction."

By now I was feeling high from a shot of Demerol. It wasn't like lying on the beach where I had time to think about the consequences of the accident. Now I was involved, even though passively, and wanted to find out what was wrong.

"Okay," Joe said. "I'm going to drill holes in either side of your head and insert a pair of tongs—they're like ice tongs—into the holes. It won't hurt. You don't have nerves in your skull, and the Novocain will take care of your scalp. Then I'm going to hang weights on you to immobilize your back and neck."

I was wheeled out of X-ray into another room. Joe shaved my head around the ears, and then I felt him make two pencil marks on both sides of my head for the holes. He shot my skull full of Novocain. I looked out of the corner of my eye, expecting to see a high-speed drill. Dismayed, I saw him pick up an old hand drill with what looked like a quarter-inch bit. I braced myself for a shock. I felt the pressure of the drill but felt no pain as it chewed its way into my head. By now the Demerol was really working, and I imagined that my whole being was inside my skull as the drill ripped into me. I could hear the bone being ground, and out of the corner of my eye I could see Joe cranking the drill. He finished one side, then the other. Then with something like toggle bolts he clamped the tongs into my head and suspended big black weights from them. When he finished, two nurses wheeled me down a long hall to a hospital room. All I saw was ceiling.

It had been about three hours since the accident, but time didn't seem to have any shape. I was still in my swimming trunks, still covered with sand. I had no idea whether it was day or night. I felt no pain, and the pull of the weights in my head was strange but not uncomfortable. I still couldn't believe what was happening to me, and I was scared. Mary was waiting for me in my room. She told me that she had called her parents in New York and that they would be out soon. When her parents arrived, I couldn't tell from their eyes how bad off I was. I didn't have to. I knew. We tried to talk, but I drifted off to sleep.

I hiked up three flights of stairs, Mary opened the door. She was pretty but looked even younger than I had expected. She took my arm while we waited for a taxi. She did it easily, as if we were old friends. My confidence soared out of all proportion to the gesture. It was the tip-off, I said to myself. She likes me. Her simple move established an intimacy and quickly did away with most of the awkwardness of a blind date. And she seemed to be saying that we'd make it.

I don't remember what we talked about, but we talked a lot, not rushed, not manic, but still afraid of pauses. Sometime during dinner I realized I was eating mechanically, shoveling food into my mouth but not tasting. I was working hard to impress her, and if I was at a loss for words and needed time to think, I'd pick up a piece of meat and chew slowly and thoughtfully, buying time for myself. Or if she said something she seemed to think deserved a laugh and I didn't, I would slip her a tight grin that appeared to have great meaning. Later we went to a bar on the East Side and talked until early morning.

I suppose we talked about all the things people talk about on a first date. She'd been raised in New York and I in Los Angeles. She'd gone to private schools and to Sarah Lawrence, I to public schools and to U.C.L.A. She was a researcher at *Newsweek*; I made documentary films. She was twenty-two and I was thirty-four. She liked older men, and I liked younger women. And we were both Jewish, even though Pleshette sounds French and Willis like a black athlete.

Our second date was on a Sunday afternoon in Central Park. It was late March and the first warm day of the year, the kind of day before the trees begin to blossom, when the earth is still soft and wet, when the sunlight is thin and winter is still present but mixed with the promise of spring. We ate hamburgers and hot dogs at the zoo. She looked beautiful to me, slim and young. She talked almost compulsively about herself, the way people who have been terribly lonely and inside themselves for a long time talk. Another neurotic chick, I said to myself, strung-out and unhappy, mixed up about life and love. But it wasn't that way at all. She was simply talking out her own sense of discovery and growth.

I spent most of our third date trying to get her into *her* bed without success and the fourth date trying to get her into *my* bed with success. Apparently it did matter whose bed it was. I was still some kind of intruder in her apartment, that newly found symbol of independence. By summer we were what my Aunt Edith might call "an item."

That summer is only a few years ago, but it seems like twenty. What I remember most clearly is an overwhelming sense of joy and completeness when we were together that got stronger as the year went on. I traveled a lot that summer, working on a new film. I'd return to New York to rich days and joyful nights with Mary.

That summer we spent long, hot weekends on Long Island. We stayed in a tiny guest house that belonged to an elderly couple and spent days and nights on the beach. We body-surfed together. We began with the tiny waves that break late but roll a long way, high onto the shore. I taught Mary how to get out in front of them, to keep her head up and then ride the wave all the way onto the beach, where we were left covered with sand as the water rolled back to the sea. Then I taught her to go after the big ones, the wave "outside," the wave beyond the others. I showed her how to spot the dangerous ones, the waves that have no water underneath them, that crush down on you or flip you around so that you hit the sand instead of being cushioned on a bed of water. When we saw the right one, we'd run to catch it while it was still swelling.

Everyday things took on new meanings. Yet because we were together they became invested with an overall common meaning. Our concept of time itself changed because we were living to a new and different rhythm. Those tiny boxes of time—eating, sleeping, loving, working, and playing—with which we define our days became blurred around the edges and in the center as well. Eating became a time to share new experiences together and took on a sensuousness of its own. We went to bed to make love and slept only to restore ourselves. Waking in the morning was to make more love. And our work, the days' triumphs and frustrations, added to the whole we shared.

In the fall Mary moved in with me, and neither of us was seeing anyone else. We both thought about marriage but didn't talk about it . . . not until the following spring.

It was a beautiful San Francisco day. We were on the last leg of a month's holiday—three weeks in Mexico, a few days in L.A. with my family, now San Francisco.

We took the cable car to Fisherman's Wharf. I had planned this day to pop the question to Mary. We walked down to the wharf for a lunch of cracked crab. I tried projecting what I would say and how it would feel to ask Mary to marry me. The problem was that we'd been living together for so long that I didn't know what I should say. It only made me nervous to think ahead, so I decided to say whatever came into my mind at whatever moment I considered appropriate.

I ordered wine and asked that it be brought to the table before lunch, and then, still distracted by what I might say, made small talk. I decided to wait until after lunch when I could order brandy or champagne.

But I felt like a kid on Christmas Eve, who wants to sleep so the night will pass quickly, but who's so excited that he can't and the night seems as if it will never end. Our meal felt that way to me. I couldn't wait any more. I took my wine glass, raised it toward Mary, and tried to catch her eye. I coughed, and she looked up and put some crab in her mouth and waited for me to say something. "I . . ." I began. "Mary . . . will you marry me?" She blushed like a virgin and, still with her mouth full of crab, said, "Yes." We both started laughing, laughing like crazy people, and we both had tears in our eyes.

CHAPTER 2

MARY

It had been such a perfect day. It felt like the first day of summer—clear blue sky, a hot direct sun, so hot that you could actually feel your already tan skin burn. And the waves were perfect for body-surfing. Jack and I arrived at the beach at eleven thirty and, looking for a comfortable place to camp, saw a group of friends, a family whom I have know all my life. They greeted us warmly and congratulated us on our engagement.

I relished this summer, our first house, our plans to get married in the fall. I had never been so happy, completely secure, and yet, in a peculiar way, acutely aware of life's fragility, as though intense happiness reminded me of our mortality. And I have always loved the sea, have always identified it with the happiest moments of my childhood summers on Cape Cod. Our friends' daughter reminded me of myself as a child. Her hair was bleached-out by the sun, her smooth backside was bare and tan, and she exuded freedom, running around the open beach, taunting the waves.

After twenty minutes in the sun we decided to go in for a swim. Both Jack and I have always loved to body-surf, but I had grown more cautious with age and had been frightened by a riptide the day before. But that was yesterday, and today the waves were big, and there was no undertow.

Today was different. There is nothing more exhilarating than riding a wave, catching it at the perfect moment just before its swell turns into a cascading crest, fighting to stay out in front. I had always admired Jack's talent for catching the biggest or smallest wave, swimming with it and then riding it to the shore. I'm lazy and usually dive under as many as I ride in. I also chicken out. But today we were drunk with the ocean and sun. We stayed in the water until we were chilled, then baked on the beach and went back in the water again.

Jack decided to jog down the beach, and when I saw him in the distance ready to turn back, I ran to join him. We would take one last swim before leaving. The waves were getting bigger, and we both had one or two perfect rides. Then I dove under a breaking wave and, when I surfaced, turned to see where Jack was. I saw nothing but foam. Then his head popped up and he cried for help. I tried to run toward him and felt as though I were part of an anxiety dream where you try to run but cannot move your legs. But this wasn't a dream. The water fought my efforts to reach Jack quickly, and for a second I felt panic and heard myself cry his name.

It made no sense. It could have been me or either of our friends who had been swimming with us all day. Thank God for the people on the beach. I could never have pulled Jack out by myself. And the irony, I found out later, was that the curly-haired man who helped me did not know how to swim. And then there was Stanley, an elf of a man with sun-bleached hair and skin the color of molasses, who maternally brushed the sand away from Jack's eyes and kept telling him that everything was going to be all right.

I remembered looking down at my body in the shade of the ambulance. My skin was smooth and brown, my breasts full, the bikini a little too small. Walking into the hospital, I felt naked and vulnerable. Everything was cool and clean inside, medicinal, sterile, but not unkind. I felt again I was part of a bizarre anxiety dream, the kind where you find yourself in a crowded restaurant having lunch with impressive-looking strangers and realize you are completely naked. I walked slowly next to Jack's stretcher, holding his hand. An X-ray technician, realizing I was uncomfortable, handed me a white coat.

The X-ray showed nothing. Possibly, the doctors said, the vertebrae in the lower spine had dislocated and snapped back into place. Possibly. But Jack still couldn't move. I felt no relief.

I had to speak with the policeman who had accompanied us from the beach to the hospital. I saw the curly-haired man who had helped me pull Jack out of the ocean just an hour before walking toward me, our car keys and my red beach dress in his hands. I thanked him and asked if he would write his name down on a piece of paper.

The policeman rechecked the information I had given him on the beach. Yes, we were to be married in October and had rented a house for the season. I had debated for a split second on the beach telling the police that we were married because I was petrified that they might separate us. The same policeman, blond and baby-faced, was the first to diagnose Jack's "problem" as a broken neck, but I had still not made a connection between that and paralysis. I was touched by the policeman's concern. He wished us luck, mentioned a case of a man whose house had fallen on top of him, had been paralyzed, and was walking a year later. . . .

They shaved Jack's head around his ears. He was describing what he could and couldn't feel to a nurse. I couldn't believe he was unable to move. He looked so healthy, his chest a dark rust color and his arms and shoulders muscular.

They were going to put Jack into traction, and Dr. Spinzia explained that he would have to stay in the hospital for approximately six weeks. Six weeks! Jack was supposed to teach a night course at Columbia. What about his work . . . and I would have to arrange something with the office. I was still part of a scheduled existence where time is punctuated by plans, and fictitious futures are marked neatly into black books and calendars. I tried to call my father from the hospital, but he wasn't home. I left a message with his service: "Call immediately. There's been an accident."

A tall, horsy-looking blonde asked me to fill out an admission form for Jack. "I wonder how long Jack'll have to stay here," I said. "We're supposed to be married in October."

"Oh, don't worry," she said. "I bet you'll be a beautiful fall bride." She paused, but I didn't say anything. "Dr. Spinzia's a superb orthopedic surgeon, really outstanding." I didn't care. I wanted to go home and have the barbecue dinner we had planned.

My father called. I told him that we had been body-surfing, that Jack had been thrown by a wave and couldn't move, that the attending physician was a man named Joseph Spinzia.

"Are you all right?" my father said in his scratchy voice.

"I'm fine," I said. I felt better just hearing his voice. Ever since I was a little girl I always trusted my father, always went to him to discuss my problems. He was direct and honest but never cold. He was a doctor, but my father first. "Papa, don't worry about me. I'm really okay."

"Mama and I will drive out tonight," he said. "You stay at the hospital and figure we'll be there in around three hours."

A nurse warned me that Jack would be bleeding where the tongs were drilled into his head, but that everything was all right. Visiting hours were over, but no one said I had to leave. I walked to Jack's room and saw two nurses wheeling him toward me. Jack was asleep and I watched his belly heave up and down. The wounds in his head were still trickling in an irregular drip, like water from a broken faucet. He woke up for a moment but was too drugged to speak. I told him I would be close by. At that moment I saw my mother and father walking toward me. For the first time since the accident, I felt my throat constrict and my eyes fill up with tears. There was nothing to say. We just embraced.

I led Papa into Jack's room. Jack's eyes slowly opened and he smiled. My father put his hand gently on Jack's arm.

"Wow," he said softly, "you're really done up good. Are you in a lot of pain?"

Jack told him no and tried to explain what had happened. Papa told him not to speak, that he had looked up Dr. Spinzia before driving out and that he was a good man and also that the Southampton Hospital was very good. His presence, his gaze, his tone were comforting. My mother came in for a short visit, and then my father said we should go, that Jack should get some sleep.

I was glad my parents were with me, and yet their presence seemed strange. The little farmhouse in the middle of a green lawn in the middle of potato fields was Jack's and my first house together, and it embodied all my hopeless romanticism about being in love, getting married, and having babies. My father and mother in city clothes looked pale and tired. I realized that all I was wearing was my beach dress and that my tanned skin had a film of salt on it.

My mother and I went upstairs to make up the double bed in one of the extra rooms. When Jack and I had taken the house the previous March, we'd discussed how we would have friends out to share the weekends. It was a perfect house, simple, old-fashioned. It even smelled like the house I had lived in for fifteen summers on Cape Cod. Jack had laughed at my enthusiasm, my ability to rationalize anything I wanted badly enough. Yes, he loved the house, too, but he loved my childish joy about having it even more. It seemed ironic that now my mother and I were making hospital corners for a hideous emergency.

She wanted to sleep with me downstairs, but I wanted to be alone. I gave my father an alarm clock and kissed him good night. He didn't tell me not to worry. Mama and I went into the miniature green living room to talk. The room was so tiny, the furniture so small that anyone over five feet tall looked like a giant who had invaded a doll's house. I had stopped smoking a year before but found myself chain-smoking my mother's cigarettes. She told me I shouldn't start again. I told her that I didn't care. I suddenly realized I hadn't called Jack's parents in California.

I found Jack's black notebook and looked up their number. I stared at his handwriting. He had written all those notes, names, addresses, and phone numbers, and now he couldn't even move his fingers. I dialed his parents' number and his mother answered the phone. She was so happy to hear my voice that my immediate response was good-natured calm, as if I had forgotten why I was calling. "There's been an accident," I heard myself telling Libbie. "We were body-surfing this afternoon and Jack was thrown by a wave and hurt himself. . . ." There was no hysteria or dramatic silence from her end of the phone. She wanted to know if he was in the hospital, whether he had broken anything. I told her that he was in traction, that the X-rays showed no fractures, that he wasn't in pain but that he couldn't move. I told her my parents were with me, that Papa had investigated the hospital and doctor, and I would call her the next morning to keep them posted.

The conversation was brief and, in an eerie way, detached. I hung up the phone and went back into the living room to rejoin my mother. The phone rang and it was Libbie again. Something had begun to sink in. I went over the details again, de-emphasizing the paralysis and re-emphasizing how good the care had been so far. The more rational I became in describing the accident, the more removed I felt from crisis. But as soon as I hung up the phone for the second time, I was swept up in a sea of exhausted nausea. I had to sleep.

When you have shared the same bed with someone for a long time, there is a special feeling of loneliness and dislocation when he is gone. I was scared to turn out the light, afraid of sleep and of waking up alone. I took off my red beach dress and stared at myself in the mirror. The light in our powder-blue bedroom was soft and yellow, and my skin and hair looked golden. The contrast between the suntanned and the white parts of my body accentuated my hips and made my breasts look round and firm. It was almost as if my own image comforted me, as if I were celebrating my own health and ability to move at will as much as I was indulging in vacant narcissism.

I stretched my arms out to touch Jack's side of the bed. The sheets were cold on his side, but I could still smell his scent on the pillows. I thought of him in the hospital fastened by his head to a contraption that looked like a giant spit. I knew he was safe in the hospital, that I would see him the next morning, but that something had come abruptly to an end. I started talking to myself: "Everything's going to be all right; Jack, I love you. Please, God, let everything be all right."

As I said the words I started to cry.

CHAPTER 3

JACK

I awoke and a young black man in a white uniform was standing next to me. I asked him what time it was. He told me eight o'clock in the morning and that he had let me sleep an extra hour. I was still in my swimming trunks, still sandy. It flashed through my mind why the hell they hadn't taken my trunks off. At the time it didn't seem to matter. I was lonely and depressed and felt totally disoriented. It was Monday morning. I should be at work, but here I was in a hospital with no idea of how seriously I was hurt.

I couldn't turn my head sideways, and my neck was stretched so far back by the tongs and weights that I couldn't bend my head forward. I was staring straight up at the ceiling. The young man was leaning over me so that I could see him.

"What's your name?" I said.

"Clive. I'm a nurse's aide."

"Can I have something to drink? I'm thirsty as hell."

"I don't know," he said. "I'll ask. In the meantime this will help," and he rubbed my parched lips with a cotton swab that had been soaked in a sugary lemon substance. I licked my lips; it quenched my thirst a little but compounded the already awful morning taste I had in my mouth.

I told Clive, and he brought me some mouthwash in a cup with a straw. He tried to hand it to me. I instinctively reached for it but couldn't grip the cup. So he held it while I sipped, rinsed my mouth, and spit it into a metal tray, getting most of it on my chin. A nurse came in and said it was all right for me to have liquids, so Clive gave me a container of milk and a glass of orange juice.

The room I was in was very small. The walls were light green. The ceiling was made of large, white perforated plasterboard. My frame was next to the door and there was a large window on my right that faced the corridor. I could vaguely see the window but couldn't see out of it. My roommate, who was moaning softly to himself in his sleep like a hurt animal, was on my left. Next to him was a small window. I could see the light coming through but couldn't see out of it either. Not even the sky.

Joe came into the room. "How do you feel?" he said.

"About as good as anyone can feel under the circumstances, I guess." It was true. I didn't hurt. I didn't feel sick. The tongs in my head didn't bother me, although they did feel a little strange. And I had no urge to go anywhere since I couldn't move. I was worried that they hadn't identified the trouble yet.

"What do you think is wrong with me?"

Joe pressed his hand on my belly. "Why you can't move? I don't know. But gas is accumulating in your belly. We're going to have to put a tube, a Levine Tube, down into you to suck it out."

A few minutes later a doctor, who, I thought, was Chinese or Filipino, came into the room.

"Relax," he said. "This might be a little uncomfortable, but it won't hurt."

He began pushing the tube into my nostril, but he hit a membrane and the tube got stuck. Then he tried the other side, but the tube got stuck again. He started to push harder.

"That hurts!" I yelled. He didn't say anything. He just kept wiggling and pushing the tube. I started to panic. Then the tube somehow cleared the nasal passage.

"Swallow," he said, as he began shoving it down my throat and into my stomach. As soon as it was in, a brownish fluid began to flow out of me into a jar near my bed.

Then the doctor pulled out another tube and told the nurse to take down my swimming trunks.

"Relax," he said again. "This won't hurt."

"What are you doing?" I said.

"I'm going to insert this tube through your penis and into your bladder so that it will automatically drain."

I felt the tube go in, but there was no real pain. I could see the doctor's arms slowly pushing the tube farther and farther in. I waited for the pain. There was none. I felt the tube bend with my penis. I felt one final push and then the doctor looked as if he were tying the tube off, securing it to something.

21

I felt something, I thought. That's good.

Then a nurse brought in another bottle on a stand with a tube attached and inserted a needle into my arm—intravenous feeding.

About mid-morning Clive and a couple of nurses came in. They took what looked like soft and furry sheepskins and covered me from my chin to my toes.

"What are you doing?" I said.

"We're going to turn you onto your stomach. If you're on your back too long, you'll get bed sores."

Then Clive and one of the nurses picked up a large metal frame and placed it on top of me. My face was exposed except for my chin and forehead, which were supported by canvas straps. They strapped the top frame to the one I was lying on.

"Just like a ham sandwich," one nurse laughed. "Okay, now, we're going to turn you. Just relax and it won't hurt at all."

I didn't say anything. I felt strangely secure strapped in like that. Only the Levine Tube was a little uncomfortable. With Clive at my head and a nurse at my feet, they slowly began turning the entire frame like a spit. I tensed and my body slid a little sideways. My neck moved and I felt the bullets of pain shoot through my shoulders and into my arms. I screamed in pain, and they quickly finished the turn. When I was on my stomach, the pain stopped. I was staring down at the floor, my head supported by the two canvas straps, which were cutting into my chin and forehead.

"Get me out. Hurry," I pleaded.

They took the top frame and sheepskins off my back. That helped a little.

"How do you feel?" Clive asked.

"I slipped when you turned me. I think you hurt my neck." I could hardly talk. The straps kept cutting into my face and the Levine Tube was still very uncomfortable. I wanted to be turned back. "The straps hurt," I said.

Clive tried to adjust them for me, but it didn't help.

"Turn me back," I grunted. "I can't take any more."

"You've got to try it a little longer," the nurse said. "You've only been over five minutes and you must stay on this side for at least two hours."

Two hours. The pressure from the straps was killing me, and the Levine Tube was pressing against my larynx so that I could hardly talk. I tried to relax but couldn't. The sweat was pouring off me. A couple of nurses walked out of the room.

"Don't leave. Turn me back."

"Five more minutes."

I tried to wait but couldn't. "Turn me," I screamed. I felt Clive putting the sheepskins on my back and strapping me into the frame. "Tighter," I ordered. Then they began turning me. I slipped again. The pain was excruciating. Finally I was on my back and the pain stopped. They unstrapped me and lifted off the frame and sheepskins. I lay there, staring at the ceiling, exhausted, gasping for breath. "The pain is incredible," I said to one nurse. "I slip around when you turn me. I want to see Joe."

"It's Dr. Spinzia's orders—every four hours."

"I don't care. I want to talk to him."

"He'll be by later." They all began to leave.

A nurse came in and told me that I was purposely put in this room because it was across from the nurses' station and that if I needed anything, I just had to yell. Then she left. The panic mounted. What if they didn't hear me? I waited about three minutes and yelled, "Nurse." With the tube in my throat, it was hard to yell. Nobody answered. "Nurse. Nurse." More time passed and then a nurse appeared. "What do you want?" she said.

"What time is it?"

"About ten."

I waited for Mary.

CHAPTER 4

MARY

It was just beginning to be dawn when my father woke me. He wanted me to lead him to the highway back to New York as he is notoriously bad at following directions in a car. I walked outside. The air was clean and cold and the sky a thin, ethereal blue. My feet were wet with dew and covered with freshly cut grass. My senses seemed anesthetized. I had an incredibly empty feeling, a hole in the pit of my stomach. The morning was beautiful but joyless. I was awake but still asleep, so out of touch with how I felt that I methodically and efficiently wiped the morning mist from the windshield, started the car, and led my father to the Montauk Highway. I was even careful to use my direction blinkers and keep an eye on Papa through the rear-view mirror. We waved good-by to each other. On the way back to the house I saw the sun rise over the flat horizon of potato fields.

When we had first started coming out for weekends in late May, the potato plants were tiny green specks. From the bathroom window I could see the perfectly straight rows rush toward the sand dunes like a series of railroad ties and converge at what looked like a single point in the distance. As the plants got fuller, the geometry of the landscape softened.

I knew that I wouldn't be able to see Jack for hours and that it was still too early to call the city, so I tried unsuccessfully to fall asleep again. I thought about what I would say to Jack's boss and how I would manage to complete the files I was preparing for *Newsweek*. Just three days before, I had spent a hot, sticky day at Grossinger's interviewing some of the actors in *Taking Off* for a story on Czech film directors in New York. That day was vivid in my mind but felt millions of miles away.

I heard my mother puttering around in the kitchen. She thought I was still asleep and was trying to make as little noise as possible. I joined her in the kitchen and she asked me how I had slept.

"Mary, you must eat something," she said. Her dark brown eyes reflected her concern, immediate and maternal—I had to have something in my stomach. I agreed but could only manage to swallow half an English muffin and some coffee.

I looked at the plastic clock over the icebox and realized that Jack's boss at NET was probably at work. Bill accepted the collect call without hesitation. It was unusual for me to call him, but his voice was friendly.

"Jack's been in an accident," I said. "He's in the Southampton Hospital in traction. They don't know exactly what's wrong—we don't know how long he'll be away from the office."

As I was mouthing the words, I started to shiver, not from cold but from intense nervousness. I knew how excited Jack was about the new show that was to debut in January. It was important to him.

"Oh, my God," Bill said over and over. He kept telling me to tell Jack not to worry about work, that everything would be taken care of and that he would let the rest of the staff know what had happened.

I knew exactly how I felt about my own responsibilities to work. I would let the office know what had happened, would somehow finish my work on the story, but would stay near Jack for as long as I had to. At that point, I truly believed that there was a good chance that I'd be back in the city in about ten days, working at the very least on a part-time basis. As I heard the *Newsweek* operator answer the phone I began to shiver again. I wanted to speak to my immediate boss, the warm, pint-sized den mother of researchers whom I've always had a special feeling for, but she wasn't there. So I talked with another editor.

"This is Mary," I said. "I'm out on the Island and wanted to tell you that my fiancé has been badly hurt and is in the hospital."

Dead silence on the other end of the phone.

"I will finish my files today and give them to my mother. She can drop them off at the office early tomorrow . . . but I will not be in until we know more."

At this point he responded with a hollow, "Yes?" I could tell that he didn't believe me. He thought I was making up a story to get out of work, so I went into more detail, hoping he would believe me, but not really caring. I refused to play for sympathy, but I heard my voice crack and felt my eyes well up with tears.

"Listen, Jack can't move, and I don't think I will be back in New York for a week . . . I just don't know . . . maybe not for longer than that."

There was another silence but shorter and a little less suspicious than before.

"Well," he said matter-of-factly, "at least he's not a paraplegic, is he?"

"No, he's not a paraplegic. He's a quadriplegic."

Visiting hours didn't start until one o'clock, but by noon I couldn't wait to see Jack. I started to walk down the long green corridor that was now filled with sunlight and realized my legs were moving faster and faster, until I actually broke into a trot. I peered into Jack's room and hesitated a moment before going in. There was a tube in his nose.

Jack called my name. Somehow he knew I was there even though he couldn't see me. I bent over him and kissed his lips. His face was a mass of freckles. His wonderful blue eyes looked tired, and his healthy color seemed a fraud of nature. He had a sheet draped over him, and as I lifted it I thought it strange that he was still wearing bathing trunks. I saw a plastic tube that ran from his penis to a plastic sack partially filled with urine. Nothing had bothered me before—not the blood, not the tongs in his head, not even the tube in his nose. But the sight of that plastic tube in his penis made my stomach sink.

I didn't want him to think I was upset, so I casually asked him whether the catheter hurt him. He said it didn't, and I pretended that I was glad. My mind started to race. It *should* have hurt him to have something stuck into his penis. A friend's father who had kidney stones had described the pain of having a catheter inserted into him as excruciating.

I quickly told Jack that I had spoken to his boss, who had been wonderful. Jack's eyes looked straight ahead. He was thinking, not depressed, just thinking.

"Maybe they should get someone else," he said. "They need a healthy producer."

I told him to shut up, that he was being stupid. There was always that possibility, but now it was much too early to know and he shouldn't torture himself thinking about it.

I spent a good part of the day making a list of things Jack wanted done—making calls, breaking dates, taking care of a world we were no longer a part of. I was tense with waiting. The doctors had taken new films of Jack's neck but still couldn't determine what was wrong. Not knowing made the wait more trying.

I had to call Jack's parents. My God, it was only four o'clock and I felt as if it should be getting dark already. I never felt panicked around Jack, but as soon as I entered that dirty, cream-colored phone booth, my heart started to beat at twice its normal rate. And then there was nowhere to sit, and I clutched the dimes, the yellow, now tattered piece of legal paper, my cigarettes, matches, and stub of a pencil, all the while trying to dial the operator.

Finally I got through to Jack's parents, and his brother Dick answered. I was so happy to hear his voice. My instinct was to kid him as I had so often done before, but his voice was almost foreign to me, and the shock of hearing the sadness in his tone frightened me. I told him what was going on—nothing—but that the doctor seemed extremely capable. Dick hardly spoke. He seemed numb. I wanted to hang up the phone.

Night finally came, a clear, cold night for July. I walked into Jack's darkened room. He was asleep. I touched his arm, lightly ran my fingers across his chest.

"Hi, doll," he whispered. "How ya doin?"

"I love you, Jack. Everything is going to be all right."

He closed his eyes again and smiled. I didn't want to leave him but knew that he had to rest. Anyway, the loudspeaker in the hospital was already announcing the end of visiting hours. I kissed his cheek and told him that I would be back before I left the hospital. He heard me but kept his eyes closed. I knew he wasn't in pain and that he wasn't really sick, but his stillness spoke to me of danger.

I heard my name being announced on the loudspeaker. Someone was calling me long distance. I didn't recognize the voice or the name on the other end of the phone, but whoever it was was nervous and excited.

"Look, Mary, I'm a friend of Jack's brother Dick." The voice seemed disembodied, disconnected from a familiar face. "I'm a psychiatrist, and my brother-in-law is a neurosurgeon. I don't like what Dick tells me. It sounds like Jack's in bad shape and time is crucial now."

My head began to pound. Who was this person and why was he trying to shake me up? Why was he intruding?

"Listen, I know you're under a great strain, but why haven't they done a myelogram?" He stopped as though my silence indicated that he was upsetting me. "I wouldn't call if it weren't Jack's bod that is racked up."

I didn't know what a myelogram was, but the word bod really infuriated me. Jack's bod. What did he know about Jack's bod?

"My father has been checking up on everything that's going on, and they are doing everything they can," I said curtly.

The voice interrupted me. "I understand," he said, "but it's a small hospital and . . ."

He was three thousand miles away, had no idea what was happening, and was trying to tell me that I should be scared. I was scared. I was petrified. I knew that he was calling because he was concerned and that his intentions were good, but his call seemed rude and pointless, almost a cry of fire in a crowded theater, and I resented him utterly and completely.

"There is nothing we can do now," I said, trying to gain control. "Jack can't be moved, and the neurosurgeon is coming tomorrow."

When I hung up the phone I was shaking. I looked up to see who had put his hand on my shoulder and saw my older brother, John. The sight of him, the surprise and emotional thanks that he was near me, made me want to cry. I knew he should have been in New York rehearsing a show. "Oh, John," I heard myself say, "it's all so awful."

I felt myself beginning to weaken, as much from exhaustion as from the lurking fear that Jack wasn't going to be all right. Mama lovingly put her blue cardigan around my shoulders as we drove toward East Hampton to find a place to eat. We drove in silence, and I thought how easily my mother would set the wrongs of my life right when I was a little girl.

We stopped at a restaurant that had been decorated to look like a barn. The place was almost empty, and the candlelight and flowers on the tables reminded me of the depressing ambience of a dinner party where half the guests have forgotten to come. I still wasn't hungry, but Mama insisted I eat. The sight of the food on my plate made the lump in my throat swell. I tried to swallow, but the lump wouldn't go down. The tears rolled into my mouth as I talked.

"Oh, it isn't going to be all right," I sobbed. "I just have a terrible feeling that Jack's in danger. I just know it . . . I don't know. But I feel it."

The salty taste of my tears seemed to produce more tears. I tried to wipe my eyes with a napkin, and my brother and mother listened calmly. They seemed to know that silence was a greater solace for me than optimistic words.

"Why do you feel so sure?" my mother asked.

"I know . . ." I hesitated and tried to control my crying. "I know because of the catheter. I know because they don't catheterize a man unless it's serious." I hesitated again, frightened to admit what I knew was an even worse sign. "And Jack said it didn't hurt him when they put the tube in his penis."

My mother said it didn't hurt her when she was catheterized for her gall-bladder operation.

"But you don't have a penis," John said.

We all laughed—even me, for a moment.

When we got home, I remembered that I had to type up some files for *Newsweek*. I was exhausted and couldn't have cared less about work, but I knew that I had promised, and that was that. John offered to type for me if I read the interviews aloud. I hoped they would take my mind off Jack, but they seemed so irrelevant. How differently I felt then, I thought to myself. How close I was to what was going to happen that weekend, yet how unsuspecting. It takes only a second to change or end a life. It takes longer than that to create one. I couldn't blame anyone for what happened, and it was still too early to feel cheated. Maybe I was lucky there was no one to blame, but I found myself cursing a God I hardly believed in.

I didn't cry myself to sleep that night, but I lay awake for hours. Something had come abruptly to an end. I knew that even then. There is a special conceit lovers share, as though their happiness makes them superior to the rest of the world. And, in a way, this superiority is both real and illusory. We felt protected by our love, almost immune. Yet there was an early awareness that our love, like any love, was "two solitudes that bordered and saluted each other." I remembered a discussion we had had, lying peacefully in each other's arms. We were separate human beings, strong and vital, who had chosen each other because life was fuller that way. And we knew that if something happened to one of us the other would go on. And then I remember we stopped and stared into each other's eyes. The thought of having to survive without the other was deeply disturbing but not frightening. We never said, "But nothing will happen," maybe we never even thought it. But we wished it.

When I awoke the next morning, I started to weep. Now I realized how alone I was; I was so frightened. No matter what my dreams had been the night before, sleep always came as a relief, a momentary escape from the harshness of the days, what I knew would stretch before Jack and me. When I'm happy, I welcome the days as though each morning were a microcosmic rebirth, a new chance . . . a new day. But when I opened my eyes that morning, my very soul seemed weighted in yesterday and the day before that, until my thoughts took me back to the ocean on that July 12. "Oh, why did it have to happen?" I asked myself.

CHAPTER 5

JACK

Mary was smiling when she came in and gave me a kiss. If the tubing bothered her, she didn't show it. I tried to tell her about their turning me that morning, but I could see she didn't understand. She said she'd called work for me and that Bill had been wonderful and had said not to worry about anything. I asked Mary to call my secretary and have her break or shift all my appointments to someone else. She left to make the call, and I thought about work.

The show wasn't due to go on the air until January. This was only July, but we'd already been working on it for six weeks. What should I do? I thought of a film producer I'd known in Canada who had broken his leg and had his staff assemble every day in his hospital room to screen and go over the film. I hardly felt like doing that even if it had been possible. Maybe they should get somebody else for the job. But I didn't know anything. Joe still hadn't found the cause of my paralysis, so I decided to wait.

That afternoon Joe came in. "I want to take another X-ray," he said. "There's an area of your neck we haven't been able to get a clear picture of. We'll do it in here so we won't have to move you."

A machine was wheeled into my room. Joe stood at my feet and grabbed my hands, which were lying by my sides.

"You're thick in the shoulders," he said. "I'm going to try to pull them down and out of the way, so we can get pictures of C-6, C-7, the two lowest cervical vertebrae. Ready?"

"Ready."

"Okay. Relax," he said and began pulling on my arms.

I tensed as he pulled. I felt those bullets shooting down my arms. I screamed. But Joe kept pulling while the X-ray was taken. Then he let go. He left with the technicians. A few minutes later he returned.

"We still can't get a clear picture," he said. "But as far as I can tell, nothing's broken."

Later that day Joe told me that if nothing changed by evening he was going to call a neurosurgeon in on my case.

"What's his name?" I asked.

"Dr. Sengstaken . . . Dr. Robert Sengstaken."

I told Joe about the pain in my neck and arms when they turned me. He said it might be painful, but that it wasn't doing any damage and that I had to get off my back and onto my stomach every four hours.

That night the older man in the bed next to mine was alternately moaning and delirious. I couldn't see him because the curtain around his bed was drawn, but when the nurses tried to roll him onto his side to bathe him he screamed in pain, swearing at them, begging them to stop, yelling that he couldn't stand it. I wanted to yell at them to stop, too, but I didn't. They got him over on his side and bathed him. Then they rolled him back while he begged them to go slowly. When the nurses left, I tried to talk with him, but it was impossible. When the night nurse, Swanee, came in, I asked her who he was.

"You're in with a celebrity," she said. "He's been written up in all the newspapers. He's a famous jewel thief—eighty years old. Tried one job too many, chief. Got caught out here in one of these swank houses, panicked, fell down a flight of stairs, and broke his hip."

Toward morning he woke up. "Where am I?" he said.

"You're in the Southampton Hospital," I answered.

"What am I doing here?"

"You're pretty badly hurt. I think you've got a broken hip. You fell down some stairs, and they brought you here. You've been delirious for the day and a half I've been here."

"I shouldn't be here at all," he said. "I was in a hospital in Baltimore. I've been kidnapped. Call the FBI. Please call the FBI."

I wanted to laugh but couldn't. He was delirious. I was paralyzed. But I thought if I could keep him talking, maybe he'd tell me where he'd hidden his money. "Listen," I said, only half kidding. "I can't call the FBI. But maybe if we pay the nurses off, they'll call them. But I don't have any money."

"I don't either," he said. "Call the FBI."

"You must," I said. "You've made all this money."

"I don't have any money. Call the FBI," he insisted.

I felt like a cop grilling a burglary suspect. I kept at it for another few minutes, but he stuck to his story and kept asking me to call the FBI. It was ludicrous. I couldn't believe what I was doing, so I finally gave up and tried to change the subject. But he only babbled on about being kidnapped, so I just shut up and tried to sleep.

Joe looked different when he came in to see me the next day. The uncertainty was gone. He'd made up his mind about something.

"I've talked to Dr. Sengstaken," he said. "He's coming out here tonight. We're going to try to get a better X-ray, and if we can't, we'll take a myelogram. We inject a fluid into the spine and then trace it."

Neither Mary nor I said anything, and I think our silence made Joe defensive. He repeated that he didn't want us to think he was stubborn or inflexible and that we could still call in our own doctor if we wanted to. After Joe left, Mary said she had already spoken to her father and that he had heard of Sengstaken and thought he was excellent.

CHAPTER 6

MARY

John arrived at around five and was talking with Jack when I thought I saw a man who must be Sengstaken. I remember that he looked tremendous to me, maybe six feet three inches tall, and handsome in a roughhewn way. When I saw him go into the nurses' station and look at what I thought was Jack's chart, I was sure it was he. I wanted to introduce myself. I wanted him to know who I was—Jack's girl and a doctor's daughter. I wanted him to be nice, but he seemed different from anyone, any doctor, I'd ever met. He was wearing an ugly summer suit, the type that shines too much, a yellow-brown fabric that borders on being cheap even though it isn't. He was wearing an almost aqua-colored shirt that I thought particularly unattractive. The clothes looked as if they belonged to another man, maybe a salesman. But I watched Sengstaken move, and even from a distance he commanded respect. He hardly spoke and seemed to move with incredible swiftness, but never seemed harried or rushed. When I saw he was alone, I walked over to him. "Dr. Sengstaken," I said meekly. "I'm Mary Pleshette, Jack's fiancée."

He shook my hand, and I remember that I felt dwarfed by him as his huge hand enveloped mine. He didn't say anything. He didn't smile. I felt the same kind of fear I'd experienced on the beach—I might be separated from Jack. I might be pushed out.

"Excuse me," he said and shifted his attention to Jack's chart. I watched him scan the information as if he already knew what had to be done. He never sat down, never wasted a move. Everything about him seemed to say, "Let's get going."

Joe arrived from nowhere. I saw him by Sengstaken's side. He was nervous and uncomfortable, as though Sengstaken's authority disturbed him. I wasn't allowed inside the X-ray room, but I tried to stand close by so I could hear what was happening. Sengstaken's voice was serious but kind. I thought I heard him tell Jack to relax. When he walked from the X-ray room to a small office nearby, I tried to accompany him from a distance. I dreaded their telling me to go away. They never did.

I never took my eyes from Sengstaken. They had taken two films and still couldn't get a good picture of Jack's neck. Sengstaken was annoyed with the X-ray technician.

"You'll have to do better than this," he said.

Then they smiled when they clipped the third X-ray up against a lighted milky glass frame.

"We really got it," one doctor said.

"We sure did," Joe responded, and he seemed delighted too.

I thought everything was fine. They couldn't be so happy if it was bad. But I didn't really know, and I turned to John in the hope that he would understand what everything meant. He just raised his eyebrows quizzically. No one said anything.

Sengstaken turned to me and said, "Would you mind coming in here?"

I followed him into a small blue conference room and watched him clip the X-ray of Jack's skull and neck onto a long lighted board. It was a side view. John was standing next to me.

"What is it?" I blurted out. I was frightened again. I waited for Sengstaken to speak, and I stared at the picture of an unfamiliar, surrealist skeleton that was Jack. "It looks very bad," Sengstaken said. "He's broken and dislocated his sixth and seventh vertebrae."

He pointed with the eraser tip of a pencil. He helped me count as he moved the pencil downward.

"One, two, three, four, five . . . you see . . . they're all in place."

He didn't have to help me any more. Six and seven were at least a half-inch out of place, shoved forward toward Jack's jaw. There was a brief silence, and I could feel everyone's eyes glued to me, waiting for me to say something. I was sitting now, and I was numb. I felt suspended, almost weightless, as though I were floating in an alien world.

"Will Jack be able to walk again?"

Sengstaken was sitting on a desk top with his feet on a chair. His eyes were cold.

"No. He will probably never walk again."

The words seemed to echo in my head. I felt lost, completely alone. I felt as if I were drowning, or maybe I had already died. I saw my own eyes staring at me—vacant, pleading eyes.

"Why? Why are you so sure?"

Sengstaken came over and sat down next to me. He pointed to the X-ray and said in a soft, calm voice, "The spinal cord runs through the vertebrae. When Jack hit his head, those two vertebrae were pushed forward against the cord and hooked on to each other. The cord was probably severed or, if not, irreparably bruised and torn." He waited for me to say something. But I didn't. "You see, the spinal cord is like a telephone cable, and like the individual lines that run through it, the nerves carry messages from the brain to the muscles." Again he paused for a moment and then went on. "But unlike a telephone cable, once the spinal cord is torn, it can't be mended. . . . The result is permanent paralysis."

It was irreversible. Jack was paralyzed from the neck down. I quietly, almost politely, asked Sengstaken to stop. "Please. Just let me cry."

I buried my head in my arms and for the first time in three days wept without any desire to hold back. I felt my shoulders sag, my breast heave, and I held on to Sengstaken's left hand that was resting on the table in front of me. I pressed it to my forehead and felt myself gripping onto it. No one spoke, and Sengstaken made no effort to draw away from me. I felt him hold the back of my head in his right hand, and at one point he smoothed my hair. I told him I'd be all right.

"Is there any chance he will recover?" I asked meekly.

Sengstaken shrugged and said, "I seriously doubt it . . . but there are always miracles."

Nobody said anything for a few moments. Then Joe said, "I don't agree with Sengstaken." I was surprised that Joe would say this with both Sengstaken and me in the room. I looked up and saw that Joe meant what he was saying, that he wasn't trying to ease my sorrow. "I can't tell you why I feel this way, but I do. I don't think the cord has been severed."

"What are you going to tell Jack?" I asked.

Sengstaken said they wouldn't tell him anything, not unless he asked.

"How can you lie to him?" I asked.

"We won't lie to him. We will tell him everything he wants to know when he asks."

Sengstaken paused and looked sternly at me.

"He can't see you cry, Mary. He can't see that you are upset."

Sengstaken explained that they would try to unhook the vertebrae with traction, that they would add up to sixty pounds of weight to avoid having to operate. I waited while he disappeared into the X-ray room. He came back with another X-ray and quickly stuck it up on the lighted glass.

"We need another ten pounds," Sengstaken said. He went back into the X-ray room. Another ten minutes passed. He came back with another X-ray. "One of the vertebrae snapped back," he said. He had marked every X-ray with a red wax pencil in the order it had been taken, and I could see the difference in the latest picture.

"Let's add some more weight," Sengstaken said. "Maybe we can get the second one back in place." He went into the X-ray room. It seemed like an endless, monotonous parade.

I was aware that someone had walked into the room. I turned and saw my father and mother. They didn't know anything, but they knew everything. I felt like crying again but couldn't. Sengstaken and Joe came back into the room. Sengstaken shook my father's hand and stuck a new X-ray up against the light. I half listened to the conversation between Joe and Sengstaken, but nothing seemed to register any more. I dimly heard Joe say, "If we do that, we'll have to wire the sixth and fifth, and that won't work. What do you think?" It all sounded like a foreign language to me, but I was beginning to understand that the second vertebra hadn't snapped back, that whatever they were doing wasn't working. Sengstaken didn't answer immediately. Finally he broke the silence.

"We'd better get going. We have to operate."

As I approached the X-ray room, I saw Sengstaken talking with my father. I went up to them and said I was all right, that I wanted to see Jack. Sengstaken led me into the room. Jack's shoulder muscles were bulging from the stress of all those weights. He looked like a healthy animal trapped and tied down before being shipped off to a zoo.

"They're going to have to operate, baby," Jack said.

He asked Sengstaken to explain to me what was happening. He really didn't know what I knew, and I no longer wanted to tell him.

Everyone seemed to be scurrying around. Joe and Sengstaken had disappeared to get something to eat before the operation, and Jack was wheeled back to his room. A nurse came in and gave him an injection. The hospital seemed deserted, the visitors were gone, the hall lights had been dimmed, and the place stank of silence. When I looked into Jack's eyes, I wasn't frightened. He asked me to get my father.

"Do you think I have to be operated on?" Jack asked calmly. "Do you think they're doing the right thing?"

"They know what they're doing," Papa said. "They have to clean you up and straighten out those vertebrae. They have to get the pressure off the cord." He paused. "Nobody goes into the neck unless they have to. And I have confidence in Sengstaken, and Spinzia's an excellent man."

A nurse came into the room with another injection. They were ready to wheel him into the operating room. I knew the nurses wanted me to leave, but I wouldn't go. I felt riveted to Jack's side. I wanted them to go away. I wanted more time, but they started to push the hard, narrow rack out of the room. I walked next to Jack, and a second before they pushed him behind two heavy swinging doors, I asked the nurses to stop. "Please, just let me kiss him good-by," I said and didn't really understand the "good-by." I told Jack I would see him when he woke up from the operation. I told him I loved him. I told him everything was going to be all right.

My father put his arm around my shoulders as we walked out the automatic emergency doors of the hospital. I started to cry without knowing it. "Could Jack die?" I asked.

I felt my father's hand tighten around my arm. "Yes."

"I don't want Jack to die," I said to myself. "I want more than life for Jack to live." As I uttered the words, I felt immediate relief, and with relief I felt hope, and with hope a surge of strength.

CHAPTER 7

JACK

I dreamed I was calling for Mary. Then I realized I was awake and Mary was next to me. She bent down and kissed me.

I don't remember feeling pain, but Mary says that the first thing I said was how much I hurt. Then I asked her what time it was, and she told me it was after midnight.

"And the operation?"

"It went well. Everything's okay," she said.

"Where's Joe?" I asked.

"He went home."

I was hurt. I didn't understand why he wasn't there. Didn't he care? I had a lot of questions to ask him. A nurse came over to us, and Mary said she had to go. She kissed me good-by, and I fell back into a drugged sleep.

I was awakened by two nurses. It was still night, and they were covering me with sheepskins, furry sides down, from my shoulders to my feet. Then they placed the metal frame over me. They strapped it down so that I was sandwiched between the sheepskins and frames. I began to get frightened. They were going to turn me onto my stomach.

"Joe said I wasn't to be turned," I said.

"It's doctor's orders," they said, "four hours on your back, Mr. Willis, two hours on your stomach."

Two hours! I hadn't lasted ten minutes the first time. I gritted my teeth and waited for the pain as they turned me, but there was none this time, and I realized the operation must have relieved the pressure on my cord.

I lay there in the dark, staring down into blackness. The straps cut into my forehead. I tried to sleep. I couldn't. I tried thinking about work, but I couldn't concentrate. All I could feel was the straps. I heard the nurses quietly move around the darkened room. I cried out. There was no answer.

"I can hear you," I yelled. "I know you're there."

No answer.

"Turn me back. My head is killing me."

"You've only been over five minutes, Mr. Willis," one of the nurses said, and the other one came over and rubbed my back and said I had to try to take more.

For the first time I felt the total impotence of my position. I understood for the first time what it really meant to be paralyzed. My frustration gave way to rage. "Goddamn, son-of-a-bitch. Turn me. I can't stand it," I screamed.

From the darkness came the answer: "We can't. Doctor's orders. Two hours on your stomach. You've only been over ten minutes."

And then, miraculously, the nurse who had rubbed my back came out of the darkness and began placing the sheepskins on my back. I could hardly stand it. "Hurry," I said. She put the frame over my back, strapped me in, and without saying a word, rolled me over onto my back. "Get the frame off me fast."

She did and I relaxed and fell asleep. I dreamed I was running full speed down a hill. About halfway down, a fist materialized and smacked me full force right in the face. When I was a kid playing football in the street, I'd gone out for a pass and run into a lamppost and had been knocked cold. That's what the sensation was in the dream. I took a few more steps, and it hit me again and again and again.

I woke up dripping wet from my own sweat. I waited a few minutes until I calmed down and then went back to sleep. The same dream began. I was running downhill and got hit in the face over and over again. That dream is clearer to me today and more frightening than the accident itself.

I couldn't get back to sleep. I tried to piece together the events just before they operated on me. Sengstaken had told me then that two vertebrae in my neck, the lower two, were fractured and dislocated, the same two Joe had tried to get a picture of in my room the day before. They had been pushed forward and had locked together, causing pressure on the spinal cord, which accounted for the paralysis. To snap them back into place and relieve the pressure on the cord, they first had to be unhooked.

"We don't want to operate," Sengstaken said. "We'll have to roll you over for the operation, which could be dangerous."

I thought about being turned in my bed the day before and the pain in my arms. I wondered if any damage had been done then. I knew it was the wrong time to ask and that they wouldn't tell me even if they knew.

"We're going to add more weight to your head," Sengstaken said. "We're hoping to stretch you out and pull the vertebrae free of each other." He walked behind me and added weights to the twenty pounds already suspended from my head. "That's ten pounds," he said. I lay there waiting, not knowing what to expect. I felt the added weight pulling on my body but felt no pain. Then I heard a snap and said, "I think it's back in place." They took another X-ray and disappeared into another room. I waited, thirty pounds of dead weight stretching my dead body. They came back in. "Only one vertebra's snapped back," Sengstaken said. The other one was still locked. "Let's try another ten pounds."

He added the weight, and we waited, expecting another snap. After ten minutes, when nothing had happened, they took another X-ray and disappeared again. I made small talk with the X-ray technician, and Mary's father and brother came into the room.

Sengstaken came back in. He stepped behind me, and I thought he was going to add more weight. Instead, he told me to relax and put his huge hands under my shoulders and tried to stretch me out farther by lifting and pulling my head toward him. I could feel the desperation in the effort and knew we had reached the end of the line. I let him try a couple of times, and finally I said, "I guess we've had it."

"I guess so," he said. "I think we have to operate."

"Let's get on with it," I said. But first I wanted Mary to know what was happening. I made him bring her in to explain everything that had happened and what was wrong with me and why they had to operate. I wanted them to know how close Mary and I were and that it was important to both of us that we go through this together. What I didn't say was that I needed her, that she had to know what was happening because at some point we were still going to have to make a decision about whether or not we were going to be married.

The sun was finally up, and now I found myself objectifying all that was happening to me, the same as I had on the beach. I was looking down at myself, not quite believing it was happening to me. The day before, I had been happy to see Sengstaken. It meant that two days of waiting and wondering were over. I was even relieved when they finally got the X-rays and found the fractures. At least we knew what was wrong. And as crazy as it seems, I was relieved that they were operating. At least we were doing something.

But now it was the morning after the operation and I still couldn't move. The night before, Sengstaken had told me that all the damage was done to my spinal cord the second I hit my head on the sand. If my cord had been severed, the operation could relieve the pressure but could not bring back my movement.

I waited for Joe and tried to frame the questions I would ask him, like what did they find when they opened me up. But when Joe came in, I just blurted out, "Will I walk again?"

"Sengstaken doesn't think so," he said.

The blood rushed out of my head and I felt my heart sink.

"What are the odds?" I asked.

"About ten percent," he said.

"And you. What do you think?"

"I don't know," Joe said. "I'm more optimistic."

I didn't really hear him. I rushed on. "Can I fuck?"

"Probably. But you wouldn't feel anything."

"Can I have kids?"

"I don't know. An erection doesn't mean ejaculation." Joe smiled.

"Those were the same questions Mary asked."

Mary. So she already knew. I was glad because I didn't want to have to tell her. The night before, when Joe had awkwardly attempted to help us by telling us how much everyone admired the way we were acting and how we were going to need all our courage in the days ahead, it had cheered me a little to get his recognition, but now it didn't seem to help. Now I searched for answers.

Joe began talking quietly. "The odds are against you," he said. "But there's some room for hope. When we opened you up, we could see that the cord was intact."

I pressed him. "Well, then what's wrong?"

"Sengstaken's pessimistic because of the paralysis and because he ran his finger down the cord and felt an indentation. He thinks that means a whole group of nerves within the cord have been severed . . . but I don't know. It could just be a temporary indentation, like the kind you get when you sit for a long time in a chair with slats."

"When will we know who's right?" I said. "When will movement begin to return if it returns at all?"

"In around two to three weeks," Joe said. "Not before then." He paused. "Even Sengstaken doesn't know for sure if the cord was severed. If it's only badly bruised, you should begin to get return when the swelling goes down. Give yourself a chance. If you still can't move after three weeks, then . . ."

Then? What then? What was I going to do? How was I going to deal with it? I couldn't even commit suicide. I couldn't move.

CHAPTER 8

MARY

When I opened my front door on a Tuesday evening in March, I thought Jack looked older than I had imagined he would be. But I was immediately comfortable with him and almost inadvertently took his arm as we waited for a taxi. When I realized that my hand was neatly resting on his, I made a conscious effort to keep it there. I was testing myself, testing Jack. I was saying, "This is the way I am, and I'm sick to death of first-date protocol."

I wore a light blue sleeveless dress and the beige Gucci shoes I'd bought the previous summer—the shoes which I'd saved twelve dollars on by buying them in Italy but which now killed my feet. I had suspected from his phone voice that Jack wasn't from New York, and I was now sure that my suspicions were right, from the thin black tie and cloddy shoes he wore. I was disturbed that I even noticed, much less cared about his clothes, but he was unlike anyone I had ever dated. I was the one who always had a fantasy that the man I'd marry would speak fluent French and that we'd have lots of beautiful, bilingual children. Jack didn't fit that mold.

We had dinner in the Village and I talked about how I longed for a job that would utilize all my energies. Jack listened. He often leaned forward on his elbows to hear me better. He seemed interested. I talked about the newness of being on my own, the incredible difficulty of learning to be alone. I talked about my family and he spoke about his. After dinner we walked around the Village and Jack casually put his arm around me. We took a cab uptown and stopped at a bar near my apartment. Jack described his experiences, making films in the South, and I asked him whether he had been afraid. "No," he said. "I was much more frightened in Appalachia." Mississippi, Kentucky . . . AMERICA. He didn't fit the ideal image, but I liked him. I really liked him.

We were different people then, but those two strangers were a part of us. I lay quietly waiting to be called to go back to the hospital. By midnight I still hadn't received word but could wait no more.

Jack was in the Intensive Care unit, a large room with only a few beds. It was so quiet that even the sound of a footstep seemed an intrusion. A nurse in a green uniform led me to where Jack was sleeping. But he wasn't really sleeping, just resting. He looked as though he had been beaten; his cheeks were swollen, his eyes puffy and bruised. He could hardly speak, and I tried to quiet him as he struggled to talk to me.

Jack wanted to know what time it was. I told him midnight. He asked to see Joe. I told him that he'd gone home. I wanted to hold Jack's hand, to sit quietly by him and stay the rest of the night. A nurse came over to me and said I had to leave.

Jack was alive. The panic and fear had vanished. In its place was a calm, so real and solid that I understood I had passed through the nightmare and was now so firmly rooted in the present that nothing seemed to scare me. I knew nothing except that Jack was alive, and that knowledge seemed to steer me like an invisible rudder.

I drove slowly back to the house. The air was misty, and everything was quiet, still, soft. I could see the farmhouse from the road. My mother had left the kitchen light on. I parked the car and stared at the house. I was going home to my parents, and I felt a little like Emily in *Our Town*, traveling backward in time to her thirteenth birthday.

I thought about how happy everyone was the night we announced we were getting married. It was my twenty-fourth birthday, a ridiculously special day for me every year, with a family celebration that always included gifts, poems, and my favorite dinner of roast beef and a strawberry shortcake for dessert. But this birthday was golden. Jack and I had decided to surprise everybody with the news.

Jack raised his glass of champagne. "A week ago today on Fisherman's Wharf in San Francisco, over a plate of cracked crab, I asked Mary to be my wife. . . . And she said yes." No one knew whether to drink the champagne or kiss us. There was a happy commotion—my wonderful Aunt Mabel, who had once broken all the windows in her courtyard trying to kill some noisy pigeons with a slingshot, cried, my brother kissed Jack, my mother kept repeating, "Oh, how marvelous, oh . . ." and my father glowed. And once the gleeful surprise had passed, I was bombarded with questions of when and where and by whom.

I remembered the walk Jack and I had taken down a dirt road to an abandoned yellow house. "My dream house," I had told Jack as we stared at rambler rose and blackberry bushes gone so mad with growing that they had pushed their vines through windows and grew freely inside the house. "Dream house?" he said incredulously. "You're crazy. I want a place right on the beach with a big sun porch and an outdoor barbecue." Not me. I wanted a house with grass and trees and told him if he wanted his house on the beach he should move back to California. We argued, insulting each other's taste, and then laughed at how lucky we were not to have to make a decision because we couldn't afford to buy a house anyway.

I tried to hold on to the memory of that day, the way one tries to linger in the fantasy of a wonderful dream. But I could not pretend that all I remembered wasn't tainted with the ugly wounds of an accident, a stupid, pointless trick of nature. It was three o'clock in the morning by now, and Jack's parents had probably arrived at Kennedy Airport and would be at the house by six. I let my eyes close and told myself to sleep.

The last time I had seen Libbie and Lou was in Los Angeles at the tail end of our Mexican vacation. I'd been uncomfortable speaking to them long distance, but I discovered that being with them in their environment, lolling around the pool, wandering into the kitchen for a snack, was another story entirely. I began to relax with them and build a relationship based on a real affection for them rather than simply on my love for Jack, the one thing we all shared. When Jack spoke, I'd watch Lou's eyes. To say they filled up with love and admiration is corny, but that's just what I saw. He exuded pride. Libbie reminded me of my own mother, except that she was more solicitous of me because I wasn't her daughter.

I heard the car on the gravel driveway and the doors slam shut. Another sunny day that hurt my eyes. I expected Lou to be crying and Libbie to be controlled. I ran downstairs and wrapped my arms around Libbie. She was sobbing, and we stood in the middle of the kitchen quietly cradling each other. I realized how much taller I was than she and that I wasn't crying. It was the first morning in days that I hadn't cried. When Libbie pulled away, she seemed a little embarrassed, but that didn't matter, and both she and I knew it. Then I saw Lou, who gave me a big hug and said, "Hiya, my little doll. It's going to be okay." I looked into his eyes—round blue eyes with thick black lashes. He believed what he said. He wasn't crying. Sengstaken's words, "He will probably never walk again," no longer echoed in my head, but had been absorbed by my entire system, and I was just beginning to feel calm with the acceptance that Jack might not get better. And there was Lou standing in front of me, saying that everything was going to be okay.

We moved out onto the porch, which was filled with sunlight. Libbie sat quietly on the swinging couch. She clutched a handkerchief with a big L embroidered on it and occasionally wiped her eyes behind the big light-blue sunglasses she was wearing.

Lou talked nervously. He didn't care what the doctors' prognoses were.

"I've seen Jack fight," he said. "I've seen him put his foot through a shower door in anger after he lost an important ball game. He'll play ball again. He won't give in. And we know a kid—you know, Libbie—who dove into a quarry and broke every bone in his body. He was paralyzed too. He's doing just great now. He was told he'd never walk again, too. But he's walking."

The image of Jack kicking anything now, much less a shower door, was like a sick joke. The doctors said he wouldn't walk. How could Lou be so sure they were wrong? I tried to ignore what he was saying. I tried to remember what Joe had told me when I spoke to him after the operation. I'd called him before I went to sleep. I had asked him if Jack was better, and he said, "Mary. This is going to take a long time. If you go into the hospital every day expecting to see improvement, you'll go crazy. You can't expect any change, you can't expect anything."

I tried to warn Libbie and Lou that Jack would be wired with tubes and tongs, but I knew nothing could soften the shock. I knocked on the windowless door of Intensive Care, and a stocky, round-faced nurse opened it a crack. "I know we're here early," I said, "but Jack's parents just arrived from California." The nurse whispered that I should come in first and tell Jack they were here. I turned to Libbie and told her I'd be just a second and then she could go in.

Jack's eyes were open, and the swelling had begun to go down. He tried to smile. I told him that his parents were here and wanted to see him. The tube in his nose made talking difficult, but he indicated that he was glad they were here. I kissed him gently on the forehead and said he shouldn't try to talk too much. We looked at each other for a second longer, and then I realized I couldn't hog the brief time allotted visitors.

Lou and I didn't speak as we waited for Libbie to come out. We just looked at each other. Lou put his arm around my shoulders, and I wrapped my arm around his waist. We stood quietly together like two old friends who haven't seen each other for years but whose physical proximity is a comforting proof that they share something very special. The door opened, and as soon as Lou went in, Libbie embraced me, crying, "My little baby, what have they done to my little boy!"

When Lou emerged from Intensive Care, his eyes brimmed with tears, but he seemed almost buoyant. "I told him that he's going to be all right," Lou said positively. "I told him he had to fight, that he couldn't give in. I said we were all with him and that he couldn't believe everything the doctors said." Lou hesitated and looked at me. "I didn't say that the doctors weren't good, but they're going to be wrong. Look. I was told by some specialist son-of-a-bitch that I had cancer. The schmuck sent the X-rays to the house by mistake and I saw the diagnosis—carcinoma. He wanted to operate. Well, I said, just wait a minute. You're not just going to cut into me and mess around. I went to another doctor who said, 'Lou, you're as healthy as an ox!'"

CHAPTER 9

JACK

The tube in my nose and throat made breathing difficult. I tried to disregard the discomfort and think about what Joe had said. I couldn't clear my mind. Paralysis, wheelchair, Mary, sex, marriage, children, job, friends, pity. I couldn't begin to deal with it. I sank deeper and deeper into mindless depression.

A pretty young nurse came over and tried to talk with me. We kidded about something. That was a little better. She even flirted a little, which made me feel better. She made me feel as if I were still a man. Then she disappeared. When she returned, she had a flower in a glass which she placed on the floor under my face. She told me she'd gone outside to pick it for me, but I figured she'd swiped it from another patient, probably someone who'd just died.

Over on my back again. Drugged, dozing, depressed. I sensed someone was there. I opened my eyes. It was Mary. We kissed. She seemed nervous and excited. We didn't talk about what we both knew. There was no time. She said my parents were outside, waiting to see me.

My mother came in first. She looked fine but controlled. She was wearing sunglasses so I couldn't tell what was going on inside her. I had no idea what I looked like to her, except that I knew I was still tan and thought that outwardly I looked pretty healthy. I could tell she didn't know how to start. She couldn't very well ask, "How are you?"

"How was the plane trip, Mom?"

"Oh, fine, a little tiring. But we're fine."

"And Dick. How are Dick and Cece?"

"They drove us to the airport. I think they'll be here soon. . . . Jack, do you hurt very badly?"

"No, Mom. I don't hurt. It was a freaky accident, but hell, I'm going to be okay. Don't worry. I'm just very tired, and it's hard to talk."

Then, out of the corner of my eye, I saw my father. He was grinning, coming toward me with that crazy Groucho Marx lope of his, knees bent, arms swinging, skating across the floor. It was the same run, grin, and excitement he always had when he picked me up at the airport on my visits to Los Angeles. He'd shake my hand, throw his arm around my shoulders, and say, "Hiya, Jacko." He'd talk to me a mile a minute, never listening, while we picked up my bags and headed toward the car.

Now he stood at my bed and grabbed my hand and said, "Hiya, Jacko." He didn't even give me a chance to say anything. "Listen, I don't care what the doctors or anyone else says. You'll beat it. You've been a scrapper all your life. You're the guy who breaks shower doors. You're a fighter, and no matter what else, you'll fight."

I tried to smile. I tried to answer, but I couldn't. He didn't ask me how I felt or how it happened or what I thought. Nothing. He wasn't telling me to be brave or to fight. He was telling me that he *knew* I'd fight.

That night they rolled me out of Intensive Care and back to my room. My brother, Dick, and his wife, Cece, were there. I was happy to see them.

It didn't occur to me until later that the family suddenly being there meant I could have died. I never thought of it—it just seemed natural for them to be here now.

Dick is four years younger than I and was a dentist who worked in the Watts Clinic in L.A. We had always been very close as kids, and even though we lived at opposite ends of the country, we remained close. I was also crazy about Cece, who was pretty, warm, and open.

"Hey, how'd you get away from work?" I said.

"I'm not working this summer," Cece said in her soft voice. She was a teacher.

"And I just left," Dick said, flashing me that big toothy grin of his. We both wore braces when we were kids and picked up the habit of lifting our upper lip, all the way to the gums, when we smiled, so as not to get ourselves hooked onto the wires.

"Actually, I took a short leave of absence," he said.

Dick and I stared at each other for a long time. Mary and Cece stood a little behind. I wondered what I must look like to Dick and what was going through his mind. I knew that with his medical training he probably understood a lot about what was happening to me, but I didn't want to ask. I was too scared. I wanted to joke but couldn't. He looked too serious and upset. He didn't feel the need to say or do or offer anything. I had the feeling he knew exactly what I was feeling and that a part of him was attached to the tongs with me. "It took less than a second to change my life," I said, breaking the silence. Dick just nodded.

The fourth night in the hospital I had nightmares again. This time I dreamed of the wave, tumbling over and over, falling and smashing my head on the sand. I could feel my head jerk and the horrible spasms in my neck and back. I woke up scared. I thought I had lifted out of the tongs, but I hadn't. That was impossible. I closed my eyes and went back to sleep and had the same dream, falling, falling, crashing down, and the pain. It was like diving into an empty swimming pool.

I awoke and called for the nurse. Like a kid scared of the dark, I asked her to turn on the light. She said the dreams might be caused by the Demerol. Then she turned me on my stomach, and for the first time I relaxed in that position. I let my arms hang down and asked one of the aides if she had time to give me a massage. Her hands kneaded my shoulders and back muscles. I lay there staring down at the floor, the straps supporting my head. I didn't think of anything. I just let myself feel her hands.

I felt more relaxed after she turned me back. "I'm better. You can turn off the lights," I said.

"It's okay," she said, as if I were a little boy scared of the dark. "The sun is coming up."

She was right. I did feel safer with the dawn.

When Joe came in later that day, I told him about my bad trips.

"Sometimes Demerol can do that," he said. "We'll try another drug. Also, I think I'm going to change your roommate."

"Why?"

"Well, there's a young kid down the hall who'll be better company for you. The old man is out of it too much of the time, and I think you'll like this other guy. You'll be good for each other."

"It's okay with me. . . . Too bad I never found out where the old man hid his loot."

My room was so small that they had to maneuver my bed around into a corner in order to get my old roommate out and my new roommate in. Out of the corner of my eye I saw someone being rolled in. Rather, I saw an arm and leg in a cast suspended from a metal frame above his bed. Because I couldn't see the bed itself, he appeared to be hanging like a chimpanzee in the zoo. "Hi," I said. "Welcome."

"Hi," he said as they wheeled him past me, "I hear you're in really shitty shape. . . . Hey, sweetheart, Patti," he called to a nurse as soon as his bed was in place. "Where is my table and the radio? And be careful when you bring it in. My cigarettes and watch are in the drawer, and don't forget my Bermuda shorts, the checked ones, and my shirts." Then he turned his attention to me. "Hi. I'm Mike Guerin."

"Hi. I'm Jack Willis. Where you from?"

"The Bronx."

I had guessed from his voice that he was around thirty years old.

Then he said, "Hey, Jack, man, what happened to you?"

"I was flipped by a wave and broke my neck."

"Wow." He half laughed. "Ain't that a pisser? The surf did all that to you. Man, I've never heard of *anyone* getting his neck broke by a wave."

"Me either," I said. "What happened to you?"

"It's crazy, man. We got this place in Hampton Bays, lots of girls, guys, always something doing. Three weeks ago my buddy and I went out for dinner and some fun. We were driving home when I saw this guy step out

46

into the road. My buddy swerved, and that's the last thing I remember."

"You were in a coma," I said.

"A coma? Man, I didn't wake up till ten days later. I think we went off an embankment and I was thrown out of the car. And then the car rolled over onto me. They told me that when they found me, I had so little pulse they gave me the last rites."

"What happened to your friend?"

"Nothing, man. Do you believe it? He walked away without a scratch, the bastard. All he lost was his car. And I've been here three weeks."

Early the next day, when they gave me a shot and turned me onto my stomach, Mike offered me his radio.

"Hey, sweetheart, put it down by his head so he can hear. What d'ya like, Jack?"

"It's okay, Mike," I said. "You keep it. I'll just sleep."

"No. You take it," he said, and made sure the nurses put it on the floor a few feet from my head. "Hey, sweetheart," Mike said, "turn it up, will you, so I can hear it too?"

A nurse came over to my bed and gave me a shot. I closed my eyes, tired from a sleepless night, and gave in to the drug. The music from Mike's radio was blasting, but I didn't want to hurt his feelings by asking him to turn it down. I lay there, torn between telling him to turn the damn thing off and just letting it blare. Then the drug began to work, and I was somewhere between a world of sleep and a world of complete lucidity. Colors, bright and beautiful colors, filled my head. I began to hear the music, and the colors danced, changed, and flashed to the rock beat. I gave in and went with it. Part of me watched while the other part fixed on the beat and moved with the rhythms. I forgot the discomfort of the straps across my forehead and chin.

When they turned me onto my back, the white hospital ceiling was a rich blue. I forgot the music and watched the paint move across the ceiling. The texture and color looked like paint when you mix it in its can before it is completely blended. Mary, Dick, and Cece came into the room and I started to tell them about what I saw. But then they began to close in on me. My brother's smile and the look of concern in Mary's eyes made me nervous, and I closed my eyes tight, trying to stop the drug. Finally my head stopped spinning and the colors disappeared, so I opened my eyes. I looked up at the ceiling; the paint was still a rippling blue. Everyone was moving in on me, coming closer and closer to my head. I tried to explain what was happening, but I was getting more and more nervous and out of control. I asked them all to leave.

When I told Joe what had happened to me, he very cautiously asked me what my past drug experience had been. I guess he thought I was part of some wild New York scene. "Almost nothing," I said. "A little social smoking, some pot—you know. Why?"

"Because if you'd been a heavy user that might explain your extraordinary reaction to what is usually a harmless drug."

"Well, I'm not a heavy user," I said. I wasn't sure whether I convinced him of that, but he decided to give me morphine. At first I felt nothing. Then I felt a warmth, beginning in my legs, that slowly crept upward, enveloping my entire body. I felt as if I were slipping slowly into a warm tub of water.

CHAPTER 10

MARY

Dick, Cece, and I went into the conference room across the hall from Jack's room. I wanted Spinzia to talk with Dick. I wanted Dick to understand so he could explain to Libbie and Lou. And, I didn't know why, but I wanted to hear it all again. Maybe I still didn't believe it myself.

Spinzia came into the room and sat down. He was tense, but acted casual, as if he'd already done the explaining routine and would waste no time getting into hard facts. "Have you thought about a rehab hospital?" he said, and seeing the look of dismay on our faces, he went right on. "I know you're shaking your heads. But Jack is going to need a lot of care. And that care costs a lot of money. You can't just put it off."

I was struck by the notion that Joe was talking about someone else, discussing the fate of a faceless cripple. Dick slumped in his chair, but his words came quickly, without hesitation.

"Before we talk about rehabilitation, I want to know why you say you're more optimistic than Sengstaken."

"I don't think Jack's cord was severed. I think there's a chance it was badly bruised. If I'm right, he'll get return in around two to three weeks."

I looked at Dick. "Sengstaken says the odds are only ten percent, but if Jack's that ten percent, it's a hundred for us," Dick said. Cece and I smiled.

"We never know with these spinal injuries," Joe said. "There can be complications." Joe paused. "I just want you to know that I think Jack is an incredible man. I could never go through what he's going through.

Maybe I shouldn't say that, but I'm the kind of guy who gets all his relaxation from working with his hands. When I go home, I work on old cars. I get them when they're piles of junk and transform them into collectors' items. Even if Jack gets some return, the chances are slim that he'll be able to use his hands. Luckily, there is surgery that can be performed that would restore some movement in that area."

I wasn't listening. "Complications? What kind of complications?" I blurted out.

"I guess the most dangerous is pneumonia. If a quadriplegic begins to collect fluid in his lungs, he has no way of getting it out because he doesn't have the muscles to cough. And then there's the catheter. . . . If it stays in too long, he could develop strictures which would cut off his ability to urinate . . ."

"And ejaculate," I interrupted. The fear of pneumonia didn't frighten me, but the mention of strictures in his penis terrified me. I wished Joe hadn't mentioned them. He had told me too much already. Why did he have to mention strictures?

"How long can the catheter stay in before it's dangerous?" I asked.

"A pretty long time," he said, trying to be understanding. "That's the least of my worries. We can always catheterize him by inserting a tube right into the bladder, a supra-pubic catheterization."

I had stopped taking The Pill the morning after the operation. I felt a little like a novice whose outer vestments and gold wedding band are as much a symbol of abstinence as a protection against any lingering desire to sin. There seemed no point to protecting myself. My sex life had been washed out to sea with that wave, and the strange part of it all was that I felt no frustration, no physical withdrawal. If I thought of Jack's and my lovemaking, I felt a deep sadness, an empty, hollow nostalgia, but I had lost touch with my sexuality. And in a peculiar way, sex seemed irrelevant. The closeness was still there, the warmth; the need to share was now satisfied by a look, a touch, a kiss.

I felt defiant and angry, more anxious to get pregnant now than ever before. We would have a child as soon as we could. Sengstaken said we could still do that. "I'll show them," I said to myself. "I'll show them and get pregnant right away." I fantasized walking into Sengstaken's office one day, big-bellied and glowing. I even imagined Jack playing with a baby. The thought of his not being able to run or play with a child didn't frighten me. I tried to picture him in a wheelchair, surrounded by a family, our family. I focused on this idealized vision the way one looks at a collage, not concentrating on the individual parts of the painting but looking at the work as a whole. I didn't try to imagine how we would have sex. "We will do it," I said to myself. "Somehow we will make it work."

CHAPTER 11

JACK

Like a baby, I was totally dependent upon others for everything. I had to be fed, cleaned, made comfortable. I had no control over my bladder, and defecation was induced. Unlike a baby, I had the brain of a man and the memory of what I had been and also the understanding of what I might be.

I tried to scratch my nose, but like a spastic, I missed it completely. When I got close to it, I couldn't use my fingers. It felt more natural for me to scratch with the heel of my hand. I knew Mary was watching, and I wondered what she was thinking. Maybe, like me, she was remembering all those jokes we used to tell about spastics, like the boy who misses his mouth and hits himself in the forehead with an ice-cream cone. I tried not to think about the jokes. I even felt a funny kind of pride in just getting my hand close to my face, and I wondered why I hadn't tried to do it before.

I tried to concentrate on other things I could do. There was a little stand attached to the underside of my bed. I thought maybe I could read, and I asked Clive to get me a newspaper and lay it flat below me. I tried to turn the pages, but my hands were useless, paralyzed and numb. I discovered that if I bent my wrist backward, I could open my forefinger and thumb and that if I bent my wrist forward, I could force the fingers into something resembling a pinch. I tried turning the pages that way, but because my fingers were numb, I couldn't feel the paper. The head nurse, Janet LaVinio, suggested I use the heel of my hand to push the page and crumple it. Then I could dog-ear the bottom of the paper and would have something to pinch. That way, maybe, I could turn it. It took me forty-five minutes to read a quarter of the *Times*. Janet stayed with me and massaged my back and shoulders. She brought me some juice in a cup and, exhausted, I waited for her to feed it to me.

"Try it yourself," she said and placed a straw in the cup.

I tried gripping the cup between my hands. But it was heavy to lift, and I couldn't coordinate lifting the cup and placing the straw between my lips. So I picked up the straw, put that into my mouth first, then lifted the cup around the straw. When the cup was half full, it was finally light enough for me to handle, straw and all. When it was empty, I put it down on the stand, both elated and depressed by my accomplishment. I thought about how weak and uncoordinated my arms were and they weren't even paralyzed.

That night after all the visitors had gone, Joe dropped in to say hello. He had come to the hospital to check another patient. Now that he was finished, he was relaxing, his foot propped up on the chair next to my bed, puffing on a cigar. We made small talk for a while. I could tell he wanted to stay and talk but didn't know quite how to do it. I sensed he was afraid to get too close to me, afraid of straining what he thought was the doctor-patient relationship. But that's exactly what I wanted. I wanted to get as close to the guy as possible. I needed continual reassurance that he really cared for me. To do that, he had to understand me. So what I really wanted to talk about was me, but because he was unsure of himself, I knew to keep him there we'd have to talk about him.

"Pretty tough racket?" I began.

"Yeah. But I love it. The hours don't bother me, and I'm really my own man."

"What do you mean? You're here all day and night."

"Sure," he said defensively, "but I get time off. I live only five minutes from the hospital, and my office is right across the road. I work hard, but I can run home and see my kids. If patients get on my nerves, I can just knock off work a few days." He shifted his legs on the chair, unwinding a little more.

"Baloney," I said. "I've seen you here over the weekend and almost every night. It's not as good as you make it sound. You don't relax."

"But winter's soft. I get to work on my car."

"Car?"

"Yeah. I rebuild old cars. Buy them cheap and rebuild them. I like working with my hands . . . be a lot tougher on me if I was in your position."

I heard my voice rise. "What do you mean by that?"

"In my work I depend on my hands. You work with your head."

"Yeah, well, I also work with my hands and legs."

"But it'd be tougher for me to adjust."

"Bullshit. What do you think I'm going to do if I'm stuck in a wheelchair the rest of my life? I wasn't sitting on my ass—I made films, and I love sports, and what about a family?"

"Well, sports aren't important," Joe interrupted.

"Maybe not to you, but . . ."

"And maybe you can still have a family."

"Maybe. Maybe," I said, but felt depressed. He wasn't giving one inch. He wasn't telling me anything he hadn't told me before. I tried to shift gears. "Have you had other broken necks here?"

"No broken necks, but a couple of years ago we had a young guy who broke his back in an auto accident and was paralyzed from the waist down. He's still in a wheelchair, but he drives a car—hand controls."

Big deal, I thought. He thinks the worst thing about paralysis is not being able to drive a car. Nothing about not having control over your bladder and bowels or not being able to fuck or run or work. "Is he married?" I asked.

"Yeah. He has a wife. I'm not sure about kids."

After he left, I thought about what he'd said, how it would have been more difficult for him than it was for me because he worked with his hands. I thought of my numb hands. I thought of trying to caress Mary or to type a letter or to play catch or to carry an envelope home from work. I didn't want to be like a baby, dependent on others. I thought of how unfair it was, especially for Mary, that I was racked up like this. But, strangely, I didn't feel a need to talk with her about it because I knew her well enough to know that she would be totally honest with me and with herself. If she was with me, it was because she wanted to be with me, because she still loved me, not because she felt pity for me or had some misplaced sense of duty. And I also knew that when she felt that she could no longer stand it or that she didn't love me, she would leave. But for the moment I was confident—confident of the fight in her and of the love we shared.

I fell into a half sleep. I dreamed I was holding Mary. It was more than a dream. It was so real I could actually feel her. She was in bed with me. I was in a half-sitting position and she was lying against my shoulder. We kissed. I touched her. I could smell her hair and body. I could feel her softness as I stroked her hair. Her skin was wet and the odors of our sweat commingled in the hot room. We kissed some more, and I held her closely and stroked her head. I kept telling her that everything was going to be okay and she believed me. We both believed it. I woke up drenched in sweat. I was alone except for Mike in the next bed.

During the past week or so I would have worked on the new show. I knew from my secretary, who'd come out to visit, that it wasn't going well. I'd had a lot of ideas that I thought would help make it work. But now I didn't care. Now it was the weekend, and if I hadn't taken that wave, we'd be back out there at the beach. I would have gotten up and gone to town to buy a newspaper and whatever we needed for breakfast. Then I would have gone to the beach and jogged along the hard sand at the water's edge. If it was really hot, I would have gone into the ocean for a short swim, and then I would have gone back to the house to wake Mary to have some breakfast together before heading for a day on the beach.

But I wasn't having breakfast with Mary. I was staring up at the perforated tiles on the ceiling above my head in the Southampton Hospital. I was lying there sweating my ass off, waiting for the morning shift to come on, for a new hospital day to begin, for somebody to feed me my breakfast. I really was like a baby. If there was no return, I'd probably need a full-time nurse to care for me. And where I had been confident just half an hour before of Mary's and my love, I now couldn't imagine her staying with me. I couldn't imagine her changing the catheter, giving me suppositories, pushing me around in a wheelchair.

I thought of the future and of being alone. Maybe I could teach, not in New York—how could I get around the city in a wheelchair? Maybe the University of Miami, or somewhere in California—Pomona or Mills. I pictured the campus and being pushed to class and home again. I thought of what Joe and the nurses said about the spinal injury cases they knew. "Why, he can even drive a car. You know, hand controls." So I pictured myself driving, lifting myself up out of the car, being pushed up and down special ramps.

CHAPTER 12

MARY

I watched Jack sleep. The blood around the tongs was dry and black, and the hair around his ears was already beginning to grow back. His lips had a sticky film over them, and he smelled of sleep. His eyes fluttered lightly, and I wondered what he was dreaming. I looked over his body, big and silent, and tried to convince myself that he really couldn't move. I pinched his thigh, secretly hoping that it would twitch or slide away from my touch. But it stayed in place, heavy and dead. His chest didn't move with breathing, and his mouth was slightly open, the corners cracked and dry.

I longed for the time when Jack and I would be in control of our lives without the advice or hopes of all those who now surrounded us. I thought of suicide, of helping Jack kill himself. I wondered how we'd do it. Then I thought what if it had been the other way around. Maybe it would have been better, at least easier. I remembered the slow, measured words of Sengstaken when I asked him if Jack and I would be able to make love. "Jack will be able to get some kind of erection, but he won't feel anything. . . . You will have to be the active partner." What about children, could we still have children? "Yes, he could still ejaculate. Many paraplegics have children. . . ." The words rushed in front of my eyes like ticker tape. The memory of that first mention of "paraplegic" and the sickening effect it had had on me returned. If I had been the one, if I were paralyzed, I could still be made love to. I could still have a baby. I didn't think about the pain of having holes drilled into my head. All cosmetic, all vanity.

I stopped projecting. It hadn't happened to me. It had happened to a part of me, to the one person from whom I didn't want to separate myself. I wondered why the same thoughts didn't frighten me when I realized it *was* happening to Jack. I didn't project about us. I knew from the moment I said I wanted Jack to live that the future couldn't be tampered with, that what lay ahead nobody could know. Jack opened his eyes and ran his tongue over his mouth. It almost seemed a miracle that he was alive, that he was not a stranger.

Jack smiled at me, and for a moment I was reminded of the lazy, happy smiles that spread with yawns over our faces when we used to wake up together in the same bed.

"How you feeling, baby?" he said. "Come here and kiss me."

We kissed and I could tell that Jack was beginning to smell like the clean but stagnant air of the hospital. There was no odor of sweat, no smell of dirt, no overpowering scent of perfumed disinfectant. Just a different smell, one of inactivity, of no sun and no fresh air.

"How did you sleep?" I asked.

"Okay. I had some bad dreams, but I slept soundly from around five till eight. . . . What about you?"

"Pretty well, I guess. I don't have sleep problems. It's just strange sleeping alone. . . . Oh, Jack, I miss you so." I rested my head on his chest and closed my eyes. I felt him rub his arms over my hair. We didn't speak, and I wanted to crawl up onto that skinny frame and lie down with him.

Then a mousy girl in a pink nurse's aide uniform wheeled in a tray filled with aluminum-covered dishes. I timidly removed a sweaty cover and stared at Jack's lunch—a ham-and-cheese sandwich on Tip-Top Bread, suffocated by steam. Off came another cover—iceberg lettuce, topped with some tired slices of tomato, the whole salad limp and lukewarm. Dessert was a piece of cake and some Del Monte pears. Every meal began with a large glass of cranberry juice, which cleaned out Jack's kidneys and staved off infection. I broke the sandwich into quarters and began feeding it to Jack. The salad, dripping with neon-orange dressing, required more care. I had to cup one hand under the other to avoid splattering Jack's face with the sticky liquid. Jack and I began to laugh. The whole operation seemed so ridiculous that neither of us could have stood it without laughing.

Jack was usually turned onto his stomach shortly after lunch. I was just beginning to be able to bear looking at this procedure without feeling panic or nausea. I knew how painful it had been a week before, and the sound of Jack's cries made me shiver with fear and anger and frustration because I knew there was nothing I could do to stop it. Now he gave the nurses instructions, and they did their best to follow them.

The moment they turned him, I froze. Reflexively I waited for him to cry out in pain, even though he hadn't for almost a week.

As he lay on his stomach, Jack's back still looked muscular and tan. A bandage covered the incision which ran almost seven inches from the nape of his neck down his back. I'd expected a much larger bandage and a meaner-looking scar, but the surgeons cut into Jack with such artistry that the skin was healing perfectly and it looked as if someone had taken a delicate brush and painted a straight line down the center of his back.

Jack had fallen asleep again. I watched his belly rise and fall with the quiet rhythms of sleep. He lay perfectly still, never twitched or jerked. It was as if his dreams were tied down by the same invisible net that immobilized his body. At times I felt I was guarding him, protecting him from noise and sudden awakening. I'd look at his body and wonder if he'd ever move again. What does it feel like to be paralyzed, I thought in the silence of that muggy room. I tried to keep my hand in one position and pick up a paper cup. Like Jack, I'd bend my wrist to open my fingers and then bend it back to tighten my hold. But there was no way I could know or understand or feel what Jack was going through. As I started to lift the cup, I invariably felt the muscles in my fingers grip the cup in complete defiance of my simulated paralysis. With the tiniest effort, I would crush the cup with one hand into a waxy ball and throw it into a trash basket on the other side of the room.

The Willises had finally moved into a house of their own. For the first emergency nights both families had lived together; Libbie and Lou slept upstairs, as did Dick and Cece. I slept with my mother after my father returned to New York, and John slept on the living-room floor. We were still eating numerous meals together, but even that was difficult. The accident had pulled everyone together, but we couldn't really feel close. It was as if we had been lassoed and were beginning to feel the burn of the rope. There was a growing need for privacy, for being able to grieve with our own clan.

It was the first meal in a week that the two families hadn't been together. I stared at the food in front of me. My mother had done all the work, and I'd been called to the table from a nap upstairs. I managed to finish some chicken and a few teaspoons of rice, and though I could feel the food land hard somewhere in my stomach, I felt I had eaten nothing. At one point during the meal I realized that my eyes were riveted on the chicken neck which someone had picked clean. I could see the vertebrae and the exposed slippery cord that ran through it. So that's what it looks like a little. The connection both revolted and fascinated me.

I walked into the bedroom that had been Jack's and mine just a while before. I climbed up on the bed, which faced a long mirror, and stared at my image, no longer comforted by my lingering suntan, but cynically amused by my loneliness. "What a waste," I said to myself. "I thought I'd finally made it. I'd found the right guy."

Mama came into the room and immediately looked to see if I was crying. She sat down on the bed and took my hand. Before she could say anything and despite her efforts to hold back the tears, she started to weep. She tried to stifle her sobs with a Kleenex she had pulled from the sleeve of her sweater, but she was too exhausted to control herself, and I wished she would stop trying to be so strong. "Cry, Mama, go ahead. Let it all out," I said, wrapping my arms around her.

"It's so unfair." She shook her head. "You're so young and beautiful. . . ." And then she stopped herself, embarrassed to say what was really on her mind. She took a deep breath. "I shouldn't be crying. I'm your mother. I should be comforting you."

"But you are comforting me. Don't hold back. Talk it out. Then you'll feel better."

My coaxing seemed to work, and Mama let herself cry freely. For a moment I realized we were more than a mother and daughter grieving together. We were two women who understood each other because we knew what it was to love a man so deeply.

Mama looked at me and tried to brace herself against more tears. "If Jack doesn't improve, he won't want you to . . . " She stopped.

"To marry him," I finished her sentence. "We're not there yet, Mama. We don't have to decide anything now."

The next day I hesitated before entering Jack's room. At first I thought he was asleep, but then I saw that his eyes were open and that he was staring at the ceiling.

I walked over to his bed and kissed him. His eyes looked cloudy and his mouth was grimly set. I put my hand on his forehead. "What's the matter, Jack? What are you thinking about?" I asked, and tried to ignore the mounting queasiness of fear. There was a sadness, a depression, I'd never seen in him before. But I saw it now. I saw it in his eyes. Not terror, not self-pity, but the dull gnawing of insecurity, the deep bruise of doubt.

"What are you thinking?" I asked. "Tell me."

"What if I don't get return?" Jack said in a monotone, still staring at the ceiling. "They said two to three weeks. It's almost two. I haven't let it get me down. This is the first time I've really been depressed."

I realized how contagious fear was, how, as a child, the littlest hint of parental panic had terrified me, made me feel lost and dizzy. I tried to fight the dizziness, the swirling feelings of doubt and questioning. I couldn't give in. We couldn't give in. "Jack. I don't know what will happen. It will never be the same. No, we've both changed, even though I can't say how. But the most important is us. Not letting our personalities change. It's all now, all present. All I know is I love you now, that I'm here, not because it's my duty, but because I want to be here. Because I want us. I can't think about the way we were. What's the point? You can't give in to the ifs—if you hadn't taken that wave, if I hadn't wanted to go in for that swim, if you don't get return."

"But we have changed," Jack said. "You said we've changed. What do you mean, not let our personalities change?"

I knew what I was thinking. I was fighting, fighting back the fear. If Jack had doubts, they infected me. "I mean if our life together became unbearable, unhappy, joyless, I couldn't hide it from you. I wouldn't hide it from you. I mean, we can't ever play games. We never have. I can't imagine being your nurse, living a life without sex. But we've had no sex for weeks, and if someone had told me two months ago that I wouldn't make love for two days, much less two weeks, I'd have told them they were crazy. Don't you see, Jack? Maybe one day I won't love you, but now I can't imagine that because I do love you. I don't see you as a cripple because you don't see yourself as a cripple. That's what I mean about personalities changing. Maybe we won't make it. Maybe one day I'll leave you or you'll want me to go, but that thought now makes me sick. If we change, we'll be two different people. And we'll know. But now I don't know those people. I can't even imagine them."

I felt flushed and excited. It was the fight that saved me from the dejection of hopelessness. It was the deep conviction that comes from loving someone that made me rebel against the odds. Jack was smiling at me and I smiled back. What a crazy time to feel lucky, to feel proud and strong.

CHAPTER 13

JACK

I was so involved with myself that Mary was really the only person to whom I could talk. Mike and I kidded a lot and tentatively got to know each other, but we didn't really talk. And there just wasn't that much I could say to either Mary's or my family.

My parents would ask me how I was coming along, and when I said nothing was happening, they tried to hide their disappointment. The questions annoyed me. It was a reminder that nothing had happened so far. I began shutting them out in self-defense. Mary and I were building our own world, always hoping for the best, but quietly preparing for the worst.

I knew how difficult it was for my parents. I could tell they were confused. They'd flown across country to be with me, and when they arrived, they'd found there was not much they could do. Yet just having them there was good for me, though in actual fact I saw them very little. They would drop by the hospital at lunchtime with my favorite sandwich and would come by after dinner, usually with a malted or snack of some kind. It wasn't lack of imagination that kept them from doing more; it was that there was nothing else I wanted them to do.

Mary's parents were different. Obviously they felt awful about my personal tragedy. They had canceled their trip to Europe and had moved into our farmhouse to be with Mary and to help me. Norman had done everything he could to make sure I got the best care possible. Like my parents, they were with me almost every day. But there was the difference in attitude. My father was eternally, overwhelmingly confident, my mother had quiet hope (shored up completely by my father), and I felt Mary's parents were pessimistic, a pessimism born of a sense of reality.

They had to be thinking about Mary's happiness first. I wasn't their son. I was the guy whom they hardly knew, who was engaged to be married to their daughter. And who now, according to the doctors, was almost certain to be paralyzed for the rest of his life. Who could blame them, I thought, if they thought how much better it would be if Mary and I split up. And that the sooner she saw this and started a new life of her own, the better. I felt they had to be thinking that. Hell, I was thinking it.

I thought about our breaking up, but I never reached any conclusions. I still hoped for return. If I didn't get it, then we would have to decide what to do. But until that time, there was an unspoken agreement between us not to discuss either our past, which would have been too painful, or our future, which seemed too ominous. I tried to examine my feelings. Did I feel guilty about the accident? No. Did I feel guilty about Mary? No. Was I dependent on her? Yes. Was I in any way encouraging her to stay by me by making her feel guilty or playing on her sympathies? No. So the hell with it, I thought. I was giving myself from two to four weeks to see if I would get any return. All my judgments and decisions were suspended while we waited out that time together.

One morning just before the two weeks were up, Joe went through his usual flexing, twisting, and bending of my limbs. "Try to move your toes," he said.

I tried. "I can't."

He told me to concentrate. "Think about your toes. You've somehow got to get the message down from your head through your central nervous system to your toes. Just try. Keep on trying."

I closed my eyes and concentrated as hard as I could on my toes. I felt nothing and nothing happened. It was as though my head were separated from my body. When I was a kid my father tried to teach me to wiggle my ears. I'd sit for hours, jiggling my scalp, crinkling my nose and forehead to no avail. But one day I felt something, and I realized I had to reach farther back for my ears. I stopped wiggling my scalp and concentrated on my ears. All of a sudden they wiggled. I now tried to concentrate on exactly the muscle I wanted to move. I tried to move my toes for a couple of minutes but still felt nothing. Finally Joe told me to relax and walked out of the room.

A few minutes later I tried to move my toes again. I tried to get a mental picture of the nerve circuitry, to picture the location of my toe. Suddenly I heard Mike hollering. "Your toe, your big toe is moving!" It was. I could feel the connection. I couldn't see it, but if I concentrated, I could will it to move. Mike called Joe back into the room, and I moved it for him. Then all the nurses crowded into the room for a look.

"What does it mean?" I asked Joe.

"I don't know," Joe said, controlling the excitement I could hear in his voice. "You don't know. Don't kid yourself. Waiting is the name of the game. I can't predict what will happen. Just keep trying to move that toe. We'll see. We'll wait and see."

CHAPTER 14

MARY

Jack gave me a warm, glowing smile. "I have a surprise for you," he said, almost laughing.

"What? What's going on around here?" I asked.

"I can move my toe," Jack said. "I moved it late last night. . . ."

"What?" I said, not believing. "How? How did it happen? Tell me. Tell me everything."

"Joe asked me to try to concentrate on moving my toes. I tried. Shit. I broke my ass, but nothing happened. Then, just as he was out of the room, Mike started yelling. 'It's moving. Your toe is wiggling.'"

I listened, not believing. I was laughing at the ridiculousness, the hugeness, the sheer beauty of a wiggling toe. "Tell me again. Tell me everything that happened."

"I just told you." Jack was laughing too. "I called Joe back into my room and really concentrated, and he saw it move. I thought he was going to die. 'You did it,' he screamed. 'You wiggled your toe.' Mary, it's all so crazy. I can't see my feet, but I can tell when the toe moves. It's like I'm making a connection. I can't explain it."

I ran around to the foot of Jack's bed. His feet were propped up against a board. "Let me see. See if you can do it again."

"You have to move the board first," Jack said excitedly.

I stared at Jack's feet. I was concentrating so hard that my eyes hurt. I was scared to look at his face for fear of missing the sight of his toe moving. Nothing happened. And then it happened. The big toe on his left foot made a little bow and I could hear myself yelp with glee. "Oh, my God. It moved. Oh, Jack. You really moved it. Do it again. Let me see it again." I stared hard at his foot, hardly breathing, believing that silence would somehow help him to do it again. I watched that foot, the way a crowd at a circus watches a tightrope walker, silently praying, immersed in excitement and fear.

"I'm not moving it, am I?" Jack said, staring up at the ceiling.

"No. It's not moving."

"There it goes," Jack said, his eyes wide with joy, his whole face proud with accomplishment.

"You're right. Oh, Jack. You moved it again. I saw it. I really saw it. Tell me again what happened. Tell me what it all means."

"Well, you know Joe," Jack said with a smirk. "He said it might mean that I'm beginning to get return and that more will follow. But it might just be that I can wiggle my toe and that's it."

"He doesn't say more than that?" I asked.

"No."

I wanted to run home to tell everyone what had happened. "What can we tell your parents and mine?" I asked Jack.

"I guess all you can tell them is that I can move my big toe."

My mother was in the kitchen preparing lunch. I burst into the house like the kid who has no cavities in the Crest commercial. "Jack moved his toe. Papa? Did you hear? Jack can move his big toe."

They were happy but not jubilant. Their enthusiasm was guarded, and I felt the same kind of letdown one feels after telling a Great Joke which elicits only a polite chuckle instead of a belly laugh. "But it really is great news," I said to myself. "I just didn't tell it right."

I couldn't tell what it was in their eyes that disappointed me, made me sink with insecurity. I realized that I was a little girl again and that realization depressed me. I needed to please them. I needed the kind of affirmation I hadn't needed in years. I knew how fond they were of Jack, but that affection was measured by my happiness. I remembered with amusement my mother's reaction to my last boyfriend. She seemed to like him a great deal until we broke up. "I never liked that guy," she said. "I always had a feeling he was a neurotic no-goodnik." It was as though I were viewing the movement of that toe through the magnifying lens of a telescope where everything looked big and soft around the edges, while they were viewing it all through the long lens where the same objects looked razor-sharp and far away.

I didn't dare be hopeful. If I let myself think about how wonderful it would be if Jack's legs continued to come back and if he might walk again someday, I was overwhelmed by a terrible dread that some unseen force would punish me for even thinking those happy thoughts. Indulging in sanguine fantasy was a terrifying setup for disappointment. Wishing became synonymous with bad luck—"if I think about it or want it, it won't happen." I was vulnerable again.

As I left the hospital every night, I looked up at the sky and picked out the biggest and most glittering star. I would try not to blink, to keep my eyes glued to the flickering light for as long as it took me to make my wish. "Oh, please, let everything be okay. Let Jack walk again, let us be able to make love, let us be able to have babies, let him be able to use his hands." If people passed me and saw me mumbling to myself, straining my neck and staring transfixed at the sky, I didn't care. I wasn't even aware of them.

CHAPTER 15

JACK

Every chance I got I tried to wiggle my toe. Sometimes it worked, sometimes it didn't. I was stretched out flat on the frame and couldn't raise my head to see my feet, but I knew it when I moved my toe. I'd test myself by checking with Mike or Mary. I could tell when I made a connection, no matter how weak. Somewhere inside my spinal cord there was a bruised nerve or ganglion that was healing, and if I concentrated I could locate it and send a message from my brain down through the cord into the muscle that controlled my toe. And even if the muscle was tired and my toe didn't move, I knew I was sending the message down that single live passage, because somehow I "felt" it.

The night I first moved my toe, my legs began doing a St. Vitus's dance, as if they were possessed. I would lie there, my legs outstretched, perfectly straight, and then one leg or the other would jump. Sometimes just a foot moved; other times my whole leg would bend at the knee. I'd try to stop it, but I couldn't. Then I'd try to take advantage of the involuntary motion to move my legs at will. But I couldn't do that either. The movement kept me up most of the night.

Joe didn't know what caused it, and he didn't know whether it really meant anything. It still excited me because, even if it was involuntary, at least I was moving. But days passed, and nothing else seemed to be returning. I had only sporadic control of my toe, and that was really hit-or-miss. The meagerness of the return began to get me down. Joe was right. I couldn't expect anything.

For a few days I thought I'd been getting feeling in my hands. One night I thought I could move them a little. I thought I could pinch my thumb and forefinger together. I showed Joe. He grabbed my wrist and held it tightly. Then he told me to try to bend the forefinger. I couldn't. "Okay," I admitted. "I can't do it. I guess I was kidding myself, but I do think I'm getting feeling back in my right hand."

Joe just laughed. "I think you're bulling me."

He was right. I had been kidding him and myself. There was no more feeling in my hands. I began to get depressed again. Mary, too, I could tell, was disappointed, but she never said anything about it. She never asked if there was any more return. She knew I'd tell her.

One afternoon I was lying on my stomach when my father came barging into my room. He was full of enthusiasm because of the movement in my toe. I was depressed and feeling sorry for myself because there'd been no recent return. He wanted to hear all about the return, but I just turned him off by telling him that I was glad to see him but that it was too hard for me to talk on my stomach. Anyway, I wanted to sleep. I told him I'd see him that night.

When he and my mother came back to visit that night, I was talking with Mary and her younger sister, Annie, who had recently returned from Europe. My father prowled around them like a trapped animal, impatient and angry. Finally I asked everyone but him to leave. He asked me how I felt and immediately wanted to see me move my toe. His enthusiasm and optimism annoyed me. I knew it shouldn't, but I couldn't help it.

"Look," I said angrily. "You can't get too excited. It's not realistic. Just because I've got a couple of muscles doesn't mean I'll get any more. I may never walk again, and you and Mom have got to accept that. Calm down. You're not helping anybody. I may be in a chair the rest of my life. Don't you understand that?"

He apologized for pacing the room and said it was just because he was so concerned about me. After he left, I lay there thinking about him and realized I'd never really explained anything to him, had never shown him how I could move. I'd shut him out.

He came back in the next day as if nothing had happened the night before. "Hiya, Jacko. How're you feeling?"

"Dad, I've been thinking about last night. Let me explain to you what I know. If the cord isn't torn, the reason I can't move is that it's badly bruised and swollen. That's putting pressure on the nerves. It may take up to four weeks for that swelling to go down. Understand?"

He nodded.

"But we don't know whether the cord was torn or how badly it was bruised. So we're just waiting. The toe coming back is a good sign, because it means that at least one nerve is intact. But it's possible that that's the only nerve or that there are just a few others. Nobody knows."

I realized I was lecturing, but I couldn't help it. He had to be made to understand. "Mary and I are hopeful, Dad. We really are. But we're afraid to get too hopeful because we've got to be prepared for the worst. We've got to live each day as it comes. I'd go crazy if I lay here and kept asking myself why there wasn't more return. And Mary would go crazy if she got up every day expecting something to happen and it didn't. I'm trying. I'm trying all the time to make connections. And I'm hopeful. And I'll tell you as soon as something does happen. In the meantime all we can do is keep our cool, and you've got to understand that."

He nodded, his blue eyes sparkling. I knew I was getting through.

A couple of days later Joe came into my room while I was over on my stomach. He bent my right leg up from the knee and then down again, taking me through the range of motion exercises he usually performed in the mornings. Then he grasped my foot and swiveled the ankle, first to the right and then to the left. "Okay, move your toe," he said.

I tried. I concentrated on the toe on my right foot, the one that had never moved. Nothing happened.

"Relax," he said. "Try moving the left toe."

I tried and felt it move slightly.

"Good," he said, and then bent my left leg at the knee. As he started to lower it, I tried to resist him. I thought I'd been able to resist Clive a few times but was never sure. And I could never do it for Joe. But this time I felt something. Joe was pulling my leg down and I *was* resisting him, I was consciously holding my leg up.

"Are you trying to do that?" he said.

I could only grunt "yes," I was concentrating so hard on holding my leg back.

"Relax," Joe ordered, and set my leg down on the frame. Then he bent it up again. "Okay, I'm going to pull the leg down and you try to hold it back." He gripped my ankle with one hand and placed his other hand behind my knee. Slowly but steadily he began to pull my leg down toward the frame.

I concentrated on my legs and held back with everything I had. Slowly but steadily he was forcing my leg down, but I was resisting him—I could feel it. And then Joe slapped my leg on the frame.

"I felt it," Joe cried. "I felt it. I could see it flex. You've got your hamstring. You've got it." He ran outside and called in the nurse. "Watch," he said and lifted my leg. I felt him slowly push my leg down toward the bed, and I held back.

"Look. Look," he cried. "The hamstring. It's quivering."

I resisted until I couldn't any longer and let my leg fall. I lay there staring down at the floor, totally exhausted. Joe was laughing, and I could hear the nurse laughing with him.

"You've got it. You've got your hamstring. I saw it quiver. It's only a quiver, but it's a beginning, Jack, it's a real beginning."

I lay awake for another hour and said to myself over and over, "I'm going to walk. I know I'm going to walk."

CHAPTER 16

MARY

W hat did you say? You moved your leg? The whole leg?"
Jack was laughing as he described what had happened the night before. "My hamstring. Joe screamed about how I was resisting him. And then he said he could feel the muscle behind my knee. He could feel it quiver." Jack looked like he was going to cry. His lips trembled and his eyes filled with tears. He never said the word "walk," but that's what we both were thinking. This was more than a toe, the faint hint of life; this was a whole leg, a real promise. I wanted to hear it described again, just as I had when Jack first moved his toe. Hearing it repeated was like rereading an especially marvelous chapter in a book.

"He's going to walk," I thought to myself. "I bet he's really going to walk." And then I felt like weeping, as much from my recurrent, superstitious fear that because I'd said it out loud I had tempted fate, as from joy. I wrapped my arms around Jack's body and kissed him. I pressed myself against him, careful not to hit the tongs with my arms, nervous about jerking his neck in my desire to be physically close to him. I felt Jack awkwardly trying to caress my back and hair. We were both laughing and crying.

"Can I feel the muscle?" I asked, walking down to the end of Jack's bed. I pulled the sheet back and removed the board which braced Jack's feet, almost black with the dead skin of old sunburn. His right leg began to shake violently like a machine gun when it's being fired.

"A spasm," Jack said, and waited for the jerky movement to subside.

I slid my right arm underneath Jack's left leg and lifted it. It felt heavy and sinewy as I awkwardly tried to hold the back of his knee in my hand. I was shocked at how thin his legs were.

"Grab my ankle with your left hand," Jack ordered. "That's it. Now I'm going to try to push down, but don't you move."

"Okay, I'm ready when you are," I said, and watched Jack's face strain and redden in effort. Then I felt a delicate flutter in his leg, as though the muscle beneath the smooth skin behind his knee had whispered to me. "I felt it! I felt it move!" I almost cried the words.

As I drove home for lunch, I realized I was happy, actually happy. I knew that our close friends, the Wardenburgs, were coming out to visit, and I couldn't wait to tell them the good news. Jack had known Fred for ten years and had made his first film with him. I also knew that despite my parents' quiet pessimism they, too, would be happy.

I saw Chris Wardenburg holding her baby, Jason, on her lap. She was sitting on the lawn talking with my mother. I ran over to them, bursting with excitement. "I have wonderful news," I said, bending over to kiss Chris and the baby. "Jack moved his leg last night. He can move his left leg."

Both Chris and Fred were anxious to see Jack, but I sensed they were also frightened. They had no idea what to expect and, like so many friends who had been in touch only by phone, were still stunned by the first horrible reports.

Jason wasn't allowed in the hospital, so Fred stayed with him while Chris and I went in to see Jack. I went in first to make sure Jack wasn't asleep. I beckoned to Chris to come in, and she hesitated at the door as though she wanted to turn and run. But Jack's face lit up with a huge grin when he saw her, and Chris seemed pulled to him like a magnet. She bent over and kissed him.

"You look great," Jack said, completely at ease, as though he were lying on the beach or sitting in the Wardenburgs' living room in Brooklyn.

"Oh, I'm so glad we finally got here," Chris said almost in a whisper, a hospital whisper. I could tell she was upset by the tongs and Jack's pallor, but also that she really was happy to see him. I realized how strange the dark, claustrophobic room must have felt to Chris . . . to me?

Chris stayed only a short time. She said she'd wait outside the front entrance of the hospital. I told her I'd join her shortly.

"I know how badly Fred wants to see you, Jack," she said. "I'll come back. But for now I think he should have some time with you."

I watched Chris leave. I couldn't tell what she was feeling, but I knew she was confused. She must have forgotten what I had said about good news—the beginning of return—the moment she saw Jack. She must have seen only human devastation, for to the uninitiated eye Jack must have looked devastated, physically destroyed.

I waited for Fred to come in before going out to join Chris and the baby. I guessed she would want to be alone for a few minutes. Fred was less timorous and clasped Jack's hand in his. "I hear you moved a leg," Fred said. "That's great, really great."

"Not really the leg," Jack said, "just the hamstring, but it's a beginning."

"I'll leave you two alone for a while," I said, and went out into the sunny day to sit with Chris and Jason.

"What's going to happen with Jack?" Chris asked.

"Seeing him really upset you, didn't it?" I said, trying to sound understanding. I didn't want Chris to feel embarrassed or ashamed, and yet I was disappointed that Jack obviously looked so bad to her.

"I guess it did. It took a lot out of me. I feel physically drained. What a joke that *I* feel tired! Oh, I hate myself for that."

"Don't hate yourself," I said, laughing. "What did you expect? I'm with Jack every day. I'm not aware of the change. I don't know what's going to happen. Neither of us does. Originally the doctors said he'd never walk again, but now I'm not so sure. To tell you the truth, Chris, we don't talk about what we're going to do . . . because we just don't know."

The despondency many people felt after seeing Jack came simply from a lack of preparation to deal either emotionally or imaginatively with all the horrors Jack was dealing with. Every individual had his own secret dread, and I discovered that Jack became a weird human mirror to their deepest emotions and nightmares. It hadn't happened to them . . . yet. Ironically, the dread and threat of its happening to Jack was no longer. Strangely, he was freer than the rest. He had been reduced to the most basic honesty, to the purest openness . . . and many people weren't prepared for that. They came wanting to help, and left realizing that Jack had helped them, that in some strange way they had learned something new about themselves. They came expecting to listen, to be a shoulder to cry on, and left aware that they had done all the talking, all the confessing.

I went back to Jack's room. Fred and he were talking, and Mike was drunkenly raving in the background, high from his shot of Demerol. As I approached Fred and Jack, I noticed how big Fred looked. I'd known before the accident that they were about the same size, but now Fred seemed a giant. He was wearing a short-sleeved pullover, and I noticed how thick his forearms were. I had never thought I was particularly sexually attracted to him, but for a moment, seeing him standing next to Jack, I felt something stir and realized that I was reacting to the sight of a healthy man's body.

I felt embarrassed and frightened. I tried not to look at Fred in comparison to Jack. But I couldn't keep my eyes from darting back and forth between them. I saw Jack's thinness and pallor more clearly. I simply hadn't noticed the greasiness of his hair and the milky overcast of his eyes. For the first time I saw how much weight he'd lost (it was more than twenty-five pounds). It was as though his whole body had shrunk a size, like a sweater that is accidentally thrown into the washing machine and comes out familiar but totally misshapen. I would push the thoughts out of my head. I wasn't ready to deal with them. I wasn't even ready to acknowledge the repressed doubts and hidden fears. For the first time since the accident the outside world had squeezed its way into the limited but protected world of the hospital. For the first time I was seeing and judging Jack through the eyes of the past, and I was shocked by what I saw. Earlier that morning I had been elated by the movement of Jack's leg and had allowed myself the luxury of thinking about his walking. Now, compared to Fred, to normalcy, that movement seemed such a tiny thing.

CHAPTER 17

JACK

It was incredible. I was suddenly being treated like a prize race horse. Nurses kept coming into my room and massaging my legs. And I showed off to everyone.

Fred and Chris Wardenburg visited the hospital the day after I got return in my hamstring, and Mary showed me off as though I were a child prodigy, made me wiggle my toe and had them hold my leg so they could feel the hamstring quiver.

"Gee, that's great," Fred kept saying. But I could tell he was confused by our enthusiasm. I felt he was more upset by what I couldn't move than excited by what I could move. Other friends on their first visits had the same kind of reaction. They hadn't seen me when I couldn't move anything, hadn't spent the three weeks with us in desperate wait. They only saw me as I was—head shaved, tongs in my skull, immobile. They couldn't imagine where I'd been or what an achievement that toe and hamstring were, or what it meant to us.

The next day Joe tried my leg again and said it was a little stronger. I could resist him a little more. He grabbed my ankle and told me to move my foot. I tried to swivel it at the ankle, but I wasn't making a connection. It wasn't moving. I tried thinking about my knee. I tried to think about turning *it*. I tried "right" and then "left," but I wasn't making any connection there either. Then I thought about my heel, and I tried moving *it*. Again, I felt nothing, but Joe said, "You moved it. I think you moved it. Try again." So I thought about my heel again and tried to remember what I had just done. "You did it," he said. "You did it again. I saw it move. Try again." I tried, but nothing more happened.

"Put my leg down, Joe. I'm tired." He put it down and picked up the other foot. But I couldn't make it move so he tried the left one again. "Okay, move your heel," he said. I concentrated on my ankle and heel. "You did it again," he said excitedly. "That muscle is an extension of your hamstring. It all figures. You've got three down and only nine hundred muscles to go."

CHAPTER 18

MARY

After Fred's and Chris's visit with Jack, we went back to the house. "Do you have any idea what's going to happen?" Fred said. "What have the doctors said about sex? Do they think Jack'll be able to screw?"

I was shocked by his directness but tried to hide my feelings. "They say we'll be able to," I said. "But they don't know about children. . . . It's still too early to know anything definitely."

I felt Fred was freer to question me than he was Jack, and I couldn't completely blame him for his curiosity. Sex was probably the first thing everyone wondered about. The question he posed with uninhibited candor presumed a separation or distance between Jack and me, as though I were an objective bystander who could comment coolly on the fate of his friend. But I wasn't an outsider. I was part of that fate, part of the answer to these questions. "Will he be able to screw?" meant will I be able to screw. What would happen to Jack was what would happen to me.

I tried not to be angry with Fred, who, I knew, was asking these questions out of love and concern. Anyway, I reacted more violently to people who did a bad job of suppressing the same questions, like the mother of a friend who asked whether we were still planning on getting married. "What do you mean?" I said.

"Well—" she stuttered. "It's such a big decision."

"We're not rushing into it, if that's what you mean."

At least Fred came right out with it, like a child greedy for knowledge and understanding. But I realized I was more sensitive to the questions about sex than I had been earlier. Much more sensitive.

CHAPTER 19

JACK

Though I never mentioned it to Mary, I was worried about the catheter. Did it mean I would never have control over my bladder? Could it do permanent damage? And most important, how had the accident affected my reproductive organs?

Now that it looked as if my leg was coming back, what worried me most was sex. I could imagine a relationship where we couldn't have children. It would be disappointing, but we could always adopt kids. But I couldn't imagine a relationship without sex. It was so much a part of us.

Joe asked a urologist, a Dr. Weir, to examine me. The night he was expected I was tense. I wanted to know everything, but I was also afraid the news would be bad.

Dr. Weir came into my room pushing a rack with a half-dozen bottles suspended from it. The first thing he did was push his finger hard up into my scrotum.

"Does that hurt?" he asked.

"Hell, yes, it hurts."

Then he stuck my scrotum with a pin. I felt that, too. I was quietly thankful for the pain. Then he stuck me around my thighs and belly. It all felt dull. I could feel the pressure of the pin sticking me but felt no pain.

"The long nerves that run down into the penis and the prostate are intact," he said.

That's probably why I can move one leg, I thought. But does that mean if I can't move the other leg, there are nerves that have been severed?

"How come I have sensation in my penis and scrotum but not over the rest of my body?" I asked.

"I don't know. Each case is different," he interrupted my thoughts. "You know I was once paraplegic,"

"You were?"

"I caught a bullet in the spine in Korea."

"But you're fine. You can walk beautifully."

"I've still got a brace on my leg, and I limp a little."

I hadn't noticed the limp. I still couldn't detect it. I didn't know what kind of brace he had or even what it did. He was up and about, apparently normal. He was walking.

It was good to know he'd been hurt like me. I knew he understood. But it was also the first time I'd thought of myself as a paraplegic. In fact, I wasn't a paraplegic; I was a quadriplegic. The word numbed me. I suddenly saw myself as I really was.

But maybe I didn't have to be a basket case. My left leg was coming back, and Weir said I could have erections. He said the signs in my genital area were good. I pressed him about paraplegics. Weir laughed. He told me he had a couple of spinal-injury patients. "One of them's a paraplegic," he said. "He's still in a wheelchair, but he's back at work. He can drive a car and gets around pretty well by himself. His sex life is lousy. But I think his problems are as much psychological as physical because I think he's capable of normal sex."

"What about the other guy?"

"He was a quadriplegic like you. He can walk now and has a normal sex life."

"You say I will be able to have erections, but will I be able to ejaculate?"

"It's too early to tell," he said. "And that's much more complex."

"When will I know?"

"You'll have to wait."

CHAPTER 20

MARY

I knew Jack was going to see a urologist, and I was simultaneously anxious for him to have and not to have the prescribed tests. Not knowing was less and less of a comfort as time went on, but the possibility of knowing definitively that our sex life might be finished was unbearable.

"Sex isn't everything," I remembered Joe saying. "Maybe not to you," had been my silent response. Of course sex wasn't everything. But what did that mean?

Luckily I didn't know which day Dr. Weir was coming. Unaware, I walked into Jack's room one morning and saw an extra bottle attached to his bed with a cord leading ominously in the direction of his crotch. Oh, my God, I thought to myself. This is it. It's worse than I imagined.

"The urologist was here late last night," Jack said.

"Well, what happened?" I almost shouted.

"Calm down. I'm telling you. He said he was very hopeful that I'd be able to have erections. He did all these tests, one where he stuck a pin in my balls."

"And you felt it?"

"Fuckin' A I felt it! He said the long nerves to my scrotum, bowels, and penis are intact. . . . But it's still too early to know about ejaculation. That's much more complicated."

I felt myself flush and weaken at the knees. I sat down and took a deep breath, not sure of my reaction to what Jack was telling me. It was neither as bad as I had dreaded nor as good as I had hoped. I wanted it all—erection, ejaculation, perfection. I wanted to be totally reassured that sex would be just as it had been.

"What do you mean, he doesn't know about ejaculation?" I tried to be calm but I knew I sounded accusatory.

"Just what I said. The whole mechanism for ejaculating is very complicated, and there's no way he can test those nerves."

I listened intently as Jack described the series of water tests, pin tests, pressure tests, and temperature tests the doctor had performed. The fuller the description, especially of what Jack was *feeling*, the more hopeful I became.

"What did he say about the catheter? Will they take that out soon? Is it hurting you to leave it in?"

I knew I was being insistent and perhaps asking too many questions, but I couldn't help it. Jack seemed to understand my compulsive need to be reassured. I hated my obsession, my minimally disguised panic. I'd lived through a month not knowing whether Jack would ever move a muscle again. I'd watched the slow and torturous return of his left leg and waited patiently for the progressive stirrings in his right. A month before I'd been able to imagine living with a man in a wheelchair. My idealized picture of us surrounded by children had even been a comfort. But now that picture frightened me.

As I walked out of the hospital toward the parking lot, I saw Joe slamming the door of his car.

"Jack tells me that Weir's report pleased you," I said.

"Yes, it did."

I waited to see if he'd say more—I hoped something reassuring.

"You know, Mary, your feelings about Jack might change. . . . . You can't be too hard on yourself if they do. Jack is going to be a big responsibility, and you're very young."

"Don't all relationships change?" I said, feeling the bile rise in my throat. "And don't you think that Jack and I know this?" I resented Joe's de-personalizing Jack by thinking of him more as a big responsibility than as a man.

"I'm just telling you this for you," Joe said. "Very few people really know what it's like."

"We don't pretend to know," I said. "So there seems no point in worrying now about how I'll feel two months or a year from now. Who would have thought Jack would have come this far three weeks ago?"

"You're right about that," Joe said. "But remember, I was the one who had hope."

"I haven't forgotten," I said. "So why lose it now?"

Joe bit on his pipe and forced a smile. He turned and walked up the steps toward the hospital.

CHAPTER 21

JACK

One day while Mary and Norman were visiting with me, Joe came in. "You need another operation to stabilize your neck," he said. "We'll take some spongy bone from your hip and fuse it to the vertebra that's been damaged in your neck."

"When?" I asked.

"In about ten days. Afterwards I hope we will be able to move you within five or six weeks to a rehabilitation center, depending on how quickly you recover."

The idea of another operation didn't bother me. "It doesn't sound as dangerous as the first operation," I said. "You won't be working so close to the spinal cord."

Joe looked at Norman and then at me. "All operations are dangerous.

73

There's the usual risk of disease and the dangers of anesthesia. But I'll have the top specialists in the field working with me, and we'll cut the risk as much as possible." Joe paused. "But I really have to tell you there have been a number of deaths from this type of operation due to unknown causes."

"What do you mean?" I said. "People you've operated on? How many? What caused it?"

"We don't know what caused it," he repeated. "I've never had it happen to one of my patients. I've just read about it in the medical literature."

I looked at Mary, who was watching me carefully. Norman was looking at Joe but didn't say anything. As he turned to leave the room, Joe said, "Don't worry. We'll take care of you."

"Are you scared?" Mary said.

"Hell, yes, I'm scared." What I didn't say to her was that I was afraid of dying. I'd never thought of dying before the first operation. I wouldn't have thought of it now if Joe hadn't mentioned it. I didn't question the risks in any operation. I figured the doctors knew what they were doing, that the operation was mechanical and by itself not dangerous, and that they were pretty sophisticated in handling post-operative complications. Why did Joe go out of his way to frighten me?

I couldn't sleep, I lay there panicked. I thought about the operation and about death—death from unknown causes. Something doctors had no control over. I was getting angry. He might as well have said, "Don't worry, there's nothing you can do. Thousands of people die in automobile accidents every year."

What the hell did that have to do with me? So the odds were in my favor. They were in my favor when I took the wave. After all, how many people break their necks body-surfing?

CHAPTER 22

MARY

How they would take a tiny piece of bone from Jack's hip and fit it carefully into his cervical spine like a pivotal piece in a jigsaw puzzle fascinated me. I knew all operations were risky, but I was almost smug that this one would be okay.

"There have been a number of deaths from this type of operation due to unknown causes," Joe told Jack as my father and I stood around his bed. I watched Jack's eyes and then looked at Papa, who remained silent. No one said anything for quite some time, but I could feel that my father and I were holding back our anger, our desire to tell Joe what a stupid ass he was to mention death right before Jack was to be operated on. It was at moments like this that the doctor-patient relationship was nothing more than a source of frustration, and I resented Joe as a doctor even though I didn't really dislike him as a person. In fact, I rather liked him when he wasn't trying so hard to be a doctor.

The flat voice of the head nurse came over the loudspeaker: "Visiting hours are now over. All visitors must leave by nine o'clock."

I grabbed Jack's hand and brought it to my lips. I didn't want to leave. I felt helpless to soothe his fear, and seeing it in his eyes made me frightened. "It'll be all right, Jack."

"I know it will, baby. Don't worry. I'll be okay. Give me a kiss and go home and get some rest."

Papa and I walked toward the car. "What do you think about Joe's saying that business about death from unknown causes?" I said.

"He was a dope to say that," my father said in his scratchy, gruff voice. "But he's young and insecure, especially around me. We all know that any time you take a general anesthetic you're risking death, but what's the point of saying it? This operation isn't nearly as dangerous as the first. They won't be working on top of the spinal cord, and Jack's in better shape going into the operation than he was the first time."

"So you're not too worried?" I said, needing to be reassured.

"No," my father said. "It's amazing he's come this far. As long as he keeps improving . . ."

I didn't ask Papa what if he doesn't improve? I didn't want to know what he thought about that.

The alarm went off at six thirty, startling me out of a deep sleep. I could tell that it was going to be a hot day from the fuzziness of the horizon and the heaviness in the air. I didn't linger in bed any more because Jack wasn't there to linger with. And on this morning I wanted to get to the hospital by seven—a full hour before Jack would be wheeled into the operating room.

As I walked into the hospital I was struck by the amount of movement and noise at such an early hour. If I'd been dropped inside those walls with no knowledge of the time of day, I certainly wouldn't have been able to tell whether it were morning, noon, or night. Like a wind-up clock the hospital seemed to run on its own time.

I could tell that Jack had been waiting for me to arrive. He looked tired but alert with anxiety. I could see in his eyes that he was scared. I kissed Jack and felt the dryness of his lips.

"Don't you want something to drink?" I said, forgetting that you couldn't eat or drink before an operation.

Jack looked at me a little angrily. "Yeah, get me a tall gin and tonic—you know they won't let me," he said.

"You're scared, aren't you?" I said.

"Yeah. I've been awake half the night. It's crazy. Last time everyone was scared, and I didn't know it. Now they're all running around like they do every morning—same jokes, same everything, and I'm shitting in my pants."

I held Jack's hand in mine. It felt cold. "It's crazy," I said. "Because I think it's going to be okay, too. I know that's no help, but . . ."

"Yes, it is," Jack said. He looked at me and tried to smile a dry, crack-lipped smile.

Two nurses dressed in green came into the room.

I watched the bed move into the operating room—a frightening, forbidding place to me. I stood dumbly for a while, the way you stand after someone you love boards a plane and you've watched the last traces of exhaust disappear in the sky after take-off.

CHAPTER 23

JACK

The afternoon before the operation they shaved my pubic hair, part of my head, and all of my chest, down to my navel. I was reminded of the hairless male models on the covers of homosexual magazines, but now with my very white skin and skinny body I felt more like a plucked chicken.

Ann, a nurse's aide, came into the room to say hello. "Let me see what you look like, honey," she said as she slid the sheet slowly and sensuously down my body.

"Hey, me too, baby," Mike yelled.

"You get yours later, honey," she promised.

Joe had agreed to let Mary be with me right up to the time of the operation. He also agreed to give me morphine instead of Demerol after I reminded him of my previous bad trip.

I fell asleep and dreamed I was going to be operated on, but first I had to get over a twenty-five-foot wire playground fence. I started to climb over it. When I got to the top and looked down, I froze with fear, unable to move. I just clung to that fence, afraid to go forward or backward. I awoke thinking about the dream and death from "unknown causes." Finally I fell asleep again. When I awoke, Mrs. Swanson—Swanee—was there. "What time is it?" I asked.

"Around two in the morning."

"Can I have some water?"

"Sorry, chief. Nothing to eat or drink until after the operation." She told me that a part-time substitute nurse named Martha, whom Mike and I had dubbed "super-sub," had called to wish me luck and to tell me that she would be in Thursday night to take care of me. Then Swanee bent down and gave me a big kiss on the forehead. "Good luck, chief."

I awoke too early—about six o'clock—and lay there thinking nervously about the operation until Mary came in about seven.

Then they wheeled me out of my room and down to the operating room. Mary walked beside me and kissed me before they pushed me through the big swinging doors into the operating area.

"See you, baby," I said, and we kissed again.

Joe came by and introduced me to Dr. Farrell, who was going to assist him in the operation. Then they went off to have coffee and study my X-rays. A nurse with a check list asked if I had any false teeth or allergies. An aide with a clipboard asked me the same questions. I felt like I was in a Marx Brothers movie. It struck me also that I didn't remember their asking me questions before the first operation, although they must have.

The longer I waited, the more nervous I got. I hated just lying there like a lump, while people were walking by me. I wondered what they thought when they saw me there. Did they think I might die? Did they try to imagine the pain I might feel?

Once I was actually wheeled into the operating room, I felt better. I was now not only part of the scene; I was the centerpiece. Now I could participate, even if my participation was only cooperative. An intravenous tube was stuck in my arm.

"Okay. Now we're going to feed you some oxygen." A rubber mask was put over my mouth and nose. I closed my eyes and took deep breaths.

From a distance I thought I heard Joe talking to me. I tried to push through to him. Clearly I heard him say, "The operation was successful." I think I smiled, and then he said something about my legs which, if I heard, I didn't remember when I finally did come out of the anesthesia and was fully conscious in the Intensive Care unit. But by that time Joe was gone.

I hurt a little. One of the nurses gave me an injection and I felt better, even a little euphoric. The operation was over and I'd come through it successfully. I was almost smug. No thoughts now about death from unknown causes.

CHAPTER 24

MARY

Jack wants you to know that he can still wiggle his toes," a kindly, round-faced nurse told me.

"When will I be able to see him?" I asked.

"He's still pretty groggy. Give him a couple more hours. We'll move him back to his room by then."

I was excited. The operation was over and Jack was alive, wiggling his toes. I saw Joe and ran up to him. He was still wearing his white operating shoes and gown. He was glowing.

"It went beautifully, Mary. He lost very little blood, and Dr. Farrell is very optimistic."

At that moment I felt nothing but love for Joe, and instinctively kissed him on the cheek. He was surprised and pleased. He led me over to a taller man who was also wearing a surgical gown. Dr. Farrell looked older than Joe, and his manner was friendly and relaxed. I held out my hand and he shook it warmly.

"I think Jack's going to make it," he said. "I think he's going to walk. I'm not as sure about his hands—but there's still a good chance they'll come back too."

I felt elated, mesmerized by his positive prognosis. I grabbed his hand. "Thank you so much," I said. "I can't tell you how much I appreciate your help."

Farrell smiled at me. "You don't have to thank me," he said. "Jack's an extraordinary guy. . . . Joe's told me how well you both have been handling this. . . . It's you who should be thanked."

Jack was still half asleep when they wheeled him back into the room. He had a small bandage on the front side of his neck. I found out later that the incision was only two inches long and ran along a natural crease line in his neck. When it healed, the scar would be no more than a large wrinkle in his skin, a vague reminder of hard times.

Jack moaned and tried to move his hand toward his right hip. I gently lifted the sheet and saw a large gauze bandage stuck to his side with adhesive tape. There was some blood on the bandage, but it looked more like red paint than like real blood. I couldn't understand what he was saying. I bent forward to kiss his forehead and to hear him more clearly.

"My throat," he whispered. "My throat is killing me."

"Don't talk," I said. "You'll be fine. Just rest. The operation was a success. You'll be okay."

I offered him a glass of cold water. The straw slipped out of his mouth as he weakly sipped it. As he swallowed, his face tightened with pain, and I remembered my own first excruciating taste of water after my tonsils had been removed ten years before.

I watched Jack fall back to sleep. Mike, too, was sleeping, his mouth open and his head precariously balanced on the edge of his pillow. It was getting dark. The whole day had passed, and I felt strangely removed from time. I wasn't even sure what day of the week it was.

As evening wore into night, Jack's discomfort increased. I stayed by his side as much for my peace of mind as for his comfort. At eight a group of Mike's friends barged into the room. I'd seen them all before. They were always loud, bragging about all the booze they'd drunk, grass they'd smoked, and chicks they'd balled. It hadn't bothered me before—in fact, they'd been something of a diversion. But this night they really got to me; they seemed especially noisy. A small, wiry guy who looked like a spider monkey lurched into Jack's bed. A wave of hatred swept over me, and I wanted to yell but could only stare coldly at him. He apologized meekly. Jack couldn't have felt the bump, but the monkey didn't know that. I drew the curtain around the bed, hoping to block them out. But not seeing them only made their noise sound louder.

"I'll tell them to be quiet," I said. Jack nodded his head.

CHAPTER 25

JACK

When I awoke the euphoria had worn off and I ached all over. They gave me a shot, which helped a little but not much. I felt as though I'd just fought ten rounds with Muhammad Ali. I was aware of a dull ache in my hip where they had taken the bone fragment which was now fused in my neck. I had a terrible, raspy sore throat where they'd placed a tube during the operation, and it hurt me to swallow or even talk. I also felt terribly nauseated.

The next few days were awful. I felt that up to the time of the operation I was beginning to make progress, but that now I was so sick and sore I couldn't stand it. It felt like a real setback, which depressed me, which in turn depressed Mary. Joe said that by Sunday I would feel better. And on Sunday I did feel better, at least well enough to start thinking once again about the future. Now that the fusion was successful Mary and I both wanted to know how much longer I'd have to be in traction and when we could look forward to going to the Rusk Institute for rehabilitation.

The waiting became interminable. The days were long and boring. Now that the danger was past and we thought I'd walk again, Mary finally began to let down and the strain began to show. She looked tired and drawn and began to worry about details, especially money. We already owed $5,000 and were told that the Rusk Institute would cost about $1,000 a week and wasn't covered by Blue Cross. I tried to assure her that it would be okay, that only we mattered, and that we had the rest of our lives to pay off our debts. I wasn't putting on an act just to make her feel better—I really wasn't concerned about money. I had seen death—total paralysis. I had touched bottom. But now I was on my way up again. I didn't know how far I could go, nor could I imagine how hard it would be to return to a somewhat "normal" life. But getting there was the only thing that mattered. I couldn't worry about things like money.

I convinced Mary to spend more time at the beach and to nap instead of coming to be with me at dinnertime. But I was hardly ever alone. If she didn't come herself, she always made sure one of the family, hers or mine, was with me.

The physical therapist I had wasn't working out. He seemed content to take me through a range of motion exercises. He never gave me a real workout. Mary and I began working together on the sly. I showed her how to give me the resistance exercises Joe had taught me. Every day we worked for half an hour on our own. She resisted with her thin body while I pushed and pulled my arms and wrists, left leg and ankle, against her weight.

The exercises did a lot for me; physically they gave me some small sense of well-being. And we saw improvements. Each day I'd be a little stronger than the day before, until one day I'd do something remarkable like let my leg dangle off the side of the frame and then lift it up again by myself.

Or I would lie on my stomach and bend my left leg up at the knee nine or maybe ten times.

One day I suddenly wiggled the toes in my right foot, though the movement was very slight. Then I lost the connection, and for two days I couldn't move them at all. I began to lose confidence and even doubted that I'd ever moved them. But Joe said it was possible that I'd lost contact only temporarily with the nerves and in time would be able to move the foot again.

I spent all my spare time concentrating on those toes, thinking about them, trying to find the nerve circuitry that led to the muscle that could make them move. Slowly I found the nerves and began to gain control over them. I could now wiggle them on command but soon realized that that was all I could do with the right foot.

I was worried but tried not to show it to Mary. The first thing I did every morning was demonstrate to her how much stronger the left leg was getting. There was always a new trick—I'd push against her hand or pull up against her or wiggle my right toes hello. Then one day she picked up my right leg and bent it at the knee. I began pushing it out, the way I had the left leg, and it suddenly straightened out. I had to ask her to be sure. "Did my leg straighten out?"

"Yes," she said.

"Did I do it?"

"You must have. I didn't."

I wanted to try it again immediately to make sure I had done it. I couldn't feel the actual movement, but I was able to straighten the leg again. When Joe came in on rounds, he began playing with my left leg. Then he picked up the right. "Wiggle the toes," he ordered.

"Forget that," I said. "Pick up my leg and bend it at the knee—one hand on my heel and one behind my knee."

Joe got a funny look on his face—the same look Mike had described when I first moved my left leg. He tried other things with my right leg. All of a sudden I had movement in the ankle and calf. "It's there, Joe. I can feel it."

"Thanks for telling me," he said as he kept working my legs. Then he came around to the side of the bed and grabbed my hands. He told me to move my fingers, but I couldn't. There was nothing there. I heard him mumble something, more to himself than to me. "I can't believe they're not going to come back soon," he said.

"What makes you so sure?" I asked.

"I'm not, except that it looks as if you might get it all back."

I realized that was an incredible statement for him to make, but it didn't really excite me. I was now so used to waiting. Also, my hands were last on my personal priority list. I was already teaching myself to pinch by manipulating my wrist. Even if there was no return in my hands, surgery could help. Joe could transfer tendons from my elbows or wrist to my fingers, giving me at least partial use of my hands. What I cared most about now was sex and my legs.

One morning my legs spasmed. I got a terrible cramp as they contorted. I asked Mike to call for a nurse to straighten my legs out. He rang but there was no response, so he began calling for someone. I was getting more cramps. I began to try to move my legs myself. All of a sudden I did it. I lifted my left leg up in the air and bent it at the knee at the same time. Then I moved it to the left and straightened it out and set it down.

I got so excited that I practiced until my leg was too tired to move. If I can do this, I can walk, I thought, because all walking is is picking up your leg and putting it down. After the lights were out, I tried to move my left leg again, and I found I could lift it up, bend the knee, and put it down again. I wondered how long it had been there without my knowing it. What if I hadn't had the spasm and been uncomfortable? Maybe it would have been weeks before I would have discovered it and started using that muscle.

This new discovery made me even more anxious to get out of the hospital and into Rusk. I wanted to find out what muscles I did have. There was no way for me to know the extent of nerve damage to my abdomen, back, or internal organs while I was still in traction and catheterized. I did know I had my hips, however. One day when Mary and I were talking and I was lying on my stomach I decided to experiment and see if I could hump the bed. My movements were crude, my rhythm was off, and I tired quickly. But we were both elated with the promise of what that meant.

"That's it," Mary said excitedly. "Looks pretty sexy to me."

That night I ran my hands under the sheet to my groin and felt where they had shaved my pubic hair. I then ran my fingers up along my body. It was the first time I had done that since the accident. I didn't know why I was doing it, but suddenly I realized I felt a sense of wholeness. For the first time in six weeks I somehow had a sense of my entire body. I felt connected from head to toe. I was no longer a lot of disparate parts. I felt like a person.

With the feeling of wholeness came another phenomenon. The

spasticity that had occurred only in my feet and legs now racked and jerked my entire body. It seemed to begin in my lower back and extend downward through my hips and legs to my feet. I would be lying perfectly still and suddenly my entire body would spasm. I might suddenly jerk and the lower part of my body would kick or lift off the bed, or I would suddenly tense up and straighten out as if somewhere inside me were a coiled steel spring that was being pulled from opposite ends of my body.

For the first time being in traction became a nuisance. As long as I was paralyzed it didn't bother me because I never felt motivated to move. I just didn't feel like going anywhere. Nor did I get uncomfortable if I lay in one position for a long time. But now, lying in traction, fastened by the tongs, became hell. I ached from lying in one position, and I couldn't move to alleviate the pain. And worst of all, I now *wanted* to move, to get up, to go somewhere, and I couldn't.

It seemed an incredible paradox—the better I got the worse I felt, the more I was subject to fits of depression, the more I felt trapped by my environment. I tried sleeping more—something I used to do in college when I was depressed. But when I awoke I still felt tied down and trapped. I remembered a picture of Gulliver tied down by thousands of tiny ropes, his arms at his sides, his neck stretched out. That's how I felt.

CHAPTER 26

MARY

The beaches emptied after Labor Day. A steady stream of cars, piled high with bicycles, boxes, barbecues, and beach gear, had lined the Montauk Highway from Sunday night straight through to Wednesday. Long Island belonged once again to the locals and to a few hangers-on.

We'd received word from the Rusk Institute that a bed would be ready by September 15, and my family was already making plans to leave. Papa and my sister, Annie, would go the week before, and my mother and I would close the house.

Libbie had wanted to stay until we left, but we convinced her that she was needed more in Los Angeles, where Lou had been alone for a month. There was a tearful good-by, mixed with relief on both sides. We were all going home. . . .

My mother and I hung out clean, damp towels on a clothesline. The potatoes had been harvested, and the fields were dusty and dry. One strong breeze and everything was covered with dust. Looking now at those flat, dry fields, it was hard to imagine that they had been green with fat potato plants most of the summer and would be green and fat again.

"Where do you think you'll live when we get back to New York?" my mother asked.

"Live? What do you mean? I'll stay in the apartment." I really didn't understand what she was asking.

"But whose apartment? Yours and Jack's or home?"

Now I understood. There was "home," and there was Jack's and my apartment—and the two were not one and the same, at least not in Mama's eyes.

"I'll live in Jack's and my apartment. Why?"

"I just thought it would be easier for you if you lived with us," my mother said. "You won't have to worry about cooking or keeping house. . . . I just thought it would be nicer, that's all."

"No, Mama. All my things are in our apartment. I really feel that's home. I know it may be difficult, but I'm not too worried. I even look forward to being there."

My mother looked concerned and disappointed. "All right, darling. But you can always change your mind."

I waited a moment outside Jack's room. Clive stood near him and poured a large glob of white lotion on his back. I watched his huge, strong hands work the liquid into Jack's back, slowly and evenly. Jack's ribs showed through his skin, which looked especially pale next to Clive's black hands and forearms. Clive rubbed more lotion into Jack's legs, which were so thin that I was sure Clive could have wrapped his whole hand around the thigh. I watched him lift Jack's leg and bend it at the knee, gently bouncing it back and forth toward Jack's back. The muscle was so tight that I could see it twitch under the smooth skin of Jack's knee.

"Got to keep those muscles loose," Clive said. "Okay, Jack. You bring that leg up without me."

The hamstring muscle began to strain like the taut string of a bow. Clive looked on patiently, excitement and real pride filling his eyes. Jack's leg started to fall to one side.

"Come on, you can do it. Just keep it comin'," Clive said.

Jack struggled silently to keep the leg from falling. Once past the halfway mark, he was all right. I thought I saw the muscles in his lower back begin to share the burden of the leg's weight. He did it. The leg swayed a little but stayed at a firm right angle, the toes pointing toward the ceiling. It seemed so little, but I felt tremendously excited.

I bent down and kissed Jack's shoulder, which was still slippery and sweet with body lotion. Clive was immediately more formal with me in the room. In a way, I wished I'd stayed outside longer. There was a bond of love and unarticulated loyalty between them, the kind of friendship I imagined men share when they're fighting a war together.

"Guess I'd better get you over on your back," Clive said, a smile curling his lips. "Then you two can be more loving." And he broke into an embarrassed giggle. He placed the sheepskins on Jack's back, easily lifted and placed the frame on top of the sheepskins, quickly strapped Jack in tight, and with enormous grace and ease turned the contraption over.

Lying on his back, Jack let his left leg hang over the edge of the bed. "Watch this, Mary," he said and began to swing his leg back and forth, building up momentum with each swing. Then with one big heave and sigh, he let the leg fall back onto the bed.

"When did you discover you could do that?" I said excitedly.

"I've been working on it," Jack said. "I've started to try it with the right, but it's still too weak."

"Let me see it again." As I watched him swing his leg like the weighty pendulum of a big clock, I realized I'd never seen him move so dramatically. Whenever I spoke to Joe or asked him questions, I always saw how far Jack still had to go. Joe could never tell me simply what I wanted to hear—that Jack would walk.

"We still don't know if he has back muscles or how strong his hips are," was Joe's guarded professional response.

But watching Jack now, I didn't think about all the muscles he might not have. I saw movement, real muscle action. When I helped him do his exercises and felt him push against my arm, I felt real pressure, the twinges and jerks of muscles. His legs were alive, and at times like this I felt as though they'd never been dead.

CHAPTER 27

JACK

The harder I pushed Joe to set a firm date, the more stubborn he seemed to get. Finally one morning I apologized for pushing him and said I'd leave it up to him. That tack worked, as I'd known it would, and he said he understood my anxiety. Two days later he told me I could be moved the Monday after Labor Day. That night I worried that maybe he was just committing himself to a day to satisfy me and perhaps it was really too early for me to move.

I panicked a little. What if I wasn't really ready to be moved? Suppose they took me out of traction too early and I hurt my spine? I should have been laughing at myself. For three weeks I had pushed Joe to commit himself to a date and let me out of the hospital. Now that he had set the date, I was scared *he* was making a mistake. I should have laughed, but I couldn't because I was too scared.

It was Friday, three days before I was to be moved to Rusk. Joe held a small screwdriver in his hand. "This is the day," he said. "How'd you like to sit up?" He began unscrewing the toggle bolts in my head. I didn't feel any pain. One side came loose, then the other. I felt him remove the tongs from my head and sensed rather than felt that the weights, too, had been removed.

"Don't move," Joe ordered. "Don't move your head."

Joe slowly and very slightly lifted my head and slid part of a brace behind my neck. Then he gently laid my head back and fitted the front part under my chin and strapped the back and front together.

"How does that feel?" he asked.

"Okay, I guess. Maybe a little loose."

He made a couple of adjustments. "How about now?"

"Better."

I still hadn't lifted my head. But I could tell that with my chin held high and the back of my head supported and pushed a bit forward, my movements would be limited.

"Okay, " Joe said, "get him into bed."

There was some scurrying while some of the nurses went searching for an empty bed. Clive pushed my frame into the hall and placed it near the regular hospital bed. There was a brief conference about how to transfer me from the frame to the bed. Then Clive and three nurses grabbed the sheepskins on one side while Joe held my head and pulled me, sheepskins and all, onto the bed.

I felt funny in the bed. It was so soft after nine weeks in the frame, and I was so used to being forced to stare at the ceiling that I hadn't moved a muscle.

"Smile," Joe said. "You're out of traction." Everyone stood around me and grinned proudly, and I felt as if I'd just been bar mitzvahed. Then they wheeled me back inside the room.

I gingerly tried to roll onto my left side, but couldn't do it. The neck brace was a little awkward, and without wrenching myself over, I didn't have enough strength to do it easily. With my left arm I reached out and grabbed a bar on the upraised side of the bed and slowly pulled myself over onto my left side and rested my head on the pillow. I looked up and found myself staring directly into Mike's eyes. For what was probably ten seconds but seemed like ten minutes, we silently stared at each other as if we were trying to be sure we were really the same two people who had shared that room for nine weeks. We were like two blind men who have been brought together and can now suddenly see. I broke the silence first.

"Jesus. Are you thin!"

"You look worse," Mike said. "We both look like we just came out of a Japanese prison camp."

We laughed together, but I was shocked. If I looked worse than Mike, I knew I was in bad shape, worse than I'd imagined. Suddenly I realized I hadn't seen my own face since the morning of the accident.

The neck brace weighed heavily on me and didn't seem to fit quite right, but I hardly noticed it as I looked around at the room I'd never really seen. From my new vantage point, it seemed even smaller and dingier than I'd thought it was. From my bed I could now see the bright sunlight through the window and without too much trouble imagine what it felt like to be out in the hot sun, lazing in the sand or jogging along the beach. I tortured myself with those memories until Mary came in.

CHAPTER 28

MARY

The tongs. They took the tongs out," I said, looking straight and level and incredulously into Jack's eyes.

"Well, what do you think?"

"I think . . . I can't believe you're actually sitting up without those meat hooks in your head."

Jack was smiling and opened his arms to embrace me. He was wearing a neck brace and was so thin that he looked lost in the regular-size bed.

"I won't break," he said as I gingerly hugged him. "It's okay, doll. You won't hurt me."

I felt as though I were hugging a young boy. I could feel his bones. His chest was narrow, almost concave. I closed my eyes and gently passed my hands over his angular shoulders, down his skinny arms. His body felt unfamiliar.

"I'm skin and bones, aren't I?" Jack said. "They let me look at myself in the mirror and I hardly recognized myself."

I burst into tears, overwhelmed by this strange new physical closeness.

"It's not that bad, is it?" Jack said, laughing, smoothing my hair with his tightly fisted hand.

I tried to bury my head in his shoulder, but the neck brace got in the way. Then I took a deep breath and smiled back at Jack. "I'm just not used to seeing you face to face, that's all. It's so good not to have to look down at you, so good to touch you. I'll be all right. Just give me a few minutes to get used to you." I got up and walked to the foot of the bed to see Jack from a short distance. Then I walked around the bed to see him from all sides. "I guess you *are* pretty skinny," I said. "You look like the ninety-eight-pound weakling who gets sand kicked in his face."

I lay awake listening to the chirps and creaks of the country. I saw Jack's long, thin, pale face—not the face of memories, not even the face I'd grown accustomed to staring down at for nine weeks. I hadn't realized how much weight he'd lost. When he was flat on his back, he'd looked fatter, maybe because the weight of him spread him out a little, the way my thighs always look fatter when I'm sitting or lying down.

I wanted to run back to him right away. I wanted to get used to him so I could feel attracted to him again. That's what was upsetting me. I wasn't attracted to this shrunken-looking man.

I closed my eyes tightly. "Oh, please, let everything be okay," I prayed out loud. "Let everything work out and be happy and normal again." And then I reiterated my ritual list of wishes, the way most people count sheep, and tried to fall asleep.

CHAPTER 29
JACK

Mary and her mother arrived early with a box of little gifts for the hospital staff. We were going back to New York. As usual Clive fed, bathed, shaved me, and brushed my teeth. But this was the last time.

Joe had come in earlier to say good-by. "Good luck," he said. "Come back to see us."

"Thanks, Joe. Thanks for everything."

"I think you're going to be okay," he said as he left the room.

Now the room was packed with nurses and aides who had come to say good-by. Some had even come in on their day off. There was lots of kissing and hugging as all of us nervously killed time, waiting for the ambulance to arrive.

As they wheeled me down the hall, I could hear Mike complaining about the injustice of being left behind. Clive helped Mary with our belongings. For the first time in nine weeks there was nothing for him to do. I grabbed his hand just before they lifted me into the ambulance.

"I'll miss you, Clive. Thank you."

He looked at me and pulled his hand away. Finally he just wished me luck. Mary kissed him good-by and then climbed into the ambulance.

POSTCRIPT

JACK

I had been at the Rusk Institute for two weeks when I got return in the thumb and forefinger of my left hand. Shortly afterward I could also move the fingers of my right hand. Three months later, just before Christmas, Mary met me in my room at Rusk. I'd been waiting for her. We were going home. She carried my bag, and we walked out together. I was using aluminum crutches, like the kid in the Easter Seal poster.

For the next five months I attended Rusk in the mornings and went to work in the afternoons. Slowly I got stronger; slowly sex, bowel, and bladder control became more normal.

A year after the accident I quit Rusk altogether, threw away the crutches, and started to get around on a cane. I joined an exercise class and had hopes of a slow but almost total recovery.

JACK AND MARY

On September 26, 1971, one year and two months after the accident, we were married. On June 26, 1973, we had a beautiful baby girl. Her name is Sarah.

PURSUIT

THE CHASE AND SINKING
OF THE BATTLESHIP BISMARCK

A condensation of the book by

LUDOVIC KENNEDY

CHAPTER 1

It was a May evening of 1941, a time when most of Europe had yielded to Hitler, and across the narrow moat that had made and saved her, a truculent Britain faced Germany alone. To the west, across the steep Atlantic, and to the east, beyond the Vistula, the two giants marked time: their turn would come, but now they were spectators, uneasily neutral, also alone.

In the daytime, in the country, you hardly knew a war was on. Dusk was for remembrance, in cities especially, Coventry, Hamm, Hamburg, Devonport, Genoa, Brest: then the blackout curtains were drawn and the street lights doused, and the streets became like long tunnels and men and women rabbits, diving in and out of bright warrens, shutting away until morning the perils and peradventures of the night. It was like that always, even when the bombers didn't come, and when they did come, it was another story.

In a few places in Europe the lights still shone. In Stockholm, for instance, considered by some to be a dull, clean city servicing dull, progressive people, but then, like its partners in neutrality at the other end of Europe, Madrid and Lisbon, a buzzing beehive of espionage and intrigue. Here the Germans and the British had embassies and other front organizations, spied on each other, bribed Swedes and others to spy for them, touted for hot tips like how much iron ore was coming down from Narvik, and the wavebands of British radar, coded dark secrets for London and Berlin, and sent them by radio or airplane, in the trouser legs of sea cooks and the incredible memories of agents.

An unlikely man to find mixed up in all this was Captain Henry Denham, Royal Navy, who liked nothing better than sailing and racing small boats. He'd been naval attaché in Copenhagen in 1940 when the Germans overran Denmark, and getting out, had been asked to go to

Sweden to do the same. Why, he never knew: he understood no Swedish.

He reached Stockholm in June 1940 via Narvik and the North Cape, crossing the frontier to Finland with the Wehrmacht half a day behind. At first, lacking the language and contacts, it had been uphill work. But he had persevered, called on the right people, been congenial at parties, and now, a year later, had several useful informants, in the Swedish armed forces and without. He lived in a comfortable, small flat in the Riddargatan, but he met informants elsewhere, at the embassy or in the woods. He knew his flat was watched from the building opposite, and that his telephone was tapped, and he suspected bugging too.

On this evening in May Captain Denham was in his flat when the telephone rang. It was the British embassy in the Strandvägen. Colonel Roscher Lund had arrived to see him. It was urgent.

Colonel Roscher Lund was the military attaché of the exiled Norwegian government in London, a friend and colleague of Denham and the most reliable of his informants: he knew many Swedish officers, having done liaison work with their interception and cryptography service before the war. One man he knew well was Major Törnberg, himself half-Norwegian and Chief of Staff to Colonel Petersén, head of the Swedish secret service. Törnberg hated the Germans for what they had done to Norway, and felt no disloyalty to his own country in passing on to Roscher Lund information that might be useful to Britain in the prosecution of the war. Twice a week, in the evenings, Roscher Lund brought papers to Denham at the embassy: Denham made abstracts of what he thought important and Roscher Lund returned the papers to Törnberg's office before it opened in the morning. Denham and Roscher Lund referred to Petersén as 'P' to preserve his security.

Denham got out his bicycle and set off for the embassy, five minutes away on the waterfront. Never before had Roscher Lund asked for a special meeting, so he guessed something unusual was up.

At the embassy they went to Denham's office. Roscher Lund's message was brief and undramatic. It was a report from 'P''s office that two big German warships with sea and air escort had been sighted that afternoon off the south coast of Sweden. There was no indication of the source, which was in fact the Swedish cruiser *Gotland*: so delicate was the matter that not even Roscher Lund knew of it. As a result Denham doubted its reliability, and it wasn't until long afterwards that he realized that someone in 'P''s office, Törnberg probably, knowing this intelligence to be vital to Britain, had taken special, cautious steps to see that he was informed.

Roscher Lund left, and Denham drafted a telegram to the Admiralty, classified Most Immediate, graded B.3. Within an hour it had been put into cipher and was zinging its way from the Gothenburg radio masts across the North Sea to London.

Kattegat today 20th May. At 1500 two large warships, escorted by three destroyers, five escort vessels, ten or twelve aircraft, passed Marstrand course northwest. 2058/20.

The secret was out. *Bismarck* and *Prinz Eugen* were on their way. Operation *Rheinübung* had begun.

The head of Hitler's Navy was Erich Raeder, Grand Admiral in the German Fleet, a handsome square-faced man of 65. The highly intelligent son of a teacher of languages near Hamburg, Raeder was, like his parents, deeply religious. He joined the Navy in 1894, was navigator of the Kaiser's famous yacht *Hohenzollern* in 1911, then for five years was Chief Staff Officer to Admiral Hipper, commanding the scouting forces.

Raeder became head of the Navy in 1928, so that when Hitler came to power five years later there was already the nucleus of a new German fleet. First came the U-boat arm, forbidden by the Versailles Treaty, started with secret constructions in dockyards in Finland and Spain; then the far-ranging armored cruisers or pocket battleships, *Deutschland, Admiral Graf Spee, Admiral Scheer;* later cruisers and destroyers, the fast battleships or battle cruisers *Scharnhorst* and *Gneisenau*, the huge *Bismarck* and her sister *Tirpitz*. (These ships were all designed to look alike, an idea which later and quite unintentionally paid rich dividends). For years Hitler assured Raeder he need never fear a war with Britain; even in 1938 when the nightmare looked like reality he promised him another seven years' grace. So Raeder prepared his 'Z' plan, 250 U-boats, six more battleships even vaster than *Bismarck* and *Tirpitz*, and swift, light cruisers to scout for them, all to prowl about the Atlantic like hungry tigers and drive British shipping from the seas. And then a year later came war, and an unprepared Raeder found what foreigners had found before him, that his master's promises were dust.

"On land I am a hero," Hitler once said, "but at sea I am a coward." He was fascinated by battleships, talked knowingly about their technicalities, but of sea power and its influence he knew nothing. So he left things to Raeder, and of all the arms and institutions of the Third Reich the Navy was the least affected by Nazi ideas and practices. Raeder was able to impress on the Navy his own high standards of morality. He retained the old naval salute for all routine occasions; he forbade officers to become involved in party politics and dismissed the few who did, including a naval aide to Hitler; he retained, despite opposition, the Chaplain Corps of the Navy, expanded it as the fleet expanded, encouraged corporate worship. He refused to retire Jewish officers like Backenköhler, Grassmann, Rogge; and when in 1938 the infamous 'Crystal night' took place—the burning and looting of the synagogues—and outraged senior officers like Lütjens and Dönitz protested, he conveyed their protests, and his, to Hitler. Navies by their nature exist at the periphery not the center of their country's events: Raeder's rules about no politics ensured that the German Navy was insulated from the regime's grosser excesses, that its sailors mostly were straightforward, uncorrupted men.

With the coming of war in 1939 Raeder lost no time in putting his aggressive policy into action. *Graf Spee, Deutschland* and several U-boats were already on the trade routes, and in November *Scharnhorst* and *Gneisenau* put to sea. Off Iceland they sighted and sank the British armed merchant cruiser *Rawalpindi*, an action which caused some alarm in the British and French Admiralties, for no home-based German battleship in wartime had ever been this far north before. In the spring of 1940 Raeder committed most of the Navy to the invasion of Norway: the losses were heavy (at Narvik about half the entire German destroyer force) but considering the success achieved, tolerable. *Scharnhorst* and *Gneisenau* under Admiral Lütjens covered the Narvik landings from seaward and briefly engaged the battle cruiser *Renown: Gneisenau* was hit three times and several of her crew were killed and wounded. Two months later when the British were evacuating the port (and Captain Denham was struggling to cross into Sweden), the two ships returned to the same waters under Admiral Marschall and sank the aircraft carrier *Glorious* and two destroyers.

That summer the conquest of France gave the German Navy a foothold on the very edge of the Atlantic battlefield: U-boat bases were set up at Lorient, Brest, La Rochelle, St. Nazaire. German merchant raiders operating on the world's trade routes had orders to send prizes to French ports; so did *Admiral Scheer* when she left Germany in October for a five month cruise in the Atlantic and Indian Oceans. In December the heavy cruiser *Admiral Hipper* broke out, like *Scheer,* through the Denmark Straits between Greenland and Iceland, and after a brush with an allied troop convoy, put into Brest, the first German heavy warship to do so. Finally in January 1941 Admiral Lütjens again took *Scharnhorst* and *Gneisenau* north, this time to operate in the Atlantic. On passage through the Faeroes-Iceland gap, they were spotted by the British cruiser *Naiad*, retired at speed to the Arctic, refueled from a waiting tanker and a week later passed through the mists and darkness of the Denmark Straits unseen. "For the first time in our history," Admiral Lütjens signaled to his two ships on reaching the Atlantic, "German battleships have today succeeded in breaking through the British blockade. We shall now go forward to success."

In a two-month cruise, supported by supply ships and tankers, the battle cruisers sank 116,000 tons of allied shipping before turning for France: they would have sunk more if some convoys sighted had not had battleship escorts like *Rodney* and *Malaya*, which Lütjens's orders forbade him to attack. The Atlantic Battle was now mounting to a climax as successes against shipping by U-boats, warships, raiders and aircraft mounted. In March 1941 Atlantic losses were the severest so far, over 350,000 tons; in April in all theaters a record of nearly 700,000 tons. To Admiral Raeder it was clear that the tide was running in his favor: such losses could not be sustained indefinitely. Now was the time to go *banco* with all he had; and he signaled to Lütjens not to delay unduly his arrival in Brest, as *Bismarck* was almost ready for service and preparations were under way for *Scharnhorst*, *Gneisenau*, and the new heavy cruiser *Prinz Eugen* to join with her on a fresh operation in the Atlantic under his command.

She was built by Blohm and Voss of Hamburg and went down the slipway there on St. Valentine's day, 1939, the anniversary of Nelson's great coup at the battle of Cape St. Vincent. The German government declared the ceremony a state occasion. Hitler, Raeder, Keitel, Göring, Goebbels, Hess, Ribbentrop, Himmler, Bormann, von Schirach were all present on the podium, and Hitler in a speech hoped her future crew would be imbued with Bismarck's iron spirit. The bands played, the Nazi flags curled in the air, Hitler and Raeder beamed happily and a vast crowd cheered to see Bismarck's granddaughter, Dorothea von Loewenfeld, christen their greatest ship with the name of their greatest Chancellor. She was a sixth of a mile long, 120 feet wide, designed to carry eight 15-inch guns and six aircraft, with 13-inch armor made of specially hardened Wotan steel on her turrets and sides. Listed as 35,000 tons to comply with the London Treaty, she would in fact be 42,000 tons standard displacement and over 50,000 tons fully laden. There had never been a warship like her: she symbolized not only a resurgent Navy but the whole resurgent German nation.

The captain was Ernst Lindemann, aged forty-five, clever and cool, top of his term as a cadet, specialist in gunnery, chain smoker and coffee drinker, blond hair sleeked back. With him came his steward, ex-waiter of his favorite Hamburg restaurant, a man nervous about military service but happy to be taken to sea in something so large and safe. By August 24th the ship was ready to be handed over: the band played on the quarterdeck, the Nazi naval ensign was run up, *Bismarck* was commissioned into the German Navy.

On September 15th, 1940 *Bismarck* was weaned, left the crèche of Hamburg, slipped the cords that tied her to shore, and glided down the lazy Elbe towards salt water and the open sea. Warships combine uniquely grace and power, and *Bismarck*, massive and elegant, with the high flare of her bows and majestic sweep of her lines, the symmetry of her turrets, the rakish cowling of her funnel, her ease and arrogance in the water, was then the most graceful, most powerful warship yet built. No German saw her without pride, no neutral or enemy without admiration.

In the enclosed waters of Kiel Bay she underwent acceptance trials, adjusted compasses, tested degaussing gear, ran machinery and speed trials over the measured mile, worked up to 30 knots. Some trials didn't go as smoothly as expected and in the first week of December she was back in Hamburg for extensive adjustments. Here she was joined by another child of Blohm and Voss, the newly built U-boat *U.556*, which came and fitted out alongside her, ferret at the tail of a tiger. The Captain of *U.556* was Herbert Wohlfarth, known as "Parsifal" in the U-boat Service because of his fastidiousness on a prewar cruise. He was a cartoonist and a bit of a joker, though experienced and brave. This was his third command.

By March *Bismarck* was ready to take to sea again, and returned to Kiel for further trials, this time successful. Then she filled her bunkers with oil, and magazines with ammunition, and sailed east to the Bay of Danzig, to Gdynia or Gotenhafen as the Germans had renamed it, there to carry out a long program of exercises and training, away from the attention of British bombers. The great guns spoke and deafened the novices with their blast. The Arado aircraft were catapulted from their launching rails, spotted fall of shot, flew on search patrols, alighted and were recovered. Land-based aircraft with drogues passed down the ship's sides as targets for the flak crews. There were exercises in towing and being towed, in oiling from tankers while under way, in electrical failures, firefighting, damage control. Soon *Bismarck* was joined by the new heavy cruiser *Prinz Eugen*, 14,000 tons, named after the Prince of Savoy, the liberator of Vienna. Recently completed at the Germania works at Kiel, with lines so like *Bismarck's* that from afar you could barely tell them apart, she had eight 8-inch guns, and a speed of 32 knots. Her captain was a classmate of Lindemann's, Helmuth Brinkmann from Lübeck.

One day in the *Bismarck* they practiced flooding the steering gear compartment, down aft by the rudders. Ordinary Seaman Herbert Blum on damage control duty there jokingly asked his lieutenant permission not to obey orders, as if the compartment had really been knocked out, for then he and his mates would be dead. "Quite right," said the lieutenant laughing, "so you'd better play dead, put your caps on back to front, lie down on the deck and everyone will know you are bodies." After the exercise the lieutenant said, "The chances of getting a hit there are a hundred thousand against." At the time Blum didn't pay much attention to this remark; weeks later he was to remember it.

On April 2nd, 1941, just two weeks after the arrival of *Scharnhorst* and *Gneisenau* in Brest, the German naval staff issued preparatory orders. In the next new moon period at the end of the month *Bismarck*, *Prinz Eugen* and *Gneisenau* were to rendezvous in the Atlantic for a combined attack on allied shipping: *Scharnhorst* would be unable to join them because of repairs to her boilers. Unlike Lütjens's order on the previous operation which forbade him to attack a battleship escort, this time *Bismarck* had discretion to draw enemy fire, while *Gneisenau* and *Prinz Eugen* attacked the ships of the convoy. Otherwise action with enemy warships was to be avoided, the object of the operation being the destruction of merchant shipping.

Had this squadron, even without *Scharnhorst*, put to sea, it might have been disastrous for Britain—indeed it could have altered the whole course of the war. But luck was not with the Germans. Two days later there was a British bombing raid on Brest and a bomb fell without exploding into the water of No. 8 dock where *Gneisenau* was lying. The ship was moved to a mooring in the harbor, and here at 9 A.M. on April 6th she was attacked by a torpedo-carrying plane of British Coastal Command. Her pilot, Flying Officer Kenneth Campbell, a Canadian, went in low over the harbor mole, brave beyond the call of duty, shells and bullets screaming at him from every side. He and his crew crashed almost at once, but before hitting the water they released a torpedo which struck *Gneisenau* near the stern, smashed a propeller shaft, flooded two engine rooms and put the ship out of service for six months.

So what had once been a formidable force of one battleship, two battle cruisers and a heavy cruiser was reduced now to the still powerful *Bismarck* and *Prinz Eugen*. Should Raeder postpone the operation until *Tirpitz*, which had recently arrived at Gotenhafen for her own working-up exercises, was ready to join them? On balance there was little to be said for it. The longer the operation was put off, the shorter the northern nights, the less chance of breaking out unseen. America might soon be in the war against them, and the range and quality of aircraft patrolling the Atlantic were increasing monthly. Finally, on the very day that *Gneisenau* was torpedoed, the German army began pouring into Greece on its drive south towards Crete and the Eastern Mediterranean, and any diversion to prevent reinforcements from reaching Admiral Cunningham's hard-pressed Mediterranean Fleet was to be welcomed. Raeder must have reached his decision quickly, for two days later, on April 8th, Admiral Lütjens flew to Paris to confer with his old friend Karl Dönitz, the admiral commanding U-boats, about cooperation between *Bismarck* and submarines.

But on April 24th a further setback took place. A magnetic mine exploded a hundred feet from *Prinz Eugen*, damaging a coupling. Repairs would take two weeks, so the earliest the squadron could now sail was the new moon period towards the end of May. Should postponement be considered again? Raeder thought not but felt he should put his views to the Fleet Commander; and Lütjens flew to Berlin.

Günther Lütjens was then 51, a long, lean, lamppost of a man, with cropped hair like most German officers, and a dour, tight expression which some said concealed a dry sense of humor. He was a man wholly dedicated to the service, courageous, single-minded, stoical, austere, taciturn as a Cistercian monk. He was not a Nazi, gave Hitler the naval not the party salute, and always wore an admiral's dirk of the old Imperial Navy, not one with a swastika. His friend Admiral Conrad Patzig, who succeeded him as Chief of Personnel, called him "one of the ablest officers in the Navy, very logical and shrewd, incorruptible in his opinions and an engaging personality when you got to know him." Few did. To those who admired him, he was shy and withdrawn, to others aloof and remote. He believed that young officers should wed themselves to the Navy, and while Chief of Personnel was inflexible about the rule that no officer should marry until earning a certain level of pay. He practiced what he preached and didn't marry until forty, and then very happily.

Raeder asked Lütjens what he thought about postponement, and

Lütjens said he was in favor of it at least until *Scharnhorst* or *Tirpitz* was ready. But Raeder's mind was already made up and he trotted out all the reasons for not postponing. Lütjens was in Raeder's words "perhaps not entirely convinced by my views" yet agreed to accede to them. As he told Patzig later, what else could he do? Patzig also wondered what need there was for the Fleet Commander and his valuable staff to embark for what had now become a single operation. "We can't afford to lose any more Fleet Commanders," said Patzig jokingly, referring to Boehm and Marschall, both of whom Raeder had recently sacked. Lütjens agreed but said any such suggestion must come from the Admiralty planning staff, and made Patzig promise not to propose it himself. Already a sense of fatalism, that was increasingly to show itself, was beginning to color his thinking. "I realize," he said to Patzig, "that in this unequal struggle between the British Navy and ourselves I shall sooner or later have to lose my life. But I have settled my private affairs, and I shall do my best to carry out my orders with honor."

At the beginning of May Lütjens flew to Gotenhafen and embarked with the officers of his staff. The operation was given its code name, Rheinübung (Rhine Exercise), and a starting date of May 18th. On May 5th Hitler and his staff traveled to Gotenhafen by special train to inspect *Bismarck* and *Tirpitz*. Raeder did not accompany him, the first time in eight years he had not done so on such a visit. He gives no reason in his memoirs, but elsewhere he speaks of Hitler's malign influence and the ease of succumbing to his wishes. Aware of Hitler's lack of enthusiasm for surface ship operations, fears of sinkings and loss of prestige, he had not given him the squadron's exact sailing date: he may have felt that Hitler would have wormed it out of him, panicked at realizing there was less than two weeks to go, and ordered its cancellation. All Lütjens had to do if asked was to say he didn't know.

Instead of Raeder, there went with Hitler General Keitel, Chief of the General Staff, later to be hanged at Nüremberg. Captain von Puttkamer, Hitler's naval aide, was also present, as was Walther Hewel, Joachim von Ribbentrop's liaison officer at the Führer's headquarters.

At Gotenhafen ("the very hideous Gotenhafen" Hewel called it) the party embarked in the yacht *Hela* in the inner harbor, and steamed out to where *Bismarck*, massive and graceful, was lying at anchor in the roads. Perhaps even Hitler caught his breath at the sight of her. The crew were lined up on deck with Admiral Lütjens, Captain Lindemann, Commander Oels and the officers of the watch waiting at the gangway to receive him. Hitler was piped over the side, and the officers were presented to him. He then inspected the crew and the ship. In the fore gunnery transmitting station he stayed nearly half an hour listening to Sub-Lieutenant Cardinal explaining how speed, course, wind direction, and temperature were fed into the machine, how the machine came up with the right angles of deflection and elevation for the guns. It was this sort of technical talk that Hitler liked, much better than old Raeder gassing about sea power. Keitel, a gunner himself, found it absorbing too.

Then Lütjens took Hitler to his cabin, with von Puttkamer but without Keitel. Lütjens gave an account of his earlier cruise with *Scharnhorst* and *Gneisenau*, then told Hitler that this time because of *Bismarck's* superiority, he would be able to take on any convoy escort while *Prinz Eugen* attacked the merchant ships. Was there then nothing to worry about? asked the cautious Hitler. What about torpedo-carrying aircraft? Yes, agreed Lütjens, that was a worry, his biggest worry, though he thought the ship's tremendous fire power could cope with it—on another occasion he told a friend that with *Bismarck's* armor, torpedo hits would be felt as bee stings that hurt but didn't damage. He might have added what all senior officers felt: that had the intriguing Göring not denied the Navy its air arm, had the aircraft carrier *Graf Zeppelin*, lying even now in the yards at Gotenhafen, half-completed and abandoned, been accompanying him, his worries would have been considerably less. Hitler, said von Puttkamer, was pleased to find that the experienced Lütjens shared his concerns. He then went ashore in the *Hela* and inspected the *Tirpitz* in the harbor. Captain Topp begged him to allow his ship to accompany *Bismarck* on her first operation. Hitler listened but said nothing. The party then returned to the train. "Visit unbelievably impressive," Hewel wrote in his diary that night. "Concentration of force and the highest technical development."

On May 16th Lütjens reported the squadron ready to proceed from midnight on the 18th-19th, and during the next two days support ships sailed from French Atlantic and Norwegian ports to take up waiting positions.

On the morning of Sunday, May 18th Admiral Lütjens held a final conference in his cabin, attended by his staff officers and Captains Lindemann and Brinkmann. His operational brief from Admiral Carls of Naval Group Command North in Wilhelmshaven (his shore authority until he crossed the line Southern Greenland/Northern Hebrides, when it became Group Command West in Paris) recommended sailing direct to Korsfjord [now called Krossfjord] near Bergen, there anchor for the day while *Prinz Eugen*, whose radius of action was very limited, topped up with fuel, and then sail direct for the Atlantic through the Iceland/Faeroes gap. Now Lütjens said he had decided on a change of plan. The squadron would not call at Korsfjord but proceed directly to the Arctic Ocean, oil from the tanker *Weissenburg* near Jan Mayen Island, then go at high speed into the Atlantic through the Denmark Straits. Typically Lütjens gave no reason for the change.

After the conference Lütjens went in his barge to the harbor to inspect *Prinz Eugen* and her crew, but neither to them nor her officers did he say a word about the impending operation. During the rest of the day the two ships topped up with oil fuel. Earlier in *Bismarck* while cleaning the oil tanks several Polish laborers had been killed by fumes, and this may have resulted in the decision not to oil to full capacity: the ship is believed to have sailed 200 tons short. Whatever the reason it was an omission that Captain Lindemann was later profoundly to regret.

In the afternoon *Prinz Eugen* left the harbor and proceeded into the bay for degaussing trials against magnetic mines, and then *Bismarck* weighed. As the anchor came up from the Baltic seabed and the crew on the fo'c'sle hosed down the cables, the band on the quarterdeck a sixth of a mile away played *"Muss i' denn?"* ("Must I leave?"), a ballad of grief and parting. It was the first time they had played it and later it was to be criticized as a possible breach of security. People on shore watched the two ships exercising until evening when they disappeared into the dusk.

They proceeded independently through the night and at 11 the next morning rendezvoused off Arkona, the northernmost cape of Prussia, with a flotilla of minesweepers and the destroyers *Friedrich Eckholdt* and *Z.23* under the command of Captain Schulze-Hinrichs. At noon Captain Lindemann addressed *Bismarck's* crew on the loudspeaker system and told them officially what they had already guessed: that they were going on a three-month cruise in the Atlantic to destroy British shipping. He finished: "I give you the hunter's toast, good hunting and a good bag!" The news was welcomed, for it dispelled mystery, cleared the air, challenged the spirit. *Bismarck* was the most powerful warship in the world: Führer, admiral, captain had said so, they could see it too, and there was nothing in the world she and they could not do. One or two perhaps, those who had read of the British Navy's strength and traditions, looked over the side of the gray Baltic slipping astern, and wondered uneasily what the future might bring.

All that day and night the squadron sailed in formation westwards and northwards, the escorts leading, then *Bismarck* with the admiral's flag, white with a black cross fluttering at the fore, then *Prinz Eugen*. They passed through the Fehmarn Belt, skirted the eastern edge of Kiel Bay where they were joined by the destroyer *Hans Lody*, sailed through the Great Belt which divides two parts of Denmark, and on through the waters that Nelson had taken on his way to victory at Copenhagen 140 years before. At 4 A.M. a signal was received saying air reconnaissance of the British fleet at Scapa Flow had not been possible the day before because of cloud. Dawn broke to reveal a calm and empty sea, for as a security measure Group North had frozen all shipping movements in the Kattegat and Skaggerak during the squadron's passage. They had not reckoned with the *Gotland*, though, which showed up soon after, gray in the sunlight against the green of the Swedish coast, steaming on a parallel course. She kept company with the German ships for several hours; then off Marstrand they swung away to port, shaping a northwesterly course across the Skaggerak for a landfall at Kristiansand in southern Norway. *Gotland* sent a routine signal to Stockholm, and Lütjens wirelessed to Group North that he believed his presence had been betrayed.

In Kristiansand's Vesterveien a party of people were walking by the shore. They were Viggo Axelssen, a well-to-do young ship's chandler, his friends Arne Usterud, solicitor, a photographer called Wintersborg and half a dozen others. They had just been to see the launching of Axelssen's new boat, built to replace one commandeered by the authorities, and were now on the way to the local club for a celebratory dinner.

Viggo Axelssen, a bachelor, worked in the Norwegian resistance movement for the Oslo-Stavanger circuit. His job as ship's chandler gave him easy access to the port and harbor master's office where he noted things like the positions of minefields and arrival and departure of convoys. He sent coded messages via the local bus driver, Arne Moen, who hid them in a pocket in the casing of his engine, to a radio operator called Gunvald Tomstad who lived at Helle near Flekkefjord sixty miles away. The Germans knew there was a transmitting post at Flekkefjord but so far had been unable to find it. In Kristiansand only the two Arnes, Usterud and Moen, knew of Axelssen's activities.

The group stopped at the place called Runningen to admire the view. It was a still, calm evening and they could see far out to sea, beyond Oksøy lighthouse eight miles away. As they looked they saw a group of ships steaming west at high speed, the white foam curling at their bows. Wintersborg had with him an old-fashioned spyglass, and Axelssen borrowed it to look at the group closer. He saw two big, camouflaged warships which he knew must be German, with aircraft circling above and escort craft ahead, steaming urgently in the direction of the Norwegian fjords. Quietly he returned the spyglass to Wintersborg and said it was time to get along to the club.

On the way he told the others he had to call in at his office to fetch something. They took this to be a bottle of schnapps and laughed, all except Arne Usterud, who realized something was up. In his office Axelssen coded a message of twelve words, then took it along to Arne Moen before the bus left for Flekkefjord.

Late that evening the message was at Helle in Tomstad's hands. He and another agent, Odd Starheim, noted its urgency, decided there would be no time, as usually there was, to take the transmitter from beneath the hay in the barn and set it up at some remote spot. So they put it in Tomstad's "dark-room," erected the aerial and began transmitting at once. And soon a second message about Rheinübung was going out across the ether to confirm the earlier truth of what Captain Denham had said.

And on that same night, far out in the long reaches of the Atlantic to which *Bismarck* and *Prinz Eugen* were bound, Herbert Wohlfarth in *U.556* along with other U-boats got in among the homeward bound convoy H.X. 126 and sank five ships.

CHAPTER 2

At Scapa Flow in the Orkney Islands, ten miles from the north coast of Scotland across the racing waters of the Pentland Firth, lay the British Home Fleet. Scapa was ideal for guarding the approaches from the North Sea to the Atlantic, a sweep of water ten miles by eight ringed almost entirely by islands, a natural refuge for war-weary ships. Here one October night at the beginning of this war the bold Günther Prien had cocked a snook at British sea power, taken his U-boat into the Flow through a narrow, unguarded eastern channel, torpedoed and sank the battleship *Royal Oak* with huge loss of life, crept out on the ebb as unobtrusively as he had come, and returned to a hero's welcome in Germany.

Admiral Beatty called Scapa the most damnable place on earth; most of the lads agreed. The islands were heather and grass, seabirds and sheep, and across the bare face of the Flow tempests blew, often for days on end. There were no shops, restaurants, girls: just a couple of canteens to dispense warm beer, a hall for film shows and the occasional concert party, and football fields that too often fathered the signal, "All grounds unfit for play." And yet now in the summertime when the Flow sparkled blue in the morning sun and the hills of Hoy were touched with purple and green, at nighttime too when the the Northern Lights wove pale patterns over the sleeping ships, the place had a rare beauty.

It was here, while Admiral Lütjens was steaming up the Norwegian coast in his new flagship *Bismarck,* that the British admiral, Tovey, lay moored off Flotta in his new flagship *King George V.* Tovey was 56 now, a small, blue-eyed, twinkly man, last of a family of eleven. He entered the Navy at fifteen, won his spurs at Jutland commanding the destroyer *Onslow,* and helped sink the German light cruiser *Wiesbaden.* At one moment in the battle he was quite close to Raeder, and like Raeder, he was deeply religious. He was a natural leader, and radiated confidence; he could be quite fierce sometimes but it soon passed. A jokey admiral wrote of him when captain of the *Rodney,* "Captain Tovey shares one characteristic with me. In myself I would call it tenacity of purpose. In Tovey I can only call it sheer bloody obstinacy." Churchill found the same, called him stubborn, and tried to get rid of him. Tovey did what he thought right. He refused to kow-tow to titular superiors and hated "yes-men" in others. He was a civilized man who dressed well and liked good food and wine and company. Like many naval officers he would address foreigners loudly and slowly, and was often astonished to find they spoke English too. He liked Poles and Americans especially, and he adored King George the Sixth.

On board the flagship was a green telephone which, when the fleet was in Scapa, was connected to a special shore line to the Admiralty in London. It was the same line on which Jellicoe had spoken to Churchill when he was First Lord of the Admiralty twenty-six years earlier. On this telephone, in the early morning of May 21st, Tovey's secretary, Captain Paffard, and his Chief of Staff, Commodore Brind, learned from the Admiralty of Denham's signal, received during the night. To them, as to Tovey, it came as no surprise. It was known from intelligence that both *Bismarck* and *Prinz Eugen* had completed training, and one agent's report that new charts were being delivered to *Bismarck* and another's from France that battleship moorings were being prepared at Brest, made it clear her time in the Baltic was coming to an end.

There were two things to be done immediately: make an aerial search of the Norwegian fjords, which the Admiralty had already arranged, and bring the fleet to short notice for steam. A signal went out from the flagship's bridge, and from across the Flow the ships in company answered: the old battle cruiser *Hood*, 42,000 tons, for twenty-one years the pride of Britain's Navy, the biggest warship in the world; the new battleship *Prince of Wales*, sister ship of *King George V*, fresh from the builder's yard, with two turrets not yet free of teething troubles and dockyard workmen still aboard her; the brand new aircraft carrier *Victorious*, with 48 crated Hurricane fighters on board for beleaguered Malta, and due in two days' time to join the battle cruiser *Repulse* off the Clyde and escort the valuable Middle East troop convoy WS8B to the southwards; and a score of cruisers and destroyers. Men in these ships wondered what the crisis might be; some went below and flashed up second and third boilers.

During the morning Tovey spoke several times to the Admiralty on the green telephone and conferred with his staff officers in his comfortable cabin, but until he had further news there was little more he could do. He had made his dispositions.

At around noon Admiral Tovey heard that two Spitfires of the Photographic Reconnaissance Unit of Coastal Command had just taken off from Wick, across the Pentland Firth, heading for the Norwegian coast. One went east towards Oslo and the Skaggerak; the other, piloted by Flying Officer Suckling, made for the Bergen fjords.

Through the night the German squadron steamed northwards up the Norwegian coast, steering a zigzag course to avoid British submarines. At breakfast on the mess decks there was cheering news on the wireless: the day before German paratroops had made a massive descent on Crete.

Now Admiral Lütjens did the very thing he said he wouldn't do at his conference at Gotenhafen three days before: he signaled the squadron to enter the Norwegian fjords. Just before 9 A.M. off the island of Marstein the two ships entered the quiet waters of Korsfjord, the tongue of water that leads to Bergen.

What reasons caused Lütjens to reverse his decision we shall never know, for typically he left none. Whatever the reason it was as foolish a decision as that of allowing the ships to leave home waters by the Baltic rather than the North Sea. To send them by daylight through the narrow waters of the Kattegat and Skaggerak was to invite the attention of neutrals and agents, which was exactly what happened. Further, Raeder knew it; for a signal sent that very morning from Admiral Canaris, head of the *Abwehr* or Counter Intelligence Service, stated that he had proof positive of British agents' reports of the squadron's outward movements.

For the squadron, in the light of this knowledge, to be permitted to enter Bergen, the nearest Norwegian harbor to British air bases, was asking for trouble, like a burglar loitering outside his local police station.

And trouble came. At about 1:15 P.M. Flying Officer Suckling in his Spitfire, almost at the end of his search, spotted two warships 25,000 feet below. They looked like cruisers: he turned, made a run over the fjords, opened the shutter. At the time no one in *Bismarck* or *Prinz Eugen* saw him: it wasn't until fifteen minutes later that the alarm bells sounded, by which time Suckling and his happy snaps were a quarter of the way back to Wick.

At Wick the Station Intelligence Officer looked at the wet prints, assessed the ships as one battleship and one cruiser, and informed Tovey's staff. The Air Ministry agreed to an Admiralty request to mount a bombing attack that night, but the Chief of Coastal Command, Air Marshal Sir Frederick Bowhill, once a seaman himself, wanted his own staff to evaluate the photographs further. The only pilot and plane available to take them the 650 miles to London was Suckling and his Spitfire, so he climbed in again, and set off south. At nightfall he found himself short of fuel and near Nottingham, where he lived. He landed, roused a garage-proprietor friend who had a car, and drove through the blackout at 50 miles an hour to hand over the prints in the early morning. Later Admiralty and Air Ministry experts confirmed the appreciation of Wick.

At Scapa Admiral Tovey had assumed the same: and when the *Victorious* came into the Flow in the late afternoon after exercises, there was a signal at the flagship's yardarm for her captain, Henry Bovell, to come on board. Tovey asked Bovell whether his Swordfish aircrews, who had flown on board from nearby Hatston only a day or two before, were capable of mounting a torpedo attack on the ships in the fjord. Bovell said he doubted it; few had any operational experience, some had just landed on a carrier for the very first time. Tovey was left under no illusions as to the rawness and lack of sea experience of most of the carrier's aircrews.

Nor was he much happier about *Prince of Wales*. Two days before her captain, John Leach, sensing that something was afoot and not wanting to miss it, had reported to Tovey that *Prince of Wales* had completed her working up and was now ready to join the fleet as a fighting unit. In fact, as Tovey knew, her guns were far from satisfactory and civilian technicians from Vickers-Armstrong were still working on them. Now, this evening, having heard of the report from Bergen, Leach had his ship's company mustered on the quarterdeck, mounted the roof of Y turret, told them what he'd told Tovey, thanked them for their hard work during exercises, and hoped they'd acquit themselves well if and when battle came.

In *King George V* Tovey waited anxiously for further news. But now came a change in the weather. A mist settled over the sea, and it began to rain. The hours went by and a creeping fear started to gnaw at Tovey's heart: that the German ships had sailed, were even now heading towards the Atlantic where no less than eleven allied convoys were at sea. If so, there were no heavy ships to stop them. It was nine in the evening and growing dark when he made up his mind. To Vice-Admiral Holland in the *Hood* he made a signal to take the *Prince of Wales* under his orders together with the destroyers *Electra, Anthony, Echo, Icarus, Achates, Antelope,* proceed to Iceland to refuel and then take up a position southwest of the island so as to cover both the Iceland-Greenland and Iceland-Faeroes gaps.

Just before midnight the destroyers slipped their moorings in Gutter Sound and formed line ahead to pass through the Switha gate. Outside the Flow, at the edge of the Pentland Firth, they waited for *Hood* and *Prince of Wales.* On the quarterdeck of the *King George V,* which for exercise he paced so often, Admiral Tovey watched the old battle cruiser and the new battleship weigh, swing around on their engines, and glide southwards through the mist and darkness towards the Hoxa gate. *Hood* led the way, proud and elegant, Admiral Holland's flag fluttering at the fore. The crew of the gate vessel drew aside the huge underwater anti-submarine netting and the two ships passed through, the destroyers taking station ahead. Twenty-one years before *Hood* had sailed this way to Scandinavia, on the first mission of her long and wonderful career. She had been here many times since. Now she was leaving for the last time. No landsman would ever see her again.

At Kalvanes during the afternoon *Prinz Eugen* oiled from the tanker *Wollin,* the destroyers refueled from a tanker in Bergen harbor. *Bismarck,* incredibly, didn't oil at all, despite having sailed short and burned over a thousand tons since leaving Gotenhafen. It was an astonishing omission, in sharp contrast to the British Navy's wartime rules that on reaching harbor oiling took priority over everything else. Admittedly the tanker *Weissenburg* in the Arctic was only a day's steaming away, and there was little likelihood of meeting the enemy en route. Yet the decision allowed no margin for error or change; it showed an amateurishness in planning, a lack of experience of ocean warfare for which in the end Lütjens would have to pay.

Also in the afternoon crews of both ships painted out camouflage markings, substituting battleship gray to confuse them with British ships; and Lütjens and his staff closely examined the previous day's aerial photographs of Scapa sent down by special car from Bergen. Fighter planes circled the two ships continuously, "buzzing" Norwegian boats that got too near; patrol craft moved to and fro across the entrance of the fjords—Norwegians ashore noticed their crews peering over the sides. Later, when painting over the camouflage was finished, the men of both ships were allowed to laze about, sleep, read, play games on deck. Many wrote last letters home, taking care not to say where they were.

At about 7:30 *Bismarck* weighed and turned north to antiaircraft action stations. Off Bergen Schulze-Hinrichs's destroyers were waiting to take station ahead; off Kalvanes *Prinz Eugen* was waiting to take station astern. In single line the five ships steamed at 20 knots up Hjeltefjord and the Fedjeosen. At the end of the Fedjeosen they dropped the Norwegian pilot, then swung to port past the Skerries to enter the open sea.

Here the destroyers took up screening positions ahead and the ships started zigzagging. The wind was astern from the southeast; ahead there were low, dark clouds. At a little before midnight, at about the time that *Hood* and *Prince of Wales* were leaving Scapa, the ships turned due north, heading for the Arctic Ocean. Presently lookouts reported, far away to the south, enemy aircraft dropping flares and bombs over Korsfjord—good news for Lütjens, for it showed the British had no idea he had sailed. At five in the morning he dismissed Schulze-Hinrichs and the destroyers to Trondheim.

At Scapa Tovey was woken with gloomy news: because of the weather only two of the eighteen bombers that had set out from Wick during the night to bomb the German ships had found the target area. Neither had seen anything, both had bombed blind. And the latest weather reports showed a blanket of rain and mist spreading over the whole of the northern part of the North Sea. Reconnaissance aircraft that had left for the fjords before dawn had all had to turn back. From his cabin Tovey couldn't see more than halfway across the Flow.

Were *Bismarck* and *Prinz Eugen* still at Bergen or had they sailed? And what was he to do? These were the questions that tugged at Tovey's mind. The temptation to sail must have been overwhelming, but Tovey resisted it and decided to stay until he had something further to go on.

As the day wore on, the weather over Norway remained thick as ever, and the ships at Scapa stayed motionless, mute. In mid-morning Coastal Command reported all reconnaissance flights to the Norwegian coast canceled until further notice. To Tovey it must have seemed his God had deserted him. Was there *nothing* that could be done?

There was, thanks to Captain Henry St. John Fancourt, Royal Navy, commanding officer of the naval air station at Hatston, on the other side of the Flow. Hatston was used mostly as a training base. But it also had an operational squadron of Albacore torpedo planes, and when Captain Fancourt heard the German ships were in Bergen, he was given permission by Coastal Command to move these to Shetland, a hundred miles nearer Bergen, with a view to launching an attack.

For his Albacores then, as much as for Tovey and Coastal Command, Captain Fancourt wanted news of the enemy. His second in command at Hatston was one Geoffrey Rotherham, a pen-pusher now, but a trained observer and aerial navigator of long experience. Captain Fancourt asked Commander Rotherham whether in existing conditions he felt like making a trip to Bergen in one of the old twin-engine American Marylands they used for target-towing, the only suitable plane since the Albacores had left. Commander Rotherham, who reckoned his operational flying days were over, said he'd like it very much: when could they start? Noel Goddard, leader of the target-towing squadron, insisted on being pilot and a volunteer telegraphist/air gunner was soon found.

They took off at 4:30 P.M. Within minutes of their estimated landfall Rotherham signaled Goddard to go down. The clouds parted momentarily: there right ahead lay Marstein Island and its light. They flew up Korsfjord, looked into Grimstad and Kalvanes fjords and found them empty. They took a look at Bergen harbor just to be sure, racing over the housetops and docks while every gun in the place opened up at them. They ran up Hjeltefjord for a further check; then, satisfied the birds had flown, headed seawards and home.

Fearful of being shot down before Tovey heard the news, Rotherham scribbled an urgent message for the radio operator. For Tovey it was negative news but at least he was no longer completely in the dark. He signaled *Victorious*, the cruisers *Galatea*, *Hermione*, *Kenya*, *Aurora* and the destroyers *Inglefield*, *Intrepid*, *Active*, *Punjabi*, *Windsor* and *Lance* to be ready to proceed with him at 10:15 P.M. He signaled *Suffolk* to join *Norfolk* immediately in the Denmark Straits, *Arethusa* to join *Birmingham* and *Manchester* in the Iceland-Faeroes passage, and the battle cruiser *Repulse* in the Clyde to join his flag north of the Hebrides in the morning. Then, like other great commanders before him, he sat down with his staff to dinner.

Rotherham's news reached London too, and on no one did it make more of an impression than the Prime Minister, Winston Churchill. With his experience of naval affairs in two wars he knew of the fearful havoc the German squadron could cause among the Atlantic convoys, and of the effect on the war.

Yet if the British Prime Minister and his admirals knew a fraction more than they did of the German squadron's movements, the German Chancellor knew nothing at all. Raeder had long discovered that timing was the essence of his dealings with Hitler, and it wasn't until the first part of the breakout was successfully completed that he felt able to go to the Berghof, the Führer's retreat at Berchtesgaden, and in the presence of Keitel, Ribbentrop and von Puttkamer, tell Hitler the news. At first, as he feared, Hitler expressed profound misgivings and wanted the ships recalled. He was worried about American reactions, about complications connected with the coming attack on Russia, about the risk of torpedo damage from British carriers. Raeder stressed the most difficult part of the journey was now over and the naval operations staff had the highest hopes for its success; and after further discussion Hitler allowed it to proceed.

After Schulze-Hinrichs's departure on the morning of the 22nd, the squadron continued northwards at 24 knots. Lütjens was still uncertain whether to go north or south of Iceland. There was some discussion on the matter among his staff, and a signal from Group North to Admiral Dönitz warned U-boats to be prepared for either. What may have finally convinced Lütjens to stick to the original plan was the continuing poor visibility which Dr. Externbrink and his fellow meteorologists, conspicuous about the ship in flimsy white coats, predicted would last to southern Greenland. At noon Lütjens signaled *Prinz Eugen* his intentions to go direct for the Denmark Straits but not to oil from *Weissenburg* unless the weather lifted.

The decision to forego *Weissenburg* was bold in view of *Prinz Eugen*'s limited endurance and the depletion of *Bismarck*'s own stocks, but Lütjens believed it correct. His information from Group North was that British air reconnaissance was active only around the lower half of the Norwegian coast, and that while Luftwaffe reconnaissance of Scapa had not been possible the day before because of weather, monitoring of

British wireless traffic gave no indication that any British ships had sailed in pursuit or that the enemy had any idea where the squadron was.

This was faulty intelligence, but all that Lütjens had to go on. If Lütjens wanted confirmation of the wisdom of going direct to the Denmark Straits, he got it that night in a signal from Group North that although no photographic reconnaissance of Scapa Flow had been possible that day because of weather, visual reconnaissance had reported three heavy units, a carrier and several cruisers and destroyers—an exact repetition of the photographic report of the 20th, giving the impression no heavy units had sailed and the situation was unchanged. This was an example of the sometimes sloppy work of the Luftwaffe when detached on naval assignments, work which they (unlike the R.A.F.'s Coastal Command) often resented. For of the three heavy units the observer had seen on a quick swoop from the clouds, two were wood and canvas dummies (the other was *King George* V) and so it escaped Group North's attention entirely that *Hood* and *Prince of Wales* had sailed. Had Lütjens known of this, he would certainly have recast his plans and might even have turned the squadron back.

Further encouragement to push on came from a second piece of faulty intelligence—a signal from Group North that the ships of the formidable British Force H (the battle cruiser *Renown*, the carrier *Ark Royal*, the cruiser *Sheffield* and destroyers) based at Gibraltar and obviously a danger to Lütjens, were now at sea, probably en route to Crete. In fact they were all at Gibraltar.

At eleven that night, when *Bismarck* and *Prinz Eugen* were some two hundred miles northeast of Iceland, and Tovey and the main British fleet clearing Scapa Flow, Lütjens turned southwest for the first leg of his run through the Denmark Straits. In this latitude it was light all night but still foggy. It was also very cold. At four in the morning, perhaps in answer to Dr. Externbrink's pleas, the squadron went on to 27 knots. At ten they started entering the mush ice and reduced to 24.

Now the squadron was approaching the most dangerous part of the breakout, the narrow passage, at this time of year not more than thirty to forty miles wide, separating the edge of the Greenland icepack from the limits of the British declared minefield that stretched northwards from the Icelandic peninsula of Vestfirdir. Presently the pack ice came into sight to starboard. The ships turned to steer parallel to it, moving on again at 27 knots. Soon they were among the big, flat ice floes that had broken off from the pack ice and were drifting southwards. There were frequent alarms as lookouts mistook floes for ships and at times swift avoiding action had to be taken; but Lütjens maintained the speed of the fleet, knowing the next few hours were critical.

It was late afternoon when Dr. Externbrink's worst fears were realized: the weather began to clear. Ahead, for the first time in nearly thirty-six hours, there was a clear path of water between three and ten miles wide. Only to port in the direction of Iceland did a thick wall of fog still lie, yellow-gray in color, mottled with shifting patterns of white, what sailors call the ice blink, the fierce reflection of the glare from the pack ice.

On the bridge of the *Prinz Eugen* too the officers, cold in their leather trousers and winter woolies, gazed through binoculars at the transformation of this twilight world. Captain Brinkmann trained his binoculars on the thick wall of fog to port and said: "If they're in these parts, they're in there."

He was right, they were; and a little later, while Commander Busch and other officers were finishing a quick meal in the dimly lit wardroom aft, the ship's alarm bells rang.

For the men of the *Norfolk* and *Suffolk*, the three-funneled 8-inch-gun cruisers that were part of the First Cruiser Squadron, patrolling the Denmark Straits was not a popular job. One saw nothing but an agony of water, gray-green or blue-black, spume tossed, marble-streaked; heard nothing but the thunder of the seas against the sides, the yell of the wind above. Off duty men ate and slept like automatons, browsing in magazines or comics.

The captain of the *Suffolk*, Robert Ellis, was very tired. When on May 18th he got Admiral Tovey's order to oil, his ship had already been ten days on patrol in the vilest weather. He made a fast night passage to Hvalfjord on the west of Iceland, remaining on the bridge most of the time, then snatched a few hours' sleep while oiling was in progress before returning to the bridge for another night passage back. It wasn't too bad a trip, for during the ship's last refit the bridge had been "arcticized," that is, closed in and steam heated: this was luxury compared to the open bridge of the *Norfolk*.

While Captain Ellis was on his way back to the Straits, his admiral, Frederick Wake-Walker, in the *Norfolk*, was steaming to Isafjordur, a deep cleft on Iceland's northwest peninsula of Vestfirdir, to look at a new radar station: *Suffolk* was to join him there to receive final instructions. Wake-Walker was a torpedo specialist who in 1940 had superbly organized the evacuation of the British Army from the beaches of Dunkirk. A tall, impressive-looking man, very technically minded, lacking much humor or imagination, he was also a friend of Tovey. His hobbies were shooting, sketching and looking for wild flowers.

At ten on the foggy morning of May 23rd the *Suffolk* edged into the entrance of Isafjordur, the bleak cliffs of Vestfirdir towering above, and soon a signal lamp was winking from *Norfolk's* bridge. *Suffolk* was to proceed within radar distance of the pack ice opposite Vestfirdir, there patrol parallel to it in a southwest/northeast direction, each leg of the patrol to last for three hours. *Norfolk* would station herself some fifteen miles to the south of her, in case the Germans risked skirting the edge of the minefield. If nothing had been sighted by the following morning the two ships would rendezvous to check positions.

Ellis swung his ship round and made off through the fog towards the pack ice. He was in a buoyant mood, for it looked as though he might be using a new toy in which he had taken a great interest, a radar set of an improved kind which had been fitted on the last refit. Radar then was in its infancy: this set had a range of thirteen miles and covered all sectors except either side of the stern.

On reaching his patrol area Ellis found, as Lütjens was soon to find, clear water along the ice edge and good visibility over Greenland, but on the Icelandic side the fog was stretching a long way in either direction.

The afternoon passed without incident. There hadn't been a whisper of the German ships since Suckling had seen them in the Bergen fjords two days before. In that time they could have steamed over a thousand miles: they could be just over the horizon, already at the edge of the Atlantic, on their way back to Germany, at anchor in a Norwegian fjord. Everyone had his own theory; no one had a clue to work on.

It was Able Seaman Newell in the *Suffolk* who brought suspense to an end. When sweeping his sector between the beam and the stern for perhaps the fiftieth time, he saw something which for the rest of his life he would never forget—the *Bismarck*, black and massive, emerging from a patch of mist on the starboard quarter, not more than seven miles away. "Ship bearing Green One Four Oh," he shouted, as though his life depended on it, which it did, and then as the *Prinz Eugen* swam into his lenses, "*Two* ships bearing Green One Four Oh."

The *Suffolk* sprang to life. Captain Ellis ordered hard aport and full speed ahead to get into the fog. Another officer pressed the alarm bells, and all over the ship men leaped from mess bench or hammock, slid into sea boots, snatched coats and scarves, lifebelts and tin hats, raced down passageways and up and down ladders to reach their action stations. Swiftly the ship answered the helm, leaning heavily to starboard: in the wardroom where dinner had started, crockery and cutlery went crashing to the deck. On the quarterdeck Ludovic Porter, the ship's commander, took off for the bridge, "as though airborne."

It was going to take a couple of minutes for *Suffolk* to reach the fog, and everyone on the bridge watched *Bismarck* coming on at them, noted the high V of her bow wave, waited fearfully for the crash of her first salvoes. Miraculously they never came and *Suffolk* breached the fog wall unharmed. Safe inside she waited, sending out a string of enemy reports, watching the two blips on the radar scan that represented the German ships passing from right to left. When the enemy was some thirteen miles ahead—at the limit of *Suffolk*'s radar range but well within scope of *Bismarck*'s guns, she ran out of the fog and took up position in *Prinz Eugen*'s wake.

Norfolk, meanwhile, fifteen miles away inside the fog, had picked up the first of *Suffolk*'s signals: her captain, Alfred Phillips, was in his sea cabin eating cheese on toast when the Yeoman of Signals burst in with the news. Phillips at once increased speed and steered for the open water, but in his eagerness not to lose touch, he misjudged the direction and emerged from the fog to find *Bismarck* only six miles ahead, coming straight at him. This time there was no doubting her readiness. As *Norfolk* swung to starboard to get back to the safety of the fog, *Bismarck*'s guns roared in anger for the first time. On the *Norfolk*'s bridge they saw the ripple of the orange flashes and brown puffs of cordite smoke, heard the scream of the shells—a sound which some have likened to the tearing of linen and others to the approach of an express train. Admiral Wake-Walker saw the sea to starboard pocked with shell splinters and observed one complete burnished shell bounce off the water fifty yards away, ricocheting over the bridge. Great columns of milk-white water rose in the air, two hundred feet high. Five salvoes in all *Bismarck* fired before *Norfolk* regained the mist: some straddled, and splinters came on board; but there were no casualties or hits.

Now *Norfolk* waited for *Bismarck* and *Prinz Eugen* to pass, as *Suffolk* had done, and when they were decently ahead, took station on the enemy's port quarter in case he suddenly altered course to port. *Suffolk* remained more or less astern of the enemy, knowing that he couldn't make an alteration to starboard because of the ice. Sometimes the German ships could be seen far ahead. When they disappeared in mists and snow flurries, Wake-Walker relied entirely on *Suffolk*'s radar, for *Norfolk*'s set, with its fixed aerials, was to all intents and purposes useless.

Ever since *Suffolk*'s contact with *Bismarck*, she had been sending out a stream of wireless reports of the enemy's position, course and speed. But none had reached base because of icing to her aerials and it was *Norfolk's* sighting report that was first picked up by ships and shore establishments of the Atlantic command; by Admiral Tovey in *King George V*, then 600 miles to the southeast, as relieved as Churchill and the Admiralty in London that his dispositions had been correct. The man to whom the news was of greatest moment was Vice-Admiral Holland in the *Hood*, which with *Prince of Wales* and their destroyers were now only 300 miles away and steering on a converging course.

CHAPTER 3

If any one ship could be said to have been the embodiment of British sea power and the British Empire between the wars, it was "the mighty *Hood*," as Britain and the Navy called her, and for later generations it is hard to convey the blend of affection, admiration and awe in which she was held, not only at home but by hundreds of thousands throughout the world.

She was an old lady now, one of the oldest in the Navy, laid down in 1916 in the Clydebank yards of John Brown, who later built the great Queens, named after a family who had given the Navy four famous admirals. She was launched in August 1918, just three months before the Armistice, the biggest warship ever built—longer even than *Bismarck* (860 feet as compared to 828) though narrower in the beam, with—like *Bismarck*—eight 15-inch guns mounted in pairs in four turrets. Her maximum speed of 32 knots made her the fastest warship of her size in the world; going flat out it took a ton of oil to drive her half a mile. She was a beautiful ship, elegant and symmetrical like *Bismarck*, yet dignified and restrained, without the aggressive sweep of *Bismarck's* lines or the massiveness that spoke of held-back power. But she had one great defect, a lack of armor on her upper decks. *Hood* had been laid down before Jutland where three British battle cruisers were destroyed by German shells which, fired at long range, had plunged vertically through the lightly protected decks and exploded inside. All big ships built after Jutland had strengthened armor. *Hood's* armor was strengthened on her sides but not on her decks: they were to be her Achilles' heel.

Between the wars, when a quarter of the globe was still colored red for Britain, the *Hood* showed the flag, as they used to say, to the Empire and the world. She went on cruises to Scandinavia and South America, to the Mediterranean and the Pacific, to the old world and the new.

In the thirties war and talk of war was increasingly in the air. This was when *Hood* was supposed to go into dock for a long refit and have her main deck armored as it always should have been, but by now Hitler and Mussolini were in power, crisis followed crisis, and to have allowed *Hood* to go out of commission for the months needed for the alterations was unthinkable. She had a brief refit just before the war, mainly to put antiaircraft guns on her upper deck. These and other additions increased her deep load by 3,000 tons and made her aft an even wetter ship than usual; in heavy seas her quarterdeck often went under and she lay down and wallowed like a dog.

In August 1939 she put away the deck awnings and light bulbs that had been such a feature of her life for nearly twenty years, painted herself overall a dull gray, rigged blackout curtains in every passageway, took on reserve officers and men, embarked tin hats and duffel coats and morphine, and went out on patrol in the gray North Sea. Now on this May evening of 1941 *Hood* was on her way to do what she had been designed to do twenty-six years before: engage on the high seas her country's enemies in battle. The wind, from the north, was rising, and she pushed her long nose into the oncoming swell, rising and falling, wet but marvelously steady. Astern and a little on the quarter was *Prince of Wales*, ahead the screening destroyers. Two had gone to Iceland to refuel, four were left: the gunner of the *Electra*, Mr. Cain, looking at the flagship across the darkling sea, thought her never so impressive. "With *Hood* to support us we felt we could tackle anything . . . there was no beating her . . . it was inconceivable to think that anything could happen to her."

On *Hood*'s bridge stood Vice-Admiral Lancelot Holland who had come on board only ten days before. Holland was 54, a gunnery specialist, a short slim man with almost white hair. He was shy at first but companionable when you got to know him, had a wry sense of humor, was well read, very able, and intensely ambitious: one evening in his cuddy he thumbed through the Navy List with his flag lieutenant and said it was either him or Bruce Fraser for First Sea Lord.

From the wing of *Hood*'s bridge Holland looked astern at where *Prince of Wales*'s great bulk lifted and fell. He felt reassured, despite her deficiencies, to have her with him. Since leaving Scapa he had exercised the two ships in range and inclination practice and signaled tactical intentions: if *Hood* and *Prince of Wales* were together when the enemy was met, fire would be concentrated; if apart, they would fire independently and report each other's fall of shot. Radar was not to be used unless action was imminent for fear the enemy might pick up its transmissions and alter course away. Preparations had been made and now there was nothing more to do but leave things, as Nelson once said, to the Great Disposer of Events. Nearly two days had gone by without further news: tension had eased and it began to seem as though this trip, like so many others in the past, was just one more false alarm.

The bubble was pricked at four minutes past eight on the evening of the 23rd when *Hood* picked up the first of *Suffolk's* reports. With his staff officers Admiral Holland studied the chart closely, plotting *Bismarck's* position and course relative to his. Then he signaled the squadron to increase speed to 27 knots on a course of 295°, and for the destroyers to follow at best speed if they could not keep up. Over the loudspeakers the ship's companies were told that action was expected within a matter of hours.

The blast from *Bismarck's* guns when firing at *Norfolk* had put her forward radar out of action, and she was now blind ahead. A desire to have eyes in front of him and also perhaps a fear that *Suffolk*, *Norfolk* and/or *King George V* might creep up on *Prinz Eugen* in bad visibility, caused Lütjens to signal to *Prinz Eugen* to take station ahead.

Now *Prinz Eugen* was in the lead, *Bismarck* astern of her, with *Norfolk* and *Suffolk* ten to fourteen miles astern of *Bismarck*—all going at nearly 30 knots, for the weather was calm, all creaking and groaning at the strains being put upon them. Four bows churned white furrows out of the leaden sea. The water slapped against the sides with quick, sharp blows like a wet towel, then fell back, hissing and frothing like detergent on the troubled, swiftly passing surface, white on peppermint green.

As the chase settled down, some of the German crews were puzzled why the world's greatest battleship should be running away from two British cruisers; so Lindemannn and Brinkmann broadcast that their orders were to avoid action with enemy warships in order to reach the Atlantic undamaged and destroy merchant shipping. These same orders had given Lütjens discretion to turn back on meeting *Norfolk* and *Suffolk*, but thinking the British fleet was still at Scapa, he saw no reason to: when darkness came, he and his staff hoped, they would give the cruisers the slip.

But in this quiet sea his ships had no superior speed and could not get away. Often *Norfolk* and *Suffolk* were blotted from sight in snow flurries and fog patches, but when the visibility cleared, there they still were; and their situation reports to the Admiralty when decoded by the German cryptographic teams showed them aware of Lütjens's every alteration of course or speed. At first the Germans believed the British must have some sensitive, underwater, hydrophonic detection gear similar to their own; then that they were picking up German radar transmissions. It was some time before they realized that at least one enemy ship was equipped with a radar set far superior to theirs. The question of British naval radar had not been discussed in the operation orders because the German naval staff believed they had none. The discovery of it at this time and place was for Lütjens and his staff a shock.

The hours passed, the four ships continued thundering south. Once the chase had settled down, there was little to disturb its monotony save, in the British ships, the fear of losing contact; in the German ones, the hope of getting away. Near *Suffolk* a snow goose detached itself from a passing flock and kept the ship company, flying above the fo'c'sle. Some officers wanted to shoot it down to have wardroom goose for next day's dinner, but Captain Ellis, remembering the Ancient Mariner, said no.

As the long day came to an end, the visibility worsened, less because of light than an increase of snow flurries, rain showers, and mist. Soon after 10 P.M. the officers on *Suffolk*'s bridge saw *Bismarck* disappear into a rainstorm and a few moments later were horrified to see her emerging from the storm and coming straight at them—the thing they had always feared—before rain again blotted her out. *Suffolk*'s wheel was put hard over to an about turn, but as the minutes passed and no *Bismarck* appeared, they realized they had been tricked by a mirage. Luckily *Suffolk* had a few knots in hand, and after some hard steaming she made contact again.

The distance between Holland and Lütjens continued steadily to close; and far away to the southeast Tovey debated whether to signal Holland to station *Prince of Wales* ahead of *Hood* so that the better protected ship might draw the enemy's fire. In the end he decided against it ("I did not feel such interference with so senior an officer justified"). Yet before many more hours had passed, he was to wish profoundly he had.

At about this time another event occurred which, small in itself, was later to affect the outcome of the whole operation. The Admiralty in London, increasingly concerned by *Bismarck*'s southward progress and the vulnerability of the troop convoy WS8B, now two days out from the Clyde, sent a signal to Admiral Somerville in Gibraltar for Force H to raise steam for full speed. And so, two thousand miles away from Greenland's icy coasts, naval patrols went ashore in the warm Gibraltar night to comb Main Street and its bars and cinemas to tell the officers and men of the aircraft carrier *Ark Royal*, the old battle cruiser *Renown*, the 6-inch-gun cruiser *Sheffield* and their destroyers to return to their ships at once. Usually their orders took them east into sunshine and blue water, on operations against the Italian fleet or for the relief of Malta, but this time they turned west, past Tangier and the edge of Africa, then northwest towards the gray Atlantic, past the two capes of Trafalgar and St. Vincent where Nelson and Jervis had won immortality so many years before. They steered so as to meet Convoy WS8B in two days' time west of Brest and southwest of Ireland. It was a rendezvous they never kept: more dramatic things were waiting for them than that.

The men of *Hood*, *Prince of Wales* and their destroyers, told that action was expected before the night was out, felt the chill of fear in their bowels, a heightening of sensation, a quickening of the blood. They were about to undergo a novel experience, to do what the ship had been built for and they had been trained for: fight. For most, so far, war had been what for most participants it always is—boredom and discomfort, long patrols in winter weather, seeing nothing, meeting nobody, dog days in harbor when you had to listen to the radio to know a war was on. And now the moment which had lived only as an embryo in the wombs of their minds had gestated, was at the point of birth; there was absolutely no avoiding it. And everywhere men wondered—all but the very unimaginative, the very brave—how it might go for them; whether they would be mutilated, lose a hand or eye or testicles; whether they would die, in agony, or without knowing a thing about it; how they would acquit themselves. And they looked at one another, each alone in his cell, hoping, doubting that others felt the same. But none spoke, for all were ashamed of their fears.

By 9 P.M. the squadron had worked up to 27 knots, which in the rising sea was as much as they would manage. It was rougher here than where the *Bismarck* was, and the destroyers were finding it increasingly uncomfortable.

At ten the squadron began preparations for battle. In the wardroom of *Prince of Wales*, before it was turned into an emergency casualty station, Lieutenant Esmond Knight, RNVR, actor, artist and ornithologist, attended a briefing by the ship's gunnery officer. Then he went to the cinema flat, where only a few days before he had been watching

Bing Crosby, to join a queue waiting for antiflash gear, white gloves and strange white hoods like those of the Ku Klux Klan, to protect hands and faces from burns. In all the ships, officers and men went to cabins and messes and put on clean underwear and socks, a ritual the British Navy has always observed before battle to prevent wounds from infection. While there, they sat down, many of them, to write farewell notes to parents, wives, sweethearts, for no one doubted the gravity of what lay ahead.

In his cabin Esmond Knight wrote two letters, then took down pictures, photographs and other breakables and wrapped them in the bedclothes, for the blast from *Prince of Wales's* own guns would soon smash them, let alone anything *Bismarck* could do. He dressed carefully, tucked trouser legs into seaboots, put on several sweaters and a warm scarf—for his action station was in the exposed Air Defense Position above the bridge—tied a lifebelt around his chest, saw that tin hat and binoculars—a German Zeiss pair he had bought in Austria before the war—were handy, then sat down in a chair to try and compose himself. He thought of the birds he loved to watch, remembered with pleasure the sight of two fulmar petrels which had kept company with the ship all day, skimming the water one on either side, traveling at over 25 knots, yet hardly ever seeming to move their slender wings. He recalled too the mountain caps of Iceland which he had seen away on the starboard beam just before coming down, and how strangely pink they looked.

But try as he would he could not keep his mind off the coming battle. "All the time there was a persistent little voice crying out from every nook and cranny in the ship that we were to be in action before many hours, and that nothing could avoid it."

Presently the squadron went to action stations, and everywhere men closed up: in the wind and spray of the upper deck, in the fug of the engine room, in the cool and claustrophobia of shell room and magazine. Watertight doors were closed, ammunition hoists tested, communications checked, guns elevated and trained: in each of *Prince of Wales's* turrets the civilian technicians from Vickers-Armstrong, never dreaming they would be required to fight a sea battle and wishing they were snug at home in bed, stood by to keep the guns in action. Down below, men looked more carefully than usual at temperature and pressure gauges, listened more acutely to orders from the bridge, to wireless messages coming in from the ether. Cooks damped down the fires of galleys, and in sickbay and wardroom doctors and sickberth attendants sterilized instruments, prepared anaesthetics and morphine. On his way to the bridge superstructure Esmond Knight passed an ornithologist friend who shouted at him and pointed excitedly to starboard. Esmond turned, expecting to see *Bismarck* on the horizon at least, but saw instead what he and his friend had longed to see for years: bobbing contentedly on the water not a hundred yards from the ship, a Great Northern Diver.

The signals from *Norfolk* and *Suffolk* continued streaming in, and at midnight the enemy was estimated to be just over a hundred miles away. If Admiral Holland continued on his present course and speed, and the enemy on theirs, he would cross some sixty miles ahead of their track by about 2:30 A.M., thus effectually barring their passage to the Atlantic. But it would also mean going into action at high speed in the darkest period of the night, with all the uncertainty and confusion that this would involve. If on the other hand he turned north towards *Bismarck* now, he could with advantage bring action on. The two squadrons would close at a mean rate of 50 knots and should meet at around 2 A.M.; sunset in this latitude was at 1:51 A.M., so while *Bismarck* and *Prinz Eugen* would be silhouetted against its afterglow, the British ships would be in darkness and could approach rapidly and unseen from a range where *Bismarck's* shells could do the maximum damage to *Hood*, to one where *Hood* would be on terms of greater equality. The Germans would not be expecting an attack from this quarter, and so he would have all the advantage of surprise.

It was a bold plan, and might well have succeeded had not *Suffolk* temporarily lost contact. Her first signal to suggest this (it contained no enemy report) was sent at 12:28 A.M. and about the same time Holland signaled that if they had not sighted the enemy by 2:10 A.M., he would turn south until the cruisers regained contact: this was so that if the *Bismarck* had maintained her southerly course, he would still be ahead of her. An hour and a half passed without sight of the enemy or any further news from *Norfolk* and *Suffolk*, so reluctantly Holland swung his ships round and steadied on 200° or south-southwest, the course that *Bismarck* was steering when the cruisers lost contact. But he told the destroyers to continue searching to the north. In the event, he missed Lütjens by a hairsbreadth. The British ships were steering an almost perfect intercepting course and were only twenty miles away when at 1:41 A.M. the German ships altered a little to the west to follow the line of the Greenland ice pack. They passed only ten miles to the northwest of Admiral Holland's destroyers, and had the visibility then not been down to between three and five miles, they would almost certainly have been spotted.

The men of *Hood* and *Prince of Wales* had now been at action stations for more than four hours, and those not actually on duty were told they could doze at their posts. Some cradled their heads in their arms, others lolled forward on lifebelt or counter, but most were still too keyed up to lose consciousness. Not wanting battle in the first place, they had yet steeled themselves to it, and now that it had been denied them, they felt let down, oddly disappointed, and annoyed at having to make another psychological adjustment. And mixed with this was a feeling of relief, instant joy that this night at any rate they might not have to spill their blood. Those who had not liked to admit their fears could afford a few quips now that danger had receded. "Pity, there goes my V.C.!" and "Those bastards in *Bismarck* don't *know* how lucky they've been," they said, helping to take themselves and others out of their private cells, reestablish comradeship, ease the tension.

It was just before 3 A.M. that *Suffolk*, steaming south at 30 knots, signaled that she was in touch with the enemy again, and on *Hood*'s plot this showed *Bismarck* to be 35 miles to the northwest, with the British just a fraction ahead. During the past hour the two squadrons had been steaming on slightly divergent courses, Lütjens on 220°, Holland on 200°, which accounted for the now increased distance between them.

Holland signaled his squadron to steer slightly inwards, across the track of *Bismarck* and *Prinz Eugen*, and presently to increase speed to 28 knots. Battle was now as certain as anything could be, though *Suffolk*'s loss of contact and *Bismarck*'s alteration to the west had put the British at a disadvantage, for the German ships had now got so far ahead that instead of the swiftly closing "head on" approach that Holland had planned, he would have to converge at a wide angle, much more slowly. The situation was worsened when at 3:20 A.M. *Suffolk* signaled that the enemy had made a further slight alteration to the west, so that the two squadrons became almost abeam. Now there would be a very long period when *Hood* was vulnerable to *Bismarck*'s plunging shells.

To the officers and men at their action stations, the news that *Bismarck* had been found meant one more psychological adjustment; but by now they were too emotionally and physically drained, and the action was too imminent, for it to make much impact. In a way it was to be welcomed, for it meant an end to doubt; if it had to be done, let it be done and over with as soon as possible. The quarter hours ticked by while the signals from *Suffolk* and *Norfolk* showed the range gradually closing. By 4 A.M. the enemy squadron was only 20 miles to the northwest, an hour later 15 miles. At 5:10 Holland signaled instant readiness for action, and in *Prince* of *Wales* Captain Leach broadcast to the ship's company that they expected to be in action within a quarter of an hour. He was followed by the ship's chaplain's flat, metallic voice: "O Lord thou knowest how busy we must be today. If we forget thee, do not thou forget us."

Captain Leach gave an order, and a lad of eighteen, Knocker White by name, was given a pair of glasses and a spare coat, told to go aloft at once, up the swaying mast to the crow's nest, keep his eyes glued to the starboard beam, and sing out loud and clear when the enemy's topmasts came into sight. The minutes passed, agonizingly slowly. No one on the bridge said anything; every eye, every pair of binoculars was trained to starboard. There was no sound but the bows slicing the water and the wind tearing and snatching at the halyards. Then, from above, came the voice, a thin, reedy cry, but no doubting its urgency: *"Enemy in sight!"* Everyone looked up and there was Knocker White, leaning out of the crow's nest and pointing excitedly to starboard. *"Enemy in sight!"* he cried again, so there should be no mistake. On the bridge they trained binoculars in the direction of the boy's arm, as the 14-inch guns in their huge turrets and the director tower and rangefinder began swinging around too. For a few moments there was nothing to see, the bridge being so much lower than the crow's nest; then from below the rim of the horizon the tops of two masts appeared, the superstructures, the ships themselves. Black they seemed to Esmond Knight in the dawn light, black and sinister and powerful. This was the enemy, come out of its lair, and to those in the British ships who had never seen a German warship before, there was something evil in the silent, purposeful way they raced southwards, hell-bent on their mission of destruction, as if the Atlantic was suddenly theirs.

The range on sighting was 17 miles, too far to open fire accurately. How quickly would Holland close it? While most of those on *Prince of Wales*'s bridge gazed, as if hypnotized, at the enemy ships, one man had his telescope trained firmly on the flagship's yardarm. He was the Chief Yeoman of Signals, and as he watched the little colored flags run up the halyards, it was his turn to speak. "From *Hood*, sir," he shouted against the wind, "Blue four. Alter course forty degrees to starboard."

It was a big alteration and the new course meant approaching the enemy at so fine an angle that *Hood* and *Prince of Wales*'s after turrets would not be able to bear—what the First Sea Lord later called "going into battle with one hand when you have two." On the other hand it meant exposing *Hood*'s vulnerable upper deck to the enemy's long-range fire for the minimum time. Captain Leach gave the orders to the helmsman, the bows of *Hood* and *Prince of Wales* swung around, pointed more acutely across the paths of *Bismarck* and *Prinz Eugen*. The range began closing rapidly; in minutes now the battle would begin.

A rather less hectic night had been passed by the crews of *Bismarck* and *Prinz Eugen*, quite unaware of the movements of *Hood* and *Prince of Wales*. A signal from Group North made late on the evening of the 23rd that there was still no enemy operational activity discernible must have given Lütjens pause for thought when two enemy ships had been trailing him for hours and one of them was reported by his cryptographers as having the call sign of *King George V*. On the other hand these could be part of the routine patrol the British kept in these waters, and if so, and Group North's report was correct, there should be nothing further ahead of him. It was true that all attempts to shake off the shadowers, lay smoke screens, and make violent alterations of course had so far failed, but once in the Atlantic, with rougher weather and longer nights, they should be able to get clear.

In the staff medical officer's cabin in the *Prinz Eugen* Commander Busch lay down for a couple of hours, fully dressed, on the cold leather bunk. He was up again a little before midnight to prepare for the middle watch. He put on bridge coat, scarf and binoculars, crossed the anteroom leading to the captain's day cabin, now unoccupied, passed the pay office with the guard mounted outside the door, skillfully avoiding the hammocks in the passageway of those sleeping near their action stations, reached the heavy, steel door that led to the upper deck, and unbolted the clips. A flurry of snow met him, thick, white flakes that blotted out all visibility. It was in this storm, a few minutes later, that *Bismarck* and *Prinz Eugen* went on to 30 knots, and *Norfolk* and *Suffolk* lost them. Busch put his head down, groped his way along the upper deck, climbed the steel ladder to the bridge.

Commander Jasper was already there, and Paul Schmalenbach, the second gunnery officer, was handing over the watch. There was little to report. *Bismarck* was in the same position, a mile astern, and some way astern of her were *Norfolk* and *Suffolk*, whose signals to the Admiralty were being decoded and sent up to the bridge within minutes; from here they were being passed by lamp to *Bismarck*, whose own wireless office was having difficulties with reception. The radar screen ahead was clear, but there were a few small ice floes about, which meant occasional alterations of course. The captain was on his chair at the back of the bridge.

Busch looked over the edge of the curved bridge rail. The snow had stopped but the wind had freshened, and the seas were breaking over the forward gun turret and shipping the spray up and over the bridge. Relief communication ratings, earphones on heads, had taken up their positions on the wooden gratings at the feet of the gunnery commander and officer of the watch, "like hens," said Busch, "on the roost." From the earphones thin cables trailed away to a switchboard panel at the side of the bridge. Inside the armored control position the helmsman rested his hands lightly on the press buttons of the electrical steering gear, keeping his eyes fixed on the dimly lit rudder indicator and compass.

Friebe, the bridge orderly, brought round soup and coffee to ease the bitter cold. Captain Brinkmann, at the back of the bridge, sipped his, spluttered and swore. "God dammit! Someone's been throwing cigarette ends into the tureen, and I've got one. Friebe, you will be shot at dawn." The captain was always coming out with things like this and everyone liked him for it. The watch dragged on, and throughout the ship—and in *Bismarck* and in the British ships too—men's thoughts turned to what they most desired. A few days before it might have been steak and eggs, an evening on the beer, the body of a beautiful girl, but for most now it was nothing more demanding than eight hours' sleep in a warm, still bed. Captain Brinkmann thought of the Kaiserhof in Berlin and the many good meals he had had there; Busch's mind turned to his home in Steuben Square, Charlottenburg, the big block of flats and the pretty women who lived in them, the provision store near the underground station run by the ex-sailor who always dressed in white.

At 3 A.M. the *Prinz Eugen*'s wireless room picked up the first enemy report from *Suffolk* for nearly three hours, and passed it to *Bismarck*. Lütjens and his staff had noted that none of *Suffolk*'s or *Norfolk*'s signals since midnight had mentioned enemy bearings, only their own course and speed, but as the signals were coming in strongly, it was reasonable to assume the British were still in touch. Had Lütjens realized he had shaken the cruisers off, he would probably have altered course drastically to make certain of it.

At 4 A.M. a refreshed Schmalenbach reappeared to take over from Jasper and the starboard watch. There wasn't much news. It was getting lighter all the time, the sea was moderate: *Suffolk* and *Norfolk* were sending out regular reports, the radar screen was clear, the captain was sleeping in his cabin. Schmalenbach settled down to the prospect of another four hours of high speed steaming. He was joined on the bridge by Lieutenant Hane of the Luftwaffe, the senior of the ship's three aircraft pilots, who had come to sniff out the chances of his taking off that morning on reconnaissance. "Good, I would think," said Schmalenbach, "we know what's behind us, but as to what's ahead, who can tell?" Hane said he hoped they would get off; he was sick of having his leg pulled in the wardroom about the airmen's extra ration of fried eggs for breakfast.

It was about an hour later that the listening post reported the sound of screws of two fast-moving ships approaching on the port bow. The bridge checked with the radar in the foretop, but they had nothing; it was not surprising, for *Hood* and *Prince of Wales* were still more than twenty miles away, over the horizon. It was the third gunnery officer who, high up in the foretop position, saw in his rangefinder smoke far away to the southeast. Once again the alarm bells were pressed—this time the succession of long trills that warned of surface action—once again men leapt from hammocks and bunks and passageways, raced to their action stations. Captain Brinkmann was on the bridge in a flash, sending an enemy report to *Bismarck*. Schmalenbach, the expert on warship silhouettes, grabbed Weyer's *Handbook of Foreign Navies* and made for the gunnery control in the foretop. Jasper hurried there too, from his cabin below the bridge, and Graf von Matuschka, a young rangefinding officer, later to do well in U-boats. In the engine room the chief engineer, Commander Graser, switched the engines and power supply to action duty and checked the emergency lighting. From all over the ship officers and men reported to the bridge or foretop that their positions were ready for action.

In the gunnery control position they watched through the rangefinders the smoke become masts, the masts become ships, the ships take shape.

"Any idea what they are?" said Jasper.

Schmalenbach took his time in answering.

"The one on the right is more squat than the one on the left, and has a tremendous bow wave. The one on the left is obviously a more modern vessel." He paused. "I think the one on the right is the *Hood*."

In the control position they heard this with astonishment. The *Hood*? Impossible. Jasper laughed out loud. "Nonsense!" he said, "it's either a cruiser or destroyer."

"I'll bet you a bottle of champagne," said Schmalenbach, "that it's *Hood*."

"Taken," said Jasper, thinking he was on to a good thing. "Load with high explosive shell and impact fuses."

These shells were ideal for bursting on the exposed decks of lightly armored cruisers or destroyers and causing casualties among the crew.

Had Jasper believed Schmalenbach, he would have loaded with armor-piercing shell with delayed fuses, designed to penetrate *Hood*'s deck and explode inside. Indeed had Brinkmann known earlier and for certain that the ships were *Hood* and *Prince of Wales*, he would have dropped out of the line, for German Fleet orders expressly forbade cruisers to engage capital ships. Lütjens did not order him to do so because in *Bismarck* they were also confused as to the identity of the British ships: the gunnery officer Commander Schneider thought them both cruisers.

And in the British ranks there was confusion too, caused by the similarity of *Bismarck*'s and *Prinz Eugen*'s silhouettes. Assuming that *Bismarck* must be leading the enemy line, Holland signaled to *Prince of Wales*, "Stand by to open fire. Target left-hand ship."

CHAPTER 4

And so the two admirals, Lütjens and Holland, riding on their great chargers, came at each other like knights of old, with guns for lances and armored bridges for visors and pennants streaming in the wind. And beneath their feet, on the airy decks and in the warm bellies of their mounts, were their six thousand young seconds, half on either side, who felt no personal ill will towards each other at all, who in different circumstances might have played and laughed and sung together, kissed each other's sisters, visited each other's homes; but now, because of this time and place, were at each other's throats, concentrating as never before to ensure that they killed first, that their knights' lances toppled the other in the tourney.

In the gun turrets of the four ships, the first shells and cartridges and silken bags of cordite had been sent up from shell rooms and magazines far below, were even now rammed home in the barrels of each gun. The breeches had been closed and locked, the gun ready lamps were burning: the guns of *Hood* and *Bismarck* were over twenty yards long, weighed 100 tons apiece. The rangefinding ratings leaned heads forward on rubber eye cushions: the German rangefinders were stereoscopic, which meant centering the little yellow *Wandermark* on the base of the enemy's superstructure; British rangefinders were co-incidental, presenting an enemy vessel in two images which required merging into one. The British Navy had considered stereoscopic equipment after the first war, for it was deadly accurate, especially at initial ranges; but it required special aptitudes and a cool head which might be lost in the heat of the battle, so in the end they rejected it. The ranges both visual and radar were fed by electrical circuits to computers in transmitting stations deep below each bridge, along with own course and speed, enemy's course and speed, wind velocity, air density, and rate of range change. Thus programmed, the computers fed to the gun turrets an ever changing stream of directions for the training and elevation of the guns. In four gunnery control positions above each bridge, the four gunnery control officers—Schneider, McMullen, Moultrie and Jasper, saw the gun ready lamps burn in front of them, stood by to open fire.

On *Hood*'s bridge a man with headphones on his ears began singing out softly the closing ranges as given from the gunnery control position, like the conductor of a Dutch auction. And at about the same time as Admiral Holland's Chief Yeoman of Signals was hoisting the preparatory signal to open fire to *Prince of Wales*, Admiral Lütjens was ordering his Chief Yeoman to hoist JD, the signal to open fire to *Prinz Eugen*. When the range was down to 13 miles, Admiral Holland said, "Execute." The Chief Yeoman shouted to the flag deck, "Down Flag 5," Captain Kerr said, "Open fire" and in the control tower the gunnery officer said "Shoot!"

There came the tiny, tinkly, ridiculous ding-ding of the fire gong, like an overture scored for triangle. For a moment the world stood still—then the guns spoke with their terrible great roar. The blast knocked one almost senseless; thick clouds of cordite smoke, black and bitter-smelling, clutched at the throat, blinded the vision, and four shells weighing a ton apiece went rocketing out of the muzzles at over 1,600 miles an hour. To Busch in the *Prinz Eugen*, *Hood*'s gun flashes appeared as "great, fiery rings like suns," and Jasper beside him called out "Damn it, those aren't cruisers' guns, they're battleships'," just as *Bismarck*'s second gunnery officer, Lieutenant Albrecht, was telling Schneider the same. Now it was *Prince of Wales*'s turn. Esmond Knight in his air defense position was deafened by the crash of the forward turrets, felt the breath squeezed from his body, was unable to see for the smoke. As it cleared, he saw an orange ripple of fire run down the length, first of *Bismarck*, then *Prinz Eugen*.

In the tightly shut armored control position on *Bismarck*'s bridge Lütjens and his staff rocked to the roar of *Bismarck*'s opening salvo. This battle was not of his choosing, for his instructions were to shun any engagement with enemy forces not escorting a convoy, and he had delayed permission to open fire so long that there were some in *Bismarck* and *Prinz Eugen* who thought he was hoping to avoid it. But with the ice to the west of him, the two cruisers to the north, and Holland's force to the east, there was no escape; and in that situation his orders were to fight all out.

Now the shells were in the air, like flights of arrows, and men on either side, counting the seconds until their arrival, asked themselves anxiously where they would fall. Some believed they were directed to them personally, had their name on them as the saying went, and felt the first stirring of panic. "He's fired," came the agitated voice of a petty officer on *Prinz Eugen*'s bridge, and Captain Brinkmann said quietly, "Keep calm, man. Of course he's fired. Now let's see what comes of it." With a shriek and a roar the shells fell, and great geysers of water leapt in the air, high as Hiltons. *Hood*'s shells landed in the vicinity of *Prinz Eugen*, but not dangerously so; *Prince of Wales*'s were a thousand yards short of *Bismarck*. But the shells of *Bismarck* and *Prinz Eugen* were deadly accurate: they enveloped *Hood* in a curtain of splashes, while the men of *Prince of Wales* watched with horror and relief.

If Admiral Holland's plan of the night before had worked, and he had come upon Lütjens unseen, he might already have won a great victory. But now everything had gone sour on him. By steering at this angle he was denying his own force the maximum of fire power and yet giving the enemy more to aim at than necessary. He had reduced his initial superiority in heavy guns of eighteen against eight to ten against eight, which was about to be reduced to nine against eight, as one of *Prince of Wales*'s forward guns had a defect which would render it inoperative after the first salvo. Further, while the British fire was divided between *Bismarck* and *Prinz Eugen*, the German fire was concentrated on *Hood*. It would have helped if *Norfolk* and *Suffolk* had closed up on *Bismarck*, worried her from the rear and drawn the fire from her after turrets: this was Holland's intention, and orders to Müllenheim-Rechberg in *Bismarck*'s after control to keep his eyes fixed on the two cruisers show that Lütjens was expecting it. But Holland had failed to give Wake-Walker the necessary orders. The opportunity was lost.

The shells went to and fro, east and west. One from *Hood* landed just ahead of *Prinz Eugen*. The water rose in a tall, white column and, falling, drenched fo'c'sle and upperworks, smearing the lenses of periscopes and telescopes that jutted out from the armored control position on the bridge. Other splashes rose on the port bow, and Captain Brinkmann ordered the helmsman to steer towards them, knowing that salvoes never land in the same place twice. Then he opened the heavy door and went outside with Friebe to see through dry binoculars. *Prinz Eugen*'s first salvo had been a little short; now she was firing her second. Twenty seconds went by. Brinkmann saw the white fountains shoot up, some short, some over—a straddle—and then a flame leapt up on *Hood*'s boat deck amidships. "It's a hit," shouted one of Jasper's crew excitedly, "the enemy's on fire." Busch saw the fire as "a glaring blood-red rectangle which began to emit thick fumes"; Captain Leach in *Prince of Wales* as "a vast blow-lamp"; Captain Phillips in *Norfolk* as "a glow that pulsated like the appearance of a setting, tropical sun."

On *Hood*'s bridge the fire was reported by the torpedo officer as being caused by a shell burst among the 4-inch antiaircraft ammunition. Able Seaman Tilburn, one of the 4-inch guns' crews, was ordered with others to put the fire out. He was about to do so when ammunition in the ready-use locker started exploding, so they all lay flat on the deck. Then another shell, or perhaps two, hit *Hood*, killing many of the gun crews now sheltering in the aircraft hangar; and part of a body, falling from aloft, struck Able Seaman Tilburn on the legs.

Now Holland decided, whatever the risks to *Hood*, that he could no longer afford to keep half his gun power out of action. He had already made one small alteration back to port, and to bring the after turrets of both ships to bear he hoisted the signal for another. While some on *Prince of Wales*'s bridge were looking at the fire in *Hood*, and others had their eyes fixed on the enemy, one man's telescope had never wavered, despite the smoke and confusion of battle, from the flagship's yardarm. "From *Hood*, sir," shouted the Chief Yeoman of Signals as the flags went up, "Two Blue. Turn twenty degrees to port together." Captain Leach and Lieutenant-Commander McMullen heard the news with joy: now at last the four-gun after turret with its frustrated crew would be brought into action.

The executive signal came down; the two ships began to turn. Then the incredible happened. When Schneider in *Bismarck* saw the fire on *Hood*'s boat deck, he ordered an immediate broadside, and presently, and for the fifth time in four minutes, *Hood* was hidden by a curtain of shell splashes. But at least one shell of that broadside made no splash: it came plunging down like a rocket, hit the old ship fair and square between center and stern, sliced its way through steel and wood, pierced the deck that should have been strengthened and never was, penetrated to the ship's vitals deep below the water line, exploded, and touched off the 4-inch magazine which in turn touched off the after 15-inch magazine. Before the eyes of the horrified British and incredulous Germans a huge column of flame leapt up from *Hood*'s center. It was followed by a thick mushroom-shaped cloud of smoke. One of the oddest things about the explosion was that it made no noise. On *Hood*'s bridge Midshipman Dundas and Signalman Briggs heard nothing unusual, and Esmond Knight said, "I remember listening for it and thinking it would be a most tremendous explosion, but I don't remember hearing an explosion at all." As the smoke welled upwards and outwards bits and pieces of *Hood* could be seen flying through the air—part of a 15-inch gun turret, the mainmast, the main derrick. Captain Brinkmann noticed the ship's shells exploding high up in the smoke, bursting like white stars.

In all disasters, however unexpected and dramatic, there is often a moment, maybe no longer than a fraction of a second, when those about to die comprehend dimly that something unusual has happened, that things are not as they should be. On *Hood*'s bridge, after the great flame had shot up, there was time for Signalman Briggs to hear the officer of the watch report the compass had gone, the quartermaster to report the steering had gone, the captain to order a switch to emergency steering: then the ship fell sideways like a collapsing house. On the boat deck Able Seaman Tilburn was conscious of a most extraordinary vibration. He saw a man beside him killed, another's side ripped open by a splinter and the guts coming out; he went over to the side to be sick and found the deck level with the water. And elsewhere in the ship there were others calmly watching dials or adjusting levers who suddenly were aware that something very strange was happening to them, who, as they were lifted off their feet, and plates and bulkheads collapsed around them, sensed for one terrible, brief moment, no longer than it takes a flash of lightning, that death had come to fetch them.

In *Prince of Wales*, *Bismarck* and *Prinz Eugen* only a handful of men saw *Hood*'s end with their own eyes: the vast majority were below decks and to them the incredible news came on intercom and by telephone, secondhand. Some simply did not believe it. *Prinz Eugen*'s executive officer, Commander Stoos, on duty in the lower command post, hearing his captain's voice announcing the news, said quietly, "Some poor fellow up there has gone off his head." In *Bismarck*'s after transmitting station Leading Seaman Eich heard Commander Schneider's joyous shout, "She's blowing *up*," and would remember the long drawn out *"uuup"* for the rest of his life. In the after director tower Müllenheim-Rechberg heard it too, and despite orders to stick to the two cruisers, couldn't resist swinging round to see for himself. The smoke was clearing to show *Hood* with a broken back, in two pieces, bow and stern pointing towards the sky. As he watched, he saw the two forward turrets of *Hood* suddenly spit out a final salvo: it was an accident, the circuits must have been closed at the moment she was struck, but to her enemies it seemed a last defiant and courageous gesture.

Now *Prince of Wales*, turning to port to obey Holland's orders, had to go hard a-starboard to avoid the wreckage ahead, and Jasper, through *Prinz Eugen*'s main rangefinder, saw on the far side of *Prince of Wales* a weird thing—the whole forward section of *Hood*, rearing up from the water like the spire of a cathedral, towering above the upper deck of *Prince of Wales* as she steamed by. Inside this foresection were several hundred men, trapped topsy-turvey in the darkness of shell room and magazine. Then *Prince of Wales* passed; both parts of *Hood* slid quickly beneath the waves, taking with them more than 1,400 men, leaving only a wreath of smoke on the surface. "Poor devils, poor devils!" said Jasper aloud, echoing the thoughts of those around him; for as sailors they had just proved what sailors do not care to prove: that no ship, not even *Hood*, is unsinkable—and that went for *Bismarck* and *Prinz Eugen* too.

But joy and awe were both short-lived, for the battle was not yet over. Before the blowing up of *Hood*, *Prinz Eugen* had already been ordered to shift her fire to *Prince of Wales* and now *Bismarck* had to make only the smallest of adjustments to find the range too. On *Prince of Wales*'s bridge they saw the burst of black smoke from *Bismarck*'s cordite and the long ripple of orange flashes from her guns, knew this time without a doubt where they were aimed, what they were capable of doing. Yet Captain Leach was not despondent. His own guns had found *Bismarck* with the sixth salvo, straddled and hit. If everyone kept a cool head, they might win a victory yet.

The salvo fell and then there was chaos. A 15-inch shell went clean through the bridge and exploded as it went out the other side, killing everyone except the captain and Chief Yeoman of Signals, and the navigating officer, who was wounded. Young Midshipman Ince was among the dead, aged eighteen and full of promise. On the deck below, the plotting officer, unable to distinguish between hits from *Bismarck* and the firing of *Prince of Wales*'s own guns, was unaware anything had happened until blood trickled down the bridge voicepipe and dripped onto his chart.

This same shell did for Esmond Knight too. The man whose delight in life was visual things, painting pictures, watching birds, was already among the ranks of the war-blinded, and he would now never see the

Harlequin Duck or Icelandic Falcon, or anything but dim shapes again.

Now in *Prinz Eugen* there were reports from the hydrophonic detection room of torpedoes approaching. Both ships turned to comb, to steer parallel to, their tracks. As *Prinz Eugen* swung round, funnel smoke blinded Jasper in the main gunnery control, so Albrecht, the civilian from Siemens and designer of the firing mechanism for the guns, fired the after turrets himself. Now the two German ships turned back, confident, assertive, weaving in and out of *Prince of Wales*'s shell splashes, dancing and side-stepping like boxers who suddenly sense victory in the blood. *Bismarck*'s salvoes thundered out every twenty seconds, *Prinz Eugen*'s every ten. The shell splashes rose round *Prince of Wales* like clumps of whitened trees. Now the British battleship was within range of *Prinz Eugen*'s torpedoes; but just as Lieutenant Reimann was about to fire, she turned away.

For after only another twelve minutes of battle, *Prince of Wales* had had enough. She had been hit by four of *Bismarck*'s heavy shells and three of *Prinz Eugen*'s. The compass platform, echo-sounding gear, radar office, aircraft recovery crane, fore secondary armament director, and all the boats and several cabins had been wrecked. The shell that hit the crane landed just as the Walrus aircraft was about to be launched to spot fall of shot—the launching officer's hand was in the air. The wings were peppered with splinters, and as the pilot and observer scrambled out, the plane was ditched over the side to avoid risk of fire. The same splinters that blinded Esmond Knight also pierced a fresh water tank, releasing a flood of hot water onto survivors of the bridge and men on the signal deck below. One 15-inch and two 8-inch shells hit the ship below the waterline, letting in 400 tons of sea water. Another 8-inch shell found its way into a shell handling room, whizzed around several times without going off or hitting anyone, and finally took two men to throw it over the side.

Moreover *Prince of Wales*'s own gunnery was less than adequate. Although Lieutenant-Commander Skipwith, the spotting officer, had observed straddles on *Bismarck* with the ninth and thirteenth salvoes, few salvoes were of more than three guns when they should have been of five. Mechanical defects were developing continuously in the newly installed guns, and though the Vickers-Armstrong workmen in the turrets were doing wonders, they had hardly corrected one fault before another arose. It dawned on Captain Leach that not only was he engaged in a very unequal battle, but if he continued much longer, he might soon deprive the Navy of a valuable ship without inflicting further damage on the enemy. He knew that his Commander-in-Chief was four hundred miles to the southeast with *King George V* and *Repulse,* and that if *Bismarck* and *Prinz Eugen* continued on the same course, they would make contact with them early next day. If he broke off action now, joined the shadowing cruisers, overhauled the guns and repaired the damage, he would be well placed to attack *Bismarck* from the rear when Tovey came in from the east, and effect a concentration of fire power that would force the enemy to divide his.

So after having fired eighteen salvoes, *Prince of Wales* made smoke and disengaged to the southeast. As she turned, the shell ring of Y turret jammed, rendering the four guns in it inoperable. Her casualties were two officers and eleven men killed, one officer and eight men wounded. The time was 6:13 A.M., just twenty-one minutes after Admiral Holland in *Hood* had so proudly led his squadron into battle.

And when *Hood's* four destroyers reached the edge of the scene, they found only three of her survivors.

CHAPTER 5

When the crews of *Bismarck* and *Prinz Eugen* were told that *Prince of Wales* (which they mistook for *King George V;* they didn't know *Prince of Wales* was in service) had broken off action and turned away, there was much cheering and shouting, joy at victory and relief at survival. Some men left their posts and went on the upper deck to see for themselves. The two gunnery officers came in for much praise: Schneider was the center of congratulation in *Bismarck's* wardroom; in *Prinz Eugen* Jasper was called to the telephone from A turret to listen to the crew playing his favorite dance tune on a gramophone. In both ships there was a special issue of cigarettes and chocolates: everyone said the victory was a birthday present for Admiral Lütjens, who was to be 52 next day. "Report hits and casualties," Lütjens signaled to *Prinz Eugen,* and Brinkmann was happy to signal back, "None." A great jagged splinter from one of *Hood's* shells found at the base of *Prinz Eugen's* funnel brought home to her crew how incredibly lucky they had been: as Brinkmann pointed out, one of these slicing through *Prinz Eugen's* flimsy armor and exploding in the boiler room would have quickly stopped her.

Bismarck had been less fortunate. She had received three hits altogether, though Müllenheim-Rechberg and others were unaware of any until the action was over. One had carried away the captain's motor boat amidships, damaged the aircraft launching gear, and landed in the sea beyond without exploding. The second had also struck amidships, penetrating the ship's side beneath the armored belt, destroying one of the dynamoes, putting No. 2 boiler room and its two boilers out of action, wounding five men by scalding, and causing some flooding. The third and most serious hit had struck the port bow about the level of the water line, penetrated two oil tanks, and come out the starboard side without exploding. This hit not only let sea water into the oil tanks and quantities of oil into the sea, but knocked out the suction valves and cut off from the engines a further thousand tons of oil. Now for the first time Lütjens had cause to regret not having topped up from tankers *Weissenburg* or *Wollin*.

It was this, as much as anything, that determined *Bismarck's* future course of action. There is evidence that after *Prince of Wales* broke away, there was a difference of opinion between Lindemann, who wanted to finish off the damaged battleship, and Lütjens, who was determined to press on south. Lütjens must stick to his instructions, the sinking of merchant shipping, avoiding encounters with enemy warships. Even to have known that it was not *King George V* he was fighting but the raw and untested *Prince of Wales* would not have altered his decision; for to have turned and followed her would have meant exposing the squadron further to her gunfire as well as gun and torpedo attacks by *Norfolk* and *Suffolk* (and possibly other ships lying beyond the horizon), risking the lives of his ships and crews on a venture that had been expressly forbidden.

Meanwhile there was enough to think about with the damage. Because of flooding the bow was down by two or three degrees. There was a list to port of nine degrees and the starboard propeller was coming out of the water. Lindemann ordered counterflooding aft to restore the trim, and maximum speed was reduced to 28 knots. Oil from the damaged tanks continued gushing into the sea, so Lütjens signaled *Prinz Eugen* to drop back and see how much of a wake it was leaving astern. As the cruiser fell back, the battleship came up on her port side, close, so *Prinz Eugen's* men could see *Bismarck's* men clearly, saw too the great dark gash on her starboard bow where the shell from *Prince of Wales* had come out. In her wake stretched a broad carpet of oil, all colors of the rainbow, smelling strongly, a telltale sign of her presence. Brinkmann made his report. *Bismarck* turned sharply to the west and ordered *Prinz Eugen* to take the lead again.

Soon it was clear beyond a doubt to Lütjens and his staff that with one boiler room out of action, maximum speed reduced to 28 knots, serious flooding and loss of fuel and the ship leaving a pathway of oil that could be seen for miles, *Bismarck* could no longer carry out her assignment without dockyard repairs. But to which dockyard should he go? If back to Germany his nearest friendly port was Bergen or Trondheim, both a little over a thousand miles away. But this meant a return through the hazardous passages north or south of Iceland, with the enemy's air forces now fully alerted, and the possibility that further heavy British units were at sea between him and Scapa Flow (the appearance of *Hood* which Group North had reported as being in West Africa and of a *King George* class battleship had proved how little he could rely on his own Intelligence). The coast of France was six hundred miles farther, but meant longer nights and wider seas in which to shake off his shadowers, perhaps entice them over a line of U-boats, top up with fuel from one of the waiting tankers, then steam unmolested to the Normandy dock at St. Nazaire. A further advantage of this was that once repairs had been effected, *Bismarck* (with perhaps *Scharnhorst* and *Gneisenau* too) would already be poised on the edge of the Atlantic trade routes instead of having to renegotiate the perils of a second breakout from Germany. So, three hours after sinking *Hood*, Lütjens signaled Group North, together with a report on *Bismarck*'s damage and the efficacy of British radar, his intentions to release *Prinz Eugen* for independent cruiser warfare and for *Bismarck* to put into St. Nazaire.

Because of a faulty aerial or inexperienced radio personnel, neither Lütjens's signal that he had sunk *Hood* nor his later signal about making for St. Nazaire reached Germany until early afternoon. There the news of *Hood*'s destruction was seized on joyfully by Dr. Goebbels's Propaganda Ministry. In the Berlin Admiralty, though, satisfaction at Lütjens's success was tempered by despondency at news of *Bismarck*'s damage and the decision to steer for France. It was not clear to Raeder whether Lütjens intended to make for St. Nazaire immediately or after shaking off his shadowers and then oiling in mid-Atlantic.

Preparations went ahead to cover all eventualities. In Norway Schulze-Hinrichs and his destroyers were ordered from Trondheim to Bergen, U-boats detailed to patrol the Faeroes-Shetland passage, and Air Fleet 5 put on special alert. In St. Nazaire balloon barrage equipment, searchlights, and heavy and light flak units were ordered to the Normandy dock, and in other French west coast ports escort vessels were brought to short notice for steam. Air Fleet 3 and Air Commander, Atlantic, were also alerted, as were U-boat headquarters at Lorient, where Lütjens's old friend, Karl Dönitz, offered to suspend all Atlantic operations and put his entire fleet at *Bismarck*'s disposal. In April in Paris Lütjens had discussed with Dönitz the possibility of *Bismarck* drawing enemy forces over a concentration of U-boats, and now, with the two cruisers and *Prince of Wales* hard on his tail, Lütjens sent Admiral Saalwächter (Group West's commander) a signal asking for just such a concentration south of Greenland the following morning. Dönitz ordered seven boats to take up position.

The British Admiralty, meanwhile, fast recovering from the shock of the *Hood*, were also making their dispositions. From Halifax, Nova Scotia, the old battleship *Revenge*, from east of Newfoundland the old battleship *Ramillies*, from northeast of the Azores the cruisers *London* and *Edinburgh*, from west of the Clyde the battleship *Rodney* and her destroyers—all these ships were ordered to break off immediately from patrol or convoy escort or whatever they were doing and steer to intercept the German squadron. From Portsmouth a submarine was sailed to take up position outside the Biscay ports; and so vital did the Admiralty think it not to lose touch with *Bismarck* that they signaled Wake-Walker to remain in pursuit even if it meant running out of fuel: Commodore Blackman steaming north in *Edinburgh* at 25 knots was told the same. And from Washington came word that a squadron of American naval planes based in Newfoundland would search the waters south of Cape Farewell the next morning.

The nearest force to Lütjens now was that of the Commander-in-Chief, Admiral Tovey, who with *King George V*, *Repulse*, *Victorious* and five cruisers was some 360 miles to the southeast. The news of *Hood's* end had been broken to Tovey by Commander Jacobs, the fleet wireless officer, in a voice loud with emotion. "All right, Jacobs," said Tovey calmly, "there's no need to shout." Now he and his Chief of Staff, Commodore Brind, with Commander Robertson, the staff operations officer, were in the plotting room off the admiral's bridge, discussing quietly what needed to be done. Would the German admiral continue south, break out to the westward after dark, or double back on his tracks to Germany, north or south of Iceland? Tovey felt he must steer a course that covered all three contingencies.

Meanwhile, thanks to the dogged persistence of *Suffolk's* radar operators and *Norfolk's* lookouts, the shadowing of the German squadron went on. As the forenoon wore on *Bismarck* gradually dropped speed

while carrying out repairs to the bows, first to 26 knots, then 24, and
Norfolk on her port quarter found herself slowly creeping up on her
beam. *Prince of Wales* in turn had taken advantage of *Bismarck's*
reduction of speed to close the distance between herself and *Norfolk*.
Wake-Walker signaled Leach to take station astern and asked how things
were: Leach replied he was again ready for action, though still engaged in
washing down the bridge to remove the remains of the men killed there.

Soon the visibility deteriorated. *Bismarck* disappeared in the mist, and
Suffolk found herself temporarily out of radar touch. *Norfolk*, followed
by *Prince of Wales*, swished along in the mist for some time, now
completely out of contact with the enemy. Suddenly Wake-Walker had a
hunch, nothing more, that *Bismarck* had altered course to port across his
bows, and that the range between them was closing rapidly. He ordered
Captain Phillips to turn 360° to port—a complete circle—before resuming
his previous course and signaled *Prince of Wales* to follow him, thus
lengthening the distance from *Bismarck* by three or four miles. Forty
minutes later the mist cleared and revealed *Bismarck* only eight miles
away, dead ahead. She had in fact altered course to due south—a turn to
port of thirty degrees—only minutes after *Norfolk* had started to circle.
But for Wake-Walker's intuition the two ships would have closed each
other in the mist unseen, met beam to beam a mile or two apart, where
Bismarck would have blown *Norfolk* out of the water.

For Tovey the news of *Bismarck's* alteration to the south, i.e. slightly
towards him, was greatly encouraging. He and Brind made calculations
on the chart and concluded that if *Bismarck* were to maintain this course
and speed, they would be in action with her and *Prinz Eugen* early next
morning. But what if the Germans put on a burst of speed during the
night, zigzagged violently, broke away westwards or to the north? He had
only one weapon that could slow *Bismarck* down, make the action more
certain—the carrier *Victorious* and her Swordfish torpedo planes.
Captain Bovell had told him before sailing that the maximum range he
could launch an attack and get his planes back was a hundred miles. If
Victorious were to leave his flag now, steer a direct intercepting course
towards the enemy, she should be a hundred miles from *Bismarck* by
evening. A little after three in the afternoon Tovey hoisted a signal to
Rear-Admiral Alban Curteis in the *Galatea* to take *Victorious* and his
four cruisers and proceed in execution of previous orders. "Good luck,"
he made to Bovell, and perhaps only Bovell knew how much they needed
it. Then he ordered *King George V* and *Repulse* to turn forty degrees to
port to a course of a little west of south, so that if *Bismarck* herself

continued due south, there would be no danger of what sailors call "losing bearing," i.e. getting behind her. He and Brind stood and watched *Victorious*, protected by Curteis's cruisers, standing on towards the still distant enemy in a flurry of spray, become a smudge on the southwestern horizon, dip and disappear below the world's rim: from that moment she and her young aircrews were seldom out of their thoughts.

Visibility was patchy all day. The mist came and went, and at times *Bismarck* was in sight of *Norfolk* and *Prince of Wales*, at others blotted out; but away on the starboard quarter *Suffolk* had regained radar contact and held it firmly.

In the forenoon morale on board *Bismarck* remained high. Few doubted they would shake off the enemy during the night, top up with fuel from one of the waiting tankers, make good the damage, then go on to attack allied shipping. Information in big ships circulates slowly; and to Müllenheim-Rechberg and others the news that *Bismarck* was to make for St. Nazaire and *Prinz Eugen* was to operate independently came as a complete surprise.

In the early afternoon Lütjens signaled to Brinkmann his plan for the breakaway. During a rain squall *Bismarck* would make off to the west: *Prinz Eugen* was to maintain present course and speed for three hours, then steer for either of the tankers *Belchen* or *Lothringen* southwest of Greenland, replenish her tanks and proceed independently on cruiser warfare. The executive code word for the movement was to be—an ironic touch—"Hood."

This was the first news Brinkmann had had that the two ships were to part company, for Lütjens had not informed him of his signal to Group West about St. Nazaire. He remained completely in the dark as to Lütjens's intentions for *Bismarck* after she had got clear, whether to operate her also independently or, because of the damage, make for Germany or France. . The most likely explanation for this is that Lütjens had assumed *Prinz Eugen*'s wireless office had picked up his signals to Group West. But a more communicative admiral would have checked.

Before Brinkmann had time to query the situation there was an air raid warning as a plane from Iceland made contact. Soon after a rain squall came up, *Bismarck* signaled "Hood," and sheered off to the west. Twenty minutes later she was back in station, having sighted (and been sighted by) *Suffolk*, shadowing by radar thirteen miles away on the starboard quarter.

And so the chase continued south; and at about this time Admiral

Wake-Walker, batting along in the *Norfolk* ten miles astern, received from the British Admiralty a very disturbing signal.

The operations room of the British Admiralty was situated in a large, new, ugly concrete building, called the Citadel, adjacent to the old Admiralty building in Whitehall, London, close by the War Office and Nelson's column in Trafalgar Square, and just up the road from Downing Street and the Houses of Parliament. This was the heart and center of the whole British naval war effort. There was a big map of the world on one wall, one of the Atlantic on another, and pins and flags showed the constantly shifting positions of British warships and convoys, as well as the enemy surface craft and U-boats, sighted by aircraft or fixed by intelligence or radio direction finding. It was to this room that Tovey spoke on the green telephone from his flagship at Scapa. It was here that information and intelligence of all kinds, from ships, shore establishments, embassies, monitoring posts and agents all over the world flowed in; from here that operational instructions, commands, advice and situation reports to ships at sea went out. It was manned by fifteen or twenty officers and men who, ever since receiving Captain Denham's signal of *Bismarck*'s departure, had been at full stretch. The officers most concerned with important decisions at this time were Captain Edwards, Director of Operations; Captain Daniel, Director of Plans; Rear-Admiral Clayton; Commander Denning and Lieutenant-Commander Kemp of Naval Intelligence. Above them in the naval hierarchy were Rear-Admiral Power, Assistant Chief of the Naval Staff; Vice-Admiral Sir Tom Phillips, Vice-Chief of the Naval Staff; and the head of the Navy, Admiral of the Fleet Sir Dudley Pound, First Sea Lord. Any important operational signal going out from the Admiralty to the fleet at sea either originated from Pound or else had his approval.

Of all the admirals involved in the *Bismarck* operation it was Dudley Pound about whom opinion was most divided. He had had a distinguished career as flag captain of the battleship *Colossus* at Jutland, but he was now a sick man who had only become First Sea Lord because other, more senior officers had been even iller than himself. He had a tumor of the brain that was eventually to kill him and a disease of the hip that caused him pain and insomnia. Before the war, when Commander-in-Chief, Mediterranean, he was sometimes to be seen pacing the deck of the flagship in the dead hours of night: the Fleet Medical Officer thought him unfit to command in time of war but couldn't bring himself to tell the Admiralty. He was not really fit to be a wartime First Sea Lord, with all the strains of office: pain and loss of sleep at night meant that he sometimes dozed off at daytime meetings. But he was flattered by the Prime Minister's trust in him; and Churchill liked him because he was often amenable to his wishes.

Pound's besetting sin was what sailors call "back-seat driving," constantly going over the heads of appointed admirals, trying to run operations from Whitehall, thinking that he knew best. "He was neither a great tactician nor a great strategist," wrote Tovey, "but unfortunately he believed he was." Tovey's staff officers speak feelingly of the stream of instructions that came pouring down the line from him in London whenever the Fleet was in harbor, and which added to their work rather than eased it.

As the day of the 24th wore on, as morning gave way to afternoon and the German squadron continued unmolested southwards, each mile bringing them nearer to shipping lanes—and in particular troop convoy WS8B—it seemed to Churchill and others in high office a strange thing that Admiral Wake-Walker should be content to let *Prince of Wales* trail along in *Bismarck*'s wake, making no effort to reengage and slow her up. Now Pound of all people knew from the maps in the operations room the exact situation. He knew *Victorious* was on her way to launch a torpedo attack, that *King George V* and *Repulse* were closing the enemy and could be expected to make contact next morning. Nevertheless, and doubtless because of Churchill's prodding, he sent a signal to Wake-Walker asking what his intentions were about *Prince of Wales* reengaging.

Wake-Walker received the signal in the late afternoon and was much shaken. He drafted and tore up several replies before signaling that he did not consider *Prince of Wales* should reengage until other heavy ships made contact or failed to, adding he doubted whether she had the speed to force an action. Tovey, hearing this exchange of signals in *King George V*, was as pleased with Wake-Walker's reply as he was angry at the Admiralty's inquiry. Wake-Walker was doing what he wanted in keeping *Prince of Wales* in touch, but out of battle, until his arrival, and he had no desire to risk further damage to her, or the cruisers losing contact.

Later the Admiralty sent *Norfolk* and *Suffolk* a signal congratulating them on their shadowing, urging them to keep up the good work, but by this time the damage had been done. Wake-Walker told his staff he proposed to order *Prince of Wales* to take station ahead of *Norfolk*, and *Suffolk* to close in from twelve miles to the westward to five, so he could maneuver his ships as a force. His flag-lieutenant, David Kelburn, and

Norfolk's navigating officer, Norman Todd, implored him not to move *Suffolk* from where she was, as it would make shadowing more difficult. But the admiral was adamant. He was going to order *Prince of Wales* to creep up on *Bismarck*'s port quarter, attack her from astern, then retire with his force to the eastwards in the hope of luring *Bismarck* towards the Commander-in-Chief. What reason he imagined would induce *Bismarck* to go eastwards, it is hard to say, but that was his story and he was sticking to it: no more Admiralty signals were going to suggest he was lacking in offensive spirit.

In *Prinz Eugen*, meanwhile, two miles ahead of *Bismarck* and out of sight of the British squadron, Commander Busch woke in the staff medical officer's cabin from an afternoon sleep. He went on deck, found the sea rougher than in the morning—little heads of foam breaking on the gray swell—and nothing in sight but *Bismarck*, black and massive, astern. He climbed to the bridge and found Beck, the navigating officer, with a sheaf of signals in his hand, cap under arm, the wind ruffling his red hair. Jasper was sucking a boiled sweet from a bag the officer of the watch was handing round, and Brinkmann, smart in his blue battledress, was smoking his usual cigar.

They told him of the *Bismarck*'s unsuccessful efforts to get away; then, as he had the next watch, he went to the wardroom for an early dinner. Half a dozen officers were sitting at the horseshoe dining table. They picked at the food, pickled herrings and baked potatoes with bacon and onion sauce, eating mostly in silence. Busch sensed an atmosphere of depression. They were all tired and tense; the cruisers had been in touch for nearly twenty-four hours and it seemed they could never shake them off: unconsciously they were listening for the alarm bells which had been sounding on and off all day, shrill and urgent, tearing at frayed nerves. The whole of the British Navy was after them, seeking a terrible vengeance: soon other ships would arrive, and even if they disposed of them and escaped damage again, there would be others and then others to take their place. The whine and rumble of the turbine shafts racing beneath them, the vibration of deck and bulkhead, the clatter of cutlery and glasses marathon-dancing on the table, were messages that every minute and meter were taking them farther into the unknown. "If there's an alert now," said the shipwright lieutenant, echoing their thoughts, "it won't be aircraft, it'll be the other thing. And that'll be something to be getting on with."

Busch went on watch again at 6 P.M., reported on the bridge to Jasper, and noticed it was getting misty. Brinkmann, having heard no more from

Lütjens about "Hood," assumed he had abandoned the idea and was now busy drafting his own proposals.

He was about to send a signal to *Bismarck* when the flagship's own signal lamp started winking. "*Prinz Eugen* from Fleet," shouted the signalman. The message was brief, four letters only flashing across the empty sea. "Hood," sang out the signalman, and even as they watched, *Bismarck* swung away to starboard, into the mists, her main turrets already easing around towards the enemy, her antiaircraft guns thick and erect as bristles, looking to Busch like drawn swords. Slowly the mist swallowed her, all but her fighting top sliding down the sky; then that disappeared too.

A long time went by. *Prinz Eugen* drove on southwards and the mist began to clear. From astern they heard the low rumble of *Bismarck*'s guns, saw the yellow and orange flashes, brown cordite smoke welling up the sky. Men came up from mess decks and washroom, cabin and galley, crowded the guard rails to see for themselves. Briefly *Bismarck* came into sight on the northwestern horizon, still firing, militant and proud, said Busch, wearing a halo of smoke from the salvoes of her turrets. "There goes our big brother," said Jasper on the bridge. "We're going to miss him very, very much." Like Tovey watching *Hood* glide out of Scapa Flow only three days before, he and the rest of *Prinz Eugen*'s crew, passing out of this story, looked at their country's greatest warship for the last time.

CHAPTER 6

So instead of Wake-Walker initiating the action with *Bismarck* he had planned, *Bismarck* had got in first. When she disappeared into the mist, *Suffolk* was thirteen miles on her starboard quarter, easing her way over towards *Norfolk* and *Prince of Wales*. Captain Ellis had been resting his radar set and its tired crew; now he switched it on again. It was just as well—the range started coming down rapidly. When it was at ten miles Ellis put the wheel over to port and increased speed. *Bismarck* emerged from the mist, heading straight for *Suffolk*, and fired an opening salvo. The white geysers gushed up silently a thousand yards astern; later ones fell near enough to loosen rivets in the plating aft. *Suffolk* replied with nine broadsides, mostly short, and retired behind a smoke screen when Wake-Walker signaled, "Do not waste ammunition." The blast from B turret, firing aft, had smashed all the bridge windows, opening the enclosed, steam-heated bridge to icy winds and spray. *Norfolk* and *Prince of Wales* hurried over and opened fire at *Bismarck* at 15 miles: *Bismarck* fired three salvoes, *Prince of Wales* twelve before two of her guns again went out of action. "I am sure this opportunity to reengage must have had a good effect on her," Wake-Walker wrote breezily later. He hoped it had had a good effect on the Admiralty too.

Bismarck turned west, then south: Lütjens had accomplished one task in enabling *Prinz Eugen* to slip away, but if he had had hopes of getting *Bismarck* clear too, they were soon disappointed: Argus-eyed *Suffolk's* radar never lost touch. Wake-Walker formed the squadron in line ahead, *Suffolk* leading, *Prince of Wales* supporting her in the center, *Norfolk* in the rear. He felt the need to keep his ships together as a fighting force—even if it meant some sacrifice in efficient shadowing. But he assured *Prince of Wales* he did not intend her to engage *Bismarck* again until Tovey's arrival in the morning.

And so things continued as before, except that now the Admiralty sent a signal warning of U-boats, and Wake-Walker ordered the force to zigzag together, the port runs taking them away from *Bismarck*, the starboard ones back towards her. In *Bismarck* there was much satisfaction that *Prinz Eugen* had got away so cleanly, and was over forty miles away, beyond the southern horizon: all that remained now was for the flagship to slip away during the night. The optimism spread with the arrival of a signal from Saalwächter sending congratulations on the sinking of *Hood*, saying that preparations for *Bismarck's* reception were going ahead at St. Nazaire and Brest, and advising Lütjens to take off the enemy by withdrawing temporarily to a remote sea area. By steering south-south-west for the U-boat patrol line halfway between Greenland and Newfoundland, this is just what he was doing.

And then later came the announcement on the German wireless network to stand by for a special naval announcement. They knew this was not another of Dönitz's U-boat triumphs; it could only refer to them. Word was sent down to the wireless office to plug in the network to the loudspeaker system, tuning the set carefully to minimize hissing and crackling, for they were a long way from home. Everywhere on board, and in *Prinz Eugen* too, in mess deck and turret, engine room and control position, men stopped their chatter, put down cards, roused themselves from sleep, crowded round the speakers so as not to lose a word. First came the familiar voice of the announcer: "This is Berlin," and those who knew Berlin, like Busch, remembered it, and those who didn't imagined it, brave and beautiful. Then came a band playing the naval anthem, stirring enough on its own, but in this context, as an overture, overwhelming. The music ended, there was a brief pause, then the announcer read the dispatch from the Supreme Command, how the battleship *Bismarck* on a mission in the Atlantic had sunk the pride of the British Navy, the great battle cruiser *Hood*, and was now proceeding on further operations. And throughout *Bismarck* officers and men from Lütjens down to the humblest able seaman were in a turmoil of pride, for this was their victory that was being celebrated, and it was to them alone, in the wild Atlantic and two thousand miles from home, that the whole German nation was paying homage.

Yet this was the last good news in *Bismarck* for some time. For the fleet engineer officer and the ship's engineer officer had been doing their sums, and now they reported to Lütjens the seriousness of the fuel situation. The problem was this: If *Bismarck* continued on her present course, drawing the shadowers over the U-boat line, she would have ample fuel to reach *Belchen* or *Lothringen*, even to run down to *Spichern* or *Esso Hamburg* near the Azores. But say she was prevented from reaching any of her oilers; say the U-boats failed to torpedo the shadowers and she herself was unable to shake them off. Then they would be marooned in mid-Atlantic with insufficient fuel to reach France. If on the other hand they abandoned the U-boat patrol line and made for France now, there would be adequate reserves for the journey, providing nothing unforeseen happened. Looked at in that light there could be no choice. Just before 10 P.M. Lütjens signaled Group West: "Impossible to shake off enemy owing to radar. Proceeding directly to Brest because of fuel situation," and ordered Lindemann to come round from south-southwest to due south.

Meanwhile, unknown to Lütjens, the *Victorious* and her escorting cruisers were slowly closing from eastwards. Captain Bovell had hoped to be within 100 miles of *Bismarck* by 9 P.M., fly off his striking force then; but Lütjens's diversion to the west to allow *Prinz Eugen* to slip away had opened the gap and by 10 P.M. he was still 120 miles away.

There were to be nine aircraft in the attack, ancient Swordfish biplanes, "Stringbags" the Navy called them, that looked like survivors of Richthofen's Circus—their cruising speed was 95 m.p.h. and that was pushing it. Each carried a crew of three: pilot, observer, rear gunner, and an 18-inch torpedo slung below the belly. The squadron was divided into three sub-flights led by Eugene Esmonde, the squadron commander, Percy Gick, a former instructor at the Torpedo School, and "Speed" Pollard (so called because of his lethargy), all regular R.N. officers. These were the only men of experience; the others were mostly reservists, some of whom had never been in a carrier before. Earlier the twenty-seven of them had been briefed by Commander Ranald, the flight operations officer, shown silhouettes of the mighty *Bismarck*, and had explained to them the method of attack. Now, dressed in bulky flying jackets with little red lights and whistles attached, they sat about in the crews' rest room, smoking cigarettes, thumbing through dog-eared magazines. Few could concentrate on anything but what lay ahead. Soon they would be required to take off from this swaying bucket, fly over a hundred miles in a decreasing visibility to look for a moving target that might alter course at any moment, find it, attack it, survive its devastating fire power, and return in darkness to *Victorious*. The more one looked at it, the more ridiculous it seemed.

Soon after 10 P.M., at about the time that Lütjens was deciding about Brest, orders came down from the bridge for the squadron to go. The nine planes were squatting at the end of the slippery flight deck like a covey of damp partridges. The deck staff started engines, the crews clambered in and fixed the straps. The *Victorious* turned to starboard, into the northwest wind, reducing speed from 28 to 15 knots. The first plane trundled down the flight deck, took off, then the second; presently the whole squadron were airborne without mishap. They formed up on Esmonde, turned away from the ship, and set course southwest. As they were swallowed up in a rain squall Captain Bovell wondered if he would ever see any of them again.

Some thirty miles ahead of *Bismarck* when she turned to her new course, a solitary vessel with gray upperworks and a yellow mast pushed her way slowly through the evening drizzle and swell. She was the United States Coastguard Cutter *Modoc*, 1,800 tons, from 1922 until the war part of the North Atlantic International Ice Patrol. For the past three days she had been searching for boats and survivors from torpedoed ships of the H.X. 126 convoy attacked by Wohlfarth and his fellow U-boat commanders on May 20th.

Although it was to be another seven months before America entered the German war, she had already shown where her sympathies lay: with the country of which she had once been a part, whose language she shared, whose institutions had been models for her own. In March President Roosevelt declared that the defense of Britain was vital to the defense of the United States, and he authorized the Lend-Lease Act which gave to Britain millions of tons of desperately needed food and weapons of war. In April, when the first food ships left, he pledged American responsibility for the defense of Greenland, and it was to relieve her sister ship *Northland* as part of the Greenland Survey Expedition that *Modoc*, commanded by Lieutenant Commander H. Belford, U.S.C.G., sailed from Boston on May 12th.

On May 24th about 6:30 P.M. by *Modoc's* clocks she was steaming slowly northwestwards. Earlier in the day she heard by radio of the sinking of the *Hood,* and a chance meeting between *Northland* and the British corvette *Arabis* (which was taking in *Norfolk's* shadowing reports) revealed that *Bismarck* was continuing south. It seemed unlikely the chase would come her way, but earlier when she and *Northland* had entered the war zone, they had hoisted outsize United States Coastguard ensigns, illuminated themselves by night and broadcast their positions every hour, to avoid possible misunderstandings.

It was a dull, gray evening, with the wind coming from ahead, the spray falling like light rain on the fo'c'sle as the bows breasted the swell. Lieutenant Bacchus, officer of the watch, and lookouts on *Modoc's* bridge swept their glasses from beam to beam. For days now they had seen nothing but tossing seas and low, gray clouds, endured the long, slow rolling of the ship, and suffered an eternity of fatigue and boredom.

Then in an instant boredom vanished. There swam into the lenses of the port forward lookout's binoculars, as there had swum into the lenses of Able Seaman Newell's binoculars only the night before, the outlines of a giant battleship. It was the *Bismarck,* speeding south. She herself must have sighted *Modoc* at about the same time, but gave no indication of it: from Group North she had received frequent reports of *Modoc's* movements and was fully expecting her.

From below decks in *Modoc* men swarmed up to see *Bismarck* for themselves and were electrified, as others had been, at the power and massiveness and beauty of her. They had heard that she was unsinkable; looking at her they could well believe it.

This glimpse of *Bismarck* as she sailed by on her day of triumph had smashed the gray monotony of their trip like a brick through a frosted window. It was something to chew over the talk about until they got home, to tell later to families and friends. Then, from the low clouds above them, there dropped like leaves in autumn eight of the craziest looking planes you ever saw, each with two wings and struts, two fixed wheels and a single propeller, things the Wright brothers or Blériot might have flown an age ago. The planes sped off towards the *Bismarck*; from the battleship's huge upperworks the orange and yellow flak burst like fireworks, some, in Belford's words, whizzing "dangerously close to our bows." Next in hot pursuit of *Bismarck* came speeding two cruisers and another battleship.

Yet if *Modoc* had been surprised by the appearance of Esmonde and his flock (less one, which had erred and strayed), they were no less surprised by her. Flying from *Victorious* at 85 m.p.h., they had found *Bismarck* by radar an hour and a quarter later, gone back into cloud to make their attack, failed to relocate her, and made for *Norfolk* to get their bearings. From there they streaked off in the wrong direction, so David Kelburn seized a bridge signal lamp and redirected them: Esmonde's plane flashed back "O.K." Up they went into cloud, soon got another radar echo, dived down to attack *Bismarck*, and found to their astonishment *Modoc* instead. It was an unfortunate error, for it alerted *Bismarck* and took away all surprise: Esmonde's ailerons were hit when still four miles away.

In *Bismarck* they watched the approach of the Swordfish with amazement and admiration. "It was incredible to see such obsolete-looking planes," said Müllenheim-Rechberg, "having the nerve to attack a fire-spitting mountain like *Bismarck*." But attack they did. Esmonde's sub-flight came in low on the port beam, dropping their torpedoes at half a mile range: a minute later Gick's three planes attacked on the port bow. Gick himself was unsatisfied with his run-in; he turned and came in again against an inferno of fire. In *Bismarck* the din was terrific, with shells and bullets from fifty guns including the main armament firing in an unbroken stream. While Esmonde and Gick were attacking from the port side, Sub-Lieutenant Lawson of the Reserve crept round to the starboard side where he was silhouetted against the sunset, dropped his torpedo, and zoomed up to the clouds. Seconds later one of the shadowing Fulmar monoplanes which had left *Victorious* after the Swordfish observed a huge column of water shoot up amidships on *Bismarck*'s starboard side, followed by a burst of black smoke from the funnel.

Miraculously not one of the Swordfish was shot down or even badly damaged. But now they had to find their way back to *Victorious*, still nearly a hundred miles away. It was nearing 2 A.M. when Esmonde sighted a red lamp signaling from Admiral Curteis's bridge, and Bovell and Ranald, crazy with relief, heard the sound of approaching engines. *Victorious* turned into the wind and one after the other the pilots, including three who had never made a night landing before, somehow or other reached the deck. The engine of one plane, empty of fuel, cut out at the moment it was pulled up by the arrester wires. Gick's air gunner, Petty Officer Sayer, got out half-frozen: a shell splash from one of

Bismarck's 15-inch guns had knocked the flooring from under him, so that he was suspended above the sea; all the way back he kept complaining on the intercom, "Bloody draughty back here."

There was no sign of two of the Fulmars. Later Bovell was to learn that both planes had come down in the sea and that, amazingly, the crews had been picked up by passing ships.

The night wore on as the main forces slowly converged. From *King George V*, steering southwest at 28 knots with *Repulse* and destroyers, Tovey wirelessed to Wake-Walker that he hoped to meet the enemy about 9 A.M., and to *Repulse*, whose armor was even flimsier than *Hood's*, he signaled to keep 5,000 yards outside him and not to engage until the flagship had opened fire. For the men of these ships action was now only a few hours away, as it had been the night before for the men of *Hood* and *Prince of Wales*. Like them, they felt the cold hand of fear on the skin and wondered, when the time came, how it would go for them.

Because of the brush with *Modoc*, Wake-Walker temporarily lost touch with *Bismarck* and didn't sight her again until an hour after the torpedo attack, when she appeared eight miles away. *Prince of Wales* fired two salvoes: *Bismarck* replied with two, none accurate; then contact was lost again in the gathering dark. *Suffolk*, though, continued to hold *Bismarck* by radar.

In *Bismarck*, to help morale and justify the piles of empty shell cases which lay like anthills about the ship, all sorts of extravagant claims were made about damage to the Swordfish. On occasions like these men believe what they want to believe, see what they want to see.

The torpedo had done little damage. Although set to run at 31 feet, where it would tear out the ship's bowels and do the maximum injury, it was what's called a surface runner, and it struck the armored belt just below the water line; according to Ordinary Seaman Manthey it did no more than scratch the paint. The explosion went upwards, not inwards. The blast lifted some men standing near the aircraft catapult off their feet, smashed Chief Boatswain Kirschberg's skull against the hangar and killed him, and broke three airmen's legs.

Yet if the torpedo damage was negligible, there was much concern about No. 2 boiler room and the forward oil tanks, where the earlier damage had been aggravated by the high speed twisting and turning. No. 2 boiler room was now completely flooded and had to be abandoned. Forward, the collision mats and caulking had been displaced, and as the water poured in, the ship again went down by the bows. Speed was reduced to 16 knots to allow divers to go down and reset the collision mats. An hour later, sufficient repairs had been made to allow an increase to 20 knots: this was within a knot of the ship's "most economical" speed, the highest speed at which the precious fuel would last longest.

For Lütjens and his staff two things had become paramount: to abandon the somewhat leisurely course they were steering down the middle of the Atlantic and cut away direct for France as soon as possible; and secondly, and even more important, to escape the shadowing cruisers. The attack by the Swordfish meant there was an enemy carrier within a hundred miles: other planes would be back in the morning for certain, and while luck had seen them through one attack, it might not in another.

Fortunately for Lütjens a means of escape now came to hand. As the night went on, it became evident to him and his staff from the hydrophone office (which was listening to the strength and bearing of the shadower's screws), from the rangefinders, and also perhaps from the radar, that not only were there no British ships on the starboard side, but that those on the port side were continuing the zigzag observed earlier, at times coming within twelve mïles of *Bismarck*, at others increasing the distance considerably. If *Bismarck* were to turn sharply to the west and increase speed by a few knots when the British ships were going away from her, would the amazing antennae with which they seemed to be equipped notice the movement, would they follow her round as they had done on every occasion when she had tried to escape before?

There was everything to be gained and nothing to be lost by trying; and soon after 3 A.M. Lindemann ordered the helmsman to put the wheel over to starboard. Slowly the ship began to describe a huge loop, through west and northwest to north, through north and northeast to east, and three hours later she crossed her own wake and that of her shadowers, steadied on a course of 130°, almost due southeast, pointed at the northwestern corner of Spain, southwestern corner of the Bay of Biscay—pointed too, though Lütjens was not to know it, at the ships of Force H thirteen hundred miles away, battling northwards into a northwesterly gale, and at that very moment taking in a signal from the Admiralty: "Cancel my signal ordering Force H to join Convoy WS8B as escort. Steer to intercept *Bismarck*."

The crews of *Norfolk* and *Suffolk*, the captains and bridge officers especially, were near to exhaustion. In *Norfolk* Wake-Walker and Captain Phillips had been kept going by the ship's doctor on Benzedrine and black coffee. Now they agreed to split the night watches between them. In *Suffolk* Captain Ellis had no one similar to delegate authority to, and he was spending the fourth consecutive night on his bridge without sleep apart from catnaps. In addition he was lashed by gouts of wind that tore through the frames of the smashed bridge windows, and drenched by showers of spray. The radar operators, themselves tired beyond tears, kept singing out the bearings and distance of the enemy in the flat, even monotones of an Anglican priest reciting matins. It seemed as though they had been doing it since time began and would go on doing it forever. Tiredness, constant repetition, overconfidence had made them automatons, dulled to the idea of anything new. At 2:30 A.M. and again at 3, they reported echoes of two enemy ships, not knowing *Prinz Eugen* had gone. When at about 3:30 A.M. they failed to pick up *Bismarck* on the inward leg, at first no one thought greatly of it. They had lost and found her several times during the past 33 hours; soon they would find her again. But time passed and passed, and though *Suffolk* increased speed and kept on towards the west where she believed *Bismarck* had gone, there was not a sign or whisper of her. She had vanished as completely as if she had never been, and at 5 A.M. Ellis signaled to Wake-Walker: "Have lost contact with enemy."

CHAPTER 7

To Bovell in *Victorious* the news of *Suffolk*'s loss of contact was particularly galling. But all was not lost. *Bismarck*'s last reported course had been 160° or south-southeast, which seemed to Bovell a clear indication that her destination must be France, and if so, she had either made some westing before turning southeast, or swung right around and cut back across her wake. He signaled Curteis for permission to fly off seven Swordfish at first light to search towards the east and southeast, and Curteis, who shared his conclusions, approved. The aircraft were readied and lined up on the flight deck for departure at 7:30 A.M. Then at 7:16 a signal was received from Tovey ordering *Victorious*'s aircraft and escorting cruisers to search, not towards the east and northeast, but towards the west and north.

Tovey had been asleep in his bridge cabin when *Suffolk*'s loss of contact signal arrived. He went at once to the plotting room, where he was joined by Commodore Brind. Now Tovey knew as well as anyone that if *Bismarck* was still bound for France, the eastern to southern sector was where to find her. To assume she was continuing for France was a reasonable conjecture but not a certainty. There were other possibilities: that the damage she had received was so serious that she was returning to Germany by one of the northern passages; or alternatively that it was so slight that once she had lost the shadowing cruisers, she could steer northwest to the coast of Greenland to repair it, oil from a waiting tanker, and go on to attack allied shipping. Ideally Tovey would have liked to cover all points of the compass, but he had not the ships or aircraft. If one of the three routes had to be discarded, it was clearly the one to France: *Bismarck* in Brest or St. Nazaire might mean that he had failed to sink her but there she would be bottled up like *Scharnhorst* and *Gneisenau*, a target for bombers, temporarily out of harm's way; but *Bismarck* loose on the Atlantic trade routes did not bear thinking about. So he ordered a search between southwest and northeast to a depth of a hundred miles: this would cover both a breakout to the west or a return to Germany by the Denmark Straits.

At 8 A.M. that morning the situation was as follows: *Bismarck* was now east of all three British forces: northeast of Admiral Tovey's force (which had passed about 100 miles ahead of her at around 4 A.M.), southeast of Admiral Curteis's force (which had crossed her wake at around 6 A.M.), and due east of Admiral Wake-Walker's force. She was steering southeast at a speed of 20 knots while all the British ships were steering in a westerly direction, away from her. *Prince of Wales*, no longer needed to protect *Norfolk* and *Suffolk*, was on her way to join the Commander-in-Chief: she would take the place of *Repulse* which, very low in fuel and with prospects of an immediate action gone, was about to leave for Newfoundland to oil, and would search in that direction en route.

Four hundred miles to the south Captain Reid in *Ramillies*, thinking *Bismarck* was bound for an oiler near the Azores, altered course to the northwest; and east of *Ramillies* Commodore Blackman in the cruiser *Edinburgh* was also steering northwest along the track of *Bismarck* when last seen. Both these ships were on a parallel course to *Bismarck* and would (if all three continued it) pass well to the westward of her.

But 350 miles southeast of *Bismarck*, on the line of her course to Brest, was the old battleship *Rodney*, which with four destroyers was escorting the troopship *Britannic* across the Atlantic before going to Boston to refit. At this time *Rodney* was urgently in need of refit. One engine room had recently broken down twice, leaving her dependent on a single propeller.

Her maximum official speed was 23 knots, but she hadn't attained it in years. She had 500 passengers on board, drafts for the West Indies, the Falklands and Halifax, and her upper deck was stacked with crated stores for the refit.

Rodney's captain was Frederick Dalrymple-Hamilton, a big, tall Scot, owner of a property in Wigtownshire. When he first heard *Bismarck* was out, he formed a small operations committee. They met in the charthouse two or three times a day, discussed the latest moves and signals, and advised what action *Rodney* should take. After *Bismarck* was lost, they agreed that if she was bound for France, they would be excellently placed to intercept her and had best stay put and await events.

One other thing Dalrymple-Hamilton needed to do: inform Tovey and the Admiralty where he was. He was loath to make a radio signal that might be picked up by German D/F stations and passed to *Bismarck*, but it was essential.

Of the seven Swordfish which Captain Bovell had flown off at 7:30 that morning to search to the north and west, six returned to *Victorious* four hours later. But of 5H, piloted by Sub-Lieutenant Jackson, observer Sub-Lieutenant Berrill, air gunner Leading Airman Sparkes, there was no sign. *Victorious* called for a long time and the lookouts scanned the horizon; but nobody answered, nothing came. Bovell felt the loss keenly, for 5H was manned by one of his best crews.

The events which Captain Dalrymple-Hamilton and his committee had decided to wait for were not long in coming: they were not what they expected and were to have equally unexpected results. In *Bismarck* that morning, Lütjens thought he was still being followed. Why Lütjens thought this is hard to say. Whatever the reason, it was in this belief that at 6:54 A.M. and again at 7:48 A.M. he transmitted to Germany a long signal, about the efficiency of British radar, the engagement with *Hood*, damage to the oil tanks, the unreliability of *Bismarck*'s own radar—a thing he would not have dreamt of doing if he had thought he was alone, as only two days before Group North had sent a signal warning of the efficiency of British Radio Direction Finding.

In the event *Bismarck*'s transmissions were picked up by various D/F stations scattered about Britain, and the bearings passed to the operations staff at the Admiralty. They could hardly believe their luck; this was the sort of miracle they had been hoping for, the information that would give *Bismarck*'s position, show in what direction she was steering. In the

Admiralty Lieutenant-Commander Peter Kemp plotted the bearings on a gnomonic chart (the kind suitable for radio waves which follow the great circle of the earth): they were a pretty woolly set, the proximity of the D/F stations to each other and their great distance from *Bismarck* resulting in almost parallel lines, no bearings from Gibraltar or Iceland to give a nice "cross cut"; but they showed *Bismarck* to be south and east of her last reported position.

Kemp showed this to Rear-Admiral Jock Clayton, his immediate superior, suggesting the position be radioed to Tovey immediately. Clayton said not to send the worked out position, only the D/F bearings. Kemp protested it was hardly right to expect the C-in-C to do the Admiralty's homework for them in the middle of an important operation, but Clayton explained that before putting to sea Tovey and his Radio Intelligence Officer, Lieutenant-Commander Guernsey, had separately asked for bearings only and not a worked out position: Tovey had two newly equipped D/F destroyers with him and hoped that one or both would provide a cross bearing, enabling him to pinpoint where *Bismarck* had been.

So Kemp sent the bearings only and they reached the flagship soon after 10 A.M. But what Kemp and others at the Admiralty didn't know was that Tovey no longer had any destroyers, D/F or otherwise, with him: they had all left for Iceland at midnight because of shortage of fuel (of the two equipped with D/F, one had broken down with boiler trouble soon after leaving Scapa and returned to base; the other's D/F was out of action). Next, the bearings were plotted wrongly in the flagship, and as a result showed *Bismarck* to be not southeast of her last reported position, as Kemp had found her and as she really was, but *north* of it; and the only deduction to draw from this was that she had reversed course and was returning to Germany by the Faeroes-Iceland gap. Accordingly at 10:47 A.M. Tovey broadcast this position to the fleet, and *King George V, Prince of Wales, Victorious,* Curteis's cruisers, and *Suffolk* all turned northeast. Wake-Walker in *Norfolk,* away to the south, knew there were other cruisers covering the Faeroes-Iceland gap, and none except *Sheffield* to the south, so he steered as though *Bismarck* was making for France; so did *Edinburgh* and *Rodney. Ramillies,* doing all of 19 knots, also turned northeast, but she would never catch up, and soon the Admiralty ordered her to find *Britannic* and escort her to Halifax.

At 10:54 A.M., however, the Admiralty obtained another D/F fix on *Bismarck,* which confirmed her general movement towards France: this time they broadcast the plotted position and it was received in the *King*

George V at 2:01 P.M. Again at 1:20 P.M. a further fix of an enemy transmission was obtained, made on U-boat wavelength but with the strength of a surface ship: this also fitted in with *Bismarck*'s passage to France. Although it seemed strange to Tovey that *Bismarck* should start transmitting on U-boat wavelength (he was in fact right, the ship transmitting was a U-boat) it was, if true, further evidence that the enemy was making for France.

At 3:48 P.M., therefore, Tovey ordered the flagship to come around to east-southeast. But soon after this he intercepted a signal from the Admiralty to *Rodney*, canceling her earlier orders to steer for France, telling her to conform with Tovey's movements towards the Iceland-Faeroes gap. Why this signal was ever sent, when Admiralty opinion had been hardening in favor of France all day, is a mystery. One writer says Captain Edwards told him it was made at the insistence of Winston Churchill who himself believed *Bismarck* was returning to Germany. Another explanation is that it was thought essential for *Rodney* and *King George V* to join forces so as to have local superiority. The signal made no difference to *Rodney*, whose course of northeast was right whichever of the two courses *Bismarck* was steering. But to Tovey it was totally baffling. Concluding that the Admiralty were now favoring the Faeroes route, yet with all other evidence pointing to France, he gave orders for *King George V* to come around to port and steady on 080°, a compromise course betweeen the two destinations.

And so, all that morning and part of the afternoon, Tovey and Lütjens were steering away from each other, the one north of east, the other southeast, with the distance between them gradually opening.

In Brest dockyard, at a little before 8 A.M. on this same Sunday, May 25th, Lieutenant Jean Philippon of the French Navy was on his way to the Combined Navy Office where he had the forenoon watch. He was a lean, spare man with black hair, a strong hawklike face, and percipient eyes. When war broke out Philippon was first lieutenant of the submarine *Ouessant*, which arrived in Brest in February 1940 for a long refit. She was out of action when the Germans overran France and as the Panzer troops entered the town, Philippon and his fellow officers scuttled her.

For the German Navy Brest was a jewel beyond price, an advance base for submarines and surface ships on the very edge of the Atlantic battlefield; and in the wake of the occupying forces there came as admiral commanding the port the most famous of Germany's first war U-boat aces, the legendary Lothar von Arnauld de la Perière, holder of the

Kaiser's highest award for gallantry, a man of Huguenot origins, amiable character and impeccable French. His mission was to persuade the French Navy, under the terms of the Franco-German Armistice of June 24th, 1940, to collaborate with him in the administration and running of the dockyard. Luck was with him. The port's two admirals, Traub and Brohan, had already been removed to an unknown destination. The next senior officer was Captain Le Normand, an old friend of de la Perière; they had both commanded submarines in the same waters in the first war and later got to know each other as captains of cruisers. Le Normand didn't much care for being commandant of a collaborationist dockyard, but seeing in it the means of conserving the installations for France, as well as saving many sailors from the miseries of a prisoner of war camp, he accepted. The French Navy Office in the dockyard was converted into a Combined Navy Office, with de la Perière's staff on the upper floors, Le Normand's on the lower. Lieutenant Philippon was chosen by Le Normand for his staff. He told Le Normand that he would not work directly for the Germans, so he was put in charge of the dockyard's gardens.

All through the late summer and early winter of 1940 Philippon looked after the gardens diligently, but by the end of the year, when there were no more flowers to tend or vegetables to grow, he was finding his duties, or lack of them, increasingly irksome. Nor was it easy to stomach the sight of German naval officers and men strutting about the yard, German ships and submarines entering and leaving the port. On a New Year visit to his home at Puynormand, he confided his frustrations to the family doctor, an old friend, and said how he longed to do something for France. The doctor listened carefully, then before Philippon left, hinted darkly that he might expect a visitor soon. Within a few days the visitor came, the famous "Colonel Rémy," who was to head the most successful of all the French resistance groups. Would Philippon act as an agent for the British Admiralty, observe what he could in the dockyard, ship movements, garrison strength, new construction, bomb damage? Philippon was in a dilemma: he hated the British Navy for what they had done to the French fleet at Oran, yet his duties at the gardens allowed him to go anywhere without raising suspicion, and it was a challenge, not just to help the British but his fellow countrymen who had rallied to the Cross of Lorraine overseas, an opportunity to serve France. He accepted. *Bien,* said Colonel Rémy, and did he know of a good radio operator for his messages, a man that could be relied on? Philippon remembered Bernard Anquetil, a former quartermaster of *Ouessant,* now living quietly at Saumur, 250 miles away, and he gave Rémy the man's name.

And so it was arranged. Lieutenant Jean Philippon of the French Navy adopted the code name "Hilarion" and became a spy for France. He gave his messages to a brave youth named Paul Mauger, code name "Mimi," whom Rémy had recruited at Nantes. Mimi took the messages by train to Saumur; there Anquetil transmitted them by radio to England.

At the beginning of May Philippon got word that the German Navy was putting up *ducs d'Albe* or big mooring posts at Lanvéoc and near Ile Longue, with antitorpedo netting all around them. He went to look at them and concluded they must be for ships of 35,000 tons or over; *Bismarck* and *Tirpitz*, he thought, perhaps both. Once again Mimi took the train to Saumur.

And now, at eight o'clock of this Sunday morning, May 25th, Philippon entered the Combined Navy Office to take over the duty watch from his friend Jan. The night before he had heard on the radio of the sinking of the *Hood*, so he knew *Bismarck* and *Prinz Eugen* were out.

"Be on your guard today," said Jan, "the Boches are in a bad mood."

"Why?"

"I don't know, but something's up. They seem rattled."

A German lieutenant from de la Perière's headquarters upstairs came in and asked Jan to order the harbor tugs to raise steam immediately, saying they were wanted at Lanvéoc and Ile Longue for inspecting the antitorpedo netting.

There was some further conversation which Philippon didn't hear; then the German left.

"What's up?" he asked.

"The *Bismarck*'s expected Wednesday. The whole port's getting ready to receive her. There's quite a panic."

Philippon tried not to show his intense interest, asking Jan if he'd mind keeping watch a little longer, as he'd left something at home. He knew there was an express about to leave for Paris, and he hurried to the station. There was no time to find Mimi, so he scribbled in a code that Rémy had supplied for emergencies, *Bismarck expected Brest Wednesday, Hilarion*, put it in an envelope and wrote a Paris address. Then he gave it to a startled passenger, said it concerned a sick child, was a matter of life and death, and the passenger, glad to be of service, promised to deliver it in person.

And on this same Sunday, May 25th, Herbert Wohlfarth and the crew of *U.556*, still in the Atlantic, were also making their way towards France.

After the attack on Convoy H.X. 126, they had one torpedo left. Presently they sighted a straggler from the convoy, the 5,000 ton *Darlington Court*. Wohlfarth ordered an attack but on the way in his navigator, Sub-Lieutenant Souvad, said: "Captain, why waste our last torpedo on this little ship? Why not keep it for something better on the way home?" Wohlfarth considered the matter, then decided, as he put it, that the certainty of a sparrow now was better than the possibility of a pigeon later. But when they reached the firing position, something went wrong, and they had to break off and come around again. Once more Souvad suggested it might be better to keep the torpedo, but Wohlfarth had made up his mind. When they reached the firing position a second time, he fired. The torpedo hit the straggler amidships and she began to settle. Souvad turned *U.556* for France, and Wohlfarth radioed to Dönitz his position, course and expected time of arrival.

And now on this Sunday morning came a signal from Dönitz to Wohlfarth. It was a signal that made all the crew happy, lifted their morale. "Hearty congratulations on your successes," it ran. "The Führer has been pleased to approve the immediate award to you of the Knight's Cross of the Iron Cross."

In three days, thought Wohlfarth, they would be at their berth at Lorient. And then they would have a party.

And on the morning of this same Sunday, May 25th, *Bismarck* received a message from Group West. "Last enemy shadowing report was at 0313. Type of enemy signals now being sent indicates shadowing vessels have been shaken off." And so the dulled, radar-shocked minds of Lütjens and his staff realized at last that the hounds had finally lost the scent, that *Bismarck* was alone on the ocean. And officers and men who had been at action stations for thirty-six hours were able to stretch themselves, allowed to go in turn to their messes, wash and shave, get a bite of hot food. Müllenheim-Rechberg welcomed the opportunity to what he called run round a little, visit the bridge to get the latest information, meet other officers, exchange views and compare notes. And later that morning a little ceremony took place when Lütjens, who as a Commander-in-Chief in the field was empowered to grant immediate awards, decorated Leading Seaman Hansen with the Iron Cross for his brilliant handling of the ship during the attack by *Victorious*'s Swordfish.

There was another cause for celebration in *Bismarck* that morning, one that had nothing to do with the present operation. It was the admiral's birthday. He was fifty-two. His staff officers and the crew, through

Commander Oels, wished him many happy returns. There was a signal from Raeder which said: "Heartiest congratulations on your birthday. May you continue to be equally successful in this coming year," and another from the Führer, briefer, for he was worried about the damage the ship had suffered, and had premonitions about loss of prestige: "Best wishes on your birthday. Adolf Hitler."

But the admiral himself was not sharing the general joy, not allowing himself any wishful thinking. There were still nearly a thousand miles to go, and Dr. Externbrink and his colleagues held out no prospects of misty or foggy weather on the route to France. Lütjens knew, from the volume of enemy traffic being picked up by the wireless office, from the reports being sent by Group West, that the British Navy were straining every nerve to find him, that the worst was still to come. At noon, in gray mood, he addressed the crew over the loudspeaker system for the first time since leaving the Baltic. In clipped, unemotional tones he thanked them for their birthday wishes, for their part in the victory over the *Hood*. And then, because it was not in his nature to do otherwise, he spoke of the dangers and difficulties that lay ahead. "The British are massing their forces to destroy us, and we shall have another battle with them before we reach home. It may well be a question of victory or death. If we have to die, let us take with us as many of the enemy as we can."

A more imaginative admiral would have considered the effect of such words on morale. It was almost as if Lütjens wanted to infect the crew with his own fatalism, share with them the euphoria of a truly Wagnerian end. Captain Lindemann said a few words afterwards, tried to make amends with news of aircraft and U-boats that were on the way, but the damage had been done. Morale was further shaken by the sight of some officers, including those on the admiral's staff, wearing life jackets under their uniforms, when ship's orders stated they were always to be kept in their containers.

Meanwhile the crew were sent to special defense stations, four hours action stations, four hours lighter duties, four hours rest. It was a strenuous routine but it prevented people from brooding.

The day wore on. The wind increased in strength, and the sea rose, a rising sea from the northwest. It was a sea that carried *Bismarck* with it, flung her stern to this side and that, and induced a horrid corkscrewing motion that for many of the younger members of the crew, some of whom had only finished shore training six weeks before, brought on agonies of seasickness. But there were compensations. As afternoon gave way to evening and evening to night without further signs of the enemy, the hopes which had taken such a buffeting from the admiral's speech that morning began to recover. The talk on the mess decks that evening was that the admiral was wrong, they were going to make it after all.

Tovey meanwhile continued steaming east-northeast, increasingly puzzled by the contradictory signals reaching him, increasingly wondering where *Bismarck* had gone. During the afternoon the mistake in plotting the morning D/F bearings had been discovered, so apart from the Admiralty's signal telling *Rodney* to conform to his movements, all indications now were that *Bismarck* was making for France. If this was the Admiralty's appreciation too, why had they not signaled him? At 4:30 P.M., unable to contain his misgivings any longer, he signaled the Admiralty: "Do you consider the enemy is making for the Faeroes?" He had hoped for an immediate reply, but in those days it took a long time for signals to be coded, transmitted, received, decoded, answered, coded, sent back and decoded once again. An hour and a half passed. Tovey decided he could wait no longer and ordered Captain Patterson to turn southeast, signaling Whitehall accordingly.

But he turned alone, for most of his ships were desperately short of fuel. *Norfolk* had already altered course for Iceland, passing *Prince of Wales* heading for the Faeroes gap. *Prince of Wales* went on for an hour or two, then also steered for Iceland. *Suffolk* (after searching to the southwest all day) turned southeast briefly, then thought better of it and steered for Scapa. *Victorious* had enough fuel to continue, but Admiral Curteis's escorting cruisers were getting dangerously low, and with U-boats on the alert, he did not dare let her go on alone. That night her aircraft made a final search to the southeast of the morning's D/F position, but sighted nothing.

In the Admiralty meanwhile opinion was hourly hardening in favor of France; it looked more and more as if the flagship had wrongly plotted the morning D/F position. And at about the time that Tovey signaled he was turning southeast, they signaled *Rodney* for the second time that day to assume that *Bismarck* was making for France. Once again she continued on her present course, as it still covered both eventualities.

Now that France seemed certain, Wake-Walker in *Norfolk*, en route to Iceland, was in an agony of indecision, torn between his instincts to continue the chase and fear of running out of fuel. In the end instincts won. He ordered Captain Phillips to turn southeast and go on to 26 knots. Presently he sighted *Prince of Wales* again, still steering for Iceland, and he signaled "I am going towards Brest."

Now the two main adversaries, *Bismarck* and *King George V*, were steaming roughly the same course, southeast towards the Bay of Biscay, but with *Bismarck* some 150 miles in the lead. *Rodney* continued steaming slowly northeast in the hope of sighting the enemy as she crossed his presumed line of advance. Having reached it without sighting him, she too turned towards the Bay. Neither of the two adversaries knew where the other was; each side, as it waited, made dispositions to help.

Group West in Paris sent signals to *Bismarck* about preparations being made. Ships 13 and 24 were being provisioned and fueled for eight days and would sail immediately; three destroyers would escort *Bismarck* for the last lap across the Bay. Air Fleet 3 was being put at the Navy's disposal: long range aircraft would operate up to 25° West, reconnaissance planes up to 15° West, bomber formations to 14° West. At St. Nazaire buoys were in position and lights operating; pilots had been arranged: a berth was being prepared in La Pallice Roads, but should the situation demand it, Lütjens should consider putting into a Spanish port. A further U-boat patrol line was being formed, but *U.74* was unseaworthy because of damage and *U.556* out of torpedoes. Approaching this area *Bismarck* was to fly a blue pendant so that U-boats might not mistake her for a British ship.

The British too were making their dispositions. In the unlikely event of *Bismarck* making for the Mediterranean, *Rodney*'s sister ship *Nelson* was ordered to sail from Freetown to Gibraltar, and the submarine *Severn* was told to take up offensive patrol in the Straits: like Lütjens, her commanding officer was given discretion to enter Spanish territorial waters. At Coastal Command plans were made for aircraft patrols along *Bismarck*'s presumed track to Brest, starting at first light; and the Royal Air Force made the first of several mine-laying sorties to the roadsteads of Brest and St. Nazaire. But the most pressing need for Tovey that night, as he himself signaled the Admiralty, was for destroyers; for every mile that *King George V* steamed southeastwards was taking her, unescorted, into U-boat waters. In the Admiralty operations room they looked at the chart, saw the only destroyers within hailing distance were those escorting the troop convoy WS8B, *Cossack, Zulu, Sikh, Maori,* and the Polish destroyer *Piorun.* Earlier this precious convoy had been deprived of *Victorious* and *Repulse:* if its destroyers were taken, too, all that was left to guard it was one solitary warship, the antiaircraft cruiser *Cairo.* But there were no U-boats near, and in the circumstances it was a risk that had to be taken.

The officer commanding these destroyers was Captain Philip Vian, a hard, ruthless, dedicated sailor (though privately he could be quite humble and shy) who like all great commanders in war never failed to seize opportunities offered him. Vian received the Admiralty's signal in the middle of the night: *Cossack, Sikh, Zulu* to join *King George V, Maori* and *Piorun* to make for *Rodney.* Vian formed his division in line abreast, setting course east-northeast at 27 knots; the same northwesterly sea that was pushing *King George V* and *Bismarck* towards Brest hit Vian's destroyers on the beam, making them yaw violently fom side to side, leaning over so far it sometimes seemed they would never come back.

On the bridges of *King George V, Rodney* and *Bismarck,* more comfortable because enclosed, more stable because of their size, officers stood on the gratings of compass platforms, faces reflected in the dim lights of compass bowls, bracing tired bodies to the motions of the ships.

To most now, British and German, it seemed that the long day's night was almost at an end, that the great chase was all but over. Just before midnight Tovey signaled the Admiralty that he might have to reduce speed to economize on fuel, while in *Bismarck,* cruising at 20 knots, they had about enough to reach Brest. And men's thoughts turned, as those of sailors do at the end of a voyage, to how it might be when they reached harbor. In just over forty-eight hours *Bismarck's* young crew, most of whom had never been outside Germany, would find themselves in France, and because of the damage, the ship would stay there some time. What would life in Brest or St. Nazaire be like?

Rodney's crew were having similar thoughts. Soon they would be resuming their interrupted journey to Boston and the long promised refit; unlike *Bismarck's* crew they had no doubts of the welcome that awaited them.

Even the men of *King George V* could afford a few daydreams. Now that *Bismarck* had broken out, was about to join *Scharnhorst* and *Gneisenau* in France, would their presence not be required rather nearer the Biscay ports? At Plymouth, say, where there were pubs and cinemas and girls, and London only a few hours away by train.

So ran the thoughts of some sailors as in their seaborne castles they were buffeted through the night across the long Atlantic. Others, below decks, in the small privacy of bunk or hammock, dreamt of other things. Most, sooner or later, slept; but some, in *Bismarck* mostly, lay half the night in agonies of seasickness, retching until it seemed they must choke, not caring if they lived or died.

And then dawn broke over a wild gray sea that was empty of other ships and a sullen gray sky that was empty of planes. In *Bismarck* it was nearly twenty-four hours since Lütjens had made his Death or Victory speech. They were four hundred miles nearer port: of the enemy there was still no sign.

Hopes that had been rising all night rose to a new peak, and perhaps even Lütjens secretly shared them. But they were not to last. In the dead of night, about the time that Captain Vian and his destroyers were taking leave of Convoy WS8B to join the fleet, a Catalina aircraft of Coastal Command, No. Z of 209 squadron, was racing in the darkness across the trout-filled waters of Lough Erne in the northwest of Ireland. The copilot was an American serviceman, Ensign Leonard B. Smith, wearing the uniform of the United States Navy—a fact known then to a very few. The plane rose gracefully towards the stars, circled once over the sleeping countryside, set course southwestwards across Donegal Bay and Eagle Island towards the open sea.

CHAPTER 8

When on the late afternoon of the 25th the Admiralty operations staff sat down to plan the air patrols for the following day, they were somewhat despondent. Despite extensive searches by several aircraft along the most likely tracks to France and the Faeroes, nothing had been sighted.

The staff completed their proposals, and the duty captain telephoned them to Captain Charles Meynell, the Navy's liason officer with Coastal Command at their headquarters at Northwood. Meynell took them along to Air Marshal Sir Frederick Bowhill, Coastal Command's Chief. Bowhill concluded that, so far as *Bismarck*'s direct course to the French ports was concerned, they were perfectly adequate. But would *Bismarck* steer direct for the French ports? His trained seaman's mind told him (what was not evident to Admirals Pound or Phillips) that a direct course for the French ports was unlikely, that it would take *Bismarck* unnecessarily close to British airfields, result in her making a night landfall on a rocky and treacherous coast. If he was the German admiral, he told Meynell, he would steer a more southerly course, point the ship towards the north of Spain, only turn east when near the latitude of the French ports. There should be an extra patrol to cover this area. Meynell agreed and telephoned the Admiralty operations staff for approval. They agreed, provided it did not interfere with the more northerly patrols already accepted; and Catalina Z of 209 squadron was the aircraft chosen to execute Bowhill's wishes.

Ensign Leonard ("Tuck") Smith was twenty-six, a farmer's son from Higginsville, Missouri. As a lad he'd always wanted to fly. After graduation and a year of boredom in a Chicago insurance firm, he joined the naval reserve in 1938 and trained as a pilot at Pensacola, Florida. When the European war broke out he was second pilot and navigator in a squadron of Catalinas, or PBY's, based at Sand Point Naval Air Station, Seattle.

Early in 1941 Smith's commanding officer called some of the pilots together and told them the U.S. government was lend-leasing the British PBY's, volunteers were needed to go over to England and teach the British pilots how to fly them. Smith volunteered. He was sent to Washington, D.C., where he and sixteen other pilots got a different sort of briefing from the Chief of Naval Operations: "Boys, we're going to war soon with Germany and Japan. But we haven't fixed the date yet, so we want you to go over there and learn all you can about it." The volunteers flew to Bermuda where the Consolidated Aircraft Company, which built the Catalinas, was delivering them to pilots of British Ferry Command. On the morning of May 4th, 1941, they all embarked: in addition to Smith the party included Ensign Carl Rinehart, who trained with him at Pensacola, and Lieutenant Jimmy Johnson, who had already clocked 1,500 hours. Three thousand miles and twenty-four hours later, at about the time that Hitler was inspecting *Bismarck* and *Tirpitz* in Gotenhafen, they became waterborne in Greenock, Scotland.

The Americans went to London for a few days' acclimatization; then nine of them, including Smith and Johnson, flew to Lough Erne to join Coastal Command as "Special Observers." "The C.O. there," said Johnson, "informed us he was sending nine of his copilots on leave, so we became full crew members, which was quite humorous." Johnson became copilot of Catalina M of 240 squadron, Smith of Catalina Z of 209 squadron. The remaining eight Americans, including Carl Rinehart, went to Oban on the west of Scotland as "Special Observers" to 210 squadron.

Smith's fellow crewmen in Z/209 came from all over England—Sussex, Newcastle, New Barnet, Liverpool. The captain was Flying Officer Dennis Briggs, who had recently flown in the first Catalina to take part in the Battle of the Atlantic and had even survived a crash in it. "It was the blind leading the blind," said Smith. "Briggs had had plenty of operational flying but knew little about Catalinas. I knew something about Catalinas but had no experience of operational flying."

Smith found the patrols similar to those from Seattle, but longer and more arduous: the plane carried 1,750 gallons of gasoline and could remain airborne for up to twenty-eight hours. The crew took their meals with them, meat and eggs and vegetables, cooking them on a little Primus stove as they went along. They were very cramped; the noise and vibration were continuous and many plugged earholes with cotton wool to lessen the din. Each crew member did three hours at a stretch, then took an hour off in one of the four bunks aft. Fourteen days after Smith's joining, they had a very exciting trip: they just missed a mountain on the way out, were fired on by escorts of the convoy they had been sent to protect, and had a small fire on board on the way back.

That was on May 24th, the day *Hood* was sunk. The following evening they learned that *Bismarck* had escaped and were told they were to join in the search for her. They went to bed early, were roused at 2 A.M. on May 26th, and dressed in kapok-lined flying jackets and fur-lined boots.

For three hours the plane flew steadily southwestwards; then dawn broke and to those on watch came the pleasant smell of frying bacon and eggs. Some, having eaten it, wished they didn't have to wait so long for lunch. They flew on for another three hours and at 9:45 A.M. reached the area of search. Here the plane was put into automatic control. Smith moved into Briggs's seat and Briggs took over as second pilot. It was a hazy morning with poor visibility and a very rough sea. About half an hour later, flying below cloud at 500 feet, Smith pointed ahead and said, "What's that?" Briggs looked and saw about eight miles away, at almost maximum visibility, a dull, black shape, which gradually took on the contours of a large warship. Hardly able to contain his excitement, he ordered Smith to take a closer look while he moved to the wireless table to write a signal to base. Smith banked to starboard, went up into cloud, meaning to curl around to a position astern of the ship, but he slightly misjudged it; a few minutes later at 2,000 feet the clouds parted and there was *Bismarck* on the beam, less than 500 yards away. Now there was no need to question her identity: she disclosed it on her own. There were shell bursts all around them, the nasty rattle of shrapnel hitting the hull. The barrage was so fierce that a crew member off duty was knocked out of his bunk, and the rigger, washing up breakfast things in the galley, dropped two plates. Smith took violent evasive action, jettisoned the plane's four depth charges to gain height, and went on to full speed. ("Never been so scared in my life," he said afterwards). Briggs, trying

frantically to finish his message and get it off before being shot down, saw
Bismarck from the corner of his eye as one great winking flame, watched
her keel over to port as she turned to starboard under helm to avoid being
hit.

"One battleship bearing 240° five miles, course 150°, my position 49°33'
North, 21°47' West. Time of origin, 1030/26."

It was the signal for which the navies of two nations had been waiting,
the one with hope, the other with fear. In Germany it was decoded within
minutes, passed to Raeder in Berlin, Saalwächter in Paris. They had to
accept the inevitable, at least with the compensation of knowing where
Bismarck was (690 miles from Brest—though when Lütjen's own signal
reached them, there was a discrepancy in the position given of about 70
miles: Briggs was 25 miles out; Neuendorff, who hadn't had a sight for
days, nearly 80). On the British Admiralty operations room chart it could
be seen how narrowly *Rodney* and her destroyers had missed *Bismarck*
the day before—*Rodney* and her destroyers by 50 miles, *Edinburgh* by 45
miles—while that very morning Vian's flotilla had crossed her wake only
30 miles astern. At the Admiralty and in the fleet at sea (and at Coastal
Command, too, where Bowhill was giving himself a small pat on the
back) relief at *Bismarck*'s rediscovery was tempered by the knowledge that
unless she could somehow be slowed down, *King George V*, 135 miles to
the north, and *Rodney*, 125 miles to the northeast, would not be able to
catch up.

But perhaps *Bismarck* could be slowed down? Vian with his five
destroyers and twenty-six torpedoes knew where his duty lay. He altered
course towards the enemy without asking permission, then went on to
full speed. Captain Benjamin Martin in the cruiser *Dorsetshire*, with eight
torpedoes, escorting a convoy 600 miles southward, handed over escort to
the armed merchant cruiser *Bulolo*, also without permission, steering at
26 knots to get between the enemy and Brest. Perhaps both of them
remembered Nelson's dictum: No Captain can do very wrong if he lays
his ship alongside that of an enemy.

Yet the man to whom the news of *Bismarck*'s rediscovery was most
urgent, who had the best means for slowing her down, was the
commander of the force nearest to her. Vice-Admiral Sir James
Somerville, with *Renown*, *Ark Royal* and *Sheffield*, steering north, had
crossed ahead of *Bismarck*'s track earlier that morning and was now only
just over 100 miles away, between *Bismarck* and Brest.

Vice-Admiral Sir James Somerville was one of the Navy's characters, a big congenial man, full of humor and vitality. He had no pretensions to intellect, peppered his conversation with four letter words, and was a devotee of the dirty joke. (There could have been no better recipient for the signal that Admiral Cunningham sent him when, a K.B.E., he was made a K.C.B.: "Congratulations, but isn't twice a knight at your age rather overdoing it?") He maintained, says his biographer, "a school-boy-ish approach to all things, a youthful zest and sense of fun combining with an uninhibited simplicity of expression . . . an unconscious urge to be the centre [sic] of the stage and act the unorthodox admiral at all levels . . . these were important ingredients in his make-up as a leader . . . and brought him enemies as well as friends."

In 1938, when Commander-in-Chief in the East Indies, Somerville had an attack of tuberculosis and was invalided home and out of the Navy. But when war broke out he was passed fit by a Harley Street specialist and he was soon knocking at the Admiralty's door. As a radio specialist he was given a job in the Admiralty's signal division concerned with the development of naval radar; and as a result, says his biographer, "an effective surface warning set reached our warships many months, if not years, before it would have done otherwise." So *Suffolk*'s success in shadowing *Bismarck* and *Prinz Eugen* was due partly to Somerville.

His next job was to assist Admiral Ramsay at Dover with the evacuation of the British Army from Dunkirk. This involved a trip to France, where Admiral Wake-Walker was supervising the evacuation on the beaches, and going many hours without sleep. The way his health stood up convinced the Admiralty he was fit again for sea, and in June 1940, when Force H was formed to fill the naval vacuum left in the Western Mediterranean by the defeat of France, he was appointed its commander. The nucleus of this force was a carrier, *Ark Royal*, and the battle cruiser *Hood*, in which he hoisted his flag at Gibraltar.

On May 23rd, Force H returned to Gibraltar after safely flying off to Malta 48 Hurricane aircraft from *Ark Royal* and *Furious*. That afternoon, while *Bismarck* and *Prinz Eugen*, as yet unsighted, were approaching the Denmark Straits, Somerville, now in *Renown*, took Captain Talbot of the *Furious* for a walk up the Rock. "We found a little track among the scrub," he wrote, "and we sat in the sun surrounded by wild flowers . . . it was a small and very welcome bit of peace."

Early next morning Force H was on its way north. By 4 A.M. on the 25th, at about the time that *Bismarck* was shaking herself free of *Suffolk*'s radar, Somerville detached his destroyers to Gibraltar because of lack of fuel after high speed steaming. The senior officer was ordered when 150 miles clear to signal to the Admiralty Force H's position, and to ask what the situation was regarding *Scharnhorst* and *Gneisenau*. The rest of a rather worrying day was spent communicating with *Ark Royal* about next day's area of search for *Bismarck*. It was arranged that the first patrol should leave at first light.

That night the gale that was pushing *Bismarck* along on her southeasterly course hit Force H hard. At 11:15 P.M. they had to reduce to 23 knots, at 11:40 to 21 knots, and finally at 1:12 A.M. on the morning of the 26th to 17 knots. The old *Ark*, "sunk" by German propaganda so many times but still afloat, seemed to be creaking and groaning in every plate, and her captain, Loben Maund, wondered just how much more punishment she could take.

Dawn broke to show a storm-tossed sea, streaked with white foam, waves the height of four-story houses. Although *Ark Royal's* flight deck was 62 feet above the waterline, it was being drenched with spray. There were times when the forward end shipped green seas like a destroyer. Few carrier-borne aircraft had even operated in such conditions before.

But the times were abnormal too; and on *Ark Royal's* aircraft now depended whether *Bismarck* could be further slowed down. The Swordfish detailed to cover the route to Brest got safely away, and then ten others were brought up from below and ranged in line. With the ship rolling up to 30° to starboard the flight deck crews had the greatest difficulty preventing the aircraft sliding across the deck. It had been intended to fly off the planes at 7 A.M. but reduction of speed during the night had meant loss of ground. They were now scheduled to leave at 9 A.M. Just before 8:45 Captain Maund turned the ship into the wind, reduced to 10 knots: rolling gave way to pitching, the wind was like a hurricane and the fierce gusts almost tore the flimsy planes out of the deck crew's hands. Across the raging sea on the bridge of *Renown* Admiral Somerville kept his binoculars fixed on them. On the bridge of *Ark Royal* Commander Traill, the flight operations officer, looked down at the first plane due to take off and raised his green flag. He waited for what he hoped was a lull, then let the flag fall. The plane gathered speed slowly against the wind, infinitely slowly it seemed to those watching. As it lumbered past, Traill watched the goggled observer read the wind indicator on the side of the bridge, raise a gloved hand thumb upwards. Now, as the ship rose to meet the next wave, the plane was climbing skywards; then, as the wave passed, tearing like the Gadarene swine downhill towards the sea. Everyone held his breath. The plane took off, its wheels ploughed a furrow through the wavetops, and then it was airborne and clear. Jerkily, hesitatingly, the others followed. Many touched the water as they left, but all got safely away. Well, thought Maund, we've got them away . . . how do we get them back?

An hour and a half later came Flying Officer Briggs's sighting report, followed soon after by a signal saying he had lost contact. A glance at the chart showed *Bismarck* to be heading straight for the center of the Swordfish's search area; only twenty minutes later Sub-Lieutenant Hartley in Swordfish 2H sighted her. But he made the same mistake as Admiral Holland, mistook her for *Prinz Eugen*, and reported a cruiser. Seven minutes later aircraft 2F under Lieutenant Callander arrived and confirmed Briggs's report of a battleship. Which was it? It was vital to know, for a torpedo attack on a cruiser required a shallower depth setting. Somerville ordered two more Swordfish with long-range tanks to take off from *Ark Royal* and relieve 2H and 2F.

The other eight Swordfish had already been recalled to the ship to be armed with torpedoes. The *Ark* was now steaming at high speed on a parallel course to (and about 50 miles from) *Bismarck* to make up the ground lost when steering northwest to fly off. Now she turned northwest again in order to land on. The stern was still rising and falling the height of a large house, but between them the pilots and batsman gauged each approach wonderfully, managing to get the planes down on the slippery, skiddy deck. Only one misjudged completely: the stern swished up as he came in over it and smashed the plane to pieces, though the crew were unhurt. Further landings were held up while the pieces were swept over the side.

During these flying operations *Renown* remained to the east of *Ark Royal* in order to keep between *Bismarck* and France. The Admiralty, fearful of Somerville doing something rash, signaled that *Renown* was only to engage if *King George V* or *Rodney* were themselves heavily engaged. *Sheffield*, though, was not serving any useful purpose, so at 1:15 P.M. Somerville ordered her to steer for *Bismarck*, then 40 miles away, and shadow from astern. By wireless signal, he informed the Admiralty and Tovey of this, as well as *Ark Royal*, who was out of visual touch with the flagship at the time.

This wireless signal reached *Ark Royal* in cipher a few minutes later, but as it was not addressed, only repeated, to *Ark Royal*, and as other important messages were waiting to be deciphered (especially those from the shadowing aircraft), it was put on one side. When after lunch the crews of the striking force went to the Observers Room for briefing, they were not told that *Sheffield* was on her way to *Bismarck* and would be quite near her by the time they reached the scene. Their instructions were that *Bismarck* was alone on the ocean: that no other ships were anywhere near.

At 2:15 P.M. the Swordfish started coming up on the lifts. Because there was still a faint doubt as to whether the enemy was *Bismarck* or *Prinz Eugen*, the torpedoes were set to run at 30 rather than 34 feet; and they were fitted with magnetic pistols, designed to trigger off an explosion under the enemy's hull. At 2:40 P.M. engines were started up and at 2:50 P.M. the leader of the flight, Lieutenant-Commander Stewart-Moore in Swordfish 4A took off. Fourteen other planes followed without mishap, formed up and turned south towards the enemy.

An hour passed. Maund and Traill and everyone else in the *Ark* waited anxiously for news. Then a harassed signal officer dashed to the bridge, holding a copy of Somerville's signal about *Sheffield*, just deciphered.

Maund, a calm man, read it and said to the signals officer, "Make to the striking force, 'Look out for *Sheffield*.' No, there's no time to cipher it, make it in plain language. Make it now."

CHAPTER 9

All that morning and early afternoon *King George V* went corkscrewing along towards the southeast, steering a slightly converging course on *Bismarck*, cutting a bit of a corner on the route to Brest. To Tovey and his staff officers it was clear from reports of the shadowing Swordfish that little by little they were catching up. But not fast enough. By this time tomorrow *Bismarck* would be inside the range of shore-based air cover and *King George V* would have to turn back for lack of fuel. If the planned Swordfish attack failed to slow *Bismarck* down, then they must return home with *Hood*'s death unavenged and—despite all the ships and aircraft allotted to the operation—*Bismarck* still at large.

All day signals of *Bismarck*'s position continued streaming in from Coastal Command Catalinas and *Ark Royal*'s Swordfish—the second a good deal more accurate than the first.

In *King George V* meanwhile Tovey had been receiving Somerville's signals about recalling the Swordfish for arming as a striking force, then of their proposed time of departure, and finally of the successful takeoff. Now there was nothing to do but wait. It was an agonizing period but Tovey was not left brooding for long. "Ship bearing Red Seven-O," shouted one of the port lookouts. All eyes on the bridge turned to the port beam; there below the horizon were the unmistakable outlines of a warship's fighting top. Could it be *Prinz Eugen*? The alarm bells were sounded, the gun crews ran to their turrets, the great guns swung around. But now her upperworks were coming into view, there could be no mistaking them. It was *Rodney*, for Tovey and his staff a truly wonderful sight.

The course that she and her two remaining destroyers (*Somali* had returned to base to fuel) were steering was only a few degrees off that of *King George V*, so it took a long time for the two ships to converge. When *Rodney* was near, Tovey signaled, "What is your maximum speed?" and Dalrymple-Hamilton replied: "22 knots." Tovey wanted to reduce speed anyway to conserve fuel, so he hoisted, "Speed of the fleet 22 knots." *Rodney* fell in astern of *King George V*, but soon the gap between them began widening. The engine room staff was doing marvels with *Rodney*'s worn out engines—down below men were fainting—but it was still not enough. "I am afraid," Dalrymple-Hamilton signaled ruefully to Tovey, "that your 22 knots is a bit faster than ours."

It was now well after 6 P.M., and Force H and *Bismarck* were only 90 miles away. There was still no news of the Swordfish attack, although the planes had left the carrier over three hours ago, and it couldn't have taken more than an hour and a half at most to deliver the attack. What had happened, why was there no news? At 6:21 P.M. Tovey signaled the Admiralty and Somerville that unless *Bismarck*'s speed had been reduced by midnight, he would have to return to harbor for lack of fuel. *Rodney* could continue until 8 A.M. the next day without her destroyers, then she too would have to return; and in answer to Somerville's offer to join him with *Renown*, he advised him to remain with *Ark Royal*.

Another ten minutes went by, then the blow fell. From Somerville came the briefest of signals, the one they had been waiting for, but not with the news they wanted. "From Flag Officer Force H to C-in-C Home Fleet," the message ran, "Estimate no hits." That was all. Why no hits? Was it the weather or skillful avoiding action, or *Bismarck*'s flak?—or a combination of all three? Not that it mattered anymore; the pursuit had ended, the campaign was over. On the bridge nobody said anything: there was nothing more to say.

When Stewart-Moore's striking force left *Ark Royal* at 2:50 P.M. they went up into cloud, then laid off a course to take them to the enemy. Several of the planes had recently been equipped with radar, and after some forty minutes' flying they picked up a ship right ahead. The pilots had not expected to contact *Bismarck* so soon, but as they had been told at the briefing that there were no other ships near, they knew the contact must be the enemy. They dived down through the cloud, saw the outlines of a warship right ahead, and went back into cloud to get into positions for attack.

Ten minutes later Captain Charles Larcom on the bridge of the *Sheffield* saw the Swordfish approaching. He was expecting to see them, having just received Somerville's signal that they had taken off from *Ark Royal*. But there was something horribly familiar about their approach. Instead of flying past him in the direction of the enemy, they were coming at him from different directions, as he had often seen them do *when carrying out practice torpedo attacks on him*. In a flash he realized the pilots had mistaken him for *Bismarck*, rang down for full speed, and ordered the gun crews not to open fire. The first plane dropped its torpedo; Larcom put the wheel over to comb the track. A second torpedo fell and an extraordinary thing happened: it exploded in a great fountain of spray as it hit the water. The third torpedo did the same. The magnetic pistols were firing prematurely, and three others exploded in *Sheffield*'s wake. But five or six more were launched successfully, and they streaked through the water towards the ship. On the bridge Larcom listened to reports of where they were coming from and swung the wheel hard over to port or starboard. Men looked down, watched the ship's bows swing slowly round to run parallel to the tracks, and held on hard, not knowing if they would make it. Thanks to Larcom's cool ship handling they did: not one torpedo hit.

The planes set course for *Ark Royal*. On the way they got Maund's signal, "Look out for *Sheffield*," and saw a long way off Vian's gray destroyers careering in from the west. Despite some hairy moments, all planes landed safely. The pilots and observers clambered out despondently, then went to the bridge to tell their woeful tale. But Maund was sympathetic. He told them they were not to blame, to go down to the wardroom and get some supper, and to be ready for another attack in an hour's time. In one way the attack on *Sheffield* was a blessing, for it showed the magnetic firing pistols to be faulty: contact pistols with a depth setting of 22 feet were ordered instead—these would not explode unless they hit the hull. Maund informed Somerville by lamp what he was doing, and Somerville signaled Tovey and the Admiralty: "Second striking force will leave *Ark Royal* about 18:30."

In *Bismarck*, apart from the weather which brought continued discomfort to young men who still hadn't found their sea legs, it had been a day of fluctuating fortunes. There had been a nasty moment at eight in the morning when a lookout high up in the fighting top observed the topmasts of several warships passing from left to right across the northern horizon. This was Vian's flotilla, on its way to join the Commander-in-Chief; thankfully it was soon lost to sight. The arrival of Briggs's Catalina followed by the Swordfish was depressing, for it meant the enemy had found them again and that another carrier, probably *Ark Royal*, was operating not far away. But as the hours wore on—as morning gave way to afternoon and afternoon to evening—and there were still no attacks, people began to think there might not be any.

During the day signals kept arriving in the ship from Group West about further preparations to receive her. These messages gave a lift to morale, and made the crew feel they were as good as home—which they almost were, for in a few hours it would be dark and by dawn next day they would be under protection of German air cover, almost within shouting distance of France.

And then a shadow fell across the sunset, for astern of *Bismarck* where for nearly two days there had been empty sea, were now the dim outlines of a shadowing cruiser. Through the rangefinders she was identified as *Southampton* class. Almost certainly *Sheffield*, thought Lütjens, and if so the rest of Force H, *Ark Royal* and *Renown*, couldn't be far away. How Lütjens must have again regretted not fueling at Bergen or in the Arctic! Had he done so, he could have steamed four or five knots faster during the past thirty-six hours, and by now would have been a further 160 miles nearer home, almost out of danger altogether. Well, he could still fight a surface action at speed providing a tanker met him in the morning. "Fuel situation urgent," he signaled to Group West, "when can I expect fuel?"

In Paris Saalwächter was puzzled. He knew Bismarck was short of fuel, but surely not as short as all that. He had the signal repeated back to Lütjens, adding, "Text of message appears defective, as I assume you have sufficient fuel?" But he ordered the tanker *Ermland* to be sailed immediately.

Whether Lütjens intended to reply, we shall never know, for now came the sound that he had been expecting all day. "Frederiiicke, Frederiiicke, Frederiiicke," shrilled the alarm bells. "Attack by enemy aircraft imminent."

The leader of the striking force this time was Lieutenant-Commander Tim Coode, with Stewart-Moore as second in command. They and their forty-three fellow pilots, observers and air gunners had no illusions about what lay ahead; but the false attack on *Sheffield* had been helpful, showing them that flying and landing in such weather was not as hair-raising as it seemed. Further the stigma of failure they all felt at not having recognized *Sheffield*, the humiliation of having attacked one of their own ships, was something they wanted to expunge. On them now lay all the hopes of the Navy and of England, for if they could not slow *Bismarck* down, no one else could. They feared what was before them, but there was exhilaration, too, a challenge to prove themselves, show what the Fleet Air Arm could do.

At 7 P.M. Captain Maund turned the *Ark* into the wind, reducing speed to 12 knots: now the gap between her and the enemy was opening at over 30 knots. Commander Traill stood on the bridge with his green flag; below him the fifteen planes—all the Swordfish, apart from the shadowers, left in the ship—were ranged on the flight deck, engines roaring. At 7:10 P.M. the green flag went down, Coode opened his throttle, the flight deck crew with trousers billowing in the slip-stream pulled away the chocks, and for the second time that day Swordfish 5A went trundling down the slippery deck. Coode took off safely into the stormy sky: one by one the others followed.

The planes formed up in line astern, in six sub-flights of two to three planes each. This time, so there should be no mistakes, the pilots had been briefed to make for *Sheffield* and obtain from her the enemy's exact position. They sighted *Sheffield* briefly just before 8 P.M., lost her, didn't pick her up again until 8:35 P.M. Captain Larcom signaled to Coode, "The enemy is twelve miles dead ahead."

Coode led the striking force upwards with the intention of meeting them above the cloud, there splitting up so as to approach *Bismarck* from different directions, make it more difficult for her to avoid the torpedoes. But unknown to him *Bismarck* was sailing under what meteorologists call a "front," a wall of cloud reaching to beyond 10,000 feet and extending downwards almost to sea level. The little planes climbed through the gray murk to 6,000, 7,000, 8,000 feet—there was still no sign of it ending. It was clear to Coode there was now no chance of carrying out a coordinated attack, that each sub-flight must attack on its own, and he signaled the others accordingly.

As leader of the force his own sub-flight was the first to attack. Down through the gray murk they screamed together, aiming for a position astern and upwind of *Bismarck*. As the altimeter changed rapidly from 8,000 to 5,000 to 3,000 to 1,000 feet without a sign of the cloud dispersing,

Coode wondered how much longer he could continue the dive without, as he put it, running out of height. At 700 feet the three planes plus another from No. 3 sub-flight that had accidentally joined them broke through the cloud to find themselves, not as they had hoped, astern of *Bismarck* but four miles ahead of her, her great bulk lurching through the seas towards them. To attack upwind in this weather would have been suicidal, so the sub-flight banked to port and climbed back into cloud to attack from *Bismarck*'s port beam.

A few minutes later those on the bridge of *Sheffield*, twelve miles astern, saw stabs of light and the brown puffs of bursting shells on *Bismarck*'s port side. The time was 8:53 P.M. The last attack had begun.

All day *U.556* had been steering southeast, like *Bismarck* towards the coast of France, also very low on fuel. From U-boat headquarters she had been receiving messages of *Bismarck*'s position regularly and realized the pursuit was gradually coming her way. Each new signal was received with added interest, for *Bismarck* was *U.556*'s adopted baby, her special child. Across the wild sea there, where *Bismarck* was, hung a picture in her wardroom of *U.556* deflecting torpedoes from *Bismarck*, a promise, sealed with Wohlfarth's thumb print, to guard and look after her.

And then, out of the blue, without any word of warning, came the opportunity to fulfill the promise. In the evening, after supper, a lookout on the bridge reported two big warships right ahead. The officer of the watch sounded the klaxons, the bridge party scrambled below, and *U.556* dived. At thirty feet she leveled off. Wohlfarth ordered "Up periscope." When it was raised, he looked, looked again, hardly believing his eyes. The legendary *Ark Royal*, Swordfish aircraft on deck, was making straight towards him. She had no destroyer screen and was not zigzagging. The battleship on her beam (which he mistook for *King George V*; the mistake was understandable in the weather) had no screen and was not zigzagging either. It was the sort of situation U-boat commanders dream about. "I could have maneuvered in between the two of them and got them both at the same time," he wrote in his log, "*if only I had any torpedoes.*" But they had all gone on ships from the convoy H.X. 126. Why had he not listened to Souvad's plea not to waste the last torpedo on the straggler; why, when he decided to attack the sparrow, could some kind fairy not have warned him of the two eagles that lay ahead? He stood helpless at the periscope as the huge ships passed a few hundred yards from his torpedo tubes, the noise of their screws loud in the hydrophone operator's ears, watching them slowly disappear from sight.

On the admiral's bridge of the *King George V* and in the plotting room just off it, Tovey and his officers once more waited for news. They knew that in less than three hours, barring a miracle, they would have to turn for home. Everyone was very tired, physically and emotionally, and the movement of the ship did nothing to ease it.

In Tovey's plotting room the officers stood quietly around the plot, holding onto voice pipes or table edges for support, bracing stomach muscles and knees to meet the motion of the ship. Only the admiral seemed wholly cool, in command of the situation and himself, radiating confidence and serenity.

And now the buzzer from the wireless office sounded: another signal had arrived. The Fleet Signal Officer unwrapped it, read, "From the leader of the striking force. Estimate no hits." It was the final blow, though no less than what they were expecting. And yet to have come so far, to have been robbed like this at the last moment, was a bitter thing. Tovey said nothing, smiled as though his partner had just lost him the match on the last green, which in a way he had.

Although all hope had gone, the squadron steamed on. Presently another signal arrived on the admiral's bridge, this time from *Sheffield*. "Enemy's course 340°," it said. Tovey looked at it, baffled: 340° was north-northwest or directly towards them. Then he understood. "I fear Larcom has joined the reciprocal club," he said bitingly. What he meant was that Larcom had mistakenly judged *Sheffield* to be moving from right to left instead of left to right. It was a not uncommon mistake, especially at long range and in poor visibility, though hardly to be expected from so senior an officer. Poor old Larcom, everyone thought, to make such a balls-up at this time.

A few more minutes passed, in which no one knew quite what to think, then a Swordfish report confirmed *Sheffield*'s estimate of a course of north-northwest. And then *Sheffield* reported again, this time a course of north.

Now there was no doubt about it, something very serious had happened to *Bismarck*, very serious indeed. Tovey and his officers looked at each other with incredulity and joy.

Coode and his four planes dropped out of the cloud on *Bismarck*'s port beam, leveled out, pointed their noses ahead of the enemy's bow to give the necessary deflection. The whole of *Bismarck*'s port side antiaircraft armaments burst into life: tracer bullets like billiard balls, red, green, orange, white, came towards them in long, slow arcs, small caliber shells exploded all around them. They tried to remember the simple rules for attack they had learned at training school—drop torpedoes at a speed of 90 knots at a height of 90 feet at a distance of 900 yards—but in this inferno of fire it was hard to think of anything. Sub-Lieutenant Dixon-Child's plane was hit by splinters but kept going, turning away to port, downwind. The observer of the plane from No. 3 sub-flight, attacking a little after the others, thought he saw a column of water shoot up abaft *Bismarck*'s funnel but couldn't be sure: Edmond Carver, observer of Coode's plane which had reached a position on *Bismarck*'s port bow, saw nothing. He and Coode hung around some time in the low cloud and rain, saw no other attacks, assumed they were the only ones to find the target, and made to *Ark Royal* before turning for home, "Estimate no hits," the signal that was passed on to Tovey.

But the three planes of No. 2 sub-flight, led by Lieutenant "Feather" Godfrey-Faussett (so called because of his bulk), were now coming in from starboard. They'd climbed to 9,000 feet without leaving cloud, found ice forming on the wings, and turned to attack from there. Godfrey-Faussett went tearing down on a firm radar bearing. He came out of cloud on *Bismarck*'s starboard beam to find only one plane, Sub-Lieutenant Kenneth Pattisson's, still with him, the other, piloted by Sub-Lieutenant Tony Beale, nowhere to be seen. He and Pattisson went into attack, saw *Bismarck*'s starboard side erupt into smoke and light, watched the colored bullets curve towards them, heard the shell splinters tearing at the flimsy canvas covering the fuselage. But they pressed home the attack and as *Bismarck* combed the torpedo tracks, they thought they saw one hit.

While this attack was in progress, four of the five planes from No. 3 and 4 sub-flights came out of cloud astern of *Bismarck* and attacked from the port quarter. Now the enemy's port side flak opened up again and one of the planes, caught in a pattern of shell bursts, was shot through and through with splinters: the pilot and air gunner were both wounded but the plane kept flying and with the others dropped its torpedo, though none claimed any hits.

Tony Beale meanwhile had come out in clear air above the clouds, found no one there, and returned to *Sheffield* to be redirected. His observer, Sub-Lieutenant Friend, made by lamp as he had done on many a practice occasion, "Where is target?" to which Larcom replied, "Enemy bears 340°, 15 miles"—an almost pointed reminder, thought Friend, that he too should have said "enemy" not "target," and that this time it was the real thing.

Beale climbed towards cloud again, but before reaching it spotted *Bismarck* and worked his way around to her port bow. Friend thought how wicked she looked with her huge humped back, no clear break in her upperworks as in British ships. Beale turned, made a long, brave upwind attack at 50 feet, dropping his torpedo at 800 yards. Oddly *Bismarck* didn't fire until he had turned away; then, said Friend, "her decks seemed to explode into crackling flame, the sea was lashed with shot and fragments." Leading Airman Pimlott, the air gunner, fired back, less with any hopes of damaging *Bismarck* than the sheer impertinent joy of it. Friend watched for signs of a hit and was rewarded by a plume of water rising on the port side amidships. "Pimlott was dancing a small jig as I excitedly told Beale. By turning the Swordfish quickly, he too was able to see the splash subsiding. Thus, all three of us saw our hit." One of the shadowing aircraft saw it too.

The two aircraft of No. 5 sub-flight lost each other while diving. The leader, Lieutenant Owen-Smith, who saw shell bursts near him at 3,500 feet, came out of cloud at 1,000 feet and well astern of *Bismarck*, and while working around to a more favorable position on her beam, thought he saw a large column of water rise up on *Bismarck*'s starboard side, right aft, just as Godfrey-Faussett and Pattisson were withdrawing. He himself withdrew to five miles, came in very low on the beam, wheels almost brushing the wavetops, released his torpedo at just over a thousand yards: his observer didn't see or claim any hit. The other aircraft of No. 5 sub-flight made two attempts to attack from starboard, found the fire too hot, jettisoned its torpedo and retired.

The two aircraft of No. 6 sub-flight also lost each other. The leader, Sub-Lieutenant Willcocks, attacked from 2,000 yards on the starboard beam without success. The other returned to *Sheffield* for a new direction, flew back to *Bismarck* at sea level, and also attacked unsuccessfully from the same direction.

The attack had started just before 9 P.M.: it was over just before half-past. On the way back to *Ark Royal* some of the planes flew past *Sheffield*, waggled their wings, and the pilots waved. On *Sheffield*'s bridge they waved back, gave a cheer, less for any success achieved than relief at seeing them in one piece.

Hardly had the last plane disappeared from *Sheffield*'s view when *Bismarck*, emerging from a patch of mist, was seen turning to port. As those on *Sheffield*'s bridge looked at her, a ripple of flame ran down her port side, followed by a burst of black smoke. Their first reaction was surprise. It was, says one writer, as though stung to fury by the air attacks on her, *Bismarck* was seeking revenge on the only British ship she could see. The salvo fell over a mile short; someone made a disparaging remark about her shooting. But *Bismarck* had not sunk the *Hood* in six minutes for nothing. Once more the orange flashes rippled down *Bismarck*'s side, once more the black cordite fumes drifted away on the wind. Captain Larcom gave a drastic alteration of course to avoid the shells now on their way towards him. On the bridge, and among the antiaircraft crews in exposed positions on the upper deck, they waited: ten seconds, twenty, went by, each long as a prayer. At thirty seconds the sea on either side erupted with a shattering roar, long white pillars rose beside them—as high, they seemed to some, as Nelson's column. The salvo was a straddle: splinters from one shell raked *Sheffield*'s upperworks, inflicting fearful wounds among the antiaircraft gun crews. Twelve men were hit altogether, five seriously. Later three died. Larcom put the wheel over again, went on to full speed and ordered smoke. Another four salvoes fell dangerously close before the smoke blotted *Bismarck* out. Larcom, noticing that in that time the enemy had maintained his course, sent out the signal that was to so puzzle Tovey, "Enemy steering 340°."

Sheffield worked around to the west to open the range. When the smoke cleared, Larcom saw *Bismarck* far away, still steering to the north, and he sent another signal to Tovey. Then she was lost to sight. The radar was ordered to get a range and bearing on her, but now came a report that a splinter had put the radar apparatus out of action. This meant that even if *Sheffield* did sight the enemy again, she would not be able to shadow after dark. The last of the shadowing Swordfish would also soon have to break off, and then, deprived of its eyes, the Fleet would lose contact with *Bismarck* altogether. In the night she would slip away unobserved, by dawn be safe inside Luftwaffe air cover.

So ran Larcom's thoughts, and within minutes a beneficent Providence had acted on them. "Ships bearing Red One Five," shouted a lookout, and there, coming to join the fray at the moment they were most needed, were Vian's five destroyers. They made a brave sight as they steered eastward at high speed, at one moment riding the crests of the long swell, the next all but their topmasts hidden in the troughs, yawing and rolling so that it seemed they must be pushed right over, the spray falling over them like rain. "Where is the enemy?" signaled Vian, and Larcom gave him an estimated bearing and range. The little ships didn't pause in their pursuit; they swept on and past *Sheffield*, fanning outwards, disappearing to the east. Forty minutes later and just as the last Swordfish had left for *Ark Royal*, the Polish *Piorun* on the port wing signaled "Enemy in sight."

Ark Royal's striking force meanwhile had all landed safely, though it had taken them over an hour and many attempts to do it. The crews were taken off for independent de-briefing, as a result of which Maund signaled to Somerville and Tovey, "Estimate one hit amidships" and half an hour later, "Possible second hit on starboard quarter."

Leading Seaman Herzog was loader at one of the 37mm flak guns on *Bismark's* starboard side aft, when he saw two planes coming towards him. He noticed how low they were, wheels almost touching the wavetops, and how bravely they pressed home their attack, coming so near that at full depression the 37mm gun could no longer bear. At full speed *Bismarck* started turning to port. To Herzog it seemed that one of the planes was pointing amidships, the other farther aft. They dropped their torpedoes—Herzog saw them clearly—and turned away. *Bismarck* was turning to port at high speed when the hit came. On the bridge Lindemann ordered the wheel to be centered. She refused to answer to it, went on swinging to port, then began to heel sharply to starboard. In the after transmitting station, Ordinary Seaman Alfred Eich saw on the engine room indicator the ship was doing 28 knots, while the compass repeater showed she was steaming in a circle. In the after control tower Müllenheim-Rechberg looked at the rudder repeater, saw the wheel was jammed at 15° to port. Farther and farther *Bismarck* heeled to starboard, farther than ever before, so some thought she would capsize: they looked at one another with disbelief and fear, and one man voiced their thoughts, "She's sinking."

But Lindemann ordered a reduction of speed and though the ship still went on circling, she presently eased to a more or less even keel and headed into the wind. *Sheffield* came into sight to port and Schneider ordered main armament salvoes. He saw them straddle and *Sheffield* disappear behind smoke. Presently a report reached the bridge of the torpedo damage. The torpedo had struck right aft, at least twenty feet down, breached the steering gear compartments, flooding them: the three propellers were unharmed, but the rudders were jammed at 15° port. Water was also coming into the ship from where the after hydrophones had been destroyed and into the port engine room up the shaft tunnel that led to the propellers. Ordinary Seaman Blum, on damage control duty, remembered the time in the Baltic when they'd practiced damage to the steering gear compartment, how he'd had to feign dead. He remembered, too, his lieutenant saying then, "The chances of such a hit are a hundred thousand to one against."

The first thing to do was try and free the jammed rudders, which meant getting men into the flooded steering compartments. It was going to be a long and difficult business, for it meant first entering the flooded main steering compartment to unclutch the motor, then going into the flooded hand steering compartment and coupling that up.

Before the work was begun, however, Admiral Lütjens did a strange thing. Believing the rudders were beyond repair and the ship doomed, anxious to secure his own passport to Valhalla, he signaled Berlin with typical brevity: "Ship unmaneuverable. We fight to the last shell. Long live the Führer." Such heroic exultation at such a time cannot have done much to help the morale of the admiral's staff officers nor of the wireless room operators who, because of frequency problems, took nearly two hours to pass it to Group West. Elsewhere in the ship morale was high. "We had great trust in our captain and what he could do for us," said one man, "and so remained full of hope."

Presently two engineer officers, Lieutenants Giese and Richter, came aft with the carpenter's party. They shored up the bulkhead above the steering compartments, stopped the leak from the broken hydrophonic gear and got the water out of the port engine room. Commander Lehmann with two stokers in diving suits meanwhile had reached the armored hatch leading to the main steering compartment. They opened it. At once the sea water came surging and gushing into the passageway, then as the stern rose the level in the compartment dropped dramatically, and the water was sucked back into the sea. The stern fell again like a lift out of control, banged against the trough, the water came surging upwards and quickly the armored hatch was secured and battened down. No diver could possibly get down there, let alone move about and work.

So all that remained was to see if the ship could be steered southeast by propellers alone. Back on the bridge where it was almost dark Lindemann tried every combination of telegraph orders he could imagine. But whatever he tried, the result was the same: for a while the ship's head pointed more or less in the direction he wanted, then the 15° of port rudder brought the bows slowly back into the wind, towards the northwest and danger, away from safety and home. There was not a thing wrong with the engines or main armament; but this absurd 15° of port rudder made the ship helpless as a babe.

And now came further troubles to try the sore-pressed *Bismarck*. From the control and information posts about the ship reports reached the bridge that the destroyers they had sighted earlier were now surrounding them, maneuvering into position to attack. Müllenheim-Rechberg in the after control tower recognized them uneasily as Tribals, the ships that a year earlier had sunk his own destroyer, *Erich Giese*, at Narvik. Was history about to repeat itself, were they going to be successful again?

CHAPTER 10

On *Bismarck*'s course of north being trebly confirmed, Tovey at once altered south towards her. The two flagships were closing at a mean rate of over 30 knots, and he thought there might be a chance of action before the light went. But when Somerville's signal reported the critical torpedo hit on the starboard quarter, and Vian also reported he was in touch, he told his staff he would postpone attack until morning. "I shall never forget," said his secretary, Captain Paffard, "the horrified look on Daddy Brind's face." Brind feared, as all the staff did, that *Bismarck* would repair her damage and slip away in the night. But Tovey knew what he was doing: with rain squalls bringing visibility down to under a mile and a forecast of a pitch black night, it was impossible to say where anyone was and the conditions gave him no advantage; and he trusted Vian to maintain contact. All the same, said Paffard, "it was a decision that must have taken tremendous moral courage."

Tovey radioed Somerville to take Force H twenty miles south of *Bismarck* so as to be clear of his approach, while he hauled off to the northeastwards so as to remain between the enemy and Brest: before dawn he would run down to the southwestwards to engage *Bismarck* against the sunrise with the advantages of sea and wind. Then he went to his sea cabin, wrote a message for the ship's company and handed it to Captain Patterson.

To K.G.V.

The sinking of the *Bismarck* may have an effect on the war as a whole out of all proportion to the loss to the enemy of one battleship.

May God be with you and grant you victory.

J.T. 26/5/41

In *Rodney* the captain came on the loudspeakers, told them *Bismarck* was damaged, and that they and *King George V* would engage her at dawn. All over the ship men cheered to know that they would be avenging the *Hood* after all.

To the north of *King George V*, Wake-Walker in *Norfolk* was still trying desperately to catch up. Captain Phillips had reduced speed earlier to save fuel, but with the news of the Swordfish attack he went on again to full speed. To the southward the cruiser *Dorsetshire* was coming up at 28 knots. The cruiser *Edinburgh* had turned for home before hearing that *Bismarck* was crippled; at once she reversed course towards the enemy, but her fuel reserves were very low and when action was postponed until morning Commodore Blackman once more turned for Londonderry. Somerville, meanwhile, having received Tovey's message that he would postpone attack until morning, signaled to *Ark Royal*: "At what time will striking force take off? With any luck we may finish her off before C-in-C Home Fleet arrives." To which Maund, remembering *Sheffield*, wisely replied: "Not until such time as aircraft can differentiate between friend and foe."

Astern of *Rodney* the destroyers *Tartar* and *Mashona* kept station on the battleship and each other. For four days now they had had a continual buffeting, so that one officer was to write afterwards that it seemed in looking back "like one long twilit day punctuated by meals that would scarcely stay long enough on the table to be eaten."

Tartar and *Mashona* were Tribals of the Sixth Destroyer Flotilla, *Cossack, Maori, Zulu, Sikh* of the Fourth. They were the Navy's newest and biggest destroyers, completed just before the war, with their flared bows and long, sleek lines as elegant and powerful looking as *Bismarck* herself. And those appointed to command them were all seasoned men, the cream of the Navy's destroyer captains.

As in the fading light Vian and his five commanders closed in towards the elusive *Bismarck*, he had formulated what he thought his duty to be. "Firstly," (as he wrote to Tovey later) "to deliver to you at all costs the enemy, at the time you wished. Secondly to try to sink or stop the enemy with torpedoes in the night if I thought the attack should not involve the destroyers in heavy losses."

The first thing was to take up shadowing positions, casting a net around *Bismarck* from which she would not easily escape: one destroyer on each bow and quarter, *Cossack* shadowing astern.

At 11:24 P.M., half an hour after sunset, Vian ordered his ships to take positions for a synchronized torpedo attack. This was easier ordered than done. Steaming downwind it was possible to move at speed, but into it, the way *Bismarck* was going, 18 knots was the maximum without those on the bridge being drenched with spray, unable to see the enemy or where they were going. Further, despite the darkness of the night and

Bismarck's wounds, she was soon ranging accurately on the destroyers. The British believed this was by radar, and it may have helped, but Müllenheim-Rechberg saw them clearly through the powerful rangefinders. At 11:42 P.M., when *Bismarck* was still four miles away, Vian saw her silhouetted in the light of her own gunfire, fifteen seconds later heard the song of her shells, large and small: they burst all around. Splinters shot away the wireless aerials; *Cossack* turned away.

A few minutes later it was the turn of Commander Graham in *Zulu*. He too saw the white flashes of *Bismarck*'s guns stabbing the night, heard their thunder, sensed upheavals in the sea all around, as though a cluster of underwater geysers had suddenly erupted. Graham turned away. Half an hour later Commander Stokes in *Sikh*, shadowing astern, saw *Bismarck* alter course to port, let loose a salvo at him; and he also moved away.

Now, because of the darkness of the night, the frequent rain squalls, and *Bismarck*'s accurate fire, all Vian's destroyers had lost touch with the enemy. When at half-past midnight *Cossack* fell in with *Piorun* and then *Zulu*, neither where they were meant to be, he knew there was no possibility of a synchronized attack and signaled by wireless for ships to attack individually as opportunity offered.

None of the torpedoes from any of the ships hit. It would have been surprising if they had. In normal conditions the range at which a torpedo was considered to have a reasonable chance of hitting was a mile or two miles. Here they had been fired at ranges that varied between two miles and three and a half in conditions that were extremely abnormal, waves fifty feet high, a pitch black night, and an enemy whose course and speed was erratic, whose gunfire was precise.

Claims of hits were made in good faith; but the wish fathered the thought. Vian and his officers and men had been through much and believed that on them much depended: the Fleet Air Arm had scored hits on both their attacks; it would be intolerable for them not to do the same. Such thoughts were not conscious, but when men have experienced great strain, as these had, bringing themselves to within a whisker of death, they see things their eyes are reaching to see, that will justify the risks taken and prove to themselves and the world that it has all been worthwhile.

Bismarck lay stopped for the next hour or so, wallowing heavily in the waves. Soon after 2:30 A.M. she got under way again, moving slowly northwestwards. Vian got a signal from Tovey to illuminate the enemy with starshell every half hour: the admiral was to the northeastwards of

Bismarck and didn't want to bump into her in a rain squall on his run down to the westwards before dawn. The destroyers complied, but *Bismarck* opened such fire they had to withdraw.

By about 4 A.M. all the destroyers had lost touch with *Bismarck*, though they guessed she could not be very far away. At 5 A.M. Vian signaled *Piorun* by wireless to return to Plymouth, as he knew she must be very short of fuel. Commander Plawski and his crew, still searching for *Bismarck* to the southeast, were dreadfully disappointed. Unlike the British who considered the enemy as a scourge to be eradicated, a boil to be lanced, the Poles hated them with a deep, personal loathing, for their brutal conquest of Poland and for making them exiles from their own land. Further, they had ten torpedoes to the Tribals' four, which gave them a far better chance of hitting: all they wanted was to get in really close to *Bismarck*, and pump every one of them into her. To have come so near to getting their own back as this, then to be denied it, was almost unbearable. For an hour Plawski ignored Vian's order, and continued searching for *Bismarck*; then with bitter regrets, he turned for the Channel.

At 5:50 A.M. *Maori* sighted *Bismarck* again, slowly zigzagging northwest. *Sikh* also sighted her emerging from a rain squall forty minutes later. It was almost full daylight, and just before 7 A.M. at a range of four and a half miles *Maori* fired her last two torpedoes: no hits were observed.

The four destroyers took station in four sectors around the crippled battleship. Vian had done what he had promised to do—hung on to the enemy through the night to deliver him to his Commander-in-Chief in the morning. And now he sat back to wait for Tovey's arrival.

The events of that long night in *Bismarck* are difficult to record with any certainty; for by now most of the crew were near exhaustion, and later when some came to recall them, their memories were confused by subsequent events, horrors that were yet to come.

In big ships news travels slowly, unless there is an announcement from the bridge; this is especially so at action stations when men are immobile at their posts, cut off from one another. In *Bismarck* it had been broadcast that there had been a hit affecting the rudders, but it was known that men were working on it; they had faith in each other and their ship, and with many hours of darkness still ahead there was every reason to suppose the damage would be made good and they could then continue home. Meanwhile there was an action to be fought with British destroyers, instruments to be watched and tended, shells brought up from below, guns to be trained and fired. There was no time to speculate or brood; energies were needed elsewhere.

On the bridge, though, as the night went on, the seriousness of the situation became increasingly apparent. Reports from aft indicated that all attempts to free the jammed rudder had failed, that nothing more could be done: in the wireless room the growing strength of enemy signals (and whatever of their contents the cryptographic team were still able to obtain) made it clear the final reckoning could not long be delayed. It was what Lütjens had been expecting all along. "To the Führer of the German Reich, Adolf Hitler," he signaled just before midnight, "We fight to the last in our belief in you, my Führer, and in the firm faith in Germany's victory." Hitler replied from the Berghof two hours later, "I thank you in the name of the German people," and he also sent a message, perhaps at Raeder's prompting, to the *Bismarck*'s crew. "The whole of Germany is with you. What can still be done will be done. The performance of your duty will strengthen our people in the struggle for their existence." There were other messages of encouragement and farewell. Raeder signaled, "Our thoughts are with you and your ship. We wish you success in your hard fight," Admiral Carls in far away Wilhelmshaven, "We are all thinking of you with faith and pride," Saalwächter in Paris, "Best wishes. Our thoughts are with our victorious comrades." Later, to strengthen resolve for the battle ahead, Lütjens signaled Raeder, "Propose award of Knight's Cross to Commander Schneider for sinking of *Hood*." Hitler was in his study when his adjutant brought him the message, and he nodded approval. Two hours later *Bismarck*'s crew heard on the loudspeaker Lindemann's voice read out Raeder's signal to Schneider: "The Führer has awarded you the Knight's Cross for sinking the battle cruiser *Hood*. Hearty congratulations."

These messages were double-edged: they were designed to help morale but they underlined a situation in which help for morale was needed. From Group West came signals of more practical encouragement. All available U-boats were steering for *Bismarck*; the ship should transmit beacon signals for them on 852 meters and 443 kc's. Three tugs were on their way to take *Bismarck* in tow, the *Ermland* had sailed with supplies of fuel, and squadrons of bombers—81 aircraft, some remember being said—would be reaching the ship by dawn.

And yet as time went on and the course and speed of the ship remained the same, there was a smell of death in the air and some began to talk openly about what few dared to think: that with every hour that passed, the gap between themselves and *Rodney* and other enemy battleships was slowly but inevitably closing. In one engine room a man went berserk, wanted to stop the ship: Captain Junack had to telephone for a guard to take him to the doctor for sedation.

Müllenheim-Rechberg, sitting in the after control tower with one or two officers of the prize crews, said he felt "like meat on the slab waiting for the butcher's chopper." It was bad too for those whose work was over, who had no part to play in the coming battle: the flak crews, most of whose ammunition was now expended, Dr. Externbrink and his fellow meteorologists, the merchant navy captains and the prize crews, the pilots and observers of the Arado aircraft, cooks and cobblers, tailors and stewards, the bandsmen whose instruments lay unwanted in their lockers. From exhaustion these and others, all over the ship, slept: the guns' crews in their huge turrets, the supply teams at the ammunition hoists, stokers and engine room staff below, doctors and sickberth attendants in the sickbay. Lying in cots there were the stokers who had been scalded when *Prince of Wales*'s shell burst, the airmen whose legs had been broken by the explosion of *Victorious*'s torpedo, a man recovering from an emergency appendectomy. On the tables near them saws and scalpels, rubber gloves and syringes, cotton wool and bandages and ampules of morphia hinted at the frightfulness to come.

At about 5 A.M., the order was piped on the loudspeakers: "Prepare ship's aircraft for launching." Lütjens, who had few doubts about the fate of the ship in the face of the opposition now massing, wanted the ship's log saved so that Raeder might have a true record of the voyage, details of the actions, to draw conclusions for the future. He also wanted to send home the film of the sinking of the *Hood* taken by the cameraman Dreyer, and accounts of the battle written by the war correspondent Hanf.

The hangar door was opened by the deck crew, one of the aircraft lifted by crane onto the launching rails, pushed to one end and linked to the catapult gear. A pilot and observer were detailed, and they went to change into flying gear, hardly believing their luck.

The two men climbed in, the engine was started and allowed to warm up. When it was ready for takeoff, word was passed to the bridge, and Lindemann did what he could to bring the ship broadside to the wind. When the windward side, on its way up, was level with the leeward, the catapult gear operator pressed the lever that would send the Arado shooting 120 feet across the length of *Bismarck*'s beam and away into the night.

Nothing happened. The plane stayed on the rails, engine racing. Once again the officer gave the signal, once more the lever was pressed, once more the plane stayed still. Now an inspection of the gear was made and it was found the compressed air pipe was badly fractured by a splinter from one of *Prince of Wales*'s shells. The catapult mechanism was out of action.

The experts were called, but it was not possible to repair it. So the engine of the Arado was switched off, the pilot and observer who a few moments ago had been so full of joy climbed heavily out, the ship's log was taken back to the bridge, and the cans of film and copy were returned to Dreyer and Hanf. The aircraft, now useless and a fire risk, was allowed to run down the rails and into the sea. The pilot and observer walked wearily to the changing room, removed their flying gear, and rejoined the ranks of those about to die.

After *Ark Royal* and *Renown* had passed him, Wohlfarth steered on the surface for where he believed *Bismarck* to be. At 11:30 P.M. he sighted one of Vian's destroyers, dived, at 90 feet heard the screws pass over him. At midnight he surfaced, saw in the distance the flashes of *Bismarck*'s guns, and was astonished to find that by his reckoning she was sixty miles from her given position. He sent a signal to U-boat Command giving her true position for the benefit of the Luftwaffe and other U-boats, and sent out D/F signals for German shore stations to fix. Not far away Lieutenant-Commander Eitel-Friedrich Kentrat in the damaged *U.74*, hastening towards the scene, altered course when he got Wohlfarth's signal, for U-boats had a reputation for giving accurate positions.

Without torpedoes and being as low in fuel now as everyone else, all that Wohlfarth could do was keep in touch with *Bismarck* and send out regular transmissions. Once again he had been given the opportunity to fulfill his promise to protect *Bismarck* in the seas and oceans of the world; once again he was unable to do so. "It is a terrible thing to be so near," he wrote in his log, "and unable to do anything."

Another two hours went by. The flashes of *Bismarck*'s guns became more distant and sporadic; he lost her turbines on the hydrophones. With his lack of fuel he couldn't chase after her, but now in the dawn light Kentrat in *U.74* hove in sight, guided by his beacon signals. Kentrat couldn't attack either because of damage caused by a depth charge attack, but he had sufficient fuel and could take over duties as observer and reporting ship. The two boats closed to within hailing distance. Wohlfarth indicated the direction in which *Bismarck* had gone. He wished Kentrat luck. Then with heavy heart he pointed the bows of *U.556* towards Lorient. Relying on most economical use of diesels and motors, he reckoned he had just about enough fuel to reach France.

Hitler was at the Berghof that evening, entertaining guests in the big hall, watching the latest newsreels. Since the sinking of the *Hood*, Raeder had been in touch by telephone, keeping him abreast of events. After hearing of the torpedo hit by *Victorious*, Hitler telephoned Göring to ask for bombers to attack the carrier. Göring replied she was far beyond their range. When *Bismarck* was picked up again by *Ark Royal* aircraft, he got on to Göring again. The answer was the same.

Now the telephone rang once more. It was Raeder to tell him about the hit on the rudder. He took the news calmly, said his Luftwaffe adjutant, Colonel von Below, though when told that the ship was unmaneuverable, he remarked with some bitterness, "Why is our Air Force not able to do that sort of thing to the British?" Later a teletype message came from Raeder saying that gale force winds were preventing the dispatch of light forces and tugs and adding that if a press notice was thought desirable, it should read: "The battleship *Bismarck* on entering the Bay of Biscay had another brush with enemy forces and was hit by a torpedo aft"—a clear indication that Raeder believed that nothing more could be done and wanted to prepare the nation for the blow that was to come.

The guests left by side doors. Hitler took von Below to his study. He became increasingly depressed, says von Below, fretting about the effect of the loss of the ship on German prestige. Perhaps his mind went back to the happy day of the launching three years before when he had stood on the podium with the old Chancellor's granddaughter, and the crowds cheered and the sun shone and Europe was at peace. When Lütjens's signal about fighting to the last shell arrived, he dictated his replies to von Below, perhaps at Raeder's prompting. At 3 A.M. Luftwaffe headquarters rang to say the first planes had taken off to search for the ship and attack the British forces, though at the extreme limit of their range. Hitler dismissed von Below and went to bed.

While Hitler slept, Raeder and Schniewind at the German Admiralty in Berlin accepted the ship was now beyond aid, and turned their minds to the fate of the crew. At 5 A.M. Schniewind put through a call to the German naval attaché in Madrid, Captain Meyer-Döhner, to ask the Spanish naval authorities to send a hospital ship, merchant ship, or warship to the area "to render assistance." Later Captain Meyer-Döhner called back to say the cruiser *Canarias* and two destroyers would leave Ferrol in five hours' time: the British naval attaché, Captain Hillgarth, would not be informed until the ships had sailed. When Hitler heard of this request, he took Raeder to task, saying it was harmful to national prestige.

She lay there wallowing in the unrelenting seas, like a great wounded, sullen bull. The *picadors* had done their work, thrust their darts deep into flank and shoulders, taken half her power from her. Now she waited for the arrival of the *torero*, for the last trial of strength whose result was a foregone conclusion. But if she had to die, as bulls did, then she would die bravely and with dignity—that too was determined.

The destroyers had retreated out of range, were halfway to the gray horizon, so a partial standdown was piped to allow men to stretch cramped limbs, get some refreshment, walk about. Most stayed put: some, deep in sleep, never heard the pipe; others were too worn out to move. "Look out for friendly aircraft, look out for friendly submarines," chanted the loudspeaker hopefully, but this too went ignored. Nobody believed it any more. Records were played to stop people brooding. One man remembered hearing *"Warum ist es am Rhein so schön?"*—"Why is it so lovely by the Rhine?"

Müllenheim-Rechberg left the after control, made his way to the wardroom where soup was being served, took a little to warm him, and exchanged a few desultory remarks with others as unshaven and bleary-eyed as himself. Then he went to the bridge and entered the armored conning tower. Eich had been there a little earlier, had seen the captain congratulating Schneider on his Knight's Cross. Lindemann was smoking as usual, but otherwise seemed relaxed: Eich was impressed by his composure.

But things had changed when Müllenheim-Rechberg arrived. There was very little activity going on. He noticed Lindemann was wearing an inflated lifebelt, went over and saluted. Lindemann looked at him dully without returning the salute, which Müllenheim-Rechberg thought strange as he had once been his aide. "He looked like a man doomed to destruction," Müllenheim-Rechberg wrote afterwards, "dead tired, waiting patiently for the end." He moved to the chart table and saw the drunken course the ship had been steering through the night, a picture that was self-explanatory. Then he went aft, back to his post, and on the superstructure passed Lütjens and Commander Ascher, the staff operations officer, returning to the bridge. Mullenheim-Rechberg saluted, the admiral saluted back.

There is further evidence that Lindemann's once cool nerves had frayed, that his reserves of endurance were exhausted. Down in the engine room Commander Lehmann had asked Gerhard Junack to relieve him for a while on the engine room platform. There had been no engine room orders for some time, but now they rang down from the bridge: "Stop engines." At about this time Lütjens's last signal, "Send U-boat to save war diary" was sent, so it seems likely the admiral had asked for the ship to be stopped for any U-boat near to come alongside. But to stop the engines abruptly and leave them stopped was risky—they could seize up—so Junack picked up the bridge telephone and asked permission to keep the engines turning over slowly. The exasperation of the captain's reply surprised him: "Oh, do what you like! I've finished with them." It was as though Lindemann's will had broken, that after his superhuman efforts of the last five sleepless days and nights, the brilliant way in which he had sailed and fought his ship, his mind was no longer capable of answering to the situation.

At a little after eight o'clock an enemy cruiser was reported on the port bow. Lütjens and Ascher raised their glasses, recognized an old friend, the cruiser *Norfolk*, which they had first seen in the Denmark Straits three and a half days before. Now, after 36 hours' solitary high-speed steaming, she had arrived on the scene in the nick of time, as the final curtain was about to go up. She flashed her light at *Bismarck*, then veered away. A rain squall swept over *Bismarck*, and when it had cleared, her officers on the bridge saw with tired eyes two battleships dead ahead. One was *King George V* class, the other, as expected, *Rodney*.

By one in the morning Tovey and the battle fleet had got as far to the northeast as he wanted, then turned and ran down the reciprocal bearing so as to get to the westward of *Bismarck* by dawn. At about 5 A.M. they crossed twenty miles ahead of the enemy's track, but in the poor visibility failed to see the destroyers' starshells. "Throughout the night on the admiral's bridge," wrote Hugh Guernsey, "we sat, stood or leant like a covey of disembodied spirits. It was dark, windy and rainy. None of us will ever know if it was cold. About two o'clock in the morning cocoa appeared. We drank it gratefully, but it might equally have been pitch-tar; no one would have noticed." Everyone's mind was on the coming battle. Now that it was as certain as anything could be, men asked themselves, as those in *Hood* and *Prince of Wales* had asked earlier, whether by this time next day they would be alive or dead, whether wounded and how, whether they would be able to do their duty as England and the ghost of Nelson expected.

Captains Dalrymple-Hamilton and Patterson stayed on their compass platforms all night, occasionally dozing in upright chairs. Tovey was up most of the time, too, making frequent visits to the plot to see the enemy's latest position obtained by D/F bearings of Vian's destroyers (*Bismarck's* wireless office was sending out similar signals to guide U-boats to her) and attending to incoming signals. From Somerville came news that twelve Swordfish would attack at dawn; from Vian that the enemy had made good eight miles between 2:40 and 3:40 and was still capable of heavy and accurate fire; while the Admiralty, desperately worried that having got this far Tovey might now have to break off and return for lack of fuel, gave approval for him to seek sanctuary in an Irish port, where an oiler would be sent.

Dawn broke at last, "patchy rain squalls," wrote Guernsey, "a tearing wind from the northwest and a rising sea." Somerville thought the visibility too poor to risk the Swordfish attack. He was afraid of a repetition of the *Sheffield* incident and signaled Tovey he was canceling it. Tovey felt the same: with so many ships about and *Norfolk* and *Dorsetshire* approaching from north and south, he decided to stand off until full daylight, for he had no worries about the enemy escaping him now. He went to his sea cabin as Nelson had done before Trafalgar and prayed, as he put it, "for guidance and help." He had no doubts that his ships would sink *Bismarck*, but was afraid they might get terribly damaged. The longer he prayed, the calmer he felt. It was, he said, "as if all responsibility had been taken from me, and I knew everything would be all right," and he returned to the bridge refreshed and confident. About the same time his operations officer, Commander Robertson, went to his cabin to fetch his steel helmet. An astonishing sight met his eyes—four large rats running about in terror. Robertson remembered the adage about sinking ships and hoped it wasn't a bad omen.

During the night Tovey had been planning his battle tactics. Now he revealed them to Captain Patterson and his staff. *King George V* and *Rodney* would approach the enemy head-on in line abreast, six cables (three-fifths of a mile) apart. "I hoped," said Tovey, "that the sight of two battleships steering straight for them would shake the nerves of the range takers and control officers, who had already had four anxious days and nights." The two ships would close as quickly as possible to a range of between seven and eight miles, then turn and fire broadsides: *Rodney* would have discretion to maneuver on her own. Dalrymple-Hamilton, receiving this message, was grateful to Tovey for giving him the freedom of action Holland had denied to *Prince of Wales*. He thought of his son

North, at his action station in one of *King George V*'s antiaircraft directors, and hoped he would come safely through the battle. At 7:30 A.M. Tovey began to turn the fleet to port, in a long, slow arc to the eastwards, towards *Bismarck*, keeping informed of her position by D/F bearings on *Maori*. An hour later *Norfolk* came into sight dead ahead, having reached the scene of battle at the very last moment. She had mistaken *Bismarck* for *Rodney*, challenged her by lamp, only realized who it was when there was no reply, and sheered away sharply to get out of range, as she had done in the Denmark Straits four days before. Then an alert *Bismarck* had fired on her within seconds; now, rolling sluggishly in the heavy seas, she made no attempt to. Nor did *Norfolk*. "I felt it unwise to irritate her unnecessarily before she had someone else to distract her attention," wrote Wake-Walker, not realizing her days of irritation were over. As *Norfolk* increased the range from the enemy, she sighted *King George V* and *Rodney* coming in from the west, became the first visual link between the three battleships. "Enemy bears 130° 16 miles," Wake-Walker signaled to Tovey, "On tin hats!"

Tovey saw he was steering too far to the north and altered course to starboard to close. The ships came round, steadied on south. Tovey reached for his tin hat, hanging on a hook outside: when he put it on, a trickle of water ran down his face (during a rain squall some had collected in the bottom): he smiled, and those around him smiled to see their leader so relaxed. The minutes went by, Wake-Walker continuing to send reports of the enemy's position. On the bridge of *King George V* and *Rodney* officers and lookouts strained through binoculars to catch a first glimpse of the ship that for days now—it seemed like weeks—had been in the very marrow of their lives. Did she really exist? She had the same sort of grim reality as the giant in the boy's storybook. And what did she look like, this monster that had sunk their beloved *Hood*?

And then, suddenly, there she was; "veiled in distant rain-fall," wrote Guernsey, "a thick, squat ghost of a ship, very broad in the beam, coming straight towards us." "Enemy in sight" came over the *Rodney*'s loudspeakers and telephones, and all over the ship men cheered. The time was 8:43 A.M., the range twelve and a half miles. Four minutes later George Whalley in *Tartar*, walking aft along the upper deck, saw a cloud of brown smoke erupt from *Rodney*'s foremast guns, seconds later heard the rumble of her opening salvo. He ran down to the wardroom where some officers, having been at action stations all night, were sprawled asleep in every posture.

"They've found her!" he shouted. "It's begun!"

Before Rodney's first salvo had landed, the fire gong sounded in *King George V*. On the upper bridge Captain Patterson and his officers, on the lower the admiral and his officers, waited, in tin hats and with cotton wool stuffed in their ears to deaden the sound, for the flagship's opening roar. Within seconds it came, like a small earthquake, the bitter cordite fumes catching at their throats, the explosion of the charges stunning them. The compass bounded out of its binnacle, Guernsey's tin hat was blown on to the deck, and a pile of signals was sucked upwards like a tornado, scattered to the winds.

The salvoes fell as *Bismarck* was turning to starboard to bring all her guns to bear: great, white clumps rose all around her, higher than her foremast. Then it was her turn. In the British ships they saw a ripple of orange fire down the length of her, followed by a pall of cordite smoke, far blacker and thicker than their own. "Time of flight 55 seconds," announced a keen officer of the admiral's staff, and started counting off the time that was left. "For heaven's sake," said Tovey, not wanting to know the moment a shell might strike him, "shut up!" Even so they waited anxiously on the bridges of the two battleships for the salvo to arrive, the men of each hoping it was aimed at the other. They felt an instinct to duck; then the thunderbolt fell off *Rodney*'s bow, short, in a pattern of huge splashes and Guernsey and others in *King George V* breathed a sigh of relief.

At ten miles' range *Norfolk*, to the east of Tovey, joined battle with her 8-inch guns. *King George V* and *Rodney* continued firing with their foremost turrets and were soon claiming straddles and hits. But *Bismarck* was finding the range too; her third salvo straddled *Rodney*. A few splinters came aboard: one passed through the starboard side of the antiaircraft director, smashed the cease fire bell, passed through a tin hat on a hook, severed the trainer's telescope, hit the fire gong and grazed the trainer's wrist, after which the director was evacuated and the crew took shelter below. Dalrymple-Hamilton turned to port to avoid the next salvo and bring the after turret into action. "I watched *Rodney*," said Guernsey, "to see if she was being hit, but she just sat there like a great slab of rock blocking the northern horizon, and then suddenly belched a full salvo." With his own eyes he saw some of the one ton shells come whizzing out of the barrels at 1,600 m.p.h., watched them "like little diminishing footballs curving into the sky."

At a minute before nine, when the range was down to eight miles,

Tovey ordered *Rodney* and *King George V* to turn from southeast to south to bring the full weight of their guns to bear. Just before *Rodney* turned, Captain Coppinger, who was beside Captain Dalrymple-Hamilton on the bridge, taking notes of the battle, saw the burst of a heavy shell on *Bismarck's* fo'c'sle, while another sent a sheet of flame up the superstructure. After the turn, *Bismarck* was seen to be altering to starboard, too, to keep all her guns bearing, so that both forces were steaming on opposite courses, almost parallel.

Now a fourth British ship arrived to join the battle. It was the *Dorsetshire*, cutting things even finer than *Norfolk*. After 600 miles' steaming at speeds that varied between 20 and 32 knots she had sighted *Cossack* forty minutes earlier, been directed by her to the scene, and opened fire on the enemy from the south. She appeared at a useful moment, for the battleships were now steaming downwind: the funnel gases and cordite smoke hung about the bridge and around the gunnery control tower, making aiming at *Bismarck* difficult.

And now *Bismarck* shifted her fire from *Rodney* to *King George V*, spat out a salvo. Guernsey heard the whine of its approach, saw four tall fountains rise near the fo'c'sle, one short, three over. He wondered if the next would hit, found himself edging into the doorway at the back of the bridge, then, remembering it was only splash-proof plating, stepped boldly forward. On the scan in the radar office they tracked some of *Bismarck's* shells coming toward them, held them from about three miles out to half a mile in. The radar officer said it was no more alarming than seeing enemy gun flashes and the period of suspense was much less. They also tracked the flight of their own shells, but lost them at five miles out.

Only a quarter of an hour after the two ships had turned south, Dalrymple-Hamilton found *Bismarck* beginning to draw past him. If he continued on this course he would be masking the fire of *King George V* on his other side, so interpreting in the widest sense Tovey's permission for him to maneuver independently, he did what no captain of a British warship had done since the Battle of Cape St. Vincent 144 years earlier—he took his ship out of the line, and while the enemy was engaging *King George V*, turned *Rodney* right around to a course of north. Tovey, following a few minutes later, called up to Patterson: "Get closer, get closer, I can't see enough hits!"

Now *Rodney* was only four miles from the enemy and closing, so *Bismarck* shifted fire back to her. Deep down in *Rodney's* bows, more than 20 feet below the waterline, Chief Petty Officer Pollard and his crew were reloading the ship's torpedo tubes. They had fired six torpedoes during the run south, all without success, and were now getting ready to fire more. Like other parts of the ship they had suffered much from the blast of their own guns. Main lighting gone and water pouring in from a cracked pipe, they were working on three dim emergency lights and a couple of torches. Below the waterline the explosion of *Bismarck's* shells was magnified enormously, and they knew that if the deck above them was hit and the hatch buckled, they would be unlikely to get out. Now there was a noise in their ears like a thunderclap, and the compartment seemed to rise and fall. A shell from *Bismarck* had landed just off the starboard bow, jammed the sluice door of the starboard torpedo tube, and rendered it useless.

This was the nearest that *Bismarck* got to a direct hit: afterwards her fire began to fall off rapidly. Now untroubled by gases or cordite smoke, the British battleships closed the range, poured in salvo after salvo. *Norfolk*, too, was keeping up a steady fire from the east, while to the southeast *Dorsetshire*, which had previously checked fire because of the confusion of so many shell splashes, joined in again. Looking at the enemy closely it was now possible to see something of the damage done. The hydraulic power that served A turret must have been destroyed, and its two 15-inch guns were stuck at maximum depression, "drooping" said one man, "like dead flowers." The back of B turret had been blown over the side: one of its guns like a giant finger pointed drunkenly towards the sky. In the after turret one barrel had burst, leaving a stub like a peeled banana. The main director control was smashed in and half the foremast had gone over the side. Inside the hull flames were flickering in half a dozen places; the fire from the few guns still in action was increasingly ragged and spasmodic.

She was now barely crawling through the water, so to avoid U-boats which the Admiralty had warned were gathering, Dalrymple-Hamilton found himself obliged to zigzag across her bows, firing broadsides alternately from port and starboard. The range was under four miles and still closing, so that Captain Teek, in charge of X turret manned by the Royal Marines, found that the breech of his gun which had started the action down near the deck had risen almost to the roof of the turret. At one moment the foremost guns were pointing so far aft that the blast took Captain Coppinger's steel hat off his head and into a signalman, and sent his notebook flying (it was found later on the quarterdeck). At three and a half miles *Rodney* fired two more torpedoes through the undamaged port tube, neither of which hit. And still, because there was life in *Bismarck* and her flag flew, the huge shells went on being pumped into her. "I can't say I enjoyed this part of the business much," said Dalrymple-Hamilton, "but I didn't see what else I could do."

By 10 A.M. the *Bismarck* was a battered burning wreck, her guns twisted and silent, full of huge holes in her sides and superstructure through which fires glowed and flickered, gray smoke issuing from a hundred cracks and crevices and drifting away on the wind, listing heavily to port—but at the foremast her admiral's flag and at the mainmast the German naval ensign still bravely flying. In the British ships they looked at her with awe and admiration, awe that such a magnificent ship should have to be reduced to this, admiration that her crew had fought so gallantly to the end. "Pray God I may never know," said Guernsey, echoing George Whalley, "what those shells did as they exploded inside the hull." It was a thought shared by many sailors that day, one rarely expressed by airmen who incinerate cities, nor by soldiers of those they kill in tanks.

As they watched, the lifeless ship took life—the enemy in person, a little trickle of figures running aft along *Bismarck*'s quarterdeck, climbing the guardrails and jumping into the sea, unable to stand any more the inferno aboard, welcoming like lemmings death in the cool, kind sea. And presently in the British ships fire was checked, for the *Bismarck* no longer menaced anyone. Her life was almost at an end.

Admiral Somerville, just over the southern horizon, with *Ark Royal*, *Sheffield* and *Renown* (whose crew were desolate to be deprived of a share in the battle) had been listening to the rumble of gunfire for the last hour. At 9:30 A.M. *Ark Royal* had flown off twelve Swordfish to make a final torpedo attack on the enemy, but they arrived when the battle was in full spate and kept well clear. Now the gunfire had stopped. Somerville was desperate to have news, and he signaled Tovey as to whether he had finished the enemy off. The reply was surprising: *Bismarck* was still afloat, Tovey could not get her to sink by gunfire, he was discontinuing the action for lack of fuel and going home.

In fact there was nothing more for Tovey to do. Whether *Bismarck* sank now or later was immaterial: what was certain was she would never get back to port. He had already stayed ten hours longer than he had said his fuel would allow, and U-boats would soon be on the scene, if they had not reached it already. He signaled *Rodney* to form up astern and gave orders to Patterson to take the flagship home. And as he left he made a general signal to ships in company: "Any ship with torpedoes to close *Bismarck* and torpedo her."

Tartar and *Mashona* had already turned for home, Vian's ships had spent all their torpedoes; so had *Norfolk*, so had *Rodney* (firing her last two at the end of the action she claimed one hit which, if true, was the only instance in history of one battleship torpedoing another). Only one ship, *Dorsetshire*, still had torpedoes, and when Tovey's signal reached her, Captain Martin had already anticipated it. Closing in to a mile and a half on *Bismarck*'s starboard beam, she fired two torpedoes, both of which hit. She then went round the other side, at just over a mile, and fired another which also hit.

Far off now in *King George V*, halfway to the horizon, Tovey saw through his glasses the great ship slowly keel over to port until her funnel was level with the water and go on turning until she was completely upside down. He remembered Jutland and the sinking *Wiesbaden,* was already forming in his mind the words of his official dispatch: "She put up a most gallant fight against impossible odds, worthy of the old days of the Imperial German Navy." The stern dipped below the surface of the water, then the main keel: the great flared bows were last to go, and then all that was left to show where *Bismarck* had been were hundreds of men in life belts, swimming in oil and water.

<h3 style="text-align:center">CHAPTER 12</h3>

Some died early in *Bismarck* and some late, and the luckiest were those who knew nothing of it.

When the battle started, despite tiredness, morale seems to have been good. Müllenheim-Rechberg says the British ships took quite a time to find the range. When they had found it, and were hitting regularly, the fore part of the ship suffered more than aft. A and B turret were knocked out fairly early in the action, as was the main gunnery control. Of those that survived the day none at all came from the fore part, not from A and B turrets, the bridge or bridge superstructure, the charthouse and gunnery control, the magazines and shell rooms below. So we do not know how Lütjens and Lindemann, Schneider and Neuendorff, Netzbandt and Externbrink and all the other officers of the admiral's staff died. But there is much evidence of fires raging forward, both in the superstructure and below decks, and it would seem that the people who were not killed by shell bursts were burned to death by the fires or else trapped behind them, unable to get out, and drowned when the ship turned turtle.

Like Müllenheim-Rechberg, others who survived knew little or nothing of what was going on elsewhere, for they stayed at their posts, behind armor plating, until the order came to abandon ship. In the engine rooms they heard thuds and bangs distantly above them, couldn't tell the difference between their own guns firing and British hits. The lights continued to burn brightly and the engines to turn at slow speed: the only unusual thing was water slopping down from the air intakes, indicating near misses from enemy shells. Later smoke from shell bursts and fires came down the intakes, making breathing difficult, so in some compartments they put on gas masks.

Some people, like the flak crews and the merchant navy men for prizes, had nothing to do. Herzog and others of the after flak were ordered down to their mess on the after battery deck, near the barbette. It was uncomfortable sitting there, listening to the shells hitting the ship, not being able to strike back. After the forward turrets and superstructure had been hit, Chief Petty Officer Wienand, who had been talking to them of his home in Hamburg the night before, came to collect men to act as stretcher-bearers. When they had gone, Herzog opened his locker, took a couple of swigs from a bottle of *Rösenlikor* he kept there, and stretched himself out. He felt exhausted after the exertions of the last few days; presently things began to get misty. He was aware of the loudspeaker saying the admiral and Lindemann had been killed, then that Lindemann hadn't been killed, and then there was a tremendous bang and the clatter and singing of iron and metal and afterwards sounds "as though through cotton wool" of the cries of the wounded.

The duties of a few men like the medical orderlies and damage control parties took them about the ship. One damage control party was in the charge of Chief Mechanician Wilhelm Schmidt from Friedrichshafen. As they moved about, they were aware of British shells plunging down through the upper deck, sometimes the next deck too, bursting inside enclosed compartments, filling them with smoke and gases, putting out the main lights, showering splinters everywhere, twisting and buckling the ladders and doors and hatches. Some of the shells fell close to them, the splinters killing some men, wounding others. A messenger appeared to say that men were needed to fight the fire in the superstructure: those that went were all killed. Later, after the flashback in D turret, another messenger arrived with orders to flood D turret magazine, lest the ship blow up. So Wienand switched on the pump to flood the magazine, though whether the men in it got out or were drowned there or had already been killed by the flashback, no one knows.

Around 10 A.M., after C turret had packed up, but while the British ships were still firing, orders were given to prepare Measure 5, the order for placing scuttling charges, and to prepare to abandon ship. These orders came from the senior surviving officer, Commander Oels, the executive officer, from his post at the base of the superstructure. He had assumed command of the ship after the bridge had been knocked out.

There were several ways out of the command post: up a vertical ladder which ran through a narrow shaft to the superstructure, or through one of the doors in the bulkhead. Able Seaman Staat didn't fancy the ladder, went out of the port door, found the next compartment deep in water, hammocks floating about in it, the ship listing to port. He went up to the next deck, into a compartment full of yellowish-green smoke, full of wounded lying about and doctors and orderlies giving morphia injections, working so fast they were not even pausing to sterilize the needles.

He went through this compartment and up to the battery deck, into the main canteen alongside the funnel, and here he found Commander Oels and about three hundred men all struggling to get out. They couldn't go forward because of the fires raging there, and the midships hatch was jammed, so everyone was pushing and shoving to get through the narrow door aft: the canteen too was full of fumes, and those who hadn't gotten gas masks were shaken by fits of coughing.

Another man in the canteen was Herbert Blum. A few minutes earlier he had been standing beside Commander Lehmann at the damage control command post when the order came by telephone to abandon ship. He remembered how Lehmann had replaced the telephone receiver "as carefully as if it were the most fragile glass," and said to Blum and the others, as calm and friendly as ever: "You may go now," and that was the last they saw of him.

Blum made his way to a workshop behind the funnel where he and his mates used to gather. He was lying down there exhausted on the deck, when a shell burst in the next compartment. It blew the bulkhead door open and through the smoke Blum saw a wounded man being carried out and another without any arms.

So then he made his way up to the canteen and he hadn't been there long when there was a tremendous explosion. Blum saw a dazzling red ball of fire a few feet from his eyes, felt a terrible noise and agonizing pressure in his eardrums, and was flung to the ground. Staat saw it differently, as a flare, blue-green and yellow-white like phosphorus, and the after side of the funnel flaring a brilliant red.

Like Blum, Staat was thrown to the deck, momentarily concussed; after a few moments they picked themselves up, touched themselves all over, found they were unhurt. But all around was a scene of unspeakable carnage, at least a hundred dead, Oels among them, as many more wounded, some terribly: young men with bits of their faces blown away, limbs separated from bodies, splintered bones sticking through skin, blood gushing and flowing everywhere, men with stomach wounds watching their insides seep out and trying to shove them back, others vomiting with shock and disgust, the ghastly screams of the suffering.

These casualties made it easier for those untouched to get out. Staat picked his way over the dead and mutilated into the next compartment, found it almost as crowded as the one he'd left. Step by step he made his way aft. In the alleyway by the after canteen he found a ladder leading to a hatch, and with the help of five men opened it and came out on the upper deck.

Blum also managed to get to the upper deck, through a jammed hatchway, not more than two hands-breadths wide. Like Staat, Blum was horrified by what he saw, the wreckage everywhere, the huge shell holes in the deck, gray smoke rising from below, the piles of dead and wounded. A man came up to him with one hand shattered, the other carrying a field dressing. While Blum was bandaging him up, he heard screams and yells coming from the after starboard 5.9-inch turret. He went over but found the hatch into it jammed; neither he nor the men inside could open it, and he had to leave them there, trapped.

One of the crew of this turret, Ordinary Seaman Paul Hiller, was lucky. In the destroyer action during the night he'd injured himself loading and been ordered to change places with another man in the shellroom below. He didn't like this and felt trapped in such a small space so far below, but when the order came to abandon ship, he managed to get up the ammunition hoist, then through a small door on to the 'tween deck. He started to go forward but the fires drove him back. He managed to get to the battery deck and entered a compartment where the older merchant navy men for the prize crews were sitting patiently on their sea chests. A shell plunged through the compartment, bursting on the deck below. Many of the merchant navy men were wounded by splinters. Hiller called to them to follow him aft, but they just sat there silent and bleeding, waiting resignedly for the end.

In ones and twos other survivors reached the upper deck aft, some through hatches that were still free, others up ammunition hoists, a few, like Seaman Adolf Eich, up the wiring shaft from the switch room to Müllenheim-Rechberg's after control position.

Some of the last men to come up were the people in the engine room. Gerhard Junack was in the midships engine room when Commander Lehmann on the telephone gave the order for Measure 5: at the time steam was coming from the boiler rooms and all three engines were going slow speed ahead. Junack ordered his men to place explosive charges with time fuses in the cooling water intakes, and to open the seacocks. In the port engine room Werner Lust and others weren't able to do this, because the deck was flooded with water from the ventilating shafts, but in the starboard engine room the charges were laid by Mechanician Klotzschke and others. When Junack's men had lit the fuses, which had nine minutes' delay, he ordered them to evacuate the engine room and go up top. The compartment was full of fumes but the lights were still burning brightly. They were burning, too, on the armored deck, though no one was there. The firing had stopped, said Junack, and it was deathly still, quiet as a Sunday afternoon in harbor. In the silence he and his men heard the scuttling charges go off far below.

On the next deck they tried to get forward, only to be driven back by the fires. Aft on the deck above they found a group of men in the smoke wearing gas masks and life belts, wandering about, utterly confused. Junack ordered them to follow him, found a half-opened hatch, made the men take off gas masks and life belts, and they all just squeezed through, coming out on the upper deck.

By this time a lot of men had gathered on the quarterdeck, two or three hundred, said Junack, and now they were joined by Müllenheim-Rechberg and others from the after control, and by the crew of C turret, none of whom, said Hans Riedel, the leader of C turret, was even hurt. They were all horrified by what they saw: the tangled wreckage, smoke and flames, the piles of dead and mutilated, the moans of the wounded. Some helped to adjust the life belts of the less badly wounded and put them over the side; others found the screams got on their nerves and wanted to shut them up.

Junack gathered a group of men together, among them Blum, and said, "We'll give three 'Sieg Heils' and then we'll go overboard. Don't worry, comrades. I'll be taking a Hamburg girl in my arms again, and we'll all meet once more on the Reeperbahn." The Reeperbahn is Hamburg's red light district, and Blum thought, my God, how on earth does he manage to think of that and taking girls in his arms in the middle of all this? So they gave three "Sieg Heils" and a few others sang the national anthem, and then they went over the side. A few stupid ones went down the sloping deck over the port side, where the water was nearest, and were soon thrown back against the ship, knocked unconscious. The others slid down the starboard side until they reached the bilge keel, then jumped from there into the sea. Kenneth Pattisson in one of *Ark Royal's* Swordfish flying overhead, saw hundreds of heads bobbing in the water, like turnips in a field of sheep, regretted he had no dinghy to drop to them, waved in a friendly useless gesture. As he turned away he observed smoke pouring out of *Bismarck's* decks, smelt her burning, and described her main gunnery control as a torch of fire.

When the survivors were clear of the ship, she slowly rolled over away from them until she was bottom up. Müllenheim-Rechberg and Junack looked for signs of torpedo damage but couldn't see any. Staat noticed two men sitting on the upturned keel, making no effort to save themselves. The stern went under and then the rest of her, taking all their personal belongings and hundreds of dead and wounded.

The *Dorsetshire* came around from the port side where she had fired her last torpedo, lay stopped in the sea a little way off; and survivors who had wondered if they were not escaping death by shellfire for death by drowning, felt a new surge of hope: even if it meant being taken prisoner, they were going to be rescued, they were going to live.

They struck out as well as they could towards the cruiser, though with the high seas and the oil from *Bismarck's* tanks and the wounds of many, it wasn't easy. Müllenheim-Rechberg, swimming along, passed a man who said, "I've no left leg any more." Staat remembered being told that when you died of cold, you first felt it in the testicles, but it was his feet and fingers that were getting numb. After more than an hour's swimming the first of them reached the *Dorsetshire's* side, where rafts, ropes, scrambling nets, fenders, lifelines of all kinds had been let down. Müllenheim-Rechberg noticed that many men, not seamen, didn't know how to grip a straight rope, and urged them to get into ropes with bowlines. Staat's fingers were so frozen that he couldn't grip the rope at all. He seized it with his teeth and was hauled on board that way. Müllenheim-Rechberg put his foot in a bowline rope and was pulled up by two sailors. When he reached deck level he tried to grab the guardrail, was too exhausted, and fell back into the sea. He got into the same rope again, was hauled up by the same two sailors, this time took no risks, and said in immaculate English, "Please help me on board," which they did. Midshipman Joe Brooks of the *Dorsetshire* went down one of the lifelines, tried to get a bowline around a German who had lost both arms and was gripping the lifeline with his teeth: the ship rolled heavily, they both went under, Brooks never saw him again. Blum reached the *Dorsetshire's* bow, was sucked under by a sea, felt himself under the keel, then came up the other side. The waves carried him away from *Dorsetshire*, but *Maori* was lying stopped a little way off. He managed to reach her and was hauled safely up.

The *Dorsetshire* had picked up some eighty men and the *Maori* some twenty: many more were in the process of being hauled up, and hundreds more were waiting in the water when an unexpected thing happened. *Dorsetshire*'s navigating officer, Lieutenant-Commander Durant, sighted on the starboard bow two miles away a smoky discharge in the water. He pointed it out to Captain Martin and others on the bridge. No one knew what it was but the most likely explanation was a U-boat: the Admiralty had sent a warning that U-boats were on the way, and they were lucky not to have encountered any already. And if it was a U-boat, *Dorsetshire*, laying stopped in the water, was a sitting target. In the circumstances Captain Martin had no choice but to ring down for full speed, and in *Maori* Commander Armstrong did the same.

The water round *Dorsetshire*'s stern foamed and bubbled with the sudden exertion of the screws. Slowly, then faster, the ship moved ahead. *Bismarck* survivors who were almost on board were bundled over the guardrails on to the deck: those halfway up the ropes found themselves trailing astern, hung on as long as they could against the forward movement of the ship, then dropped off one by one; others in the water clawed frantically at the paintwork as the side slipped by. In *Dorsetshire* they heard the thin cries of hundreds of Germans who had come within an inch of rescue, had believed that their long ordeal was at last over, cries that the British sailors, no less than survivors already on board, would always remember. From the water *Bismarck*'s men watched appalled as the cruiser's gray side swept past them, believed then that tales they'd heard about the British not caring much about survivors were true after all, and presently found themselves alone in the sunshine on the empty, tossing sea. And during the day, as they floated about the Atlantic with only life belts between them and eternity, the cold came to their testicles and hands and feet and heads, and one by one they lost consciousness, and one by one they died.

All except five. Lieutenant-Commander Eitel-Friedrich Kentrat in *U.74* had been cruising in the area. During the morning he had sighted a cruiser and two destroyers (possibly *Dorsetshire, Maori* and another of Vian's flotilla), later got a message from Dönitz to close *Bismarck* and take off her war diary. Later still, when Kentrat learned that *Bismarck* had sunk, he got a further message from U-boat headquarters to look for survivors. He searched in the area all day, and about 7 P.M. came across the raft carrying Manthey, Herzog and Höntzsch, took them on board, gave them warm food and drink, and put them to bed. They had an adventurous voyage back to Lorient, for it was found that salt water had got into the batteries and the U-boat was unable to dive. Off the French coast, a British submarine, positioned in the area for *Bismarck's* arrival, fired five torpedoes at *U.74* which, by Kentrat taking violent avoiding action, all missed. On arrival in France the three survivors were closely questioned about the time they had left *Bismarck*, for it seemed to some it might have been before the order to abandon ship. But their stories satisfied the authorities, and having told all they knew of the *Bismarck's* last voyage, Manthey, Herzog and Höntzsch were sent on survivor's leave and then distributed to other units.

The German weather ship *Sachsenwald*, commanded by Lieutenant Schütte, passing through the general area on return from a fifty-day meteorological patrol in the North Atlantic, was also ordered to search for survivors. They sighted nothing on the 27th or the night of the 27th, but at 1 P.M. on the 28th they came across a big oil slick, and beyond it many life belts, some with bodies in them, some without, and quantities of wreckage. *Sachsenwald* and two U-boats she met searched all day but found no survivors; but at 10:35 that night, she sighted two red lights to port. Through his glasses Schütte saw a raft with two men on it, and steered towards them. One of the men shouted, "Are you German?" and when Schütte said yes, they gave a faint cheer. They were taken on board and found to be totally exhausted, for they had been tossing in the raft for two days and a night without food or drink. They had the salt washed from their faces, were given warm clothes and soup, and put in bunks. They gave their names as Otto Maus and Walter Lorenzen, and said there was another raft with men on it nearby. Although *Sachsenwald* was by now very short of food, Schütte stayed in the area all night and searched again the following day; they saw nothing but more wreckage and life belts.

At 12:45 A.M. on the morning of May 30th, he spoke to the *Canarias*, which had also been searching in the area and sighted only wreckage and bodies, five of which she had taken on board to check identity discs. At daylight both ships left the area to return to harbor, the *Canarias* to Ferrol and the *Sachsenwald* to Bordeaux.

In Britain the general reaction to the news of the sinking was one of relief rather than exhilaration. On the afternoon after the battle, in the House of Commons, Winston Churchill, not yet knowing the final outcome, told an enthralled House of events up to the beginning of the final action, then went on to other business. In the middle of the other business he was handed a note, read it, said to the Speaker: "Mr. Speaker, I crave your indulgence. I have just heard that the *Bismarck* has been sunk." Members cheered wildly, waving their order papers, thankful that the cloud that had darkened their horizon for the last five days had at last been lifted. But one member, the writer Harold Nicolson, sat silent: more than some, he saw the thing in human terms, thought of the innumerable dead, and sensed its high tragedy.

Now that *Bismarck* had been safely disposed of, it was time to think about *Prinz Eugen*; and next day Winston Churchill wrote a top secret memorandum, marked "For First Lord and First Sea Lord alone. In a locked box":

The bringing into action of the *Prinz Eugen* and the search for her raise questions of the highest importance. It is most desirable that the United States Navy should play a part in this. It would be far better, for instance, that she should be located by a United States ship, as this might tempt her to fire upon that ship, thus providing the incident for which the United States government would be so thankful.

Pray let this matter be considered from this point of view, apart from the ordinary naval aspect. If we can only create a situation where the *Prinz Eugen* is being shadowed by an American vessel, we shall have gone a long way to solve the largest problem.

But *Prinz Eugen* was unable to help Churchill and Roosevelt with their plans. After leaving *Bismarck* on May 24th she had steered for the southern group of supply ships, reached the tanker *Spichern* northwest of the Azores on the 26th with only 8 percent of fuel remaining, next day got a report from an Italian submarine of sighting five battleships steaming southwest at high speed in the *Bismarck*'s area (almost certainly Vian's flotilla), so broke off her journey to the convoy routes. On the 28th she oiled again from *Esso Hamburg*, then discovered she had serious defects in all three engines, as well as a chipped propeller blade caused by ice when going through the Denmark Straits. Captain Brinkmann therefore abandoned all further plans for commerce raiding and shaped course for Brest, which he reached safely on June 1st. Since leaving Gotenhafen *Prinz Eugen* had traveled 7,000 miles at an average speed of 24 knots.

U.556 meanwhile had also reached harbor on almost her last remaining drop of fuel: when Wohlfarth made fast alongside the submarine jetty at Lorient, he had only eighty liters left. Next day Admiral Dönitz came aboard and presented Wohlfarth with the Knight's Cross of the Iron Cross. It was an honor he was not to enjoy at liberty for long. On her next trip to the Atlantic *U.556* was sunk, and Wohlfarth and most of his officers and men taken prisoner.

In Germany, despite news of further successes by the Luftwaffe against the Royal Navy off Crete, people were as depressed by the news of *Bismarck*'s death as the British had been by the death of *Hood*—more so perhaps, for unlike the British, they had no hopes of a compensating victory. Hitler's intuitions, as often, were right: the ship symbolized the nation, reputation had become a little diminished, prestige a little dimmed. Meanwhile a special office was set up, in which thirty people were employed answering telegrams and letters from next of kin, informing them that no information could be given as to whether their son or husband had survived until returns had come in from the British Admiralty. One letter from a father said his son could not possibly have been on board, as he had been called up only a few days before *Bismarck* had sailed. Research revealed that he was a stoker in the Merchant Navy and had been drafted to *Bismarck* at the last moment as part of the prize crew. On June 7th the German Admiralty received the names of the 102 British-held survivors: with the three from *U.74* and two from *Sachsenwald*, that made a total of 107 out of a ship's company of over 2,000.

Yet if despondency was the dominant mood of the German people and relief that of the British, there were two small groups of people whose excitement knew no bounds. In Brest, when Philippon heard the news on B.B.C. radio, he ran down the Tourville steps four at a time, rushed to the French naval officers' mess—the big hall with its Louis XIV paneling—where some twenty officers were about to sit down to dinner. Slamming the door behind him, he cried, "The *Bismarck*'s been sunk!" They all turned around. "If I live to be a hundred," he wrote afterwards, "I shall never forget the expressions on their faces."

He was not the only foreigner concerned with the operations to hear that B.B.C. broadcast. A thousand miles away in Southern Norway, Viggo Axelssen, Arne Usterud and others sat drinking in the Red Room of the Kristiansand club, listening with quiet concentration to the news of the battleship's sinking. Viggo and Arne remembered the evening only seven days before when walking on the Vesterveien they had sighted *Bismarck* and *Prinz Eugen* speeding northwards, how Arne Moen had carried the message about it in the engine of his bus to Helle; and how Odd Starheim and Gunvald Torstad had sent it out from there on their transmitter. They remembered, too, how quickly the German army's D/F unit had arrived at Helle, how narrowly Torstad and Starheim had escaped detection. Now Viggo raised his glass and said, "Gentlemen!" They all stood up. Viggo said, "Thirty-five thousand tons" (*Bismarck*'s "official" tonnage). They repeated it, drained their glasses. Viggo opened the door to the dining room where other members were at their evening meal, asked them to rise too, and drink the same toast. They did; everyone knew what was meant.

And next day across the Norwegian border, in far off, spy-ridden Stockholm, no Englishman alive was more delighted than Captain Henry Denham when he received from the Admiralty this signal:

> Your 2058 of 20th May initiated the first of a series of operations which culminated yesterday in the sinking of the *Bismarck*. Well done.

EPILOGUE

In a story of such nobility and high endeavor, it is sad to have to record what follows.

Sometime during the night of May 26th, Winston Churchill, not then knowing the enemy was crippled beyond repair, became obsessed with the idea that *Bismarck* must be sunk at whatever cost to our ships. He therefore drafted or had drafted for him the following signal to Tovey:

> We cannot visualize the situation from your signals. *Bismarck* must be sunk at all costs and if to do this it is necessary for *King George V* to remain on the scene, then she must do so, even if it subsequently means towing *King George V*.

This was an extraordinary signal. To have suggested allowing the fleet flagship to run out of fuel in an area where U-boats were gathering and to which aircraft would soon be directed was to invite her certain destruction—and the deaths of the admiral, his staff, and the ship's company. Furthermore, until *Prince of Wales* was repaired, *King George V* was the only British capital ship that had both the armor and the speed to match *Bismarck*'s. If *King George V* had run out of fuel and been sunk, *Bismarck*, once repaired, would have had a more or less free hand in the Atlantic. Admiral Pound himself disagreed with the signal, and should not have approved it; but he was not always firm where Churchill was concerned, and it finally went out from the Admiralty next morning, by which time the battle was over and Tovey was on the way home.

Tovey and his staff thought the signal ridiculous: when it was read to them they laughed out loud. Later, when they had time to realize its import, they were angry. "It was," said Tovey, "the stupidest and most ill-considered signal ever made," and he told his staff that if the situation envisaged had arisen, he would have disobeyed the signal and risked court-martial. When the fleet reached harbor and the green telephone was connected to London, Pound apologized for the signal, agreed it should never have been sent out. But Tovey never forgot it.

An even more distasteful event occurred a few weeks later—one which proved that Wake-Walker was right in his suspicions on May 24th that the Admiralty were thinking him lacking in offensive spirit. Having read all the reports on the operation and studied the track charts, Pound informed Tovey that he wanted Wake-Walker and Jack Leach of the *Prince of Wales* brought to trial by court-martial for failing to engage *Bismarck* during the run south after the action with the *Hood*. Tovey was appalled, replied that the conduct of Wake-Walker and Leach was exactly what he desired—the last thing he had wanted was a premature action that might force the enemy to the westward and away from *King George V*. Pound's answer to this was that he still wished the two officers to stand trial by court-martial and if Tovey would not order it, then the Admiralty would. To this Tovey replied that if they did, he would if necessary haul down his flag as Commander-in-Chief and appear at the trial as prisoners' friend. After that, said Tovey, "I heard no more about it."

The pursuit and sinking of the *Bismarck* will remain one of the great sea stories of all time, worthy to take its place with Salamis, Lepanto, the Armada, Trafalgar, Tsushima, Jutland, Midway, the Coral Sea. It covered an immense area of ocean, from the Baltic to the Arctic, the Arctic to the Atlantic, the Atlantic to the Bay of Biscay, and all in the space of only eight days. More than 4,000 sailors, British and German, were killed. People of other nationalities were caught up in it, too: Poles, Swedes, Norwegians, Americans, French, Italians, Spanish.

Bismarck's mission came too late. Had she and her sister ship *Tirpitz* been completed a year earlier, sailed with *Scharnhorst* and *Gneisenau* for the Atlantic trade routes in the early winter of 1940–41, it might have been a different story. Split into separate battle groups, there is no knowing what damage they might have done, what effect their actions might have had on Britain's war effort. Even now it had required a huge effort by the British Admiralty, the summoning of a multitude of forces to track down this one warship: eight battleships and battle cruisers, two aircraft carriers, eleven cruisers, twenty-one destroyers, six submarines, more than 300 air sorties; and of nearly sixty torpedoes (apart from *Dorsetshire's*) fired at her, no more than three, or at the most four, hit.

It was lack of oil that was the most direct cause of Lütjens's defeat (and very nearly of Tovey's withdrawal). Had he sailed from Norway with full tanks, as he should have done, he might still, despite the hit from *Prince of Wales*, have considered turning west into the Atlantic to shake off his shadowers, then fueled from one of the waiting tankers before turning for home. Alternatively he could have steered direct for Brest at a much higher speed, one that would have outdistanced the approach of Force H. But undoubtedly luck was with the British. The hit on the rudders from *Ark Royal's* Swordfish was, as the Germans said, one in a hundred thousand.

In theory Raeder could have sent *Prinz Eugen* to sea again together with one of the battle cruisers as soon as their damage was repaired. But a number of things prevented it. First, the capture of the cipher machine from *U.110* as well as other captured intelligence meant the end of *Bismarck's* supply ships. On June 3rd the *Belchen* was sunk by the cruisers *Aurora* and *Kenya* (her crew were picked up by *U.93*); on June 4th the *Esso Hamburg* by the cruiser *London*, and the *Gonzenheim* by the cruiser *Neptune*; on June 5th the *Egerland* by the *London*; on June 12th the *Friedrich Breme* by the *Sheffield*; and on June 15th the *Lothringen* was captured by aircraft from the carrier *Eagle* and the cruiser *Dunedin*.

Despite these losses German heavy warships could still have operated in the Atlantic for shorter periods, sailing from and returning to Brest. But by now other factors had entered into consideration. The hit on *Bismarck's* rudders may have been a lucky one, but what had happened once could happen again. British air power was growing in strength daily. The combination of aircraft carriers, long-range flying boats and radar meant that once a German warship was picked up in mid-Atlantic, she would be unlikely to get away: carrier planes by day and radar at night would maintain contact until superior forces could be brought up. Hitler was quick to see this, and fearing further loss of prestige forbade Raeder to send any other German warships into the Atlantic.

That effect was the realization (reinforced by Luftwaffe successes against the British Navy off Crete) that the airplane had now made the battleship obsolete. And if that were true, there was no point at all in keeping *Scharnhorst*, *Gneisenau* and *Prinz Eugen* bottled up in Brest, a nightly target for the bombers. They must be brought home to Germany, not via the Atlantic where they might be crippled by aircraft and sunk as *Bismarck* had been, but by the shortest route available, the one that gave them the maximum air cover, up the English Channel. It was a daring idea, Hitler's originally, but the more the naval staff looked at it, the more feasible it seemed. The three ships left Brest on the night of February 11th, and despite warnings of their imminent departure by Philippon to London, were unobserved until just before entering the Narrows. Six Swordfish led by Eugene Esmonde attacked them with great courage, but the Germans had a huge air umbrella over the ships and all six were shot down: Esmonde was killed, got a Victoria Cross posthumously. Air power succeeded in the end when both *Scharnhorst* and *Gneisenau* hit mines off the Dutch coast, but all three ships reached German ports.

Unfortunately the lesson that had been learned by the Germans had to be learned afresh by the British. When the situation in the Far East began to deteriorate towards the end of 1941, Winston Churchill decided to send the now repaired *Prince of Wales* and the *Repulse* to Singapore, hoping that such a show of strength might deter the Japanese from whatever devious plans they had in mind. Pound appointed as commander of the force his deputy Vice-Admiral Sir Tom Phillips. The two ships and their escorting destroyers (*Electra* was one) reached Singapore on December 2nd. On the 7th the Japanese attacked Pearl Harbor and landed forces in Northern Malaya. On the afternoon of the 8th Phillips took the squadron northwards to attack the landing forces, but on the evening of the next day, having been spotted by Japanese reconnaissance planes, he turned back for Singapore. On the morning of the 10th, and without air protection of any kind, the squadron was attacked by waves of Japanese bombers and torpedo planes: they hit *Prince of Wales* and *Repulse* repeatedly and sank both ships.

And so it was brought home to the British, even more painfully than to the Germans, that battleships without massive air protection were sitting ducks, indeed that the day of the battleship was almost over. All four main protagonists continued to use them for the rest of the war, less to fight pitched battles than as support for ground forces and carriers.

The last battleship in service was the American *New Jersey* which went out of commission in 1972. Today the battleship and battle cruiser are almost extinct; one or two still moulder in the world's dockyards as gaunt memorials to the past. Those of us who lived with, and in, those strange, lovely, vast, mysterious creatures, remember them with pride; are proud, too, to have been at sea in their company in the week that *Hood* and *Bismarck* sailed to glory and disaster.

HOLLYWOOD

STARS AND STARLETS,
TYCOONS AND FLESH-PEDDLERS,
MOVIEMAKERS AND MONEYMAKERS,
FRAUDS AND GENIUSES,
HOPEFULS AND HAS-BEENS,
GREAT LOVERS AND SEX SYMBOLS

A condensation of the book by

GARSON KANIN

MUSEUM OF MODERN ART

MUSEUM OF MODERN ART

BROWN BROTHERS

BROWN BROTHERS

CHAPTER 1

Mr. Samuel Goldwyn and I sat alone in his throne room, looking at each other. We had met for the first time some five minutes earlier when Abe Lastfogel of the William Morris Agency had brought me in, made the introduction, and then gone.

It was a crucial moment for me. A nod of this formidable man's head could signal the beginning of my career in films. Was there anything I should be doing—could be saying—to elicit that movement? The pause stretched out.

Mr. Goldwyn, his right forefinger clamped firmly to the side of his nose, continued to study me through his small gray eyes. It was as though I were a mysterious, unopened box that had been delivered to him, and he was trying to guess the contents.

In the inflating silence I was taking him in. A large man. Why had I expected him to be small? Beautifully dressed and groomed and shod. A smooth, pink face under a finely shaped, bald dome. An impressive presence.

At last his finger came down from the side of his nose.

"Well, young man. What can I do for you? What do you want?"

"What do *you* want, Mr. Goldwyn?"

"What?"

"*You* sent for *me*, didn't you?"

"*I* sent for *you*?" he repeated, amazed.

"Certainly," I said, without breaking the rhythm. "You paid my fare out here, didn't you?"

He grinned and said, "Say, you're pretty good!" Suddenly, the grin disappeared. His piercing eyes grew smaller, intensifying the sharpness of their focus. "Well, young man, let me ask you. How would you like to learn the business?"

"I'd like it," I said.

"And get *paid* the same time."

"Sounds great."

"I'm not making a firm offer, y'understand," he added quickly. "I'm only asking."

"I understand."

"All right," he said. "Now. So tell me something about yourself."

I told him something about myself, carefully, all the while reflecting upon the curious set of circumstances that had brought me to this time and place:

I had been for several years an assistant to George Abbott, working with him on *Three Men on a Horse, Boy Meets Girl, Brother Rat, Room Service,* and other plays. After a string of failures, Mr. Abbott was enjoying a meteoric streak of success. Gossipy Broadway had it that the change in his fortunes had a good deal to do with that kid in his office. Although I did or said nothing to encourage this nonsensical idea, I confess I did or said nothing to discourage it, either.

There existed, at that time, a Broadway rivalry between George Abbott and another George—George S. Kaufman. They both wrote, both directed, both (at times) acted, both specialized in comedy, although now and again each ventured into other fields as well.

Beatrice Kaufman—Mrs. George S.—was Samuel Goldwyn's eastern representative. It was she who got the idea that I might be a valuable piece of manpower for Mr. Goldwyn in California.

That is why an odd-looking, twenty-four-year-old bundle of nerves who had been an early high-school dropout, a mediocre musician, a burlesque stooge, a stock clerk at Macy's, a drama student, a mildly successful minor New York actor, and the director of one Broadway failure, was sitting here reciting a bowdlerized version of his professional life to Samuel Goldwyn.

"That's enough," I heard him say. "I get the whole idea of you."

He rose. So did I. We shook hands, firmly.

"I'll talk to Abe," he said. "We'll see what we can work out. On some reasonable basis. How's your health?"

"Fine."

"You sure?"

"Sure I'm sure."

"Take care of it. Your health. And it will take care of you. I tell you I get more goddam sick people around me here all the time—they all got migraines and ulcers and f'Chrissake heart attacks. I seem to pick 'em."

He looked at his watch, said, "Jesus!" and propelled me out.

Abe had left a message for me to get a taxi and meet him back at his office.

On the way, I reviewed the meeting and made notes. When I reached the end and recalled Goldwyn's complaint that he always seemed to pick men with migraines, ulcers, and f'Chrissake heart attacks, it gave me pause.

"How'd it go?" asked Abe.

"He said he'd talk to you."

"He did?"

"Yes."

"That's a good sign. Now. I'm having lunch with Pan Berman—he's the head of RKO now—so you better come along. And tonight you'll have dinner with Frances and me at Chasen's with Benny Thau. He's Metro. It'll all get back to Sam, see?"

"What will?"

"These meetings with Pan and Benny. I don't want him to think—Sam—he's getting a free ride."

"Well, he paid for my trip out here, didn't he?"

"But you're not talking business with Benny or with Pan. They're not interested in you."

"Oh."

"Let me handle it, okay?"

"Okay."

The next morning, he handled it and got Goldwyn to offer me a seven-year contract starting at $250 a week for the first year, $400 the second, then in yearly stages—$600, $750, $1,000, $1,250, $1,500.

Duties? Learn the business and then we'll see. I was troubled by the vagueness of the arrangement.

"Don't worry about it," Abe advised. "Part of your job will be to *make* yourself a job. The main thing is to get in there. Get to know the business. Get to know *him*. And him, you."

My first month there was euphoric.

I had somewhere to go every morning, a pleasant office, and an efficient secretary to assist me. I had the fascinating studio world to play with; charming, witty, talented colleagues; and a library of films at my disposal.

The second month was less happy since I began to see that my chances of becoming a director were remote. One afternoon, I took the matter up with Mr. Goldwyn at his home. I thought it best to pursue it in an informal, casual way.

"There are so many tests to make next week," I said. "Would you want me to direct one or two—to help out?"

"What's the matter with you?" he said irascibly. "Jesus Christ, here you are, a young nobody, and you want to be a *test* director, f'Chrissake."

"I don't want to be a test director," I said. "I want to be a director."

"How can you be a director?" he said. "You've never directed."

"Well," I argued, "there was a time when Willie Wyler and John Ford and Leo McCarey had never directed."

"Don't you believe it," he said gravely.

The conversation ended, but not my determination.

One morning, browsing sleepily through the trade papers, I saw a story that woke me as though it were a thunderclap.

Warner Brothers announced it had bought the film rights to *Boy Meets Girl* by Sam and Bella Spewack, and were going to make it with James Cagney and their dumb blonde of the day, Marie Wilson.

Here was a happy circumstance indeed. As George Abbott's assistant, I had read the play and brought it to Mr. Abbott with my enthusiastic recommendation. He had agreed, bought it, produced and directed it. It was a great success. I had been responsible for much of the casting, was finally in the play myself. I had directed all the road companies. I knew and liked the Spewacks.

Surely Warner Brothers would want me to work on the picture in *some* capacity. Of course, I would try to get to direct it. Who could arrange it for me?

I went to see Abe Lastfogel, told him my plan. He thought my chances of getting to direct the picture were infinitesimal, but worth a try.

Later in the day, he phoned me to say that Steve Trilling was the first man to see. Trilling was then the principal assistant to Jack Warner, and greatly respected by him.

Steve Trilling turned out to be an amiable and receptive young man. I made my pitch. He saw the advantages in my scheme, but candidly pointed out the disadvantages.

"Let me say this right now," said Trilling. "There's no question in my mind that you could make a contribution to this thing. I called George Abbott in New York yesterday and he gave us a good report on you."

"You called Mr. Abbott?" I said, somehow encouraged.

"Yes," said Trilling, "I'm very thorough. I'm sure I could get you onto the picture doing something. Would you like to play your original part? You weren't bad."

"Well, as they say," I said, "I wasn't *supposed* to be."

No laugh. Trilling was all business. "Would you? *That* I think I could swing."

"Jesus, no," I said, "I'm finished with all that."

"I can't really promise you dialogue director because we've got so many contract ones of our own, and we'd run into a studio mess. Actually, it might be easier to get you the *picture* than *that* job."

"That's fine with me," I said.

"I'm going to think about this—I mean seriously," he said.

"I'll come over and direct some tests," I said. "For nothing."

"No, no," said Trilling. "We have test directors for that."

I could see I was being forced into the top spot.

There were further meetings, one with J.L. Warner himself. A rough-talking, vital man who loved to laugh.

When it began to appear that a deal of some kind might indeed be made, Abe decided to broach the subject to Mr. Goldwyn.

We went in to see him.

"I'm very busy today," said Goldwyn, as we came through the door.

"This won't take a minute, Sam," said Abe. "In fact, we won't even sit down, how's that?"

"That's good," said Goldwyn.

"What I want to ask you, Sam, is simply this. If anything came up somewhere for Gar, say like a chance to direct a picture, how would you feel about loaning him out? Naturally, I'd try to get you a good price, and Gar doesn't expect any part of it. It would just be a loan-out. The idea is that it would be a start for him, he'd get some experience. Then, of course, he'd be back here with you."

Even before Goldwyn responded, I could see it was no go.

"God damn it!" he shouted. "You think that's all I got to do is train people for other goddam studios? Let 'em train their *own* goddam people, not steal people from other studios. From me." He looked at me and pointed a finger. "You take *my* money and then you want to go and work for them!"

"That isn't it," I said. "I want to see if I can direct a picture."

"You want to see! You don't *have* to see. I'll tell you right now you *can't* direct a picture. How can you direct a picture? You never *directed* a picture."

"Don't get excited, Sam," said Abe.

"Don't tell me not to get excited!" Goldwyn shouted. "I'm in my own office, in my own studio, and if I want to get excited, I can get excited. Here's a kid comes out here, a nobody, takes my money, and then he wants to go someplace else. "

He was out of control now, completely unreasonable. There was no point in going on with it. We left.

Three more meetings on the same subject were filled with increasingly bitter exchanges.

The *Boy Meets Girl* deal fell through, but by now I had begun to believe I was ready to direct. So virulent was my germ that Lastfogel became infected and actually got me an offer from RKO. I could scarcely believe it. I had, as yet, done nothing.

All that stood in the way was the Goldwyn contract.

"He *has* to let me out," I said. "Doesn't he? I mean, what good am I to him if I don't want to be there? I can just horse around and do nothing. I don't want to do it that way. I'd rather have it amicable."

We went in to see Goldwyn again. I expressed my feelings. He looked hurt, and said, "Well, you're not the first one who stole money from me."

Abe was outraged.

"That's a *hell* of a thing to say, Sam," he said. "So I'll tell you what. You give him his release, and we'll give you back all the money you've paid him this last year."

It was Goldwyn's turn to be outraged. "You think I need the money?" shouted Goldwyn. *"F'Chrissake!* It's the *principle.* Of the thing. I wouldn't take a penny from you *or* from him. It would be from you anyway because what has *he* got? Nothing. And I'll tell you something else. He's *never* going to have anything. He's got a little talent, but he doesn't know how to use it. Bothering me, day in and day out—he wants to be a director, f'Chrissake, when I was giving him all this opportunity." He turned to me. "Listen, you don't want to be around here? Nobody's going to put you on a ball and a chain. You want a release? I'll *give* you a release."

"Thank you, Mr. Goldwyn," I said, and extended my hand before he could change his mind, and we left.

The next day Goldwyn gave me an unconditional release. That was on a Saturday. On Monday, I reported to work at RKO.

Seven months later, my first picture, *A Man to Remember,* was having a success. It was a small, inexpensive film, but, unlike the usual run of B pictures, did not insult the intelligence.

I was at last an accepted member of the Hollywood film community.

When Willie Wyler, whom I had known at Goldwyn's, took a new wife—a girl named Margaret Tallichet—he invited me to the wedding.

At the reception, I was standing at the bar with a glass of champagne in my hand when I saw Samuel Goldwyn coming toward me.

I had neither seen him nor spoken to him for almost a year. He seemed to be smiling, although with him, it was not always easy to tell.

"Hello, Mr. Goldwyn," I said. "How are you?"

"You dirty little bastard," he replied. "You dirty, double-crossing little son of a bitch."

He smiled. I did not.

"Why do you say that, Mr. Goldwyn?"

He laughed. "Because that's what you are. A little double-crossing bastard." He put his hand on my shoulder in the most avuncular way and said gently, "Why didn't you ever *tell* me you wanted to be a director?"

He clapped me on the back, too hard, spilling some of my champagne and said, "Call me up. Come over to lunch. I want to talk to you."

He was gone.

I sought out Willie Wyler and told him what had happened. "How do you explain it?" I asked.

"Well, I'll tell you," said Willie. "He believes with all his heart that you spent a year at his studio and never mentioned the subject of directing. He believes it because he *has* to. He's convinced himself that's the truth, because—don't you see?—if he admits to anybody or to himself that there you were, under contract to him, begging him every minute for a chance to direct, with him turning you down, then you go out and become a successful director for another studio, he's made a blunder. He's used bad judgment, so rather than admit this, he convinces himself you never mentioned it. That's his mentality. I think it may be one of the main reasons for his success. To himself, he's never wrong. He's a god. Not a bad thing to be, especially if you live on earth."

"What makes you think he lives on earth?" I asked.

CHAPTER 2

I n his long day, John Barrymore was considered by many to be the greatest American actor ever.

My relationship with this remarkable man began near the beginning of my own career as a film director, shortly after making *A Man to Remember*.

I was immediately assigned to a run-of-the-mill nonsense, objected, was told to do it or else, chose to do it, and suffered through it.

As I was finishing the second picture, the first one opened and was a surprise critical success, gaining much attention. At this point the front office executives looked at it for the first time. They too pronounced themselves impressed. Thus, about a month after *A Man to Remember* had been in national release, a preview was held, following which the film was re-booked into larger and more important theatres.

Pandro S. Berman, then the head of RKO, sent for me. I took the opportunity to blast my resentment of having been so cavalierly assigned to a nothing job.

Berman was entirely sympathetic and said, "Listen, I'm sorry but we'll make it up to you."

"How?" I asked. "How can you?"

"We'll let you do any picture you want next. Anything on the lot that you can put together."

As it happened there was a picture on the lot that interested me greatly. It was a shelved project called *The Great Man Votes*.

A *Saturday Evening Post* short story by Gordon Malherbe Hillman had been adapted for the screen by John Twist, one of the best writers at the studio.

I read it and was instantly captivated by its whimsical, yet powerful premise: a once-promising, cultivated scholar, now a widower with two small children, lives and works as a night watchman in a forgotten precinct in lower Manhattan. Gerrymandering has reduced the voting population of this precinct to one and that one is the night watchman, Gregory Vance. In a hotly fought mayoralty election, the outcome depends upon this particular precinct and thus on this one man. Life has kicked him into obscurity, but he is all at once being wooed by both parties and is elevated to momentary greatness but then—a surprise ending.

Shots came into focus, sights and sounds, and shortly, visualizations of the various characters. To my eye, Gregory Vance was John Barrymore and John Barrymore was Gregory Vance.

Taking Berman at his word, I went to him with the suggestion that he let me make *The Great Man Votes*. I reminded him of his promise, and after a time he agreed, saying, "Okay. If—and it's a big 'if'—if you can cast it."

"It's all cast," I said.

"Go ahead."

"John Barrymore."

"Nothing doing," said Pan, in a way that made me fear it was final.

"Why not?" I asked.

"He's not going to work on this lot," said Pan. "He's unreliable and irresponsible and impossible."

"That's all over, Pan. This new marriage of his. He's all settled down. He wants to work. Let me do it, Pan. Trust me."

"Listen," he said. "The last time we let that bastard on the lot—we didn't want him then, but this big director from New York had come out, Worthington Miner, and he kept giving me the same kind of malarkey you're giving me. 'Leave him to me,' he kept saying. 'I can handle him.' And he was handling him just fine—until one afternoon Barrymore took a whole gang of the crew over to Lucey's for lunch. He always gets very pally with the crew and they call him Jack and he calls them whatever, and they all have a lot of hijinks and nothing but fun and the picture goes in the crapper. So he took the crew to lunch and the crew came back. What the hell. They *had* to. They've got a union. But *he* didn't come back. Not that day or the next or the next. In fact, never. We had to stop it. The insurance covered some of it, sure, but not all and that's another thing. We can't get any insurance on the guy. So forget it."

I rose and said solemnly, "All right, Pan. If that's your decision, I accept it, but I must say I'm surprised. You've got a great reputation in this business as a picturemaker but more important, everyone who knows you, who's dealt with you, says that you're a man of your word. A man of honor and I'm really surprised to see you betray that idea. "

A look into his widening eyes told me I had struck home.

"*What* idea?" he blurted out.

"Well, after the rough time you people gave me about that second assignment, you promised you were going to make it up to me. You said I could do anything on the lot—"

All at once, I could no longer see him. I saw only his finger, pointing directly between my eyes.

"All right, you dumb jerk," he said. "I'm going to give you enough rope and let's see what happens."

The Great Man Votes was under way. All I had to do now was to persuade John Barrymore to do it. He could be extremely erratic, I was told.

I got Barrymore's home telephone number from his agent, remembering Mr. Goldwyn's advice to deal with principals whenever possible. I phoned John Barrymore, identified myself, and began telling him about the script.

"No, no," I heard that great voice say. "Let's not do this on the phone—a diabolical instrument, in any case. Come on over. Bring the manuscript. Although, to be perfectly candid, I prefer to have you *tell* me the story and describe the role. A movie script is so boring to read. It's like a plumber's manual, isn't it? Furthermore, I have no idea who you are but when you've told me the story, I'll have some idea as to your competence to convey it to an audience."

"When?" I asked.

"When what?"

"When can I come over?"

"Why not right now?"

I was on my way in a matter of minutes.

I had difficulty finding his hideaway house and it was precisely noon when I drove up to the front door.

I rang the bell. I heard it sound loudly inside and waited for a minute, for two, for three. I rang again. Five minutes later, I rang for a third and what I had decided would be a final time. The front door was flung open and there stood John Barrymore, the greatest actor in America, stark naked.

"Were you out there long?" he asked as I entered the house. "I'm sorry. My apologies. We don't have any servants here. They keep leaving." He looked around. "My wife should be here but she isn't. Would you like some coffee?"

"Yes, I would."

"All right, then. Why don't you go out into the kitchen and make it? It's out there somewhere. The kitchen. And there should be some coffee in it." He looked down at his nakedness and suddenly became a coy ingenue. "Would you excuse me while I slip into something more comfortable?" He minced off and up the stairs.

I found the kitchen. It was a mess, but I managed to prepare coffee. I put everything onto a tray and carried it out to the sitting room.

Barrymore sat there, beautifully dressed in slacks, slippers, a smoking jacket, and an ascot, smoking and reading the morning newspaper. He seemed surprised to see me, but said, "Oh, coffee. Fine. Put it right down there."

I felt as though I were about to be tipped.

I poured coffee for both of us and began. "This is a great honor, Mr. Barrymore."

"I should think it would be. Are you the director of this thing we're supposed to talk about?"

"Yes, sir, I am."

"Oh, I thought you might be his grandson working for him as his messenger boy."

"No," I said. "I'd like to direct this picture. That is, if you'll star in it. If you'll play the lead."

"The *lead*?" he asked sharply. I could almost see his ears prick up. "May I ask how many *other* leads there are in this opera?"

"None," I said.

He looked at me long and hard and did not speak again until he had finished his cup of coffee. Then he lit a fresh cigarette, regarded me once more, and ordered, "Tell me the story."

I did so.

I was, by that time, beginning to be fairly experienced in the business of telling (selling) stories to various players. Sometimes I told them well; more often, poorly. On this afternoon with Barrymore, I surpassed myself and realized about one third of the way through that what it takes to tell a story well is a sympathetic listener. There has never been a listener to equal John Barrymore. He took it all in moment by moment and somehow I felt him helping me.

"When do we start?" he said.

The next few days were spent in the excitement of confident preparation. Everything seemed to be falling into place. I thought it time to invite Barrymore to dinner. I phoned him. Would he and Mrs. Barrymore have dinner with me on Friday at Chasen's at eight?

"I'll be there," he said. "Let's leave her out of it, unless you'd like to buy her from me."

I pretended I had not heard this last.

That Friday night, as I walked into Chasen's at ten minutes to eight, I was simultaneously delighted and dismayed.

Sitting at the bar waiting for me was John Barrymore, not only punctual but more than punctual. What did they mean, unreliable? Irresponsible? There he was, beautifully gotten up and waving to me affably.

At the same moment, I saw Pandro S. Berman sitting with a party of friends in one of the booths. I would have preferred my first public meeting with Barrymore to have gone unscrutinized, but there it was.

I joined Barrymore at the bar. We shook hands.

"Good evening, Mr. Barrymore. I hope I'm not late."

"No, no," he said. "I'm early. I'm always early. I find it affords an opportunity for an extra ration of giggle water."

I shuddered. I hoped he did not notice.

He finished his martini, put it down on the bar, tapped the rim of the glass with a long, graceful finger. The bartender made him a second martini. I ordered Scotch. By the time I had finished my drink, Barrymore had had another. That made three, I calculated. Three that I knew of. I prayed that Pan Berman would soon leave. I looked over to his table. He was just starting his soup.

"Well," I said, "shall we order, Mr. Barrymore?"

"In a minute," he said.

I signaled the headwaiter, who recognized my desperation and brought menus at once. I ordered swiftly and unimaginatively and sat by while he consumed yet another set of martinis.

At dinner he ate, discussed the food, talked of other dinners in different places and times.

As we parted, he said, "Thanks. It was a splendid repast. I've enjoyed it."

"Thank you, Mr. Barrymore," I said.

"Mr. Barrymore!" he snorted, giving that well-known single syllable laugh of his, and was driven off by his chauffeur.

I wondered why he had reacted so oddly to being called by that name. He was more than thirty years my senior, a distinguished star. Why shouldn't I call him Mr. Barrymore? It struck me that because he had lost a certain amount of respect for himself, it embarrassed him to sense even the suggestion of it from someone else, especially a stranger. Could this be the key, I wondered, to the solution of the problem? I remembered what Pan Berman had told me about Barrymore's camaraderie with the crew.

I decided upon a stratagem.

Three days before shooting was to begin, I assembled the crew and that part of the cast which was available. I explained our mutual problem.

"Our star is John Barrymore and it's no secret to any of you, especially those of you who know him, who've worked with him, that he presents certain problems. I happen to think he's a great actor. I call him Mr. Barrymore, and I'd appreciate it very much if all of you would do the same. Now, it may seem like a small thing but I believe that one of the principal functions of a director is to create an atmosphere in which creative work can take place, and what worries me is that if we get into one of those loose work situations full of hijinks, horsing-around, laughing-it-up, everybody-topping-everybody-else, calling him Jack, and remembering all the peccadilloes, I'm not going to be able to do that. So I need your help. Let's keep it businesslike. We've got a long picture and a short schedule. Rule number one. He's Mr. Barrymore."

Throughout the twenty-four days of shooting, no one called him or referred to him as anything but "Mr. Barrymore." In a matter of days, I believe he began to think of *himself* as Mr. Barrymore.

Never before had I worked with a more thorough professional. He was never late, never objected to overtime, gave everything on every take, and was totally prepared, although he insisted upon using his notorious blackboards.

This was the one thing about his work I could not understand. I am sure he knew his part perfectly, yet he insisted upon having his man somewhere in the line of sight, holding up that blackboard.

There were, in fact, many blackboards, in varying sizes and shapes. Large ones for the long speeches; small ones for the shorter speeches; oblong ones to fit between the lights if necessary; tiny ones for single lines.

One morning, as we were about to begin, my cutter came onto the set and asked if I would make one small additional shot. It was simply an entrance to tie in two scenes. The whole shot would consist of a medium angle on an empty door. A woman comes in and knocks. The door is opened by Barrymore. She asks, "Are you Gregory Vance?" He replies, "Yes." Whereupon she enters. That would be all.

We set up the scene and I went off to get a cup of coffee. All at once I heard a furious row from the vicinity of the camera. As a rule, these flare-ups died out as swiftly as they began but this one continued. I went over to see what the trouble was.

Henry, Barrymore's blackboard man, was engaged in a violent shoving match with the principal gaffer. It was only a question of who was going to throw the first punch. I heard myself yelling.

"All right! That's enough! Hold it! Shut up *everybody!* Now *cut it out!*"

I succeeded in bringing about a temporary abatement.

"What *is* all this?" I asked.

The gaffer spoke. "Listen. I've put up with this goddam pest every day since we started, but enough is enough. He doesn't have to be in here with that goddam sliver. I need this spot for my key light and I want him the hell out of here."

Henry, a dignified old gentleman, said, "I know my job and I'm going to do it and no one's going to prevent me from doing it. My job."

I was confused. "What job? What do you mean 'sliver'?"

Henry held up a blackboard the size of a child's slate. On it was written the word "Yes."

"All right, Henry," I said. "Just relax."

I went over to Barrymore, who sat in his chair smoking and smiling.

"Could I have you in the scene, Mr. Barrymore, for just a moment?"

"Of course. Of course," he said, and joined me near the camera.

"We have a little problem," I explained. "You know the scene. We're outside here with the camera. Miss Alexander knocks on the door. You open it. She says, 'Are you Gregory Vance?' You say, 'Yes.' She walks in and that's it."

"Fine," said Barrymore. "What seems to be the trouble?"

"Well," I explained, "Henry here seems to feel that he has to be standing here with this little slate that says 'Yes.'"

"Oh, by all *means!*" said Barrymore.

I did not grasp his meaning at once. "You mean it's all right for him *not* to be here. Is that it?"

"No, no," said Barrymore. "I'd like to have him there. With his slate."

I was losing patience, struggling for control. "But let's be reasonable, Mr. Barrymore. All she asks is, 'Are you Gregory Vance?' And you *are,* so what else could you possibly say?"

Barrymore thought for a long moment, then looked at me and said, "Well, I could say 'No,' and *then* where would you be?"

We found a spot for Henry and his slate.

His acting technique was flawless.

When, toward the end of the picture, his part called for him to recite the final touching lines he did them perfectly on the first take, with the aid of a medium-sized blackboard.

"That's it," I said. "Print it." He beckoned to me. I went over to him at once. "Yes, Mr. Barrymore?"

"Would you like one with a little juice?" he asked.

"Juice?" I repeated, confused.

"Juice," he said. "A little eye juice?"

"Oh," I said, "I wouldn't have thought so. I always think that when the actor cries the audience probably doesn't. It's when the actor seems to be holding back tears that the audience is more likely to supply them. They like to cry *for* him, in a way."

"Oh," he said. "Very well."

I could see he was disappointed. I went on. "Still, no harm in trying. Let's do one."

"Good," he said, brightly. "Then you can decide."

We rolled again. He recited once more. To take best advantage of the effect, I had arranged for the camera to dolly in toward him very slowly. As the camera approached him, the tears began to flow, splashing off his cheekbones.

"Cut!" he shouted, waving his palm at the lens.

I thought for a moment that the camera mechanics had disturbed him. Not at all. He looked at me. "Too much juice," he said. "I'm sorry. I apologize for my excess. May we do one more, please?"

"Of course," I said.

Another take. This time there were tears but they were discreet tears, one small one falling out of the right eye and when that was halfway down his face, a large one from the other eye. I watched him, agape, and forgot to say "Cut." The scene ended somehow. Applause.

"What did you think?" he asked.

"It looked fine," I said. "Surprisingly fine."

He frowned. "Did you like that little one first and then the big one or would it be better with the big one first and then the little one?"

I was content with two satisfactory takes in the can but I confess that by then I was riveted by this display.

"Yes," I said. "That would be *much* better. First the big one and *then* the little one."

"All right," he said. "But for that, you better move in a little quicker."

The camera operator nodded and said, "Okay."

The next take. We all watched, no longer interested in the scene or in the shot, not even concerned about the face. We were concentrating on the trick of the tears.

"Roll 'em."

He did not disappoint us. First the big one, then almost at the end, when we had given up hope, the little one melted out of his other eye.

Later, I discussed it with him.

"Oh, Christ!" he said. "It's nothing. Don't confuse it with acting. It's a trick, like being able to blush." He blushed.

"The crying thing is nothing. All women can do it. And kids. Kids bring on tears to get what they want. And when they've got what they want, they stop. That's how I learned to do it. When I was about seven, I watched Ethel do it, and Lionel, and that gave me the idea. I went off into the bathroom for an hour or so every day and practiced. When you've been doing something for fifty years, you're bound to get pretty good at it. But it isn't acting. It's crying. Doesn't mean a damn thing."

A year or so before his death in 1942, John Barrymore was clowning away the last of his days in some foolishness in Chicago when he collapsed on the stage shortly after a performance began.

The news reached Hollywood quickly. There were rumors of a stroke, a few claimed to have heard that he was dead. I tried to reach him by phone, and, unable to do so, I sent a telegram of enquiry. The next morning, I had a message from him. It read: DON'T WORRY. FOR A MAN WHO HAS BEEN DEAD FOR FIFTEEN YEARS I AM IN REMARKABLE HEALTH. LOVE. MR. BARRYMORE.

CHAPTER 3

Ever since I can remember, the girls of America have shared a dream: To be a movie star. To be in the movies.

"You ought to be in pictures."

"Anybody can be in the movies. It's how they photograph you."

"My legs are as good as Elizabeth Taylor's."

"All you need is one good break. Look at Lana. Just happened to be sitting at the right soda fountain, the right time. If not, where'd she be today?"

The legend of You Too Can Be A Movie Star is one of the myths of our time.

The power of the dream is largely generated by the fact that every now and then it comes true.

It came true for a slightly chubby, very peppy blonde from Indiana named Jane Peters, later known as Carole Lombard.

"I think that 'e' made the whole fuckin' difference," she said to me one day, during the time I was directing her in *They Knew What They Wanted*. (It should be noted that this was Carole's normal style of speech. She used the full, juicy Anglo-Saxon vocabulary; yet it never shocked, never offended because she was clearly using the language to express herself and not to shock or offend.)

She was the only star I have ever known who did not want a dressing room on the set. What little makeup she used, she put on herself. She preferred to look after her own hair. All she asked for was a chair and a small table. There she would be, twenty minutes or half an hour before she was due, ready and able. I never knew her to fluff a line. She liked everyone and everyone adored her. She was happy.

I thought her a fine actress, one of the finest I had ever encountered. She was completely untrained, had never appeared on the legitimate stage. She came to Hollywood from Fort Wayne, Indiana, became a child actress, and later went to work for Mack Sennett as one of his bathing beauties. But the movies were growing, the business was burgeoning, and there was room at the top for a beautiful, talented girl.

"Isn't it crazy?" Carole said one day over coffee in my trailer. "I just think about that husband of mine all the time. I'm really stuck on the bastard. That's *something*, isn't it?"

"Not so remarkable," I said, "considering he's Clark Gable, and sixty million other women are stuck on him. Now if you happened to be stuck on *me*, that would be news. "

"And what's ridiculous is that we made a picture together for Wesley Ruggles, over at Paramount. Pretty good picture, too. *No Man of Her Own*. And we worked together and did all kinds of hot love scenes and everything. And I never got any kind of a tremble out of him at all. You know, he was just the leading man. So what? A hunk of meat."

"So then what?"

"Well, about three years ago, Jock Whitney gave this party, and it said you had to wear white. And the first thing struck me was a hospital. So I got my doctor to get me what somebody in a hospital would wear. One of those white things that ties in the back, you know, with your ass out and a white mask over my face and a bandaged head. And I even got a white stretcher and a white ambulance and I drove up in the white ambulance and I had myself carried in to Jock's party on a white stretcher, by two dressed-in-white interns. I was a smash. And for some reason, this got to ol' Clark. He thought it was hot stuff. Who knows? Maybe with all that white he thought I was a virgin or something. Believe me. I wasn't. If you want the truth, I don't think I *ever* was! I'm really stuck on the son of a bitch."

"You ought to make another picture together."

"Yeah. We talk about that sometimes. But I don't know. We also talk about chucking the whole thing. He's nuts about the ranch, the whole twenty acres. We both like it. The horses and the animals. You ought to see Clark run a tractor. And we shoot. I think maybe we *could* give it up. Of course, I don't know if we've got enough dough. I know *I* haven't got much. I wonder if *he's* got any?"

"Why don't you ask him?"

"Yeah, I think I will. Tonight."

"We didn't have too simple a time getting going—me and Clark—because when we first started messin' around, he was tied up elsewhere and so was I, sort of. So we used to go through the God-damnedest routine you ever heard of. He'd get somebody to go hire a room or a bungalow somewhere on the outskirts. Then the somebody would give him a key. Then he'd have another key made, and give it to me. Then we'd arrange a time and he'd get there. Then I'd get there. Or I'd get there, then he'd get there. Then all the shades down and all the doors and windows locked, and the phones shut off, and then we'd have a drink or sometimes not. He's not much of a bottle man. And we'd get going. And that's how it went on for quite a time. Finally, he got unglued and I did too, and we thought what the hell, we might as well get married. But would you believe it? After we were married, we couldn't ever make it unless we went somewhere and locked all the doors and put down all the window shades, and shut off all the phones! Even now, swear to God, we've been married all this time, he still goes around putting down window shades and locking doors. Don't you love it?"

"I love *you*," I said.

In December 1941, Clark Gable had been appointed chairman of the Hollywood Victory Committee. In this post, he had assigned Carole Lombard to go to Indiana and open a bond drive in Fort Wayne. She had had a great success and was returning to California with her mother. On January 16, 1942, at 7:23 P.M., the plane crashed into Table Rock Mountain, about thirty miles southwest of Las Vegas.

CHAPTER 4

Garbo. I saw her first in *Flesh and the Devil* with John Gilbert. She made an indelible impression on me and I saw her for countless days and nights afterward.

I saw her not long ago on Madison Avenue in New York, walking along under an umbrella, stopping from time to time to look aimlessly into a shop window.

Can it be that after almost fifty years she has lost not one jot of her magical beauty? As a figure, as a presence, as a screen personality, she was and is so arresting that it is hard to believe she has not made a film since 1941. Can it be? *Thirty-three years?*

She always worked with dedication: felt, thought, projected, communicated, listened, and talked.

Greta Garbo saved her personality for her work. She was never a scintillating dinner companion or an avid partygoer.

I recall a Sunday luncheon at George Cukor's in honor of an unmarried British couple, recently arrived in Hollywood. The girl was to play Scarlett in *Gone with the Wind;* the man to play Maxim de Winter in *Rebecca.* Vivien Leigh and Laurence Olivier. Among the guests was Greta Garbo. I had never met her and disgraced myself by staring at her for three and a half hours.

Shortly after lunch, Greta Garbo and Laurence Olivier strolled away into Cukor's beautiful gardens. They were deep in serious conversation.

From afar we could see him talking and her listening. Then *she* talked and *he* listened. She laughed, soundlessly. They stopped. He gesticulated. She looked surprised, asked another question. He replied, underlining the reply with expansive gestures. In the fading light of the cloudy afternoon, it all began to seem like a scene from a silent film.

I found it entertaining but the beauty at my side had a distinctly different reaction. Vivien Leigh was smoldering in the flames of irritation, anger, and jealousy. She was hardly accustomed to being anything less than the most beautiful creature in any assemblage. Thus, the presence of Garbo unnerved her, and the idea of Garbo in deep, intimate conversation with her husband-to-be was a further annoyance.

"Look at him," she said tightly. "He's behaving like a ninny."

"Well, I would be too, in his position," I said.

"Oh, *would* you!" she said, using five musical tones.

"You have to admit," I said, "she's a pretty spectacular number."

"I don't have to admit anything of the sort," said Vivien. Her tight little face suddenly changed expression. Her beautiful smile illuminated her visage as she said, "Ah, *there* you are! *Bonne promenade?*"

I turned and saw that Garbo and Olivier had returned.

Less than five minutes later, we were in my car, Vivien, Larry, and I, and I was driving them home. Our departure had been so swiftly and gracefully engineered by Vivien that I could remember none of its details.

At my side, the most romantic couple in the world was having a spat.

"—the last time I *ever* go to lunch with *you!*" said Vivien. "Do you hear? The last. I'd rather *starve*."

"Now be reasonable, Puss—"

"Hah!" she said.

"What does that mean?"

"It means," said Vivien, "that I'm fed up with that David Copperfield performance."

"Oh my God," said Larry. "Will you give it a rest?"

"Floating around the garden like some moonstruck ninny."

"She asked me if I would like to walk a few steps," said Larry. "What was I to say?"

"Did you try 'no'?" asked Vivien.

"Of course not."

"Why not?"

"I was being polite. It's as simple as that."

I laughed, hoping it might prove to be contagious and that the whole small contretemps would dissolve in gaiety. I was wrong. They both turned on me.

"Shut up!" said Larry as Vivien said, "What's so funny?"

They turned to each other again and continued the set-to.

"What was so enthralling?" asked Vivien.

"Enthralling?"

"That conversation. What was it about?"

"All right!" Larry shouted. "If you insist. I'm about to *tell* you what it was about."

"Thank you," said Vivien. "And do not dissemble, if you please. You know what a rotten liar you are and how I always know when you're lying."

"I have no intention of lying this time," said Larry. "There's no need."

"Ah!" said Vivien. "Then you admit that sometimes you *do* lie?"

"Jesus, Puss!" he said, pained. "How many battles do you expect me to fight at once?"

"Go on about your enthralling little tête-à-tête with your new enthusiasm, Miss Greeta Garbo."

"Here it is!" cried Larry, with the air of a man broken down by the third degree and about to confess all. "We began to walk and she said, 'This is a nice garden.'"

"'Yes,' I said. 'It *is* a nice garden.'"

His imitation of her voice and accent was uncanny. Since I was keeping my eyes on the road, it was easy for me to get the impression that the account which followed was a replay of the conversation. It was almost as though Miss Garbo had joined us on the front seat.

"'We have gardens in Sweden.'

"'Yes, you must have.'

"'Do you have nice gardens in England?'

"'Yes, we have *many* nice gardens in England.'

"'In some of our Swedish gardens, we grow fruit. Apples.'

"'We have apples in England, too.'

"'And strawberries?'

"'Yes. Very good strawberries.'

"'Do you have oranges?'

"'No. No oranges. But we have peaches.'

"'We have peaches in Sweden.'

"'Oh, I'm *so* glad! And do you have nectarines?'

"'No. No nectarines. . . . Cabbages.'

"'Yes. We have cabbages, too, but not in our gardens, unless, of course, you'd call a kitchen garden a garden.'

"'Yes. I think I would.'

"'Gooseberries?'

"'What are gooseberries?'

"'Gooseberries. You know. To make gooseberry jam with. Or a pie. Or a gooseberry fool.'

"'What *is* a gooseberry fool?'

"'Well, it's the same as a *raspberry* fool or a *damson* fool, except that it's made with gooseberries.'

"'Do you have artichoke?'

"'We have them but I don't think we grow them. We import them. However, we do have asparagus.'

"'We have asparagus, too. But no Cranshaw melon.'

"'Nor do we.'

"'Cranshaw melon is good.'

"'Watermelon is good.'

"'And cantaloupe?'

"'I don't like cantaloupe,'

"'I like this garden. It's a nice garden.'

"'Yes, it is. A very nice garden.'

"And that was it until *you* said, 'Ah, there you are. Let's go home.'"

Nothing more was said until I swung off into the driveway of their house on Camden Drive.

We all sat quietly until Vivien said, "I don't believe one bloody word of all that."

"No," said Larry. "I didn't think you would."

It was not my place to say anything, but *I did* believe it. Every bloody word.

What it indicated to me was that inventing conversation, making charming small talk, and forming opinions was not generally her mode of expression. Greta Garbo's art was akin to music, in which the expression vented goes beyond words.

Garbo was one of the figures who brought to the screen an idealization of womanhood so overpowering that it captured the imagination of the moviegoing public the world over. At Metro, it was common knowledge that Garbo pictures were never significantly successful at the box office in the United States, but they did so well in Europe that they were worth making. Very few Garbo pictures lost money.

The story of *Camille* has always strained credibility, but when Garbo played it, it became believable.

After *Flesh and the Devil*, she made *Love*, *The Divine Woman*, and *The Kiss*. This was to be her last silent film. Sound came. The talkies. A revolution. Careers collapsed.

At Metro, someone came up with an inspired idea. Eugene O'Neill's *Anna Christie* for Garbo. "Garbo Talks!" read the streamer on the billboards and ads.

The effect of her first line, spoken in that husky, sensuous and thrilling voice—"Gif me a whiskey!"—was immense. She became, with that film, a greater star than she had ever been in the silents.

Garbo's career now moved from strength to strength. *Romance, Susan Lenox, Mata Hari*, Pirandello's *As You Desire Me, Grand Hotel, Queen Christina, The Painted Veil, Anna Karenina, Camille, Conquest, Ninotchka*. Then, in 1941, came a mechanical, incomprehensible film finally titled *Two-Faced Woman*.

There were many difficulties on this production. Shooting was stopped several times. Garbo thought, long before it was finished, that the film would be a disaster.

When her fears were realized, she took it badly and decided not to work for a time, perhaps to renew herself. The sabbatical lengthened and lengthened, projects came up but failed to materialize for one reason or another. After a long and difficult career she had lost the drive and energy necessary to sustain it and we have not seen her in a new film on the screen since.

In 1941, when Garbo ended her career, she was thirty-six years old. In a well-ordered professional life, her greatest triumphs would have lain before her.

CHAPTER 5

For most of the 69 million (or so) Americans who were alive on that day, September 14, 1895, was unexceptional.

Grover Cleveland was serving his second but nonconsecutive term as President of the United States. The wounds of the Civil War were healing slowly. Children of six and seven worked in fields and factories. The rich were extremely so; the poor, desperate.

It was at this time that Sammy Goldfish, a thirteen-year-old orphan, arrived. He had come from Warsaw, Poland, by way of Hamburg, Germany; Birmingham, Manchester, and London, England. He had entered the United States through Canada because of quota restrictions.

On that day, although America had countless theatres, music halls, cabarets, and tent shows everywhere, there did not exist, anywhere in the country, a single motion-picture theatre.

Forty-five years later there were 19,032 motion-picture theatres and an industry that produced some 700 feature films each year to supply them, and no individual in this industry was more important or more powerful than Samuel Goldwyn, who had metamorphosed out of young Sammy Goldfish.

His story bears careful consideration on two counts. First, it is the epic of the American film industry from cradle to almost grave. Second, in Goldwyn's case, at least, the promised land provided the opportunity it had promised, and he responded with energy, enterprise, imagination, and unflagging effort.

The thirteen-year-old proceeded without delay to Gloversville, New York, because the people who had befriended him in England chanced to be glovemakers.

In Gloversville he set to work, learning the trade and acquiring a working knowledge of the English language. According to Goldwyn, he did not become a craftsman.

"I never got the hang," he explained. "Maybe because I wasn't too interested. In life, you got to be too interested. I mean, interested. If not, nothing. Even so, I got to be pretty good—not bad—on setting a thumb, though."

He was possessed of a restless nature and envied the natty salesmen he saw coming to the Kingsborough Hotel and going out into the great world beyond.

He resolved that *he* would become a salesman and wear those highly polished, pointed shoes, fancy cravats, fashionable derbies, and would smell of Lilac Végétal, the way they did.

By the time he was eighteen, he had become an English-speaking glove salesman covering the New England territory.

"I had it on my mind to be a salesman," he recalled. "I wanted to go around and see people, meet people. Listen, I love people. Why not? Look what people did for *me* . I asked him and asked him—Mr. Lehr the boss—and at first he laughed at me, at my English. But listen—it got better fast—better than *his*, even. I was going to night school every single day. So—sixteen and a half years old, I said to him one time, to Mr. Lehr the boss—I said, 'Listen. Give me the worst territory. Give me a place you can't sell and let *me* try to sell.' So finally—maybe to get rid of me, he gave me a territory. The worst. In New England. The Berkshires. Pittsfield, Mass. They had a big store there that never bought a thing from Lehr. I went there. They looked. Nothing. I went back a few days later and you know what I did? I told the buyer in that store there my story. I told him this was my chance and if I failed I was finished. You know what he did? He gave me an order—for three hundred dollars—and I don't think he even liked the merchandise. I hear them talk sometimes—in a story conference—about Yankees—those tight, mean, hard Yankees and I always get mad. I tell them they don't know what the hell they're talking, f'Chrissake. I think of that fellow in Pittsfield. How he took pity on me and helped me out. So that started me.

"I built up that territory from the worst to maybe the best," he boasted. "So when New York City opened up—Mr. Lehr the boss—gave it to me. A few years later, you know what I was? A sales manager. But for a different company. Time went by and the next thing, I was a partner in the business. I had a drawing: fifteen thousand a year. That would be like today maybe seventy-five. You could go f'Chrissake in those days to Delmonico's and get the best steak for maybe a dollar and a quarter."

As he recalled those days, his small eyes grew larger, his age fell away, his energy increased.

"The glove business was all right, sure. Fine. But I began to find out about *other* businesses—better ones. I saw that my chance would be better in some *new* business—because in the established ones it was first of all hard to get in with no connections—and what connections did I have? No, I could see my best chance was in some *new* business where I could start out even and have some kind of a fighting chance."

"And was that when you met Lasky?"

"No. First I met his sister. Jesse Lasky's sister. Blanche. She was once an entertainer. In the vaudeville. Then in the costume business. We started going around together. A good person. She always was. We got married later—after I met Jesse. Her brother. He was then in the vaudeville, too. A booker. And I was the one explained him how a new business was our best bet." He chortled happily, remembering. "You should have seen the things he came up with! All kinds of mining propositions. And tamales. He said they were very big in California and we should introduce them to New York. Can you imagine it? Me in the tamale business? And once he was sure we should go in the pectin business.

"And then around Union Square, Herald Square—a few places—like stores—started in to show moving pictures. And everybody went. A novelty. Have you noticed how people like novelties? Miniature golf. A novelty. The gramophone when it first came out. Brownie cameras. Moving pictures. To tell you the truth, I wasn't too interested. Then somebody—I think Blanche, maybe—told me it was an invention by Thomas Alva Edison and then I wanted to see it. He was one of my idols—Edison. What a brain! What a mind! The things he thought up. When I heard he only slept four hours, *I* started in only sleeping four hours—but I didn't do too good. I became a wreck." He laughed heartily. "I went to five, then six. But I never went back to eight, I tell you. On account of Thomas Alva Edison. So I went to see these moving pictures. No stories, y'understand. No situations even. Just trains going. And people jumping. Horses. I liked it right away."

"And went into it? The business?"

"No, no. It wasn't even a *business* yet. It was just a—you know—a novelty. A sideshow. Not a business. No theatres. A few little companies—one of the first ones I can remember was the Universal Film Manufacturing Company—and they made these little movies—two, three minutes. Then Jesse started in to sell these little movie strips. That's how we got to know about it from the ground up—from the beginning. The very beginning."

"And then did *you* go into it, too?"

"A little later. After I left the gloves. And it didn't take me long—one, two, three—I said to Jesse, 'This is nothing, this peddling. What the hell's the difference if it's gloves or vaudeville acts? Or moving pictures? Peddling is peddling. We should *make* the product. Let somebody *else* do the peddling.'"

I often heard Samuel Goldwyn tell the story of their first production. He never changed it for effect; never embellished it, as most raconteurs do; never deviated from the facts as he remembered them. It was almost a set-piece, and I believed every word of it.

"All of a sudden," he said, "it *was* a business. There was this one came out, *The Great Train Robbery*. This must've been nineteen-oh-three, or maybe four. A fellow named Porter made it. Not a story, but a situation. A drama. And the *big* thing was—I pointed out to Jesse—there was something you couldn't do on the stage! In a way it made me mad, because I loved the theatre and I don't like to see anybody taking advantage of it. Still and all, we saw we had a chance. I put in some money. Jesse some, and Blanche, too, and another fellow—a backer—Arthur S. Friend. And even then I knew the important thing was—the story. Nobody could tell me different *then*. Nobody can tell me different *now!* So the first thing we did with our money was we bought a story. A play. It was not a terrific success. A terrific success we couldn't afford, but it was good. The name of it was *The Squaw Man*. The next thing we started in looking for a director and there was this fellow, Bill DeMille—William C. DeMille—and Jesse knew him from the vaudeville. So we went to him with the property and we asked him would he direct it. Well, you should have heard the man. He *hated* the movies and he thought any actor did it was a disgrace to his profession and that the movies were going to hurt the theatre or kill it and he practically threw us out. Then a couple days later, he called us up and recommended his brother, Cecil. That's right. Cecil B. DeMille. And he came around and we made the deal with him—one hundred dollars a week—and the next thing we started going around trying to raise the money. We had to raise about thirty thousand dollars to make the picture, and you can laugh if you want, but in those days to raise the thirty was harder than today to raise thirty *million*. But we did it and we made it. In Flagstaff, Arizona. It took eleven days. That was the shooting schedule. Eleven days. I'd like to see Willie Wyler with an eleven-day schedule someday. It takes him sometimes eleven days to decide where to put the camera for the first shot of the day. So anyway, we shot the picture in Flagstaff, Arizona, on account of Indians and in Hollywood, California, on account of cameramen. And cameras. And then it was put together and we took it to Philadelphia to show it to this man who had a little distribution chain. It was one of the first. And this man said all right, he'd look at it, but with an audience—so he could tell the reaction. So in one of his little theatres down there, we put it on one night—and, so help me God, even to this day when I tell about it, when I think about it I feel sometimes like I'm having a heart attack because the picture started in jumping all over the screen. Just jumping and blurring and once in a while for three or four seconds it would stand still and then it would start jumping again, and the people started in whistling and stamping their feet and laughing. And I was running to find the projection booth to stop it, but I couldn't find it. And after a while he stopped it himself—the projectionist—and we went up to the booth to see what happened and the projectionist started in explaining everything, but I didn't understand. It was something wrong with the sprocket holes. They were all different and not the same like they were supposed to be. The theatre man, he didn't even want to talk to us. A couple of amateurs, he figured. And you should have seen us on that train home from Philadelphia, with the tin cans of film on our laps. I don't think we said—Jesse or me—three words the whole way home. . . .

"There it was. All our money, and all our investors' money, shot. Listen, I'm not ashamed to say it. I cried—and Jesse cried, too, but what good was that gonna do? Well, the next day, we started in to try to see what could be done and everybody was putting the blame on everybody else. You know how it is in the movie business. They *still* do it. Everybody blames everybody else. The cameraman, the lab, the actor. What it was, was DeMille had to use different cameramen with different cameras. Pathé, Edison, Lumière. And they didn't match. And he didn't know it. Or *we*. Finally, by luck, we found this film technician. In Philadelphia. By the name of Sig Lubin. So we're on the train again. But we had to raise some more money and you can imagine how easy *that* was. We hocked everything. Gave up most of our interest but we had to save that picture. Our first picture. And Sig Lubin, he came through for us. He saved us—and when that picture went on and didn't jump around, it was damn good. In fact a hit. We were in business. . . .

"We put together this company. Cecil—Jesse and me—B. DeMille. We called it 'The Jesse L. Lasky Feature Play Company.' Jesse was the president. I was the treasurer and the general manager, and Cecil was the something. I can't remember. And we signed up Geraldine Farrar, from the Metropolitan Opera. We gave her twenty thousand dollars. To make three pictures. In eight weeks. Everybody thought we were crazy."

"But why Geraldine Farrar? She was an opera singer. The main thing she could do was sing, and you weren't going to use *that* on the screen."

"I'll tell you. This was an idea Cecil B. DeMille had. He was very smart—young and smart—and he noticed something. What he noticed was he noticed how most of the stage actors didn't act *big* enough. Now you got to remember the movies then were not too clear, sometimes they would be grainy and sometimes the focus would not be in focus. In certain places, sometimes the screen would go dim, and sometimes because there weren't enough regular theatres, they couldn't get it dark enough, so on the screen it was sometimes hard to see. So Cecil figured out that one way to get around this was for everybody who acted for the camera, they should act pretty big. But there were some of them, these stage actors, who they didn't want to do that. So Cecil said, 'In the opera, everybody acts big, with big gestures and big expressions on their faces.' So that's how he got the idea that opera people would be good. For on the screen. Dim or dark or whatever. Big enough would be the answer. And that Geraldine Farrar! My God, she was beautiful anyway. So it was a good idea. And we went on like this for two, three years."

"Excuse me," I said, "but how come it was called 'The Jesse L. Lasky Feature Play Company'?"

"Well, he got together—Jesse—most of the financing," said Goldwyn. "And that's how he wanted it. So we let him have it. Listen, I didn't care. In those days, I didn't realize how important it is to make your name. Anyhow, for me in that time, the main thing was to get into the business. But then, well, what can I tell you? Partners. That's why I've never had partners. If you have one partner, that's already trouble. When you have two partners, you might as well go kill yourself. And Jesse started to get very ambitious. We had a lot of competitors, and one of the worst ones—I mean, *best* ones—was Zukor. Adolph Zukor. He had a company. The name of it was 'Famous Players.' And Jesse got the idea that if we would merge our two companies, we would really have some power. So the merger went through and that's how it became Famous Players-Lasky Corporation. So now I had *three* partners and I couldn't stand it. So I got out. I sold out my stock. And I tried to put something together myself, but I wasn't ready. So there were these two men I loved and I respected very much. They were no doubt the finest theatrical producers in New York. Brothers. Edgar Selwyn and his brother Archie. And we formed our company and for the name of it, we decided to take half of each name. Half of my name, Goldfish, and half of their name, Selwyn, and so we called it the Goldwyn Pictures Corporation. It came out Goldwyn because we wanted to put our names together—and listen, it was the only way to do it. Archie—he was the jolly brother—I remember he said, 'Another way to do it is to call it *Selfish* Pictures, Incorporated.'

"I remembered what Cecil said about opera people. So we signed up Mary Garden. She was the greatest of them all. We decided to do one of her big opera parts. It was *Thaïs*. To tell you the truth, it didn't turn out too good. But we got a lot of publicity out of it. It was a religious subject, you know. And they showed it in the Vatican. Right inside of it. The first movie in history to be shown at the Vatican. . . . Then, in Europe—I used to go to Europe—I saw this wonderful picture, *The Cabinet of Dr. Caligari*. And we bought it to release in America. And we showed it at the Capitol Theatre. And what a flop *that* was! People asked for their money back, but it used to get great reviews, and today they call it a classic. . . . I put in four years with that company. With that sonofabitchin' company. I was with it longer, but for four years I was the president. And I nearly killed myself. And then I got out of it. It was too hard. Partners. Partners. Not only the Selwyns, but we even had a board of directors. And it was no good. And I made up my mind never again partners. And that's the way it's been. I've never had any partners."

"Was that when all that trouble about you using your own name came up?"

"Sure. By then, I'd gone to court and changed my name to Goldwyn. It was more dignified. More American. A man with a name like Goldfish, people make fun of it. And then when I left the Goldwyn company, I sold out, and I decided I'm going to form my own company. That's when they said I couldn't use my name. My own name. It took a year in court. And that great, great judge, Judge Learned Hand, he handed down the decision where it said I could use 'Samuel Goldwyn Presents,' except under it, it had to say, 'Not now connected with the Goldwyn Pictures Corporation' in the same size type. He was a great judge, like I said, but that was a God damn foolish decision. Because it looked ridiculous on the billing. But then, the next year came *another* merger and the Goldwyn company merged with the Metropolitan and L.B. Mayer and they formed the Metro-Goldwyn-Mayer. M-G-M. And that's when I made the deal with them that I could say 'Samuel Goldwyn Presents' and not have anything under. On the billing."

Many years later, there was Hollywood talk that a merger was being considered involving M-G-M and Samuel Goldwyn. It was rumored that

Goldwyn insisted that if the merger went through, the company be known as Metro-Goldwyn-Mayer and Goldwyn.

It would not have worked out in any case. Goldwyn was clearly a loner. Had he not been, the story of United Artists would have been different.

The original formation of United Artists, dedicated to the freedom of film expression, involved D. W. Griffith, Douglas Fairbanks and Mary Pickford, Charles Chaplin, and Samuel Goldwyn. What should have been a perfect partnership disintegrated because each member of the combine was a loner, and none more than the incomparable Chaplin.

CHAPTER 6

Artists create art forms. In exceptional cases, the form creates the artist. Charles Spencer Chaplin is the outstanding exemplar of the latter case.

Charlie Chaplin invited imitation. At children's dress-up parties there would be more Charlies than Indians. Little girls especially were attracted to the idea of the trousers, mustache, and derby.

Growing up, we identified with him on a more serious, social plane. He was all of us: downtrodden, kicked-around, treated unfairly by life and by fate. His enemies, like ours, were the bosses of the world, the bigger-than-us guys, the cops, and all other forms of authority. Charlie could outsmart them, he could charm them.

As in the case with all original creators, Charles Chaplin's working life was an amalgam of arrogant self-confidence and deflating self-doubt. With *The Great Dictator,* his worries proliferated along with his ideas. In 1938 to joke about Adolf Hitler was no joke. It was a nervous world in which anything might happen at any given moment. There might come a sudden time when Hitler might prove to be an impossible subject for comedy. A film takes a long time to make, especially when it is being made by a perfectionist. *The Great Dictator* would take perhaps a year and a half. What if Hitler were to die in the interim? What if he were assassinated? What if the United States went to war against him? (An unlikely thought but one that had to be considered.) These questions and many more were constantly under discussion.

Yet, there was something magnetic and irrresistible about the subject and Chaplin's creative juices were flowing. Several times he abandoned the project completely. Each time he returned to it.

His closest collaborators, his friends, and the rest of us who were casual acquaintances, rode with him up and down the roller coaster of vacillation. One night, I was at dinner with him and Paulette Goddard, his wife, who was urging him to go forward with his project. He stared at his uneaten food, bit his lip, and said, "I don't know. I just don't know. It's such a risk. Such a *risk.*"

"Everything's a risk," said the beautiful Paulette.

Then one night, at his house, the evening was growing duller by the minute. Political pontification by swimming-pool intellectuals filled the air.

Suddenly Chaplin was into it.

"We open," he said, "in a little barbershop in the ghetto. Outside, storm troopers are patrolling." He became two storm troopers patrolling. "Inside the shop . . . "

His performance was spellbinding. He transferred each image, each sound from inside his brain to the collective mind of his listeners. Everyone there that night saw the film, complete.

The Great Dictator went into production and I did not see my friend for almost two years. When he worked, he worked, and had no time, no interest in such nonsense as friends.

When *The Great Dictator* was to open in New York, I contrived to be there and told Charlie so. He got me a ticket for the opening at the Capitol Theatre and invited me to the various festivities.

It was a tremendous success, but one detail in the film troubled me.

After the opening, after the party, after the move of a dozen or more stragglers to the Oak Room of the Plaza Hotel, it was getting late. But Chaplin, excited and stimulated by the events of the opening, was hardly ready for bed. He wanted to talk.

"Let's get the hell away from here," he said. "I hate it. All this ostentatious show of wealth and power. Let's go down to the East Side, to the pushcart market. That's where real life is."

"It's two-thirty in the morning, Charlie," I reminded him. "The pushcart peddlers are all asleep."

We were standing in front of St. Patrick's Cathedral. This structure, too, like the Fifth Avenue shops, offended him. We turned left and walked toward Third Avenue.

We entered P.J. Clarke's, crossed into the back room, and sat down at a table. It was after hours but insiders or Chaplins could still get a drink. We ordered. Chaplin looked at me seriously.

"What didn't you like about it?" he asked.

I laughed loudly. Too loudly.

"Never mind the stage laugh," he said. "Yours stinks. You're no actor. What don't you like about it?"

"Charlie," I said, "I know you're not entirely reasonable tonight. Why should you be? You've just had the triumph of your life and I'm sure it's hard to take it all in, but for the past three hours or more, along with everybody else, I've been telling you that it's your greatest picture, your greatest performance—greatest *two* performances—that it's sure to be a world-wide smash . . . Didn't you hear me?"

"I heard you," he said, "and there was something about it you didn't like."

I could see it was no use, so I said, "All right. If you insist. I wish you'd let me think about it for a day or two. I'd probably come up with the answer myself."

"What's the question?" asked Chaplin.

"Well, just this. In the picture you do the most fantastic imitation of Hitler—no. Imitation's the wrong word. Caricature—maybe even caricature is wrong. It's a portrait beyond a portrait, like a Goya, where you can see the soul of the subject coming through the canvas. Your impression of Hitler makes it possible for us to understand Hitler and what he's about. You certainly had the look of him and the sound of him and all his gestures and facial expressions and posturing and attitudes. The uniforms, the mustache. Everything."

"Yes, yes," said Charlie, impatiently.

"Everything but the hair," I said. "That's what I couldn't quite understand. You kept your own curly hair and didn't bring that forelock brushed down against the forehead. That would have completed the reflection. Wait a minute! Even as I talk I'm getting it. Was it because you wanted a kind of blending of the Hitler image with the Chaplin image? Is that why you left out that one detail?"

"No," he said, crossly. "Of course not."

"Oh. Then why? Why didn't you provide that one last touch?"

Chaplin was tense with anger. "Well, God damn it!" he said righteously. "Why should I? I was using that makeup before *he* was."

The coming of sound was disastrous to the art of Charlie Chaplin. He had trained an audience to understand every subtle nuance of his pantomime, and had given more joy than any other figure in the arts of his time. Suddenly, the medium changed, and the greatest pantomimist in the world would be called upon to talk.

The problem was not his alone. Other great figures of the silent screen were similarly affected. John Gilbert, the most attractive and magnetic leading man of the day, proved to have a high, squeaky voice that ended his career almost overnight. Certain suave sophisticates sounded like Brooklyn truck drivers. It was a hard time.

Chaplin, after due consideration, decided to ride out the storm by ignoring it. There were many who thought the talkies were a temporary novelty that would soon pass and that the art of the film would return to its true form—moving pictures.

In the midst of the talkie revolution, he made *City Lights*, one of his finest films. Daringly, audaciously thumbing his nose at progress, he made it as a silent film. Even now it seems perfect.

CHAPTER 7

Hollywood and the Hollywood system have not produced a finer picturemaker than Billy Wilder of Vienna, Austria. Even his failures are the failures of a master.

Wilder began as a journalist, was a cub reporter at an early age, and worked for several Viennese publications.

"I worked on *Die Stunde* for a while. It wasn't such a bad job. One day I did some interviews for a Christmas number——Arthur Schnitzler, Alfred Adler, Richard Strauss, and Freud. All in one day. Not a bad job. Later on, when I left Vienna and went to Berlin like a schmuck, I worked on the *B.Z. am Mittag* for a while. But everybody wanted to be in the movies in those days. My way was to write scripts. I wrote thirty or forty. In those days my schedule was about one a day. It's a little slower now."

"And when did you go to Paris?"

"In 1933," says Billy. "It wasn't my idea, it was Hitler's. I hated Paris at first. I couldn't seem to get laid. So instead, I worked. And eventually sold a script. And then kept writing. I was only there about a year, and kept dreaming about Hollywood. Finally, I took off. What did I have to lose? And all of a sudden, there I am at Paramount, writing. There was one small handicap. I didn't have any English, so I kept writing in German, and some of my pals who were a little ahead of me would translate my stuff into English. I had a look at one of those translations a couple of years ago and I almost had a massive coronary. Then came Brackett and that changed everything."

Brackett means Charles Brackett, then one of Paramount's best writers. Brackett and Wilder became the most successful writing team in Hollywood. Their first collaboration was on *Bluebeard's Eighth Wife*. The director was Ernst Lubitsch. Gary Cooper and Claudette Colbert starred and the picture was memorable.

In 1942 Billy Wilder felt ready to take on the responsibility of direction, and did a Ginger Rogers picture called *The Major and the Minor*. He and Brackett collaborated on the screenplay.

"Nineteen forty-four," says Wilder, "was 'The Year of Infidelities.' Charlie produced *The Uninvited*. I had nothing to do with it. Instead, I wrote *Double Indemnity* with Raymond Chandler. Because he asked me. Terrific book, and what a writer! It was quite an experience, the whole thing. Then Charlie and I got together again for *The Lost Weekend*—but I don't think he ever forgave me. He always thought I cheated on him with Raymond Chandler. He got very possessive after that."

In the next development, Charles Brackett became their producer and Wilder continued to direct. From this producing-directing-writing team came *Five Graves to Cairo*, *The Emperor Waltz*, *A Foreign Affair*, and, finally, *Sunset Boulevard*. With this film, perhaps their most notable, the partnership came to an abrupt end.

Some years later, on a rainy Sunday in Bel Air, the dying Charlie Brackett talked about it.

"I never knew what happened, never understood it, we were doing so well. But we met one morning, as we always did, and Billy smiled that sweet smile of his at me and said, 'You know, Charlie, after this, I don't think we should work together any more. I think it would be better for both of us if we just split up.' I could say nothing. It was shattering. And Billy—you know how he is, bright and volatile—got right into the business of the day, and we said no more about it. But it was such a blow, such an unexpected blow, I thought I'd never recover from it. And, in fact, I don't think I ever have. It was just that I loved working with him. It was so stimulating and pleasant. And such fun, you know. I never gave a thought to working with anyone else ever. Don't you think it was odd? What he did? There was no reason. We liked each other, even our wives liked each other. We had our disagreements, of course, but they were always professional, never personal. And I don't think in all our years together, in all those pictures we made, I don't think we ever had a serious quarrel."

"Well, you made some terrific pictures together, Charlie, and in the end, that's what counts, isn't it?"

After the breakup, Brackett went to Twentieth Century-Fox as a writer-producer and did *Titanic, The King And I, Ten North Frederick, Journey to the Center of the Earth, State Fair,* and many others.

During a studio upheaval and reorganization the new administration canceled Brackett's contract on a technicality, saying, "Sue us." He had been at the studio for thirteen years and still had about two years left on his contract.

Billy Wilder, without previous announcement, called a press conference and made a statement in which he said, "In view of the treatment accorded Charles Brackett at Twentieth Century-Fox—" He then spelled out the details. "Therefore, I cannot imagine any self-respecting artist, whether director, writer, actor, producer, or musician, going to work for Twentieth Century-Fox under its present administration."

The statement was widely circulated and Twentieth Century-Fox was greatly upset. They contacted Wilder and gave him their side, but he was unregenerate. Brackett was paid off in full. Wilder remained loyal to his friend to the end. It was simply a question of a man deciding he wanted to be on his own, that being part of a team—no matter how successful—was not fulfilling.

Billy Wilder was taking a long time between pictures, longer than usual. I observed that the time between lengthened with each interval. During one of our quiet, late-afternoon talks, I asked, "What is it, do you suppose, Billy, that slows us down so? There was a time around here when top directors made two pictures a year, sometimes three. Now we can't even count on one a year from guys like you. What is it? Have you slowed down? Or is it the whole business?" He was silent, seemed to be thinking.

"I don't know about you—but let me tell you about me. Did you ever—when you were a kid—get a Brownie camera for a present?"

"Of course. I was born in Rochester, New York. Where the Brownie was born."

"Okay. Then you remember how you got the wonderful little magic black box and the roll of film and the book of instructions. And you loaded the camera and began to turn the roll—yes?—and there came first that hand pointing, and then dots, and finally—Number One! And you started. Focus, click. Turn the knob. Number Two. Focus, click. You could hardly wait to turn it to Three. And do you remember how when you got to Four or Five, you began to realize that there were only eight on the roll—so you got more careful, selective—and you waited for something really worth photographing. And sometimes you kept that roll in the Brownie for a week before you finally clicked your last picture on the roll."

"I remember," I said.

"Well, that's how it is with me. In the beginning, sure. One picture after another. But now—I feel I'm getting to the end of the roll. What is it?—three more, two more, *one* maybe? That's why I'm so careful before I click it."

Billy Wilder's first picture following the breakup, *Ace in the Hole*, must have given him pause. It was a failure. The word around town was he had blundered in splitting with Brackett. There was talk they were on the verge of being reunited.

Billy had other ideas. He bought a Broadway success, *Stalag 17*, about adventures in a World War II prison camp. Those of us who saw in him an original creative force were disappointed. No matter how well he did *Stalag 17*, it would not be a Billy Wilder picture.

This did not concern him. He was interested in success. He followed this with another Broadway hit, *Sabrina*. The picture did well. Next, he made *The Seven-Year Itch* with Marilyn Monroe. Another success, but not a Billy Wilder picture.

On the crest now, he inexplicably made *The Spirit of St. Louis*. It was costly and unsuccessful.

To shake off the dust of failure, he went to Paris and began work on *Love in the Afternoon*. It had been both a novel and an earlier film, but it became a Billy Wilder movie. The reception for it was mild. He reached for something sure-fire again, and made *Witness for the Prosecution*. His friends wondered why.

Then came *Some Like It Hot*, which many consider his best film. This, too, had been done earlier, but Wilder made it his own.

The following year came *The Apartment*. This was an original story by Wilder, with a screenplay by himself and I.A.L. Diamond.

Billy says, "I'll tell you where it came from. It came from Noël Coward. When I saw that beautiful picture of his, *Brief Encounter*, my God, it hit me hard. And what a job David Lean did! I thought about that picture endlessly, the way you do about a picture that has an emotional impact on you. I finally had that story completely digested. Then I began to brood about one of the undeveloped characters, the guy who owns the apartment. And I thought, Now there's a really interesting character. A guy lives in an apartment, and he loans it out to somebody for the purposes of love. And, feeling as I do about business and about the competitive system, I thought, What if there's this little schnook, this eager beaver in a big company, trying to get ahead and he can't do it, until it comes out that he lives in this little apartment, and all the executives start to want to borrow it for their little *cinq-à-septs* and, what the hell? I don't have to tell you, that was enough, I was off and running. I wonder if I ever remembered to thank Noël Coward!"

The next year, Wilder made *One, Two, Three.* He and Diamond did the screenplay from a play by Ferenc Molnár.

"Don't ask me why," he says, "but I just got the feeling I wanted to make a picture again in Germany. And when I got Cagney interested, that was good enough for me. For me, there's never been anybody better on the screen. Also, I happen to think Coca-Cola is funny. A lot of people didn't. Maybe that's why the picture bombed out. I still think it's funny. And when I drink it, it seems even funnier."

Irma La Douce, his next picture, had begun as a small musical in Paris. Wilder bought it, and changes began.

"I have nothing against music," he says, "but the more I went into that story, the better I thought it was. And for me, the numbers got in the way. So, first, one of them went, then another one went, and, one day, I made the decision, and we threw the whole score out and made it a straight picture. We used some of the music for underscoring, but that was all. I think it worked out very well. The truth is, I personally earned more out of that picture than any other picture I ever made. That doesn't mean it was the best. It just means I made the most money. And I enjoyed making it, too."

Billy Wilder's recent output has been uneven, but interesting, and he remains as able a filmmaker as there is. His admirers are waiting for him to choose a stimulating subject, get excited, and provide once again a Billy Wilder picture.

CHAPTER 8

Men of size are full of surprises. One of Samuel Goldwyn's greatest charms was his unpredictability.

He once arrived in New York and phoned me.

"Say," he said, "I've just been reading *The New York Times,* about this wonderful English ballet company."

"Yes, " I said. "The Sadler's Wells. They're at the Met."

"I have to see that," he said. "Get tickets and we'll go. I'll pay for them."

"All right," I said. "When would you like to go?"

"When? What do you mean, 'when'? Tonight."

"Well, I'm not sure I can get tickets for *tonight*."

"Why not?" he said. "You just told me you could get tickets."

"Let me see what I can do."

Fortunately, I was able to acquire seats and was not at all surprised when I found myself canceling the plans I had made for that evening.

We took Goldwyn to dinner, but he was too excited to eat. As we entered the Metropolitan Opera House, he kept looking around and shaking his head in wonder.

"Hasn't changed," he said. "It never changes. Isn't it wonderful to have some things that don't change? I remember coming here and sitting way up high. Caruso and Mary Garden and Geraldine Farrar. What artists they were!"

It was one of the great nights. Margot Fonteyn in *Giselle*. I could not help but observe Goldwyn and his reaction to what was taking place on stage. He was leaning forward in his seat, his hands clasped tightly. His lips were parted, and his small eyes had grown large.

During intermission, Goldwyn sat perfectly still, not wanting to talk or to step out to the lobby. He seemed to be digesting what he had seen and heard.

The *pas de deux* with Fonteyn and Robert Helpmann brought tears to Goldwyn's eyes. When it was over, he applauded and cheered. He got out his handkerchief, wiped his eyes, and blew his nose. At the end, he was the first one on his feet applauding and shouting "Bravo!"

"It was great," said Goldwyn at supper. "It was just great. I have to send that girl flowers. Remind me."

"Could I ask you something, Mr. Goldwyn?"

"Certainly," he said.

"Why did you want to see this tonight? Are you thinking of her for something in a picture? Or the company? Or what?"

I had hurt his feelings. "I wanted to see it," he said, "because I wanted to see it. Everything in my life isn't connected with my business. Do you think that? Is that what you think of me?"

"No, but I just wondered."

"The ballet," he said, "is something I've always loved. Maybe because when I first ran away from Poland—wherever I was, in Hamburg, in London, in America, I would love to go to the theatre. But mostly I had trouble with the language. So I started in to love the ballet wherever I was. Now, of course, I understand the language, but I still love the ballet, especially when it's great. Like tonight. She was wonderful—that Lynn Fontanne. The best I ever saw. Call me up tomorrow and remind me to send her some flowers. Some beautiful flowers."

I had reason to recall the evening a year or so later, in Hollywood. The American Ballet Theatre arrived to play an engagement. I was working at Columbia at the time and invited Harry Cohn to the opening.

"The opening of what?" he asked.

"The American Ballet Theatre," I replied.

"I can't stand ballet."

"Why not?"

"Because I don't like it where everybody chases everybody and nobody catches nobody."

A marked contrast, I reflected, between Cohn and Goldwyn, outwardly alike in many respects. The differences between them were small, yet vital.

"Harry," I said. "You've got no class."

"Who needs class? I've got money. That's *better* than class."

"I'm not so sure," I said.

"You think *you've* got class?" he demanded. "Your *wife's* got class. Not you."

"Who needs class," I said. "I've got money."

"You haven't got that either," he said. "Don't kid me."

"How do you know?" I asked.

"Because," he said, craftily, "if you had money, would you be working for a bum like me—with no class? I'll tell you who had class. Aly Khan."

"Come on, Harry," I said. "Let's talk seriously. I don't think I can define class, neither can you, neither can anybody."

"You're wrong again," he said. "I'll tell you about class. It was in the South of France and Aly was married to Rita Hayworth, and he'd bought the most beautiful château down there. I think he bought it from Lady Mendl. And he gave a party, A big dinner dance down there. Black tie and everything. Rita was pregnant. And out on this kind of terrace, they put down a dance floor. Right on the water. You know, overlooking. And it was really unbelievable, but the whole evening went on and Aly—you know how he loved to dance—and of course Rita Hayworth was about the best dancer there was—listen, for all I know, that's why he married her—and he danced with everybody. First this one and then that one and he danced with everybody but Rita. Who was his wife. I remember I said to Joan, 'It's like that song John Golden once wrote, "I Can Dance with Anybody but My Wife."' So Joan said to me, 'Maybe Rita's not *supposed* to dance. After all, she's six months' pregnant.' But finally—now you talk about class—finally, when Aly, the host, had danced with every woman there, there were about eight, he called the butler over and said something to him and the butler went out and in a few minutes all the lights on the terrace started to get dim. Because the butler was dimming them. And they got dimmer and dimmer until there was just a kind of a glow. And then Aly nodded to the little orchestra and they started to play a slow foxtrot. It was 'Night and Day,' and then he went over and got Rita. And he danced with her for the rest of the evening. And with nobody else. And if you don't think that's class, then you don't know what the hell you're talking about."

It is easy to understand why this event would appeal to Harry Cohn. For one thing, he admired its showmanship. For another, like most roughnecks, he admired gentlemen. Above all, he wanted to be one but had no notion of how to go about it.

This was a quality he shared with Sam Goldwyn. The difference was that Goldwyn made it.

CHAPTER 9

The making of a motion picture is an enterprise that requires at least a million decisions—great and small—to see it from conception to completion. A successful film is one on which most of the decisions have been correct; an unsuccessful film is the opposite. It comes down to the question: Who makes the decisions?

Professor Albert Einstein and his wife were being interviewed by the world press on the occasion of their golden wedding anniversary. They were asked the routine question: "To what do you attribute the success of your marriage?"

Professor Einstein took his wife's hand in his and replied, "Well, when we were first married fifty years ago—*Gott im Himmel!*—fifty years—we made a pact. It was this. That in our life together I would make all the *big* decisions and she would make all the *little* decisions. And we have kept to it for fifty years. That, I think, is the reason for the success of our marriage." Then he looked up, and added, "The strange thing is that in fifty years there hasn't yet been one big decision."

Things have changed, but in Hollywood until the 1950's, the final decisions, great and small, were made by the front offices, or by surrogates of those exalted founts of wisdom.

The head of the studio or the vice president in charge of production had his way. No writer, no star, no director of that period had the final say. Important directors were often replaced in mid-picture. Worse, they sometimes completed their work, only to have it taken out of their hands, recut, reshaped, and even reshot by the front office.

I have known many Hollywood producers and studio heads. Some are literate, sensitive, intelligent men. Others are two-fisted, business-oriented politicians. Still others are lucky idiots.

Harry Cohn was the founder and, until his death, head of Columbia Pictures. He was courageous, stubborn, energetic, ruthless, amiable, comical, attractive, gregarious—but above all, tough.

He had fought his way out of the hopelessness of poverty and had moved on to the periphery of show business. Because his innate talent lay in the area of salesmanship, he became a song plugger. Song pluggers were one of the principal means by which songs were promoted in the days before television, radio, and an extensive recording industry. They worked for the music publishers, and it was their job to get the publishers' songs performed in vaudeville, music halls, cabarets, restaurants, saloons, and stores. Most of them were performers of a sort. They would go around town, stand up, and sing the song.

Harry Cohn built a $400-million motion-picture empire but he was not as proud of it as he was of the fact that he alone had made a hit out of "Ragtime Cowboy Joe." Snapping his fingers on the afterbeat, he would begin to sing the catchy, bouncy words.

In mid-chorus he paused. "I liked that song. Liked! I *loved* it. Would you believe it? I would sometimes sing it fifty, sixty times a night. I'm talking about all over New York. Rector's, Shanley's, Reisenweber's, in dressing rooms, in agents' offices. I knew it was catchy and I knew if I plugged it enough, it would have to catch on. I was right. It did. Do you realize people still play it? And sing it? Even now? And you know how long ago I'm talking? Forty-five years. He taught me somethin', that 'Ragtime Cowboy Joe.' He taught me if you believe in somethin' and you stick with it and with what you believe in, no son of a bitch around is going to get ahead of you."

Harry Cohn was given to expressing himself with great vehemence. As he railed at his staff one morning about an unavoidable accident, an associate sitting close to him said, "Take it easy, Harry—you'll get an ulcer."

"I don't get ulcers," shouted Cohn. "I *give* 'em!"

There are many who worked with him across the years who would testify to the accuracy of this statement.

Norman Krasna was an early adversary. Young Krasna had written a play called *Louder Please* which was produced on Broadway and was something of a success. He returned to the studio in minor triumph, hoping for a great promotion, a plum assignment, or a raise. None of these was forthcoming. In an effort to break his contract, Krasna took to hectoring Cohn on every occasion.

Once, in the dining room, Cohn announced to the table, "I'm going to London next week."

"Take me with you, Mr. Cohn?" asked Krasna.

"You? What the hell do I need *you* for?"

"Interpreter?" suggested Krasna.

On another occasion, Cohn told his staff he was leaving for New York. In those days such trips were made by train. Krasna spoke up. "This time, Mr. Cohn, you've *got* to take me with you because on trains you have to write out your order for your meals."

"So what?"

"So what?" screamed Krasna in his high voice. "*You* can't write. You'll starve to death!"

Harry Cohn seemed to thrive on friction. He believed instinctively that it was only out of hostility, conflict, and abrasiveness that superior work could be created.

Harry enjoyed nothing more than he did a feud, a battle or a fight. Since he was not given to compromise, he achieved his share of hostilities. Perhaps the most intense and lengthy of his wrangles was the one that involved Jean Arthur.

Jean Arthur was unique and irreplaceable. She hardly needed a part written for her since she always brought along her own enchanting personality. She was one of Columbia Pictures' greatest assets and starred for Cohn in a brilliant series of films, including *Mr. Deeds Goes to Town,* *You Can't Take It With You,* and *Mr. Smith Goes to Washington.*

But she and Cohn did not often see eye to eye on material. Early in 1941, after Jean had turned down four of the pictures Cohn had offered her, he placed her on suspension and it appeared they were permanently deadlocked.

I was in the Army at the time, having recently been drafted, and stationed at Fort Monmouth, New Jersey. Jean and her husband, Frank Ross, were in New York for an extended stay. They were close friends, and I saw them every time I got a leave and came to New York.

From time to time, in order to strengthen his case, Harry Cohn would send Jean a script or a story or a book. She asked me to read some of this material for her. It seemed clear from the quality of the submissions that Cohn was simply going through the motions, that he would be horrified if by any chance Jean were to accept one of these scripts. Were this to occur, I believed he would find a way of pulling out.

I suggested to Jean and Frank that one way out of the dilemma would be for them to find a piece of suitable material and offer it to Cohn.

"He'd turn it down," said Jean.

"But what *if?*" I insisted. "What if you offered him a shooting script for nothing? Now that's something he couldn't resist."

"Maybe," Frank agreed.

"Sure," said Jean, "but where do we get one of those?"

"That's the next step," I said. "Let me think."

At Fort Monmouth, I had made a friend—a gangly charmer from California, named Robert Wallace Russell. He occupied the bunk next to mine, but for the first week or so of our proximity, we exchanged no more than a morose grunt now and again. Morale was low.

At 3:15 one morning, I awoke from a nightmare in which I had become a paratrooper who knew that when his turn came, he would not be able to jump. As I opened my eyes, I saw my bunkmate sitting on the edge of his cot, fully dressed, pressed, and carefully groomed. He simply sat, apparently thinking. It was a rare sight.

I raised myself on an elbow, squinted at him, and asked, "What's the matter, buddy? Can't you sleep?"

He looked back at me through his always-droopy eyes and replied, seriously, "It's my dreams. They *bore* me."

I knew at once we were going to be friends.

Bob had been trained in architecture; had gone to work for Walt Disney; had written fiction, plays, and screenplays; was an accomplished documentarian; and had written an impressive monograph on the subject of the dynamic screen, offering imaginative ideas for changing the size and shape of the conventional screen.

Some time later, when we were both placed on detached service to the New York headquarters of the film division of the Office for Emergency Management, we rented a small but ridiculously expensive house in New York—a reaction against our ghastly months in the barracks.

It occurred to me that Bob might assist in the Jean Arthur situation. I asked Frank Ross if he and Jean would be prepared to pay $25,000 for that screenplay we were looking for. I was delighted when Frank agreed, since a solution of Jean's problems might also be a solution to ours. Ours was that we were flat broke, drawing Army pay, and borrowing heavily.

At dinner that night, I said to Bob, "Listen, how would you like to make twenty-five thousand dollars?"

Bob chewed his lamb chop slowly and did not reply. Woolgathering, I diagnosed, and achieved his attention with a snap of my fingers in front of his nose.

"Bob!" I repeated with increased projection.

There was a long pause during which he regarded me fretfully. Then he asked, "Would it be hard work?"

We eventually developed something out of an idea for a play Bob had once had: a girl in an overcrowded city rents half of her apartment, for economic reasons, to an elderly gentleman. The elderly gentleman, in turn, rents half of his half to an attractive young man. Now all three are sharing a single apartment. Take it from there.

A weekend trip to Washington, D.C., proved to be the catalyst for the completion of the story. Wartime Washington was the ideal city for the situation. We returned to New York and wrote, with youthful speed and laughing all the way, a screenplay that Bob titled *Two's a Crowd*. This was delivered in due course to Jean Arthur and Frank Ross, who responded as we had hoped they would.

We could not imagine Harry Cohn turning it down, especially since he was going to get it free of charge. On the other hand, we could not imagine him, hostile as he was toward Jean, sitting down to read a script she had submitted. He would probably toss it routinely to a reader for a swift report, and who knew where that might lead?

When I learned accidentally from a film editor at Columbia that Harry Cohn was coming to New York, an idea struck me.

Although we had never met, I phoned Harry Cohn. He took my call and could not have been more cordial—until I mentioned Jean Arthur.

"Jean Arthur!" he shouted. "Don't talk to me about any goddam Jean Arthurs. If they were all like her there wouldn't be any *pictures*. She don't want to work, she only wants to aggravate *me*. You know how many scripts she's turned down? In a row?"

"Seven," I said.

"How the hell do you know that?" he asked.

"She told me."

"She did, huh? *Nine!* She's a liar on top of everything else. Not seven. Nine."

"All right," I said. "Nine. I'll tell her."

"Don't tell her. Stay out of this. Why don't you mind your own business?"

"Well, look, Mr. Cohn. I'm just trying to—"

"Harry," he said, firmly. "Not Mr. Cohn. Harry. Call me Harry. You're not that young and I'm not that old."

"All right, Harry. Listen. A friend of mine—terrific writer— and I have written a screenplay, and we've sold it to Jean."

"Are you nuts?" he shouted. "Sold it to *Jean!* Who's Jean? What *is* she? A studio? A producer? What's she going to do with it? Sit on it? She can't work for anybody, any place—except for me. What the hell is *she* going to do with a screenplay?"

"Well, I'll tell you, if you'll calm down," I said.

"I'm calm. Go ahead."

"She's going to give it to you."

"What do you mean 'give'?" he asked suspiciously. "What does she mean?"

"For nothing. Free. If you like it, it's yours."

He was thoroughly rattled by this unexpected strategy.

I went on. "And you're wrong about her not wanting to work. She does. More than anything."

"A script for *nothing?*" asked Cohn, in all disbelief.

"There's only one condition—" I began.

"I knew it!" he shouted exultantly.

Even over the telephone I could sense his resistance stiffening.

"Very simple," I said quietly. "I want to come over and read it to you. I think it's great and so does Jean and so does Frank. It's a comedy. Hilarious. And romantic. It's about wartime Washington and it's got three terrific parts and—"

"What do you mean, 'read it to me,' you stupid bastard? What do you think? I can't read?"

"All right, Mr. Cohn," I said. "Never mind."

"Wait a second," he said.

I hung up.

It was a calculated risk, but in the circumstance I thought it worth taking. In five minutes my phone rang.

"I have Mr. Cohn for you," said a breathless operator.

"Fine," I said. "Put him on."

His voice was icy as he said, "I think we got cut off."

"No," I said. "I hung up."

"You hung up on me?" he asked. "Is that what you're trying to tell me?"

"I thought our conversation was over, Harry. I thought we both hung up."

"I did," he said. "What do you think? I'm gonna sit there hold an empty phone like a schmuck? I hung up."

"That's what I said. We both hung up."

This seemed to satisfy him.

"Okay," he said. "So when do you want to come over and read that crap out loud?"

"How about tomorrow morning?" I asked.

"All right," he said. "Come on up to my office."

"Ten o'clock," I said.

"Don't be late. And we'll see."

I rehearsed the reading with my cohorts and at ten o'clock the following morning presented myself at the offices of Columbia Pictures.

I was shown into Mr. Cohn's office. He had gathered a small group of his executive assistants. Having met only his voice, so to speak, the rest of him surprised me. I found him attractive, magnetic, and charming. He was beautifully dressed and every detail of his appearance showed care.

After a few empty amenities and casual introductions, Cohn said, "Okay, go ahead. They all know what it's all about, these guys."

I took the script out of my briefcase and said, "It's called *Two's a Crowd.*"

"Don't worry about it," said Cohn. "We can change it."

Again I recognized a crucial moment.

"Before I begin," I said, "there's just one thing I insist on and that is—"

"Don't *ever* use that word around *me*," said Cohn, tightly. "'Insist.' Nobody does." He looked around the room. "Tell him," he added.

"How about 'request'?" I asked.

"Request all you want," said Cohn.

"I'd just like the opportunity of reading this to you from beginning to end without interruption."

"Go ahead," said Cohn.

I began to read.

Almost at once, I noticed a few smiles. At one point there was a little laugh, then a big laugh led by Cohn. I reached the end of the opening and was about to begin on the body of the script when Cohn held up a hand and said, "Hold it."

I was annoyed, looked at him and said, "I thought we agreed—"

"I'll take it," said Cohn.

"What?"

"You heard me. I'll take it. I'm no dummy. I know pictures. Any picture starts like that I'll take it."

"But you don't even know the story."

"Sure I do. You told it to me on the telephone."

"I did?"

"You told me all I got to know."

He rose. "This is great. Tell Ross to come in here and we'll fix it up. And I'll tell you another thing. I don't take nothin' for nothin'. I'll make a deal with him. Some kind of a deal. It's going to be a swell picture."

We shook hands again and I was out on Seventh Avenue before I knew it, without the script, looking for a telephone to convey the news to Jean.

The picture was beautifully made by George Stevens not long afterward. Starring Jean, Joel McCrea, and Charles Coburn, it proved to be Columbia's greatest success that year.

True to his word, Cohn changed the title to *The More the Merrier*. Untrue to his word, he never reimbursed Jean Arthur for any part of the twenty-five thousand she paid to Russell. My own part in it remained anonymous because I was still under contract to RKO. No matter. It was a joyous affair all around.

Moreover, it taught me the trick of selling Harry Cohn screenplays. From that day forward I made it a point to read scripts to Cohn, a move he accepted cheerfully. He did not always buy what I read to him, but he always gave me a fair chance.

One of the scripts I read aloud to Harry and his wife, Joan, during an evening at his home was *The Marrying Kind*, which I had written in collaboration with my wife, Ruth Gordon. After dinner, the reading went extremely well with both Mr. and Mrs. Cohn offering congratulatory punctuation from time to time. Less welcome was another sort of punctuation the evening offered. This came in the form of telephone calls from Cohn's broker, his bookie, two or three agents, and several mystery guests.

It made for a rocky evening but at the end Cohn accepted the material.

Under the influence of Somerset Maugham and the accounts of his Spartan working discipline, my wife and I were attempting to follow his good example.

Despite the fact that we were theatre-oriented people, accustomed to late nights and late risings, we changed all that—rose at seven, got to work by eight, worked until noon, and then got ready for lunch. After lunch we would drive down to our offices, then located in the St. James Theatre building on West Forty-fourth Street.

One evening, as we were driving down, I noticed that Ruth was uncharacteristically depressed. I tried to cheer her up using a few proven methods, but on this day they all failed. As we traversed Columbus Circle I noticed an enormous sign which was blank except for a square of rental information in its center.

"You know what I'm going to do?" I said brightly. "I'm going to rent that sign and have 'RUTH GORDON' painted on it in the biggest letters it will hold. How would you like that?"

Not a sound. Apparently she had not even heard. We continued down to the office. An hour later, Ruth told me she was going out to walk.

I was still thinking of that sign on Columbus Circle and began to wonder what it actually would cost. I had no idea, and phoned the rental agency to inquire.

To my surprise it turned out to be about $200 a month. I had thought it was going to be ten times that. I then found out what it would cost to have it painted. This, too, was within practical limits. I became giddy as I felt myself moving toward the fruition of this nutty idea. By evening, I thought better of it.

The look on my wife's face when I described what I had been planning to do as a surprise told me I had made the correct decision in abandoning it. But the notion stayed in my head and without meaning to do so, I began to plot a fiction involving such an act.

What if there were an attractive, but discouraged young man who has been beaten down by the city? He had come to New York a year earlier, confident he would make good somehow, that he would make a name for himself, that he would get there. It has all gone wrong and he has just about decided to take what is left of his savings and go back home. He walks around in Central Park, dejected. At Columbus Circle he looks up and sees that empty sign. He decides upon one final satisfying gesture. He rents the sign and has his name emblazoned upon it. One thing leads to another, and in the way of our world he becomes a celebrity, one of those who is famous for being a celebrity. Now where? Perhaps he runs for office and gets elected and so on and so on. I played with the idea for a few weeks and finally had, in my head, what I thought was a solid story.

We were asked to come up to Boston to see a friend's play. On the way up I told Ruth my story. She listened carefully, intently, then said, "It's good but it's wrong."

"What do you mean, wrong?"

"Wrong sex," she said. "Think how much better that story would be if a *girl* did it. A girl makes it whimsical and special and audacious. If a man does it, he's just being pushy or dumb."

"I don't agree with you," I said.

"All right. But it feels like Judy Holliday to me."

"Fine," I said, "but it's going to be Danny Kaye."

A few days after we returned from Boston, I decided I was ready to turn my story into a screenplay. I began to write and even now I cannot explain how it was that my young man turned into a young woman, that Danny Kaye changed his name to Judy Holliday, and *A Name for Himself* became *A Name for Herself*.

When it was finished, I handed it to Ruth and said, "I've done that movie about the fellow who puts his name up on the sign in Columbus Circle."

"Good," she said.

When she had read it, she said, "I like it very much. Who do you see as the fellow?"

"Judy Holliday," I replied.

"Yes," she said. "He'd be good."

We went to Hollywood to present it to Harry Cohn. We assembled in the library of his home on Crescent Drive: Harry with his cigar, Joan with her knitting, my wife with her confidence, and me with my nerves.

I finished the reading and Harry responded with special enthusiasm because he needed a picture for Judy Holliday.

I had not directed a commercial film since *Tom, Dick and Harry* just before the war but I was anxious to do this one on several accounts. First, I enjoyed working with Judy Holliday. Second, the film could probably be made in New York. Also, it would be the first time I had ever directed anything of my own for the screen, and I was eager to learn if such an undertaking was practical. I insisted on doing the final cut myself.

Cohn made a fair offer for the screenplay and an overgenerous offer, I thought, for the direction. However, he dismissed my major condition out of hand.

The agents argued with him for several days and reported to me that it was no use. Cohn would not yield on this point.

The argument went on serving only, as do most arguments, to make each adversary cling more firmly to his own view. I finally sold the script to Harry Cohn and went to Europe for three years. I realized, sadly, that for the moment, there was no place in Hollywood for me.

"Listen," Cohn said to me one Sunday afternoon, "anybody tells you they're a starmaker, tell 'em they're a knucklehead. I broke my ass tryin' to make a star out of Kim Novak. So what happens? She turned out to be Kim Novak. I tell y', I gave 'er the best scripts, the top directors, I brought in Jean Louis, and other terrific designers, hairdressers, makeup people, coaches. And if she had to sing, we dubbed her. And if she had to dance, we tricked it. She was a beautiful girl, she was willing, too. We put her in one picture after another. Nothing, nothing, nothing. She had talent, mind y'. In fact, she was good. But, God damn it, she didn't have that one thing, that plain one thing makes a star. Kim Novak. Jesus. Her name was Marilyn Novack, but everybody would've thought we were trying to make it sound like Monroe. So we picked 'Kim.' And we did a big campaign on 'er, and then we started 'er out in a movie with the name *Pushover*. Beautiful little blonde. How old could she have been at the time? Twenty-three, twenty-four? Sound good? Nothing. Then we stuck her with Judy Holliday and Jack Lemmon in *Phffft* by George Axelrod. Is *that* bad? I figured workin' alongside of Judy some of the talent, some of the magic might rub off, right? Nothing. So then we put 'er with Sinatra yet in *The Man with the Golden Arm*. Preminger. The picture was sensational, Sinatra came through like Gangbusters—but her? Nothing. Then the biggest hit in the world, *Picnic*. She struck out in that one, too. *Jeanne Eagels*. Well, maybe that was a mistake. Then we gave her *Pal Joey*, *again* with Sinatra. *Bell, Book and Candle*. And I tell y' about now I began to give up because I began to see that she was okay, this kid, but no star. No. The public just didn't grab onto her. . . . Look, I've tried it before. Sometimes it works, so you get the idea you're doing it. But that's the bunk. It's always the *public* who's doing it."

"I'm inclined to agree with you, Harry," I said. "I remember an evening some time ago when L. B. Mayer—considered quite a starmaker, huh?—came over to Ruth and me in a restaurant in New York. And he sat down and said to us, 'Why don't you people write a picture for Howard Keel? We're building him, so we can use material. He's going to make Bogart and Tracy and Gable and all those other bums look sick in a couple of years. They're old men, they're on the way down, but Keel, he's going up like a rocket.'

"Well, nobody can deny that Keel is a gifted fellow—handsome, tall, good actor, splendid singer. But that big breakthrough never happened."

"Listen," said Cohn. "L.B. was good—as good as the best—as me or Goldwyn or J.L.—anybody. But we none of us are God. And only God can make a tree."

"A tree?" I asked. "I thought we were discussing stars. So what's a tree got to do with it?"

"You didn't let me finish. That's another thing with you. Always buttin' in, interrupting. What I was sayin' was, 'Only God can make a tree, and only the public can make a star!' Satisfied?"

"Yes."

"Yes? Well, you're *still* wrong. My property department can make the best goddam tree you ever saw!"

"But not a star."

"But not a star."

CHAPTER 10

Every movie star is a leading character in a fairy tale. Once upon a time (July 16, 1911, in Independence, Missouri), a little girl was born. She was christened Virginia Katherine McMath. While she was still young, her mother and father were divorced. Her mother resumed her maiden name, Lela Rogers, and took little Virginia to Hollywood. Lela tried without success to break into the movie business as a scenario writer. Virginia, aged six, was offered an acting contract. Her mother turned it down.

They moved to Texas. Lela went to work for *The Fort Worth Star* as a reporter, later became its theatre critic. Virginia Katherine began to dance, sing, mimic, and act on the local amateur show-business scene. Before long she was signed as a substitute dancer by Eddie Foy, who was touring his act.

The Charleston struck, a dance craze such as had never before been known. The vitality of the dance suited Virginia's style perfectly. She became an expert. Charleston contests were being held everywhere. Virginia won them all, and minor fame as well. An enterprising vaudeville producer put together an act around her. "Ginger and Her Redheads." Virginia Katherine McMath was no more. Ginger Rogers Charlestoned her way across Texas, through Oklahoma, across the Midwest and found herself, eventually, at the Oriental Theatre in Chicago.

One week, a comedian named Jack Pepper was on the bill. His real name was John Edward Culpepper, but he thought Jack Pepper more suitable. He found Ginger Rogers pretty suitable, too, and in 1929 she became Mrs. Jack Pepper. The marriage lasted no more than two years.

She did a musical short with Rudy Vallee called *Campus Sweethearts*, but no one seemed to take notice. She went to New York and worked constantly in clubs, in vaudeville. Out on the road. Fairs.

She landed a small part in a Broadway musical called *Top Speed*, and made an impression. This led to her first feature picture, a Paramount film shot in the East, *Young Man of Manhattan*. She played a supporting part opposite Charlie Ruggles, sang a song called "I've Got *It* but *It* Don't Do Me No Good," and spoke that unforgettable line—"Cigarette me, big boy!" It was echoed through the 1930's.

More movies, then Broadway again: George Gershwin's *Girl Crazy*. In this, at long last, she made an enormous hit. Her career was under way. For Pathé, she made *The Tip-Off*. Then came *The Suicide Fleet*, *Carnival Boat*, *The Tenderfoot*, *Hat Check Girl*.

"I did anything in those days," Ginger recalls. "I just wanted to stay an actress. I did second leads and third leads and straight pictures and musicals and mysteries. The truth is I don't even remember all the pictures I made. They'd just say, 'Go to Stage Eleven,' and hand you some script and you'd learn it and go on and do it and a lot of the time I didn't even know the *name* of the picture. Then it happened. Finally. That great, wonderful, unbelievable accident—getting together with Fred Astaire. I was under some kind of a nothing contract to RKO, and Thornton Freeland was going to do a musical."

"When was this?"

"About nineteen thirty-three, I think. Or thirty-four. Gene Raymond was the leading man and Dolores Del Rio was the leading lady. And there were these two small parts. They didn't really tie in as I remember but they knew we could do a number. The idea in those days was to get an idea for a dance, and then they'd have somebody write a song for it. Well, in this picture—*Flying Down to Rio*—it was 'The Carioca,' by Vincent Youmans, and what a song that was!

"Fred hadn't been having too great a time in pictures either. Of course, he was a star on Broadway teamed up with his sister, Adele, but even though he had done these tremendous shows on Broadway, they didn't cotton to him out here. They made a test and Fred once told me that the report on his test read, 'Can't act. Slightly bald. Dances a little.' But because they were thinking of doing musicals, RKO signed him and right away loaned him to M-G-M to do one little number in *Dancing Lady* with Joan Crawford. Then *Flying Down to Rio* —'The Carioca'—hit for both of us."

"I'll say," I said. "I'll never forget it. It tore up the screen. Nobody'd ever seen a dance team like that. Not on the screen, anyway."

"And we were off," she said. "They saw right away what they had and Pan Berman bought one of Fred's big hits, *The Gay Divorce*, with that Cole Porter score. 'Night and Day.' My God, was *that* something! You remember how they had to change the title of the picture because the Hays Office wouldn't let them call it *The Gay Divorce?* So it had to be *The Gay Divorcée*. Anyway, that was a real hit for us, and the dance they stuck in that one was called 'The Continental.' Then we did *Roberta*, and after that Irving Berlin wrote *Top Hat* for us. Those were some days. I don't think I ever worked so hard in my whole life. That Fred. He never stopped till he dropped. And that's how he made you feel, too. A lot of wonderful things've happened to me, but that was the greatest. All we thought about was the work and making each picture better than the one we'd done before."

The Astaire-Rogers output was carefully marshaled. They made a picture a year for a time. No more. In between, Ginger made other pictures, usually straight, while Fred and Hermes Pan brooded about numbers for the next Astaire-Rogers.

Ginger was ever ambitious and courageous.

John Ford was on the RKO lot preparing to make *Mary of Scotland* with Katharine Hepburn and Fredric March. The studio had bought the successful Maxwell Anderson play and was planning it as one of its most important productions of the year.

In Anderson's version of the story, there is a small but showy part—Queen Elizabeth. Anderson had taken the dramatic license of giving Mary and Elizabeth a great scene together, although history has no record of their meeting. Anderson's point was that they *should* have met.

Ginger had seen the play in New York. Perhaps because she envisioned herself stealing the picture with a comparatively small part, she went to Pandro Berman and announced that she wanted to play Queen Elizabeth.

He said no, but Ginger did not get where she was by taking no for an answer. She persisted. He argued against it, saying he had no intention of putting one of his big stars into a small part.

"There are no small parts," said Ginger loftily. "Only small actors."

Pandro had never heard this old theatre chestnut and was momentarily impressed.

"I'll tell you what I'm willing to do, Pan," she said, "and you can't turn me down on this because I'm asking it as a personal favor and one of these days you're going to be asking *me* for a favor. So what I'm asking is this. Let me make a test for it. Okay?"

"Okay," said Berman wearily.

Ginger did not insist upon making the test immediately. She wanted time to prepare. She engaged Constance Collier to coach her. She asked Mel Berns, head of the RKO makeup department, to work with her.

Berns went all the way. He shaved part of her head, painted an Elizabethan face on her, and shot some makeup tests secretly on a weekend without letting anyone know he was doing it.

On another weekend, the test itself was made, with full makeup and costume and other players. The story is that they put a phony name on the slate. Constance Elliot. When the test came on in the projection room, everyone went wild.

"Sign that girl!"

Later, they found that the object of their enthusiasm was their own Ginger Rogers.

It was left to Berman to talk her out of the idea.

One of Ginger's successes was *Stage Door.* George S. Kaufman and Edna Ferber had written the play, and following its Broadway run the film rights were acquired by RKO. By the time Gregory LaCava, the director, and Morrie Ryskind, the screenwriter, had finished, the result was something like a distant cousin to the original *Stage Door.* A rough cut was shown to Kaufman.

"Have you any suggestions?" he was asked.

"Only one," he replied. "I think under the circumstances you ought to call it 'Screen Door.'"

Another Kaufman title idea comes to mind. Howard Hughes was spending a part of his fortune in an attempt to make a star of Jane Russell. He succeeded to the extent that she was well known to the public even before she made her first film. Each publicity still revealed more of her capacious major endowment. When at last the film was ready for release, it seemed that every twenty-four sheet in New York bore that famous, reclining figure and its beckoning bosom over the title *The Outlaw.*

Walking down Broadway, George and I counted five such billboards.

"They've got the wrong title on that picture," he said.

Ever the straight man for him, I asked, "And what is the *right* title, George?"

"They ought to call it," he replied, "'A Sale of Two Titties.'"

In Ginger's day, stars had power. She had been at RKO as one of their most important contract stars for seven years.

Sometime after she left RKO, she went to Paramount to do *Lady in the Dark*. Paramount and RKO were neighboring studios but since each lot involved several acres, distances were considerable. At RKO, Ginger had always had her own suite of dressing rooms, improved and refurbished and enlarged each year to keep her happy. Finally, it was a large establishment with a kitchen, bedroom, sitting room, hairdressing and makeup room, wardrobe and fitting room, and so on. At Paramount they tried to outdo RKO and furnished her with a spacious bungalow in addition to an impressive trailer to use as a portable dressing room, and a special rig for location days.

One day, the director, Mitch Leisen, was shooting a fantasy sequence, with a cloud effect. The floor would never be seen. The dance number was going to be done in and around the mist.

The special-effects men were in charge. They are among the Hollywood elite, difficult to replace: technicians with mysterious secrets. This time, even they were having their problems. The area was huge, three connected sound stages. The special-effects men had never attempted to cloud as large an area as this and apparently did not have sufficient equipment. By the time they had finished clouding the last part, the first part had begun to disappear.

Work continued all morning. Miss Rogers was ready, made up, and rehearsed, the playback track was ready, as was the chorus, but the clouds were not. Finally, Leisen broke for lunch. The special-effects men stayed and tried to figure out new ways to proceed.

A little after three in the afternoon—the company dispirited at not having made a shot all day—the special-effects men and the cameramen pronounced it ready.

Ginger started for the set but stopped and said to Leisen, "I'll be right back."

"What're you *talking* about?"

She leaned closer to him and said, "I'm sorry, Mitch, but I've got to go."

"Jesus, Ginger!" said Leisen. "We've been working for seven hours. It's all set. It's delicate. Critical. Couldn't you just do it once?"

"I *have* to go to the *bathroom*, Mitch," said Ginger tightly.

"Couldn't you—couldn't we just make the one shot, honey? Just one?"

"Mitch, I've got to *dance* in it and everything. I've got to go."

"All right, Ginger. But listen, for God's sake, will you hurry up?"

Leisen informed the special-effects men that they would have to hold the effect for a few minutes. They were lying all over the sound stage with gas masks on and slowly pumping the clouds in.

"Keep pumping it in. Don't let it go. Keep it even."

Every few minutes the camera operator had to wipe the oil off the lens. The extras were ready and standing by.

"Nobody leave the set, now!" shouted Leisen. "We're going to shoot this in about one minute, one minute and a half."

The minute did indeed get to be a minute and a half. Then five. Ten. Fifteen. Twenty minutes later it was hopeless.

"All right. Kill 'em."

The effort had gone for nothing. The company and the crew sat and waited. About forty-five minutes later Ginger came sailing on the set.

Mitch Leisen, who had aged several years in the forty-five minutes, looked at her and said, "Where the hell have you been?"

"Don't talk to me like that," said Ginger. "I have a perfect right to go to the bathroom."

"It took you forty-five minutes to go to the bathroom?" he asked outraged. "Where the hell did you go?"

"Why, to RKO," she said logically.

Mitch Leisen began to laugh uncontrollably.

When he told me about it he said, "We never did get the shot that day. In fact, we didn't get it for another two or three days. But that thing with Ginger, it was sort of a Pavlovian thing. They'd given her this beautiful dressing room at Paramount and she had a sensational portable, but she was accustomed to her own pot, that's all. She'd been seven years in that dressing room at RKO, and we found out later that she wasn't using the Paramount accommodations at all. First thing in the morning, she'd go to her own old rooms at RKO and get made up and dressed and then she'd drive through the gate from one lot onto the other lot, and that's how she worked it. So naturally when she had to go to the bathroom, she went back to her old studio. I mean, she was a *star* when she was a star."

CHAPTER 11

In a business as complex, as diversified as the film business, agents and agencies are frequently important as catalysts, go-betweens, and matchmakers. Looking back on it all, I find that there are a larger number of agents I admire than there are producers. Agents have frequently been helpful and creative, even imaginative.

I am convinced that we would never have known the joy of Marilyn Monroe had it not been for an extraordinary agent named Johnny Hyde.

He had what used to be called "a roving eye." When finally it lit on an obscure, unemployed, struggling film actress named Marilyn Monroe, the roving stopped. Johnny Hyde, at that time a senior partner in the William Morris Agency, and a multimillionaire, was about fifty. He fell in love with Marilyn, and she fell in love with him.

His belief in her future as a screen personality was every bit as passionate as his love for her.

I was subjected to a barrage of pressures and arguments having to do with her suitability for the leading role of Billie Dawn in *Born Yesterday*, which I had sold to Columbia Pictures.

Finally, after a month of scheming, Marilyn Monroe did make a test for the part. Those who saw it thought it was excellent. But Harry Cohn, the head of the studio, did not trouble to take the six steps from his desk to his projection room to look at her.

Despite Cohn's indifference, and Johnny's failure to get anyone in a key position to see Marilyn through his eyes, he persisted. It was with no little embarrassment that I once said to him, "Johnny, you're a darling fellow and a wonderful agent, but you certainly are a bore on the subject of Marilyn. Give it a rest, will you?"

"You'll see," said Johnny, pointing up at me. "You'll *see!* They'll *all* see. This kid has really got it. It's not just her looks, although everybody admits she's a knockout, but she's got the spirit. And she's funny. And a hell of an actress. And what's more important, she wants to do it. She wants to get there and be somebody. And people who have that kind of drive, nobody can put them down. Nobody."

"All right, Johnny," I said. "All *right*."

Johnny Hyde prevailed upon his friend John Huston to let Marilyn test for the part of Louis Calhern's mistress in *The Asphalt Jungle*. Huston responded to her, spotted her beautifully in the film, and she made an impression.

It was Marilyn's luck, and his, and ours, that Joseph L. Mankiewicz was also a client of the William Morris Agency. At Twentieth Century-Fox he was preparing *All About Eve*. Johnny read the script and found a small but effective part that he thought would be right for Marilyn. He badgered Mankiewicz until Mankiewicz agreed. Then the Twentieth Century-Fox front office vetoed the idea.

Johnny did not give up, took it to the top, which at that time meant Darryl F. Zanuck. Again luck. Zanuck owed Johnny a favor and Johnny called his note. Marilyn got the part in *All About Eve* as George Sanders' girl friend, a minor actress described in the picture as "a graduate of the Copacabana School of Dramatic Art."

"It wouldn't have happened, any of it," she once said to me, "if not for Johnny. When I did *The Asphalt Jungle*, it was like that was some kind of a discovery. But Jesus, I'd been knocking around, and I mean knocking around, for about six years before that, modeling and everything. And finally Howard Hughes got interested. That was nothing. And then Twentieth and getting kicked out. And then Columbia, and that turned out another nothing. And did you see me in *Love Happy* with the Marx Brothers? I was good in that, but nobody knew it. And *A Ticket to Tomahawk*. I swear I was getting ready to give up and maybe learn to be a negative cutter like my mother or something—at least make a living. And that's when Johnny Hyde happened. Look, I had plenty of friends and acquaintances—you know what I mean, acquaintances? And, sure, I played the game the way everyone else was playing it. But not one of them, not one of those big shots, ever did a damn thing for me, not one, except Johnny. Because he believed in me."

"He loved you," I said.

"I know it. And I loved him."

Those luminous eyes moistened as she continued. "You know what a creep town this is and, naturally, when I was living with Johnny, it was like I was doing it because he could do me some good. He was the first kind man I ever met in my whole life. I've known a few since, but he was the first. And smart. When he died like that, all of a sudden, I really thought maybe my whole life was over, too. But just before he died, he got me this contract with Twentieth, a second one. And without him around to promote me—It's something I don't know how to do. I mean, I know how to put my body over, but I don't know how to put *myself* over. Does that make sense?"

She went on. "So after then, it was practically nothing but loan-outs and cheesecake. And I don't know what would've happened if it hadn't of been for that whole thing with the bare-ass calendar."

"What whole thing?" I asked. I knew the story, but I wanted to hear it from her.

"Well, somebody in the modeling business told me they were going to make some art calendars. And it was for a lot of money, which I needed at the time. And when I got there, they wanted me to pose in the nude. So I said, 'Nothing doing!' So they upped the ante, and finally I took a drink and thought, What the hell. This guy, the photographer, he told me that for a calendar in color, they were going to do it with a lot of silk screen and a lot of retouching and he said, 'Listen, nobody's ever going to know it's you by the time we get finished. After all, you look like a lot of other bimbos and *they* look like *you*, so if the subject ever comes up, you can just say it's *not* you.' Well, anyway, we did it. And he was right, it hardly *did* look like me. And I guess nothing would've happened about it, except when I got to be a little well known, these bastards who owned the rights to the calendar started putting it out by the millions. And, of course, said it was me. My new agent, I thought he was going to drop dead, and, of course, the studio was upset. And then my press agent came up with that great line, you know, when they ask me if, during the posing, I had anything on. And I said, 'Yes, the radio.' And all of a sudden, even those dumbheads at the studio began to see that it wasn't such bad publicity. It was sort of good publicity because it was kind of sassy. So that's when they stuck me right across the top of that whole *Niagara* billboard and, I don't know, things sort of got going from there. But I tell you again, it wouldn't have happened without my Johnny Hyde. None of it."

Marilyn Monroe was starring in *How to Marry a Millionaire*. The screenplay had been written by Nunnally Johnson, who, in self-defense, was also producing the picture. Marilyn had a short, but complicated scene to shoot, involving breakfast in bed and a simultaneous phone call. The director, Jean Negulesco, explained the routine patiently. Marilyn listened patiently. They rehearsed for about an hour, but she appeared to be getting more and more confused.

Negulesco decided to shoot the scene and pray. Maybe something would happen. When everyone was ready, and the lights, and the camera, they began the scene. Again, Marilyn became hopelessly confused, answering the phone before it rang, drinking out of the coffee cup before she had filled it and so on.

"Cut!"

"One more."

The one more became six more, sixteen more, twenty-six more, and still the shot had not been made. Something went wrong each time. It was approaching six o'clock and Negulesco could already hear the production office explosions when they saw on the sheet that not a foot of film had been produced all afternoon. He was desperately anxious to make this one shot at least. He kept trying. No success. He sent for

Nunnally Johnson and asked if perhaps something could be done to simplify the scene. Johnson simplified it. They tried two more takes, then decided to give up. It was six o'clock. Time had run out.

Negulesco sank down in his chair and put his head into his hands.

Marilyn sat up in bed, looking bemused. Nunnally Johnson, a warm and benign figure, went up to Marilyn, took her hand, and said, "We'll do it in the morning, honey. Don't worry about it."

"Don't worry about what?" asked Marilyn.

Nunnally reports that he dropped her hand in astonishment.

CHAPTER 12

"Can I see you a minute? A *half* a minute, Grouch?"

Groucho Marx put down his cards (he didn't have anything anyway), picked up his cigar, and got up from the table.

There were few who could achieve this instant response. Harry Ruby was one of them. He was perhaps Groucho's oldest friend.

Groucho followed Harry out onto a secluded terrace of the Hillcrest Country Club.

Harry looked to his right, his left, then over his shoulder.

"Get goin'," said Groucho, in his celebrated nasal monotone. "You're beginning to look like George M. Cohan in *The Tavern.*"

Harry stepped closer to Groucho.

"Shall we dance?" asked Groucho. He took Harry into his arms and began a waltz.

Harry disengaged himself roughly and said, "Cut the comedy, Grouch, this is serious."

"What is?"

"I'm in a situation, and you've got to do me a favor."

"Sure, Harry, if I can."

"Look, it's a quarter to twelve. At three o'clock, I've got two girls coming to the bungalow."

(The bungalow was Harry's "studio" in South Beverly Hills; ostensibly a workplace, actually an assignation point.)

Groucho regarded him. "You're sure it isn't three girls at two o'clock?"

"I mean it, Grouch. It was a misunderstanding and now I can't get out of it without a whole lot of trouble. What am I going to do with two girls?"

"Harry, what do you want from me? Let me go back to the game."

"The hell with that game!" shouted Harry. "I'm offering you a better game. A matinee. A foursome."

"Harry, let me ask you something. Do you know how old I am?"

"Not exactly, no." Groucho looked right, left, and behind him, in imitation of Harry's earlier moves. Then he said softly, "Fifty-nine."

"So what? I'm two years older."

"Three."

"Two."

"Three!"

"Two!"

"Four."

"Three."

"All right."

"So?"

"So I'm through, Harry. I'm finished with that foolishness."

"You should be at your peak," said Harry.

"That's about all I *can* do," said Groucho, "is peek. Don't get me wrong, Harry. I'm not bitter. I've had my share, nice while it lasted. Now I'm interested in other things. Books, and so on."

Harry looked at him with compassion and said, "Listen, my old friend, you're just like *I* was about two and a half years ago. Then, thank God, my doctor sent me to this specialist."

"In what?" asked Groucho.

"In power. He gave me this shot, and the same day—*the same day,* mind you—"

"Yes?"

"I *functioned.* And, since then, I take a shot a week, sometimes two, and I live. And I want *you* to live too, Grouch. Hear me out. This is my plan. Let me call the doctor, this doctor. I'll make an appointment. Then we'll have a bite, you and me, and we'll drive down. He'll give you the shot. And three o'clock, you'll see."

"Harry, for God's sake, you're embarrassing me."

But Harry Ruby, a persistent man, persisted. He continued to talk, to sell. In time he had hypnotized Groucho and had him in his car, speeding down Wilshire Boulevard to the Wilshire Medical Building.

In the parking lot, Groucho hesitated again. But Harry, artfully describing the joys that lay immediately ahead, led him into the building and propelled him into the big elevator, peopled with wheel-chair cases, the very old, babes in arms, bandaged heads, and one trembling victim of Parkinson's disease.

Harry, troubled that Groucho might bolt at any moment, held on to his arm tightly. When the elevator was full, the operator closed the doors and the gate and called out, "Floors, please. Speak up."

"I can't get a hard-on!" shouted Groucho. "What floor is that?"

Harry Ruby swears that the elevator went up fourteen floors without stopping, then came down, one floor at a time, bouncing.

Hollywood was a raunchy, hip, swinging community. Can it be that its wild private life was a revolt against its overcensored public life?

American whorehouses are not, by and large, as interesting as the French, Japanese, or Scandinavian varieties. However, I found one in Hollywood when I went there to live and work that was *more* than interesting. It was, in fact, enthralling. It contained elements of the best and the worst of Hollywood—glamour, vulgarity; aesthetics, commercialism; originality, imitation; heady eroticism, covert pornography; art, industry; industry, art. It had charm, wit, color, imagination, talent, a sense of professionalism, and offered—above all—Stars.

Cut the word "whorehouse," an unsatisfactory label for what it is meant to describe. Is there another, a better word? Brothel? Worse. Bordello? No, none of these suggests any such establishment I have ever known, and certainly not that alluring oasis high in the Hollywood Hills.

My wife once brightly observed that the residential architecture of the movie capital is composed of a series of replicas of the finest homes in each of a thousand cities and towns.

"It stands to reason," she said. "When you make good, you want to live in a house exactly like the one that impressed you early in life. The best one in town: Dayton, Ohio. Or Providence. Or Prague. Look around. See what I mean?"

If this is true, then Mae's house was built by a Southerner who made good. It was a spacious Greek-revival structure with stately columns and wide porches and even a porte-cochere. A rolling, well-tended lawn in front; in back, a topiary garden.

Johnny Hyde introduced me to Mae and her pleasure palace during my first week in Wonderland. He and his nephew-assistant took me and Rita Johnson (another new client) to a preview of *The Awful Truth* at Pantages on Hollywood Boulevard.

The evening began with cocktails at the Beverly-Wilshire. From there we were driven in an agency limousine to The Brown Derby on Vine Street. Endless hellos and wavings and table-hoppings went on as I ate what had been ordered. At one point in the course of the frenetic activity, I found myself sitting and eating all alone. My agent had taken Rita across the room to present her to Darryl F. Zanuck. His nephew had been summoned to a nearby booth by a single imperious gesture of Adolphe Menjou's head.

I looked around the room, feeling light-headed. Could it be the alcohol, to which I was then unaccustomed? One martini and a half a glass of beer could not produce the euphoria I was experiencing. No. The cause of my inebriation was the near-presence of all these film celebrities in the flesh. Barbara Stanwyck. Gary Cooper, for God's sake! Jimmy Durante and Bing Crosby and Joan Crawford. I stared and stared.

The others returned. We finished dinner in a gulp and joined the sudden exodus. It was almost as though a cue had been given for everyone to leave.

We all streamed half a block to the theatre.

There again, myriad contacts—spoken and pantomimed.

At last, the film. A hit for everyone. Irene Dunne, Cary Grant, Leo McCarey.

Sidewalk talk. The limousine parade.

We are at Ciro's. Another drink. Scotch, this time. We stay less than half an hour. I wonder why we came in the first place. I learn later that Ciro's after a preview is *de rigueur.*

We go to The Clover Club, a posh gambling house. Roulette, *chemin de fer,* blackjack.

Rita is given some chips. She plays and loses. I decline, explaining that I do not know how to play. The nephew loses.

It is getting late. Rita has an early interview. The nephew takes her home, sends the car back.

Johnny Hyde is a big winner at the roulette wheel. His delight is contagious. We drink some more. I am beginning to feel the effects.

Johnny Hyde had turned into my buddy.

He looked at his watch and said, "I don't think it's too late. Do you?"

"For what?"

"To go on up to Mae's. Come on. It's only like a quarter to twelve."

"What's Mae's?"

"You don't know Mae's?" he exclaimed, making me feel like a bumpkin.

"No."

"Oh, baby!" he said, and began to laugh. "Have *you* got something coming! You mean to tell me you've never even *heard* of Mae's?"

"I've heard of it *now*," I said. "But I still don't know what it is. A club?"

"A *club?*" He laughed again. "Well, yeah. I guess you could call it that. You sure in hell can't get in unless they *know* you. In fact, she doesn't go for drop-ins, not even the ones she knows, but once in a while I get away with it. I tell you what. Order us another round. I'll give her a buzz." He started off, turned and came back. "Who's your favorite movie star? Female, I mean."

"Several," I said.

"Name *one*," he insisted. "Come on. There's got to be *one* comes to mind."

"Barbara Stanwyck," I said.

"Right," he said. "Barbara Stanwyck. I'll see what I can do for you. I mean, what *Mae* can."

He moved off, giggling excitedly.

I ordered a whisky sour for him, plain Perrier for myself. Something told me I was going to need my wits about me in the hours to come.

Johnny rejoined me, took a sip of his drink, grinned, and said, "We're all set. She wasn't sure about Barbara, though. She's going to try. But just in case—I mean in case not—who's your second favorite?"

"Greta Garbo," I said.

"Not a chance."

"Why not?" I asked, by now emboldened.

"Because she's not there, you cluck, that's why not. She never *has* been. Not so far as *I* know, anyway."

"Katharine Hepburn," I said.

"Come *on!*" he said, irritated and impatient.

"What's a matter?"

"Katharine Hepburn," he said as though pronouncing the name of a deity. "What're *you*, *nuts?*"

"You asked me favorites," I said stubbornly. "So I told you. So don't yap at me."

"*Favorites*, sure," he said. "But *possibles*. Don't be unreasonable. *Jesus!*"

I became reasonable. We went on to Mae's. Winding up through the Hollywood Hills—up up up through the thinning, rarefied air—I wondered what awaited me at the top. Who? Barbara Stanwyck? Bette Davis? Carole Lombard?

I could hardly wait.

We stood before the imposing main door. Johnny rang the doorbell. I heard chimes sound from within. The door was opened by a stunning, coffee-colored maid, wearing a black uniform and a lace apron and cap.

"Good morning, Della," said Johnny.

"Miss West is in the library," she said. "Would you join her there, please?"

Miss West. Mae's! My head snapped around to Johnny on a delayed take. My obvious astonishment delighted him.

As we moved through the antebellum atmosphere, my sense of disorientation was sharpened.

Greater astonishments lay ahead.

We moved into the formal, paneled library, its shelves replete with fine bindings.

My experienced theatre eye indicated to me that the room had been lighted by an expert. David Belasco himself could hardly have improved upon the soft glows and the strategically placed spills. It did not occur to me until much later that the entire establishment was arranged in half-light, and that this was essential to the success of the fantastic enterprise.

Near a gently burning flame in the fireplace, in a large armchair with a matching footstool, sat a vision of Mae West, wearing, I could have sworn, the gown she had worn five years earlier in the nightclub scene of *Night after Night* when the innocent ingenue, wide-eyed at the spectacle of Mae West's dripping jewels, exclaimed, "Goodness!" And Mae said, "Goodness . . . had *nothin'* tuh do with it!"

On a board before her, she was playing what appeared to be a complex form of solitaire. Beside her, on a small end table, stood the largest brandy snifter I had ever seen, about one-third full. Could she lift it?

Had I not been in wine, and overexcited; had the makeup been less skillful and the lights brighter, I suppose I would have seen at once that the woman in the chair was not actually Mae West, but a remarkable facsimile, a *pasticheuse*.

However, the surrounding mood was such that it was impossible not to play the game. The necessary suspension of disbelief was instantaneous. I was thrilled to be in the presence of—and about to be presented to—"Miss Mae West," the great Paramount star and, obviously, the Madam of this establishment.

"Hullo, 'Chollie,'" said her nose. "Glad t'see yuh. *Real* glad."

Johnny went to her, leaned over and kissed her hand.

"'Miss West,'" he said. "I'd like you to meet my friend 'John Smith.'"

I came forward.

"This is a great honor, 'Miss West,'" I said, sounding like someone else.

She offered her hand. I took it.

She squinted at me, and asked, "Y'wouldn' be, I s'pose, '*Captain* John Smith'?"

"No," I said. "I'm sorry. He was my great-great-grandfather."

"Mmm," she said. "I knew 'im well. He was great-great, all right."

So. It was going to be one of *those* nights. Trading toppers. I wished that I was less fatigued.

"What can I offer you genimen t'drink?" she asked.

"Scotch soda," said Johnny.

"Just soda," I said.

"Sorry," she said. "We don't happen t'have any of that."

"Water?"

"That neither."

"Nothing?"

"That's what we've got the *least* of, sonny." (Was she annoyed?) "Have a drink," she commanded.

"All right, 'Miss West.' Same as him."

"Fine. Call me 'Mae.'" She turned to the hovering Della. "Got that?"

"Yes, ma'am."

Della left.

"The first rule of the house," said "Mae," "is no lushes and no teetotalers. I don' know which is the worse."

"A lush teetotaler!" cried "Charlie."

"Y'got it!" purred "Mae."

Della was back (already?) with the drinks on a tray. She served "Charlie," then me.

"Mae" picked up her brandy glass—she *could* lift it!—and raised it.

"Your health 'n' strength, men."

We drank. The Scotch was superb. How could I find out what brand it was?

"I'm sorry, 'Chollie,' but 'Irene' isn't in tonight. She had to go to her preview."

"I know," he said. "We were there."

"How was it?" asked "Mae."

"Smash," said "Charlie."

"Great," I said.

She looked at me, critically, and inquired, "Y'mean great, or *Hollywood* great?"

"Well," I said, deflated, "*you* know."

"Sure," she said. "I don' mean t'be a pain about it—but I'm a writer, don't y'know, and words are important t'me. I write all my own stuff. That's why it's so good."

Was this a whorehouse I was in? I wondered. As I was wondering, "Alice Faye" came into the room.

I had unaccountably finished my drink and been served another. This time I was not so sure it was *not* Alice Faye.

"Hi, 'Alice,'" said "Charlie."

"Hello, sugar," she said.

They kissed, lightly and politely.

"Mae" spoke. "This is 'Mr. Smith,' 'Alice.' 'Miss Faye,' 'Mr. Smith.'"

"How do you do?" she said.

"How do you do," I echoed.

We touched hands.

I said, "I'm really delighted to meet you, 'Miss Faye.' I saw some stuff the other night on *Alexander's Ragtime Band*. The cutter's a friend of mine. You were marvelous. Better than ever."

"Thank you," she said demurely. "That 'Blue Skies.' Isn't that some *wonderful* song?"

"Wonderful," I said.

I was now living an inch or two off the ground and the entrance of "Barbara Stanwyck" did not reduce my elevation.

Greetings. Another introduction. Another drink.

We are in the long, impressive living room. A grand piano at one end. A pianist who, in the circumstances, looks to me like Teddy Wilson.

"Alice" sings. "Night and Day" from *The Gay Divorcée*.

I am alone in the room with "Barbara." We talk of the theatre, of her hit in the play *Burlesque* with Hal Skelly. I did not see it, but pretend that I did and hope she does not suspect I am lying.

Later, in her room, I study the stills all around. She is with Neil Hamilton in *The Bitter Tea of General Yen*, with John Boles in *Stella Dallas*, with Preston Foster in *The Plough and the Stars*, and alone in *So Big*, the Warner movie in which she first captivated me.

The five of us are in the library again. Elegant little sandwiches and champagne. Tender goodnights. Promises to meet soon.

Eddie is waiting in the driveway with the car. "Charlie" or Johnny or whatever the hell his name is talks all the way home. I do not listen. I am fully occupied in digesting the experience.

At the very last moment, I remember to say, "Thank you."

I never became a regular at "Mae's." The fees were far beyond my means. But from time to time, "Charlie"/Johnny would take me up there, and I found that there were others who were acquainted with "Mae" and with "Mae's."

More often than not, I went along only as a nonparticipating hanger-on. "Mae" and the girls did not seem to mind. I was young and eager to please, and full of conversation.

The girls. In addition to "Barbara Stanwyck" and "Alice Faye," I met "Irene Dunne," "Joan Crawford," "Janet Gaynor," "Claudette Colbert" (speaking beautiful French), "Carole Lombard," "Marlene Dietrich," "Luise Rainer," "Myrna Loy," and "Ginger Rogers." But *never*, as had been earlier indicated, "Greta Garbo" or "Katharine Hepburn."

There were, needless to say, cast changes from time to time. Stars faded and fell away. New stars appeared. Novas. A stage star, say Margaret Sullavan, would come out, make a success and settle down. Before long, "she" could be seen at "Mae's."

I came to know a good deal about "Mae's" unique institution as the months went by. The large house contained fourteen suites. There were four maids. The excellent food was prepared by Marcel, a French chef, assisted by his Dutch wife. The pianist played on weekends only. The basement contained the unique makeup, hairdressing, and wardrobe departments.

The wardrobe mistress turned out to be a dear Jewish lady from the Boyle Heights section, the mother of an assistant director who was, later, to work with me. She had spent years in the wardrobe departments of Metro, and Twentieth, as well as Western Costume, and had many valuable contacts. Often she would buy clothes from the studios, then remodel them to fit the girls at "Mae's."

On other occasions, she would watch current films with a sketch pad on her lap and draw what she saw. Her reproductions of the work of Adrian, Orry-Kelly, Irene, Howard Greer, and other leaders of the Hollywood fashion world were excellent. It was not uncommon to see a dress on Myrna Loy in one of the *Thin Man* pictures and later the same night, see it on "Myrna Loy" at "Mae's."

Two beautiful young men—a couple—were, respectively, the house hairdresser and makeup man. They quarreled often and acrimoniously, but did superlative work. It was this team that was mainly responsible for the amazingly accurate likenesses upstairs.

"Mae" had, in the manner of the Hollywood upper crust, a projection room. Here were shown old films (by request), previews ("Mae's" contacts were solid), and often break-up reels and tests.

One of these was Paulette Goddard's test for *Gone with the Wind*. "Paulette" arranged the screening. The girls, along with the rest of us, were most impressed. (Only "Margaret Sullavan" seemed, understandably, less than enthusiastic. After all, *"she"* was up for the part, too.) When, eventually, Vivien Leigh was signed to play Scarlett, the girls were stunned, said nothing, and "Paulette" was unavailable for a week.

This was not in itself unusual. There were frequent absences. The most common reply to the question, "Where's 'Myrna' tonight?" (Or "Claudette"? or "Jean"?) was: "Oh, she's on location." Often the information would jibe with items in *The Hollywood Reporter* or in *Daily Variety*—those morning harbingers that started every movie person's day.

The "trades," as they are known, were much in evidence at "Mae's." Her girls were trained to read them daily and carefully, in order that they might be able to converse convincingly with the clients.

And they did. The house was invariably filled with gossip, rumors, innuendoes, reports, inside info on movies or the people who made them, and on the homes some of them owned. A surprising amount of the information at "Mae's" was accurate.

There was the intriguing case of the husband of a Big Name who shall be nameless. He had to deal with a difficult marital problem, because Big Name was convinced that during those periods of time when she was shooting, she had to abstain absolutely from all sexual activity. She was not getting any younger, she pointed out, and those close-up lenses could be cruel—no matter how soft the focus or how kind the diffusion.

One Monday morning, following a splendidly wild Sunday night, she had overheard the cameraman, Joe Ruttenberg, mutter to his gaffer, "Jesus! I think the only way to shoot her today is through an Indian blanket!"

That did it.

She made her resolution of abstinence and held to it from then on. She was disciplined, as are all long-lasting stars, and although she loved her husband, she loved her career equally.

The trouble was that she was under contract to one of the major studios, which meant that she averaged about three pictures a year, each of which shot for approximately seven weeks. This meant that for some twenty-one weeks each year her husband was—so to speak—on his own.

He told me all this late one night in the bar at "Mae's," and added, "I'm telling you—I swear to God—if I hadn't wandered into this place one afternoon—Gene Fowler told me about it, but I thought he was giving me a heart-to-heart—you know how he is—full of pranks. Anyway, I dropped up and—God Almighty!—when 'she' walked in, I damn near keeled over. I mean, I thought it was *her!* And three martinis later, I *knew* it was. So my problem got solved. I mean to say, I'm not like some of these town tomcats around this town. I'm a one-woman man, and that's it. And as far as I'm concerned, I've never cheated on my wife, not once, not in eleven years. That's how I am."

That's how he was.

A single experience of my own was equally weird. I was directing *They Knew What They Wanted,* starring Carole Lombard and Charles Laughton.

I was a young Hollywood bachelor, and like everyone else who ever came into contact with Carole Lombard, I fell. The fact that she was married to Clark Gable did not seem to deter my fantasies. She was everything I had always wanted a girl to be: beautiful, funny, talented, imaginative, able, warm, dear, and no-nonsense.

I found myself touching her at every possible opportunity, and when those opportunities did not arise, I invented some. I was, to put it mildly, bedazzled by this golden girl—although I knew I was in a hopeless situation.

Then my brother married. His friends gave the customary prenuptial stag dinner. When it ended, part of the group, by prearrangement, repaired to "Mae's."

And in came "Carole." I took her aside and we talked for a long time. We discussed the stuff we had shot that day, and I explained what we were going to do on the following day. She *loved* my ideas. We panned Laughton. She told me she was thinking of leaving Clark. A clash of careers. I told her I thought she was doing the wise—the *only* thing. She asked me if I was hungry. I said yes. She suggested we have supper up in her suite. I told her I thought that was a great idea. The rest is a Glorious Technicolor, out-of-focus, slow-motion dream.

The next morning, I was the star of our little on-the-set ritual. Carole Lombard and Frank Fay and I had fallen into the habit of meeting in my trailer every morning right after the first shot for coffee and conversation. Our meetings soon developed a theme of sorts. We agreed that we would each tell—in precise, unsparing detail—what we had done the night before. Often, there was little to tell; more often, I suspected Frank of soaring invention; Carole and I usually played it straight.

I told of my visit to "Mae's," of my encounter with "Carole," leaving out nothing.

My account was punctuated by Carole screaming with laughter, "I'll die! I'll die. Wait till I tell Clark! Jesus, no, I better not. He'll go there! I'll die! I'll die!"

A friend from the East came to visit. He was a journalist, a columnist, and interested, of course, in Hollywood put-down material. He did not get it from me. I was, by then, a Hollywood patriot.

One night, at the Trocadero, my friend began to expatiate upon the dull and colorless nightlife my new town had to offer. I disagreed. We began to argue.

When it became clear I was losing, I said, "Excuse me."

I went to the phone and called "Mae."

Within half an hour, we were sitting around the bar up there with "Myrna," "Claudette," "Ginger," and "Paulette."

My friend looked as though he had been issued a mouth that wouldn't shut.

Later, much later, we were having a sandwich and nightcap with "Mae." I could hear the wheels of my friend's writing machinery clicking fitfully in his head. He was frowning. I could guess the problem that occupied him. What a story! But if he wrote it, who would (in 1938) publish it? And say it did in some way manage to get published, who would believe it?

Still, his newspaperman's drive could not be braked. He began to ask questions; small, large; discreet, indiscreet. "Mae" answered them all.

Finally, there was a pause. Information was being digested along with the superlative club sandwiches and beer.

My friend took a breath and plunged back in.

"'Miss West'—" he began.

"Call me 'Mae,'" said "Mae."

"Really?" he asked.

"'Fcawss," she said. "I'm *pahsh*'l to genimen of the press."

My friend blinked. "I know y'," "Mae" continued. "Seen y'pitcha many times. Read y'stuff sometimes."

"Oh," he said.

"Did y'think I bullieved you're 'Jay Gatsby,' f'cryin' out loud? Anyway, I happen t'know *he's dead*."

She looked at me reproachfully. I had indeed introduced my friend as Fitzgerald's hapless hero.

"Go ahead, Jimmy," she said, now on a new footing.

"Well, what I was going to ask—'Mae'—was just—"

He hesitated, feeling less free now that his anonymity had been shattered.

"Go ahead, fella," she urged. "We're all friends here."

"Well," he said, "do all your girls—I mean every one—do they all do—well, *everything?*"

In the circumstances, his blush seemed out of place.

"Whaddaya mean *everything?*" asked "Mae" as if she didn't know.

"I mean, you know, right down the line?" He winced at his own clumsy locution. "I mean—"

"Mae" rescued him.

"Okay," she said, "I know what y'mean. Y'got no business askin' such a thing. It's—y'know—pretty innamit after all. But now that y've ast . . . Every one of my girls here does *everything.*" She paused, looked off. "Except, of course, that stuck-up little 'Janet Gaynor'!"

Jimmy never did write about "Mae." It would have seemed a betrayal of sorts. Even now, several wars later, I wonder if *I* should be doing so. No matter. "Mae's" is no more. A condominium stands on the site and what good is that?

"Mae's" was most certainly the most memorable—well, I suppose "whorehouse" is the word, but somehow it did not then, and does not now, seem to fit "Mae's."

CHAPTER 13

A *nd the winner is—"*
We all waited for the voice on the radio to continue. Suddenly Einstein's incomprehensible theory of relativity became crystal clear. It was taking only a few seconds for Brod Crawford to open the envelope. He would then read the name of the winner. Those few seconds seemed like an hour to some and like a year to others, depending upon their involvement in the results.

It was 1951, and the annual ritual sponsored by the Academy of Motion Picture Arts and Sciences had not yet become the present-day television spectacular which is viewed worldwide, they say, by over 600 million people. The event had progressed from the first modest hotel banquet to a ceremony that was being broadcast for only the tenth time.

As it happened, many of the nominees as well as other interested parties were in New York. Among them José Ferrer, nominated for his performance in *Cyrano*; Gloria Swanson for *Sunset Boulevard*; Judy Holliday for *Born Yesterday*.

Ferrer and Miss Swanson were acting together on Broadway in a revival of *Twentieth Century*. Other nominees who were in New York were Celeste Holm, Sam Jaffe, Thelma Ritter, and George Cukor. José Ferrer decided to give an after-theatre party in New York at La Zambra Café. Most of his fellow nominees attended.

In Hollywood the presentations were being made at the RKO Pantages Theatre. In New York about 300 people were gathered listening to the results on an amplified radio. When José Ferrer was announced the winner, the little crowd went wild. The ABC radio network cut in from Hollywood to pick up his acceptance speech. It was packed with emotion, since Ferrer had been under a cloud of suspicion as a result of having been subpoenaed by the House Un-American Activities Committee.

He said, "This means more to me than an honor to an actor. I consider it a vote of confidence and an act of faith and, believe me, I'll not let you down."

In Hollywood, Helen Hayes officially accepted the Oscar for him.

. . . "*And the winner is—*"

The words were frozen in the smoky air.

During the pause, I looked across the room and watched Judy. She appeared to be remarkably calm. Did she care? Beside her sat Gloria Swanson, smiling a professional smile. She leaned toward Judy and whispered something in her ear. Judy nodded.

Later, I asked Judy about that whisper. She told me that Miss Swanson had said, softly, "One of us is about to be very happy."

As the pause stretched out, I reflected upon the curious set of circumstances that had brought Judy to this time and place.

I had written *Born Yesterday* in London during the war for my friend Jean Arthur. When eventually she read it, she was not enthusiastic about the play, and even less enthusiastic about the idea of herself in the leading role.

I made the mistake of talking her into it. Rehearsals were almost immediately fraught with difficulties and compromise. Jean had been a movie star for some years and had become highly adept at projecting her enormously attractive personality, but less skilled in creating a character. It was soon clear that we were going to get, not Jean Arthur as "Billie Dawn" but "Billie Dawn" as Jean Arthur.

I decided, under pressure from the management, to settle for this condition. Commercial considerations outweighed artistic ones. But Jean grew increasingly restive. An actress playing a part for which she does not feel suited is as uncomfortable as one wearing a badly fitted dress. Still, we struggled our way through rehearsals, hoping—as theatre people are wont to do—that it would all come right on the night.

It almost did. The first tryout performance in New Haven was half-triumphant. It looked as if there was a show in there somewhere. I expected that Jean would be, along with the rest of us, sufficiently encouraged to work toward the fulfillment of the promise.

Instead, she wrote me a note asking to be replaced as soon as possible and insisting that five important lines and two vital scenes be omitted from the next performance. Trouble.

The producer was Max Gordon, a strong manager of the old school, who was not prepared to give it all up without a fight. He used all of his considerable wiles to keep Jean Arthur from resigning. Changes were made. Some for the better, some not. By the time we opened in Boston, we had neither gained nor lost ground.

The on-stage and off-stage tensions began to affect Jean's health. She missed performances.

After two rocky weeks, we moved to Philadelphia for a scheduled Tuesday-night opening. Jean did not appear at the Monday rehearsal and on Tuesday morning, Max Gordon and I were summoned to her suite at the Hotel Warwick and were told by Dr. Barborka, who had flown in from Chicago, that in his considered medical opinion Jean Arthur could neither open that night nor play the Philadelphia engagement.

"What's the matter with her?" asked Max.

"Nervous exhaustion," said the doctor.

"Me, too," said Max. "Have you got something you can give me for it?"

The doctor explained that Jean was under sedation and that he planned to take her back to Chicago, where he would have her admitted to the Passavant Hospital for an indefinite period of time. Clearly, there was nothing more to say. We left.

From the time Jean asked to be replaced, I had begun to consider other actresses. Three prospects turned me down without consideration. Two others had come to New Haven, and one to Boston, and all had declined.

Max Gordon sent for his general manager, Ben Boyar, and began to discuss the agonizing details of closing.

I began again going over the list of possibilities, wondering if any of them were worth a second try. I recalled that during a rehearsal in New Haven, I had mentioned something about my difficulties to Mainbocher, who had designed Jean's clothes.

"Do you know Judy Holliday?" asked Main.

"From The Revuers?" I asked. "Sure, she's very good."

"What about *her?*" he asked.

"Well, she's terrific, Main, but not for *this.*"

"Oh," he said. "I saw her in a bit last season in *Kiss Them for Me.* One scene. She played a little San Francisco tart. Superlative."

"I didn't see that," I said.

"Pity," said Main.

I had long respected Mainbocher's theatre acumen. So, on the way from Boston to Philadelphia, I had stopped in New York and met with Judy Holliday and her agent, Belle Chodorov.

Judy, teamed with Betty Comden and Adolph Green and Alvin Hammer (and sometimes Leonard Bernstein at the piano), had made an impact on the New York cabaret scene. Judy was a standout; pert, versatile, comical, talented. But as we talked that Sunday afternoon in New York, she did not look anything like the girl I had in mind. Rattled and dispirited, I was making the common mistake of looking for a type rather than an actress.

Max and Ben were still discussing the closing. The economics of storing the scenery as against abandoning it was the topic.

"Listen," I said suddenly. "Let's try Judy Holliday."

"Who?" asked Max.

"Judy Holliday," I said.

"What are you talking about?" said Max, impatiently. "That fat Jewish girl from The Revuers? No. Like Dick Rodgers said one time at an audition, 'This show is *by* Jews and *for* Jews, but it can't be *with* Jews!'"

"She's not so fat," I said. "And, come to think of it, not so Jewish. But she's funny and a hell of a good actress."

"How do you know? She's never done anything in the theatre."

I repeated Mainbocher's account. Max had seen her in that play.

He nodded and said, "She was damn good. But I don't know. For this, a big part like this, a star part?"

Economics again. Ben Boyar sagely pointed out that it would, in fact, cost no more to play out the Philadelphia stand than it would to close.

. . . *"And the winner is—"*

Judy Holliday came down to Philadelphia late that afternoon. We had arranged for a room for her at the hotel. She had neither seen the play nor read it. I gave her a copy of the script and she went up to her room to read it. Two hours later, we met. She nodded her head, tentatively.

"The only thing is," she said, "when?"

"Whenever you're ready," I said.

"Saturday night," said Max.

Judy looked thunderstruck.

"I *couldn't!*" she said.

"Saturday night," said Max.

Judy shook her head in terror.

"Let's go to work," I said, "and then we'll see."

I hustled Judy out of the room, took her upstairs to her room, and said, "Leave it to me. First, the words. That's the main thing. Learn the words. If there's anything we can do to help—a stage manager or anything like that, let me know."

"Okay," said July. "By the way. It's a good play."

The next three days were unreal. We hardly ever left the Locust Street Theatre. The rest of the company was all that one could hope for: helpful, cooperative, and warm. Mainbocher arrived and redid the clothes. Paul Schmidt of Elizabeth Arden's came down and, late one night, in Judy's bathroom, changed her hair from what it was to the unique reddish-blonde that was to remain her trademark for years to come.

From the first day, almost the first hour, it was plain that we were in luck. Judy was creating the character before our eyes.

We opened on Saturday night. Judy had rehearsed less than four days, as opposed to the customary four weeks. She gave a near-perfect performance. The show was an instantaneous success and was not to play to an empty seat for the next three years.

Harry Cohn, that hard-headed, single-minded original, responded to the show personally (I wonder if he ever realized that the leading male role, Harry Brock, had been named after him?) and he wanted it.

The trouble was, he and I were not speaking at the time. I had informed his New York representative that although the play was for sale, it was not for sale to Harry Cohn.

"You mean that?" he asked.

"I certainly do," I said, and added gratuitously, "Not for a million bucks."

This conversation was duly reported to Harry Cohn. Two months later he acquired the film rights to *Born Yesterday*—for a million bucks.

When the time came to make the picture, he accepted my suggestion of George Cukor as director, but that was all. He wanted me to write the screenplay "as a labor of love." When I refused, he engaged other screenwriters to do the job, paying them twice what I had asked, but winning his point. I was later to work out the screenplay with George Cukor for nothing.

My suggestion that he do the picture with the excellent New York company, or at least with Judy Holliday and Paul Douglas, was ridiculed.

"What's the matter with you?" said Cohn. "I've got Broderick Crawford here under contract. He just got an Oscar for *All the King's Men*. And he's perfect for the part."

"Yes, but not as good as Paul Douglas."

"No? Then how come you offered it first to Crawford and he turned you down?"

He had me there.

"And the girl. Yours? For the stage, all right, but for the screen, I've got Rita Hayworth under contract. I've got Lucille Ball. Maybe I'll go for Alice Faye or Stanwyck. I mean, Jesus, this is no B picture here. I paid a lot of money for it. In fact, *too* much."

No amount of persuasion was effective.

We began the long and complex strategy of building up a part in *Adam's Rib*, which my wife and I were writing for Tracy and Hepburn at Metro. The idea was to have Judy play it as a sort of screen test which Cohn had refused to make for *Born Yesterday*.

The strategy succeeded with the help of Katharine Hepburn, Spencer Tracy, and George Cukor.

Judy scored decisively in *Adam's Rib*. Cohn, to his credit, recognized her quality and signed her to repeat her stage role in the film.

. . . *"And the winner is*—Judy Holliday for *Born Yesterday!"*

Gloria Swanson blanched, recovered at once, leaned over, embraced Judy Holliday, and kissed her.

Judy was truly astonished. She had not expected to win.

In Hollywood Ethel Barrymore accepted Judy's Oscar. At La Zambra Café in New York the excitement was so intense that the ABC crew failed to make the necessary connections and although Judy made a touching little speech, it was neither broadcast nor heard by more than a few people at her table.

Thus through the quiet defection of one star and the fading brilliance of another, a new star was indeed born. Judy Holliday went on to make a string of successes: *The Marrying Kind, It Should Happen to You, The Solid Gold Cadillac* (in which she was at last reunited with Paul Douglas), and *Bells Are Ringing*.

She was an unlikely type for movie stardom but made it by dedicated use of extraordinary talent. Her death in 1965 at the age of forty-two deprived the screen of one of its most uniquely gifted artists.

Many Hollywood producers were called, or called themselves, "independent," but Samuel Goldwyn was the only truly independent producer I ever knew. He purchased this independence expensively by putting up his own money to produce his films.

Other so-called independent producers, and even the majors, borrowed money from banks, from institutions or from private lending sources, at high interest rates, giving up, of course, pieces of the finished product. Goldwyn used his own money, often losing it. But when he made a success the profits were all his.

He fought the distributors and exhibitors, believing them to be largely parasitic, and at one time undertook the complicated method of hiring a theatre and exhibiting the picture on his own.

Once, I heard him talking to the house manager of a theatre in Chicago which he was using for the release of *The Best Years of Our Lives*. He was giving all sorts of instructions, many of which I did not understand. I heard him say, "Well, then, the only thing you got to do is put a chaser on. Get some kind of a chaser. Or I'll have somebody here get you one. You know, like a two-reel travelogue about Denmark or something like that. And you see that you use it. If we don't get a turnover, we're not going to get a gross." He hung up.

"What's 'a chaser'?" I asked.

Goldwyn laughed. "My God," he said, "you're taking me back. You know, you wouldn't believe it, but there was a time when the whole movie business practically was chasers. You see, they had these vaudeville houses and on rainy nights, or cold nights, or sometimes if they happened to have a couple of good acts, somebody would buy a ticket and go in, and maybe stay for two or three shows sometimes. Say, listen, I remember not so long ago, M-G-M, they were telling me what they were going to do at the Capitol. In New York City. They had this movie, *Babes In Arms*. Remember that? Dick Rodgers and Hart?"

"Of course."

"Well, it turned out good and they wanted to break all the box-office records in the history of the Capitol Theatre. They thought this would be a good exploitation thing for later, if they could say to the exhibitors, 'This picture broke every record in the history of the Capitol Theatre.' So Arthur Freed was at my house one night and he was telling me about what they were going to do, to break all the records of the Capitol Theatre. He said that Mickey Rooney and Judy Garland—they were the two stars of the picture—and they were great. And Arthur said to me, 'We're going to send Mickey and Judy to make personal appearances at the Capitol. We're going to play six shows a day and seven on weekends, and we're going to have Mickey and Judy make a personal appearance at every single show. Not long. Maybe they'll just come on for, say, ten minutes, and maybe do a couple of numbers and talk to the audience, but we'll be able to say: 'In person Mickey Rooney and Judy Garland,' and what the hell? They're so young, they can *do* seven shows a day. They'll just stay in the theatre and go on.' And I said to him, 'Arthur, you're making a big mistake. This is a strong picture, and if you play enough shows at the Capitol you will break the records. This personal-appearance thing is not so good, and anyway, it'll take up too much time. You could put in an extra show without the personal appearance. And there's another reason.' But Arthur wouldn't listen to me and he said, 'No, no. It's all been decided.' And they went ahead and they did it. Do you know what happened? The first two days not only they didn't break any records, but they had practically the lowest gross the Capitol had had in years, for those first two days."

I was puzzled. "But how could that be?"

"This was such a great attraction, this fine picture and this personal appearance, that people bought a ticket and they went in and stayed for two, three shows. Like if they went in two or three of them together, one of them would go out and buy some candy or popcorn or food, or go to the bathroom, and the other ones would save his seat, and then they would come back and they would sit through a second show and sometimes these kids sat through a third show. So instead of each seat being sold several times, during the morning, it was only sold once."

"Well, I'll be damned!"

"What they should have done—what I wanted to tell Arthur to do—was to run this on a schedule basis. One show, then you clear the house. Then another show. Nowadays you can do that. In the old vaudeville days, the ones I was telling you about, they didn't know how to do that. And it was too complicated. So what they used to do was, they used to buy a movie from us—like a two-reeler, sometimes a one-reeler—usually terrible, and at the end of the last vaudeville act, they would put this movie on. And people hated it so much they would leave the theatre. That's why they got to call them 'chasers.' You still have them. All those shorts and those travelogues, and that junk they put on between the shows. To get people out of the theatre. So that's what I was just now telling him in Chicago he has to do."

One tends to think of the Goldwyn output as being the best of the Hollywood product, and to some extent, it generally was. "A Goldwyn Picture" came to mean a quality product.

The fact is that Samuel Goldwyn, like everyone else in the business, had more failures than successes. Perhaps, overall, six failures for every success.

But workers in the arts are, thank fortune, remembered for their successes and not for their failures.

No producer was ever more courageous or more daring than Goldwyn. All the more credit to him that he continued to work and to produce well into his eighties. Even then, he was vigorous and ambitious and driving.

A good part of this remarkable condition stemmed from the fact that he took great care of himself. He respected himself as a being and attended to his body as he would to any other possession.

He always presented himself as a careful, successful arrangement of elegant details. I am not certain how all this was accomplished but I suspect that Frances Goldwyn had a good deal to do with it. Since she was *Mrs.* Goldwyn, she took pride in *Mr.* Goldwyn. One noticed his shirts and ties and socks. His manicure.

The last time I saw him, he was nearing ninety and his health had quite suddenly broken down. He was irritated and irritable, impatient and outraged—yet there was not a single wrinkle on his cherubic face. Mrs. Goldwyn once told me that Sam believed in facial massage and arranged to have one virtually every day of his life.

"In his case, at least," she said, "it seems to have worked, doesn't it?"

I cannot believe it was that alone.

There was the matter of diet. He was always a careful, sensible eater.

One evening I was dining with him at Le Pavillon in New York. The famous dessert wagon was rolled by, bearing confections and pastries and delectable creations.

Goldwyn watched it, sighed, and said, "Every time I see that, it's like they're wheeling away the body of an old friend of mine!"

He drank moderately, sensibly.

As to smoking, he had a nerve-testing custom. He smoked one cigarette each day. No more, no less. The cigarette would be produced after dinner, ceremoniously lit, carefully smoked, and enjoyed, and that was it until the following evening. How many are capable of a similar discipline?

Throughout the years, he made a point of taking various forms of exercise, usually combining them with business activities.

Back in the days when I worked for him, he would sometimes send for me at six o'clock, as the studio was closing, and say, "Get in the car and ride home with me. There are a few things."

The first time I did so, and the chauffeur took off, I wondered how I was going to get back to the studio. The thought never occurred to Goldwyn. From his point of view, I was being honored in some way.

He asked me about the daily doings around the studio, ever avid for any scrap of information. What did I think about the day's rushes? Why was Willie so slow? Was there some way to force those goddam actors to learn their lines before they came on the set? Did I know anyone in New York who would be good for the part of the press agent? He was getting sick and tired of these same old Hollywood faces in every picture.

All at once the car pulled up to the curb. The chauffeur got out, came around, and opened the door. Goldwyn got out. I followed. We were at the top of The Strip, where Sunset Boulevard divides.

Goldwyn strode off and I was soon making every effort to keep pace with him. He continued his questioning. My mind was only half on the answers. I was trying to calculate the distance I was being asked to walk. I was not overly familiar with the geography of Beverly Hills at that time, but I figured it out to be about a mile from his home at 1200 Laurel Lane. A mile! And some of it uphill. Should I protest? Impossible. My estimate was off. It turned out to be two and a half miles, precisely. Goldwyn had measured it and by walking from his house to this spot every morning and back again every evening, he put in his five miles.

Goldwyn was much taller than I am, with longer legs and a greater stride. I had a hard time keeping up with him and often felt as though I were running.

Forty minutes later, we reached the house. I was exhausted, he was exhilarated.

He thanked me, said goodnight, and disappeared into the house.

I stood for a moment, regaining my breath and wondering what to do next, when my second-hand Buick came through the gate, driven by my secretary, Jean.

"Pretty good," I said. "But how did you—?"

"Al, the driver. He phoned me and told me. He says Mr. Goldwyn does it all the time. So Al always calls, either somebody with the guy's car or a cab or something."

Tycoons do not concern themselves with unnecessary details—such as how is someone else going to get home.

That was 1937. Years passed. A war or two came and went. I returned to Hollywood for a short stay.

Driving to the Beverly Hills Hotel early one evening, I saw him. The same erect figure, the same long stride, and beside him a small young man bouncing along in an awkward attempt to keep apace. Was it still me, I wondered? Some leftover form of me?

For Samuel Goldwyn, not much had changed across the years. He had found a practical plan of life and work, and there was no need to deviate from it.

About that beautiful home on Laurel Lane. Mrs. Goldwyn recalls:

"For a long time we thought of building a house of our own. Sam had never really had one. But of course it's a project, isn't it? And there never seemed to be time. Then one day we had lunch with Joe Schenck at his place and afterward, sitting out on the patio—they hadn't begun calling them lanais yet, thank God—Sam suddenly looked up at this hill and said, 'That's a nice hill up there. That would be a nice place to have a house.' It was a casual, throwaway remark, nothing more. So I was good and surprised when we left at Sam insisting I drive up to this hill. Well, you know what Beverly Hills is, especially in this area and it took me what seemed like hours to find a way to it—but I did, eventually. And we padded around in the underbrush and I ruined my shoes and stockings but Sam was like Balboa discovering the Pacific. Something about the spot drew him to it and he couldn't rest until we'd taken title to it. And the day *that* happened, he said to me, 'Now darling, I want you to go ahead and build our house. That's your job. You go ahead and you do it and I don't want to mix in because I don't know how to build a house.' And I said, 'Neither do I, Sam.' And he said, 'Sure you do.' That was all. He never discussed architects with me, or plans or specifications or costs. As a matter of fact, I soon learned that he didn't want to discuss it at all. He was afraid it would distract him from his work at the studio. So in the year that the house was in progress, the subject hardly ever came up. Oh, he was aware, of course, that it was going on—but that was about it. Well, if you've ever built and furnished a house, I don't need to tell you. It was a full-time effort, what with the house and grounds and landscaping. Pool. Tennis court. And then the carpeting and drapes and furniture. Mind you, this was all from scratch. Well. Finally, finally, finally. It was ready. As ready as I could make it. And staffed. And full of flowers. And ready. So one evening, I picked Sam up at the studio. The driver knew my plan, so nothing more needed to be said. We drove off. It had been a rough day at the studio, I gathered. Sam looked absolutely harassed. Anyway, we drove along and when we reached Coldwater Canyon, the driver turned right and Sam began to yell, 'Where're you going? Where's he going?' And

I said, 'Take it easy, Sam. It's all right.' But he didn't like it and said, 'I don't want to go for any joy rides tonight. I'm tired. I want to go home.' And I took his hand and got his eyes and said, 'That's exactly where we *are* going, Sam. Home.' Well, he began to get the idea—that at last, after all this time and this long wait and tremendous expenditure of time and money and energy—our home was finished, ready. He looked as though he couldn't believe it was happening, and he held onto my hand tightly, tightly. We drove up the hill to Laurel Lane and into the driveway and there it was. I thought it was the most beautiful house in Beverly Hills—in fact, I still think so. And we sat for a moment and I said, 'We're home, darling.' Now from this point on, Sam behaved like a man in a dream—and in a way that's what it was. We went to the door and the maid opened it and curtsied. Sam offered his hand and they shook hands. He went in and began floating about—looking, looking. I don't know what he was thinking—but as I watched him, I was all choked up—and I was thinking of that penniless little orphan boy of thirteen coming to this strange country, wondering what would happen to him, going to Gloversville and working, then later New York and the struggles and the disappointments—and that awful disaster of the first picture—and the near-bankruptcies—and now here he was on top of the world—and the master of this beautiful home. And I began to follow him around. He didn't say a word. He went through every room, looked into the closets, saw the projection room and the paintings on the walls, the dining room—we'd set the table with the best silver and china and linen—the grand kitchen and finally he started up the stairs and I let him go by himself—because it was the upstairs part I was really proud of. It had been conceived and designed and executed out of my understanding of him. And I was confident he'd be pleased with his bedroom and bathroom and dressing room, study, gym—all his things that were and always would be the heart of the house. I wanted him to take it all in by himself. So I waited downstairs, knowing full well that what he would find up there would thrill him. Then I heard his voice—excited—shouting 'Frances! *Frances!*' And I rushed into the front hall just knowing he was going to have trouble expressing his joy—and there he stood at the top of the stairs and I looked up and he yelled again, 'Frances!' And I said, 'Yes, darling. What is it?' And he said, 'There's no soap in my soap dish!'"

Mrs. Goldwyn tells this affectionately and it always gets the expected laugh, but it is more than simply anecdotal to me.

It expresses perfectly the characteristics that went into the making of the man Samuel Goldwyn.

As he moved about his remarkable new home he must have appreciated it, but basically, he was not looking for what was right, but for what was possibly wrong, and in time, he found it.

No soap in the soap dish. There are some who see in the account a petty ingrate. Others make the valid point that when a man has invested a million and a half dollars in a residence he is entitled to soap in the soap dish.

By the mid-1960's, Samuel Goldwyn had become set in his ways and in his tastes. He had, after all, been producing pictures for over forty years and was frozen into certain attitudes. He had little artistic resilience, and could not accept the opening up of the screen to the new sense of morality and behavior and expression.

It made him angry. One night, at his home, in the middle of a screening, a nude turned up on the screen for no more than a fleeting moment. Goldwyn rushed to the front of his projection room and began shaking his fist at the screen.

"Get off!" he said, "Get off! Stop the picture. I don't allow such filth in my house. Stop the picture!"

Mrs. Goldwyn calmed him down, got him back into his seat. The picture did not stop.

The incident, however, provided Goldwyn with a theme for a discourse when the movie had come to an end.

"They'll go on their ass, f'Chrissake, with that kind of dirty filth. People don't want dirty filth. Not real people. Not most people. Sure, maybe here or there a few degenerates. And pimps. *They* like to see filth. Filth likes filth—but who makes more money than Disney? Nobody. Walt Disney. Clean family pictures. People go into filth—into the filth business—they go on their ass. I've seen it happen a thousand times. They think they can get away with this and with that and for a couple of minutes, all right, so maybe they do. You think we'd have had to have the goddam Hays Office—Will Hays—and all that nonsense, all that trouble and expense, if not for these dirty bastards with their goddam filth? They're going to ruin the whole goddam business."

Samuel Goldwyn was always sensitive to changing trends and methods and fashion—whether he approved of them or not.

Those who deal with the mass audience tend to become cynical as they search for the lowest common denominator of appeal.

At one time there was general agreement in the Hollywood front offices that the average filmgoer had a twelve-year-old mind. But what is average? It has been truly observed, "The average man is unusual." And has not this mind aged across the years, along with everything and everyone else?

In any case, the collective mind of an audience is something else again. Whatever the shortcomings of individuals may be, when they are bound together in the shoulder-to-shoulder theatre experience they become one, great, sensitive supermind.

In this important matter Goldwyn did not run with the pack. Having long been himself a member of the mass, he had respect and admiration for it.

He retained much of his innocence, which may well have been the principal reason for his lasting success. Whatever his shortcomings—intellectual, moral, or emotional—his love affair with people as a whole flourished until his death at ninety-two.

His philosophy was expressed in my presence one evening.

Harold Mirisch had invited a group of friends to a private preview at his home. The film was *The Thomas Crown Affair*, starring Steve McQueen and Faye Dunaway.

After dinner, we gathered in the projection room. Mirisch, a nervous man, rose, faced the small audience, and began a complex introductory speech. He explained that what we were about to see was a rough-cut, that the opening of the film was still in the cutting room being assembled by the director, Norman Jewison.

"But let me explain it to you the best I can," said Harold, and began a long, involved dissertation on the subject of the preparations for a bank robbery.

Billy Wilder interrupted. "But it sounds like a lot of boring exposition, Harold. You really think you need all that? On the front of the picture?"

"Yes," said Harold, tightly. "I'm *sure* we do."

"Why?"

"Because it's a very complicated plot with a lot of characters and we're worried the public won't understand it."

"Sit down, Harold," said Samuel Goldwyn. "And stop worrying. The public is f'Chrissake smarter than *we* are!"

STATE TRUCK DRIVER   CAR SALESMAN

ESSOR OF COMMUNICATIONS   RECEPTIO

IVE SECRETARY   HOOKER   COPY CHIE

GENT   INSTALLMENT DEALER   GARBA

CRITIC   BARBER   COSMETICS SALESWO

HOTEL CLERK   BAR PIANIST   BANK

ER READER   SUPERMARKET CHECKER

NIZER   MAIL CARRIER   PIANO TUNER

RY OWNER   PUBLISHER   PROOFREADE

UPATIONAL THERAPIST   BABY NURSE   C

E NURSERY ATTENDANT   STONE CUTTER

PHOTOGRAPHER   MODEL   PUBLIC SC

RNATIVE SCHOOL TEACHER   EX-SALESM

UCK DRIVER   TELEPHONE SOLICITOR   H

TRIAL INVESTIGATOR   YACHT BROKER

TS PRESS AGENT   EX-PRESIDENT OF CON

WORKING

PEOPLE TALK ABOUT WHAT THEY DO ALL DAY
AND HOW THEY FEEL ABOUT WHAT THEY DO

A condensation of the book by
STUDS TERKEL

INTRODUCTION

This book, being about work, is, by its very nature, about violence—to the spirit as well as to the body. It is about ulcers as well as accidents, about shouting matches as well as fistfights, about nervous breakdowns as well as kicking the dog around. It is, above all (or beneath all), about daily humiliations. To survive the day is triumph enough for the walking wounded among the great many of us.

The scars, psychic as well as physical, brought home to the supper table and the TV set, may have touched, malignantly, the soul of our society. More or less. ("More or less," that most ambiguous of phrases, pervades many of the conversations that comprise this book, reflecting, perhaps, an ambiguity of attitude toward The Job. Something more than Orwellian acceptance, something less than Luddite sabotage. Often the two impulses are fused in the same person.)

It is about a search, too, for daily meaning as well as daily bread, for recognition as well as cash, for astonishment rather than torpor; in short, for a sort of life rather than a Monday through Friday sort of dying. Perhaps immortality, too, is part of the quest. To be remembered was the wish, spoken and unspoken, of the heroes and heroines of this book.

There are, of course, the happy few who find a savor in their daily job. But don't these satisfactions, like Jude's hunger for knowledge, tell us more about the person than about his task? Perhaps. Nonetheless, there is a common attribute here: a meaning to their work well over and beyond the reward of the paycheck.

During my three years of prospecting, I may have, on more occasions than I had imagined, struck gold. I was constantly astonished by the extraordinary dreams of ordinary people. No matter how bewildering the times, those we call ordinary are aware of a sense of personal worth—or more often a lack of it—in the work they do.

WORKING THE LAND

ROBERTO ACUNA, FARM WORKER

I walked out of the fields two years ago. I saw the need to change the California feudal system, to change the lives of farm workers, to make these huge corporations feel they're not above anybody. I am thirty-four years old and I try to organize for the United Farm Workers of America.

His hands are calloused and each of his thumbnails is singularly cut. "If you're picking lettuce, the thumbnails fall off 'cause they're banged on the box. Your hands get swollen. You can't slow down because the foreman sees you're so many boxes behind and you'd better get on. But people would help each other. If you're feeling bad that day, somebody who's feeling pretty good would help. Any people that are suffering have to stick together, whether they like it or not, whether they be black, brown, or pink."

According to Mom, I was born on a cotton sack out in the fields, 'cause she had no money to go to the hospital. When I was a child, we used to migrate from California to Arizona and back and forth. The things I saw shaped my life. I remember when we used to go out and pick carrots and onions, the whole family. We tried to scratch a livin' out of the ground. I saw my parents cry out in despair, even though we had the whole family working. At the time, they were paying sixty-two and a half cents an hour. The average income must have been fifteen hundred dollars, maybe two thousand.

This was supplemented by child labor. During those years, the growers used to have a Pick-Your-Harvest Week. They would get all the migrant kids out of school and have 'em out there pickin' the crops at peak harvest time. A child was off that week and when he went back to school, he got a little gold star. They would make it seem like something civic to do.

We'd pick everything: lettuce, carrots, onions, cucumbers, cauliflower, broccoli, tomatoes—all the salads you could make out of vegetables, we picked 'em. Citrus fruits, watermelons—you name it. We'd be in Salinas about four months. From there we'd go down into the Imperial Valley. From there we'd go to picking citrus. It was like a cycle. We'd follow the seasons.

After my dad died, my mom would come home and she'd go into her tent and I would go into ours. We'd roughhouse and everything and then we'd go into the tent where Mom was sleeping and I'd see her crying. When I asked her why she was crying she never gave me an answer. All she said was things would get better. She retired a beaten old lady with a lot of dignity. That day she thought would be better never came for her.

One time, my mom was in bad need of money, so she got a part-time evening job in a restaurant. I'd be helping her. All the growers would come in and they'd be laughing, making nasty remarks, and make passes at her. I used to go out there and kick 'em and my mom told me to leave 'em alone, she could handle 'em. But they would embarrass her and she would cry.

My mom was a very proud woman. She brought us up without any help from nobody. She kept the family strong. They say that a family that prays together stays together. I say that a family that works together stays together—because of the suffering. My mom couldn't speak English too good. Or much Spanish, for that matter. She wasn't educated. But she knew some prayers and she used to make us say them. That's another thing: when I see the many things in this world and this country, I could tear the churches apart. I never saw a priest out in the fields trying to help people. Maybe in these later years they're doing it. But it's always the church *taking* from the people.

We were once asked by the church to bring vegetables to make it a successful bazaar. After we got the stuff there, the only people havin' a good time were the rich people because they were the only ones that were buyin' the stuff . . .

I'd go barefoot to school. The bad thing was they used to laugh at us, the Anglo kids. They would laugh because we'd bring tortillas and frijoles to lunch. They would have their nice little compact lunch boxes with cold milk in their thermos and they'd laugh at us because all we had was dried tortillas. Not only would they laugh at us, but the kids would pick fights. My older brother used to do most of the fighting for us and he'd come home with black eyes all the time.

What really hurt is when we had to go on welfare. Nobody knows the erosion of man's dignity. They used to have a label on canned goods that said, "U.S. Commodities. Not to be sold or exchanged." Nobody knows how proud it is to feel when you bought canned goods with your own money.

I wanted to be accepted. It must have been in the sixth grade. It was just before the Fourth of July. They were trying out students for this patriotic play. I wanted to do Abe Lincoln, so I learned the Gettysburg

Address inside and out. I'd be out in the fields pickin' the crops and I'd be memorizin'. I was the only one who didn't have to read the part, 'cause I learned it. The part was given to a girl who was a grower's daughter. She had to read it out of a book, but they said she had better diction. I was very disappointed. I quit about eighth grade.

Any time anybody'd talk to me about politics, about civil rights, I would ignore it. It's a very degrading thing because you can't express yourself. They wanted us to speak English in the school classes. We'd put out a real effort. I would get into a lot of fights because I spoke Spanish and they couldn't understand it. I was punished. I was kept after school for not speaking English.

We used to have our own tents on the truck. Most migrants would live in the tents that were already there in the fields, put up by the company. We got one for ourselves, secondhand, but it was ours. Anglos used to laugh at us. "Here comes the carnival," they'd say. We couldn't keep our clothes clean, we couldn't keep nothing clean, because we'd go by the dirt roads and the dust. We'd stay outside the town.

I never did want to go to town because it was a very bad thing for me. We used to go to the small stores, even though we got clipped more. If we went to the other stores, they would laugh at us. They would always point at us with a finger. We'd go to town maybe every two weeks to get what we needed. Everybody would walk in a bunch. We were afraid. (Laughs.) We sang to keep our spirits up. We joked about our poverty. This one guy would say, "When I get to be rich, I'm gonna marry an Anglo woman, so I can be accepted into society." The other guy would say, "When I get rich I'm gonna marry a Mexican woman, so I can go to that Anglo society of yours and see them hang you for marrying an Anglo." Our world was around the fields.

I started picking crops when I was eight. I couldn't do much, but every little bit counts. Every time I would get behind on my chores, I would get a carrot thrown at me by my parents. I would daydream: If I were a millionaire, I would buy all these ranches and give them back to the people. I would picture my mom living in one area all the time and being admired by all the people in the community. All of a sudden I'd be rudely awaken by a broken carrot in my back. That would bust your whole dream apart and you'd work for a while and come back to daydreaming.

We used to work early, about four o'clock in the morning. We'd pick the harvest until about six. Then we'd run home and get into our supposedly clean clothes and run all the way to school because we'd be late. By the time we got to school, we'd be all tuckered out. Around maybe eleven o'clock, we'd be dozing off. Our teachers would send notes to the house telling Mom that we were inattentive. The only thing I'd make fairly good grades on was spelling. I couldn't do anything else. Many times we never did our homework, because we were out in the fields. The teachers couldn't understand that. I would get whacked there also.

School would end maybe four o'clock. We'd rush home again, change clothes, go back to work until seven, seven thirty at night. That's not counting the weekends. On Saturday and Sunday, we'd be there from four thirty in the morning until about seven thirty in the evening. This is where we made the money, those two days. We all worked.

I would carry boxes for my mom to pack the carrots in. I would pull the carrots out and she would sort them into different sizes. I would get water for her to drink. When you're picking tomatoes, the boxes are heavy. They weigh about thirty pounds. They're dropped very hard on the trucks so they have to be sturdy.

The hardest work would be thinning and hoeing with a short-handled hoe. The fields would be about a half a mile long. You would be bending and stooping all day. Sometimes you would have hard ground and by the time you got home, your hands would be full of calluses. And you'd have a backache. Sometimes I wouldn't have dinner or anything. I'd just go home and fall asleep and wake up just in time to go out to the fields again.

I remember when we just got into California from Arizona to pick up the carrot harvest. It was very cold and very windy out in the fields. We just had a little old blanket for the four of us kids in the tent. We were freezin' our tail off. So I stole two brand-new blankets that belonged to a grower. When we got under those blankets it was nice and comfortable. Somebody saw me. The next morning the grower told my mom he'd turn us in unless we gave him back his blankets—sterilized. So my mom and I and my kid brother went to the river and cut some wood and made a fire and boiled the water and she scrubbed the blankets. She hung them out to dry, ironed them, and sent them back to the grower. We got a spanking for that.

I remember this labor camp that was run by the city. It was a POW camp for German soldiers. They put families in there and it would have barbed wire all around it. If you were out after ten o'clock at night, you couldn't get back in until the next day at four in the morning. We didn't know the rules. Nobody told us. We went to visit some relatives. We got back at about ten thirty and they wouldn't let us in. So we slept in the pickup outside the gate. In the morning, they let us in, we had a fast breakfast and went back to work in the fields.

The grower would keep the families apart, hoping they'd fight against each other. He'd have three or four camps and he'd have the people over here pitted against the people over there. For jobs. He'd give the best crops to the people he thought were the fastest workers. This way he kept us going harder and harder, competing.

When I was sixteen, I had my first taste as a foreman. Handling braceros, aliens, that came from Mexico to work. They'd bring these people to work over here and then send them back to Mexico after the season was over. My job was to make sure they did a good job and pushin' 'em even harder. I was a company man, yes. My parents needed money and I wanted to make sure they were proud of me. A foreman is recognized. I was very naïve. Even though I was pushing the workers, I knew their problems. They didn't know how to write, so I would write letters home for them. I would take 'em to town, buy their clothes, outside of the company stores. They had paid me $1.10 an hour. The farm workers' wage was raised to eighty-two and a half cents. But even the braceros were making more money than me, because they were working piecework. I asked for more money. The manager said, "If you don't like it you can quit." I quit and joined the Marine Corps.

I joined the Marine Corps at seventeen. I was very mixed up. I wanted to become a first-class citizen. I wanted to be accepted and I was very proud of my uniform. My mom didn't want to sign the papers, but she knew I had to better myself and maybe I'd get an education in the services.

I did many jobs. I took a civil service exam and was very proud when I passed. Most of the others were college kids. There were only three Chicanos in the group of sixty. I got a job as a correctional officer in a state prison. I quit after eight months because I couldn't take the misery I saw. They wanted me to use a rubber hose on some of the prisoners—mostly Chicanos and blacks. I couldn't do it. They called me chicken-livered because I didn't want to hit nobody. They constantly harassed me after that. I didn't quit because I was afraid of them but because they were trying to make me into a mean man. I couldn't see it. This was Soledad State Prison.

I began to see how everything was so wrong. When growers can have an intricate watering system to irrigate their crops but they can't have running water inside the houses of workers. Veterinarians tend to the needs of domestic animals but they can't have medical care for the workers. They can have land subsidies for the growers but they can't have adequate unemployment compensation for the workers. They treat him like a farm implement. In fact, they treat their implements better and their domestic animals better. They have heat and insulated barns for the animals but the workers live in beat-up shacks with no heat at all.

Illness in the fields is 120 percent higher than the average rate for industry. It's mostly back trouble, rheumatism and arthritis, because of the damp weather and the cold. Stoop labor is very hard on a person. Tuberculosis is high. And now because of the pesticides, we have many respiratory diseases.

The University of California at Davis has government experiments with pesticides and chemicals. To get a bigger crop each year. They haven't any regard as to what safety precautions are needed. In 1964 or '65, an airplane was spraying these chemicals on the fields. Spraying rigs they're called. Flying low, the wheels got tangled on the fence wire. The pilot got up, dusted himself off, and got a drink of water. He died of convulsions. The ambulance attendants got violently sick because of the pesticides he had on his person. A little girl was playing around a sprayer. She stuck her tongue on it. She died instantly.

These pesticides affect the farm worker through the lungs. He breathes it in. He gets no compensation. All they do is say he's sick. They don't investigate the cause.

There were times when I felt I couldn't take it any more. It was 105 in the shade and I'd see endless rows of lettuce and I felt my back hurting . . . I felt the frustration of not being able to get out of the fields. I was getting ready to jump any foreman who looked at me cross-eyed. But until two years ago, my world was still very small.

I would read all these things in the papers about Cesar Chavez and I would denounce him because I still had that thing about becoming a first-class patriotic citizen. In Mexicali they would pass out leaflets and I would throw 'em away. I never participated. The grape boycott didn't affect me much because I was in lettuce. It wasn't until Chavez came to Salinas, where I was working in the fields, that I saw what a beautiful man he was. I went to this rally, I still intended to stay with the company. But something—I don't know—I was close to the workers. They couldn't speak English and wanted me to be their spokesman in favor of going on strike. I don't know—I just got caught up with it all, the beautiful feeling of solidarity.

You'd see the people on the picket lines at four in the morning, at the camp fires, heating up beans and coffee and tortillas. It gave me a sense of belonging. These were my own people and they wanted change. I knew this is what I was looking for. I just didn't know it before.

My mom had always wanted me to better myself. I wanted to better myself because of her. Now when the strikes started, I told her I was going to join the union and the whole movement. I told her I was going to work without pay. She said she was proud of me. (His eyes glisten. A long, long pause.) See, I told her I wanted to be with my people. If I were a company man, nobody would like me any more. I had to belong to somebody and this was it right here. She said, "I pushed you in your early years to try to better yourself and get a social position. But I see that's not the answer. I know I'll be proud of you."

All kinds of people are farm workers, not just Chicanos. Filipinos started the strike. We have Puerto Ricans and Appalachians too, Arabs, some Japanese, some Chinese. At one time they used us against each other. But now they can't and they're scared, the growers. They can organize conglomerates. Yet when we try organization to better our lives, they are afraid. Suffering people never dreamed it could be different. Cesar Chavez tells them this and they grasp the idea—and this is what scares the growers.

Now the machines are coming in. It takes skill to operate them. But anybody can be taught. We feel migrant workers should be given the chance. They got one for grapes. They got one for lettuce. They have cotton machines that took jobs away from thousands of farm workers. The people wind up in the ghettos of the city, their culture, their families, their unity destroyed.

We're trying to stipulate it in our contract that the company will not use any machinery without the consent of the farm workers. So we can make sure the people being replaced by the machines will know how to operate the machines.

Working in the fields is not in itself a degrading job. It's hard, but if you're given regular hours, better pay, decent housing, unemployment and medical compensation, pension plans—we have a very relaxed way of living. But the growers don't recognize us as persons. That's the worst thing, the way they treat you. Like we have no brains. Now we see they have no brains. They have only a wallet in their head. The more you squeeze it, the more they cry out.

If we had proper compensation we wouldn't have to be working seventeen hours a day and following the crops. We could stay in one area and it would give us roots. Being a migrant, it tears the family apart. You get in debt. You leave the area penniless. The children are the ones hurt the most. They go to school three months in one place and then on to another. No sooner do they make friends, they are uprooted again. Right here, your childhood is taken away. So when they grow up, they're looking for this childhood they have lost.

If people could see—in the winter, ice on the fields. We'd be on our knees all day long. We'd build fires and warm up real fast and go back onto the ice. We'd be picking watermelons in 105 degrees all day long. When people have melons or cucumber or carrots or lettuce, they don't know how they got on their table and the consequences to the people who picked it. If I had enough money, I would take busloads of people out to the fields and into the labor camps. Then they'd know how that fine salad got on their table.

COMMUNICATIONS

SHARON ATKINS, RECEPTIONIST

A receptionist at a large business establishment in the Midwest. She is twenty-four. Her husband is a student. "I was out of college, an English Lit. major. I looked around for copywriting jobs. The people they wanted had majored in journalism. Okay, the first myth that blew up in my face is that a college education will get you a job."

I changed my opinion of receptionists because now I'm one. It wasn't the dumb broad at the front desk who took telephone messages. She had to be something else because I thought I was something else. I was fine until there was a press party. We were having a fairly intelligent conversation. Then they asked me what I did. When I told them, they turned around to find other people with name tags. I wasn't worth bothering with. I wasn't being rejected because of what I had said or the way I talked, but simply because of my function. After that, I tried to make up other names for what I did—communications control, servomechanism. (Laughs.)

I don't think they'd ever hire a male receptionist. They'd have to pay him more, for one thing. You can't pay someone who does what I do very much. It isn't economically feasible. (Laughs.) You're there just to filter people and filter telephone calls. You're there just to handle the equipment. You're treated like a piece of equipment, like the telephone.

You come in at nine, you open the door, you look at the piece of machinery, you plug in the headpiece. That's how my day begins. You tremble when you hear the first ring. After that, it's sort of downhill—unless there's somebody on the phone who is either kind or nasty. The rest of the people are just non, they don't exist. They're just voices. You answer calls, you connect them to others, and that's it.

I don't have much contact with people. You can't see them. You don't know if they're laughing, if they're being satirical or being kind. So your conversations become very abrupt. I notice that in talking to people. My conversations would be very short and clipped, in short sentences, the way I talk to people all day on the telephone.

I never answer the phone at home. It carries over. The way I talk to people on the phone has changed. Even when my mother calls, I don't talk to her very long. I want to *see* people to talk to them. But now, when I see them, I talk to them like I was talking on the telephone. It isn't a conscious process. I don't know what's happened. When I'm talking to someone at work, the telephone rings, and the conversation is interrupted. So I never bother finishing sentences or finishing thoughts. I always have this feeling of interruption.

You can think about this thing and all of a sudden the telephone rings and you've got to jump right back. There isn't a ten-minute break in the whole day that's quiet. I once worked at a punch press, when I was in high school. A part-time job. You sat there and watched it for four, five hours. You could make up stories about people and finish them. But you can't do that when you've got only a few minutes. You can't pick it up after the telephone call. You can't think, you can't even finish a letter. So you do quickie things, like read a chapter in a short story. It has to be short-term stuff.

I notice people have asked me to slow down when I'm talking. What I do all day is to say what I have to say as quickly as possible and switch the call to whoever it's going to. If I'm talking to a friend, I have to make it quick before I get interrupted.

You try to fill up your time with trying to think about other things: what you're going to do on the weekend or about your family. You have to use your imagination. If you don't have a very good one and you bore easily, you're in trouble. Just to fill in time, I write real bad poetry or letters to myself and to other people and never mail them. The letters are fantasies, sort of rambling, how I feel, how depressed I am.

I do some drawings—Mondrian, sort of. Peaceful colors of red and blue. Very ordered life. I'd like to think of rainbows and mountains. I never draw humans. Things of nature, never people. I always dream I'm alone and things are quiet. I call it the land of no-phone, where there isn't any machine telling me where I have to be every minute.

The machine dictates. This crummy little machine with buttons on it—you've got to be there to answer it. You can walk away from it and pretend you don't hear it, but it pulls you. You know you're not doing anything, not doing a hell of a lot for anyone. Your job doesn't mean anything. Because *you're* a little machine. A monkey could do what I do. It's really unfair to ask someone to do that.

Do you have to lie sometimes?

Oh sure, you have to lie for other people. That's another thing: having to make up stories for them if they don't want to talk to someone on the telephone. At first I'd feel embarrassed and I'd feel they knew I was lying. There was a sense of emptiness. There'd be a silence, and I'd feel guilty. At first I tried to think of a euphemism for "He's not here." It really bothered me. Then I got tired of doing it, so I just say, "He's not here." You're not looking at the person, you're talking to him over the instrument. (Laughs.) So after a while it doesn't really matter. The first time it was live. The person was there. I'm sure I blushed. He probably knew I was lying. And I think he understood I was just the instrument, not the source.

Until recently I'd cry in the morning. I didn't want to get up. I'd dread Fridays because Monday was always looming over me. Another five days ahead of me. There never seemed to be any end to it. Why am I doing this? Yet I dread looking for other jobs. I don't like filling out forms and taking typing tests. I remember on applications I'd put down, "I'd like to deal with the public." (Laughs.) Well, I don't want to deal with the public any more.

I take the bus to work. That was my big decision. I had to go to work and do what everyone else told me to do, but I could decide whether to take the bus or the El. To me, that was a big choice. Those are the only kinds of decisions you make and they become very important to you.

Very few people talk on the bus going home. Sort of sit there and look dejected. Stare out the window, pull out their newspaper, or push other people. You feel tense until the bus empties out or you get home. Because things happen to you all day long, things you couldn't get rid of. So they build up and everybody is feeding them into each other on the bus. There didn't seem to be any kind of relief about going home.

One minute to five is the moment of triumph. You physically turn off the machine that has dictated to you all day long. You put it in a drawer and that's it. You're your own man for a few hours. Then it calls to you every morning that you have to come back.

I don't know what I'd like to do. That's what hurts the most. That's why I can't quit the job. I really don't know what talents I have. And I don't know where to go to find out. I've been fostered so long by school and didn't have time to think about it.

My father's in watch repair. That's always interested me, working with my hands, and independent. I don't think I'd mind going back and learning something, taking a piece of furniture and refinishing it. The type of thing where you know what you're doing and you can create and you can fix something to make it function. At the switchboard you don't do much of anything.

I think the whole idea of receptionists is going to change. We're going to have to find machines which can do that sort of thing. You're wasting an awful lot of human power.

I'll be home and the telephone will ring and I get nervous. It reminds me of the telephone at work. It becomes like Pavlov's bells. (Laughs.) It made the dogs salivate. It makes me nervous. The machine invades me all day. I'd go home and it's still there. It's a very bad way to talk to people, to communicate. It may have been a boon to business but it did a lot to wreck conversation. (Laughs.)

A PECKING ORDER

JILL TORRANCE, MODEL

*S*he is a photographer's model, high fashion. Her face is a familiar one in magazine ads as well as on television commercials. She has been engaged in this work for eight years. She earns the city's top rate: fifty dollars an hour.

I do whatever kind of products anyone wants. This week I had a job for some South American product. They said, "We want you to be sexy, coy, pert, but not too effervescent." It always means the same smile and open eyes. For forty-five minutes they tell you what they want. They explain and explain and you sort of tune out and do the same thing.

There are a lot of people there: the person who has the product, the man from the ad agency, a couple of people from the photography studio, the stylist, who poses your dress to make sure it hangs right . . . suddenly there are a dozen people standing around. Each is telling you to do something else. You know they are even more insecure than you. You pretend you're listening and you do what you'd planned to do in the first place. When you've worked before a camera long enough, you know what they want even though they don't.

At first you work very hard to try to discover different looks and hairdos. After a while, you know them all. Someone once asked me, "Why do high-fashion models pose with their mouths open? They look like they're catching flies." (Laughs.) This look has been accepted for a long time. They want everything to be sexy, subtle or overt. After a while, it's automatic.

Now the natural look is in. Jumping up and down or staring out there . . . What's natural about looking into space? They want you natural but posed. (Laughs.) How can you feel natural with three pounds of make-up, in some ridiculous costume, standing there and looking pretty? What they think of as being natural is very phony.

You never know from day to day. I did a job for a snow blower in Michigan. It's a little machine that ladies are able to push to get snow out of the way. It was ten below. We flew over at five thirty in the morning. I had my long underwear on, but I forgot to wear my heavy shoes and I froze my feet. You're either doing fur coats in 110 degrees in the summer or bathing suits in the winter. I do whatever they ask me. I take the money and run.

Someone will call you at seven in the morning and say be ready at eight thirty. Can you be there in forty minutes? You're a basket case trying to get your wardrobe together and be there on time. You're having a cup of coffee, suddenly the phone rings and you have to run. It's terrible. Somehow you manage to make it on time. I'm very seldom late. I'm amazed at myself.

I'd like to say I'm sick and can't make it, but I seldom turn something down unless I think it's really awful. Usually I'm just rushing and do the job. I feel guilty if I say no. When you're working for one agency, they expect you to be on call. Otherwise the client may think you're too pampered.

You go out of your house with your closetful on your arm. Different colors and shoes to match and purses and wigs. Every time I get a taxi, they think I'm going to the airport. They're upset when I'm going ten blocks away. I've never found one to help me in or out of a cab. And I'm a good tipper. So I've developed these very strong muscles with one shoulder lower than the other from carrying all the wardrobe about.

In the middle of the winter it's really horrendous, because you're fighting all the people to get a taxi. I have three or four pieces of luggage. It's pretty heavy. Then I struggle out of the cab and upstairs to the studio. You're supposed to look fresh and your hair is supposed to be sparkling. By the time you get there, you're perspiring like crazy, and it's difficult to feel fresh under all those hot lights when you've had such a struggle to get there.

What's your first reaction when the phone rings in the morning and it's a job call?

Oh, crap.

I hadn't set out to be a model. I worked as a receptionist in a beauty shop during high school. This was in South Dakota. A woman who had worked for Eileen Ford and had been in *Vogue* and *Harper's Bazaar* said to me, "Why don't you go to New York and be a model?" I didn't know what a model was. I thought they were dummies in catalogues. I thought the people in the photographs were just cutouts. I didn't think they were really people. I paid no attention to advertising.

I wanted to go to college, but I had saved only three hundred dollars. So I went to New York at eighteen. I had never put anything on but lipstick and had never worn high-heeled shoes. I walked up and down Lexington Avenue for three hours 'cause my room at the 'Y' wasn't ready. I didn't dare turn left or right. I just kept walking. A hamburger in South Dakota was twenty-five cents and in this drugstore suddenly it was a dollar and a quarter.

At Eileen Ford, they told me I was too long-waisted and that maybe I should think about something else, and it was too bad since I had come all the way from South Dakota. I was so green.

I looked in the telephone book. Huntington Hartford had just bought this agency. So I went there. I was so bashful I couldn't even give my name to the receptionist. About a half an hour later, this guy who had just taken over the agency—he'd been a male model—came in. He was the first man I'd seen in New York, close up. I was just staring at him. He said, "You! Come into my office!" I thought I had really been discovered. He probably called me because I was staring at him and he liked himself a lot. (Laughs.)

A week or two later there was a cocktail party. I'd never had a drink in my life. They said you should be there at five o'clock. At five I was the only person there. They asked me what I wanted to drink. I didn't know. I said, "Bourbon and water is really nice." It was awful. The party was for Sammy Kaye. I'd never heard of Sammy Kaye.

The guy just wanted us to be there. He was having fifteen of his favorite models over. You just go. No pay. If there's an opening at a photography studio or whatever you go, because advertising people are there and you should be seen and you should make sure they remember your face. All the ridiculous things . . . That's what happens to a lot of girls who go into modeling. They're very vulnerable. They don't know what they're doing. Usually they come from very poor families. This seems glamorous. Most of the girls I met were from Ohio or Indiana or some place like that.

I had fifty cents left in my pocket when I got my first job. I worked two hours and made sixty dollars. It was absolutely incredible to me. I pinned a corsage on a guy. It was some hotel ad in a trade magazine. It was a very silly shot that was terribly simple. I was getting all this money for smiling and pinning a flower on a guy. It didn't turn out to be that simple.

Most people have strange feelings about standing before a camera. You have to learn to move and make different designs with your body. Some girls know how to puff their nose in and out to make it change or their lips or cheekbones. They practice in front of a mirror.

Usually you're competing with anywhere from thirty to sixty girls. They're cattle calls. Sometimes they take you in ten at a time. You wait from forty-five minutes to an hour before you're called. They narrow it down and ask for three or four to come back. It's like going out on a job interview every day. Everybody is very insecure. You walk into a room and see thirty beautiful girls and say, "What am I doing here?" Immediately you feel you should leave. But you think you might get three out of fifteen jobs, so . . .

There's no training needed, no kind of background. People spend thousands of dollars going to charm schools to learn make-up. It's ridiculous. They just take money from young girls. You learn while you're working. I didn't think it was funny the first few years because I was so nervous. After you relax, you see how absurd it all is.

I've always had a problem gaining weight. I told a photographer I had gained two pounds. I was happy about it. The agency said, "She's too fat, tell her to lose weight." They wouldn't have known if I hadn't told them.

I think the shyest people get into show business or modeling. They were wallflowers in their classes. You never really feel at ease and you force yourself to do things not natural to you. It's always something that you really aren't, that someone else wants you to be.

You feel like you're someone's clothes hanger. One day someone will say you're great. In the next studio, they'll say you're terrible. It changes from minute to minute: acceptance, rejection. Suddenly it doesn't mean anything. Why should you base your whole day on how you look in the morning?

My feelings are ambivalent. I like my life because it does give me freedom. I can have half a day off to do things I like. I couldn't do that if I had a normal job. I could never be a secretary. I make as much money working three hours as a secretary makes in a week. If I had to sit in an office for eight hours a day filing, I would find that more degrading than modeling. I don't look down at secretaries. Most are talented women who could do better jobs than their bosses probably, but will never get the chance—because they're women.

I'd probably join women's lib, but they don't believe in make-up and advertising, so I couldn't very well go to their meetings as I am. At school, where I'm studying photography, they said if I had any interest in women's lib I wouldn't be modeling. I was trying to tell them women are so underpaid that I couldn't earn a comparable wage at any other job. They disagreed, but in the next breath they were talking about something they'd seen advertised and wanted to buy the next day.

I feel guilty because I think people should do something they really like to do in life. I should do something else, but there is nothing I can do really well. I'm established and make a steady living, so it becomes pretty easy. It's not very fulfilling . . . but I'm lazy, I admit it. It's an easier thing to do.

You stop thinking when you're working. But it does take a lot of nervous energy because the camera goes one, two, three very fast, and you have to move very fast. There's a *kind* of thinking about what you're doing. If your left knee is at the right angle . . .

I usually don't tell people that I model. I say I'm an actuary or something. You're a celebrity because your picture is in a magazine or there's the negative connotation. If strippers or whores are arrested, they usually say, "I'm a model." There's also the thing about models being free and easy. I've never had the problem of men making passes at me. I've always managed to maintain a distance. I would never have become a model had I known . . .

Mrs. Paley—what's her name? Babs Paley—said the greatest thing is being very thin and very rich. I'm afraid that turns me off. I don't like to look at my pictures. I don't like to ride by and see some advertisement and tell everyone that's me.

Most models, after one or two years, can't be very interested in it. But they get involved with money, so it's difficult for them to quit. And there's always the possibility of the commercial that's going to make you twenty thousand dollars at one crack. You can work very hard all year on photos and not make as much as you can on two television commercials.

Male models are even worse. They're always talking about that lucky streak. They're usually ex-beach boys or ex-policemen or ex-waiters. They think they're going to get rich fast. Money and sex are the big things in their life. They talk about these two things constantly. Money more than sex, but sex a lot. Dirty jokes and the fast buck. You see this handsome frame and you find it empty.

I go off into my own world most of the time. It's difficult for me to talk with the others, because most people I work with are very conservative and play it safe. I usually get emotional, so since I'm not going to change them and they're not going to change me, we sort of talk about everyday gossip. You end up smiling and being nice to everyone. You can't afford not to be.

POSTSCRIPT: *"When I visit that Baptist family back home, they ask if I drink and what do I drink. When I say, 'Seven-Up,' they don't believe me. When I come home once a year, I try to make my people happy or bring them gifts. Probably like the guilty father who brings gifts for his children . . ."*

ROBERTA VICTOR, HOOKER

S he had been a prostitute, starting at the age of fifteen. During the first five or six years, she worked as a high-priced call girl in Manhattan. Later she was a streetwalker . . .

You never used your own name in hustling. I used a different name practically every week. If you got busted, it was more difficult for them to find out who you really were. The role one plays when hustling has nothing to do with who you are. It's only fitting and proper you take another name.

There were certain names that were in great demand. Every second hustler had the name Kim or Tracy or Stacy and a couple of others that were in vogue. These were all young women from seventeen to twenty-five, and we picked these very non-ethnic-oriented WASP names, rich names.

A hustler is any woman in American society. I was the kind of hustler who received money for favors granted rather than the type of hustler who signs a lifetime contract for her trick. Or the kind of hustler who carefully reads women's magazines and learns what it is proper to give for each date, depending on how much money her date or trick spends on her.

The favors I granted were not always sexual. When I was a call girl, men were not paying for sex. They were paying for something else. They were either paying to act out a fantasy or they were paying for companionship or they were paying for somebody to listen to them. They were paying for a *lot* of things. Some men were paying for sex that *they* felt was deviant. They were paying so that nobody would accuse them of being perverted or dirty or nasty. A large proportion of these guys asked things that were not at all deviant. Many of them wanted oral sex. They felt they couldn't ask their wives or girl friends because they'd be repulsed. Many of them wanted somebody to talk dirty to them. Every good call girl in New York used to share her book and we all knew the same tricks.

We know a guy who used to lie in a coffin in the middle of his bedroom and he would see the girl only once. He got his kicks when the door would be open, the lights would be out, and there would be candles in the living room, and all you could see was his coffin on wheels. As you walked into the living room, he'd suddenly sit up. Of course, you screamed. He got his kicks when you screamed. Or the guy who set a table like the Last Supper and sat in a robe and sandals and wanted you to play Mary Magdalene. (Laughs.)

I was about fifteen, going on sixteen. I was sitting in a coffee shop in the Village, and a friend of mine came by. She said: "I've got a cab waiting. Hurry up. You can make fifty dollars in twenty minutes." Looking back, I wonder why I was so willing to run out of the coffee shop, get in a cab, and turn a trick. It wasn't traumatic because my training had been in how to be a hustler anyway.

I learned it from the society around me, just as a woman. We're taught how to hustle, how to attract, hold a man, and give sexual favors in return. The language that you hear all the time, "Don't sell yourself cheap." "Hold out for the highest bidder." "Is it proper to kiss a man good night on the first date?" The implication is it may not be proper on the first date, but if he takes you out to dinner on the second date, it's proper. If he brings you a bottle of perfume on the third date, you should let him touch you above the waist. And go on from there. It's a market place transaction.

Somehow I managed to absorb that when I was quite young. So it wasn't even a moment of truth when this woman came into the coffee shop and said: "Come on." I was back in twenty-five minutes and I felt no guilt.

She was a virgin until she was fourteen. A jazz musician, with whom she had fallen in love, avoided her. "So I went out to have sex with somebody to present him with an accomplished fact. I found it nonpleasurable. I did a lot of sleeping around before I ever took money."

A precocious child, she was already attending a high school of demanding academic standards. "I was very lonely. I didn't experience myself as being attractive. I had always felt I was too big, too fat, too awkward, didn't look like a Pepsi-Cola ad, was not anywhere near the American Dream. Guys were mostly scared of me. I was athletic. I was bright, and I didn't know how to keep my mouth shut. I didn't know how to play the games right.

"I understood very clearly they were not attracted to me for what I was, but as a sexual object. I was attractive. The year before I started hustling there were a lot of guys that wanted to go to bed with me. They didn't want to get involved emotionally, but they did want to ball. For a while I was willing to accept that. It was feeling intimacy, feeling close, feeling warm.

"The time spent in bed wasn't unpleasant. It just wasn't terribly pleasant. It was a way of feeling somebody cared about me, at least for a moment. And it mattered that I was there, that I was important. I discovered that in bed it was possible. It was one skill that I had and I was proud of my reputation as an amateur.

"I viewed all girls as being threats. That's what we were all taught. You can't be friends with another woman, she might take your man. If you tell her anything about how you really feel, she'll use it against you. You smile at other girls and you spend time with them when there's nothing better to do, but you'd leave any girl sitting anywhere if you had an opportunity to go somewhere with a man. Because the most important thing in life is the way men feel about you."

How could you forget your first trick? (Laughs.) We took a cab to midtown Manhattan, we went to a penthouse. The guy up there was quite well known. What he really wanted to do was watch two women make love, and then he wanted to have sex with me. It was barely sex. He was almost finished by the time we started. He barely touched me and we were finished.

Of course, we faked it, the woman and me. The ethic was: You don't participate in a sexual act with another woman if a trick is watching. You always fake it. You're putting something over on him and he's paying for something he didn't really get. That's the only way you can keep any sense of self-respect.

The call girl ethic is very strong. You were the lowest of the low if you allowed yourself to feel anything with a trick. The bed puts you on their level. The way you maintain your integrity is by acting all the way through. It's not too far removed from what most American women do—which is to put on a big smile and act.

It was a tremendous kick. Here I was doing absolutely nothing, *feeling* nothing, and in twenty minutes I was going to walk out with fifty dollars in my pocket. That just made me feel absolutely marvelous. I came downtown. I can't believe this! I'm not changed, I'm the same as I was twenty minutes ago, except that now I have fifty dollars in my pocket. It really was tremendous status. How many people could make fifty dollars for twenty minutes' work? Folks work for eighty dollars take-home pay. I worked twenty minutes for fifty dollars clear, no taxes, nothing! I was still in school, I was smoking grass, I was shooting heroin, I wasn't hooked yet, and I had money. It was terrific.

After that, I made it my business to let my friend know that I was available for more of these situations. Very shortly I linked up with a couple of others who had a good call book.

Books of phone numbers are passed around from call girl to call girl. They're numbers of folks who are quite respectable and with whom there is little risk. They're not liable to pull a knife on you, they're not going to cheat you out of money. Businessmen and society figures. There's three or four groups. The wealthy executive, who makes periodic trips into the city and is known to several girls. There's the social figure, whose name appears quite regularly in the society pages and who's a regular once-a-week John. Or there's the quiet, independently wealthy type. Nobody knows how they got their money. I know one of them made his money off munitions in World War II. Then there's the entertainer. There's another crowd that runs around the night spots, the 21 Club . . .

These were the people whose names you saw in the paper almost every day. But I knew what they were really like. Any John who was obnoxious or aggressive was just crossed out of your book. You passed the word around that this person was not somebody other people should call.

We used to share numbers—standard procedure. The book I had I got from a guy who got it from a very good call girl. We kept a copy of that book in a safe deposit box. The standard procedure was that somebody new gave half of what they got the first time for each number. You'd tell them: "Call so-and-so, that's a fifty-dollar trick." They would give you twenty-five dollars. Then the number was theirs. My first book, I paid half of each trick to the person who gave it to me. After that, it was my book.

The book had the name and phone number coded, the price, what the person wants, and the contact name. For four years I didn't turn a trick for less than fifty dollars. They were all fifty to one hundred dollars and up for twenty minutes, an hour. The understanding is: it doesn't get conducted as a business transaction. The myth is that it's a social occasion.

You're expected to be well dressed, well made up, appear glad to see the man. I would get a book from somebody and I would call and say, "I'm a friend of so-and-so's, and she thought it would be nice if we got together." The next move was his. Invariably he'd say, "Why don't we do that? Tonight or tomorrow night. Why don't you come over for a drink?" I would get very carefully dressed and made up . . .

There's a given way of dressing in that league—that's to dress well but not ostentatiously. You have to pass doormen, cabdrivers. You have to look as if you belong in those buildings on Park Avenue or Central Park West. You're expected not to look cheap, not to look hard. Youth is the premium. I was quite young, but I looked older, so I had to work very hard at looking my age. Most men want girls who are eighteen. They really want girls who are younger, but they're afraid of trouble.

Preparations are very elaborate. It has to do with beauty parlors and shopping for clothes and taking long baths and spending money on preserving that kind of front that gives you a respectable address and telephone and being seen at the right clubs and drinking at the right bars. And being able to read the newspapers faithfully, so that not only can you talk about current events, you can talk about the society columns as well.

It's a social ritual. Being able to talk about what is happening and learn from this great master, and be properly respectful and know the names that he mentions. They always drop names of their friends, their contacts, and their clients. You should recognize these. Playing a role . . .

At the beginning I was very excited. But in order to continue I had to turn myself off. I had to disassociate who I was from what I was doing.

It's a process of numbing yourself. I couldn't associate with people who were not in the life—either the drug life or the hustling life. I found I couldn't turn myself back on when I finished working. When I turned myself off, I was numb—emotionally, sexually numb.

At first I felt like I was putting one over on all the other poor slobs that would go to work at eight-thirty in the morning and come home at five. I was coming home at four in the morning and I could sleep all day. I really thought a lot of people would change places with me because of the romantic image: being able to spend two hours out, riding cabs, and coming home with a hundred dollars. I could spend my mornings doing my nails, going to the beauty parlor, taking long baths, going shopping . . .

It was usually two tricks a night. That was easily a hundred, a hundred and a quarter. I always had money in my pocket. I didn't know what the inside of a subway smelled like. Nobody traveled any other way except by cab. I ate in all the best restaurants and I drank in all the best clubs. A lot of people wanted you to go out to dinner with them. All you had to do was be an ornament.

Almost all the call girls I knew were involved in drugs. The fast life, the night hours. At after-hours clubs, if you're not a big drinker, you usually find somebody who has cocaine, 'cause that's the big drug in those places. You wake up at noon, there's not very much to do till nine or ten that night. Everybody else is at work, so you shoot heroin. After a while the work became a means of supplying drugs, rather than drugs being something we took when we were bored.

The work becomes boring because you're not part of the life. You're the part that's always hidden. The doormen smirk when you come in, 'cause they know what's going on. The cabdriver, when you give him a certain address—he knows exactly where you're going when you're riding up Park Avenue at ten o'clock at night, for Christ sake. You leave there and go back—to what? Really, to what? To an emptiness. You've got all this money in your pocket and nobody you care about.

When I was a call girl I looked down on streetwalkers. I couldn't understand why anybody would put themselves in that position. It seemed to me to be hard work and very dangerous. What I was doing was basically riskless. You never had to worry about disease. These were folks who you know took care of themselves and saw the doctor regularly. Their apartments were always immaculate and the liquor was always good. They were always polite. You didn't have to ask them for money first. It was always implicit: when you were ready to leave, there would be an envelope under the lamp or there'd be something in your pocketbook. It never had to be discussed.

I had to work an awful lot harder for the same money when I was a streetwalker. I remember having knives pulled on me, broken bottles held over my head, being raped, having my money stolen back from me, having to jump out of a second-story window, having a gun pointed at me.

As a call girl, I had lunch at the same places society women had lunch. There was no way of telling me apart from anybody else in the upper tax bracket. I made my own hours, no more than three or so hours of work an evening. I didn't have to accept calls. All I had to do was play a role.

As a streetwalker, I didn't have to act. I let myself show the contempt I felt for the tricks. They weren't paying enough to make it worth performing for them. As a call girl, I pretended I enjoyed it sexually. You have to act as if you had an orgasm. As a streetwalker, I didn't. I used to lie there with my hands behind my head and do mathematics equations in my head or memorize the keyboard typewriter.

It was strictly a transaction. No conversation, no acting, no myth around it, no romanticism. It was purely a business transaction. You always asked for your money in front. If you could get away without undressing totally, you did that.

It's not too different than the distinction between an executive secretary and somebody in the typing pool. As an executive secretary you really identify with your boss. When you're part of the typing pool, you're a body, you're hired labor, a set of hands on the typewriter. You have nothing to do with whoever is passing the work down to you. You do it as quickly as you can.

What led you to the streets?

My drug habit. It got a lot larger. I started looking bad. All my money was going for drugs. I didn't have any money to spend on keeping myself up and going to beauty parlors and having a decent address and telephone.

If you can't keep yourself up, you can't call on your old tricks. You drop out of circulation. As a call girl, you have to maintain a whole image. The trick wants to know he can call you at a certain number and you have to have a stable address. You must look presentable, not like death on a soda cracker.

I looked terrible. When I hit the streets, I tried to stick to at least twenty dollars and folks would laugh. I needed a hundred dollars a night to maintain a drug habit and keep a room somewhere. It meant turning seven or eight tricks a night. I was out on the street from nine o'clock at night till four in the morning. I was taking subways and eating in hamburger stands.

For the first time I ran the risk of being busted. I was never arrested as a call girl. Every once in a while a cop would get hold of somebody's book. They would call one of the girls and say, "I'm a friend of so-and-so's." They would try to trap them. I never took calls from people I didn't know. But on the streets, how do you know who you're gonna pick up?

As a call girl, some of my tricks were upper echelon cops, not patrolmen. Priests, financiers, garment industry folks, bigtimers. On the street, they ranged from *junior* executive types, blue-collar workers, upwardly striving postal workers, college kids, suburban white collars who were in the city for their big night, restaurant workers . . .

You walk a certain area, usually five or six blocks. It has a couple of restaurants, a couple of bars. There's the step in-between: hanging out in a given bar, where people come to you. I did that briefly.

You'd walk very slowly, you'd stop and look in the window. Somebody would come up to you. There was a ritual here too. The law says in order to arrest a woman for prostitution, she has to mention money and she has to tell you what she'll do for the money. We would keep within the letter of the law, even though the cops never did.

Somebody would come up and say, "It's a nice night, isn't it?" "Yes." They'd say, "Are you busy?" I'd say, "Not particularly." "Would you like to come with me and have a drink?" You start walking and they say, "I have fifteen dollars or twelve dollars and I'm very lonely." Something to preserve the myth. Then they want you to spell out exactly what you're willing to do for the money.

I never approached anybody on the street. That was the ultimate risk. Even if he weren't a cop, he could be some kind of supersquare, who would call a cop. I was trapped by cops several times.

The first one didn't even trap me as a trick. It was three in the morning. I was in Chinatown. I ran into a trick I knew. We made contact in a restaurant. He went home and I followed him a few minutes later. I knew the address. I remember passing a banana truck. It didn't dawn on me that it was strange for somebody to be selling bananas at three in the morning. I spent about twenty minutes with my friend. He paid me. I put the money in my shoe. I opened the door and got thrown back against the wall. The banana salesman was a vice squad cop. He'd stood on the garbage can to peer in the window. I got three years for that one.

I was under age. I was four months short of twenty-one. They sent me to what was then called Girls' Term Court. They wouldn't allow me a lawyer because I wasn't an adult, so it wasn't really a criminal charge. The judge said I was rehabilitable. Instead of giving me thirty days, he gave me three years in the reformatory. It was very friendly of him.

I once really got trapped. It was about midnight and a guy came down the street. He said he was a postal worker who just got off the shift. He told me how much money he had and what he wanted. I took him to my room. The cop isn't supposed to undress. If you can describe the color of his shorts, it's an invalid arrest. Not only did he show me the color of his shorts, he went to bed with me. Then he pulled a badge and a gun and he busted me.

He lied to me. He told me he was a narc and he didn't want to bust me for hustling. If I would tell him who was dealing in the neighborhood, he'd cut me loose. I lied to him, but he won. He got me to walk out of the building past all my friends and when we got to the car, he threw me in. (Laughs.) It was great fun. I did time for that—close to four years.

What's the status of the streetwalker in prison?

It's fine. Everybody there had been hustling. It's status in reverse. Anybody who comes in saying things like they could never hustle is looked down on as being somewhat crazy.

She speaks of a profound love she had for a woman whom she'd met in prison; of her nursing her lover after the woman had become blind.

"I was out of the country for a couple of years. I worked a house in Mexico. It had heavy velour curtains—a Mexican version of a French whorehouse. There was a reception area, where the men would come and we'd parade in front of them.

"The Mexicans wanted American girls. The Americans wanted Mexican girls. So I didn't get any American tricks. I had to give a certain amount to the house for each trick I turned and anything I negotiated over that amount was mine. It was far less than anything I had taken in the States.

"I was in great demand even though I wasn't a blonde. A girl friend of mine worked there two nights. She was Norwegian and very blonde. Every trick who came in wanted her. Her head couldn't handle it all. She quit.

"*That was really hard work. The Mexicans would play macho. American tricks will come as quickly as they can. Mexicans will hold back and make me work for my money. I swear to God they were doing multiplication tables in their heads to keep from having an orgasm. I would use every trick I knew to get them to finish. It was crazy!*

"*I was teaching school at the same time. I used Alice in Wonderland as the text in my English class. During the day I tutored English for fifth-and-sixth-grade kids. In the evening, I worked in the call house.*

"*The junk down there was quite cheap and quite good. My habit was quite large. I loved dope more than anything else around. After a while I couldn't differentiate between working and not working. All men were tricks, all relationships were acting. I was completely turned off.*"

She quit shooting dope the moment she was slugged, brutally beaten by a dealer who wanted her. This was her revelatory experience. "It was the final indignity. I'd had tricks pulling broken bottles on me, I'd been in razor fights, but nobody had ever hit me." It was a threat to her status. "I was strong. I could handle myself. A tough broad. This was threatened, so . . ."

I can't talk for women who were involved with pimps. That was where I always drew the line. I always thought pimps were lower than pregnant cockroaches. I didn't want anything to do with them. I was involved from time to time with some men. They were either selling dope or stealing, but they were not depending on my income. Nor were they telling me to get my ass out on the street. I never supported a man.

As a call girl I got satisfaction, an unbelievable joy—perhaps perverted—in knowing what these reputable folks were really like. Being able to open a newspaper every morning, read about this pillar of society, and know what a pig he really was. The tremendous kick in knowing that I didn't feel anything, that I was acting and they weren't. It's sick, but no sicker than what every woman is taught, all right?

I was in *control* with every one of those relationships. You're vulnerable if you allow yourself to be involved sexually. I wasn't. They were. I called it. Being able to manipulate somebody sexually, I could determine when I wanted that particular transaction to end. 'Cause I could make the guy come. I could play all kinds of games. See? It was a tremendous sense of power.

What I did was no different from what ninety-nine percent of American women are taught to do. I took the money from under the lamp instead of in Arpege. What would I do with 150 bottles of Arpege?

You become your job. I became what I did. I became a hustler. I became cold, I became hard, I became turned off, I became numb. Even when I wasn't hustling, I was a hustler. I don't think it's terribly different from somebody who works on the assembly line forty hours a week and comes home cut off, numb, dehumanized. People aren't built to switch on and off like water faucets.

What was really horrifying about jail is that it really isn't horrifying. You adjust very easily. The same thing with hustling. It became my life. It was too much of an effort to try to make contact with another human being, to force myself to care, to feel.

I didn't care about me. It didn't matter whether I got up or didn't get up. I got high as soon as I awoke. The first thing I'd reach for, with my eyes half-closed, was my dope. I didn't like my work. It was messy. That was the biggest feeling about it. Here's all these guys slobbering over you all night long. I'm lying there, doing math or conjugations or Spanish poetry in my head. (Laughs.) And they're slobbering. God! God! What enabled me to do it was being high—high and numb.

The overt hustling society is the microcosm of the rest of the society. The power relationships are the same and the games are the same. Only this one I was in control of. The greater one I wasn't. In the outside society, if I tried to be me, I wasn't in control of anything. As a bright, assertive woman, I had no power. As a cold, manipulative hustler, I had a lot. I knew I was playing a role. Most women are taught to *become* what they act. All I did was act out the reality of American womanhood.

THE COMMERCIAL

RIP TORN, ACTOR

He came to the big city from a small town in East Texas. Because of some manner, inexplicable to those who hire actors, he has been declared "troublesome." Though he has an excellent reputation as an actor, he has—to many producers and sponsors—a "reputation" as a person.

"I have certain flaws in my make-up. Something called rise-ability. I get angry easily. I get saddened by things easily. I figured, as an actor, I could use my own kind of human machinery. The theater would be the place for my flaws to be my strengths. I thought theater was kind of a celebration of *man, with situations that reflected man's extremely comic and extremely tragic experiences. I say, 'Yeah, I can do that. That's the way I see life.' Since I feel, I can use my feelings at work. In a lot of other types of work I can sweat—I sweat as an actor—but I can't use my feelings. So I guess that's why I became an actor. But I found out that's not what they want. (Laughs.) They want you to be their Silly Putty."*

Actors have become shills. I remember doin' a television show, oh, about ten years ago—I haven't worked on network television for about eight years. I was smokin' a cigar. I was playing a Quantrell-type character, so I had a long Cuban cigar. I got up on a horse and we had to charge down a hill. It was a long shot. The director and the producer both hollered, "Cut! Cut! What're you doin' with that cigar in your mouth?" I said, "I don't naturally smoke cigars, but I'm doing it for the role. They didn't have cigarettes during the Civil War." They said, "You don't understand." I said, "Oh, now I do understand. But this isn't a cigarette program." The sponsor was Pontiac. But this show had resale value. They didn't want a Civil War character smoking a cigar because they might resell it to a cigarette company and my act might damage their commodity. They insisted I get rid of the cigar. We're nothin' but goddamned shills.

An actor is used to sell products primarily. There's good money in that. More than that, actors have become shills for politicians, even for some I like. I remember one of them talking of actors as political commodities. They want an actor to be the boss's boy.

I don't have any contempt for people who do commercials. I've never been able to get even that kind of work. A friend of mine gave me a name, somebody to see. She said, "You'll have to shave your beard." This was long before beards and long hair were "in." I said, "It's only a voice-over, what difference does it make?" She said, "You won't get in." So I went up to read a Brylcreem commercial. There must have been forty people in the control booth. There usually are about five. It was as if everybody from all the offices of the agency were there. I didn't get the job. They came to look at the freak. I went around and read about three or four commercials. They liked what I did, but I never got any work.

I don't know, maybe you don't bow to them correctly. If I could learn that certain kind of bow, maybe I'd try it. It's like the army. There's a ruling in the army called "insubordination through manner." You don't do anything that could really be said, "I'm gonna bring that man up on company punishment. I'm gonna throw the book at 'im." It's his manner.

He'll be saying, "Yes sir" and "No sir." But there's something within his corporal being makes you say something in his manner is insubordinate. He doesn't really kiss the golden spot in the right way. There's something about him. In a horse you say, "He hasn't quite been broken." He doesn't quite respond immediately to command or to the reins.

Years ago, when I worked in Hollywood, someone said, "You don't understand. This town is run on fear. You don't appear to be afraid." Everyone has some kind of fears. I don't think the antithesis of love and happiness is hatred. I think it's fear. I think that's what kills everything. There's nothing wrong with righteous anger. But if you speak straight to them, even the sound is strange. I don't know how to deal with this . . . I went to a party. A big producer gave it. It was alongside the pool. Must have been 150 people there. They had a diving board up in a tree. I remember when I was a kid, I could dive off a thing like that and do a double flip. Somebody said, "You never did that in your whole life." I said, "I guess I could do it now." He said, "That could be arranged." They got me some trunks. I said, "We might as well make a bet on this. I'll bet you a dollar." I should have bet him a grand. All the people at this party watched me. I got up there and I did it. The guy very angrily gave me a dollar and nobody would speak to me the rest of the night. It was as if I'd done some offensive thing. He was some bigwig and had meant to humiliate me. By showing him I wasn't bullshitting, I had committed some social gaffe. I should have taken the insult and said, "I guess you're right." I was never able to do that.

A few years later, I was reading a Pan Am commercial. The man who wrote it came out of the control booth and said, "I remember you. I remember you around that pool in Hollywood. You thought you were pretty big in those days, didn't you? You don't remember *me*, do you?" I guess he was one of those who didn't talk to me that night. He said, "You may not think artistry hasn't gone into the writing of this material. I want to tell you that twenty lines of this commercial has more thought, more artistry, more time spent, more money spent than is spent on your usual Broadway play." I said, "I believe you." Then he said, "Give us a voice level, please." I said, "Pan Am flies to—" He cut me off. "When you say that word 'Pan Am'—" I said, "I'm just giving you a voice level. I'm not giving you a performance yet." So I tried again. And he said, "Not much better." He just wanted to cave my head in. Do you think he was getting even for my social gaffe? (Laughs.) Me being me?

Who's running things now? The salesman. You must be a salesman to reflect that culture, to be a success. People that write commercial jingles make more money than people that write operas. They're more successful by somebody's standards. That somebody is the salesman and he's taken over. To the American public, an actor is unsuccessful unless he makes money.

At my grandfather's funeral, one of my uncles came forward and said to me, "No matter what you've become, we still love you. We would like you to know you have a place with us. So why don't you stop that foolishness and come home?" They look upon me as a failure.

The myth is: if you do commercials and you become financially successful, then you will do artistic work. I don't know who's ever done it. People say, "You've had your chance." I was offered over sixty television series. But I always looked upon 'em as shills for products.

A lot of young actors come up and say, "I have respect for you because you never sold out." I've sold out a lot of times. We all have to make accommodations with the kind of society we live in. We gotta pay the rent. We do whatever we can. I've done jobs I wasn't particularly proud of. You do the best you can with that. You try to make it a little better for your own self-respect. That's what's changed in the nature of work in this country—the lack of pride in the work itself. A man's life is his work.

Why, you don't even have the kind of carpenters . . . He says, "Aw, fuck it." You know they're not even gonna countersink something when they should. They don't have the pleasure in the work any more. Even in Mexico, there was something unique about the road work. The curbing is not laid out by machine, it's handmade. So there's little irregularities. That's why the eye is rested even by the curbing in Mexico. And walls. Because it's craftsmanship. You see humanity in a chair. And you know seven thousand didn't come out in one day. It was made by some man's hand. There's artistry in that, and that's what makes mankind happier. You work out of necessity, but in your work, you gotta have a little artistry too.

CLEANING UP

ROY SCHMIDT, GARBAGE MAN

They call us truck loaders, that's what the union did. We're just laborers, that's all we are. What the devil, there's no glamour to it. Just bouncin' heavy cans around all day. I'm givin' the city a fair day's work. I don't want to lean on anyone else. Regardless if I was working here or elsewhere, I put in my day. We're the ones that pick up the cans, dump 'em in the hopper, and do the manual end of the job. There's nothing complex about it.

He is fifty-eight. His fellow crew members are fifty and sixty-nine. For the past seven years he has worked for the Sanitation Department. "I worked at a freight dock for two years. That was night work. It was punching me out. At the end of the week I didn't know one day from another. I looked for a day job and landed this."

In this particular neighborhood, the kids are a little snotty. They're let run a little too loose. They're not held down in the way they should. It's getting a little wild around here. I live in the neighborhood and you have to put up with it. They'll yell while you're riding from one alley to another, "Garbage picker!" The little ones usually give you a highball, seem to enjoy it, and you wave back at 'em. When they get a little bigger, they're liable to call you most anything on the truck. (Laughs.) They're just too stupid to realize the necessity of the job.

I've been outside for seven years and I feel more free. I don't take the job home with me. When I worked in the office, my wife would say, "What was the matter with you last night? You laid there and your fingers were drumming the mattress." That's when I worked in the office. The bookkeeping and everything else, it was starting to play on my nerves. Yeah, I prefer laboring to bookkeeping. For one thing, a bookkeeping job doesn't pay anything. I was the lowest paid man there.

Physically, I was able to do more around the house. Now I'm too tired to pitch into anything heavy. I'll mow the lawn and I'll go upstairs and maybe catch a TV program or two, and I'll hit the hay. In the winter months, it's so much worse. After being outside all day and walkin' into a warm house, I can cork off in a minute. (Laughs.) The driver has some protection, he has the cab of the truck. We're out in the cold.

You get it in the shoulders and the arms. You have an ache here and an ache there. Approximately four years ago, I put my back into spasms. The city took care of it, put me in a hospital for a week. That one year, it happened twice to me—because of continual lifting. The way one doctor explained it to me, I may be goin' thirty days and it's already started. It's just on the last day, whenever it's gonna hit, it just turns you upside down. You can't walk, you can't move, you can't get up.

I wear a belt, sort of a girdle. You can buy them in any orthopedic place. This is primarily to hold me in. This one doctor says I'm fairly long-legged and I'm overlifting. The men I work with are average height. I'm six three, I was six four when I went in the army but I think I've come down a little bit. It's my own fault. I probably make it harder on myself with my way of lifting. I've been fairly well protected during the past four years. I haven't had any days off because of it. I wouldn't want to face it again, I'll tell you that.

It's a fifty-gallon drum you lift. I'd say anywhere from eighty pounds to several hundred pounds, depending on what they're loaded with. We lift maybe close to two hundred cans a day. I never attempted to count them. They surprise you every once in a while. They'll load it with something very heavy, like plaster. (Laughs.)

I always said you can read in a garbage can how a person lives. We have this Mexican and Puerto Rican movement in this area. You find a lot of rice and a good many TV dinners. They don't seem to care about cooking too much. I can't say that every family is like that. I never lived with 'em.

I wear an apron over this. By the time you get two or three days in these clothes they're ready for the washer. Working behind the truck, you never know what might shoot out from behind there—liquid or glass or plastic. There is no safety features on the truck. When these blades in the hopper catch it and bring it forward, it spurts out like a bullet. Two years ago, I was struck in the face with a piece of wood. Cut the flesh above the eye and broke my glasses. When I got to the doctor, he put a stitch in it. I had the prettiest shiner you ever seen. (Laughs.) It can be dangerous. You never know what people throw out. I've seen acid thrown out.

They tell you stay away from the rear of the truck when the blade's in motion, but if you did that throughout a day, you'd lose too much time. By the time the blade's goin', you're getting the next can ready to dump.

You don't talk much. You might just mention something fell out of the can or a word or two. Maybe we'll pull in an alley and they'll take five minutes for a cigarette break. We might chew the fat about various things—current events, who murdered who (laughs), sensational stories. Maybe one of the fellas read an article about something that happened over in Europe. Oh, once in a while, talk about the war. It has never been a heated discussion with me.

I'm pretty well exhausted by the time I get through in the day. I've complained at times when the work was getting a little too heavy. My wife says, "Well, get something else." Where the devil is a man my age gonna get something else? You just don't walk from job to job.

She says I should go to sixty-two if I can. I have some Social Security comin'. The pension from the city won't amount to anything. I don't have that much service. Another four years, I'll have only eleven years, and that won't build up a city pension for me by any means.

It'll be just day to day. Same thing as bowling. You bowl each frame, that's right. If you look ahead, you know what you're getting into. So why aggravate yourself? You know what we call bad stops. A mess to clean up in a certain alley. Why look ahead to it? The devil. As long as my health holds out, I want to work.

I have a daughter in college. If she goes through to June she'll have her master's degree. She's in medicine. For her, it'll be either teaching or research. As she teaches, she can work for her doctorate. She's so far ahead of me, I couldn't . . .

I don't look down on my job in any way. I couldn't say I despise myself for doing it. I feel better at it than I did at the office. I'm more free. And, yeah—it's meaningful to society. (Laughs.)

I was told a story one time by a doctor. Years ago, in France, they had a setup where these princes and lords and God knows what they had floating around. If you didn't stand in favor with the king, they'd give you the lowest job, of cleaning the streets of Paris—which must have been a mess in those days. One lord goofed up somewhere along the line, so they put him in charge of it. And he did such a wonderful job that he was commended for it. The worst job in the French kingdom and he was patted on the back for what he did. That was the first story I ever heard about garbage where it really meant something.

POSTSCRIPT: *Several months after the conversation he sent me a note: "Nick and I are still on the job, but to me the alleys are getting larger and the cans larger. Getting old."*

MAGGIE HOLMES, DOMESTIC

What bugs me now, since I'm on welfare, is people saying they give you the money for nothin'. When I think back what we had to come through, up from the South, comin' here. The hard work we had to do. It really gets me, when I hear people . . . It do somethin' to me. I think violence.

I think what we had to work for. I used to work for $1.50 a week. This is five days a week, sometimes six. If you live in the servant quarter, your time is never off, because if they decide to have a party at night, you gotta come out. My grandmother, I remember when she used to work, we'd get milk and a pound of butter. I mean this was pay. I'm thinkin' about what my poor parents worked for, gettin' nothing. What do the white think about when they think? Do they ever think about what *they* would do?

She had worked as a domestic, hotel chambermaid, and as "kitchen help in cafés" for the past twenty-five years, up North and down South. She lives with her four children.

When it comes to housework, I can't do it now. I can't stand it, 'cause it do somethin' to my mind. They want you to clean the house, want you to wash, even the windows, want you to iron. You not supposed to wash no dishes. You ain't supposed to make no beds up. Lots of 'em try to sneak it in on you, think you don't know that. So the doorbell rings and I didn't answer to. The bell's ringin' and I'm still doin' my work. She ask me why I don't answer the bell. I say, "Do I come here to be a butler?" And I don't see myself to be no doormaid. I came to do some work and I'm gonna do my work. When you end up, you's nursemaid, you's cook. They puts all this on you. If you want a job to cleanin', you ask for just cleanin'. She wants you to do in one day what she hasn't did all year.

Now this bug me: the first thing she gonna do is pull out this damn rubber thing—just fittin' for your knees. Knee pads—like you're workin' in the fields, like people pickin' cotton. No mop or nothin'. That's why you find so many black women here got rheumatism in their legs, knees. When you gets on that cold floor, I don't care how warm the house is, you can feel the cold on the floor, the water and stuff. I never see nobody on their knees until I come North. In the South, they had mops. Most times, if they had real heavy work, they always had a man to come in. Washin' windows, that's a man's job. They don't think nothin' about askin' you to do that here. They don't have no feeling that that's what bothers you. I think to myself, My God, if I had somebody come and do my floors, clean up for me, I'd appreciate it. They don't say nothin' about it. Act like you haven't even done anything. They has no feelin's.

I worked for one old hen on Lake Shore Drive. You remember that big snow they had there? [The week of Chicago's Big Snow-In beginning January 25, 1967.] Remember when you couldn't get there? When I gets to work she says, "Call the office." She complained to the lady where I got the job, said I was late to work. So I called. So I said, in the phone (shouts), *What do you want with me?* I got home four black, beautiful kids. Before I got to anybody's job in the morning I see that my kids are at school. I gonna see that they have warm clothes on and they fed." I'm lookin' right at the woman I'm workin' for. (Laughs.) When I get through the phone I tell this employer, "That goes for you too. The only thing I live for is my kids. There's nothin', you and nobody else." The expression on her face: What is this? (Laughs.) She thought I was gonna be like (mimics "Aunt Jemima"): "Yes ma'am, I'll try to get here a little early." But it wasn't like that. (Laughs.)

When I come in the door that day she told me pull my shoes off. I said, "For what? I can wipe my feet at the door here, but I'm not gettin' out of my shoes, it's cold." She look at me like she said: Oh my God, what I got here? (Laughs.) I'm knowin' I ain't gonna make no eight hours here. I can't take it.

She had everything in there snow white. And that means work, believe me. In the dining room she had a blue set, she had sky-blue chairs. They had a bedroom with pink and blue. I look and say, "I know what this means." It means sho' 'nough—knees. I said, "I'm gonna try and make it today, *if* I can make it." Usually when they're so bad, you have to leave.

I ask her where the mop is. She say she don't have no mop. I said, "Don't tell me you mop the floor on your knees. I know you don't." They usually hide these mops in the clothes closet. I go out behind all these clothes and get the mop out. (Laughs.) They don't get on their knees, but they don't think nothin' about askin' a black woman. She says, "All you—you girls . . . " She stop. I say, "All you *niggers*, is that what you want to say?" She give me this stupid look. I say, "I'm glad you tellin' me that there's more like me." (Laughs.) I told her, "You better give me my money and let me go, 'cause I'm gettin' angry." So I made her give me my carfare and what I had worked that day.

Most when you find decent work is when you find one that work themselves. They know what it's like to get up in the morning and go to work. In the suburbs they ain't got nothin' to do. They has nothin' else to think about. Their mind's just about blowed.

It's just like they're talkin' about mental health. Poor people's mental health is different than the rich white. Mine could come from a job or not havin' enough money for my kids. Mine is from me being poor. That don't mean you're sick. His sickness is from money, graftin' where he want more. I don't have *any*. You live like that day to day, penny to penny.

I worked for a woman, her husband's a judge. I cleaned the whole house. When it was time for me to go home, she decided she wants some ironing. She goes in the basement, she turn on the air conditioner. She said, "I think you can go down in the basement and finish your day out. It's air conditioned." I said, "I don't care what you got down there, I'm not ironing. You look at that slip, it says cleanin'. Don't say no ironin'." She wanted me to wash the walls in the bathroom. I said, "If you look in that telephone book they got all kinds of ads there under house cleanin'." She said the same thing as the other one, "All you girls—" I said same thing I said to the other one: "You mean niggers." (Laughs.)

They ever call you by your last name?

Oh God, they wouldn't do that. (Laughs.)

Do you call her by her last name?

Most time I don't call her, period. I don't say anything to her. I don't talk nasty to nobody, but when I go to work I don't talk to people. Most time they don't like what you're gonna say. So I keeps quiet.

Most of her jobs were "way out in the suburbs. You get a bus and you ride till you get a subway. After you gets to Howard, you gets the El. If you get to the end of the line and there's no bus, they pick you up. I don't like to work in the city, 'cause they don't want to pay you nothin'. And these old buildings are so nasty. It takes so much time to clean 'em. They are not kept up so good, like suburbs. Most of the new homes out there, it's easier to clean."

A commonly observed phenomenon: during the early evening hour, trains, crowded, predominantly by young white men carrying attaché cases, pass trains headed in the opposite direction, crowded, predominantly by middle-aged black women carrying brown paper bags. Neither group, it appears, glances at the other.

"We spend most of the time ridin'. You get caught goin' out from the suburbs at nighttime, man, you're really sittin' there for hours. There's nothin' movin'. You got a certain hour to meet trains. You get a transfer, you have to get that train. It's a shuffle to get in and out of the job. If you miss that train at five o'clock, what time you gonna get out that end? Sometimes you don't get home till eight o'clock . . ."

You don't feel like washin' your own window when you come from out there, scrubbin'. If you work in one of them houses eight hours, you gotta come home do the same thing over . . . you don't feel like . . . (sighs softly) . . . tired. You gotta come home, take care of your kids, you gotta cook, you gotta wash. Most of the time, you gotta wash for the kids for somethin' to wear to school. You gotta clean up, 'cause you didn't have time in the morning. You gotta wash and iron and whatever you do, nights. You be so tired, until you don't feel like even doin' nothin'.

You get up at six, you fix breakfast for the kids, you get them ready to go on to school. Leave home about eight. Most of the time I make biscuits for my kids, cornbread you gotta make. I don't mean the canned kind. This I don't call cookin', when you go in that refrigerator and get some beans and drop 'em in a pot. And TV dinners, they go stick 'em in the stove and she say she cooked. This is not cookin'.

And *she's* tired. Tired from doin' what? You got a washing dryer, you got an electric sweeper, anything at fingertips. All she gotta do is unfroze 'em, dump 'em in the pot, and she's tired! I go to the store, I get my vegetables, greens, I wash 'em. I gotta pick 'em first. I don't eat none of that stuff, like in the cans. She don't do that, and she says she's tired.

When you work for them, when you get in that house in the morning, boy, they got one arm in their coat and a scarf on their head. And when you open that door, she shoots by you, she's gone. Know what I mean? They want you to come there and keep the kids and let them get out. What she think about how am I gonna do? Like I gets tired of my kids too. I'd like to go out too. It bugs you to think that they don't have no feelin's about that.

Most of the time I work for them and they be out. I don't like to work for 'em when they be in the house so much. They don't have no work to do. All they do is get on the telephone and talk about one another. Make you sick. I'll go and close the door. They're all the same, everybody's house is the same. You think they rehearse it . . .

When I work, only thing I be worryin' about is my kids. I just don't like to leave 'em too long. When they get out of school, you wonder if they out on the street. The only thing I worry is if they had a place to play in easy. I always call two, three times. When she don't like you to call, I'm in a hurry to get out of there. (Laughs.) My mind is gettin' home, what are you gonna find to cook before the stores close.

This Nixon was sayin' he don't see nothin' wrong with people doin' scrubbin'. For generations that's all we done. He should know we wants to be doctors and teachers and lawyers like him. I don't want my kids to come up and do domestic work. It's degrading. You can't see no tomorrow there. We done this for generation and generation—cooks and butlers all your life. They want their kids to be lawyers, doctors, and things. You don't want 'em in no cafés workin' . . .

When they say about the neighborhood we live in is dirty, why do they ask me to come and clean their house? We, the people in the slums, the same nasty women they have come to their house in the suburbs every day. If these women are so filthy, why you want them to clean for you? They don't go and clean for us. We go and clean for them.

I worked one day where this white person did some housework. I'm lookin' at the difference how she with me and her. She had a guilt feeling towards that lady. They feel they shouldn't ask them to do this type of work, but they don't mind askin' me.

They want you to get in a uniform. You take me and my mother, she work in what she wear. She tells you, "If that place so dirty where I can't wear my dress, I won't do the job." You can't go to work dressed like they do, 'cause they think you're not working—like you should get dirty, at least. They don't say what kind of uniform, just say uniform. This is in case anybody come in, the black be workin'. They don't want you walkin' around dressed up, lookin' like them. They asks you sometimes, "Don't you have somethin' else to put on?" I say, "No, 'cause I'm not gettin' on my knees."

They move with caution now, believe me. They want to know, "What should I call you?" I say, "Don't call me a Negro, I'm black." So they say, "Okay, I don't want to make you angry with me." (Laughs.) The old-timers, a lot of 'em was real religious. "Lord'll make a way." I say, "I'm makin' my own way." I'm not anti-Bible or anti-God, but I just let 'em know I don't think thataway.

The younger women, they don't pay you too much attention. Most of 'em work. The older women, they behind you, wiping. I don't like nobody checkin' behind me. When you go to work, they want to show you how to clean. That really gets me, somebody showin' me how to clean. I been doin' it all my life. They come and get the rag and show you how to do it. (Laughs.) I stand there, look at 'em. Lotta times I ask her, "You finished?" I say, "If there's anything you gotta go and do, I wish you'd go." I don't need nobody to show me how to clean.

I had them put money down and pretend they can't find it and have me look for it. I worked for one, she had dropped ten dollars on the floor, and I was sweepin' and I'm glad I seen it, because if I had put that sweeper on it, she coulda said I got it. I had to push the couch back and the ten dollars was there. Oh, I had 'em, when you go to dust, they put something . . . to test you.

I worked at a hotel. A hotel's the same thing. You makin' beds, scrubbin' toilets, and things. You gotta put in linens and towels. You still cleanin'. When people come in the room—that's what bugs me—they give you that look: You just a maid. It do somethin' to me. It really gets me.

Some of the guests are nice. The only thing you try to do is to hurry up and get this bed made and get outa here, 'cause they'll get you to do somethin' else. If they take that room, they want everything they paid for. (Laughs.) They get so many towels, they can't use 'em all. But you gotta put up all those towels. They want that pillow, they want that blanket. You gotta be trottin' back and forth and gettin' all those things.

In the meantime, when they have the hotel full, we put in extra beds—the little foldin' things. They say they didn't order the bed. They stand and look at you like you crazy. Now you gotta take this bed back all the way from the twelfth floor to the second. The guy at the desk, he got the wrong room. He don't say, "I made a mistake." You take the blame.

And you get some guys . . . you can't work with a fightin' 'em. He'll call down and say he wants some towels. When you knock, he says, "Come in." He's standing there without a stitch of clothes on, buck naked. You're not goin' in there. You only throw those towels and go back. Most of the time you wait till he got out of there.

When somethin's missin', it's always the maid took it. If we find one of those type people, we tell the house lady, "You have to go in there and clean it yourself." If I crack that door, and nobody's in, I wouldn't go in there. If a girl had been in there, they would call and tell you, "Did you see something?" They won't say you got it. It's the same thing. You say no. They say, "It *musta* been in there."

Last summer I worked at a place and she missed a purse. I didn't work on that floor that day. She called the office. "Did you see that lady's purse?" I said, *"No, I haven't been in the room."* He asked me again, Did I . . . ? I had to stay till twelve o'clock. She found it. It was under some papers. I quit, 'cause they end up sayin' you stole somethin'.

You know what I wanted to do all my life? I wanted to play piano. And I'd want to write songs and things, that's what I really wanted to do. If I could just get myself enough to buy a piano . . . And I'd like to write about my life, if I could sit long enough: How I growed up in the South and my grandparents and my father—I'd like to do that. I would like to dig up more of black history, too. I would love to for my kids.

Lotta times I'm tellin' 'em about things, they'll be sayin', "Mom, that's olden days." (Laughs.) They don't understand, because it's so far from what's happening now. Mighty few young black women are doin' domestic work. And I'm glad. That's why I want my kids to go to school. This one lady told me, "All you people are gettin' like that." I said, "I'm glad." There's no more gettin' on their knees.

WATCHING

VINCENT MAHER, POLICEMAN

Each child has a dream. I had two. One was to be a marine and the other was to be a policeman. I tried other endeavors but I was just not cut out for it. I am a policeman. It is one of the most gratifying jobs in the world.

He is thirty-nine. He lives apart from his family—a wife and three children: two boys, fifteen and twelve, and a girl, fourteen. He presently directs traffic in Chicago's Loop. He had previously been a member of the Tactical Unit. Due to a personal grievance, he had resigned from the force. For a time, he worked as a bartender—disconsolately. "I had a deputy chief come in and a commander. They said, 'Vince, you're a cop. Get your fanny back on the job.' I came back on the job and I'm happy."

Two of his uncles had been on the force in New York City, as was his father, "until he lost his trigger finger in a railroad accident." As he reflects, past and present fuse.

I make an arrest on someone who commits a crime of violence. I have to resort to a physical type of arrest to subdue him, I might have to shoot the person. I'm chastised for being brutal. It's all right for him to do what he wants to do against myself or legitimate people, but in no way I can touch him. I don't see the justice.

I've been accused of being a bigot, a hypocrite, and a few other niceties. I'm a human being with a job. I judge people on face value. Just because a guy wears long hair doesn't make him a radical. Just because he's black—I'd *rather* work in a black neighborhood. They need me more than the white. White neighborhoods are not as involved in actual crime, the dirtiness, as they are in poor neighborhoods. I don't mean blacks alone. There are Southern whites that come up here, they live in jungles. So do the Puerto Ricans.

The white man, he wants me to write an illegally parked car or write the neighbor next door for his dog defecating on the grass. I don't dig this. This is not my kind. I lived in a jungle, I've come from a jungle. In those early days, nobody knew the word nigger. There was no hate. You came and went as you pleased. I've seen kids come out of a bad neighborhood, some become priests, some become policemen, others go to the penitentiary. I don't believe what some judges say: because of environment, this is the way it is. I wasn't born with a silver spoon in my mouth. I never finished high school. I finished the hard way—Uncle Sam and I. I should be a crook because I came out of a slum neighborhood? My dad was a Depression kid. I saw him when he was making four dollars a week, supporting four kids and a wife. (Laughs.) That's why I became a policeman.

I'm in traffic now—semi-retirement. (Laughs softly, ruefully.) All I ever wanted was detective and I couldn't make it. When I was on the Tactical Force, I just couldn't wait. I used to work my days off. I felt I was really functioning as a police officer. I get out there and infiltrate, to find out why, when, and where. We need an element to get out there. I'm not saying it's the greatest thing in the world, but it's necessary. It's an evil because crime is evil. Why do these people who preach liberalism and pacifism require walls around their houses? They need these buffers. That's what we are, buffers.

If there was a crime pattern working, we'd go out and find out who, what, when, and clean it up. We would roam the street as citizens, rather than marked as policemen. We'd wear neat and presentable suits. You can hear a lot more when you're sitting in a group of hippies or you're sitting in a restaurant. That's how I used to operate. I'd pick up information. Nobody knew I was a policeman.

I don't believe in entrapping. To entrap is to induce someone to commit a crime. The prostitute was a great source of information. This is funny, but I'd rather have a prostitute working the street. This is her trade and it's been going on since Adam and Eve. If I were President, I'd legalize it. As long as she's operating, I don't have to worry about someone being raped or a child being molested. They render a service as long as they're clean and don't hurt people.

I used to call the girls at two in the morning and say, "I need four or five for the night." And they'd say, "Okay Vince, we'll be here. Come back in about two hours." They'd all be lined up and I'd lock 'em up. I'd grab one of the broads off the street and I'd say, "Charlene, you'd better hustle because I'm coming back later and if I catch youse around—boom—you're gonna get nailed. The beef is on."

The good suffer for the faults of the bad. You get one hooker out there that's a bad one, starts jackrolling, working with a pimp, you've got a bad beef. As long as the broads are operating and nobody's hurt . . . If Sam wants to go out and get something strange, he's gonna go, I can't put a ball and chain on this man. His own conscience has got to be his guide.

I don't discriminate, black or white broads. They were good to me.

They were my source of information. They can go places where my eyes and ears can't go. The best eyes and ears the policeman has got is the street, because the blue is known even when you don't have it on. So you send your other people out.

When they get pinched, they're not hurt so much. When they put up a twenty-five-dollar bond, they know I'm not gonna be in court and they get their money back and they're back on the street. They take the bust and it's a cover for them.

There was a gang of thieves in Old Town. At the time, there was sixty or seventy unsolved robberies. They were working in conjunction with prostitutes. They'd rob the trick. They would sometimes cut, beat, or shoot the victim. My two partners and I set out one night and I was the decoy. I was picked up by two prostitutes. I took on four guys in a gun battle. One guy stuck a shotgun in my stomach and it misfired. The other guy opened up on me with a .38. I killed the man with the shotgun, wounded the other guy, and took the other two. I *volunteered*. I was decorated for it and given a chance to make detective. But I didn't make it.

I'm human. I make mistakes like everybody else. If you want a robot, build machines. If you want human beings, that's what I am. I'm an honest cop. I don't think any person doing my job could face the stuff I face without losing your temper at one time or another. I've used the word nigger, I've used the word stump-jumpin' hillbilly, I've used vulgarity against 'em. It depends on the element.

I've never studied psychology, but I apply it every day of my life. You can go into an atmosphere of doctors and lawyers and educators and get a point across verbally. They understand. You can also work on the South or West Side [black neighborhoods], where you can talk your fool head off and get nothing. They don't understand this nicety-type guy. So you walk with a big stick. Like the adage of a mule: He's a very intelligent animal, but in order to get his attention you have to hit him on the head with a stick. Same thing applies on the street.

You walk up to some of these people and they'll spit in your face. If you let them, then I've lost what I am as a policeman, because now I've let the bad overrule me. So I have to get physical sometimes. It isn't done in a brutal sense. I call it a corrective measure. You get these derelicts on the street. I've dealt with these people for years. You whack 'em on the sole of the foot. It isn't brutal, but it stings and he gets the message: he's not supposed to be sleeping on the street. "Get up!" You get him on his feet and say, "Now go on back to junk heaven that you live in and get some sleep." Someone coming down the street sees me use the stick on the sole of his foot is gonna scream that I'm brutal.

There were five gentlemen standing on the corner, all black. One guy stepped in front of my car, and said, "You white mother so-and-so, you ain't goin' nowhere." Bleep-bleep on the horn. I say, "Listen fella, move!" He didn't move. The challenge was there. I'm alone. I'm white. And he's one of these people that read in the magazines: Challenge the policeman. I got out of the squad car and I told him, "You . . ." (Hesitates.) I rapped to him in his tongue and he understood. I called him everything in the book. I said, "Get up off the curb or you're gonna go to jail." He made a very emphatic point of trying to take me physically. It didn't work. When his four buddies saw him go on the ground, I got the message across: I'm the boss on the street. If you're the jungle cat, I'm the man with the whip and the chain. If that's the way you want to be treated, I'm gonna treat you that way. If you want to be physical, mister, you better be an awful good man to take me.

From now on, I'd walk up and down that street and the guys'd say (imitates black accent), "Hiya mister po-lice, how ya doin'?" I don't care if you're yellow, pink, or purple, I'm a policeman and I demand respect. Not for me as an individual, but for what I represent. Unfortunately, the country's going the other way. They'll be throwing bricks and bottles at you and you'll be told don't do anything, they're merely expressing themselves.

Now this bit about advising people of their constitutional rights. I have been doing that for years. Nobody had to tell me to do it. I did it because I felt: Listen, baby, you open your big mouth and anything you tell me, I'm gonna use against you. I didn't come right out and say, "Sir, I must advise you of your constitutional rights." I didn't stand there and let them go bang-bang and stick-stick with a blade while I'm tellin' 'em. I'm just as much a policeman to the black man as I am to the white man, to the yellow man, to the liberal, to the conservative, to the hippie or whatever. I choose no sides.

I was respected as good cannon fodder. But where do I lack the quality of leadership? This is what bugs me. Is there something wrong with me that I can't be a leader? Who is to judge me? I've had guys on this job that have begged to work with me as a partner. If that doesn't show leadership . . .

Remember when you were a kid and the policeman took you across the street? What is he doing in essence? He's walking you through danger, is he not? Okay, I do the same thing. If I take you by the hand and walk you through Lincoln Park, nobody's gonna mess with you. But if I don't take you and walk you through the park, somebody's gonna mug you. I protect you from the dangerous elements. All these do-gooders that say, "Oh yeah, we respect you"—you have the feeling that they're saying yes with their mouth, but they're laughing at you. They don't respect me.

I'd love to go out on the college campus and grab some of these radicals. It's more or less a minority. When you apply logic and truth and philosophy, they cannot come back at you. You cannot fight truth. Who's being brutal? Before I make an arrest, I'll tell the guy, "You have a choice. You could be nice and we'll walk. If you become combative, I'm gonna have to break some bones. You forced the issue."

Oh yeah, the Democratic Convention. (A show of hurt appears, in the manner of a small boy's pout.) There was this radical garbage piece of thing, dirty, long-haired, not a human being in my book, standing by the paddy wagon. Not a mark on him. He spotted the camera and disappeared. In thirty seconds he came back. He was covered with all kinds of blood. He's screaming into the camera, "Look what they did to me!"

Lincoln Park. This group was comin' down on me. I'm by myself. They're comin' down the hill, "Kill the pig! Off the pig!" Well, I'm not a pig. There's only one of me and a whole mess of them. Well, *c'est le guerre*, sweetheart. I folded my arms, put my hand on my .38. I looked at them and said, "What's happening?" They stopped. They thought I was gonna pull out my weapon and start blowin' brains out. I didn't lose my cool. I'm a policeman, I don't scare. I'm dumb that way. (Laughs.) These kids were incited by someone to do something. They said, "Those guys up there with the cameras." I blame the media.

There's a picture in the Loop—*Sweet Sweetback's Badasss Song*—it is strictly hate-white. Nobody pickets that. You can imagine an anti-Negro flick? These people can get away with anything they want. But if you try it, zero, you'll get nailed. The radicals and the black militants, they're the dangers. They could be standing here on the street corner selling this Black Panther thing. (Imitates black accent), "This magazine is fo' de black man." He wants to off the pig. And I'm standing there. How do you think I feel? You know what off the pig means? Kill the pig. I look at them and I laugh. I'd like to break his neck. But I'm a policeman, a professional. I know the element they are. They're like the Nazi was with the Germans. The SS. No good.

To me, when I was a kid, the policeman was the epitome—not of perfection—was a good and evil in combination, but in *control*. He came from an element in the neighborhood and he knew what was going on. To me, a policeman is your community officer. He is your Officer Friendly, he is your clergyman, he is your counselor. He is a doctor to some: "Mr. Policeman, my son just fell and bumped his head." Now all we are is a guy that sits in a squad car and waits for a call to come over the radio. We have lost complete contact with the people. They get the assumption that we're gonna be called to the scene for one purpose—to become violent to make an arrest. No way I can see that. I am the community officer. They have taken me away from the people I'm dedicated to serving—and I don't like it.

The cop on the corner took you across the street, right? Now, ten o'clock at night, he's still there on the corner, and he tells you to get your fanny home. He's not being nice. The next time he tells you, he's gonna whack you with the stick. In the old days, if you went home and told your dad the cop on the corner whacked you with a stick, you know what your father did? He whacked you twice as hard. He said, "You shouldn't've been there. The policeman told you to go home, go home." Today these kids defy you.

I handed one parent a stick. I said, "Lady, when I leave this room and you don't apply that stick to this young lady's mouth, I will. I'll also sign charges against you for contributing to the delinquency of this child. You don't know how to be a parent." If I was sitting at a table with my father and threw a temper tantrum, I got knocked on my rear end. When I was picked up I was told, "You eat it, 'cause it's there." The law is there.

Take an old Western town. I just saw a thing with Richard Widmark on TV, which I thought was great. A town was being ramrodded by baddies. So they got ahold of this gunfighter and made him their sheriff, and he cleaned up the town. A little hard, but he was a nice guy. He got rid of the element and they told him he could have the job for as long as he wanted it. Then the people that put him in got power and they became dirty. They wanted things done and he said no. He wound up getting killed. This is what I feel about me and these do-gooders. They get power, I'm in their way.

I'm the element that stands between the legitimate person and the criminal. Years ago, he wore a .45 and he was a gunfighter and he wasted people. Okay, I don't believe in killing everybody. But I do believe we've gone overboard. They can shoot a guy like crazy but we cannot retaliate. I'm a target for these people. Go ahead, vent yourself. That's what I'm here for, a whipping boy. I'm not saying life in itself is violent, but I deal in the violent part of life.

There *is* a double standard, let's face it. You can stop John Doe's average son for smoking pot and he'll go to jail. But if I stop Johnny Q on the street and his daddy happens to be the president of a bank or he's very heavy in politics or knows someone, you look like a jerk. Why did you arrest *him?* Do you know who he is? I could care less who he is. If he breaks the law, go.

I made a raid up at the beach. The hippies were congregating, creating sex orgies and pot and everything. The word went out, especially about hitchhiking. Okay, we used to raid the beach and lock everybody up, didn't care who they were. One fella told me, "I'm gonna have your job. My father is out on the lake with the mayor." I said, "Fine, when you go to court bring your father *and* the mayor. But as far as I'm concerned, mister, you're doing a no-no, and you're going to jail."

We knew pot was involved. They were creating a disturbance. It was after eleven o'clock at night. You got rules and regulations for one reason—discipline. I consider the law as rules and regulations—in the military, on my job, or as citizens. They were puncturing tires, breaking antennas off cars, throwing bottles, fornicating on the beach—everything! Hitchhiking was impeding traffic. So I started locking them up for hitchhiking. All of a sudden, lay off! The citizens made a peace treaty with them. I'm the one who gets chastised! I did the job the citizens wanted me to do, right? All of a sudden, "Hey dummy, lay off!"

Jealous? Never. No way. I'm not prudish in any way, shape, or form. I'm far from being a virgin. (Laughs.) You're not a marine to be a virgin, no way in the world. But I don't believe in garbage. Sex is a beautiful thing. I dig it. But to exploit it in such a fashion to make it garbage, that to me is offensive. Jealousy, no way. I look at those people out there as I would be going to the zoo and watching the monkeys play games. That doesn't turn me on. They're all perverted people. I don't believe in perversion. They're making it strictly animal. Monkeys in the cage. I believe in one man and one woman.

Do all long-haired guys bug you?

I don't want my sons to have it. Now, the sideburns I wear because I do TV commercials and stuff. I'm in the modeling field.

He moonlights on occasion—modeling, appearing in industrial films, selling insurance, and driving semi-trucks. "I'm not necessarily ambitious. I do it because I like it. I jump in a truck and I'm gone to Iowa, Ohio, Kentucky. It's a great kick for me."

But I don't like long hair. If it's your bag, do it, but don't try to force it on me. A long-hair person doesn't bother me, but when you see that radical with the mop and that shanky garbage and you can smell 'em a block away, that bothers me.

A few years ago there was this hippie, long-haired, slovenly. He confronted me. Don't ever confront me when I tell you to move. That's a no-no. To make a long story short, I—uh—(laughs) I cut a piece of his long hair off and I handed it back to him. With a knife. It was just a spontaneous reaction. He was screaming "brutality." Anyway, a couple of weeks later I was confronted by this nice-looking fellow in a suit, haircut, everything. He said, "Officer, do you recognize me?" He pulled out this cellophane packet and handed it to me, and there was his hair in it. (Laughs.) I said, "That's you?" And he said, "Yeah. You showed me one thing. You really care about people. I just had to go out and get a job and prove something to you." That kid joined the Marine Corps.

Sometimes I feel like a father out there. You don't really want to paddle your kid's rear end. It hurts you ten times more than it does him. But you have to put the point across, and if it becomes necessary to use a little constructive criticism . . . I will think of my father a lot of times. No way did he spare the rod on my rump. And I never hated him for it, no way. I loved him for it.

My sons adore me. My wife can't understand this. If they do something wrong in my presence—(mumbles) even though I don't live in that house—they get punished. My wife said, "You're so hard with them at times, yet they worship the ground you walk on." When I used the belt on them I'd always tell them why. They understand and they accept it. My oldest boy is now on the honor rolls at Notre Dame High School.

He gets a little stubborn. He'd confront me with things: "I want to wear my hair long." You want to wear your hair long, get out of my house. You know what it represents to me. Till the day you are twenty-one and you will leave my jurisdiction, you will do as I tell you. You understand?" "Okay Dad, you're the boss." That's all there is to it. There's no resentment, no animosity. It's just an understanding that I lay the law down. There are rules and regulations.

But I'm not a robot, I think for myself. One thing bugs me. Burglary is a felony. If a burglar is trapped and becomes physical and is shot to death, that's justifiable homicide. Mayor Daley made an utterance—shoot to kill—and they—click—blew it up. I don't think he meant it literally.

I can't shoot an unarmed person. No way. Anyway, knowing people, they'll say, "Forget it, we're insured." So why should I get involved over an insurance matter? I would love to go after people who perpetrate robberies or hurt other people. A theft, granted it's a crime, but most of the people it hurts is the insurance company. Robbery is hurting a person.

I prefer going after robbery more than homicide. When a guy commits murder, he's usually done. He's caught and goes to the penitentiary or the chair. But a guy that commits robbery doesn't usually get caught the first time, second, third time. He's out there over and over again. I want to grab the guy that's hitting all the time, instead of the guy that's doing the one shot. I love risk and challenge. Driving a semi down the road is challenging. You never know what's going to happen. (Laughs.) Some guy passes you, cuts you off, you're jack-knifed. You blow a tire, you're gone. I don't like a boring life.

When I worked as a bartender, I felt like a non-person. I was actually nothing. I was a nobody going nowhere. I was in a state of limbo. I had no hopes, no dreams, no ups, no downs, nothing. Being a policeman gives me the challenge in life that I want. Some day I'll be promoted. Somebody's gonna say, "Maher has had it for a long time. Let's give him something." Some sort of recognition. I've proven myself. I don't think it's necessary for a man to prove himself over and over and over again. I'm a policeman, win, lose, or draw.

I'm in this Loop traffic. I don't even consider this a job. It's like R&R, rest and recreation. My day today is like—(whistles) it's a no-no. It's nothing, I get up, I eat, and I blow the whistle. It's not very exciting. I'm looking at it now as a fellow who goes to the office and he's not very enthused. Because I wear a uniform people that are garbage will say I'm a pig. They don't look at me and say, "This is a human being." They look at my dress. I'm a representative of the law, of you, the citizen. You created my job, you created me. To you, I am a robot in uniform. You press a button and when you call me to the scene you expect results. But I'm also a man. I even have a heart. (Laughs.)

PAULINE KAEL, FILM CRITIC OF *The New Yorker*

Work is rarely treated in films. It's one of the peculiarities of the movies. You hardly see a person at work. There was a scene in *Kitty Foyle*, with Ginger Rogers. It wasn't really well done, but it was so startling that people talked about it. Any kind of work scene that has any quality at all becomes memorable. The automat sequence in *Easy*

Living, the Preston Sturges film. It was done many years ago, yet people still talk about it. It's amazing how rarely work life gets on the screen.

Television now offers us this incredible fantasy on hospital work. In the movie *The Hospital* you really saw how a hospital worked. (Laughs.) The audience recognized the difference. They started laughing right from the very first frames of that film. Because we all know the truth: Hospitals are chaotic, disorganized places where no one really knows what he's doing. This pleased the audience as a counterview of the television hospital's cleanliness and order.

Just think of Marcus Welby. All those poor, sad people are going to this father figure for advice. You know actually that you go to a doctor, he tells you nothing. You're sent to another doctor. The screen doesn't show how we actually feel about doctors—the resentment because of the money they make, the little help they give us.

Movies set up these glamorized occupations. When people find they are waitresses, they feel degraded. No kid says I want to be a waiter, I want to run a cleaning establishment. There is a tendency in movies to degrade people if they don't have white-collar professions. So people form a low self-image of themselves, because their lives can never match the way Americans live—on the screen.

I consider myself one of the lucky ones because I really enjoy what I do. I love my occupation. But I've spent most of my life working at jobs I hated. I've worked at boring office jobs. I never felt they were demeaning, but they exhausted my energy and spirit. I do think most people work at jobs that mechanize them and depersonalize them.

The occasional satisfaction in work is never shown on the screen, say, of the actor or the writer. The people doing drudge jobs enjoy these others because they think they make a lot of money. What they should envy them for is that they take pleasure in their work. Society plays that down. I think enormous harm has been done by the television commercial telling ghetto children they should go to school because their earning capacity would be higher. They never suggest that if you're educated you may go into fields where your work is satisfying, where you may be useful, where you can really do something that can help other people.

When I worked at drudge jobs to support the family I used to have headaches all the time, feeling rotten at the end of the day. I don't think I've taken an aspirin or a pill in the last twenty years. The one thing that disturbs me on television is the housewife, who's always in need of a headache remedy from tension and strain. This is an incredible image of the American woman. Something terrible must be going on inside her if she's in that shape. Of course, she's become a compulsive maniac about scrubbing and polishing and cleaning—in that commercial.

Housewives in the movies and on television are mindless. Now it takes a lot of intelligence to handle children and it's a fascinating process watching kids grow up. Being involved with kids may be much more creative than what their husbands do at drudge jobs.

To show accurate pictures, you're going to outrage industry. In the news recently we've learned of the closing of industrial plants—and the men, who've worked for twenty years, losing out on their pensions. Are you going to see this in a movie? It's going to have to be a very tough muckraking filmmaker to show us how industry discards people. Are you going to have a movie that shows us how stewardesses are discarded at a certain age? And violate the beautiful pact that the airlines have with the movie companies, where they jointly advertise one another?

We now have conglomerate ownership of the movie industry. Are they going to show us how these industries really dehumanize their workers? Muckraking was possible when the movie companies were independent of big industry. Now that Gulf & Western, AVCA, Trans-America, these people own the movie companies, this is very tough. Are you going to do muckraking about the record industry, when the record from the movie grosses more than the film itself?

It's a long time since we've had a movie about a strike, isn't it? You get something about the Molly Maguires, which is set in the past, but you don't see how the working relationship is now. I'd be interested in seeing a film on Lordstown.

THE DEMON LOVER

PHIL STALLINGS, SPOT-WELDER

He is a spot-welder at the Ford assembly plant on the far South Side of Chicago. He is twenty-seven years old; recently married. He works the third shift: 3:30 P.M. to midnight.

"I start the automobile, the first welds. From there it goes to another line, where the floor's put on, the roof, the trunk hood, the doors. Then it's put on a frame. There is hundreds of lines.

"The welding gun's got a square handle, with a button on the top for high voltage and a button on the bottom for low. The first is to clamp the metal together. The second is to fuse it.

"The gun hangs from a ceiling, over tables that ride on a track. It travels in a circle, oblong, like an egg. You stand on a cement platform, maybe six inches from the ground."

I stand in one spot, about two- or three-feet area, all night. The only time a person stops is when the line stops. We do about thirty-two jobs per car, per unit. Forty-eight units an hour, eight hours a day. Thirty-two times forty-eight times eight. Figure it out. That's how many times I push that button.

The noise, oh it's tremendous. You open your mouth and you're liable to get a mouthful of sparks. (Shows his arms.) That's a burn, these are burns. You don't compete against the noise. You go to yell and at the same time you're straining to maneuver the gun to where you have to weld.

You got some guys that are uptight, and they're not sociable. It's too rough. You pretty much stay to yourself. You get involved with yourself. You dream, you think of things you've done. I drift back continuously to when I was a kid and what me and my brothers did. The things you love most are the things you drift back into.

Lots of times I worked from the time I started to the time of the break and I never realized I had even worked. When you dream, you reduce the chances of friction with the foreman or with the next guy.

It don't stop. It just goes and goes and goes. I bet there's men who have lived and died out there, never seen the end of that line. And they never will—because it's endless. It's like a serpent. It's just all body, no tail. It can do things to you . . . (Laughs.)

Repetition is such that if you were to think about the job itself, you'd slowly go out of your mind. You'd let your problems build up, you'd get to a point where you'd be at the fellow next to you—his throat. Every time the foreman came by and looked at you, you'd have something to say. You just strike out at anything you can. So if you involve yourself by yourself, you overcome this.

I don't like the pressure, the intimidation. How would you like to go up to someone and say, "I would like to go to the bathroom"? If the foreman doesn't like you, he'll make you hold it, just ignore you. Should I leave this job to go to the bathroom I risk being fired. The line moves all the time.

I work next to Jim Grayson and he's preoccupied. The guy on my left, he's a Mexican, speaking Spanish, so it's pretty hard to understand him. You just avoid him. Brophy, he's a young fella, he's going to college. He works catty-corner from me. Him and I talk from time to time. If he ain't in the mood, I don't talk. If I ain't in the mood, he knows it.

Oh sure, there's tension here. It's not always obvious, but the whites stay with the whites and the coloreds stay with the coloreds. When you go into Ford, Ford says, "Can you work with other men?" This stops a lot of trouble, 'cause when you're working side by side with a guy, they can't afford to have guys fighting. When two men don't socialize, that means two guys are gonna do more work, know what I mean?

I don't understand how come more guys don't flip. Because you're nothing more than a machine when you hit this type of thing. They give better care to that machine than they will to you. They'll have more respect, give more attention to that machine. And you *know* this. Somehow you get the feeling that the machine is better than you are. (Laughs.)

You really begin to wonder. What price do they put on me? Look at the price they put on the machine. If that machine breaks down, there's somebody out there to fix it right away. If I break down, I'm just pushed over to the other side till another man takes my place. The only thing they have on their mind is to keep that line running.

I'll do the best I can. I believe in an eight-hour pay for an eight-hour day. But I will not try to outreach my limits. If I can't cut it, I just don't do it. I've been there three years and I keep my nose pretty clean. I never cussed anybody or anything like that. But I've had some real brushes with foremen.

What happened was my job was overloaded. I got cut and it got infected. I got blood poisoning. The drill broke. I took it to the foreman's desk. I says, "Change this as soon as you can." We were running specials for XL hoods. I told him I wasn't a repair man. That's how the conflict began. I says, "If you want, take me to the Green House." Which is a superintendent's office—disciplinary station. This is when he says, "Guys like you I'd like to see in the parking lot."

One foreman I know, he's about the youngest out here, he has this idea: I'm it and if you don't like it, you know what you can do. Anything this other foreman says, he usually overrides. Even in some cases, the foremen don't get along. They're pretty hard to live with, even with each other.

Oh yeah, the foreman's got somebody knuckling down on him, putting the screws to him. But a foreman is still free to go to the bathroom, go get a cup of coffee. He doesn't face the penalties. When I first went in there, I kind of envied foremen. Now, I wouldn't have a foreman's job. I wouldn't give 'em the time of the day.

When a man becomes a foreman, he has to forget about even being human, as far as feelings are concerned. You see a guy there bleeding to death. So what, buddy? That line's gotta keep goin'. I can't live like that. To me, if a man gets hurt, first thing you do is get him some attention.

About the blood poisoning. It came from the inside of a hood rubbin' against me. It caused quite a bit of pain. I went down to the medics. They said it was a boil. Got to my doctor that night. He said blood poisoning. Running fever and all this. Now I've smartened up.

They have a department of medics. It's basically first aid. There's no doctor on our shift, just two or three nurses, that's it. They've got a door with a sign on it that says Lab. Another door with a sign on it: Major Surgery. But my own personal opinion, I'm afraid of 'em. I'm afraid if I were to get hurt, I'd get nothin' but back talk. I got hit square in the chest one day with a bar from a rack and it cut me down this side. They didn't take X-rays or nothing. Sent me back on the job. I missed three and a half days two weeks ago. I had bronchitis. They told me I was all right. I didn't have a fever. I went home and my doctor told me I couln't go back to work for two weeks. I really needed the money, so I had to go back the next day. I woke up still sick, so I took off the rest of the week.

I pulled a muscle on my neck, straining. This gun, when you grab this thing from the ceiling, cable, weight, I mean you're pulling everything. Your neck, your shoulders, and your back. I'm very surprised more accidents don't happen. You have to lean over, at the same time holding down the gun. This whole edge here is sharp. I go through a shirt every two weeks, it just goes right through. My coveralls catch on fire. I've had gloves catch on fire. (Indicates arms.) See them little holes? That's what sparks do. I've got burns across here from last night.

I know I could find better places to work. But where could I get the money I'm making? Let's face it, $4.32 an hour. That's real good money now. Funny thing is, I don't mind working at body construction. To a great degree, I enjoy it. I love using my hands—more than I do my mind. I love to be able to put things together and see something in the long run. I'll be the first to admit I've got the easiest job on the line. But I'm against this thing where I'm being held back. I'll work like a dog until I get what I want. The job I really want is utility.

It's where I can stand and say I can do any job in this department, and nobody has to worry about me. As it is now, out of say, sixty jobs, I can do almost half of 'em. I want to get away from standing in one spot. Utility can do a different job every day. Instead of working right there for eight hours I could work over there for eight, I could work the other place for eight. Every day it would change. I would be around more people. I go out on my lunch break and work on the fork truck for a half-hour—to get the experience. As soon as I got it down pretty good, the foreman in charge says he'll take me. I don't want the other guys to see me. When I hit that fork lift, you just stop your thinking and you concentrate. Something right there in front of you, not in the past, not in the future. This is real healthy.

I don't eat lunch at work. I may grab a candy bar, that's enough. I wouldn't be able to hold it down. The tension your body is put under by the speed of the line . . . When you hit them brakes, you just can't stop. There's a certain momentum that carries you forward. I could hold the food, but it wouldn't set right.

Proud of my work? How can I feel pride in a job where I call a foreman's attention to a mistake, a bad piece of equipment, and he'll ignore it. Pretty soon you get the idea they don't care. You keep doing this and finally you're titled a troublemaker. So you just go about your work. You *have* to have pride. So you throw it off to something else. And that's my stamp collection.

I'd break both my legs to get into social work. I see all over so many kids really gettin' a raw deal. I think I'd go into juvenile. I tell kids on the line, "Man, go out there and get that college." Because it's too late for me now.

When you go into Ford, first thing they try to do is break your spirit. I seen them bring a tall guy where they needed a short guy. I seen them bring a short guy where you have to stand on two guys' backs to do something. Last night, they brought a fifty-eight-year-old man to do the job I was on. That man's my father's age. I know damn well my father couldn't do it. To me, this is humanely wrong. A job should be a job, not a death sentence.

The younger worker, when he gets uptight, he talks back. But you take an old fellow, he's got a year, two years, maybe three years to go. If it was me, I wouldn't say a word, I wouldn't care what they did. 'Cause, baby, for another two years I can stick it out. I can't blame this man. I respect him because he had enough will power to stick it out for thirty years.

It's gonna change. There's a trend. We're getting younger and younger men. We got this new Thirty and Out. Thirty years seniority and out. The whole idea is to give a man more time, more time to slow down and live. While he's still in his fifties, he can settle down in a camper and go out and fish. I've sat down and thought about it. I've got twenty-seven years to go. (Laughs.) That's why I don't go around causin' trouble or lookin' for a cause.

The only time I get involved is when it affects me or it affects a man on the line in a condition that could be me. I don't believe in lost causes, but when it all happened . . . (He pauses, appears bewildered.)

The foreman was riding the guy. The guy either told him to go away or pushed him, grabbed him . . . You can't blame the guy—Jim Grayson. I don't want nobody stickin' their finger in my face. I'd've probably hit him beside the head. The whole thing was: Damn it, it's about time we took a stand. Let's stick up for the guy. We stopped the line. (He pauses, grins.) Ford lost about twenty units. I'd figure about five grand a unit—whattaya got? (Laughs.)

I said, "Let's all go home." When the line's down like that, you can go up to one man and say, "You gonna work?" If he says no, they can fire him. See what I mean? But if nobody was there, who the hell were they gonna walk up to and say, "Are you gonna work?" Man, there woulda been nobody there! If it were up to me, we'd gone home.

Jim Grayson, the guy I work next to, he's colored. Absolutely. That's the first time I've seen unity on that line. Now it's happened once, it'll happen again. Because everybody just sat down. Believe you me. (Laughs.) It stopped at eight and it didn't start till twenty after eight. Everybody and his brother were down there. It was really nice to see, it really was.

NED WILLIAMS, STOCK CHASER

I done the same job twenty-two years, twenty-three years. Everybody else on that job is dead.

He has worked for the Ford Motor Company from 1946 to now. His wife is a seamstress. They have six children. In the parlor of his two-story frame house he acts out his life, his work. He cannot sit still. He moves about the room, demonstrates, jabs at the air in the manner of an oldtime boxer. He has a quickness about him—for a moment, in the guest's mind, is the portrait of the agile little forward who led Wendell Phillips High School's basketball team to triumphs in the late twenties.

I started out on truck tires. I made sixty to eighty jobs a day, and this is all times six. We put in six days a week. A job's a whole truck. And six tires to a truck, plus spare. There was a trick to putting the rim in, so that it had a little click. You had to be very fine to know. So you would put this clip around and then you stand over it, and I would just kick it over—boom!—in there. This I had to learn on my own. Didn't nobody teach me this. I'd take this tire, roll it up, I'll lay it right beside. I'd come back, get another tire, put it on, get another tire, put it on . . .

He indicates a photograph on the end table. It is a young Ned Williams, smiling, surrounded by a whole wall of tires. He is wearing gloves.

After you mount it, you just don't leave them there on the floor. We had to put air in 'em, and then roll 'em on to little stalls. And these tires come on racks. I'd go get 'em, and you can't reach in the rack and grab any tire. You got 7/15's, you got 6/15's, you got 7/18's, you got 10/20's.

I could knock down five tires like that. Just take my left hand, guide 'em with my right. If you don't get production, you're out of there. I got my skill playin' basketball. Gotta speed it up. You had a quota, startin' time in the morning and another in the afternoon. At that time there was two of us, then they cut it down to one.

Bend and reach—like a giraffe. I had to jump all the time. Sometime I had to climb. I continually told 'em to lower the racks. They wasn't supposed to put but seventy-five on the racks. But they put 125, 140, 150. And it's up as high as you could get up on a ladder. A lot of times you pull a tire around like that (feverishly he relives the moment in pantomime)—it might go around your glasses, around your head. Some got hurt.

I wish I had a penny for every time I jumped. You really don't have time to feel tired. I'm tired, yeah, but I got a job to do. I had to do it. I had no time to think or daydream. I woulda quit. (Laughs.) Worked on the line till about two years ago.

I'm arrogant. Not too much now. Before I was. The only way I could object is—don't do it. When I get tired, I come in there with one of my mean days . . . I didn't care if they let me go and they knew it. I was proud of my work. Just don't push me. I was born here.

For the first four hours I worked there I was gonna quit. I had been addressed just the wrong way. I just came out of service. This foreman, he walked around like a little guard. Shoot me in the back, I was doin' the best I could. I had never been on an assembly line in my life. This thing's moving, going. You gotta pick it up, baby. You gotta be fast on that. He was like a little shotgun. Go to the washroom, he's looking for you.

He was pushing. Somebody's pushing him, right? After I went and ate, I felt pretty good. I said, "I'm gonna defeat him." I worked under him for ten years. That man sent me a Christmas card every Christmas. We had a certain layoff in 1946. He said, "I'm gonna get some job for you here." That's when I got into tires. See, I been here four hours now and he's on my back. I came back in the afternoon, after that he was love and kisses. I wanted to do a job really.

I had a sense of responsibility. I been to the Green House many times, though, man. That's for a reprimand. You goofed. How I goofed? Say I'm runnin' 400 jobs, 450. I can look at that sheet, and after you look at that paper so long you may read the same thing twice, right? I'd be reprimanded. It's fast work, but they didn't see it. You can do twenty years of right and one hour of wrong and they'd string you.

If somebody else is treated bad, I'll talk for him. Maybe he don't have sense enough. They say, "Tend to your own business." My business is his business. He's just like me. When a foreman says to me it's none of my business I say, "If I was in the same shoe, you'd try to do that to me, but you better not. No, they ain't never gonna get me till I'm down and dead."

Sometimes I felt like I was just a robot. You push a button and you go this way. You become a mechanical nut. You get a couple of beers and go to sleep at night. Maybe one, two o'clock in the morning, my wife is saying, "Come on, come on, leave it." I'm still workin' that line. Three o'clock in the morning, five o'clock. Tired. I have worked that job all night. Saturday, Sunday, still working. It's just ground into you. My wife tap me on the shoulder. Tappin' me didn't mean nothin'. (Laughs.)

Sometimes I got up on my elbows. I woke up on a Sunday goin' to work. We were working six days a week then. I still thought it was another workday. My wife, she sees me go in the bathroom. "Where you goin'? Come back." I got washed up, everything. "Where you goin'? You got a girl this time of the morning?" I said, "What? What girl? I'm just goin' to work." She says, "On Sunday?" I said, "Today's Sunday? Jesus Christ!" A mechanical nut. Yet, honest to God, I done that more than once. Nineteen fifty-four I know I done it twice.

I was sleeping in front of an American Legion post. I had more than a few drinks. This was Sunday. Somebody says, "Go home." I thought they said, "Go to work." Whoosh! I had a brand-new 1955 Montclair Merc and I whoosh! I cut out of there. I went out to the plant and drove all the way to the gate and got there, and I don't see no cars. I don't know what, baby.

It just affected all the parts of my life as far as that go. I'm looking at the fellas been here longer than me. They the same way, worse. I talk to 'em every day, and I hear fellas that got forty-two years, thirty-seven years, thirty-five years. Mechanical nuts.

The union does the best they can. But if the man has a record, there's nothin' union can do. They put the book on the table and he gets his time off, maybe a week, maybe three days, maybe three weeks. It's no paid vacation.

Some of the younger guys are objectin', oh yeah. They got nothin' to lose. Just like my boy I got hired out there. Some of 'em are twenty, twenty-two, ain't got no wife, so they don't worry about it. They don't show up on Monday, they don't show up on Tuesday. Take 'em to the Green House. Give 'em a week off, they don't care. If I could figure 'em out, I could be a millionaire and just sit on the porch out here. I could retire right now if I could figure 'em out.

If I had my life to live over again, it would be the first thirty-five years of my life. I didn't do nothin'. I don't like work, I never did like work. There's some elderly people here right now who looked at my mother and said, "I never thought that boy would work." My hands were so soft, like a sponge. Went to a manicurist twice a week. I always wore gloves at work. I didn't want to get my hands messed up.

I am a stock chaser now for the audit area. I get all the small parts you need, that I carry on a bicycle—like a mirror or chrome or door panels. I get 'em as quickies, 'cause I'm on the sell floor. This job is ready to go. Been doin' this last two years. Up front. There's hardly anybody there that's under twenty years' service. That's old folks home.

It's a cut in pay. I have what you call a nonpromotion job. It's easier work, I don't have to bend down now. It ain't right, but this is what you live under. I was a good worker, but I suffered that for this. Say you lose $1.20 a day. I come home and I can still play volleyball.

I don't feel tired, just older. I haven't talked in my sleep since I got off that job. I don't bring nothin' home now. I got the keys to the bicycle and that's it. (Laughs.) I don't worry about it till I get there.

Is the automobile worth it?

What it drains out of a human being, the car ain't worth it. But I think of a certain area of proudness. You see them on that highway, you don't look and see what model it is or whose car it is. I put my labor in it. And somebody just like me put their area of work in it. It's got to be an area of proudness.

WHEELER STANLEY, GENERAL FOREMAN

I *'m probably the youngest general foreman in the plant, yes, sir." He was invited to sit in the chair of the plant manager, Tom Brand. "I'm in the chassis line right now. There's 372 people working for us, hourly. And thirteen foremen. I'm the lead general foreman."*

He grew up in this area, "not more than five minutes away. I watched the Ford plant grow from when I was a little boy." His father is a railroad man and he is the only son among four children. He is married and has two small children.

He has just turned thirty. He appears always to be "at attention." It is not accidental. "I always had one ambition. I wanted to go in the army and be a paratrooper. So I became a paratrooper. When I got out of the army, where I majored in communications, I applied at Illinois Bell. But nobody was hiring. So I came out here as an hourly man. Ten years ago. I was twenty."

I was a cushion builder. We made all the seats and trim. I could comprehend it real easy. I moved around considerably. I was a spot-welder. I went from cushion to trim to body shop, paint. I could look at a job and I could do it. My mind would just click. I could stand back, look at a job, and five minutes later I can go and do it. I enjoyed the work. I felt it was a man's job. You can do something with your hands. You can go home at night and feel you have accomplished something.

Did you find the assembly line boring?

No, uh-uh. Far from boring. There was a couple of us that we were hired together. We'd come up with different games—like we'd take the numbers of the jeeps that went by. That guy loses, he buys coffee. I very rarely had any problems with the other guys. We had a lot of respect for each other. If you're a deadhead when you're an hourly man and you go on supervision, they don't have much use for you. But if they know the guy's aggressive and he tries to do a job, they tend to respect him.

I'm the kind of guy, if I was due for a raise I'm not gonna ask for it. If they don't feel I'm entitled to it, they're not gonna give it to me. If they think I'm entitled to it, they'll give it to me. If I don't deserve it, I'm not gonna get it. I don't question my boss, I don't question the company.

When I came here I wanted to be a utility man. He goes around and spot relieves everybody. I thought that was the greatest thing in the world. When the production manager asked me would I consider training for a foreman's job, boy! my sights left utility. I worked on all the assembly lines. I spent eighteen months on the lines, made foreman, and eighteen months later I made general foreman—March of '66.

A lot of the old-timers had more time in the plant than I had time in the world. Some of 'em had thirty, thirty-five years' service. I had to overcome their resentment and get their respect. I was taught one thing: to be firm but fair. Each man has got an assignment of work to do. If he has a problem, correct it. If he doesn't have a problem, correct him.

If an hourly man continued to let the work go, you have to take disciplinary action. You go progressively, depending on the situation. If it was me being a young guy and he resented it, I would overlook it and try to get him to think my way. If I couldn't, I had to go to the disciplinary route—which would be a reprimand, a warning.

If they respect you, they'll do anything for you. If they don't, they won't do nothin' for you. Be aggressive. You have to know each and every man and know how they react. I have to know each and every one of my foremen. I know how they react, all thirteen.

There's a few on the line you can associate with. I haven't as yet. When you get familiarity it causes—the more you get to know somebody, it's hard to distinguish between boss and friend. This isn't good for my profession. But I don't think we ever change much. Like I like to say, "We put our pants on the same way." We work together, we live together. But they always gotta realize you're the boss.

I want to get quality first, then everything else'll come. The line runs good, the production's good, you get your cost and you get your good workmanship. When they hire in, you gotta show 'em you're firm. We've got company rules. We've got about seventeen different rules here at Chicago Ford Assembly that we try to enforce from the beginning.

The case begins with a reprimand, a warning procedure. A lotta times they don't realize this is the first step to termination. If they've got thirty years' service, twenty years' service, they never realize it. There's always a first step to termination. If you catch a guy stealing, the first step is a termination. In the case of workmanship, it's a progressive period. A reprimand, docked time—three days, a week. Then a termination.

You mean discharge?

Discharge. This isn't always the end. You always try to correct it. It's not directly our responsibility to discharge. It's a labor relations responsibility. We initiate the discipline and support the case for a discharge.

Guys talk about the Green House . . .

I never call it a Green House. This is childish. It never seemed right to me: "I'll take you to the Green House." You wanted to tell a guy in a man's way, "If you don't do better, I'll take you to the office." Or "We'll go to labor relations to solve this thing." It sounds a lot more management. Not this: "I'm gonna take you to the Green House."

When you worked on the line, were you ever taken to the . . . office?

No. I didn't take no time off and I always did my job well, wore my glasses and everything. I don't think I've missed three days in the last five years. My wife likes to nag me, because if she gets sick I pick up my mother-in-law and bring her over. "You stay with my wife, she's not that bad. I'm going to work."

Dad never missed work. He worked hard. He used to work a lot of overtime. He'd work sixteen hours. They'd say, "He gets his wind on the second shift." He started off as a switchman. Now he's general yard master. He's been a company man all his life. I always admired him for it.

Do you feel your army training helped you?

Considerably. I learned respect. A lotta times you like to shoot your mouth off. You really don't know how to control your pride. Pride is a good attribute, but if you got too much of it . . . when it interferes with your good judgment and you don't know how to control it . . . In the army, you learn to shut up and do your job and eat a little crow now and then. It helps.

There's an old saying: The boss ain't always right but he's still the boss. He has things applied to him from top management, where they see the whole picture. A lot of times I don't agree with it. There's an instance now. We've been having trouble with water leaks. It doesn't affect the chassis department, but it's so close we have to come up with the immediate fix. We have to suffer the penalty of two additional people. It reflects on your costs, which is one of my jobs. When the boss says pay 'em, we pay 'em. But I don't believe our department should be penalized because of a problem created in another department. There's a lot of pride between these departments. There's competition between the day shift and the night shift. Good, wholesome competition never hurt.

Prior to going on supervision, you think hourly. But when you become management, you have to look out for the company's best interests. You always have to present a management attitude. I view a management attitude as, number one, a neat-appearing-type foreman. You don't want to come in sloppy, dirty. You want to come in looking like a foreman. You always conduct yourself in a man's way.

I couldn't be a salesman. A salesman would be below me. I don't like to go and bother people or try to sell something to somebody that they don't really want, talk them into it. Not me. I like to come to work and do my job. Out here, it's a big job. There's a lot of responsibility. It's not like working in a soup factory, where all you do is make soup cans. If you get a can punched wrong, you put it on the side and don't worry about it. You can't do that with a five-thousand-dollar-car.

There's no difference between young and old workers. There's an old guy out here, he's a colored fella, he's on nights. He must be fifty-five years old, but he's been here only five years. He amazes me. He tells me, "I'll be here if I have to walk to work." Some young guys tell you the same thing. I don't feel age has any bearing on it. Colored or white, old or young, it's the caliber of the man himself.

In the old days, when they fought for the union, they might have needed the union then. But now the company is just as good to them as the union is. We had a baseball meeting a couple of nights ago and the guys couldn't get over the way the company supported a banquet for them and the trophies and the jackets. And the way Tom Brand participated in the banquet himself.

A few years ago, it was hourly versus management—there was two sides of the world. Now it's more molded into one. It's not hourly and management; it's the company. Everybody is involved in the company. We've achieved many good things, as baseball tournaments, basketball leagues. We've had golf outings. Last year we started a softball league. The team they most wanted to beat was supervision—our team. It brought everybody so much closer together. It's one big family now. When we first started, this is '65, '66, it was the company against the union. It's not that way any more.

What's the next step for you?

Superintendent. I've been looking forward to it. I'd be department head of chassis. It's the largest department in the plant.

And after that?

Pre-delivery manager. And then production manager and then operation manager is the way it goes—chain of command. Last year our operation man went to Europe for four months. While he was gone I took the job as a training period.

And eventually?

Who knows? Superintendent, first. That's my next step. I've got a great
feeling for Ford because it's been good to me. As far as I'm concerned,
you couldn't ask for a better company. It's got great insurance benefits
and everything else. I don't think it cost me two dollars to have my two
children. My son, he's only six years old and I've taken him through the
plant. I took him through one night and the electricians were working the
body hoists. He pushed the button and he ran the hoist around and he
couldn't get over that. He can now work a screw driver motor. I showed
him that. He just enjoyed it. And that's all he talks about: "I'm going to
work for Ford, too." And I say, "Oh, no you ain't." And my wife will shut
me up and she'll say, "Why not?" Then I think to myself, "Why not? It's
been good to me."

I like to see people on the street and when they say, "I got a new Ford,"
I ask how it is. You stop at a tavern, have a drink, or you're out for an
evening, and they say, "I've got a new Ford," you like to be inquisitive. I
like to find out if they like the product. It's a great feeling when you find
someone says, "I like it, it rides good. It's quiet. Everything you said it
would be."

Have you heard of Lordstown, where the Vega plant is?

I like to read *The Wall Street Journal*. I'd like to invest some in Wall
Street. I'd like to learn more about the stock market. Financially, I can't
do it yet—two small children . . . I read the entire Lordstown article
they had in there. I think the union was unjustified. And I think
management could have done a better job. A hundred cars an hour is
quite excessive. But again, you're building a small car and it's easier to set
a line up. But I understand there was some sabotage.

I think the president of the union is only twenty-nine years old. I
imagine he's a real hardheaded type of individual. He's headstrong and he
wants his way. If I was working with him, we'd probably be bumpin' heads
quite a bit. I've been known to be hardheaded and hard-nosed and real
stubborn if I have to be.

I won a scholarship at Mendel High School, but I couldn't afford the
books. At the time, my family was pretty hard up. So I went to Vocational
High and it was the biggest mistake I ever made. I was used to a Catholic
grammar school. I needed Catholic schooling to keep me in line 'cause I
was a pretty hot-tempered type.

I'm the type of guy, sometimes you gotta chew me out to let me know you're still around. If you didn't, I might forget and relax. I don't like to relax. I can't afford it. I like to stay on my toes. I don't want to get stagnant, because if do, I'm not doing anybody any good.

(He studies his watch. It has all the appurtenances: second, minute, hour, day, month, year . . .)

I refer to my watch all the time. I check different items. About every hour I tour my line. About six thirty, I'll tour labor relations to find out who is absent. At seven, I hit the end of the line. I'll check paint, check my scratches and damage. Around ten I'll start talking to all the foremen. I make sure they're all awake, they're in the area of their responsibility. So we can shut down the end of the line at two o'clock and everything's clean. Friday night everybody'll get paid and they'll want to get out of here as quickly as they can. I gotta keep 'em on the line. I can't afford lettin' 'em get out early.

We can't have no holes, no nothing.

If a guy was hurt to the point where it would interfere with production, then it stops. We had a fella some years ago, he was trapped with body. The only way we could get him off was to shut the line off. Reverse the belt, in order to get his fingers out. We're gonna shut the line to see that he don't get hurt any more. A slight laceration or something like that, that's an everyday occurrence. You have to handle 'em.

What's your feeling walking the floor?

Like when I take the superintendent's job, if he's going on vacation for a week. They drive what they call an M-10 unit. Their license plate is always a numeral 2, with a letter afterwards: like 2-A, 2-D—which reflects the manager's car. When he's on vacation and I take his job, all his privileges become mine for a week. You're thirty years old and you're gonna be a manager at forty. I couldn't ask for nothing better. When I take the car home for a week, I'm proud of that license plate. It says "Manufacturer" on it, and they know I work for Ford. It's a good feeling.

Plant manager Tom Brand has returned. Wheeler Stanley rises from the chair in soldier-like fashion. Brand is jovial. "In traveling around plants, we're fortunate if we have two or three like him, that are real comers. It isn't gonna be too long that these fellas are gonna take our jobs. Always be kind to your sweeper, you never know when you're going to be working for him." (Laughs.) Wheeler Stanley smiles.

He had been hauling steel *"out of the Gary mills into Wisconsin. They call this a short haul, about 150 miles in radius."* He had been at it since 1949 when he was nineteen years old. *"I figure about 25 hundred trips. Sounds monotonous, doesn't it?"*

Most steel haulers are owner-operators of truck and trailer. *"We changed over to diesel about fifteen years ago. Big powerful truck. You lease your equipment to the trucking companies. Their customers are the big steel corporations. This is strictly a one-man operation."*

Since the wildcat strike of 1967 he's been an organizer for the Fraternal Association of Steel Haulers (FASH). *"Forty-six months trying to build an association, to give the haulers a voice and get 'em better working conditions. And a terrific fight with the Teamsters Union."*

Casually, though at times with an air of incredulousness, he recounts a day in the life of a steel hauler.

I'll go into the steel mills after supper. Load through the evening hours, usually with a long waiting line, especially years ago before the Association started. We'd wait as high as twelve, fifteen hours to get loaded. The trucking companies didn't charge the corporations for any waiting time, demurrage—like they did on railroad cars.

We get a flat percentage no matter how much work we put in. It didn't cost the trucking company anything to have us wait out there, so they didn't charge the steel outfits anything. They abused us terribly over the years. We waited in the holding yard behind the steel mill. The longest I've ever waited was twenty-five hours.

You try to keep from going crazy from boredom. You become accustomed to this as time goes by—four hours, eight hours, twelve hours. It's part of the job to build patience. You sit in the cab of the truck. You walk a half mile down to a PX-type of affair, where you buy a wrapped sandwich in cellophane or a cup of coffee to go. You sit in the mill by the loader's desk and watch the cranes. You'll read magazines, you'll sleep four hours, you'll do anything from going nuts. Years ago, there was no heat in the steel mills. You had to move around to keep from freezing. It's on the lakefront, you know.

Following the '67 wildcat strike, the trucking companies instituted a tariff that said four hours we give the steel mill for nothing, the fifth hour we begin to charge at $13.70 an hour. We get seventy-five percent of that or ten dollars. And when we deliver, they got four free hours at our point of delivery. So we start every day by giving away eight potential free hours. Besides your time, you have an investment ranging from fifteen to thirty thousand dollars in your truck and trailer that you're servicing them free. The average workingman, he figures to work eight hours and come home. We have a sixteen-hour day.

If I were to go in the mill after supper, I'd expect to come out maybe midnight, two o'clock in the morning. The loading process itself is fifteen to thirty minutes. Once they come with the crane, they can load the steel on it in two or three lifts. Maybe forty-five to fifty thousand pounds.

We protect it with paper, tie it down with chains and binders, tarp it, sign our bills, move toward the gate. It takes you fifteen to twenty minutes to get to the front gate. I must weigh in empty and weigh out loaded. Sometimes, even though you're all loaded, tarped down, and everything, you get on the scale and you're off-weight. If you scale in at twenty-five thousand pounds empty and you come out weighing seventy-two thousand pounds, you're five hundred, six hundred pounds off the billed weight. You have to go back and find out who made a mistake. Let's say it's over the one percent they'll allow. They have to weigh everything again and find out that some hooker made a paper mistake. Prior to '67, we never got paid a penny for it.

Years ago, we ran through city streets, alongside streetcars, buses, and what have you. It was a two-hour run from the mills of Gary to the North Side of Chicago. Some seventy-six traffic lights. Every one of them had to be individually timed and played differently. If you have to stop that truck and start it, it's not only aggravating and tiring, but you'd wear out the truck twice as fast as you would if you made those lights. It was a constant thing of playing these lights almost by instinct.

This is all changed with the expressways. It's just as if automation had entered the trucking business. Now you pull out of U.S. Steel in Gary and you don't have a light until you drop off at the expressway in the city of Milwaukee. It's a miracle compared to what it used to be. So much easier on yourself, on your equipment.

A stop at the Wisconsin state line, a place to eat. Big trucks stop there. Maybe meet a bunch that have been in the steel mill all night. Coffee-up, tell all the stories, about how badly you're treated in the steel mill, tell about the different drunks that try to get under your wheels. Then move towards your destination and make the delivery at seven o'clock in the morning. We're talking about thirteen hours already. My routine would be to drop two days like this and not come home. Halfway back from Milwaukee take a nap in the cab at a truck stop. You use the washroom, the facilities, you call your dispatcher in Gary, and pick up another load. Went home for a day of sleep, wash up, get rejuvenated, live like a human being for a day, come back to the mill after supper, and be off again. During the last ten years almost everybody bought a sleeper truck. It has facilities behind the seat. If you were to get a hotel room every night you were on the road, why, you'd be out of business shortly.

On weekends, if you're lucky enough to be home, you're greasing the truck and repairing it. It's like a seven-day week. There's nobody else to do the work. Years ago, the rate of truck repair was five dollars an hour. Today it's eleven, twelve dollars an hour. You do ninety percent of the work yourself, small repairs and adjustments.

I would make two round trips to Milwaukee and pass within four blocks of my house and never go home. You can't park a big truck in the neighborhood. If the police have anything to do with it, you can't even park on an arterial street more than an hour. It's a big joke with truckdrivers: We're gonna start carrying milk bottles with us. Everywhere we go now, there's signs: No Truck Parking. They want you to keep that thing moving. Don't stop around here. It's a nuisance; it takes up four spaces, which we need for our local people. You're an out-of-town guy, keep moving.

If I chose to park in the truck terminal, I'd have an eight-mile ride—and I don't think I'd be welcome. The owner-operator, we're an outcast, illegitimate, a gypsy, a fella that everybody looks down on. These are words we use. We compare ourselves to sailors: we sail out on the highways. The long-distance hauler is gone for a week, two weeks, picking up a load at one port, delivering it to another port.

You get lonely not talking to anybody for forty-eight hours. On the road, there's no womenfolks, unless there's a few waitresses, a couple of good old girls in the truck stop you might kid around with. They do talk about women, but they don't really have the time for women. There's a few available, waitresses in truck stops, and most of them have ten thousand guys complimenting them.

There's not much playing around that goes on. They talk of women like all guys do, but it's not a reality, it's dreaming. There's not these stories of conquest—there's the exceptional case of a Casanova—because they're moving too much. They're being deprived of their chance to play around. Maybe if they get more time, we'll even see that they have a little more of that. (Laughs.)

Truckers fantasize something tremendous. When they reach a coffee stop, they unload with all these ideas. I've seen fellas who build up such dreams when they come into a truck stop they start to pour it out, get about three minutes of animated description out of it, and all of a sudden come up short and realize it's all a bunch of damn foolishness they built up in their minds. It's still that they're daydreaming from the truck. He builds a thing in his mind and begins to believe it.

You sit in a truck, your only companionship is your own thoughts. Your truck radio, if you can play it loud enough to hear—you've got the roar of the engine, you've got a transmission with sixteen gears, you're very much occupied. You're fighting to maintain your speed every moment you're in the truck.

The minute you climb into that truck, the adrenaline starts pumping. If you want to have a thrill, there's no comparison, not even a jet plane, to climbing on a steel truck and going out there on the Dan Ryan Expressway. You'll swear you'll never be able to get out the other end of that thing without an accident. There's thousands of cars and thousands of trucks and you're shifting like a maniac and you're braking and accelerating and the object is to try to move with the traffic and try to keep from running over all those crazy fools who are trying to get under your wheels.

You have to be superalert all the time. Say I'm loaded to full capacity, seventy-three thousand pounds. That's equivalent to how many cars—at four thousand pounds a car? I cannot stop. I got terrific braking power. You have five axles, you'll have fourteen tires on the ground, you got eight sets of brakes. You have to anticipate situations a block ahead of you. You're not driving to match situations *immediately* in front of you. A good driver looks ahead two blocks, so he's not mousetrapped into a situation where he'll have to stop—because you can't stop like a car's gonna stop. You're committed. It's like an airplane crossing the ocean: they reach that point of no return. Your commitment's made a hundred, two hundred yards before you reach the intersection. It's really almost impossible.

You have to get all psyched up and keep your alertness all the time. There's a lot of stomach trouble in this business, tension. Fellas that can't eat anything. Alka-Seltzer and everything. There's a lot of hemorrhoid problems. And there's a lot of left shoulder bursitis, because of the window being open. And there's a loss of hearing because of the roar of the engine. The roar of the engine has a hypnotic effect. To give you an idea of the decibel sounds inside a cab, nowadays they're beginning to insulate 'em. It's so tremendous that if you play the radio loud enough to hear above the roar and you come to a tollgate and stop, you have to turn it down it's screaming so loud. You could break your eardrums. And the industrial noises in the background . . . I'm sure his hearing's affected. There was a survey made of guys that transport cars. You've heard the loud metal noise, where the different parts of the gates comes together. They found these fellas have a great loss of hearing. It's one more occupational hazard. There has been different people I've worked with that I've seen come apart, couldn't handle it any more.

I'll tell you where we've had nervous breakdowns, when we got in this '67 thing, the wildcat. We've had four people associated with us in Gary have had nervous breakdowns. And at Pittsburgh, they've had several. The tension of this labor thing, forty-six weeks, is real strong. The tension's even greater for a guy with a family to support . . .

There seemed an unusual amount of fellas having problems with their family, with the wife in particular. They're average guys with their wives going through the change and so forth. Really, that's an awful problem for the wife because she has to raise the kids, she has to fight off the bill collectors on the phone. She can't even count on her husband to attend a graduation, a communion, any kind of social function. She's just lucky he's home Christmas and New Year's. He's usually so darn tired that he'd much rather be home sleeping than getting ready to go out Sunday night.

Sure, truckers eat a lot of pills. It's a lot more prevalent than I thought. I heard fellas say they get a better price on bennies if they buy them by the thousand. We know a lot of individuals we consider hopheads off on benzedrine. A couple of guys I know are on it, even though it's on the weekends when they don't need to stay awake. It's become a habit.

The kids call 'em red devils. In trucking, they call it the Arkansas Turnaround—or whatever your destination is. A lot of 'em are dispensed by drugstores on prescription for weight control. So their wife gets the pills and the old man ends up usin' 'em to keep awake, because they're a benzedrine base. It'll be the little black ones or the little red ones . . .

They'd like to pick up the kids, hitchhikers, if it weren't for the prohibitions. I think the biggest transporters of hippies would be the owner-operators, because they want company. For years you didn't see a hitchhiker, but now with the hippie, with kids traveling across the country, every interchange has got a bunch of long-haired, pack-sacked kids hitchhiking from one end of the country to the other. It's a reborning . . .

It's a strange thing about truckers, they're very conservative. They come from a rural background or they think of themselves as businessmen. But underneath the veneer they're really very democratic and softhearted and liberal. But they don't *realize* it. You tell 'em they're liberal and you're liable to get your head knocked off. But when you start talking about things, the war, kids, when you really get down to it, they're for everything that's liberal. But they want a conservative label on it. It's a strange paradox.

In the steel mill, the truckdriver is at the absolute bottom of the barrel. Everybody in that mill that is under union contract has some dignity, has some respect from management. If he's the fella that sweeps the floor, he has job status. The man in the crane, if there's no work for his crane, he doesn't have to do anything. If the fella that pushes the broom in Warehouse Four, if he's got everything groomed up, they can't tell him, "No, you go and do another job."

Now comes the steel hauler. Everybody in that mill's above somebody, from top management down. At the bottom of the ladder, there's the hooker on your truck. He wants to feel that he's better than somebody. He figures I'm better than this steel hauler. So you get constant animosity because he feels that the corporation looks down on this steel hauler, and he knows he can order him around, abuse him, make him wait. It's a status thing. There's a tremendous feeling.

The first couple of years when I got abused, I howled and I yelled and I did my dance: "You can't do this to me." After a few years, I developed a philosophy. When I scream, it gives them pleasure, they can put it to me. They're sadists. So the average steel hauler, no matter how abused he is, you always give them that smile and you leave it go over your head. You say to yourself: One day my time will come. If you don't take this philosophy, you'll go right out of your mind. You cause an incident, you're barred from the mill. It's such a competitive business that you dare not open your mouth because your company will be penalized freight—and you get it in the neck. You try to show 'em a cockiness like you could care less.

Over a number of years, your face becomes familiar. It breaks the ice. The loader considers you an old-timer, he has some identity with you. You might find, on rare occasions, friendship. The loader is the foreman on the shift for truck loading. He has a desk in between all the piles of steel and he lays out the loads that are gonna be placed on the truck. If the hookers see the loader's giving you respect, they'll accept you.

The newer people get the most grief, do the screaming, and get the worst treatment. Younger fellas. The fella that comes into this business that's over forty takes his life's savings and buys a truck because somebody told him there's big money to be made and he wants to get in his own business. If you last the first five years, you last the worst hardships. Success means you survive. If you don't make a dime on your investment, but you're still in business after five years, we say he's a regular. Those first five years is your biggest nut to crack. You don't know the ropes, you don't know how to buy and service your truck reasonable, you make all the mistakes. Fifty percent turnover in our business every year. They drop out, lose their trucks. That's the only reward: in your mind, you feel you're in business.

There's been a change since the '67 wildcat. It spread across the country like wildfire. We're respected in a lot of places now because they know we stand up and fight for our rights. As much as it was a money problem, it was a problem of dignity.

Ninety percent of the fellas were Teamster Union members, but you'd never know it. Outside of the dues money they take out of your check, they did absolutely nothing. They did less than nothing. We know that a few telephone calls by high Teamster officials to steel mill officials could have changed our picture completely. If they would call up and say, "Look, you're abusing our people and if you don't straighten it out we're gonna do something about it." They could put one man down there at U.S. Steel, for instance, and say, "I'm a Teamster official. We're asking you guys not to load in this mill until they treat you fairly." In twenty-four hours we'd be getting loaded out there so fast we couldn't keep our hat on our head.

But they're establishment. They're interlocked with the steel mills and the trucking companies. They don't even know who their members are. Our guess is between twenty and thirty thousand steel haulers. Nobody can come up with the figures. A Teamster official was maybe a truckdriver twenty-five or thirty years ago. Fought the good fight, built the union, got high on the hog. So many years have passed that he doesn't even know what a truck looks like any more. He now golfs with his contemporaries from the trucking companies. He lolls about Miami Beach at the Hollywood Hotel that they own. To him, to have a deal with a truckdriver is beneath his station. It's awfully hard when you get to the union hall to talk to a Teamster official. They're usually "busy." That means they're down at the Palmer House, at the Steak Restaurant. It's a hangout for 'em.

Truckdrivers used to spend ninety percent of their time bitchin' about how they got screwed at the mill, how they got screwed by the state trooper. Troopers prey on truckdrivers for possible violations—mostly regarding weight and overload. It's extremely difficult to load a steel truck legally to capacity. If you're a thousand pounds over, it's no great violation but you have to get around the scales. At regular pull-offs, they'll say: Trucks Must Cross Scales.

You pull in there and you find, lo and behold, you're five hundred or a thousands pounds over. You've got to pay a ticket, maybe twenty-five dollars, and you have to move it off. This is a great big piece of steel. You're supposed to unload it. You have to find some guy that's light and break the bands on the bundle and transfer sheets or bars over on the other truck. Occasionally it's something that can't be broke down, a continuous coil that weighs ten thousand pounds. You work some kind of angle to get out of there. You wish for the scale to close and you close your eyes and you go like hell to try to get out of the state. You have a feeling of running a blockade in the twenties with a load of booze. You have a feeling of trying to beat the police. Or you pay the cop off.

Most state troopers consider truckers to be outlaws, thieves, and overloaders. The companies and the union don't try to upgrade our image. They don't go to the police departments and say, "Stop abusing our members."

Everybody's preying on the trucker to shake him down. The Dan Ryan is unbelievable. They're working deals you couldn't believe, that nobody would care about, because they're out-of-state truckers. Who cares what happens to them? What would you think of a trucker coming up the Dan Ryan for the first time? He's coming from Pittsburgh with an overload. He approaches the South Side of the city and it says: All Trucks Must Use Local Lanes. But the signs aren't well enough marked and he's out in the third lane and gets trapped. He can't get over because of the other cars, he goes right up the express lane. Well, there's cops down there makin' their living off these poor guys. They pull him over and they say, "Hey buddy, you're out where no trucks are supposed to be. We're gonna have to lock you up." They go through their song and dance about they're horrified about how you've broken the law, endangering everybody. And they're hinting around that maybe you want to make a deal.

Maybe you don't want to make a deal? Oh, you have to make bond and appear in court, that's twenty-five dollars. If you've got an out-of-state chauffeur's license, they'll take your chauffeur's license. So if you're going to come up with a ten, he'll hold court right there and he'll tell you never do it again. But if you're gonna be hardheaded—I'm gonna fight this thing—he'll say, "Okay, we're gonna take you in the neighborhood out here and we're gonna park your truck and we're gonna take you over to the station in a squad car." I can't swear to it, but there's a story goin' around that these cops are working with the people in the neighborhood. So you park your car out on those streets. While you're at the station making bond you come back and there ain't much left to your truck. The tires are gone, the cab's been broken into, the radio's gone. That's what happens to thousands of truckdrivers.

The cops tell you, "You get back on your truck any way you know how." Because they don't want to be there when you see your truck. You take a cab over there and there you stand. Now you call the copper, this official paragon of law and order, and he tells you, "How am I gonna find out who wrecked your truck and stole everything off?" A truck tire costs a hundred dollars. You're liable to come back from the station, trying to fight your ticket, to have four hundred-dollar bills gone right off the trailer.

Why the devil do you do it, right? There's this mystique about driving. The trucker has a sense of power. He has a sense of responsibility too. He feels: I know everything about the road. These people making mistakes around me, I have to make allowances for them. If the guy makes a mistake, I shouldn't swear at him, I shouldn't threaten him with my truck. You say, "That slob can't drive. Look at that dumb woman with her kids in there. Look at that drunk." *You've* got status!

Every load is a challenge and when you finally off-load it, you have a feeling of having completed a job—which I don't think you get in a production line. I pick up a load at the mill, going to Hotpoint in Milwaukee. I take a job, and I go through the process. You have a feeling when you off-load—you see they're turning my steel into ten thousand washing machines, into a hundred farm implements. You feel like your day's work is well done when you're coming back. I used to have problems in the morning, a lot of heartburn, I couldn't eat. But once I off-loaded, the pressure was off. I met the deadline. Then I could eat anything.

The automobile, it's the biggest thing in the country, it's what motivates everybody. Even that model, when they drape her across the hood of that car . . . In the truck stop, they're continually talking about how they backed into this particular place in one swing. The mere car drivers were absolutely in awe. When you're in that truck, you're not Frank Decker, factory worker. You're Frank Decker, truck owner and professional driver. Even if you can't make enough money to eat, it gives you something.

There's a joke going around with the truckdrivers. "Did you hear the one about the hauler that inherited a million dollars?" "What did he do with it?" "He went out and bought a new Pete." "Well, what did he do then?" "He kept running until his money ran out." Everybody knows in this business you can't make no money. Owning that big Pete, with the chrome stacks, the padded dashboard, and stereo radio, and shifting thirty-two gears and chromed wheels, that's heaven. And in the joke, he was using up the inheritance to keep the thing on the road.

You have to figure out reasons to keep from going crazy, games to try to beat yourself. After a number of years, you begin to be a better loader. They come with a thirty-thousand-pound coil. If you set it down on the truck three inches forward or backward of where it's supposed to be, you're misloaded. So there's a challenge every time you load. Everybody's proud of that. At the truck shop they'll flash a weight ticket: "Take a look at that." They've loaded a balanced load.

Now as we approach '67, I've about had it. I'm trucking seventeen years. There's nothing left to do. I never dreamt that our hopes of getting together some day was gonna come true. It was just a dream. I'll finish out the year, sell off my truck and trailer, and I'm gonna build a garage up at the Wisconsin-Illinois state line. I'm gonna service trucks in there. The guys needed a garage where they could get work done. The commercial garages—you got a bunch of amateurs working on your truck. To be an owner-operator, you gotta be a mechanic. I had a three-car garage when I was seventeen. So I was gonna build this garage . . .

But I met an old-timer I'd seen around for years. This was at Inland Steel on a Thursday night. One of my last hauls—I thought. We sat for about six hours waiting to get loaded. He said to me, "Did you hear about the rumble going on down in Gary?" He showed me this one-page pamphlet: "If you're fed up with the Teamsters Union selling you out and all the sweetheart contracts and the years of abuses, go in front of your union hall Monday morning at ten o'clock. We're gonna have a protest."

Friday I talked to everybody. "We're finally gonna do something. We've been talkin' about it for years . . ." I couldn't get anybody to talk to me. "Ah, hell, that's all you ever talk about."

Well, Monday morning I went out to Gary. There was twenty guys picketing. We didn't get much help through the day. We decided to go to the steel mills and intercept our people, who were coming in from all over the country with their trucks. You got the picture? Ninety percent of the guys didn't know where the union was at. For years, they paid dues as an extortion. They're hurting. Most of 'em are one paycheck away from the poorhouse. So we went there and tried to tell 'em, "Park your truck and come and picket." Well, it turned into something because the time was ripe. Everybody knew something had to happen.

We picketed for eight days on the mills. It built till we had five hundred, six hundred guys—most of 'em from out of town. Parked their trucks all over town. We hung on them gates. Sometimes we'd get down to two, three guys and we thought it was all over. But there's a new carload of guys come in from Iowa or from Detroit or from Fremont, Ohio, or something. They'd heard about this rumble that was going on and they come to help.

We picketed the steel mills and we talked to any steel haulers that come in, told them not to load, to join the picket line. Some of the haulers tried to run you down. You'd have to jump for your life. Other guys would come up and they wouldn't know what to do. They recognized a lot of faces. We met each other in truck stops for years. You know the guy—Tom, Dick, or Harry. But you never knew much more about him than just a service stop. We began to build relationships down here with these guys we'd seen for years, but we didn't know where they lived or anything else. They'll say, "What kind of truck you drive again?" They recognize you by your truck, see?

So we're having meetings. The guys call from Detroit. They shut down Armco Steel or Great Lakes Steel. Then we heard they're picketing at Pittsburgh and finally they're picketing in Philadelphia. And then we heard they blew up two trucks with dynamite in New Jersey. The Jersey crowd, they're always rough. It spread clear from here to the east coast. And it went on for nine weeks.

Steel mills got injunctions out against us. They took us into court and locked us up and everything else. The Teamsters helped the steel mills and the carriers to try to get us back to work. They came out in cars: a company official, a Teamster official, a marshal—pointing out who we were to serve papers on. They were working together.

Everybody's telling everybody: "They'll go back to work. They're all broke. They can't last more than a couple of weeks." But we hung on and we hung on, you know. (He swallows hard, takes a deep breath.) Some of the guys didn't go home at all. We raised money by going around asking truck stops and truck dealers and tire dealers to donate money and help us. A lot of 'em were dependent on us and knew we were poor payin' and knew that maybe if they helped us out we could start gettin' in better shape and start to pay our bills.

Truckdrivers are known as an awful lot of deadbeats. They live off credit and lay on everybody. Deprive their family, two legs ahead of the bill collectors, charge fuel at the new guy's station that's givin' credit to everybody and then, when they run up a big bill, they'll go by. All to keep that truck going. I don't think they're worse responsible than anybody else. But they get in a position like a businessman: you owe everybody and his brother and you start writin' paper and you try to survive. You get in deeper and deeper and deeper . . .

So we formed an organization—the Fraternal Association of Steel Haulers, FASH. We organized like hell, leading up to the contract time again. We went on a nationwide strike because we didn't hardly scratch the door the first time. This time we asked the Teamsters Union to represent us, which they never did before. Fitzsimmons promised in the agreement he'd set up a committee to meet with us. He sent us the very thieves that had locals where the steel haulers had members. These guys had vested interests to keep things the way it was. We met with 'em a couple of times and saw they weren't about to do nothin'.

So we demanded Fitzsimmons meet with us—not that we thought he'd do anything. He's nothing but a dirty old man shuffling along and filling a hole for Hoffa. But we did feel we could get recognition if we'd meet with him. Nothing doing. He wouldn't even talk with us. He sent a big bully, that's Hoffa's right hand, the head of the goons, guy with a prison record as long as your arm. He started tellin' us all he's gonna do for the steel haulers. We said, "You ain't doin' nothin' for us." We told him we didn't have to listen to his baloney. He said, "What do you want?" We told him we want the International to give us charters for steel locals. We want to have elections and we want to elect our own people. We want autonomy. And then we told him, "We want you and your crooked pals to stay ten miles away from any of our halls." He said he'd take the message back, and that's where it stands now.

We'd become aware, checking our rates with the Interstate Commerce Commission and the Department of Labor, about their misuse of our pension fund. A nine-hundred-million-dollar pension fund that got about a billion finagled away. That's our pension. We don't have the freightside driver's feeling for good old Jimmy Hoffa. They don't care how much he steals. That ain't us. That's our pension money in that fund. He belongs in jail, a lot of 'em do.

In January '70, we went out on strike to reinforce our demands for recognition. We filed with 167 companies that employed steel haulers under Teamster contract. When the hearings began in Pittsburgh, there were thirty-seven lawyers from the carriers and Teamsters and two of our attorneys—one guy and another guy helping out. The hearings lasted sixteen days. It cost the Teamsters $250,000 for their legal costs. There was ten thousand pages of testimony. The National Labor Relations Board ruled against us. We think it was a politically inspired ruling. Nixon was playing footsie with Fitzsimmons. We were fighting the mills, the union, the carriers, the President. Who else is there left?

I talked with a fella who sold trailers. He said, "You guys are nuts. You've taken on all these big people. You don't have a chance." But there's just one thing—we feel that we're a revolution. There's people's power here and truck power. And there's a lot of people in the Teamsters Union watchin' us. If they start to see that we don't get our heads busted, that we're tough enough to lead, they're gonna come out of the woodwork. *They* all want to know where their pension money went. What's wrong is that they're all scared.

We did extremely well till this last strike. We didn't make it in the strike. There were some defections in our ranks. They voted to go back to work. We were about gonna grab that brass ring when we dropped it. So there's been a lot of disillusionment on the part of a lot of guys. But we gained so much in these three years that a lot of guys are stickin'.

We're treated with quite a bit more respect, I'll tell ya, than we were before 1967. Sure, we're havin' problems. The Teamsters are trying to get the carriers to blackball us, trying to control the steel haulers. But they know they've lost us. We have membership stickers on the trucks. The sticker alone sometimes gets 'em loaded twice as fast. What they'll say, "You better load that guy, he belongs to that outfit and you don't load him you're gonna have to pay for it." We got a good reputation.

Our people are very cynical. They are always suspicious of leadership sellin' 'em out. They've seen the Teamsters. They gotta pay their dues whether they're workin' or not. So they turn on us. They're supercritical—every little thing. Between the day the strike started until March '68, I didn't pull a load of steel—that's eight months I didn't draw a penny. I been, since then, on a fifty-dollar-a-week salary, full-time for FASH, out of the Gary office. Had one guy tell me, "You only get fifty dollars a week, but that's how Hoffa started." Had another guy tell me, "I wouldn't have anybody that dumb working for fifty dollars a week to represent me." The cynicism is unbelievable.

First thing they figure, These guys are after soft, cushy jobs. They're after Hoffa, they're after the same thing we've been taken advantage of. What you have to do is rebuild confidence. These people don't trust nobody. They don't even trust themselves no more. "You're workin' in a crooked system and you gotta be a crook." So the guy figures, I wouldn't do it for anybody else, why this guy? Another typical thing is: It won't work. You can't beat 'em. They're too big. The Teamsters are too big. The steel mills are too big. Everything's against us. If you fight it, you get hurt.

You gotta re-educate 'em, you gotta climb up on the cross every day. What you build, eventually, unfortunately, is a following that will follow you no matter what you do. That's why you end up with Hoffa, with them sayin', "I don't care if Jimmy stole a million dollars, he's okay with me." It's a shame that people are that much sheep.

We're not getting the grass-roots backing we'd like to have. They're too busy, they go to their families. Sometimes I wonder why I'm in this thing. But it's rewarding. There's nothing like dealing with people, dealing with situations. It's like a crash course to educate yourself. It's something I really enjoy doing because it's something I thought should have been done all these years. After eighteen years of trucking, a change to do this work . . .

If I thought I could hand-tailor a job that I'd like to do, it's this job I'm doing right now. I never worked so hard at anything in my life. Most of this forty-six months has been seven days a week. I get weary but I never get tired of doing the job. I'm enjoying every minute of it. We're up against a lot of big people, big corporations. It has the feeling of playing chess with the top contender. It can affect people's lives, even people that don't even know.

If you win, the stakes are high. It's not just whether you're gonna make a buck. All of a sudden, you feel catapulted into these levels of decision-making that I never dreamed I'd ever reach. All of a sudden, you're no longer the guy smiling and putting up a front and waiting all the time in the truck. All of a sudden, you found your own sense of self-respect. The day's finally here. Now.

APPEARANCE

EDWARD AND HAZEL ZIMMER, HAIR STYLISTS

Mr. Edward *is a beauty salon in a suburb close to a large industrial city. "She works with me. Twenty years we've been here almost. They demand more from a hair stylist and you get more money for your* *work. You become like a doctor becomes a specialist. You have to act accordingly—I mean be Mr. Edward."*

At a certain point she joins the conversation.

Some people go to a barber shop, you get an old guy, he hasn't kept up to date with the latest styles, newest cuts. They're in a rut. They cut the same thing no matter what's in. A barber should be a hair stylist himself. There's some male beauty shops, they deal more in your feminine men and actors. Most actors prefer going to a beauty shop because a barber might just give you the same old cut and you might look like the janitor down the street or the vice president of a bank. Appearance is importance.

There are beauty operators, there's hairdressers, and there's hair stylists. A hair stylist is more than a beauty operator. Anybody can fuzz up hair, but you ask them, "Do I look good in this Chinese look which is coming in now, Anna May Wong?"—they don't know.

You have to sense the value of your customer. If the jewelry is a little better and she's accustomed to services, such as maids, her husband makes a good dollar. If you're getting a woman with five kids and her husband's a cabdriver—which is no fault in that—she is not the kind that's gonna come in here every week. Or the little lady down the street, who lives with her cats and dogs or even her husband, who doesn't care. They say, "Just set it nice. I can't wash my hair because of my arthritis." They're not fussy. You say to the beauty operator you employ, "You take Mrs. Brown because she's not fussy." You pick out the fussy one that's been around, they've been to Acapulco, Hawaii. They expect a little more from you than the beauty operator. Then you become the stylist. You have to know which customers are for whom and which are not.

The name counts. Kenneth does Mrs. Kennedy's hair—Onassis. I never saw Jacqueline Kennedy's hair when it looked anything worthwhile. Sometimes she wears a wig. Just because she came to him, this put him on a pedestal. If the Queen of England came to my place, I'd have to hire fifteen more people. They'd all come flocking in. A social thing.

The hairdresser cashes in on some of it. You'll never get this in the smaller beauty shops. You have to be a hair stylist to attract ones with money. A hair stylist can get fifteen dollars for a haircut, whereas the beauty operator, she'll get only three. Now your hairdresser is in the middle.

What makes a man become a hair stylist is different from what makes a woman become one. For women it's an easy trade. They learn this when they are twelve years old, making pin curls at home. But a man, it takes a little different approach. Jacqueline Kennedy, in a book her maid or someone wrote, said, when security police found out that two employees in the White House were homosexual, she ordered them fired. She said, "I don't want my sons to be exposed to this type of people because they're liable to grow up to be hairdressers." Not all hairdressers are homosexually inclined. Some enjoy the work more if you enjoy women.

The most important thing for a hairdresser, male, he has to dominate the woman. You can sense when you're not dominating the customer. She can tell you, "I want two rollers here." She becomes the stylist and all you become is the mechanical thing with the fingers.

In the field of beauty work, you got to have personality. I'd say one-fifth is personality. Be able to sell yourself. Your approach, your first word, like, "Good morning, the weather we're having." A man has to have a personality where he's aloof. He has to act like—without a word: Don't tell me, I'm the stylist. You expect more from Mr. Edward and you get it. If a woman needs a hair style, he says, "Madame, what you need is a little more color. I will fix it up." He doesn't do it. He will call his assistant. And he will tell her, "I want curls here, I want this, I want that." And she says, "Yes, Mr. Edward." I don't dirty my hands with the chemicals. I'm the stylist. Your symbol right there, the male. You're giving yourself a title. Otherwise, you're gonna be nothing but a flunky. Being a male, it's important you must have this ego.

Everybody expects the hairdresser to be a prototype, to have a black mustache, slick Hollywood-type or feminine. I could spot one a mile away sometimes if they're feminine. On the other hand, I know someone you'd never know he was a hairdresser. He's owned five shops at one time, a married man with a family and he's bald. I'm not gonna hide the point that I'm a beauty operator.

I used to go to a tavern around here. I met this guy. He didn't know I knew he was a cop. He knew I was a hairdresser. He was drunk. He says to me, "You're a queer." I says, "How could you tell by looking at people?" He says, "The way you twist your mouth." I said, "You're drunk and you're a cop." He says, "How do you know I'm a cop?" I says, "Just the way you look and act." Right away, he says, "Aaahhh!" I said, "If you didn't have a gun, how much authority would you pull around here? Anybody can do your job. You can't do mine. It takes skill." Right away he avoided me. He was an idiot. I do a lot of policemen's wives' hair. I always mention that he called me a queer. This other woman's husband says, "Wait'll I see him. I'll bash him in the face."

After an interval in the army he met his wife at a dance. She was working in a beauty parlor. "I said, 'I think I'll be a hairdresser.' She says, 'You wouldn't last two days.' I says, 'Hell I won't.'" He studied beauty culture. "I had my suitcase and my white jacket. I felt like an idiot. I saw these feminine young men dancing around, and these little old ladies waiting for me. They lay down and undress and you gotta rub their back and around their chest. What you learn in beauty school is nothin'. You don't learn how to handle people. My father-in-law always says, 'You do nothing but a lady's work.' But it's hard work, psychologically hard. You gotta perform a little better than a female."

Hair stylists, even if they're married, are called Miss This or Miss That. They don't seem to go much for the last name. Mr. Alexander of Paris or Mr André. Mr. Edward. That should go over bigger than Eddie's Beauty Shop. It's a little flat, see? Sometimes these young fellas who are on the feminine side lean on a feminine name. He calls himself Mr. Twinkie or something. This fella we had working here, he tried to hide the fact that he was feminine. He called himself Mr. Moran.

HAZEL: The name became important when the male entered the business. They built a reputation on their name. They use it rather than call a salon by some idiotic or nondescriptive name. A woman might call the shop Vanity Fair or Highlight. For a man, it's more important that he retains his name.

What are you called?

HAZEL: Hazel.

EDWARD: She's just called Hazel.

HAZEL: I worked for Mr. Maurice in Florida and all of us were known as Miss. He renamed me Miss Rena because he didn't like Hazel.

Do you feel less when you're called by your first name?

HAZEL: Never. I never felt inferior to any of my customers. Even though sometimes they try to make you feel that way. I think I would quit a long time ago if I ever felt any inferiority.

EDWARD: I would not stand humiliation. It's not openly when a woman gets hostile against you and says, "If you're a hair stylist, you're below me." Many wealthy people will hire a hair stylist and haul them around and they will carry their suitcases. It really looks la-de-da, you might say elite, where she's going to the airport with her hairdresser and her poodles and her dressmaker all following after her like the Queen of Sheba. This is a form of humiliation. But the guy don't care. She's paying him well and he builds his name. And she's using his image to make herself.

HAZEL: The less important or average-intellectual customer is the one that tries to humiliate you more. Where she can suddenly go to the hairdresser weekly. These kind of people try to depress your importance. She'll ask for something that you may not have heard that term. So she'll say, "Oh, you don't know!" But people who have been around, if they don't like what you do, they go to another place. It's the average-intellectual individual who's apt to come in and show her importance and try to decrease yours. I'm very good at putting them in their place.

EDWARD: There was some humiliation when I was newer. I didn't rub hard enough. "Oh, just don't bother any more! Just have Hazel do it." The beginning hairdresser could be very embarrassed by a customer. The customer says, "Oh, just leave my hair alone! Comb this out for me, get this idiot away from me!" Because the person was green. There are times when the woman will take the comb and say, "Give me that thing!" This is an insult. When she says, "This is good enough!" and you're not happy with it. Some hairdressers will blow their fuse and throw the comb on the floor and say, "I wouldn't touch you with a fourteen-foot pole." Verlaine was like that. He threw customers out of the door with wet hair. He was eccentric that way.

But I still feel we are servants. A servant to the public, like a doctor. Not a servant that does housework. I didn't mean in that class. Just because you're a great hair stylist, win prizes—anybody can buy a trophy and put it in his window. But he becomes a star, arrogant. Some people say, "I won't take this crap any more." If they give you a hard time, all you say, "Look lady, I'm sorry, this is the way I think it should be. If I can't please you, you'll have to find someone else." But you don't argue and throw brushes around like some of these guys. You may see ads in the papers for hairdressers: No stars, please.

We hired this one guy, he was going to hair coloring school. He was using our place to practice with his hair colors. One day he took a very prominent customer of ours. He colored her hair red. She's out in the car crying. She says, "I can't go home like this. My husband'll kill me." I said, "I thought you wanted to be a redhead." She says, "All I asked for was a rinse." I brought her back. By this time he was packing his bag. I didn't have to fire him. He just simply walked out. He took a woman and being another genius, he's gonna make something of her. You don't take it upon yourself.

You have to put in a thousand hours in beauty school to get your license. The average hair stylist, dresser, beauty operator has an equal amount of schooling as a practical nurse. You have to know blood, you have to know diseases. You have to know everything that pertains to the human body so you can understand why hair grows.

Styles are basically the same since the bob. What can you do with hair? It's like cooking chop suey. By adding more mushrooms or less. Styles repeat themselves over and over again, like women's clothes. You always go back to something.

We used to get fifty dollars for a permanent. Like silver-blonding. Years ago, a wife wouldn't think of going to a grocery store with blonde hair. 'Cause what is she? A show girl? Light hair only went with strippers, prostitutes, and society women. In order to silver-blonde in those days, you would use a lot of ammonias and bleaches and the woman would have to come back two or three times before it got light enough to be a silver blonde. This cost fifty, sixty dollars a treatment. So the average *hausfrau* and her husband, he'd say, "What are you workin' as a cigarette girl or something? You're a mother, you got four kids, you're insulting me in church, you look like a hoozy." But today all girls look like hoozies.

HAZEL: They have commercialized it and came out with all these gadgets, and put work that should be done in a shop into home. You can buy a comb that cuts hair. You can buy a permanent. They should have strictly remained professional. The manufacturers got greedy and they commercialized hairdressing, whereas they make it so easy it can be done at home. So you can't command the prices you did a number of years ago. Today they sell these kits, and if you can read you can do it. It has hurt the poorer sections mostly. More wealthier neighborhoods, it hasn't hurt them bad. Most of these women, they don't want to take the time.

Once in a while a hairdo will disturb me because I feel I didn't do it quite right. I'll brood over it for a little while. I like to feel I've done the best on each one every day. Once in a while I'll flunk. (Laughs.)

EDWARD: You feel like a doctor who has a patient who died on the operating table. You're concerned. What went wrong? Why didn't I get that right? A beauty operator wouldn't care. I enjoy the work. I'd do it again even if I made less money.

We have lost young people in the beauty shop. The average person we work on is over twenty-five. The olden-time mother would never stand to see her daughter with that straight gappy look. She looks like a witch on Halloween night. Today it's the style for young people.

I have a girl come in the shop: how can I straighten her hair? There was one time, a woman with hair like that, she was something on a broom.

Even her mother would say, "Why the hell don't you go to the beauty shop and get the hair out of your mouth?" Today you can't tell a child . . .

In my opinion, the men are getting more feminine and the women are getting more masculine. If a boy and a girl walk down the street together and his hair is as straight as hers, he'll get a permanent at home. The one with the straight hair is usually the girl and the one with the wavy hair is the guy.

It's due to our permissive society. There was a time, once, September rolled around, they were forced to go to the barber shop or beauty parlor and get it clipped for school. Otherwise, the teacher sent them home. Today you have a whole society where a young man can go on the street, raise a beard, wear crazy clothes, he can wear one shoe off and one shoe on, and no one bothers to look at him.

HAZEL: It has regressed.

Do you disagree with customers on occasion?

EDWARD: I often disagree with customers—depends on who she is and what authority she has. I lost a customer once because she was from Germany and this other customer happened to be from a very, very pronounced Jewish family. She said she wouldn't buy a Volkswagen because of what they did to our people. And the woman said, "What did I do? I was a child." Next thing you know, she called her a Nazi. So here I'm bound to lose one customer. The one I favored, the one I hoped I didn't lose, was the one that paid the most money and had the most service. But I felt sorry for the other girl. I took sides only for monetary reasons.

DOC PRITCHARD, HOTEL CLERK

W*e're in a Manhattan hotel near Times Square. It is an old, established place of some three hundred rooms. Its furnishings are quite simple, unpretentious. There are permanent guests as well as transients.*

He is a room clerk, on the 8:00 A.M. to 4:00 P.M. shift, five days a week. He's been at this work twenty-two years. "I not only room people, I do cashiering, checking out, cashing checks, all that sort of thing. The day goes pretty fast. Before you can say, 'Jack Robinson,' it's time to go home. (Laughs.) It's difficult at times." (Laughs.)

I begin at eight in the morning. I have to have a smile on my face. Some mornings that's a little difficult. The first thing you run into is people checking out from the night before. You might get a slight lull and then people begin arriving. They're like little bees. You're concentrating on what you're doing. It's a little difficult to have that smile all the time.

Clerks are really underpaid people. It is one of the lowest paid jobs in the United States. I think they should put out more money for a good hotel clerk. If you get a fellow on the front desk who has got a good personality and can get along with people and he's on his toes, I mean really serving the guests, I mean really getting out there and encouraging them to come back—the hotel has to be halfway decent too. Then I think you've got a clerk that's woth two hundred dollars a week.

They don't get that. It's difficult sometimes for them to get along with just one job. A great many of 'em moonlight. Or they work a couple extra nights in another hotel. A great many actors went into this. They did it just to eat between jobs. This was before the unemployment check. Many show people worked in hotels. They'd do it until the next part came along. Then they'd quit. So nobody really cared.

I doubt if a hotel clerk really commands a heck of a lot of respect. I've had people talk to me just like I was some sort of dog, that I was a ditchdigger, let's say. You figure a fellow who comes to work and he has to have a cleanly pressed suit and a white shirt and a tie on—plus he's gotta have that big smile on his face—shouldn't be talked to in a manner that he's something so below somebody else.

It affects me. It gives you that feeling: Oh hell, what's the use? I've got to get out of this. Suddenly you look in the mirror and you find out you're not twenty-one any more. You're fifty-five. Many people have said to me, "Why didn't you get out of it long ago?" I never really had enough money to get out. I was stuck, more or less.

In a lot of hotels, the cashiering is done by a certain person and the rooming is done by the clerk. Here I do everything. At times I even act as manager, because if the manager's out, you have to take hold. There's a good deal of bookkeeping. It can get quite confusing. I've had fellows from universities come in. I would try to break them in. They couldn't make head nor tail out of being a room clerk. The one thing you must remember: Forget what happened yesterday and let tomorrow take care of itself. It's today you're working. Everything you do has to come under this date. So many look back two days and post back two days and this is how we get fouled up. (Laughs.)

There's pressure when you're doing it all. There is tension, quite a bit of tension. On a busy day I'll go home and it takes me about an hour and a half to unwind. I just want to sit there and pick up a book or a paper or something. Just get away from it all.

My legs are quite tired. I'm on my feet the whole time. In doing these jobs I don't have much of a chance to sit down. You're moving back and forth and pivoting. Ofttimes through the day I take a walk in front of the desk.

The thing I don't like about it is you're trapped—in a small area eight hours a day. You're behind the desk. We had a grill on our desk and I asked them to take it away, because I felt like I was in jail. The other side is open, wide open, where you can talk with the guests. But this cage was near the cash. I told it to more than one guest. There's a glass there now and a sign: Please go to the front.

When I broke in, it was shortly after World War II. Hotels were much busier. I've worked most of 'em. I've even worked resort hotels. You might work two or three months, then you got to trudge out and look for another job. I'd rather work in a commercial house like this. Here you got things set winter through summer.

You see a lot. I'm not a nosy person. I don't care what another person is doing. It's none of my business. I've found out that people who do worry about what a guest is doing, nine times out of ten they're wrong. Especially when you're dealing with people in the arts. Many times it's pertaining to business, has nothing to do with what that person who thinks like Archie Bunker thinks is going on. I've got enough to worry about what I do without worrying about what somebody else does.

The clerk in a hotel is rarely tipped. The bellboys, rather, get all the tips. A fellow that comes into the hotel to do a little cheating will always tip the bellboy heavily. The boy can't help him at all, in any way, shape, or form. It's the clerk who watches his mail, watches his messages, and watches who comes in and out to see him. It's really the clerk who covers for him. But he never seems to realize that. If the manager wishes that he be ejected from the hotel, it's the clerk who can save him. The bellboys couldn't do a thing for him.

The clerk knows what's going on. The fellow relies on the bellboy to keep his mouth shut. The bellboys never keep their mouth shut. The first guy they tell is the clerk, when they come back—if the clerk doesn't already know it. (Laughs.) Occasionally you will get people who seem to know their way around. They will throw the clerk a couple of bucks or a five-dollar bill now and then.

We're not getting any young blood. There's no incentive. I don't blame 'em—to be tied up in one spot. There's not as many hotels as there used to be. A great many of the two-hundred-, three-hundred-room houses are being torn down or they're turned into office buildings. All that's left are a few old stand-bys. There's the big hotels, monstrosities. There is no homey feeling. You're just a lonely traveler. If you go down to the bar, you don't know who the hell you're gonna run into. Your information clerk will probably be a nineteen-year-old college girl or boy. He doesn't know a thing about hotels. He could care less. He wouldn't even have an idea what you did for a living. These hotels are going to be missed.

Everybody's in a rush: "Will you *please* hurry up with my bill? I'm in a hurry, I gotta catch a plane." It's a shame, because we could live in such a relaxed society . . .

I'm getting a little older. Can't take it the way I could twenty years ago. Sometimes you just sit and ponder the day. You get a lot of laughs. (Laughs.) A fellow walked in one morning, he wanted to know if I had seen his wife. He took a picture out of his pocket and held it up. He said, "If you see her, tell her I was looking for her." It was a picture of a nude woman. (Laughs.) You get a lot of laughs.

I have about nine years to go until sixty-five. My hope is that I'll be in good condition, so I can do two or three days' work at least in hotels. I know I'll miss people. You always have the idea that you're gonna better yourself. You think, Gee, I wonder if I could write a book or just exactly what I could do. I think I could have done a lot better than being a clerk.

COUNTING

NANCY ROGERS, BANK TELLER

A t twenty-eight, she has been a bank teller for six years. She earns five hundred dollars a month.

What I do is say hello to people when they come up to my window. "Can I help?" And transact their business, which amounts to taking money from them and putting it in their account. Or giving them money out of their accont. You make sure it's the right amount, put the deposits on through the machine so it shows on the books, so they know. You don't really do much. It's just a service job.

We have a time clock. It's really terrible. You have a card that you put in the machine and it punches the time that you've arrived. If you get there after eight-forty-five, they yell and they scream a lot and say, "Late!" Which I don't quite understand, because I've never felt you should be tied to something like a clock. It's not that important. If you're there to start doing business with the people when the bank opens, fine.

I go to my vault, open that, take out my cash, set up my cage, get my stamps set out, and ink my stamp pad. From there on until nine o'clock when the bank opens, I sit around and talk to the other girls.

My supervisor yells at me. He's about fifty, in a position that he doesn't really enjoy. He's been there for a long time and hasn't really advanced that much. He's supposed to have authority over a lot of things but he hasn't really kept informed of changes. The girls who work under him don't really have the proper respect that you think a person in his position would get. In some ways, it's nice. It's easier to talk to him. You can ask him a question without getting, "I'm too busy." Yet you ask a question a lot of times and you don't get the answer you need. Like he doesn't listen.

We work right now with the IBM. It's connected with the main computer bank which has all the information about all the savings accounts. To get any information, we just punch the proper buttons. There are two tellers to a cage and the machine is in between our windows. I don't like the way the bank is set up. It separates people. People are already separated enough. There are apartment houses where you don't know anybody else in the building. They object to your going into somebody else's cage, which is understandable. If the person doesn't balance, they'll say, "She was in my cage." Cages? I've wondered about that. It's not quite like being in prison, but I still feel very locked in.

The person who shares my cage, she's young, black, and very nice. I like her very much. I have fun with her. She's originally from the South. She's a very relaxed type of person. I can be open and not worry I might offend her. I keep telling her she's a bigot. (Laughs.) And she keeps saying, "There are only three kinds of people I dislike—the Italians, the Polacks, and the Jews." (Laughs.) I'll walk up to her and put my hands on her shoulder and she'll say, "Get your hands off me, white girl, don't you know you're not supposed to touch?" It's nice and relaxed kind of—we sit around and gossip about our boyfriends, which is fun.

A lot of people work there I don't know. Never talk to, have no idea who they are. You're never introduced. I don't even know who the president of the bank is. I don't know what he looks like. It's really funny, because you have to go have okays on certain things. Like we're only allowed to cash up to a certain amount without having an officer okay it. They'd say, "Go see Mr. Frank." And I'd say, "Who's that? Which one? Point him out." The girl who's the supervisor for checking kept saying, "You don't know who he is? You don't know who he is? He's the one over there. Remember him? You waited on him." "Yeah, but I didn't know what his name was. Nobody ever told me."

I enjoy talking to people. Once you start getting regular customers, you take your time to talk—which makes the job more enjoyable. It also makes me wonder about people. Some people are out working like every penny counts. Other people, it's a status thing with them. They really like to talk about it. I had a man the other day who was buying some stock. "Oh well, I'm buying fifty thousand dollars' worth of AT&T, and I'm also investing in . . ." He wouldn't stop talking. He was trying to impress me: I have money, therefore I'm somebody.

Money doesn't mean that much to me. To me, it's not money, it's just little pieces of paper. It's not money to me unless *I'm* the one who's taking the money out or cashing the check. That's money because it's mine. Otherwise it doesn't really mean anything. Somebody asked me, "Doesn't it bother you, handling all that money all day long?" I said, "It's not money. I'm a magician. I'll show you how it works." So I counted out the paper. I said, "Over here, at this window, it's nothing. Over there, at that window, it's money." If you were gonna think about it every minute: "Oh lookit, here's five thousand dollars, wow! Where could I go on five thousand dollars? Off to Bermuda—" You'd get hung-up and so dissatisfied of having to deal with money that's not yours, you couldn't work.

People are always coming in and joking about—"Why don't you and I get together? I'll come and take the money and you ring the alarm after I've left and say, 'Oh, I was frightened, I couldn't do anything.'" I say, "It's not enough." The amount in my cash drawer isn't enough. If you're going to steal, steal at least into the hundreds of thousands. To steal five or ten thousand isn't worth it.

It's joked about all the time. Sometimes it's kidded about if you do have a difference. Maybe I was paying out a hundred dollars and two bills stuck together and I gave him $110 instead. A lot of times people have come back and said, "I think you gave me ten dollars too much." Like they didn't want me to get in trouble. "She won't balance today and here I am sitting with ten dollars she doesn't have." It's really nice to know people are honest. Quite a few are. Anyway, we're bonded, we're insured for that. The bank usually has a slush fund for making up differences one way or the other.

I've never been held up. We have a foot alarm, one that you just trip with your toe. At the other place, we had a button you push, which was immediately under the counter. Some people, you get a funny feeling about. Like I don't think that's his passbook, it's probably stolen. Most of the time you're never right. (Laughs.)

One of the girls who works here was held up. She just gave the man the money he wanted. (Laughs.) Which is all you can do. She went up to our head teller to get more money. She said, "Mr. Murphy, I was just held up." He said, "Oh sure, uh huh, ha, ha, ha." She said, "No, really I was." (Laughs.) He said, "Ooohhh, you really were, weren't you?" (Laughs.) Like wow! I don't think they ever caught the person. She didn't give him all that money. She just gave him what she had in one part of the drawer and didn't bother to open the other drawers, where most of that cash was stored.

I really don't know what I'd do. I don't think I'd panic too badly. I'd be very nervous and upset, but I'd probably do exactly what the man wanted. If possible, trip the alarm, but that's not going to do much good. I'd give him the money, especially if he had a gun in his hand or even giving the slight implication . . . Money's not worth that much. The bank's insured by the government for things like that, so there's no real . . . It'd be exciting, I guess.

A lot of younger girls who are coming in now, they get pushed too fast. If you've never done it before, it takes time just to realize—you have to stop and think, especially if it's busy. Here I am doing three different things. I am taking money out of these people's accounts and putting part of it into checking and he wants part of it back, plus he wants to cash a check, and he asks for a couple of money orders. You got all these things that you have to remember about—that have to be added and subtracted so everything comes out right.

You force yourself into speeding up because you don't want to make people wait. 'Cause you're there for one reason, you're there to serve them. Lots of times there's somebody you know back there and you want to get rid of these people so you can talk to him. (Laughs.)

In a lot of cases, as far as males, you're gonna be asked out. Whether you accept or not is something else. I met quite a few people in the bank who I've gone out with. Sometimes relationships work out very nicely and you become good friends with these people and it may last for years. My social life is affected by my job, oh sure. A customer coming in and saying, "I'm giving a party next week, would you like to come?"

Some places kind of frown on it. But most of them have no control.

One fella I met at the bank, he was from an auditing firm, who I went out with for a short while. He said, "Don't tell anybody. We're not supposed to go with anybody from the bank we work for." That's weird, for a job to carry over into your private life.

Banks are very much giving in to desexualizing the women who work there, by putting uniforms on them. Trying to make everybody look the same. In one way it's nice, it saves on clothes. In another way, it's boring, putting on the same thing almost every day is—ech!! Some I've seen aren't too bad, but in some places they're very tailored and in drab colors. Uptight is the only word I can think of to describe them. The place I worked before, it was a navy-blue suit and it was—blach!! (Laughs.)

Most bank tellers are women because of the pay scale. It's assumed that women are paid a little bit lower than men. (Laughs.) There are only two men that work in the area, aside from my supervisor. The head teller, who's been there for years and years and years, and a young fella in charge of all the silver. For most men it's a job that doesn't offer that much kind of advancement. You'd have to be the type that would really just enjoy sittin' back and doing the same thing over and over again. A transaction is a transaction is a transaction.

Some days, when you're aggravated about something, you carry it after you leave the job. Certain people are bad days. (Laughs.) The type of person who will walk in and says, "My car's double-parked outside. Would you hurry up, lady? I haven't got time to waste around here." And you go—"What???" You want to say, "Hey, why did you double-park your car? So now you're gonna blame me if you get a ticket, 'cause you were dumb enough to leave it there?" But you can't. That's the one hassle. You can't say anything back. The customer's always right.

Certain people who are having a bad day themselves feel they must take it out on you: "What are you doing there?" "Why are you checking that?" "Why did you have to do that?" You calmly try and explain to them, "That's what's required." You can't please 'em. They make sure you're in as nasty a mood as they are. (Laughs.)

We have quite a bit of talk during coffee breaks. There's speculation: "Do you think this is what happened?" There was a girl who was let go this week. Nobody was told as to the why or wherefore. Nobody really still knows. They keep coming through the bank saying, "We don't want rumors started about such-and-such." But they don't explain it. She doesn't exist any more totally. She's no longer here.

The last place I worked for, I was let go. I told the people I worked with, "If anybody asks, tell them I got fired and give them my phone number."

One of my friends stopped by and asked where I was at. They said, "She's no longer with us." That's all. I vanished.

When it happened, it was such an abrupt thing. I hadn't really expected it. I was supposed to be an example so that these things wouldn't occur any more. One of the factors was a man I wasn't getting along with. He worked out at the desk. He was—how can I put it?—he was a very handsy person. He was that way towards everybody. I didn't like it. He'd always pick out a time when you were balancing or you were trying to figure something out. You didn't want to be interrupted. At other times, you wouldn't mind, you'd laugh it off.

The reason I was given for being fired was that I was absent too much and had been tardy too often. But I think there was really another reason. The girl who was supervisor was leaving and I was next in seniority. I just don't think they were going to let me go further.

With her the job was everything, it was her whole life. She would stay there till seven in the evening if something went wrong, and come in on Saturdays if they asked her to. When I was done—I'm sorry, I was done for the day.

And I was very open about being different. It started when one of the girls had brought in a little sticker-thing for Valentine's Day. I thought they were cute. So I had just taken a couple of hearts out of one and put it on my name sign on the window, 'cause I liked it. There was never anything really said except "How come that's there?" And I said, " 'Cause I like it." A lot of customers'd come in and say, "Wow! She had hearts on her window, she must be a nice girl." It gave them an opportunity to have something to say instead of just feeling they didn't know you and didn't quite know what to say. I think the bank didn't care for that too much. They want everybody to be pretty much the same, kind of conservative, fitting into the norm. I think that was the real reason I was let go.

I think a lot of places don't want people to be people. I think they want you to almost be the machines they're working with. They just want to dehumanize you. Just like when you walk in in the morning, you put the switch on and here you are: "I am a robot. This is what I do. Good morning. How are you? May I help you?" I hate having to deal with people like that.

In some way, I feel my job's important. Especially when you work with people who are trying to save money. It's gratifying for them when they give you the stuff and you mark in their book and there it is—wow! I've accomplished this. And you say, "I'm glad to see you again. You're really doing well." Most of these people here work in restaurants downtown and are secretaries. Lower middle class and a lot of blacks come in this bank. They're a lot more friendly than some of your other people, who are so busy trying to impress one another.

They don't even recognize you. It's like I'm almost being treated as a machine They don't have time to bother. After all, you're just a peon. I had a black man come up to my window and say, "It's really nice to see somebody working in a place like this who's even halfway relevant." And I thought—wow! (Laughs.) I had my hair up like in little ponytails on the side and just had a pullover sweater and a skirt on and wasn't really dressed up. I was very taken aback by it. It's the first compliment I had in a long time. It's nice to be recognized. Most places, it's your full name on the window. Some places just have Miss or Mrs. So-and-so. I prefer giving my whole name so people can call me Nancy. (Laughs.) They feel a little more comfortable. Certain officers you refer to by their first names. Other people you don't. Some people you would feel kind of weird saying, "Hey, Charlie, would you come over here and do this for me?" Other people you'd feel strange calling them by their proper name. All men who sit at the desk in the office you refer to as Mister. Okay, he's a vice president, he must be called Mr. So-and-so. Whereas you're just a teller. Therefore he can call you by your first name. Smaller banks tend to be more friendly and open.

When I tell people at a party I work for a bank, most of them get interested. They say, "What do you do?" I say, "I'm a teller." They say, "Oh, hmm, okay," and walk away. I remember getting into a discussion with one person about the war. We were disagreeing. He was for it. I wasn't getting angry because I thought he has his right to his point of view. But the man couldn't recognize that I had the right to mine. The thing finally was thrown at me: "What do you mean saying that? After all, who are you? I own my own business, you just work in a crummy bank." It doesn't compute. Like, unless you're capable of making it in the business world, you don't have a right to an opinion. (Laughs.)

My job doesn't have prestige. It's a service job. Whether you're a waitress, salesperson, anything like that—working directly for the public—it's not quite looked on as being prestigious. You are there to serve them. They are not there to serve you. Like a housemaid or a servant.

One of the girls said, "People who go through four years of college should have it recognized that they have achieved something." A man said, "Don't you think someone who becomes an auto mechanic and is good at it should also be recognized? He's a specialist, too, like the man who goes to be a doctor." Yet he's not thought of that way. What difference? It's a shame that people aren't looked at as each job being special unto itself. I can't work on a car, yet I see people who can do it beautifully. Like they have such a feel for it. Some people can write books, other people can do marvelous things in other ways . . .

FOOTWORK

BABE SECOLI, SUPERMARKET CHECKER

She's a checker at a supermarket. She's been at it for almost thirty years. "I started at twelve—a little, privately owned grocery store across the street from the house. They didn't have no cash registers. I used to mark the prices down on a paper bag.

"When I got out of high school, I didn't want no secretary job. I wanted the grocery job. It was so interesting for a young girl. I just fell into it. I don't know no other work but this. It's hard work, but I like it. This is my life."

We sell everything here, millions of items. From potato chips and pop—we even have a genuine pearl in a can of oysters. It sells for two somethin'. Snails with the shells that you put on the table, fanciness. There are items I never heard of we have here. I know the price of every one. Sometimes the boss asks me and I get a kick out of it.

You sort of memorize the prices. It just comes to you. I know half a gallon of milk is sixty-four cents; a gallon, $1.10. You look at the labels. A small can of peas, Raggedy Ann. Green Giant, that's a few pennies more. I know Green Giant's eighteen and I know Raggedy Ann is fourteen. I know Del Monte is twenty-two. But lately the prices jack up from one day to another. Margarine two days ago was forty-three cents. Today it's forty-nine. Now when I see Imperial comin' through, I know it's forty-nine cents. You just memorize. On the register is a list of some prices, that's for the part-time girls. I never look at it.

I don't have to look at the keys on my register. I'm like the secretary that knows her typewriter. The touch. My hand fits. The number nine is my big middle finger. The thumb is number one, two and three and up. The side of my hand uses the bar for the total and all that.

I use my three fingers—my thumb, my index finger, and my middle finger. The right hand. And my left hand is on the groceries. They put down their groceries. I got my hips pushin' on the button and it rolls around on the counter. When I feel I have enough groceries in front of me, I let go of my hip. I'm just movin'—the hips, the hand, and the register, the hips, the hand, and the register . . . (As she demonstrates, her hands and hips move in the manner of an Oriental dancer.) You just keep goin', one, two, one, two. If you've got that rhythm, you're a fast checker. Your feet are flat on the floor and you're turning your head back and forth.

Somebody talks to you. If you take your hand off the item, you're gonna forget what you were ringin'. It's the feel. When I'm pushin' the items through I'm always having my hand on the items. If somebody interrupts to ask me the price, I'll answer while I'm movin'. Like playin' a piano.

I'm eight hours a day on my feet. It's just a physical tire of standing up. When I get home I get my second wind. As far as standin' there, I'm not tired. It's when I'm roamin' around tryin' to catch a shoplifter. There's a lot of shoplifters in here. When I see one, I'm ready to run for them.

When my boss asks me how I know, I just know by the movements of their hands. And with their purses and their shopping bags and their clothing rearranged. You can just tell what they're doin' and I'm never wrong so far.

The best kind shoplift. They're not doin' this because they need the money. A very nice class of people off Lake Shore Drive. They do it every day—men and women. Lately it's been more or less these hippies, livin' from day to day . . .

It's meats. Some of these women have big purses. I caught one here last week. She had two big packages of sirloin strips in her purse. That amounted to ten dollars. When she came up to the register, I very politely said, "Would you like to pay for anything else, without me embarrassing you?" My boss is standing right there. I called him over. She looked at me sort of on the cocky side. I said, "I know you have meat in your purse. Before your neighbors see you, you either pay for it or take it out." She got very snippy. That's where my boss stepped in. "Why'd you take the meat?" She paid for it.

Nobody knows it. I talk very politely. My boss doesn't do anything drastic. If they get rowdy, he'll raise his voice to embarrass 'em. He tells them not to come back in the store again.

I have one comin' in here, it's razor blades. He's a very nice dressed man in his early sixties. He doesn't need these razor blades any more than the man in the moon. I've been following him and he knows it. So he's layin' low on the razor blades. It's little petty things like this. They're mad at somebody, so they have to take their anger out on something.

We had one lady, she pleaded with us that she wanted to come back—not to have her husband find out. My boss told her she was gonna be watched wherever she went. But that was just to put a little fright in her. Because she was just an elderly person. I would be too embarrassed to come into a store if this would happen. But I guess it's just the normal thing these days—any place you go. You have to feel sorry for people like this. I like 'em all.

My family gets the biggest kick out of the shoplifters: "What happened today?" (Laughs.) This is about the one with the meat in her purse. She didn't need that meat any more than the man in the moon.

Some of 'em, they get angry and perturbed at the prices, and they start swearin' at me. I just look at 'em. You have to consider the source. I just don't answer them, because before you know it I'll get in a heated argument. The customer's always right. Doesn't she realize I have to buy the same food? I go shopping and pay the same prices. I'm not gettin' a discount. The shoplifters, they say to me, "Don't you want for something?" Yes, I want and I'm standing on my feet all day and I got varicose veins. But I don't walk out of here with a purse full of meat. When I want a piece of steak I buy a piece of steak.

My feet, they hurt at times, very much so. When I was eighteen years old I put the bathing suit on and I could see the map on my leg. From standing, standing. And not the proper shoes. So I wear like nurse's shoes with good inner sole arch support, like Dr. Scholl's. They ease the pain and that's it. Sometimes I go to bed, I'm so tired that I can't sleep. My feet hurt as if I'm standing while I'm in bed.

I love my job. I've got very nice bosses. I got a black manager and he's just beautiful. They don't bother you as long as you do your work. And the pay is terrific. I automatically get a raise because of the union. Retail Clerks. Right now I'm ready for retirement as far as the union goes. I have enough years. I'm as high up as I can go. I make $189 gross pay. When I retire I'll make close to five hundred dollars a month. This is because of the union. Full benefits. The business agents all know me by name. The young kids don't stop and think what good the union's done.

Sometimes I feel some of these girls are overpaid. They don't do the work they're supposed to be doin'. Young girls who come in, they just go plunk, plunk, so slow. All the old customers, they say, "Let's go to Babe," because I'm fast. That's why I'm so tired while these young girls are going dancin' at night. They don't really put pride in their work. To me, this is living. At times, when I feel sick, I come to work feelin' I'll pep up here. Sometimes it doesn't. (Laughs.)

I'm a checker and I'm very proud of it. There's some, they say, "A checker—ugh!" To me, it's like somebody being a teacher or a lawyer. I'm not ashamed that I wear a uniform and nurse's shoes and that I got varicose veins. I'm makin' an honest living. Whoever looks down on me, they're lower than I am.

What irritates me is when customers get very cocky with me. "Hurry up," or "Cash my check quick." I don't think this is right. You wait your time and I'll give you my full, undivided attention. You rush and you're gonna get nothin'. Like yesterday, I had two big orders on my counter and I push the groceries down, and she says, "I have to be somewhere in ten minutes. Hurry up and bag that." You don't talk that way to me or any other checker.

I'm human, I'm working for a living. They belittle me sometimes. They use a little profanity sometimes. I stop right there and I go get the manager. Nobody is gonna call me a (cups hand over mouth, whispers) b-i-t-c-h. These are the higher class of people, like as if I'm their housekeeper or their maid. You don't even talk to a maid like this.

I make mistakes, I'm not infallible. I apologize. I catch it right there and then. I tell my customers, "I overcharged you two pennies on this. I will take it off of your next item." So my customers don't watch me when I ring up. They trust me. But I had one this morning—with this person I say, "How are you?" That's the extent of our conversation. She says to me, "Wait. I want to check you." I just don't bother. I make like I don't even know she's there or I don't even hear her. She's ready for an argument. So I say, "Stop right there and then. I'll give you a receipt when I'm through. If there's any mistakes I'll correct them." These people, I can't understand them—and I can't be bothered with their little trifles because I've got my next customer that wants to get out . . .

It hurts my feelings when they distrust me. I wouldn't cheat nobody, because it isn't going in my pocket. If I make an honest mistake, they call you a thief, they call you a ganef. I'm far from bein' a ganef.

Sometimes I feel my face gettin' so red that I'm so aggravated, I'm a total wreck. My family says, "We better not talk to her today. She's had a bad day." They say, "What happened?" I'll look at 'em and I'll start laughin', because this is not a policy to bring home your work. You leave your troubles at the store and vice versa. But there's days when you can't cope with it. But it irons out.

When you make a mistake, you get three chances. Then they take it out of your pay, which is right. You can't make a ten-dollar mistake every week. It's fishy. What's this nonsense? If I give a customer ten dollars too much, it's your own fault. That's why they got these registers with the amounts tendered on it. You don't have to stop and count. I've never had such mistakes. It happens mostly with some of these young kids.

Years ago it was more friendlier, more sweeter. Now there's like tension in the air. A tension in the store. The minute you walk in you feel it. Everybody is fightin' with each other. They're pushin', pushin'—"I was first." Now it's an effort to say, "Hello, how are you?" It must be the way of people livin' today. Everything is so rush, rush, rush, and shovin' Nobody's goin' anywhere. I think they're pushin' themselves right to a grave, some of these people.

A lot of traffic here. There's bumpin' into each other with shoppin' carts. Some of 'em just do it intentionally. When I'm shoppin', they just jam you with the carts. That hits your ankle and you have a nice big bruise there. You know who does this the most? These old men that shop. These *men*. They're terrible and just *jam* you. Sometimes I go over and tap them on the shoulder: "Now why did you do this?" They look at you and they just start *laughin'*. It's just hatred in them, they're bitter. They hate themselves, maybe they don't feel good that day. They gotta take their anger out on somethin', so they just *jam* you. It's just ridiculous.

I know some of these people are lonesome. They have really nobody. They got one or two items in their cart and they're just shoppin' for an hour, just dallying along, talkin' to other people. They tell them how they feel, what they did today. It's just that they want to get it out, these old people. And the young ones are rushin' to a PTA meeting or something, and they just glance at these people and got no time for 'em.

We have this little coffee nook and we serve free coffee. A lot of people come in for the coffee and just walk out. I have one old lady, she's got no place to go. She sits in front of the window for hours. She'll walk around the store, she'll come back. I found out she's all alone, this old lady. No family, no nothin'. From my register I see the whole bit.

I wouldn't know how to go in a factory. I'd be like in a prison. Like this, I can look outside, see what the weather is like. I want a little fresh air, I walk out the front door, take a few sniffs of air, and come back in. I'm here forty-five minutes early every morning. I've never been late except for that big snowstorm. I never thought of any other work.

I'm a couple of days away, I'm very lonesome for this place. When I'm on a vacation, I can't wait to go, but two or three days away, I start to get fidgety. I can't stand around and do nothin'. I have to be busy at all times. I look forward to comin' to work. It's a great feelin'. I enjoy it somethin' terrible.

GRACE CLEMENTS, FELTER, LUGGAGE FACTORY

S he is a sparrow of a woman in her mid-forties. She has eighteen grandchildren. "I got my family the easy way. I married my family." She has worked in factories for the past twenty-five years: "A punch press operator, oven unloader, sander, did riveting, stapling, light assembly . . ." She has been with one company for twenty-one years, ARMCO Corporation.

During the last four years, she has worked in the luggage division of one of the corporation's subsidiaries. In the same factory are made snowmobile parts, windshield defrosters, tilt caps, sewer tiles, and black paper speakers for radios and TV sets.

"We're about twelve women that work in our area, one for each tank. We're about one-third Puerto Rican and Mexican, maybe a quarter black, and the rest of us are white. We have women of all ages, from eighteen to sixty-six, married, single, with families, without families.

"We have to punch in before seven. We're at our tank approximately one to two minutes before seven to take over from the girl who's leaving. The tanks run twenty-four hours a day."

The tank I work at is six-foot deep, eight-foot square. In it is pulp, made of ground wood, ground glass, fiberglass, a mixture of chemicals and water. It comes up through a copper screen felter as a form, shaped like the luggage you buy in the store.

In forty seconds you have to take the wet felt out of the felter, put the blanket on—a rubber sheeting—to draw out the excess moisture, wait two, three seconds, take the blanket off, pick the wet felt up, balance it on your shoulder—there is no way of holding it without it tearing all to pieces, it is wet and will collapse—reach over, get the hose, spray the inside of this copper screen to keep it from plugging, turn around, walk to the hot dry die behind you, take the hot piece off with your opposite hand, set it on the floor—this wet thing is still balanced on my shoulder—put the wet piece on the dry die, push this button that lets the dry press down, inspect the piece we just took off, the hot piece, stack it, and count it—when you get a stack of ten, you push it over and start another stack of ten—then go back and put our blanket on the wet piece coming up from the tank . . . and start all over. Forty seconds. We also have to weigh every third piece in that time. It has to be within so many grams. We are constantly standing and moving. If you talk during working, you get a reprimand, because it is easy to make a reject if you're talking.

A thirty-inch luggage weighs up to fifteen pounds wet. The hot piece weighs between three to four pounds. The big luggage you'll maybe process only four hundred. On the smaller luggage, you'll run maybe 800, sometimes 850 a day. All day long is the same thing over and over. That's about ten steps every forty seconds about 800 times a day.

We work eight straight hours, with two ten-minute breaks and one twenty-minute break for lunch. If you want to use the washroom, you have to do that in that time. By the time you leave your tank, you go to the washroom, freshen up a bit, go into the recreation room, it makes it very difficult to finish a small lunch and be back in the tank in twenty minutes. So you don't really have too much time for conversation. Many of our women take a half a sandwich or some of them don't even take anything. I'm a big eater. I carry a lunch box, fruit, a half a sandwich, a little cup of cottage cheese or salad. I find it very difficult to complete my lunch in the length of time.

You cannot at any time leave the tank. The pieces in the die will burn while you're gone. If you're real, real, real sick and in urgent need, you do shut it off. You turn on the trouble light and wait for the tool man to come and take your place. But they'll take you to a nurse and check it out.

The job I'm doing is easier than the punch presses I used to run. It's still not as fast as the punch press, where you're putting out anywhere to five hundred pieces an hour. Whereas here you can have a couple of seconds to rest in. I mean *seconds*. (Laughs.) You have about two seconds to wait while the blanket is on the felt drawing the moisture out. You can stand and relax those two seconds—three seconds at most. You wish you didn't have to work in a factory. When it's all you know what to do, that's what you do.

I guess my scars are pretty well healed by now, because I've been off on medical leave for two, three months. Ordinarily I usually have two, three burn spots. It's real hot, and if it touches you for a second, it'll burn your arm. Most of the girls carry scars all the time.

We've had two or three serious accidents in the last year and a half. One happened about two weeks ago to a woman on the hydraulic lift. The cast-iron extension deteriorated with age and cracked and the die dropped. It broke her whole hand. She lost two fingers and had plastic surgery to cover the burn. The dry die runs anywhere from 385 degrees to 425.

We have wooden platforms where we can walk on. Some of the tanks have no-skid strips to keep you from slipping, 'cause the floor gets wet. The hose we wash the felter with will sometimes have leaks and will spray back on you. Sometimes the tanks will overflow. You can slip and fall. And slipping on oil. The hydraulic presses leak every once in a while. We've had a number of accidents. I currently have a workman's comp suit going. I came up under an electric switch box with my elbow and injured the bone and muscle where it fastens together. I couldn't use it.

I have arthritis in the joints of some of my fingers. Your hands handling hot pieces perspire and you end up with rheumatism or arthritis in your fingers. Naturally in your shoulder, balancing that wet piece. You've got the heat, you've got the moisture because there's steam coming out. You have the possibility of being burnt with steam when the hot die hits that wet felt. You're just engulfed in a cloud of steam every forty seconds.

It's very noisy. If the tool man comes to talk to you, the noise is great enough you have to almost shout to make yourself heard. There's the hissing of the steam, there's the compressed air, a lot of pressure—it's gotta lift that fifteen pounds and break it loose from that copper screen. I've lost a certain percentage of my hearing already. I can't hear the phone in the yard. The family can.

In the summertime, the temperature ranges anywhere from 100 to 150 degrees at our work station. I've taken thermometers and checked it out. You've got three open presses behind you. there's nothing between you and that heat but an asbestos sheet. They've recently put in air conditioning in the recreation room. There's been quite a little discussion between the union and the company on this. They carry the air conditioning too low for the people on the presses. Our temperature will be up to 140, and to go into an air-conditioned recreation room that might be set at 72—'cause the office force is happy and content with it—people on the presses almost faint when they go back. We really suffer.

I'm chairman of the grievance committee. We have quite a few grievances. Sometimes we don't have the support we should have from our people. Sometimes the company is obstinate. For the most part, many of our grievances are won.

Where most people get off at three, I get off at two o'clock. I have an hour to investigate grievances, to work on them, to write them up, to just in general check working conditions. I'm also the editor of the union paper. I do all my own work. I cut stencils, I write the articles, copy the pictures. I'm not a very good freehand artist (laughs), so I copy them. I usually do that in the union office before I go home and make supper. It takes about five hours to do a paper. Two nights.

(Laughs.) I daydream while I'm working. Your mind gets so it automatically picks out the flaws. I plan my paper and what I'm going to have for supper and what we're gonna do for the weekend. My husband and I have a sixteen-foot boat. We spend a lot of weekends and evenings on the river. And I try to figure out how I'm gonna feed twenty, twenty-five people for dinner on Saturday. And how to solve a grievance . . .

They can't keep the men on the tanks. We've never been able to keep a man over a week. They say it's too monotonous. I think women adjust to monotony better than men do. Because their minds are used to doing two things at once, where a man usually can do one thing at a time. A woman is used to listening to a child tell her something while she's doing something else. She might be making a cake while the child is asking her a question. She can answer that child and continue to put that cake together. It's the same way on the tanks. You get to be automatic in what you're doing and your mind is doing something else.

I was one of the organizers here (laughs) when the union came in. I was as anti-union in the beginning as I am union now. Coming from a small farming community in Wisconsin, I didn't know what a union was all about. I didn't understand the labor movement at all.

Before the union came in, all I did was do my eight hours, collect my paycheck, and go home, did my housework, took care of my daughter, and went back to work. I had no outside interests. You just lived to live. Since I became active in the union, I've become active in politics, in the community, in legislative problems. I've been to Washington on one or two trips. I've been to Springfield. That has given me more of an incentive for life.

I see the others, I'm sad. They just come to work, do their work, go home, take care of their home, and come back to work. Their conversation is strictly about their family and meals. They live each day for itself and that's about it.

I tried to get my children to finish vocational school. One of the girls works for a vending machine company, serving hot lunches. She makes good. One of the daughters does waitress work. One of the girls has gone into factory work. One of the boys is in a factory. He would like to work up to maintenance. One girl married and doesn't do any work at all. My husband is a custodian in a factory. He likes his work as a janitor. There's no pushing him.

This summer I've been quite ill and they've been fussin' about me. (Laughs.) Monday and Tuesday my two daughters and I made over sixty quarts of peaches, made six batches of jam. On Wednesday we made five batches of wild grape jelly. We like to try new recipes. I like to see something different on the table every night. I enjoy baking my own bread and coffee cake. I bake everything I carry in our lunch.

My whole attitude on the job has changed since the union came in. Now I would like to be a union counselor or work for the OEO. I work with humans as grievance committee chairman. They come to you angry, they come to you hurt, they come to you puzzled. You have to make life easier for them.

I attended a conference of the Governor's Commission on the Status of Women. Another lady went with me. We were both union officers. Most of the women there were either teachers or nurses or in a professional field. When they found out we were from labor, their attitude was cold. You felt like a little piece of scum. They acted like they were very much better than we were, just because we worked in a factory. I felt that, without us, they'd be in a heck of a shape. (Laughs.) They wouldn't have anything without us. How could we employ teachers if it wasn't for the factory workers to manufacture the books? And briefcases, that's luggage.

I can understand how the black and the Spanish-speaking people feel. Even as a farmer's daughter, because we were just hard-working poor farmers, you were looked down upon by many people. Then to go into factory work, it's the same thing. You're looked down upon. You can even feel it in a store, if you're in work clothes. The difference between being in work clothes going into a nice department store and going in your dress clothes. It is two entirely different feelings. People won't treat you the same at all.

I hope I don't work many more years. I'm tired. I'd like to stay home and keep house. We're in hopes my husband would get himself a small hamburger place and a place near the lake where I can have a little garden and raise my flowers that I love to raise . . .

JUST A HOUSEWIFE

JESUSITA NOVARRO

She is a mother of five children: the oldest twelve, the youngest two. "I went on welfare when my first husband walked out on me. I was swimming alone, completely cuckoo for a while. When I married this second man, I got off it. When he started drinking and bringing no money home, I had to quit my job and go on welfare again. I got something with this welfare business and I don't like it."

She is working part-time as an assistant case aide at a settlement house in the neighborhood. The director "says I'm doing real good and can have a job upstairs with a little bit more money. It's only four hours, because in the afternoon I want to be with my children. They're still small."

She has just come home from the hospital where she was treated for a serious illness. On this hot August afternoon—it is over a hundred degrees—the blower in the kitchen isn't doing much good. The three children in the house are more fascinated by technology—the tape recorder—than the conversation, though they are listening . . .

I start my day here at five o'clock. I get up and prepare all the children's clothes. If there's shoes to shine, I do it in the morning. About seven o'clock I bathe the children. I leave my baby with the baby sitter and I go to work at the settlement house. I work until twelve o'clock. Sometimes I'll work longer if I have to go to welfare and get a check for somebody. When I get back, I try to make hot food for the kids to eat. In the afternoon it's pretty well on my own. I scrub and clean and cook and do whatever I have to do.

Welfare makes you feel like you're nothing. Like you're laying back and not doing anything and it's falling in your lap. But you must understand, mothers, too, work. My house is clean. I've been scrubbing since this morning. You could check my clothes, all washed and ironed. I'm home and I'm working. I am a working mother.

A job that a woman in a house is doing is a tedious job—especially if you want to do it right. If you do it slipshod, then it's not so bad. I'm pretty much of a perfectionist. I tell my kids, hang a towel. I don't want it thrown away. That is very hard. It's a constant game of picking up this, picking up that. And putting this away, so the house'll be clean.

Some men work eight hours a day. There are mothers that work eleven, twelve hours a day. We get up at night, a baby vomits, you have to be calling the doctor, you have to be changing the baby. When do you get a break, really? You don't. This is an all-around job, day and night. Why do they say it's charity? We're working for our money. I am working for this check. It is not charity. We are giving some kind of home to these children.

I'm so busy all day I don't have time to daydream. I pray a lot. I pray to God to give me strength. If He should take a child away from me, to have the strength to accept it. It's His kid. He just borrowed him to me.

I used to get in and close the door. Now I speak up for my right. I walk with my head up. If I want to wear big earrings, I do. If I'm overweight, that's too bad. I've gotten completely over feeling where I'm little. I'm working now, I'm pulling my weight. I'm gonna get off welfare in time, that's my goal—get off.

It's living off welfare and feeling that you're taking something for nothing the way people have said. You get to think maybe you are. You get to think, Why am I so stupid? Why can't I work? Why do I have to live this way? It's not enough to live on anyway. You feel degraded.

The other day I was at the hospital and I went to pay my bill. This nurse came and gave me the green card. Green card is for welfare. She went right in front of me and gave it to the cashier. She said, "I wish I could stay home and let the money fall in my lap." I felt rotten. I was just burning inside. You hear this all the way around you. The doctor doesn't even look at you. People are ashamed to show that green card. Why can't a woman just get a check in the mail: Here, this check is for you. Forget welfare. You're a mother who works.

This nurse, to her way of thinking, she represents the working people. The ones with the green card, we represent the lazy no-goods. This is what she was saying. They're the good ones and we're the bad guys.

You know what happened at the hospital? I was put in a nice room, semiprivate. You stay there until someone with insurance comes in and then you get pushed up to the fifth floor. There's about six people in there, and nobody comes even if you ring. I said, "Listen, lady, you just find out what's the matter with me so I can get the hell out of here."

How are you going to get people off welfare if they're constantly being pushed down? If they're constantly feeling they're not good for anything? People say, I'm down, I'll stay down. And this goes on generation to generation to generation. Their daughter and their daughter and their daughter. So how do you break this up? These kids don't ask to be born—these kids are gonna grow up and give their lives one day. There will always be a Vietnam.

There will always be war. There always has been. The way the world is run, yes, there will always be war. Why? I really don't know. Nobody has ever told me. I was so busy handling my own affairs and taking care of my children and trying to make my own money and calling up welfare when my checks are late or something has been stolen. All I know is what's going on here. I'm an intelligent woman up to a certain point, and after that . . . I wish I knew. I guess the big shots decided the war. I don't question it, because I've been busy fighting my own little war for so long.

The head of the settlement house wants me to take the social worker's job when I get back to work. I visit homes, I talk to mothers. I try to make them aware that they got something to give. I don't try to work out the problems. This is no good. I try to help them come to some kind of a decision. If there's no decision, to live with it, because some problem doesn't have any answer.

There was one mother that needed shoes, I found shoes for her. There was another mother that needed money because her check was late. I found someplace for her to borrow a couple of dollars. It's like a fund. I could borrow a couple of dollars until my check comes, then when my check comes I give it back. How much time have mothers left to go out and do this? How many of us have given time so other mothers could learn to speak English, so they'll be able to go to work? We do it gladly because the Lord gave us English.

I went to one woman's house and she's Spanish speaking. I was talking to her in English and she wouldn't unbend. I could see the fear in her eyes. So I started talking Spanish. Right away, she invited me for coffee and she was telling me the latest news . . .

I would like to help mothers be aware of how they can give to the community. Not the whole day—maybe three, four hours. And get paid for it. There's nothing more proud for you to receive a check where you worked at. It's yours, you done it.

At one time, during her second marriage, she had worked as an assembler at a television factory. "I didn't care for it. It was too automatic. It was just work, work, work, and I wasn't giving of myself. Just hurry it up and get it done. Even if you get a job that pays you, if you don't enjoy it, what are you getting? You're not growing up. (Taps temple.) Up here."

The people from the settlement house began visiting me, visiting welfare mothers, trying to get them interested in cooking projects and sewing. They began knocking on my door. At the beginning I was angry.

It was just like I drew a curtain all around me. I didn't think I was really good for anything. So I kind of drew back. Just kept my troubles to myself, like vegetating. When these people began calling on me, I began to see that I could talk and that I did have a brain. I became a volunteer.

I want to be a social worker. Somebody that is not indifferent, that bends an ear to everybody. You cannot be slobberish. You cannot cry with the people. Even if you cry inside, you must keep a level head. You have to try to help that person get over this bump. I would go into a house and try to make friends. Not as a spy. The ladies have it that welfare comes as spies to see what you have. Or you gotta hide everything 'cause welfare is coming. There is this fear the social worker is gonna holler, because they got something, maybe a man or a boyfriend. I wouldn't take any notes or pens or paper or pencils or anything. I would just go into the house and talk. Of course, I would look around to see what kind of an environment it is. This you have to absorb.

I promised myself if I ever get to work all day, I'm going to buy me a little insurance. So the next time I go to the hospital I'll go to the room I want to go. I'm gonna stay there until it's time for me to leave, because I'm gonna pay my own bill. I don't like to feel rotten. I want my children, when they grow up, they don't have to live on it. I want to learn more. I'm hungry for knowledge. I want to do something. I'm searching for something. I don't know what it is.

THE QUIET LIFE

DONNA MURRAY, BOOKBINDER

S *he has been binding books for twenty-five years. Among her clients have been the University of Chicago, the Arboretum, the Art Institute, and private collectors. Her reflections are somewhat free associative in nature.*

"I didn't even really become a bookbinder. It happened because we had so many books. I inherited this great big library from my father, and John [her husband, an artist and professor of art] had many, many art books that were falling apart. We had acres of books, and I thought this was the thing to do: I'll put these books together and make them fit. So I began a sort of experiment and I enjoyed it very much. I became a bookbinder because I had nothing else to do."

At first no one taught me. I wasn't doing much of anything. Then a *marvelous* woman, who's a brilliant artist, gave me a *marvelous* frame that her father made for her, for sewing books and that sort of thing. So I learned to sew books. They're really good books, it's just the covers that are rotten. You take them apart and you make them sound and you smash them in and sew them up. That's all there is to it.

I have a bindery at home, it's kind of a cave, really. It's where you have your gear—a table where you work, a cutter, a press, and those kinds of things. You have a good screw press, a heavy one that presses the books down. A binder's gear is principally his thumbnail. You push, you use your thumbnail more than anything else.

I mustn't pose as a fine binder because I'm not. That's exhibition binding, gold tooling. You roll out this design and you fill it with egg white. Then you cover it with pure gold leaf. I enjoy restoration very much—when you restore an old book that's all ragged at the back. You must make a rubbing of the spine. The spine's all rotten, so you put that aside and you turn back the pages *very carefully*. That's what I enjoy most of all.

Obviously I don't make much money binding books, but it's very cozy work. Carolyn [Horton, her mentor] and I did simple, necessary things for the university. We bound precious pamphlets in a way that preserved them. Incunabula—books printed before 1500. Architectural works and something of the Latin poets.

Those made of vellum are usually just rotten in the back. Vellum's a wild thing, the hide of a calf or a lamb. It's treated with acid. The pages are falling apart. You take them out if you can and you wash them, de-acidify them in a certain solution. Then you fold them together and press them in your press.

Some of my private customers have very splendid collections, beautiful bindings you'll never see again. I have very specific, lovely clients. One, who's no longer living, had a magnificent collection of Stevenson and Dickens, first editions.

I go to the house and take my equipment, oils and paints and a certain binder's paste. And a painter's drop cloth. There's a beautiful Oriental rug, and indeed you may not drop anything on it. You set up a card table and book ends and that's about it, really.

We calculate the books. We make a point of being sure that the books go back exactly where they were before. We look at each book and pull it out and test it for tears. Almost everybody pulls books out by their tops, and they're always broken. Torn from beautiful leather bindings. In dusting books, you never touch them inside. The dust only goes to the top. People who pull them out with the idea of dusting them—it's just ridiculous. It only destroys the book.

My assistant takes the cloth for me, and then we line up the books. She dusts the tops. You always dust from the spine out, cleaning the book. Then you use the *marvelous* British Museum formula, potassium lactate. It's swabbed on the books to put back in the leather the acids that were taken out, that were in the hide in the beginning. They've been dried out completely and all the salts have been destroyed. So we swab all the leather goods with this potassium lactate. A very little swab, and let it sink in. Then these books are polished and put back on the shelves. It preserves books that could never exist in this climate after five years.

It's an arduous thing, but I suppose it's important because if that kind of thing didn't happen, the books would just disintegrate. Father's library did. Especially in the city with its very high potency of sulfur dioxide, which eats up the books. The hideous air, the poisonous air of the city. People love to have whole sets of Dickens or Mark Twain or Dumas—the kinds of popular acquisitions in our mothers' age, when they filled up their shelves. The books in Chicago are disintegrating to a most appalling degree in comparison to the books of the same issue in Lake Forest. It's been going on for years. It destroys them. It eats them up. Terrible.

I usually arrive at about ten thirty. I work as long as it pleases me. If I fill up the table and the books are oiled, I often leave at four or six. I might work for one client two or three weeks. In the case of Mrs. Armour's books, it was a matter of six months. She had a superb collection stored in the old house. It took two days to unpack the crates. Her mother was a collector of exceedingly marvelous taste. It was undeniably one of the most beautiful collections of books I've ever seen. Not only in the binding, but in the selection. It was kind of wonderful to be there at that moment.

I wouldn't want to bind anything that was flimsy. You have to think of what's inside. If you're binding a book about a big idea—Karl Marx! (laughs)—you obviously would accommodate a binding, wouldn't you? The idea of the binding should reflect what's inside. The books at the Arboretum are among the most interesting. Some of them are sixteenth- and seventeenth-century books, marvelous herbals. Beautiful, beautiful books. Flower papers. There is no special way you relate your own taste, your reflections.

If they're the *marvelous* trees of Japan—oh dear, oh dear. I was reared in California where I saw the redwoods that are now being systematically destroyed. And there's some redwood trees in Japan that relate to what you're thinking, oh dear (softly). You must be very clever with a binding and give it the dignity it deserves. Because the pages are so full of stunning, *fantastic* things that say, This is life. So what do you do with a binding like that? I don't know. You just give it a strength. If it's leather or it's cloth or it's paper, you give it strength, an indication of what is inside.

I only enjoy working on books that say something. I know this is an anathema to people who insist on preserving books that are only going to be on the shelves forever—or on coffee tables. Books are for people to read, and that's that. I think books are for the birds unless people read them.

That's what I discovered when I worked in Florence after the big flood. I came in the summer. John and I lived there and he worked there during his first sabbatical. I loved that city so much. And when someone from the Biblioteca Nazionale asked me to come . . .

It would be *darling* to look into books when you're working on them, lured by them—but obviously you can't. You'd never finish your work. I can read books on my own time. I feel very strongly about every book I pick up. It's like something alive or—or decadent, death. I wouldn't for one moment bind *Mein Kampf,* because I think it's disgusting to waste time on such an obscenity. Are you offering me a million dollars to bind that? Of course not.

I adore the work. It's very comforting. The only thing that makes me angry is that I'm almost all the time on the outside rather than on the inside. I'd like to be reading them. But I do think working in my house and being comfortable and doing something you feel is beneficial—it is important, isn't it?

I'm just a swabber. (Laughs.) I'm not an artist. I just use aniline dyes, so they won't be hurting the leather. Aniline's a natural dye, and that's about it. It isn't very skilled work. It's just knowing what books need, if you want to preserve them. It's just something you do. A mechanic takes care of a tire, and he knows . . .

Oh, I think it's important. Books are things that keep us going. Books—I haven't got much feeling about many other things. I adore the work. Except sometimes it becomes very lonesome. It's nice to sit beside somebody, whether it's somebody who works with you or whether it's your husband or your friend. It's just lovely, just like a whisper, always . . . If you were really brainy, you wouldn't waste your time pasting and binding. But if you bind good books, you make something good, really and truly good. Yes, I would like to make a good book hold good and I would like to be involved in a pact that will not be broken, that holds good, which would really be as solid as the book.

Keeping a four-hundred-year-old book together keeps that spirit alive. It's an alluring kind of thing, lovely, because you know that belongs to us. Because a book is a life, like one man is a life. Yes, yes, this work is good for me, therapeutic for old age . . . *just keep going* with the hands . . .

BROKERS

RAY WAX, STOCKBROKER

*H*e *has been a stockbroker on Wall Street for several years. He lives in an upper-middle-class suburb on the outskirts of New York City. He is married, has two grown children.*

"*I really believed when I was growing up that somehow I would score. As a kid—I was no more than twelve—I'd get up at five o'clock in the morning and go to an open market where they sold cakes in an open stall. It was so goddamned cold you had to cut the goddamned cakes with mittens. I made four, five dollars a day. That was a lot of money in those days. I worked. I felt good about it.*

"*I was a golf caddy at fourteen. I used to carry two sets of golf bags for eighteen holes for $2.50. I guess it's a ten-dollar bill today. You really earned your pay when you went through eighteen holes. If the caddy master liked you, maybe you did thirty-six holes.*

"*I felt even though there was money in the house, I was supposed to work. I was supposed to earn something. It was one of the things you had to do. If you did, it was supposed to make you feel good. I was a good caddy and I felt good about it. I felt that somewhere along the line someone would recognize that I had that special gleam. Horatio Alger—which is a crock of shit.*"

For twenty years he engaged in all sorts of enterprises and "*I was generally successful. Then I lost interest or I thought the promise had gone out of it and I went on to something else. In the late fifties I had exported cars to South America. I was doing a million dollars a year and sort of ran out of steam. My one virtue was I didn't rip anybody off. For a while I thought I could live in South America. And I found out that the whole world was rigged. They didn't want me to do anything legit."*

What kept you from becoming a millionaire?

"I just wasn't . . . I wasn't facile enough. I was bright enough to do the things I had to do to make a good living, but I really didn't come up with the big score. And . . . (Pause.) Well, there was a limit to what I was prepared to do to make money in a crazy way. But that's no good. You're supposed to do everything you have to do to make money. I guess at some point there's a limit. You either demean yourself or change yourself or something happens where you become something else. Later, when I owned a hotel, the only way I could survive is if I let a pimp put four broads in the bar. I passed. I couldn't do it. I eventually lost the hotel."

He became a land speculator. "I kinda ran out of money, because land takes a lot of money. I became a real estate broker in self-defense. I began to peddle land. I sold land to builders. I realized they were just one cut above running a candy store. Within a couple of years I was building houses and building them better than anybody's ever built them before. I really had some kind of responsibility to build a house that was a good house. Until I began to run out of land . . ."

I loved building houses. It's really a marvelous thing. You work with people that work with their hands. When the carpenters come in to work, goddamn it, they're good. When the bricklayers came in, they gotta know their job. I had a roofer, a Norwegian or whatever the hell he was—when he went up on that fuckin' roof and he bucked that stuff there, man, you knew you were gonna have the best roof you ever had on a house. I didn't cheat on the house. I sold my own houses, wouldn't turn them over to an agent. I enjoyed doing that more than anything I ever enjoyed in my life. I don't know why I didn't continue it.

I was kind of driven. I had to go on doing something else. I couldn't see myself building a development of fifty, a hundred houses, little boxes. I couldn't get the kind of plots where I could put five, six houses on one or two acres, to build a house with enough nuances. The challenge went out of it after a while.

I invested in a hotel. It had 101 keys. I got fascinated with hotels, the operation of it, how it was put together, who came, who went. I came out with a quarter of a million and I built my own hotel—alongside the World's Fair grounds. We did the biggest job of any motel at the fair. In two years the fair was a shambles. The area was a desert, death. I walked away with a whole skin, but gave the hotel back to the bank.

While I was fiddlin' around with the hotel I began to play the market. I got lucky at some point and made about a hundred thousand dollars. That convinced me I could make this my way of life. I thought it would be a nice way to live. I began to study to be a stockbroker. I passed the exam. You learn the ethical side of the business, what you can and can't do. It's all mumbo jumbo.

The New York Stock Exchange has 1,066 members. I always think of it as the Norman Invasion. These are William the Conquerors. The 1066 is one of the greatest clubs in the world. A seat on the exchange costs anywhere from a hundred thousand dollars in bad times to a half a million in good times. These guys didn't pay that price of admission without deciding that they're gonna take care of each other, protect their own. They're the guardians of all the stock. They're the specialists. They dole out these stocks to each other and they have the edge. They become the bookies on all the stocks. This is the only wheel in town.

I really thought of the market as a sort of river. Money running to the sea. I figured all I had to do is just stand on that bank and lower a bucket every once in a while and take a little bit of that out. I didn't care how much these gentle gentiles, with those little briefcases under their arms, took back to Larchmont or how much went up to Westport. I figured they're gonna let me lower my bucket. But they don't let anybody lower a bucket.

I'm afraid the work of a stockbroker is superfluous. He did have a function at one time, when little people were allowed in the market and given a chance to share in part of the goodies. The market really is a game played by very skilled people, who accumulate stocks at low levels so they can be distributed at high. The market is rigged. Knowledgeable people buy certain stocks, whether they have intrinsic value or not, and at some later hour the public is told these stocks represent good values and should be purchased. By the time Joe Blow goes in, the people who've created this atmosphere go out. For every dollar made in the market, a dollar has been lost. The pros make it, the 1066 boys.

The brokerage firms need some people to make this whole machine work. Somewhere in this pattern of things is the stockbroker. Here's where I come in. We're all hooked in. I'm watching every transaction. Everything that happens in the market I see instantaneously. I have a machine in front of me that records and memorizes every transaction that takes place in the entire day. It's called a Bunker-Ramo. It's really a television screen that reproduces the information from a master computer that sits in New Jersey. Within a fraction of a second, when I press for the symbol I want, it goes to the central computer and it automatically comes back. When I take my hand from the machine, the screen in front of me is already reproducing the information.

I watch eighteen million, twenty million shares pass the tape. I look at every symbol, every transaction. I would go out of my mind, but my eye has been conditioned to screen maybe two hundred stocks and ignore the others. I pick up with my eyes Goodrich, but I don't see ITT. I don't follow International Tel, I'm not interested in that. I don't see ITT, but I do see IBM. There are over thirty-two hundred symbols. I drop the other three thousand. Otherwise I'd go mad. I really put in an enormously exhausting day.

It's up at six thirty, I read *The New York Times* and *The Wall Street Journal* before eight. I read the Dow Jones ticker tape between eight and ten. At three thirty, when the market closes, I work until four thirty or five. I put in a great deal of technical work. I listen to news reports avidly. I try to determine what's happening. I'm totally immersed in what I'm doing. For the amount of work and intelligence I bring to this job, I'm not being properly compensated. I make a routine living now. The only compensation is like me against the machine. I'm trying to use my intelligence against the wheel. I'm a fuckin' John Henry fightin' this goddamned steel drill, and I'll probably die with my hammer in my hand. (Laughs.) Because I don't want to buy the package. Maybe I'm wrong, but I want to get there my own way. It's very difficult, that's God's truth.

The market moves to destroy you. It says, Play it your way, sucker, buy the package. Believe in the American Dream, buy the hundred time multiple, believe in IBM, and if you doubt it, God help you. Don't ever question what you're doing.

People go to the race track. When there's fifty thousand people at the track, 49,990 are there to lose money. It's kind of a self-flagellation. There's maybe ten people in that park who are pros, who've been there at six in the morning and clocked the horses, who've felt the turf and talked to the jockey or stable boy. They're the professional gamblers. They're there for just one reason—to make money. The 49,990 other slobs, they're there to lose. I don't have to tell you about horses.

People who go into the market are committed to losing money. They don't blame the broker. They don't blame the machine, which is rigged. against them. The moment you buy a stock, you're hooked. You're gonna pay a commission on the way in or on the way out. Normally that's a sizable percentage. The stock has to move up at least a point and a quarter for you to get even. If you bought a stock at $50, it has to move to $51.35 before you'd get even. You're being humped before you even get around the corner. The moment you buy that stock, you're a loser.

What I try to do to justify my existence is to understand how it works. I took courses. I took in every lecture. I subscribed to services. I do charting. I'm almost like that gambler who clocks the horse at six in the morning on the workout when they blow that horse out. But I'm really on the outside lookin' in. Somebody else has rigged the race and knows who's gonna win it. And somebody else knows what stock's gonna go. I'm sure every stock has a group that decides when they're gonna go and when they're gonna get off. All you can hope to do when you see that train moving—there's the theory of the moving train . . .

When the train begins to move, all you can do is see it move and hope to get on. You don't know when the train slows down until after the big boys have jumped off. You're gonna get on ten points after they did and get off ten points after they did. If you can discern the direction of the train . . .

Maybe if I was twenty, twenty-five years and I just came out of Harvard Business School and I believed this bullshit, which is packaged and wrapped . . . Wall Street, Madison Avenue. The people even look the same. They really believe in their invulnerability. They believe their own success story. I don't believe it. (A rueful chuckle.) That's a hell of an argument to be a broker. In a crazy way I do a service. I try to give such customers as I have a rational explanation for an investment. I try . . . (Sighs wearily.)

Look, we've got eighty billions of dollars worth of money floating around in Europe. It's nonconvertible. We've fucked every country in the world. We've got every central bank in the world with dollars up to their ass. They can't do anything with it. We said to 'em, "We're the Texans." The world belongs to Connally. He told 'em in effect, "Live with that money. We've bought your companies, we've taken over your economies, we've given you dollars that are spurious. Don't blow the whistle on us, because the whole fuckin' sky is gonna come down, Chicken Little. Maybe two, three years from now, if the spirit moves us, we may talk about the convertibility of the dollars into gold. In the meantime, Fuck ya. Put those dollars in our treasury notes, buy our stocks, do somethin' with 'em. But don't come back to me to redeem 'em, because they're worthless." We fucked the world.

I've seen 'em do this. I buy gold, I buy silver. It's the only thing that's real. You can't buy gold in this country. We don't dare. If we let

Americans buy gold, everybody'd be diggin' up his fuckin' back yard and buryin' gold bullion in it. 'Cause he knows the fuckin' thing's real.

(A long pause.) I try to perform a function that has some meaning. I try to take somebody's money and not make shit out of it. If a banker's taking your money and giving you five percent and he's earning twelve percent on it, there should be a better way for the little man to participate. He should do a hell of a sight better than giving it to an insurance company or a bank. It shouldn't be that rigged. He should have a chance to get a fair return on that money. He's worked for it. Somebody else shouldn't be able to use that money and get a twelve percent return while paying the little guy five in front.

The real money made in the market is being made by people with real wealth. I'll say, "If you give me five thousand dollars, I can make you a ten percent return. If we're pretty good, maybe I can get you twenty percent. If it's a smash, maybe we'll double it." But the only way you're gonna make a million dollars is to start with a million dollars.

People who have money in the market have consistently had money. The great wealth in this country has bought Johnson & Johnson, has bought IBM. They never sold a share. To this day, sixty-six percent of the stock is owned by people that never sold a share. They bought General Motors in 1930, they never sold it. They didn't put it in the banks at four percent return. They live on the return. They never sell the principle.

I'm trying to use my intelligence, which I've exercised in other businesses. But it's like wrestling with an octopus. Too many things that I can't control are happening. I can tell you what happened after the fact, but it's very difficult to tell you before the fact. The market never really repeats itself exactly in the same way day after day. There is similarity over the years. Jesse Livermore, a legend, went broke three times. But he was so valuable to the Street, he created so much excitement that the fraternity, the 1066 club, gave him the money to put him back in business. His manipulation in the market, his activity, created additional sales every day. Other people became excited and involved. Yet this man, with all his experience, continually got wiped out. He was bucking something bigger than he was. Ultimately he was destroyed and killed himself. He lost touch with even the reality he knew.

It's really an illusion. It's only real because enough people believe it's real. The whole market is based on a premise—potential growth. You can put any kind of multiple on a stock. If a stock earns a dollar a year, it sells for a hundred. It's selling at a hundred times its earning capacity. If you believe the stock is a reflection of some future experience, that you can invest in a hundred times its earning capacity and that you will subsequently benefit, you qualify as a true believer. But the moment you question that premise, the whole thing collapses like a house of cards. You have to buy this whole crazy fiction or there would be no market.

IBM, Eastman Kodak, Xerox, these are called growth stocks. And they're held by every major institution, every pension fund, every university. This is the backbone. Nobody questions the basic premise that these stocks will continually get better. Polaroid over the past four years has had an earning growth of minus eleven. But because they've got a camera that is unique, they pretend they will expand at an infinite rate. As long as you believe that, you can pay 130 for Polaroid, as it was today. You'll pay anything as long as you believe this American Dream that growth is forever. But the people who make this market, at some bad hour they're gonna sell Polaroid at 130 to shnooks like you and me. And they're gonna pick it up again at 65 and start the whole process all over. They've done it continually.

Some people know me over a period of years and have allowed me to handle their business. I've created new business on solicitation, depending on how good my track record is. The function of a broker is to try to get his account to trade. The real money is never made by selling stock. A broker's lifeblood, the only money he makes, is by generating commissions. Most money is made by getting people to turn their portfolios, their stocks, over three, four, five times a year. If you're really unethical—cynical, the milder word—you may get 'em to turn their stocks over ten times a year or fifteen times. There's a name for it.

Brokers merely are ribbon clerks. They're order takers. They do very little if it's a big house. It's a profession that's in its decline. Everything is being committed to computer, to systemized tapes. There are houses now on the Street that say, "Don't you ever make a decision. We have a computer that tells you what to do to your customer, to buy and to sell." At some point the function of a broker may be relegated to some girl who sits at a phone and repeats what the computer has told the customer to buy and to sell. I see Wall Street being reduced to kind of a supermarket. The biggest houses will be swallowing the others. You'll wind up with four or five houses and not many more than half a dozen.

There are houses that guarantee if you utilize the machine, you'll get five or ten trades a year out of your customers. They'll put him in a stock and they'll take him out. Beautiful. But in actual practice, when the market goes sour, the machine breaks down. It can't take care of the vagaries. The machine can't account for an economic crisis or a world depression. The machine can't account for a military adventure in Vietnam. It's a robot. It can do what the programmed tape tells it to. But it can't account for the extraordinary world we live in.

People like me start out with a feeling that there's a place for them in society, that they really have a useful function. They see it destroyed by the cynicism of the market. A piece of worthless stock can be given glamour and many people may be induced to buy it. Excitement, public relations. The people can be wiped out with the absolute cynicism that brings those who conceived it to the top.

Can you imagine? I really felt I could buck this machine. When I began, I was sure I could win. I no longer have that confidence. What's happening is so extraordinary. It's so much bigger than I am.

I'm just trying to go along for the ride. I have little to do with it. They believe the game because they know how the cards are gonna be dealt. I don't believe the game because I know the cards are stacked. After being told about fiscal responsibility, they know the treasury's gonna spew out all kinds of dollars, and all kinds of money's gonna be made available to the corporations for them to put in the market. This is a contradiction. This is where the thing breaks down.

I can't say what I'm doing has any value. This doesn't make me too happy. If I could learn in some way to live with the wheel—but I can't. If I make an error and it costs the customer money, it's as though it were my money. This is extraordinary. The average broker lives to generate commissions and he goes home as though he were selling shoelaces or ties. He doesn't carry the goddamn market with him. I carry it like it was a monkey on my back. Man, I wake up in the middle of the night remembering what I did right or wrong. That's no good.

When I built the houses, I hired a bricklayer, I hired the roofer, I determined who put the goddamned thing together. And when I handed somebody a key, the house was whole. I made it happen. I can't do it in the market. I'm just being manipulated and moved around and I keep pretending I can understand it, that I can somehow cope with it. The truth is I can't.

The broker as a human being is being demeaned by the financial community. His commissions are being cut. I joined the Association of Investment Brokers—we number about a thousand members as against forty thousand brokers—which tries to think of itself as though it were the Pilots Union. The terrible thing is we don't fly planes. We handle the fuckin' phone and punch out digits on something that translates from a computer. We pretend we have status in the community, but we're expendable.

The brokerage firms just cut our commission again, while they increased their own rate by forty-two percent. The SEC approved a new set of commission rates. The SEC is just an arm of the stock exchange. They put their people in it. Like every regulatory agency, it serves the exchange and pisses on the public. The commissions for the houses are larger, but I make no more than I made before. This happened in every firm on the Street. It's as though they went out and played golf together and agreed on it.

In this rip-off, we're treated with contempt by the members of the stock exchange. You're being told you're not a useful member of society. They're really saying, "If you make too big a noise, we're gonna have a girl take the orders and the machine'll do the rest. You're better off to let us make your decisions. Don't attempt to use your intelligence. Don't attempt to figure out what's happening, if you know what's good for you."

Oh, I'll continue to cope. (Laughs.) I'll continue to struggle against the machine. I'll continue with my personal disillusionment. (Laughs.) Oh, I'd like one morning to wake up and go to some work that gave me joy. If I could build houses all over again, I would do it. Because when it's finished, somebody's gonna live in it, and the house is gonna be built and it's gonna be there after I'm gone. (Pause.) Ahhh, fuck it!

BUREAUCRACY

DIANE WILSON, PROCESS CLERK

S*he works for the OEO. "This is a section called PM&S. I can't for the life of me ever remember what it means. Sometimes they change it. They reorganize and you get another initial. (Laughs.)*

"I'm a processing clerk. There are three of us in this one department. We send grants to grantees after field reps have been out to see these poverty-stricken people. The grantees are organizations of the poor. Maybe the Mobilization Center in Gary, where I live—Grand Rapids Poverty Center, something for senior citizens, a day care center. They give 'em all names.

"We mail 'em out forms to sign so they can get the money from

Washington. When they return the forms to us there's another process we go through. We have a governor's letter and a package in an orange folder that we send out to him. He has to give his consent. We have a little telegram we type up. He approves it or he doesn't. We send it on. That makes it official. There's a thirty-day waiting period. After that time we send out the package to Washington . . .

You wish there was a better system. A lot of money is held up and the grantees want to know why they can't get it. Sometimes they call and get the run-around on the phone. I never do that. I tell the truth. If they don't have any money left, they don't have it. No, I'm not disturbed any more. If I was just starting on this job, I probably would. But the older I get, I realize it's a farce. You just get used to it. It's a job. I get my paycheck—that's it. It's all political anyway.

A lot of times the grantee comes down to our audit department for aid. They're not treated as human beings. Sometimes they have to wait, wait, wait—for no reason. The grantee doesn't know it's for no reason. He thinks he's getting somewhere and he really isn't.

They send him from floor to floor and from person to person, it's just around and around he goes. Sometimes he leaves, he hasn't accomplished anything. I don't know why this is so. You can see 'em waiting—so long. Sometimes it has to do with color. Whoever is the boss. If you're in the minority group, you can tell by their actions. A lot of times they don't realize that you know it, but this has happened to you.

So this person was standing out there. He had come to offer something. He was from out of state. The secretary told this boss he had someone waiting. He also had someone in the office. He could've waited on the grantee and got him on his way quick. But he closed the door in the young man's face and the young man stood there. That went on for about forty-five minutes. The secretary got tired of seein' the man standin' there, so she said, could she help him? Was it somethin' he just wanted to give the man? He told her yes. She took it, so he wouldn't stand there. That was all he was gonna do, give it to him. I thought this was awfully rude. This boss does this quite often. I don't know if he does it on purpose. I know if it's an Indian or a black or a Latin he does this.

Life is a funny thing. We had this boss come in from Internal Revenue. He wanted to be very, very strict. He used to have meetings every Friday—about people comin' in late, people leavin' early, people abusin' lunch time. Everyone was used to this relaxed attitude. You kind of went overtime. No one bothered you. You did your work.

Every Friday, everyone would sit there and listen to this man. And we'd all go out and do the same thing again. Next Friday he'd have another meeting and he would tell us the same thing. (Laughs.) We'd all go out and do the same thing again. (Laughs.) He would try to talk to one and see what they'd say about the other. But we'd been working all together for quite a while. You know how the game is played. Tomorrow you might need a favor. So nobody would say anything. If he'd want to find out what time someone came in, who's gonna tell 'em? He'd want to find out where someone was, we'd always say, "They're at the Xerox." Just anywhere. He couldn't get through. Now, lo and behold! We can't find *him* anywhere. He's got into this nice, relaxed atmosphere . . . (Laughs.) He leaves early, he takes long lunch hours. We've converted him. (Laughs.)

After my grievances and my fighting, I'm a processing clerk. Never a typist no more or anything like that. (Laughs.) I started working here in 1969. There was an emergency and they all wanted to work overtime. So I made arrangements at home, 'cause I have to catch a later train. Our supervisor's black. All of us are black. We'll help her get it out so there won't be any back drag on this. Okay, we all worked overtime and made a good showing.

Then they just didn't want to give us the promotion which was due us anyhow. They just don't want to give you anything. The personnel man, all of them, they show you why you don't deserve a promotion. The boss, the one we converted—he came on board, as they call it, after we sweated to meet the deadline. So he didn't know what we did. But he told us we didn't deserve it. That stayed with me forever. I won't be bothered with him ever again.

But our grievance man was very good. He stayed right on the case. We filed a civil rights complaint. Otherwise we woulda never got the promotion. They don't want anybody coming in investigating for race. They said, "Oh, it's not that." But you sit around and see white women do nothin' and get promotions. Here we're working and they say you don't deserve it. The black men are just as hard on us as the white men. Harder. They get angry with you because you started a lot of trouble. The way I feel about it, I'm gonna give 'em all the trouble I can.

Our boss is black, the one that told us we didn't deserve it. (Laughs.) And our union man fighting for us, sittin' there, punchin' away, is white. (Laughs.) We finally got up to the deputy director and he was the one—the white man—that finally went ahead and gave us the promotion.

So we went from grade 4 clerk-typist to grade 5 processing clerk.

We had another boss, he would walk around and he wouldn't want to see you idle at all. Sometimes you're gonna have a lag in your work, you're all caught up. This had gotten on his nerves. We got our promotion and we weren't continually busy. Any time they see black women idle, that irks 'em. I'm talkin' about black men as well as whites. They want you to work continuously.

One day I'd gotten a call to go to his office and do some typing. He'd given me all this handwritten script. I don't know to this day what all that stuff was. I asked him, "Why was I picked for this job?" He said his secretary was out and he needs this done by noon. I said, "I'm no longer a clerk-typist and you yourself said for me to get it out of my mind. Are you trying to get me confused? Anyway, I can't read this stuff." He tells me he'll read it. I said, "Okay, I'll write it out as you read it." There's his hand going all over the script, busy. He doesn't know what he's readin', I could tell. I know why he's doing it. He just wants to see me busy.

So we finished the first long sheet. He wants to continue. I said, "No, I can only do one sheet at a time. I'll go over and type this up." So what I did, I would type a paragraph and wait five or ten minutes. I made sure I made all the mistakes I could. It's amazing, when you want to make mistakes, you really can't. So I just put Ko-rec-type paper over this yellow sheet. I fixed it up real pretty. I wouldn't stay on the margins. He told me himself I was no longer a clerk-typist.

I took him back this first sheet and, of course, I had left out a line or two. I told him it made me nervous to have this typed by a certain time, and I didn't have time to proofread it, "but I'm ready for you to read the other sheet to me." He started to proofread. I deliberately misspelled some words. Oh, I did it up beautifully. (Laughs.) He got the dictionary out and he looked up the words for me. I took it back and crossed out the words and squeezed the new ones in there. He started on the next sheet. I did the same thing all over again. There were four sheets. He proofread them all. Oh, he looked so serious! All this time he's spendin' just to keep me busy, see? Well, I didn't finish it by noon.

I'm just gonna see what he does if I don't finish it on time. Oh, it was imperative! I knew the world's not gonna change that quickly. It was nice outside. If it gets to be a problem, I'll go home. It's a beautiful day, the heck with it. So twelve-thirty comes and the work just looks awful. (Laughs.) I typed on all the lines, I continued it anywhere. One of the girls comes over, she says, "You're goin' off the line." I said, "Oh, be quiet. I know what I'm doin'. (Laughs.) Just go away." (Laughs.) I put the four sheets together. I never saw anything as horrible in my life.

I decided I'd write him a note. "Dear Mr. Roberts: You've been so much help. You proofread, you look up words for your secretary. It must be marvelous working for you. I hope this has met with your approval. Please call on me again." I never heard from him. (A long laugh.)

These other people, they work, work, work and nothing comes of it. They're the ones that catch hell. The ones that come in every day on time, do the job, and try to keep up with everybody else. A timekeeper, a skinny little black woman. She's fanatic about time. She would argue with you if you were late or something. She's been working for the government twenty-five years and she hadn't gotten a promotion, 'cause she's not a fighter.

She has never reported sick. Some days I won't come. If it's bad outside, heavy snow, a storm, I won't go. You go the next day. The work's gonna be there. She thinks my attitude is just terrible. She's always runnin', acts like she's scared of everybody. She was off *one* day. She had a dental appointment. Oh, did the boss raise hell! Oh, my goodness! He never argues with me.

The boss whose typing I messed up lost his secretary. She got promoted. They told this old timekeeper she's to be his secretary-assistant. Oh, she's in her glory. No more money or anything and she's doing two jobs all day long. She's rushin' and runnin' all the time, all day. She's a nervous wreck. And when she asked him to write her up for an award, he refused. That's *her* reward for being so faithful, obedient.

Oh, we love it when the bosses go to those long meetings, those important conferences. (Laughs.) We just leave in a group and go for a show. We don't care. When we get back, they roll their eyes. They know they better not say anything, 'cause they've done nothing when we've been gone anyhow. We do the work that we have to do. The old timekeeper, she sits and knits all that time, always busy.

I've been readin'. Everything I could on China, ever since he made that visit. Trying to see how people live and the ideas. It changed me a lot. I don't see any need for work you don't enjoy. I like the way the Indians lived. They moved from season to season. They didn't pay taxes. Everybody had enough. I don't think a few should control everything. I don't think it's right that women lay down and bear sons and then you have a few rich people that tell your sons they have to go and die for their country. They're not dying for their country. They're dying for the few to stay on top. I don't think that's necessary. I'm just tired of this type of thing. I just think we ought to be just human.

ORGANIZER

BILL TALCOTT

My work is trying to change this country. This is the job I've chosen. When people ask me, "Why are you doing this?" it's like asking what kind of sickness you got. I don't feel sick. I think this country is sick. The daily injustices just gnaw on me a little harder than they do on other people.

I try to bring people together who are being put down by the system, left out. You try to build an organization that will give them power to make the changes. Everybody's at the bottom of the barrel at this point. Ten years ago one could say the poor people suffered and the middle class got by. That's not true any more.

My father was a truckdriver with a sixth-grade education. My uncle was an Annapolis graduate. My father was inarticulate and worked all his life with his hands. My uncle worked all his life with his mouth and used his hands only to cut coupons. My father's problem was that he was powerless. My uncle's problem was that he was powerless, although he thought he was strong. Clipping coupons, he was always on the fringe of power, but never really had it. If he tried to take part in the management of the companies whose coupons he was clipping, he got clipped. Both these guys died very unhappy, dissatisfied with their lives.

Power has been captured by a few people. A very small top and a very big bottom. You don't see much in-between. Who do people on the bottom think are the powerful people? College professors and management types, the local managers of big corporations like General Motors. What kind of power do these guys really have? They have the kind of power Eichmann claimed for himself. They have the power to do bad and not question what they're told to do.

I am more bothered by the ghetto child who is bitten by rats than I am by a middle-class kid who can't find anything to do but put down women and take dope and play his life away. But each one is wasted.

I came into consciousness during the fifties, when Joe McCarthy was running around. Like many people my age—I'm now thirty-seven—I was aware something was terribly wrong. I floundered around for two years in college, was disappointed, and enlisted in the army. I was NCO for my company. During a discussion, I said if I was a black guy, I would refuse to serve. I ended up being sent to division headquarters and locked up in a room for two years, so I wouldn't be able to talk to anybody.

At San Francisco State, I got involved with the farm workers movement. I would give speeches on a box in front of the Commons. Then I'd go out and fight jocks behind the gym for an hour and a half. (Laughs.) In '64, I resigned as student body president and went to Mississippi to work for SNCC. I spent three years working in the black community in San Francisco.

At that point, I figured it was time for me to work with whites. My father was from South Carolina. We had a terrible time when I visited—violent arguments. But I was family. I learned from that experience you had to build a base with white people on the fringe of the South. Hopefully you'd build an alliance between blacks and whites . . .

I came to East Kentucky with OEO. I got canned in a year. Their idea was the same as Daley's. You use the OEO to build an organization to support the right candidates. I didn't see that as my work. My job was to build an organization of put-down people, who can *control* the candidates once they're elected.

I put together a fairly solid organization of Appalachian people in Pike County. It's a single industry area, coal. You either work for the coal company or you don't work. Sixty percent of its people live on incomes lower than the government's guidelines for rural areas.

I was brought in to teach other organizers how to do it. I spent my first three months at it. I decided these middle-class kids from Harvard and Columbia were too busy telling everybody else what they should be doing. The only thing to do was to organize the local people.

When I got fired, there were enough people to support me on one hundred dollars a month and room and board. They dug down in their pockets and they'd bring food and they'd take care of me like I was a cousin. They felt responsible for me, but they didn't see me as one of them. I'm not an Appalachian, I'm a San Franciscan. I'm not a coal miner, I'm an organizer. If they're gonna save themselves, they're gonna have to do it themselves. I have some skills that can help them. I did this work for three years.

The word organizer has been romanticized. You get the vision of a mystical being doing magical things. An organizer is a guy who brings in new members. I don't feel I've had a good day unless I've talked with at least one new person. We have a meeting, make space for new people to come in. The organizer sits next to the new guy, so everybody has to take the new guy as an equal. You do that a couple of times and the guy's got strength enough to become part of the group.

You must listen to them and tell them again and again they are important, that they have the stuff to do the job. They don't have to shuck themselves about not being good enough, not worthy. Most people were raised to think they are not worthy. School is a process of taking beautiful kids who are filled with life and beating them into happy slavery. That's as true of a twenty-five-thousand-dollar-a-year executive as it is for the poorest.

You don't find allies on the basis of the brotherhood of man. People are tied into their immediate problems. They have a difficult time worrying about other people's. Our society is so structured that everybody is supposed to be selfish as hell and screw the other guy. Christian brotherhood is enlightened self-interest. Most sins committed on poor people are by people who've come to help them.

I came as a stranger but I came with credentials. There are people who know and trust me, who say so to the others. So what I'm saying is verifiable. It's possible to win, to take an outfit like Bethlehem Steel and lick 'em. Most people in their guts don't really believe it. Gee, it's great when all of a sudden they realize it's possible. They become alive.

Nobody believed Pike County Citizens' Association could stop Bethlehem from strip mining. Ten miles away was a hillside being stripped. Ten miles away is like ten million light years away. What they wanted was a park, a place for their kids. Bethlehem said, "Go to hell. You're just a brunch of crummy Appalachians. We're not gonna give you a damn thing." If I could get that park for them, they would believe it's possible to do other things.

They really needed a victory. The had lost over and over again, day after day. So I got together twenty, thirty people I saw as leaders. I said, "Let's get that park." They said, "We can't." I said, "We can. If we let all the big wheels around the country know—the National Council of Churches and everybody start calling up, writing, and hounding Bethlehem, they'll have to give us the park." That's exactly what happened. Bethlehem thought, This is getting to be a pain in the ass. We'll give 'em the park and they'll shut up about strip mining. We haven't shut up on strip mining, but we got the park. Four thousand people from Pike County drove up and watched those bulldozers grading down that park. It was an incredible victory.

Twenty or thirty people realized we could win. Four thousand people understood there was a victory. They didn't know how it happened, but a few of 'em got curious. The twenty or thirty are now in their own communities trying to turn people on.

We're trying to link up people in other parts of the state—Lexington,

Louisville, Covington, Bowling Green—and their local issues and, hopefully, binding them together in some kind of larger thing.

When you start talking to middle-class people in Lexington, the words are different, but it's the same script. It's like talking to a poor person in Pike County or Mississippi. The schools are bad. Okay, they're bad for different reasons—but the schools are bad.

The middle class is fighting powerlessness too. Middle-class women, who are in the Lexington fight, are more alienated than lower-class women. The poor woman knows she's essential for the family. The middle-class woman thinks, If I die tomorrow, the old man can hire himself a maid to do everything I do. The white-collar guy is scared he may be replaced by the computer. The schoolteacher is asked not to teach but to baby-sit. God help you if you teach. The minister is trapped by the congregation that's out of touch with him. He spends his life violating the credo that led him into the ministry. The policeman has no relationship to the people he's supposed to protect. So he oppresses. The fireman who wants to fight fires ends up fighting a war.

People become afraid of each other. They're convinced there's not a damn thing they can do. I think we have it inside us to change things. We need the courage. It's a scary thing. Because we've been told from the time we were born that what we have inside us is bad and useless. What's true is what we have inside us is good and useful.

In Mississippi, our group got the first black guy elected in a hundred years. In San Francisco, our organization licked the development agency there. We tied up two hundred million dollars of its money for two years, until the bastards finally came to an agreement with the community people. The guy I started with was an alcoholic pimp in the black ghetto. He is now a Presbyterian minister and very highly respected.

I work all the way from two in the morning until two the next morning seven days a week. (Laughs.) I'm not a martyr. I'm one of the few people I know who was lucky in life to find out what he really wanted to do. I'm just havin' a ball, the time of my life. I feel sorry for all these people I run across all the time who aren't doing what they want to do. Their lives are hell. I think everybody ought to quit their job and do what they want to do. You've got one life. You've got, say, sixty-five years. How on earth can you blow forty-five years of that doing something you hate?

I have a wife and three children. I've managed to support them for six years doing this kind of work. We don't live fat. I have enough money to buy books and records. The kids have as good an education as anybody in

431

this country. Their range of friends runs from millionaires in San Francisco to black prostitutes in Lexington. They're comfortable with all these people. My kids know the name of the game: living your life up to the end.

All human recorded history is about five thousand years old. How many people in that time have made an overwhelming difference? Twenty? Thirty? Most of us spend our lives trying to achieve some things. But we're not going to make an overwhelming difference. We do the best we can. That's enough.

The problem with history is that it's written by college professors about great men. That's not what history is. History's a hell of a lot of little people getting together and deciding they want a better life for themselves and their kids.

I have a goal. I want to end my life in a home for the aged that's run by the state—organizing people to fight 'em because they're not running it right. (Laughs.)

THE SPORTING LIFE

EDDIE ARROYO, JOCKEY

There was an accident at the track today and I don't know really how the boy came out. At Hawthorne today. His horse fell and he just sailed. I don't know if he was conscious or not. The ambulance picked him up.

He is a jockey, unmistakably, and has been at it for about six years. He's had a good share of win, place, and show at race tracks out East, in the South, as well as in his home territory, Chicago. For "better than six months" of the year, he's a familiar man on a horse at Hawthorne, Arlington, and Sportsman's Park. "The first couple of years I rode, I didn't miss one day. I'd finish in Florida and took a plane and rode here the next day or whenever a track was open. I worked ninety-nine percent of the year."

He is twenty-eight. Though born in Puerto Rico, he's considered a Chicago home town boy, having attended high school and junior college here. "They said I was too small to be a baseball player, so why don't you try to be a jockey? I read how much jockeys made, so I figured I'll give it a try. Now that I've become a jockey, you're always worried about playin' ball and gettin' hurt. You have to be at such a peak that you're afraid to do anything else. So I quit anything else but riding.

"To the people it's a glamorous job, but to me it's the hardest work I ever held in my life. I was brought up tough and I was brought up lucky. Keeps me goin', I love it. I like the glamour, too. Everybody likes to read about themselves in the papers and likes to see your name on television and people recognize you down the street. They recognize me by my name, my face, my size. You stick out like a basketball player. I think we're all self-centered. Most of us have tailor-made clothes and you can see it—the way you carry yourself."

I been having a little problem of weight the last three weeks. I've been retaining the water, which I usually don't do. I'm not losing it by sweating. My usual weight's about 110, with saddle and all. Stripped naked, I'm about 106½. Right now I weigh 108. If I try to get to 106, I begin to feel the drain, the loss of energy. But you waste so much energy riding that I eat like a horse. Then I really have to watch it.

I've learned to reduce from other riders who've been doing it for twenty-some years. They could lose seven pounds in three hours, by sweating, by just being in the hot box. All the jockeys' rooms have 'em. Or you can take pills. It weakens extremely. It takes the salt out of your body and you're just not completely there.

Riding is very hazardous. We spend an average of two months out of work from injuries we sustain during the year. We suffer more death than probably any other sport. I was very late becoming a jockey, at twenty-two. They start at sixteen usually. At the age of sixteen, you haven't enough experience in life to really see danger. At twenty-two, you've been through harder times and you see if you make a wrong decision you might get yourself or somebody else hurt. When you're sixteen you don't really care.

I been lucky until last year, almost accident-free. My first accident last year came in February, when I broke the cartilage in my knee in a spill, warming up for a race. The horse did somethin' wrong and I fell off of him and he run over me—my knee—and tore the ligaments in my ankle, broke my finger, bruises all over. About three months later I fell again. I had a concussion, I had lacerations in the temple, six stitches, and I had a fracture in the vertebrae in my back. (Indicates a scar.) I just did this Saturday. A horse threw me out of the gate right here on my nose. I had all my teeth knocked out. (Laughs.)

His mother, who is serving coffee, hovers gently nearby. As she listens, her hand tentatively goes toward her cheek. The universal gesture. Toward the end of the evening she confides softly concerning her daily fears. She hopes he will soon do other things.

The most common accident is what we call clippin' of another horse's heels. Your horse trips with the other horse's heels, and he'll automatically go down. What helps us is the horse is moving at such a momentum, he falls so quick, that we just sail out into the air and don't land near the horse. We usually land about fifteen feet away. That's what really helps.

You put it off as casual. If I were to think how dangerous it is, I wouldn't dare step on a horse. There's just so many things that can happen. I'll come home with a bruise on my arm, I can't move it. I have no idea when it happened. It happened leaving the gate or during the race. I'll pull a muscle and not know how it happened. I'll feel the pain after the race. Your mind is one hundred percent on what you're doing. You feel no pain at that moment.

I'd say the casualty rate is three, four times higher than any other sport. Last year we had nine race track deaths, quite a few broken backs, quite a few paralyzed . . .

A real close friend of mine, he's paralyzed. Three days after I fell, he fell. Just a normal accident. We all expected him to get up and walk away. He's paralyzed from the waist down. It's been a year and some months. We had a benefit dinner for him. Gettin' money out of those people—track owners—is like tryin' to squeeze a lemon dry.

He gets compensation if he's a member of the Jockeys' Guild or the Jockeys' Association. Of the two thousand or more jockeys, about fifteen hundred belong to the guild. I'm the representative here in Chicago. The guild comes up with fifty dollars a week and the race track gives us fifty.

Only fifty bucks compensation! We don't have a pension plan. We're working on one, but the legislature stops us. They say we're self-employed. They put us in the same category as a doctor. There are old doctors, but there are no old jockeys.

Some tracks still object to the guild. A lotta time the tracks get so hazardous that we refuse to ride on 'em. They usually wait till two or three riders fall, then they determine the track's hazardous. Sometimes nothin' happens to riders, other times they break bones. The rains, the cold weather, sometimes it freezes and there are holes. It's plain to see it's just not fit for an animal or a human being to work on these conditions.

Bones break a little casual. You get used to it, a finger . . . What most breaks is your collarbone. I fractured it. I could name you rider after rider, that's the first thing that goes, the collarbone.

I prep horses for a race. Three days before, I'll go a half mile with the horse I'm gonna ride, or three-eighths of a mile. The owner wants me to get the feel of the horse. I do this day in and day out through the year. So I'm a good judge of pace. He knows I'm not gonna let a horse go three seconds too fast. He might loose all his energies out, and when the race comes up he's empty. I'll average two or three in the morning. Most of the time I'll just talk to the man and he'll tell me, "How did my horse run the other day?" or "I'm gonna ride you on this horse and he likes to run this way." I don't work for one man. I ride for anyone that wants me.

If I ride within the first four races, I have to be back at twelve-thirty. The first race is two-ten. They want you at least an hour and a half before. You have about a good thirty, forty-five minutes to get dressed, get your weight down, get prepared, read up on the charts of the horses that are gonna ride that day, plus your own. You look for speed.

You know their records, because more or less you rode against them before or rode them themselves. Does he like to go to the front? Does he like to come from behind? Does he like to stay in the middle? Does he like to go around? Does he like to go through? Then the trainer will tell you how he likes his horse rode. If he's a good trainer, he'll tell you the habits of the horse, even if they're bad habits. A bad habit are horses that lug in, that like to ride around instead of inside, that don't break too good. It makes it more dangerous—and a little more difficult to win races. There's more ways of getting beat.

You have only a minute and ten seconds sometimes to do everything you have to do. The average race is three-quarters of a mile, and they usually are a minute and ten or a minute, eleven. You make the wrong decision, that's the race. You really don't know where you're gonna lay or how the horse is gonna react from one race to the other. Your first thing is to get him out of the gate. You have to look for position. Where can I be? There's ten, twelve other horses that would like to have the same position. There's maybe six horses that want to go into the lead. The other six might come from behind. You can't be all in the same place at the same time. You have to wiggle your way around here and there.

You ride around, you find the race is half-over. If you're layin' near the leaders, you're gonna wait a little later to move. If you're way back there, you have to move a little earlier, because you have a lot of catching up to do. Here's what makes riders. You must realize there are other jockeys as capable as you are in the race. So you must use good judgment. You have to handicap which horses are gonna do what in front of you. Which ones are gonna keep runnin' and vacate that space that you can flow through. Or which are stoppin' and you have to avoid.

You must know the other jockeys, too. They all have habits. I know jockeys I can get through and jockeys that don't let you. I have a habit. I've been known as a front running rider, that I can save a horse better. I got a good judge of pace when I'm in front. But I feel I'd rather ride a horse from behind. A horse is competitive. It's his nature to beat other horses. That's all they've been taught all their lives. Usually at three years old they start going in pairs. When they start gettin' ready in the morning workouts, we're matchin' 'em up against each other. You can see the little babies, two years old, they are trying to beat each other, just their instinct. One tries to get in front of the other, just like a little bitty game. One will get so much in front and he'll wait. The other will get in front. And they'll go like that. They're conditioned to it.

Sure the animal makes a difference, but if you have two horses alike you have to beat the other rider. You have to wait for his mistakes or his habit. I've learned patience. I know other people's habits a lot better than mine. I'm sure they know mine a lot better than they know theirs.

If a jockey's in trouble and he hollers for help, that other rider has to do everything in his power to help—whether it's gonna cost him the race or not. One possibility: there's horses all around him, he's in the middle, he can't control his horse. So he's gonna run into another horse, he's gonna clip the other horse's heels. If he does this, he's gonna fall and the people behind him are gonna fall over him. That's what happened today.

You see him or he hollers "I can't hold my horse!" You just move out, let him out, so he can take his horse wide. Most jockeys'll do this even if it'll cost 'em the race. Not all. Some that are just interested in winning . . . They're frowned on. They have very little friends among other riders. You don't give them the benefit of the doubt. I know a lot of riders that had me in trouble and I've asked for help, and I felt they coulda done a lot more than they did. No conscience. At the same time, they been in trouble and I did everything possible to help. I had to stop ridin' a horse to protect another rider. What's worse is seein' another rider make a mistake and you have to protect him. You *have* to do it.

People of the racing world are a close fraternity. "We work together, we travel together. The whole shebang moves over from one state to another. We automatically seek each other out. We're good friends."

The wages consist of ten percent of the horse's purse. If it's $4,500, you get about $450. About ten percent of the win. The smallest purse here is $2,500, so you win $250. You get a straight wage for place or show. For second place, it would be fifty or fifty-five. Third money is forty, forty-five. For the out money, fourth or under, it's thirty, thirty-five dollars.

We have agents. My agent works only for me. I pay him twenty-five percent of my gross earnings. It's quite a bit, but he's worth it. An agent is very important in a jockey's success. He gets your mounts. He has the right to commit you to ride a horse and you have to abide by it. He tries to get you on the best horse he can. He has to be a good handicapper. He has to be a good talker. And he has to be trustworthy, that the owners can trust him. There's an awful lot of information related from the trainer to the agent to the jockey, which you wouldn't want someone else to find out. Some agents are ex-jockeys, but not too many. They're connected with racing, father to son and so on. Racing has a habit of keeping their own.

You go to the barn and start as a hot walker. He's the one that walks the horse a half-hour, after he's been on the track for his training, while he drinks the water. About every five minutes, you gotta do about two or three swallows. Then you keep with him until he's completely cooled down, until he's not sweating any more. You do this every day. You might walk six, seven horses, which starts building your legs up. We all started this way. There's no short cuts.

From walkin', I became a groom—one that takes care of horses. That's a step up. He usually takes care of three or four horses all day. He cleans them, he massages their legs, takes care of the stalls.

I went from groom to exercise boy, another step higher. Now you're riding a horse. You first start walking, getting used to the reins, getting used to the little bitty saddle. You might walk for a week around shed row. They usually pick an old horse, that's well-mannered. From then, you graduate to goin' on the track.

The first day you go to the track, it's really hilarious. Because there's somethin' about a galloping horse there's no way to prepare for it. No matter how much exercise you do, you're not fit. I went clear around this mile and an eighth track. When I got up to the back side where they pulled me up, my legs were numb. I couldn't feel any more. I jumped off the horse, there was nothin' there to hold me up. I went down right to the ground. I sat there a half-hour, right where I landed. They made a lot of fun out of it. It happens to everybody.

Some days I'll ride seven, eight. Some days two or three. You feel it at the end of the day. Sometimes I come home, I just collapse. I could sleep right through the next day. You're lucky when you have horses that want to run. Other times you have to do all the work. It's easier to have a free-running horse. You don't have to do very much but kinda guide him along and help him when the time comes. But if you get a horse that doesn't want to run, you're pretty tired after three-quarters of a mile.

To be a jockey you must love the horse. There's a lot of times when I lose my patience with him. There's just certain horses that annoy you. There's no two alike. They have personalities just like you and I do.

Distant-U, the filly, she's beautiful. She's a little lady. She looks like a lady, petite. Except she's a little mean, unpredictable. I've gotten to like her and I know how she likes to be rode. I don't know if she knows me, but I know her, exactly what she likes me to do. The horse can tell it right away. When I sit there with confidence she'll be a perfect lady. If you don't have confidence, the horse takes advantage of it.

Willie Shoemaker's the greatest. He has the old style of the long hold. He has a gift with his hands to translate messages to the horse. He has the gift of feeling a horse's mouth. But it's a different style from ninety percent of us. We've gone to the trend of the South American riders. They ride a horse's shoulder instead of a horse's back. They look a hundred percent better. Most riders have now changed over, mixed the two together.

Latin American riders are dominating the sport. They're hustlers and they've had it tougher than American riders. They come from very, very poor people. They have a goal they want to reach, bein' the tops. The American rider, he's satisfied makin' a livin', makin' a name for himself. He's reached a plateau and he's stayed there. While the other fella is just pluggin' away . . .

There's some prejudice from riders, but most jockeys become very good friends after they get to know each other. But most is from the officials. I couldn't believe it. The stewards are prejudiced against Spanish riders. I have not felt it because I was brought up here. Home town boy makes good. But the Spanish ones . . . two riders commit the same infraction, one's penalized, the other isn't. One's Spanish, the other isn't. Once in a while, okay, but it's repeated again and again. It has a prejudice.

Sometimes I feel people don't treat you as they should. Other times they treat you a little too well. They get a little pesty. Lotta times you want to be by yourself. They don't realize I spent fifteen minutes combin' my hair and they come along and the first thing they do is muss it up. They'll put their arm around you and buy you a drink, and you can't drink. You have to ride the next day. You turn the drinks down and right away, they'll say, "This kid is too good for me." If I was gonna accept every drink that was offered to me, I'd be as big as a balloon.

I have a lot of friends who are horse players, but I've never been approached by undesirables, gangsters. I've been approached by other riders. I'd say racing has changed a little bit from the days when they were notorious. Riders now make enough money where they don't have to cheat. Any race I win, I'm gonna make two, three hundred dollars. For me to take a chance of losing my license, it don't make sense. A rider is more apt to take it when the money isn't there.

It's incredible to see jockeys as honest as they are, for the conditions they come from. If you could see conditions on the back side, the way people have to live. The barn area, it's bad now like it was twenty years ago. The filth I had to live in, the wages I had to work for, the environment I was with, with alcoholics and whatnots. To come out of there . . . I was twenty-two, I was set in my ways. But friends of mine, when they were thirteen, fourteen years old, lived through this and made good citizens of themselves. It's *incredible* to believe that people could come out of there and become great athletes and great individuals. You figure, they'd be no good.

The guild is workin' for better track conditions, better rooms for where we ride at. I think only four or five tracks have jockey quarters that are clean and livable. Here's an organization, they're bettin' a million dollars a day and you get a newspaperman come in and interview you. You're embarrassed to have him walk in there. It's filthy. We drag all that mud in from the track. You figure they would have someone to keep it clean. They don't. The same furniture . . . there hasn't been much change.

In the barn, we have the tack rooms, where the grooms and the hot walkers live. A hot walker earns sixty dollars a week. He can't afford an apartment, he lives in the tack room. They have two cots. It's almost like a stall. You can put a horse in there if you wanted. A groom makes about $100. The exercise boys earn a little more, about $150. So they usually get apartments. I really don't know what the average jockey gets. I average around sixty thousand a year. I don't know if we average more than three or four years. I have no idea how long I'll continue. I wish I could ride another ten years, but . . . My ambition is to win the Kentucky Derby. It's still the most honored stake of all. I've come awful close two or three times to riding in it. I'm riding for Mr. Scott now. Say he comes up with a colt that's a two-year-old that I ride and I'll ride him next year and this horse works his way to the Derby. I have worked my way up there with him. Mm-hmm, could happen.

Through experience you know what to do. Whether the stick will make him run, whether hand riding, whether hittin' him on the shoulders, hittin' 'em on the rear, whistling or talkin' to 'em. You try everything. If one doesn't work, you try the other.

I'm pretty relaxed now, but when I first started riding—the night before a big stake, I'd get very little sleep. You lost two, three pounds from just nervousness, just by going to the washroom and thinking about it. Especially when you run one of the favorites. You have to fight this. I have to really get rid of the butterflies or I'm really gonna make a big mistake. Actually just mind over matter. Concentration.

What I've learned as a jockey sometimes drive me crazy. I've gotten where I could look at animals and see personalities in them. Most of what I've learned is patience. It comes with love of the horses. A lot of times a horse will do something that could even get me hurt. At first you want to hit him, correct him. But then you realize he's just an animal. He's smart but not smart enough to know that he's hurting himself and is gonna hurt you. He's only doin' it because it's the only thing he knows how to do.

Let me tell you somethin'. Animals got traits from humans. You put a nervous person around a nervous horse and he becomes a nervous horse. It's helped me to understand humans, too. By understanding the horse, the animal himself, his moods, his personality, his way of life, his likes, his dislikes—humans work the same way—you have to accept them for what they are. People do things because it's the only way they know. You try to change them to your way of thinking, but you have to accept people the way they are.

POSTSCRIPT: *"I would like to see the sport treated differently. I would like to see the politicians out of it. I would like to see the states own all the tracks. People that own the tracks now are draining them . . ."*

JEANNE DOUGLAS, TENNIS PLAYER

She is a professional tennis player. She is twenty-two. She travels nine months of the year as a member of the Virginia Slims Professional Women's Circuit. "It's Women's Lib, you've come a long way baby. Yeah. There's been quite a discussion about a cigarette company sponsoring a sporting event. What can you say? Some of the girls smoke, some don't. It's just a way of promoting tennis. We're not promoting smoking."

When the women organized their own circuit, they were blacklisted by the United States Lawn Tennis Association. "The officials of USLTA are very well-to-do businessmen, who've never paid their way to Wimbledon. I always paid my way. It's like the tournament is run for them, not the players." The schism occurred because "women's prize money was less than half of the men's. For Forest Hills men were getting six thousand dollars and the women would get sixteen hundred. Billie Jean is Women's Lib. She hit the roof." It was touch and go until Philip Morris came along. "They own Virginia Slims. They couldn't advertise on TV any more, so they put money into Virginia Slims tennis circuit."

The circuit: Long Beach to Washington, D.C., to Miami to Richmond. "People in town come out. Married couples. The blue collar will come maybe once a week. The upper class comes every night. Tennis is spreading. But I'm getting tired of living out of a suitcase and having my clothes wrinkled. That I hate. I love playing tennis.

"I started playing when I was eleven years old. My whole family plays. We're a huge tennis family. My uncle was like ten in the United States. My mom took it up after she was married. She got ranked twenty-fifth in southern California, which is one of the best places to play tennis. She works in a pro shop at our tennis club. She pushed me and I really resented it at first. But she made me play to the point where I was good enough to like it."

It's pure luck that I was born when I was born. Now there's professional tennis. There wasn't before. It's a business now. Just like a dentist. You go at it training-wise, exercises, running. Match-wise, girls are now cheating. (Laughs.)

It's not maybe really cheating. We have umpires and linesmen. The other day an umpire made a call against my opponent. It was very close. He called it "out." I'm not gonna go against the umpire. Maybe in amateur days I would say, "Hold it. I thought that was good." I may have said, "Play two, take it over." I'm not gonna do that now and nobody's gonna do it. When you were amateur, you were more open. Winning now is everything.

The first time I encountered it, I was just out of the juniors. It was doubles. There was no way we were gonna beat the others, they're world class players. Okay, I hit the ball down the center. On a clay court it kicks the back line. It's taped. You can see it shoot off. It's the first game of the whole match and they spend five minutes looking at the mark. "It's out! It's out!" My partner says, "If it's that close, let's play two." No. This was typical of the whole match. They were top players. It wasn't even gonna be close. But nobody's giving away one little inch.

Players tend to be more superficial now. Before you were more friendly. You'd write back and forth and have a good time. Now you don't have good friends. You're on the court and the people are just having fits, losing tempers. People are now so competitive for money you just don't want to get involved personally. You get on the court and how can you beat your best friend type of thing. Kind of a lonely life.

I want to be good, and this is the only way. But when there is money, the competition is so tough. There are like sixty-five women in the world, beating their heads against the wall every week, just playing against each other just week after week. It's really a hard life and getting a little shaky. Quite a few girls have gone home. The tops are getting the glamour—Billie Jean says, "We're the ones who bring the crowds."

That's why I've got to keep improving. I'll never be a tennis bum. We have them among the girl players, too. Someone who's not making it and just won't let go. They go to tournaments . . . They're kinda down on themselves. It's a sad life to be not advancing. When I stop improving I'll go into something else. Something better—like about six-foot-three. (Laughs.)

I grew up fast, I was very awkward. I really didn't like the game. My mom paid me twenty-five cents an hour to play. There's five children in my family. We all play tennis. My oldest brother's been number one for UCLA two years in a row. He's twenty-third in the United States.

We subscribe to *World Tennis* magazine. You see pictures of people in Wimbledon. I said, "I'd never see those people in my life." I got pretty good and I started to travel. I was on the Junior Wightman Cup Team for three years. I quit school—I was gonna major in design at UCLA—and went to Australia, South Africa, France, Italy, and I played in Wimbledon. Financially it was tough. You pay your own way. You get token prize money. Then Virginia Slims came up. It's just lucky timing.

My mom wanted it for me because she never could play tennis. She's been to all the teas and just felt she accomplished nothing with her life. I go to these houses and stay with these housewives and it blows my mind that all they do is plan dinner and take care of the kid. They don't do anything, these ladies. I do want to get married and have a family, but I do want to *do* something.

There's zero social life. I get romantically involved about twice a year and wreck my tennis to death. There's this French girl who was like number three in the world a couple of years ago. When she's having a great love life she's just playing fantastically.

My brother goes on the circuit too. We compare notes all the time. It's different for men. The townies come out. It never ceases to amaze me how they can sit and watch a tennis match in ninety degrees heat with false eyelashes on, make-up, hair spray, and not one drop of sweat. The guys pick 'em up. It's harder for girls to go out on a one-night. It's gotten to a point where I only go out with guys that I've met before. You can be friendly and have a good time, but you hate to be put-upon. I'm just not that kind of girl. I'm not a prude, but I'm not going to go to bed with some guy just while I'm in town.

Male athletes are just big studs. The girl tennis players used to laugh. A couple of Australians got this little game they play. They'd pick up girls and they'd rig it up so one guy would watch from the next room—and give points. They kept track. They made it a contest. These townies had no idea what these guys were pulling off. They would just pick up one girl after another after another. It was a mechanical-type thing.

Through tennis I've met fantastic people. When I'm home I teach fantastically wealthy people in Rolling Hills. They live behind gates, they have guards, they have private courts. I'm teaching a man who owns his own jet, and he's giving me a ride home from New York so I don't have to pay the airfare type of thing.

I have a sponsor, he's paying my way. Last year I barely made it. My mom has paid for all of my tennis. A lot of parents support the girls, work. It's much better with a sponsor. Last year, before each tournament, I calculated how far I had to get and my next plane ticket and everything. I was so uptight. We have to pay our own airfare.

Why can't Virginia Slims pay your fare?

They can't afford it at this time. The only thing we're guaranteed is to be able to play in the tournament. And maybe win prize money.

Suppose you don't win?

You just lose. You don't get anything. You get hospitality. My sponsor gets paid back everything he spent. After he's gotten paid back, we split fifty-fifty. This year I made my five hundred dollars' profit so far, so I'm way ahead of the game. One girl has a sponsor who gets ninety percent of every prize money check she gets until he's paid back. At the time I was so excited. But now it's coming out where it's not such a good deal.

My sponsor's a race track driver. I'm so impressed with him. He's been written up in *Time* magazine. He's such an unbelievable man, and he's so impressed with me.

If I go out with guys that aren't sports-minded, I feel like a jock. The whole conversation, there's nothing to go on. You go out with a baseball player or something, you carry on a normal conversation. But this one guy can't get it out of his mind. A female athlete is just so new. It's just like a kid growing up to be an astronaut. This was never before. It's amazing how little girls come up and ask for your autograph. They say, "Oh, I want to grow up and be a Virginia Slims tennis player, just like you." That just blows my mind. One of the greatest things happened to me. I was at a basketball game and someone asked me for an autograph. I mean, I'm not a Billie Jean King.

I meet these fantastically wealthy people I would never have a chance to meet before. A dentist, he goes to a cocktail party, who's gonna talk about your teeth? If you're a tennis pro, everybody can talk. There's a common bond. It's kind of neat to be able to talk to someone instead of having a feeling like a housewife: How do I ever talk to Billie Jean?

In a way it's an ugly wealth, too. Gaudy diamond rings, impressing each other. At Miami Beach I stayed at the Jockey Club. I lucked out, and three of us got to stay like on an eighty-five-foot yacht. They all had such disrespect for each other, but they had respect for us. It's something money couldn't buy.

Before Virginia Slims I was interested in a lot more things. I wanted to travel and learn languages. I can speak Spanish and a little French. Every country I've been in, I stayed in people's homes. You talk to them and find out much more about a country. Now it's making money.

I'm really trying to zero in and make a business out of it, 'cause all of a sudden it's big business. It never occurred to me before. So I'm trying to change my ways. I'd like to be able to endorse some rackets or shoes, do commercials, make a lot of money. I'm not a materialist like my father. He hasn't been in favor of tennis. He'd always say, "Okay, when are you going to be a secretary and make some money?" He's like a sunny day friend. When I'm winning—great! He loves publicity. I'm his daughter. But if I'm losing, "Be a secretary, get the money." He can't even see the way he changes. I couldn't care less about him. I want to be independent. Money means freedom.

If I get married and have a daughter, I would push her into something, like my mom did me. I think kids should be pushed. Okay, pushed is a crummy word. Kids should be guided. I stayed at a house a couple of weeks, the kids were fat. They didn't do anything after school, just watch TV. It's like they were dying. I would prefer athletics. I would push her to the point where she's good. If she still didn't like it, I wouldn't push her.

Junior tennis is like a world of its own. The parents usually take the kids, because they can't drive. This is like stage mothers. There's like tennis mothers. There's quite a few fathers that are obnoxious, too. These people sit on the sidelines and coach from behind the baseline. My mom's never come out to see me, though she's watching my little sister . . .

My second brother, who had a scholarship to Long Beach State, does not enjoy competition. He plays an hour a day just to make my mom happy. If he was serious, he'd be really good. He goes out and enjoys playing, and he won't get upset. He'll come home and my mom will say, "How'd you do?" He'll say, "I lost four and four. I should have won." She'll say, "Why didn't you win? Why didn't you start coming to the net?" And he'll just laugh and say, "I didn't think of it." It upsets my mom. He isn't that keen to win. He just enjoys playing. This I don't understand, because I've very competitive.

My little sister, who's ten years old, she was on the cover of *Tennis World* when she was four. She's great. She's been playing since she was two. She's done clinics all over California, with my coach. Usually you begin about five or six. So I started kind of late. I'm thirteen years older than she is, but she has more incentive. She knows exactly where she can go. She's number one in the Ten and Under.

She has not lost a match in her eight years—ever. She started playing tournaments when she was seven years old. It's going to be interesting to see how my little sister takes defeat . . .

IN CHARGE

DAVE BENDER, FACTORY OWNER

It is a newly built, quite modern factory on the outskirts of a large industrial city. Scores of people are at work in the offices. Sounds of typewriters and adding machines; yet an air of informality pervades. He has come into his private office, tie askew; he's in need of a shave. We have a couple of shots of whisky.

"I manufacture coin machine and vending machine parts—components. We also make units for amusement devices. We don't know what they're gonna do with it. We have ideas what they might. I have about two hundred employees. I never counted. They're people. We have tool and die makers, mold makers, sheet metal, screw machine, woodwork, painting, coil winding. You name it, we got it."

I just stay in the background. Myself, I like making things. I make the machinery here. I'm not an engineer, but I have an idea and I kind of develop things and—(with an air of wonder)—they *work*. All night long I think about this place. I love my work. It isn't the money. It's just a way of expressing my feeling.

When we started here we were strictly in the pinball game part business. I kept adding and adding and adding and never stopped. Finally I got into the jukebox end of it. Of course, slot machines came in and then slot machines went out. Never fool with Uncle Sam. When they said no slot machine parts, they meant it and I meant it too. I don't want them checking up on us. You can live without it. We make so many different things. A little of this, a little of that. Not a lot of any one thing.

I made a machine that makes plastic tubes. It becomes like a parasite. It runs through 250 feet a minute, five tubes at a time. I made it with a bunch of crazy ideas and junk I found around the place. I can sell that machine for twenty thousand dollars. If I dress it up and put flowers on it, you can sell it for much, much more.

I was a no-good bum, kicked out of high school. I went up to a teacher and I said, "If you don't pass me, I'll blow your brains out." I stole a gun. (Laughs.) I was kicked out. It was my second year. I did some dirty things I can't talk about. (Laughs.) When I was thirteen years old I took a Model T Ford apart and put it together in the basement. I did some crazy things.

When I talk to people about plastic I take the position *I'm* the plastic and how would I travel through the machine and what would I see. Maybe I'm goofy. In business I take the position: where would I be if I were the customer? What do I expect of you? Some people are natural born stinkers. I try to find a way to get to them. You can break down anybody with the right method.

I sell all I make. I don't know what to do with 'em. (Laughs.) They use 'em for packaging. I work with wood, plastic, metal, anything. I work with paper. Even at home. Sunday I was taking paper and pasting it together and finding a method of how to drop spoons, a fork, a napkin, and a straw into one package. The napkin feeder I got. The straw feeder we made already. That leaves us the spoon and the fork. How do we get it? Do we blow the bag open? Do we push it open? Do we squeeze it down? So I'm shoving things in and pushing with my wife's hair clips and bobby pins and everything I can get my hands on. I even took the cat's litter, the stuff you pick up the crap with (laughs), even that to shove with the bag, to pull it open. This is for schools, inexpensive packaging. It sells for about a penny a package. Plastic. In a bag, the whole darn thing. So what can I tell you?

Everybody is packaging the stuff. Their method is antique. My method is totally automatic. I know what my competitors are doing. I never underestimate 'em, but I'm ten steps ahead of 'em. I can meet them any way they want. But not to cut their heart out. We all have to make a living.

I started this whole damn thing with forty dollars. In 1940. I borrowed it. In 1938 I was a big dealer. I was the greatest crap shooter in the world. (Laughs.) I was makin' rubber parts and plunger rods for the pin games. Then the war broke out in '41. Where do you get the rods? I took a hacksaw and went to the junkyards. Remember the old rails that went up and down on the beds? I cut that out and made plunger rods. I did some crazy things.

I started with a couple of people. I made fifteen dollars a week for myself and I didn't even have that. Oh boy, oh boy, I tried everything. Making work gloves. I was eighteen, I went into the coal business. I borrowed two hundred dollars from my brother. Suddenly I had four trucks. I got sick and tired of coal and gave my father the keys for the four trucks and I said, "Pa, it's your business. You owe me zero." What else did I do? Oh God, making things. Making a factory. I love making.

Business to me is a method of engineering. Even in advertising. I've always wondered why they don't get people for what they really are. Like this Alka-Seltzer commercial. I operate business the same way—in getting to the people. What are we other than people?

Even during the war, I never took advantage of a price. I used to sell something for thirty-five cents. During the war I still sold it for thirty-five cents. A customer said, "Dave, I'll never forget you." They're liars. They did forget soon afterward. I never took anybody. I built my business on that. My competitors came and they went and I'm still at it. I'm bigger now than ever.

I hope to be going public. So I have to show an increase. That's the name of the game. I have workers been here twenty-seven, twenty-eight years. I feel I owe them something. I don't know how to compensate them. At least if I go public, I can offer them stock. I'd like to repay people. This is a way of saying thank you.

I was offered all kinds of deals which I turned down—by big vending companies. It would be beautiful for me. I walk away with a million many times over. So what? What about these poor devils? I'll fire 'em all? Huh?

To them, I'm Dave. I know the family. I know their troubles. "Dave, can you give me a dollar?" "Dave, how about some coffee?" I'll go to the model maker and talk about our problem and we'll have a shot of whisky. Ask him how his wife's feeling. "Fine." He wants to put something for his home, can I make it? "Sure." They all call me Dave. When they call me Mr. Bender I don't know who they're talking to. (Laughs.)

I love mechanics. All my fingernails are chopped off. I washed my hands before you came in. Grease. Absolutely. I get into things. You stick a ruler here or a measure here. I want this, I want that.

I'm here at six in the morning. Five thirty I'll leave. Sometimes I'll come here on Sunday when everybody's gone and I'll putter around with the equipment. There isn't a machine in this place I can't run. There isn't a thing I can't do.

They tell me it don't look nice for the workers for me to work on the machine. I couldn't care less if I swept the floors, which I do. Yesterday some napkins fell on the floor from the napkin feeding machine. I said to the welder, "Pick up the napkins." He says, "No, you pick it up." I said, "If you're tired, I'll pick it up." So I'm pickin' 'em up.

The workers say: "You're the boss, you shouldn't do this. It's not nice. You're supposed to tell us what to do, but not to do it yourself." I tell 'em I love it. They want me more or less in the office. I don't even come in here. If I do it's just to get my shot of booze with my worker and we break bread, that's all. When they call me Mr. Bender, I think they're being sarcastic. I don't feel like a boss to 'em. I feel like a chum-buddy.

I know a lot of people with money and I have very little to do with them. They're a little bit too high falutin' for me. I think they're snobs. They're spoiled rotten, their wealth. I won't mention names. I was born and raised poor. I had zero. I'm a fortunate guy. Whatever I got I'm thankful for. That's my life. I just like plain, ordinary people. I have a doctor friend, but outside of being a doctor, he's my swear-buddy. We swear at each other. A guy who works in the liquor store is my friend. Some of the workers here are my friends.

You're the boss of these people . . .

(Hurt) No, I just work here. They say, "Dave you should give us orders.

You shouldn't be pickin' up napkins." Oh, don't misunderstand me. I'm not the easiest guy in the world. I swear at 'em. I'm a stubborn son of a gun. When I finally get my idea straight, I'm rough. I know what I want, give me what I want. But I do have enough sense to know when to leave 'em alone.

Don't you feel you have status in being a boss?

Ooohhh, I hate that word! I tell people I don't want to hear another word about who I am or what I am. I enjoy myself eleven hours a day. When I get home I take my shoes off, get comfortable, pinch my wife's rear end, kiss her, of course, and ask her what she did today. I try not to take my problems home. I have problems, plenty, but I try to avoid it.

Saturdays and Sundays are the worst days of the week. It's a long weekend because I'm not here. I bum around, see movies, go to somebody's house, but I'm always waiting for Monday. I go away on a vacation, it's the worst thing in the world. (Laughs.) My wife got a heart attack in Majorca, Spain. She was in the hospital. I was there six weeks. It was the first real vacation I ever had. I finally went fishing. Here I am drinking wine, eating oranges and cheese, tearing the bread on the boat, had the time of my life. I told my wife it took her heart attack to get me to enjoy a vacation. (Laughs.)

Retire? Hell no. I'd open up another shop and start all over again. What am I gonna do? Go crazy? I told you I love my work. I think it's some form of being insecure. I've always worried about tomorrow. I worried and I fought for tomorrow. I don't have to worry about tomorrow. But I still want to work. I *need* to.

Today I worked all day in the shop with the model maker, two tool makers, and a welder. I don't have neat blueprints. I don't have a damn thing. All I have is this. (Taps at his temple.) I'll take a piece of paper. I can't even make drawings. I'm measuring, taking off three-eighths of an inch or put on two inches here. It's the craziest piece of iron you ever saw. I never saw anything like this in my life. But I saw it working the other day.

When I get it fabricated it'll be a packaging machine. You'll see arms going up and down, gears working, things going, reelers and winders, automatic everything. I know it could be patented. There's nothing like it. It's unique. This is all in my mind, yes sir. And I can't tell you my telephone number. (Laughs.)

I never tell people I'm the boss. I get red and flustered. I'm ashamed of it. When they find out—frankly speaking, people are parasites. They treat you like a dirty dog one way, and as soon as they find out who you are it's a different person. (Laughs.) When they come through the front door—"I want you to meet our president, Mr. Bender"—they're really like peacocks. I'd rather receive a man from the back door as a man. From the front door, he's got all the table manners. Oh, all that phony air. He's never down to earth. That's why I don't like to say who I am.

My wife's got a friend and her husband's got a job. If only they stopped climbing down my back. I do so many wrong things. Why don't you tell me to go to hell for the things I do? I deliberately see how far I can push them. And they won't tell me to go to hell, because I'm Dave Bender, the president. They look up to me as a man of distinction, a guy with brains. Actually I'm a stupid ass, as stupid as anybody that walks the street.

I'm making a machine now. I do hope to have it ready in the next couple months. The machine has nothing to do with helping humanity in any size, shape, or form. It's a personal satisfaction for me to see this piece of iron doing some work. It's like a robot working. This is the reward itself for me, nothing else. My ego, that's it.

Something last night was buggin' me. I took a sleeping pill to get it out of my mind. I was up half the night just bugging and bugging and bugging. I was down here about six o'clock this morning. I said, "Stop everything. We're making a mistake." I pointed out where the mistake was and they said, "Holy hell, we never thought of that." Today we're rebuilding the whole thing. This kind of stuff gets me. Not only what was wrong, but how the devil do you fix it? I felt better. This problem, that's over with. There's no problem that can't be solved if you use logic and reason the thing out. I don't care what it is. Good horse sense is what it's known as. With that you can do anything you want—determination, you can conquer the world.

MA AND PA COURAGE

GEORGE AND IRENE BREWER, NEIGHBORHOOD MERCHANTS

It is a grocery and gift store. "We got a sign out front: 10,000 items. We got all your cigarettes, ice creams, novelties. All your paints, crayons, school supplies. Drugs—not prescription, just your headache—remedies, alcohols, peroxide, and your bandages. Then we go into jewelry, which is now just costume. Before, we used to have diamonds. But the clientele didn't care for 'em. We have sundry, your hair goods, your sewing things, needles, threads, and buttons. Greeting cards . . . Ma, pa stores are foldin' fast because they don't have enough variety. Like chain stores, where they can get everything and anything they want.

"We started out toys and hobbies. Then I put milk in. I said, 'Honey, that's gonna be the ruin of us. We're gonna become a slave to it.' Then they started hollerin' for bread. Then they wanted lunch meat. Then they wanted canned goods. So it became the old country general store."

They have owned the business for fourteen years. "Before that," says George, "my folks had it since 1943." He has since expanded it. We're in the living quarters behind the store: five rooms, including one for "meditation." There are all manner of appliances and artifacts including a player piano. To the rear is a two-car garage.

Their fourteen-year-old daughter is minding the store. Their eldest daughter, twenty-one, lives elsewhere. Their son, nineteen, has been in the army three years. A dog, "mixed terrier," wanders in and out.

It is one of the oldest blue-collar communities in Chicago: Back Of The Yards. Though the stockyards have gone—to such unlikely places as Greeley, Colorado, and Clovis, New Mexico—the people who live here are still working-class. But there have been changes. "This used to be an oldtime Polish, Lithuanian neighborhood. Now it's more young, mixed, Puerto Ricans, hillbillies. Blacks are movin' closer, nothing here yet, but closer. It's not as clannish as it used to be. In the old days if you offended one, you'd have the whole block mad at you. Now it don't matter. The next will come in and take the place of him."

IRENE: We used to know ninety-five percent of our customers by name. Now it's hardly anyone we know by name any more. You could walk down the street at six in the morning and you'd see these Polish women out with their brooms and they'd be washin' the concrete down, fixin' the alleys. You don't see too much of this any more.

GEORGE: The personal touch. "How's the kids?" "How's this one?" "How's that one?" "Work goin' okay?" "Sorry to hear you lost your job." All this sort of thing—gone.

It's more of a transient deal, even though they live in the neighborhood. They're so flighty you don't know who's livin' where. You can't even trust somebody who's come in for six months, because they just up and turn that fast. We would cash checks and give 'em credit and carry 'em along. As the area changed, you'd get stuck with bad debts. So

451

we've eliminated cashin' checks due to the fact that we have thirteen hundred dollars worth of bad checks. We allow a little bit of credit to old stand-bys for about a week.

IRENE: If we take a chance and cash a check that does bounce, we find 'em walkin' on the other side of the street. They don't want to acknowledge they're in the neighborhood—for a measly five dollars. The people, they've changed in such a way it's unbelievable. We had magazines and books, but we took 'em out two years ago because the theft was so bad.

GEORGE: We had thirteen hundred dollars of books stolen in the last three months of the last year we handled books. A lot of cases with food. Women would open their purse and drop lunch meat in it. I caught a guy one evening puttin' two dozen eggs in his Eisenhower jacket.

IRENE: I was standin' at the bread rack there. I see this guy tryin' to stuff the *second* dozen eggs down his jacket, with a zipper and to the waistline. (Laughs.) He was havin' a tough time gettin' that second dozen in. I said, "Hey, hon, some guy's stealin' two dozen eggs back here." George's runnin' around and all the other customers are lookin' at one another. No one knows who's got the eggs.

GEORGE: I'm runnin' around one way and he's comin' around the other. I said, "Where is he?" He said, "Here I am." (Laughs.) He gave 'em back. The customers would come in and tease and say to Irene, "Hey, you want to search? I got eggs." (Laughs.)

IRENE: Nylons were stolen. Now we'll lock the door after eleven and only let the ones we know in. Forget it, there isn't many that you know any more. We were always open to midnight, all through the years. We used to work in the store to two, three in the morning and leave the door open. Now we can't wait to bolt the door at night, it's so bad. I take a chance when I open it. It's hard to tell any more by looks who's all right and who isn't. Some of 'em are the worst lookin' people but they're really all right when you get talkin' to 'em.

GEORGE: The worst lookin' hippie things that come in the door are so polite and some of 'em, the ones that are very well dressed, are so ignorant. When the folks had this store, it was all family. This is not too much a ma and pa area any more. The ones that are left close at six. They're scared to death.

IRENE: We've had several holdups. It was around eleven-fifteen at night, three young people came with ski masks over their face. Two guys and a girl.

GEORGE: I'm checkin' out and they put the gun to the side of my head.

I said, "Aw, go to hell." I thought it was the kids in the neighborhood horsin' around. I look up—they backed us around the jewelry counter. The front part was more expensive stuff, high-class, diamonds, gold rings. They scooped off the cheap costume jewelry off the back shelf. I said, "Damn it, leave me somethin' for the next time you come in." They said, "Okay, okay," and they backed off. (Laughs.) We've had several holdups since then. I don't worry too much about it.

IRENE: When Martin Luther King was killed, you can imagine the tension. I was alone here. People were panicky. They were announcing on the radio and television that people should be off the street at eight o'clock at night. The stores were forced to close. Our youngest was nine and was instigator of our selling a lot of food that night. She would say, "We may not be here tomorrow because there'll be a riot tonight and they might come in the neighborhood. You better get all you can get. Stock up now." She was half-hysterical and she put the fear in everyone else. They cleaned out the refrigerators, all the food. I couldn't ring it up fast enough. The police came by three times tellin' me to close the store. We really made a haul that night.

When she was three years old she'd come out in the store. We had girlie books on the rack. The guy would stand there lookin' at *Playboy*. She'd come up behind him on a ladder and hold a crucifix in front of him. That was too much for him. He had to fold the book. (Laughs.)

GEORGE: We used to open at six in the morning. One day, one mother come in hollerin' I shouldn't sell Johnny penny candy on the way to school. Next day, another mother come: Susie shouldn't have bubble gum because she's got fillin' in her teeth. Another come. So I says, "Listen, I'm not gettin' fringe benefits of bein' married to you. If you can't handle your children—I'm doin' this for your convenience so you can get things for your breakfast. I won't open till they're in school." So now I don't open till around ten-thirty.

There usually isn't that much sleep. We used to average two, three hours. That went on for ten years that way. Now we get on an average of four hours. Sometimes you have time to eat breakfast. In the morning I mop the floors, haul fifteen, twenty cases of soda from the basement, throw it in the cooler. For the first three hours you have your variety of salesmen, your bread men and your milkmen. You might open with a $200 bank in the morning. By two in the afternoon, you've paid out $197 and taken in $6. Then your evening trade starts. We switch hours between meals. I wouldn't say we're tired at the end of the day, we just drop. (Laughs.)

453

Seven days a week. Sundays we're open from 7:00 to 10:00 A.M., close to go to church, have dinner, and reopen at four to midnight. We started goin' out for dinner because they would come to the window (mimics high-pitched voice): "I gotta have a greeting card." "I need a quart of milk." We couldn't eat our dinner in peace.

IRENE: Some people think ownin' a store is real easy. All you have to do is stand there and sell it. They say, "What's your old man doin', sleepin'?" He hardly ever sleeps. Movin' all the stock, the refrigerator's blocked up, cleanin' all those drains, he hauls all the groceries home, cuts up boxes, moving all the time.

GEORGE: I usually say to her, "Hi, good-by." That's the extent of our conversation.

IRENE: After twelve o'clock we unwind for an hour, but we're so exhausted we fall asleep. It's always been a rough life, but we've made a decent living out of it and raised three children and have never gone without.

Our boy was almost the ruination of us. He supplied the whole neighborhood with everything and anything they wanted. He could never say no. The kids pressured him: "You get me that or we'll beat you up." He was haulin' the soda out as fast as we could bring it in. We almost went bankrupt with the boy. When he was in his first year high school he had nothin' on his mind but army. So when he reached the age we signed papers for him.

GEORGE: Chain stores don't bother me. People gotta have a place where they can run for a loaf of bread, a dozen eggs, or somethin' for a snack, a pint of ice cream or a bottle of soda. Instead of goin' in the chain store and standing in line. The cold indifference. They still get the personal touch here, the chatter back and forth, the gossip and the laughter.

IRENE: George and I like to kid with the customers. He horses around with the women and flatters them, no matter what they look like. I'll kid the guys.

GEORGE: A new customer come in, she got shocked. I said, "Still love me like you never did?" She said, "I beg your pardon. I love only my husband." (Laughs.) We have a standard joke. People come in and buy a box of Kotex, we'd say, "Use it here or take it with you?" They'd get all shook up. (Laughs.)

IRENE: Prophylactics, there's another joke. A man would come in at night and say, "Is your husband here?" I'd just know, and they'd turn so red, like a woman askin' a man for Kotex.

What I notice is a big change in the people's attitudes. They come in and they may look grouchy. I'd say, "Hi, how are you?" They used to answer, "Hi." Now they look at you like I'm nuts. They think you're crazy because you say hello to them. It's more like a big city now than a small neighborhood.

Years ago, every Halloween we'd give about five hundred dollars' worth of toys away. We'd have several hundred kids out front. We would drop balloons from the upstairs windows with tickets in 'em. They would turn the tickets in and get prizes. When the neighborhood changed, the parents would start grabbin' the balloons and steppin' on the kids. So we just cut it out.

GEORGE: Actually, this is a gold mine. We're on the main drag. People on this side of the street don't want to send the children on the other side. Your main trade here is all the little darlings who want "one of dem, one of dese, one of dose." Penny candy. They come in, three cents, and it takes them twenty minutes to make up their minds.

IRENE: They say, "How do you have the patience to stand and wait on those kids?" It's really difficult, but if you allow yourself to get uptight, you look bad in front of your customers. So we just shrug our shoulders.

We've seen people now that are married and divorced who were in grammar school when we came in, have got two and three children. They were miserable little kids and George taught most of 'em manners. They'd come in: "Gimme change for a dollar." He'd teach 'em to say, "Could I please have change for a dollar?" Some of 'em, you wonder where the teachings are at home.

GEORGE: One of the things in a ma, pa store you have to put up with—mothers use it as a baby sitter. It's much easier for a mother to give the child a penny and go to the store. It takes a kid ten minutes to walk to the store, ten minutes in the store, and ten minutes back. Mom says, "You're a good boy, here's another penny." So for two cents an hour they got a baby sitter. In the course of the day you'll have the same monster in eight, ten times a day. A penny at a time.

IRENE: It's unbelievable what we go through. All through the years we've had all sorts of telephone calls during the night. Not so much any more, because we don't have our name in the book like we used to. We had so many goofy calls. They call and ask if we have Prince Albert and I say yes and they'd say, "Let the poor guy out of the can." Those kind of jokes. Oh, a lot of people will stand around waitin' for papers and they talk about bingo and they complain about the blacks who take all their parking areas. We have to hear all that.

GEORGE: They used to hang around more. But now I don't allow anybody to drink soda or eat food in the store. I put the opener outside. Keep it movin'. Otherwise, it'd be just a regular hangout.

IRENE: They come in in droves, six, seven teen-agers at a time. One or two might buy and the rest circulate through the store and they'll rob you blind. You have to sort 'em out right away. "How many want to buy? The rest of you leave, please." You have to be a little rude.

GEORGE: When I first came in here, some of the punks, we call 'em, some of the neighborhood rowdies, I'd pick out a leader of the group. I'd take 'em down to the health club where I was workin' out. I'm in condition, liftin' weights. You take these young guys who think they're real tough, you put 'em through calisthenics and their bodies would ache for a week. (Laughs.) The next time they'd have a little more respect for you. Now I got into karate and I worked up to a black belt. They found out about that and they got a healthy respect for me. (Laughs.)

IRENE: A lot of people come in and make comments: "How come you're drivin' such an old car? What's the matter? You got so much money you're hoarding it. You can't buy a new car?" Then we would buy a new car: "Oh boy, you're really makin' it off us poor people." There's no pleasin' 'em nohow.

When prices go up, people come in the store and they throw the items on the counter and they blame us. Eggs go up ten cents a dozen and they act like it's us that raised them. Actually, we make two cents on a gallon of milk. You can't tell them that. They can't understand that anyone could make so little. They say, "Now you're a buck richer." They're so used to having items raised that the resentment is much more. They slam the door and they cuss at you. They gotta blame somebody so they blame us.

GEORGE: When we first opened the store, our insurance was $398 a year. Now it's jumped to $1,398. They say you're in too high a risk area. Your lights have went up, your gas, all your utilities. Your mark-up on your profit has decreased. Like Hostess cakes—they raise an item a penny, it costs you a penny more. You're getting a less percentage on the return. At one time, you were makin' a twenty-two percent mark-up with a five percent overhead—which would leave you a seventeen percent profit. Now they squeeze you down to a twelve percent mark-up if you're lucky. With costs up, your overhead is ten percent, now you're workin' on two percent profit. Instead of coming out of the hole, you're going into the hole. It's impossible to survive unless you're doing something else on the side.

We've been turned in for everything. We had a raid here. It was a set-up deal. A couple of crooked cops had some guy bring in cans of lunch meat. The guy said he's goin' out of business and he had a couple of cases. I got a good price off of him. I set it in the aisle. About a half an hour later in walks these two guys. "That's stolen merchandise. What else you got that's stolen?" They went through the house. "We're gonna have to take your television. We're gonna have to take this. This is stolen. That's stolen. Give us a thousand dollars and we'll leave you alone."

We were new at this thing and got scared. So I went out and borrowed the money and gave it to these guys. I took the license number of their car and reported it. They put us through a lie detector test. They didn't want to believe us. We had to go to the police show-up and things like that. During this time cop after cop was comin' in raiding us with search warrants, just harassment, one thing after another. All the time, we were waitin' to identify these guys at the show-up.

The phone'd ring all night long, with heavy breathing and all. They worked on the family and stuff like that. We had health inspectors, building inspectors, fire inspectors, all the harassments of the city that you could get. Just because we turned in a couple of cops. They were hushing it up all down the line.

IRENE: One day, nine or eleven plainclothesmen come in and started goin' through the store, tearing stuff out and everything. He has a search warrant that we had a printing press and we're supposed to be printing false credit cards and false ID cards. They tore the place upside down, up in the attic, in the basement. What really took the cake, they came in looking for these pornography books. They said some woman in the neighborhood reported us that we were selling to children. They put me in a state of shock. What we were selling were those coin saver books.

By the time we went to IID [Internal Investigation Division of the Chicago Police Department], we just dropped it. We said we couldn't identify them. Then everything quieted down.

GEORGE: Of course you're always lookin' for a buck on the side. Years ago fireworks were illegal. It was a beautiful setup. The police were shakin' down the peddler on the street and bringin' it in here and sellin' it to me. (Laughs.) I would turn around and sell 'em on the counter—on the open counter. Sky rockets, Roman candles, the whole works. They would get calls that we were sellin' illegal fireworks. They'd call us and say, "We gotta make a raid on you. Put everything away." So they'd come in and say, "I don't see nothin', do you, Joe?" "No, I don't see nothin'."

It's such a rat race. We were becoming stagnant in the area. We were

457

getting to be puppets. We were ruining our sense of being. We were ruining our vocabulary. What do you hear in here? "You got dat?" "You got dis?" "You got dose?" You find yourself talking like the trade that comes in, especially with the area degenerating as it is. You begin to feel like you're not progressing in life.

We decided we had to do something to enlighten ourselves. To be mentally active besides physically active. So we got into the psychic field. I did palmistry before. We went to hypnosis classes. Irene went into more development in hand reading and I was teaching hypnotic principles. She's a staff member at the psychic center.

IRENE: We're both ordained as reverends by the IGAS—International General Assembly of Spiritualists. It's a nondenominational church. George takes people in that have hang-ups and problems. In the meditation room here.

GEORGE: The work is confining. In our spare time, between midnight and six in the morning, I built the whole upstairs. Made the attic into the girls' dorm. We own the building, us and the finance company. (Laughs.)

IRENE: The tension is so great—you got to watch 'em all the time. Turn your back, they're fillin' their pockets. We've had people fake injuries here and try to collect. By the end of the day you're talkin' to yourself.

GEORGE: This is where the psychic center has helped us a lot. We can come in here and just lay down for fifteen minutes and bein' able to relax. It's equal to an hour's sleep of somebody else's time.

I hope we won't be doing this forever. If we can unload it, we have hopes to get into the psychic field, in a resort area, a rest home, retreat type of thing, where people can develop a finer awareness of theirself.

POSTSCRIPT: *There is a sign on the wall of the apartment: "Great Spirit, grant that I may not criticize my neighbor until I've walked a mile in his moccasins."*

REFLECTIONS ON IDLENESS AND RETIREMENT

JOE ZMUDA, EX-SHIPPING CLERK

He lives by himself in a tidily kept basement apartment on Chicago's West Side. There is a large-screen TV set with a vase of daisies on top of it. A small radio is on the table. An electric fan keeps things fairly cool *on this hot July day.* "Three weeks from now I'll be seventy-five years old." *Ten years ago he voluntarily retired.*

"I was a shipping clerk for twenty-five long years. The firm went kerflooey. Then I put in fifteen years at a felt works. I was operating a cutting machine. Before that, I was a roving Romeo. I worked as a kid before they asked for your birth certificate. Box factories."

Some people told me, "Joe, you got your health and you shouldna done it." But it was too late. I don't know why I retired. It's just a habit, I guess. (Sighs.) Yeah. I have no regrets.

The first two years, I was downhearted. I had no place to go, nothin' to do. Then I gave myself a good goin' over. You can't sit at home like that and waste your time. So I kept travelin'. I went to see one of my old friends. Two days later, I'd go see another one. Three days later, they'd both come over and see me. That's the way life went.

The day goes pretty fast for me now. I don't regret it at all that I've got all this time on hand. I'm enjoying it to the best of my ability. I don't daydream at all. I just think of something and I forget it. That daydreaming don't do you any good. What the heck, there's no reason to have a grouch on or be mad at the world. Smile and the world smiles with you, that's an old slogan.

I live on a pension and social security. I don't get much pension because I only put in fifteen years at that place. I get thirty-six dollars a month from there and I get $217 from Social Security. If I manage my money, I'm fifteen, twenty dollars to the good every end of the month.

(He reaches for a looseleaf book on the nearby shelf. He reads from it.) Here's cash on hand and here's my list of expenses. They're painting our church, so I contributed seven dollars. That was July first. The next day the grocery was $6.12. Gas and electric for the month was $16.48. Miscellaneous was $2.22. I don't remember what that was for. Rent is (mumbles) so-and-so. Dr.—that's not doctor, that's drink—$6.80. That's an awful, awful big bill for drink. Last Sunday, lodge meeting, $5.73. I have to keep track. If you don't, who in the hell will? If you come to the twenty-fifth of the month and you ain't got any money . . .

I stay up till one o'clock every night. I sleep late. I get up between nine and ten thirty in the morning. The first thing you do is take ahold of the coffee pot handle and you find out it's empty, so you gotta make coffee. Then I take that goddarn pipe and I fill it with tobacco, and the day is started. I just had three soft boiled eggs about a half-hour ago. I just about wiped my chin when you come in.

459

I linger around till about one and one thirty. Right now I can't go out much because I just got this cataract operation about three weeks ago. I still can't look at the sun. They're fittin' me for new glasses. I can see that picture. I can see that flower. The vision is comin' back to me real nice. I have no difficulty watchin' television.

In the evening I like to turn on the news for a half-hour or so. That Watergate's gettin' on everybody's nerves lately. I don't even understand what it's about, to tell you the truth. They say politics is politics. I'm tired of it. Tonight I suppose I'll listen to the White Sox game and lay around. At ten o'clock the Cubs will go on television. They play San Francisco. On Sunday I'll go to church.

I like baseball. I can listen to baseball on the radio and television and I don't get tired of it. In the wintertime I love bowling on television. Oh, I love that bowling. I remember one year we went out to Mundelein, Illinois. That's the only place in my life I was bowling on the outside. Believe it or not, I bowled on those wooden alleys.

During the summer I used to go fishin' an awful lot. I had a brother-in-law, he was a great fisherman. For ten long years we spent two or three weeks in Hayward, Wisconsin. We had the nicest times ever. And then come back home and wait for next year. On the first day of December, 1961, he was drivin' to work and had a heart attack. He smashed into a car, he hit a post, and he ran right into a tavern, and that was that.

Just about ten years ago I went to a golden jubilee wedding. My mother's only living sister's daughter. What an affair that turned out to be, somewheres in Elmhurst. Believe it or not, there was a dozen scrap books on two tables. It brought back memories of my grandfather, my grandmother, my mother, sisters, and all. And now all of that's gone. I call some of my relatives now and then. I got quite a number of them. I usually take a little ride to the cemetery to visit my wife's grave. And I go to the other cemetery a week or so later to see my folks' grave, and that's that.

Sunday evenings my landlord—I've known him since childhood—he likes to shoot pool. I do too. We don't shoot pool for nothin'—a buck a game. Sunday I beat him three in a row and he was crying' about it all the way: "You dirty dog." (Laughs.)

I go to the tavern Saturday or Sunday. I meet my old gang there. There's another fella, may his soul rest in peace, he died about six months ago. He liked pool very much. I'd beat this guy and he'd start hollerin', "That nasty old man beat me again." (Laughs.)

There are times when we make a foursome. Each guy takes a coin, tosses it up, and you pick your partner that way. You lose, you buy the drinks. If you win, you get the drinks for nothin'. There's conversation in-between. I liked pool when I was a kid and I still like it today. I won't say I'm a sharpie. I won't challenge Minnesota Fats, but I'll play the average guy in the tavern.

Like Sunday, we had a lodge meeting. There was seven of us. Each guy puts two dollars in the pot and we drink the rest of the afternoon with that. I like about three or four shots a week, and three, four games of pool and that's my evening.

The tavern I go to is just three blocks away. I walk there, but I'm driven home by my landlord. So we don't have to worry about gettin' held up. The idea is you gotta be careful so you don't keep all your money in your wallet. Sometimes you gotta put a ten spot behind the collar. I got held up in this neighborhood on the twenty-second of March about four years ago. I'm glad they didn't beat me. They took the money but they gave me my wallet back. I was so scared I didn't even know they put it in my shirt.

I have two friends that are living on the South Side, just about a block away from the National Biscuit Company. I get a big thrill out of it when I go by there. Boy, you should see the nice aroma from that place.

I go by my cousin, he stood up at my wedding. I spend two, three hours with him and he says, "I'm gonna call Whitey." He's another retired man. He's got that goddamn habit. He's at the park every day in the week watchin' them pinochle players and card sharks. My cousin calls him up, he comes over, and we start shooting the baloney all over again.

Like I say, when we were young fellas, there used to be one of them amusement parks. I'll never forget that place as long as I live. I had an occasion to take my girl friend out there. That was about 1920. They had that ride they called the Big Dipper. That thing went up and then down and up again. She had a great big white hat and a great big wide brim and she had what they call a stole, some fur piece. When that goddarn thing went down, she like fainted. I had to hold her. I had to hold her hat. I had to hold her fur piece. I had to hold myself. When we got off, the words she used are not allowed to be printed. Outside of that, she was a sweet kid. About fifty-three years ago. This is what we talk about.

Another man that stood up at my wedding, he's also retired. But he has asthma or something. Believe it or not, he pulled out a grocery bag about that big and he said, "Joe, here's what I got to compete with." He just dumped the contents out and he had about twelve different bottles of medicine. He says, "Joe, you don't know how lucky are are."

Sometimes when I get kind of wild, I take a train and go out to Glen Ellyn by my daughter. I surprise her because I hate to impose on people. I got two granddaughters. When I go out there, how they beg me, "Grandpa, stay for dinner." I say, "Not this time. I'm goin' home by train the same way I came out." Occasionally I stay there.

There's two Slovenian families across the street. They're brothers-in-law. They love to come to the tavern with their wives and have a drink or two. One of them got a real beautiful voice and he loves to sing. So we start singing in the tavern and their wives join in. Believe it or not, we dig up songs that are fifty years old.

I go to fires every once in a while. That fire we had on Milwaukee Avenue about three months ago, that was supposed to start in the morning. I was there at four o'clock that afternoon. I was surprised that goddarned all the windows was broke and yet the smoke was comin' out there heavy as hell, but you don't see the flame. They had about thirty units there. You get the news on the radio. I was gonna go to that Midway Airport accident. My two friends, they said, "Joe, you can't see nothin' there no more. That's all cleaned up, leveled off and everything." They work fast on that.

I tell you what I did see. In 1915 I was workin' as an errand boy. I saw that Eastland disaster about two minutes after it happened. I was right on the bridge when it toppled over. You should hear the screams. I was chased off. That was that Western Electric picnic outing. Seven hundred or something was drowned.

I usually go to the Exchange Bank downtown just to get myself a nasty headache. I have a brother there. He makes up packages of dollar bills in a canvas bag and puts a wire around. One-dollar bills come four hundred in a package. Sometimes he's got stacks about two foot long and two foot wide and three foot high. You can imagine he's got a couple of million there. That's the headache.

This coming December, it'll be three years I made the trip to California. I got a sister out there. I stayed out there over the Christmas holidays and we went to Disneyland. Believe it or not, honest to God, I didn't think such beautiful things existed in this world of ours. It was somethin'.

I'm hopin' to be around here for at least five more years. I don't care. Twenty more years? Oh God, no. When people get old, they get a little bit childish.

I have a very, very good, darn good memory. I'll tell you another one. On the eighteenth of June, 1918, I went to a dance. Another guy and me.

There was two girls dancin'. They were sisters. He grabbed one, so I grabbed the other. You know what they played. (Sings) Smile a while, you bid me sad adieu. I kissed that girl on the cheek. She told the world and me, "If I don't marry you, Joe, I'll never marry another person in this world." She was seventy years old last week. I called her up, wished her a happy birthday, and that's all. I could've married her, but—

I know a lot of songs. Sometimes when I'm washin' dishes, that's when the old time songs come to you. (He sings "Pretty Baby.")

That's all. That's over. There's more I know. I pride myself with that. Many of my friends will tell you, "If there's anything you want to know, ask Joe."

THE AGE OF CHARLIE BLOSSOM

CHARLIE BLOSSOM, EX-COPY BOY

He is twenty-four years old, of an upper-middle-class family. His father and grandfather are both doctors. His parents are divorced; each has since re-married. He attended a college on the west coast for one year, dropped out, and has been on his own ever since. "My main concern was political activity. I was then supported by my parents. It was a struggle for a lot of people I knew, whether to continue taking money from their parents."

His long hair is be-ribboned into a ponytail; his glasses are wire-rimmed; his mustache is scraggly and his beard is wispy. He is seated on the floor, having assumed the lotus position. The account of his life, adventures— and reflections—is somewhat discursive.

My first job was in a dog kennel, cleaning up the shit. It was just for a couple of days. My first real job was in a factory. I was hired to sweep the shit off the floor. They saw I was a good worker and made me a machine operator. I was eighteen and a conscientious objector. I told 'em at the factory I didn't want to do any war work, any kind of contract with any military institution. I tried to adhere to my politics and my morality. Since that time and through different jobs I've been led into compromises that have corrupted me.

They said, "You don't have to do any war stuff." They were just not telling me what it was, figuring I'd be cool. I was going along with it because I wanted to keep my job. I didn't want a confrontation. I was punching out some kind of styrofoam. It was for some burglar alarm or something weird. You twist it around and ream it out. I was getting really angry about it. It's just not worthy work for a person to be doing. I had a real battle with myself. If I had any real guts, I'd say, "Fuck it," and walk out. I would be free. All this emotional tension was making me a prisoner. If I would just get up, I would put this down and say, "This is bogus, it's bullshit, it's not worthy. I'm a *human being*. A man, a woman shouldn't have to spend time doing this"—and just walk out. I'd be liberated. But I didn't.

One afternoon I was sorting out the dies and hangin' 'em on a pipe rack. In order to make room to hang more up, I had to push 'em like you push clothes in a closet. It made a horrible kind of screeching sound—metal on metal. I was thinking to myself—somewhat dramatically—This is like the scream of the Vietnamese people that are being napalmed. So I walked over to the foreman and I said, "Look, no longer is it enough not to do war work. The whole plant has just not to do any kind of work associating with killing people of any kind. Or I'm not gonna work at all." It was sort of like a little strike. I said, "I'm going home." He said, "Yeah, come back in a day or so." So I came back in a day or so and some high-up guy said, "Maybe you better look for another job." I said, "Okay." That was my first real job.

I worked in VISTA for a couple of years. I got assigned as a youth worker, with no real supervision, no activities. I just collected my paycheck, cashed it, and lived. I suppose I did as good as anyone else with a structured job. Freeing myself of a lot of thought habits, guilt, and repressiveness. Getting better acquainted with my own feelings, my own sensations, my own body, my own life. After they fired me, I worked with guerrilla theater. I worked for a leftist printer. It didn't work out. I didn't have a car, didn't have money. Couldn't get a job. Not that I was really trying. Finally I was recommended for a job as copy boy on a Chicago paper.

I had very long hair at that time. It was halfway down my back. In order to get the job, I tied it up in such a way that it was all down inside my shirt. From the front it looked like a hillbilly greaser kind of haircut. The kind like Johnny Cash has. I borrowed some ritzy looking clothes, advertising agency clothes.

I went down to the paper and I talked to this guy and told him how much I wanted to be a journalist. It sounded like some Dick and Jane textbook. A lot of people like to pretend that's the way the world is. He liked me. He thought I was bright and hired me. I had a tie on.

Within a couple of weeks after working there, I reverted to my natural clothes. I was bringing organic walnuts and organic raisins and giving it away. Coming to work was for me a kind of missionary kind of thing. Originally I was gonna get some money and leave, but I had to get involved. So I tried to relate.

After a couple of weeks, the editor called me into this office. He said, "Read this little speech I wrote and tell me what you think of it." It was just a bunch of platitudes. Objectivity was the one thing he mentioned. I started telling him stuff: I think a newspaper should be this, that, and the other thing. We talked about an hour. I thought we were in fine agreement, that he was eating it up. I was paraphrasing exactly what he said. In the business world, you gotta play the game. I was leading around to asking for a scholarship.

We were exchanging rhetoric about how wonderful a newspaper is as a free institution and all this bullshit. *All of a sudden* he said, "I was walking through the office last week and I said, 'Who is that dirty, scummy, disgusting filthy creature over there?' And I was told that's one of our new copy boys. I was told he was bright and energetic."

He was talking about *me!* That struck me as a weird way of relating to somebody. He started by saying that clothing is unimportant, "so that's why I'm asking you to change your clothes." It was just so bizarre. I told him, "Look, now that I've got a job, I'll buy fancy clothes, I'll rent an apartment, I'll take a shower." He seemed pleased, but he wanted me to cut my hair. I balked at that. He rose from his desk and stood up. The interview was over. He said blah, blah, blah, blah and hustled me out of the office. I was very shaken by it and went out and cried. Or maybe I didn't cry at that time. But once he was pissed off at an assistant editor and took it out on me and yelled, "You got to look like a young businessman tomorrow or you're out!" That's one time I'm pretty sure I did cry, 'cause I just don't know how to relate to it.

I was enjoying my job, because I was answering the phone most of the time. People would call up and complain or have a problem. I'd say, "This is a capitalist newspaper and as long as it's a capitalistic newspaper it's not gonna serve you, because its purpose is not to serve you. It's purpose is to make money for its owner. If you want some help . . ." And I'd refer them to the Panthers or the *Seed.* People were very grateful. They'd say, "Thank you very much." After they talked to me forty-five minutes or so, they'd say, "I'm glad I talked to you. I didn't know the Panthers were like that."

Were there any complaints?

About what?

About your—uh—commentary and suggestions?

No complaints, no hassles. I was very polite. At that stage of the game, I was in a very mellow mood. I was giving organic raisins and walnuts and sunflower seeds to everybody—to reporters and rewrite men. I was bright and cheerful and everything. The city editor was very short and rude to people that called up and hung up and stuff like that. I'd say, "That's a *person* on the phone." I used to walk around the office and say, "How can grown people spend their time doing this?" I got into long raps. I actually got one, who'd been a reporter for twenty years, to seriously question himself: Am I doing anything worthwhile? I liked doing this, to persuade people to think. It was my contribution to the world. That's why I told people who called for help that they should write letters or call up the editor or come down and take over the paper. A lot of people responded very well to those suggestions.

And no complaints about your persuasions . . . ?

(A throwaway.) Sometimes. What finally happened was — I was involved in a severe personal relationship and I really got obnoxious. I was very alienated and very hostile. I stopped bringing in organic food. I started taking a couple of hours off on my dinner break—which is very cool. I'd grab two, three beers and smoke a joint or two on my break. The grass and beers put me in a very mellow state. The straw broke when somebody called up and the reporter hung up on him. The guy called back and I answered the phone. I got real mad at the guy, too, and called him a bigot, racist, and hung up on him, too. The guy complained. And I was the one who got in trouble. It was a big thing, with the editor coming down on me for my attitude on the phones. I guess he found out about those other calls. I couldn't understand his anger. I was just trying to convey my feelings to the people.

My fantasies all spring at the paper was getting a machine gun and coming in and shooting them. Getting psychedelic hallucinogens and putting them in their drinks. Getting a gun and walk into the editor's office and shooting him. Maybe pointing the gun at him first and say, "Okay, how do you face your death?" I saw a Japanese movie once where two guys met their deaths in two different ways. That's the kind of fantasies I had, cutting 'em up with knives.

Other people's fantasies, from what I could observe, were sexual. They were not connected with the political realities. They would look at the young women—attractive by white, bourgeois standards, the ones with long blonde hair and miniskirts—and draw erotic stimulation.

There was one hired as a copy girl, through some uncle who had pull, and within a month she was an editorial assistant. There were two copy boys that had worked there for a couple of years, that were married and had kids, and weren't getting fucking paid as editorial assistants.

A copy boy is a kind of nigger. You stand around in a room full of people that are very ego-involved in a fantasy—they think they're putting out a newspaper. These are the reporters and editors. Somebody yells, "Copy!" Sometimes they yell, "Boy!" You run over—or you walk over—and they give you a piece of paper. You take that piece of paper someplace, and you either leave it there and go back to waiting around or you get another piece of paper and bring it back to the person that originally called you.

The other thing you do is go down, when the editions come off the press, and you get three hundred copies of the paper on a big cart and you wheel it around and put one on everybody's desk. And stuff like that. "We've got a pack of photographs to pick up at Associated Press, go over and get it." "Somebody's in town making a speech, go and get it." Or, "Take this over to city hall and give it to the reporter that's over there . . ."

Copy boys are also expected to do editorial assistant's work. That's answering the phone and saying, "City Desk." If it's a reporter, you connect him with the editor or whatever. If an individual is calling about a story that says, "Continued on page seven," but it's not on page seven, I look through the paper until I find where the story is and tell him. Or I go get clips out of the library. You take one piece of paper and exchange it for another. It's basically bullshit.

When I first worked there, I ran. They'd say, "Copy!" and I'd run. Nobody noticed. It didn't make any difference. Then I started walking. Why the fuck should I run for them? This spring, I started to shuffle. That's when the people started to complain about me. I started in February 1970, and I was fired May 20, 1971. I was out with hepatitis for six months.

Want to know why I was ultimately fired? I had a pair of shoes, the soles were loose. I didn't want to spend money on shoes. I was taking home seventy bucks a week and saving fifty. I wasn't hanging around the paper because that was my destiny. I was just some little pinball that had dropped in a slot. I was there because a bunch of accidents put me there. I also had a will and an energy and I was moving. I was in motion, creative.

I wanted to have a computer at the paper. I wanted an arrangement where you could get up in the morning and call up and say, "Okay, this is Charlie. I can work on Tuesday, Thursday, Friday, and Saturday in the evenings. And on Wednesday morning. I absolutely cannot work Wednesday evening." Everyone would be calling up and the computer would put it all together. They would call back and say, "Okay, these are your hours this week." 'Cause it doesn't make any difference who shows up, the way they run the paper. These are the kinds of ideas I had. I wanted decision-making in the hands of the people who did the work. I wanted to fuck capitalism.

I saw those things in terms of classes. The seventh floor was the executive. The fourth floor was the middle class—editorial, reporters, and all that. The ruling class had their offices there too, not up with the executives. I used to see Marshall Field in the hall. I was thinking, If they kill Bobby Seale, maybe I should get a gun and come in here and shoot Field. Maybe that's a reason for me to keep this job. I'm not accomplishing anything else here. I don't want money. Money isn't worth it.

What would you accomplish by killing Marshall Field?

Oh well, you can't look at it as accomplishing anything. Like one of the editors told me, "If you behave yourself, you won't get fired." I wanted to take a baseball bat and smash his head in, except I wanted to do it with my hands. He made me so angry. Here is this motherfucker, who is comfortable, he's not struggling—in truth, there's not a hell of a lot for him to struggle about, 'cause he's a fuckin' marshmallow in a bag of marshmallows. He's a nice guy. I mean, I like him. But he's a fuckin' marshmallow.

Your shoes, the soles were loose . . .

Yeah. What I did was put glue on 'em. And then somebody suggested I put tape on 'em. So I did. People kept suggesting that I buy shoes. I kept saying, "No. I don't want to buy shoes. These shoes are fine." There was no reason for me to stay in their culture.

Still I was making friends with different people. I was trying to get the foreign editor to do an article about opium that the CIA is responsible for bringing into this country as heroin. I read it in *Ramparts*. They just laughed at it. A week later, another paper ran a column by Flora Lewis about the *Ramparts* article. I was incensed by these pigs. This guy thinks he's my friend. I mean, I like him a lot. He's really a nice person. I don't know if I would get any pleasure from shooting him up with a .50-caliber machine gun and seeing his body splatter to pieces. I'd be emotionally disturbed by an act of destruction as total as that. But I would get some satisfaction out of it, because of the rage I feel towards these guys. The way they wrote about the demonstrations and the Panther grand jury. I'm so enraged by these swine . . . They pretend they're liberals. They pretend to be concerned. They never fight over an issue. This editor told me, "I fight every day for space." God!!

I had my most hostile fantasies on the job. I just reached a point where I just didn't want to hand out the fucking newspaper. I wanted to burn it. It's like you get a job in a prison. It's the only job in town. Your job is to go around the cells and hand out a washcloth. I don't want to be just handing out washcloths. You begin to realize this guy that's locked up is just another human being. Maybe I could help him out. I'll bring him cigarettes. I think that was the real reason I passed out organic walnuts and raisins. And my thoughts.

The job was also a corrupting thing. I realized I could get a lot of free books, a lot of books came in to review. And records, I could cop records. You sort of be nice to this guy because he'll give you the records. I was getting corrupted.

How pitiful these people are! They kept telling me I should try to keep the job. It was security. I could look at these guys that worked twenty, thirty fucking years, and they were telling me if I cut my hair and wore different clothes, I would be like them. They don't want to have to say, "Jesus! I blew it! I'm sixty years old and I've wasted it all." I'm not stupid. I can work. I'm lazy, most of us are. But we're lazy because we've got nothing worthwhile to do. I lost a year of my life working there. Was it worth it?

I'm saying godly things, that's what it's all about. How can we get that boot to step three inches over to the left or the right, so it won't trample that flower. Look at these rich motherfuckers who don't know shit. We don't have a society in which you work because you're tricked, cajoled, manipulated, or pressured into it.

How many jobs in this country consist of locking things or counting things, like money—the banks, the cashiers. Or being a watchman of some kind. Why in the hell do these jobs exist? These jobs are not necessary to life. This guy I was talking to yesterday said, "Money makes the world go around. Brothers kill each other over money." And that's true. I pointed to the sun. "What makes that go around? You're not gonna tell me money makes that go around." So there's something else besides money. You can't eat money, you can't fuck money, you can't do nothin' with money except exchange things. We can live without money. We can live with people and grow food and build a table and massage a neck that has a sprain . . .

Your shoes, you had them taped . . .

Oh yeah. You wanna know why I was ultimately fired? I'm very interested in Oriental stuff. Sometimes I fantasize about being a samurai, especially after I see a Japanese movie. So I used to sit Japanese-style on my knees on the floor. (At this point, he shifts from the lotus position to that of a samurai.) I'd pick a quiet corner of the room.

(Softly, hardly audible) The city room . . . ?

In front of the desk of the religion editor. I thought it was appropriate. Sitting and breathing. People tried to ignore it. Some people thought I was meditating. I said, "Sure I'm meditating." I don't know what meditation is exactly, so I would be reluctant to call it that. I used to do this, before, on the floor of the mail room. One day a guy objected because he thought if a guy came in wheeling a thing, he wouldn't be able to see me. I showed him I could move extremely quickly. That put his fears to rest.

One day the head librarian, he's such an ass-hole—I really hate to call people ass-holes because they're all nice. I'm more obnoxious than a lot of people I call ass-holes. But he's the kind of guy only interested in himself, which to me is a very outdated point of view. I mean, if you study Zen or ancient philosophy, they all say the same thing, and that is that no man is an island. Okay, so he came in and said, "Don't sit like that." I said, "Why not? I'm not bothering anybody." He said, "I don't want you to."

I said, "Man, let me explain . . ." He said, "Do you want me to talk to the editor?" I said, "No, no, no, don't talk to him, he'll fire me." So he said, "I don't want you sitting there, it looks just terrible." I said, "Okay, I won't sit in the corner, I'll sit in the middle of the room." He said, "No, no, no, don't do that either." So I left. I went down and sat in front of the desk of the religion editor.

About a week or so later—one of my stops with the paper is the public relations office. There was a vase with some flowers in it. So I sat down in the chair and looked at the flowers in it—maybe five minutes, six at most—and I got up and left. A couple of days later, the editor called me into his office and says, "I got three complaints I want to discuss with you. One was from the librarian. He told me about your sitting on your knees and I told him if you ever do that again to throw you out. The second is about you and the flowers. They complained you disrupted the office." I said, "I was sitting there with my back straight and breathing (breathes slowly, deliberately, deeply) instead of (gasps frantically)—right?" *That disrupted them?*

In a way I did disrupt. It's the kind of thing Gandhi or Thoreau or Christ would say. If you really want to strike a blow at the corruption of society, come into eternity. I have to concede that a human being who sits down and meditates—tries to get in touch with God or whatever—is the most threatening fucking thing of all. On a physical plane, I wasn't interfering with them at all. But the fact that I sat with my back straight and most people at their jobs don't sit with their backs straight, that's weird. They looked at me and they felt guilty. I wasn't trying to irritate them. I wasn't trying to throw any magic their way. I was just looking at the flowers.

Most of all, I wanted to be touched by these flowers. I stroked a couple of petals really gently. I was trying to reach out and say, "Hey plant, I know you're here in this office and it's probably a drag and you're lonely. But I love you." I took a couple of petals that had fallen off the table and put them in my pocket.

The third complaint . . . ?

. . . was about my shoes. He said, "It's entirely unacceptable to have tape on your shoes."

Were you fired because of the shoes, looking at the flowers, or assuming the samurai position?

No. On Monday morning I called up the paper and said I'd be fifteen minutes late and I was fifteen minutes late. Tuesday morning I called and said I'd be fifteen minutes late and I was fifteen minutes late. He said that was entirely unacceptable. Se he gave me a written memo.

So that was it?

No. Originally they pissed about my clothing. I said, "When I wore my good clothes they got ruined here, tearing against the typewriters. You ought to provide some kind of smocks." Surprisingly, he accepted the idea and gave us smocks. Hell, it was hot and it was summertime. So I started wearing just the smock and no shirt. And he said that was entirely unacceptable. "Suppose somebody comes in and sees you. This is a business office."

Nobody complained about my work except the head copy boy, and I made a deal with him. I said, "Let me do all the paper rounds and I won't be in the city room." I hated the way they treat you in the city room.

I got great satisfaction from the paper rounds, far more than going to a library or hanging around the city room. I'd go down and fill up the cart and that fucking thing's heavy. I'd have to push it and it would take strength and I'd sweat. It's like 250 or 300 papers to go around on each edition. I liked it 'cause I sweated and I got into conversations with people. I'd get done and I would say, "I did something."

I'd do the rounds and go sit outside in the flower garden. After a week or so, the head copy boy said, "Look, the other copy boys see you sittin' around while they're working and it makes them uptight." I said, "Okay, I'll come back, do more work, but I won't do *all* the paper rounds." They were uptight not because they saw me sitting around—because dealing with these reporters, these pigs, who called them "Boy!" all the time, *they* wanted a chance to get out.

(Mumbles) Then it wasn't the shoes or the samurai position or the flowers or being late . . . ?

No. I was going through all this upset. I said to the head copy boy, "I'm going through all this weirdness and I haven't gone to lunch. I might as well leave early." People do that kind of shit all the time. Come five o'clock, I started getting my stuff together and changing. I would come to work in blue jeans and change into a pair of pants and a shirt. At the end of the day I could change back into blue jeans. At five thirty, I would just (snaps fingers) walk out the door.

At five thirty somebody walked in and said to me, "Here are some clips. Can you go and get 'em?" I said, "No, I'm leaving." Another copy boy says no, too. The next morning the editor came to me and said, "You left early . . . blah, blah, blah, blah . . . And you refused to get the clips." I said, "Let me explain." And he said, "That's entirely unacceptable. This is the straw that broke the camel's back." To me it was more like the one that broke the pig's back.

I had been thinking for months, What will I do when I get fired? Will I smoke a joint in the city room? Will I meditate in the library? I wanted to do something to show, Hey, I'm better than you motherfuckers. I'm getting fired because I'm different. I don't want to be a cipher. I was thinking, How could I show that? By kidnapping Marshall Field? By shooting him? I had to think fast, so I looked at the editor and said, "I hope you can live with the conditions you're creating." And I just turned around and walked out and started to cry.

He hurried after me and said, "Wait a minute. I'm not creating these conditions, you are." I said, "No, no, no, I'm not the one that has the power. You're the one that has the power." I walked out of there. Then I hung around the office most of the day selling copies of *Rising Up Angry*. (Laughs.)

I've gotten myself on unemployment. They were nice to me the first few times, then a woman told me to get a number. I wanted to tell her, Fuck you. I can wait outside your apartment and knock you over the head and steal your money. Fuck your money. It's not your money in the first place. It's mine. I worked for it. And if you don't give it to me, I don't give a fuck, 'cause I'll live anyway. When I was younger and applied for a job and the guy wouldn't give me a reason for not hiring me, I would say, "It's okay." I wouldn't yell at him, "You're a racist pig." I'd think, Fine. Mao Tse-tung will hire me to kill you. Or I could be a bank robber. But that bitterness, I don't like being bitter. I'm a pacifist.

I have picked a career for myself. I want to practice the kind of traditional medicine that is more spiritually oriented than modern Western medicine. I want to learn herbs and massage and things like that, and meditation. I don't want to be dependent on other people. This notion of self-reliance is peculiar today. The frontiersman lived by his own effort. Today nobody does that. I want to be a frontiersman of the spirit—where work is not a drag.

BUD FREEMAN, JAZZ MUSICIAN

He is sixty-five years old, though his appearance and manner are of William Blake's "golden youth." He has been a tenor saxophone player for forty-seven years. Highly respected among his colleagues, he is a member of "The World's Greatest Jazz Band." It is a cooperative venture, jointly owned by the musicians, established jazz men.

"I'm with the young people because they refuse to be brainwashed by the things you and I were brainwashed by. My father, although he worked hard all his life, was very easy with us. Dad was being brainwashed by the

people in the neighborhood. They'd come in every day and say, "Why don't your boys go to work?" So he made the mistake of awakening my brother at seven thirty. I pretended to be asleep. Dad said, "You're going to get up, go out in the world and get jobs and amount to something." My brother said, "How dare you wake us before the weekend?" (Laughs.) I don't recall ever having seen my father since. (Laughs.)

I get up about noon. I would only consider myself outside the norm because of the way other people live. They're constantly reminding me I'm abnormal. I could never bear to live the dull lives that most people live, locked up in offices. I live in absolute freedom. I do what I do because I want to do it. What's wrong with making a living doing something interesting?

I wouldn't work for anybody. I'm working for me. Oddly enough, jazz is a music that came out of the black man's oppression, yet it allows for great freedom of expression, perhaps more than any other art form. The jazz man is expressing freedom in every note he plays. We can only please the audience doing what *we* do. We have to please ourselves first.

I know a good musician who worked for Lawrence Welk. The man must be terribly in need of money. It's regimented music. It doesn't swing, it doesn't create, it doesn't tell the story of life. It's just the kind of music that people who don't care for music would buy.

I've had people say to me: "You don't do this for a living, for heaven's sake?" I was so shocked. I said, "What other way am I going to make a living? You want to send me a check?" (Laughs.) People can't understand that there are artists in the world as well as drones.

I only know that as a child I was of a rebellious nature. I saw life as it was planned for most of us. I didn't want any part of that dull life. I worked for Lord and Taylor once, nine to five. It was terribly dull. I lasted six weeks. I couldn't see myself being a nine-to-five man, saving my money, getting married, and having a big family—good God, what a way to live!

I knew when I was eight years old that I wasn't going to amount to anything in the business world. (Laughs.) I wanted my life to have something to do with adventure, something unknown, something involved with a free life, something to do with wonder and astonishment. I loved to play—the fact that I could express myself in improvisation, the *unplanned*.

I love to play now more than ever, because I know a little more about music. I'm interested in developing themes and playing something creative. Life now is not so difficult. We work six months a year. We live around the world. And we don't have to work in night clubs night after night after night.

Playing in night clubs, I used to think, When are we going to get out of here? Most audiences were drunk and you tended to become lazy. And if you were a drinker yourself, there went your music. This is why so many great talents have died or gotten out of it. They hated the music business. I was lucky—now I'm sixty-five—in having played forty-seven years.

If jazz musicians had been given the chance we in this band have today—to think about your work and not have to play all hours of the night, five or six sets—God! Or radio station work or commercial jingle work—the guys must loathe it. I don't think the jazz man has been given a fair chance to do what he really wants to do, to work under conditions where he's not treated like a slave, not subject to the music business, which we've loathed all our lives.

I've come to love my work. It's my way of life. Jazz is a luxurious kind of music. You don't play it all day long. You don't play it all night long. The best way to play it is in concerts. You're on for an hour or two and you give it everything you have, your best. And the audience is sober. And I'm not in a hurry to have the night finish. Playing night clubs, it was endless . . .

If you're a creative player, something must happen, and it will. Some sort of magic takes place, yet it isn't magic. Hundreds of times I've gone to work thinking, Oh my God, I hate to think of playing tonight. It's going to be awful. But something on a given night takes place and I'm excited before it's over. Does that make sense? If you have that kind of night, you're not aware of the time, because of this thing that hits you.

There's been a lot of untruths told about improvisation. Men just don't get up on stage and improvise on things they're not familiar with. True improvisation comes out of hard work. When you're practicing at home, you work on a theme and you work out all the possibilities of that theme. Since it's in your head, it comes out when you play. You don't get out on the stage and just improvise, not knowing what the hell you're doing. It doesn't work out that way. Always just before I play a concert, I get the damn horn out and practice. Not scales, but look for creative things to play. I'll practice tonight when I get home, before I go to work. I can't wait to get at it.

I practice because I want to play better. I've never been terribly interested in technique, but I'm interested in facility. To feel comfortable, so when the idea shoots out of my head I can finger it, manipulate it. Something interesting happens. You'll hear a phrase and all of a sudden you're thrown into a whole new inspiration. It doesn't happen every night. But even if I have a terrible night and say, "Oh, I'm so tired, I'll go to sleep and I'll think of other things," the music'll come back. I wasn't too happy about going to work last night because I was tired. It was a drag. But today I feel good. Gonna go home and blow the horn now for a while.

Practicing is no chore for me. I love it. I really do love to play the horn alone. They call me the narcissistic tenor (laughs), because I practice before the mirror. Actually I've learned a great deal looking in the mirror and playing. The dream of all jazz artists is to have enough time to think about their work and play and to develop.

Was there a time when you were altogether bored with your work?

Absolutely. I quit playing for a year. I met a very rich woman. We went to South America to live. We had a house by the sea. I never realized how one could be so rich, so unhappy, and so bored. It frightened me. But I did need the year off. When I came back, I felt fresh.

The other time was when I had a band of my own. I had a name, so I no longer worked for big bands. I was expected to lead one of my own. But I can't handle other people. If I have a group and the pianist, let's say, doesn't like my playing, I can't play. I don't see how these band leaders do it. I can't stand any kind of responsibility other than the music itself. I have to work as a soloist.

I had this band and the guys were late all the time. I didn't want to have to hassle with them. I didn't want to mistreat them, so I said, "Fellas, should we quit?" I wouldn't let them go and stay on myself. We were good friends. I'd say I'd quit if they didn't come on time. They started to come on time. But I wasn't a leader. I used to stand by in the band! A bit to the side. (Laughs.) Now we have a cooperative band. So I have a feeling I'm working for myself.

I don't know if I'll make it, but I hope I'll be playing much better five years from now. I oughta, because I know a little bit more of what I'm doing. It takes a lifetime to learn how to play an instrument. We have a lot of sensational young players come up—oh, you hear them for six months, and then they drop out. The kid of the moment, that's right. Real talent takes a long time to mature, to learn how to bring what character you have into sound, into your playing. Not the instrument, but the style of music you're trying to create should be an extension of you. And this takes a whole life.

I want to play for the rest of my life. I don't see any sense in stopping. Were I to live another thirty years—that would make me ninety-five— why not try to play? I can just hear the critics: "Did you hear that wonderful note old man Freeman played last night?" (Laughs.) As Ben Webster says, "I'm going to play this goddamned saxophone until they put it on top of me." It's become dearer to me after having done it for forty-seven years. It's a thing I need to do.

CATHLEEN MORAN, HOSPITAL AIDE

She is nineteen years old.
What is your work?

Makin' beds and bed pans and rotten stuff like that.

What are you called?

Nurse's aide, dumb aide.

Presently she is working at a middle-class hospital. It's her third. Her previous jobs were lower-middle-class and upper-middle-class institutions. She has been at it since she was fifteen.

I really don't know if I mind the work as much as you always have to work with people, and that drives me nuts. I don't mind emptying the bed pan, what's in it, blood, none of that bothers me at all. Dealing with people is what I don't like. It just makes everything else blah.

How often do you work?

As least as possible. Two days on a weekend, just to get me through school, like money for books and stuff. We start to work at seven, but I get up as late as possible, get everything on and run out the door. I ride my bike to work. I usually have someone punch me in, 'cause I'm never on time. You're gonna think I'm nuts, but I do my work well. If I come a quarter after seven, they're surprised. They don't mind, because I get my work done before the allotted time. I won't have anybody saying I did something lousy. I don't know why.

We get on the floor and you have to take thermometers and temperatures or you have to weigh people or pass water, and you go in the rooms, and they yell when you get 'em up so early in the morning. Then they don't want to get out of bed when you weigh 'em. They complain, "How come the water wasn't passed earlier?" "We couldn't sleep all night with the noise." Or else you'll walk in the room and you'll say, "Hello," and they'll say, "Good morning, how are you?" So I'll say, "Fine," and some of 'em will say, "Well, gee, you're the one that's s'posed to be asking me that." They don't even give you a chance.

I really wonder why I do have such a rotten attitude towards people. I could care less about 'em. I'll do my work, like, you know, good, I'll give 'em the best care, but I couldn't care less about 'em. As far as meeting their emotional needs, forget it. That's why (a little laugh) I don't think I should go into nursing.

I work on a floor that's geriatric. Old people and psychiatric, so there's never anyone in their right minds. They're out of it or they're confused. After you pass out trays, and there's rarely a tray that has everything on it, they start hollering, "I didn't get two sugars," and then you spend half the time running to all the rooms gettin' all their stuff. Then you have to feed all of them, and half the patients are out of it and they spit stuff at you and they throw their food. They throw their dishes on the wall and floor. And I hate feeding patients that are always coughing. They cough right at ya. (Laughs.) That I don't mind, cleaning stuff up. It's just that you're s'posed to calm 'em down and talk to 'em, forget it. I won't be bothered.

I used to work in a hospital, it was more of a cancer ward. Young women, men. I got along great with the men, they could care less. But I always hated working with the women. They drive you nuts. I really can't sympathize with 'em unless sometimes, rarely, I think, What if I was in their place? Like the younger girls, they want you to feel sorry for them. I just can't feel that. Some of 'em are okay, but they're always crying. That doesn't depress me. I have no feelings at all. A lot of nurses come in and they sit with the patients and they talk with 'em. Forget it.

A patient will be in pain and they'll be crying. They put the nurse's light on and want to talk and stuff. I really don't care. It's rotten, you know? Lots of times I try to think as to why I have this attitude. I really think it was from my background in boarding school.

Living in a dorm with kids all the time, you didn't have to be accepted, but you always had to be on top—or else you'd be pushed around and all that. At Maryville I never really was close with anybody. Couldn't afford to be or else you got hurt. So I just turned everybody off. I just kept to myself. I was there from when I was just three until I was sixteen.

There were kids whose parents had money, but they didn't want 'em for some reason. When we first went out to high school, everybody started calling us orphans. I couldn't understand that, because they had money, they had clothes, they had parents to come to see 'em. But there were a few who didn't have parents.

My mother, she makes about six thousand dollars a year. She really couldn't afford to take care of me at home. When I was born my dad took off. He was an alcoholic. My mother was also an alcoholic. I was raised in Maryville from loneliness and stuff. My mother always came to see me, no matter what the weather was.

In the eighth grade you had to get stupid to survive, no kiddin'. I wouldn't let anybody push me around. I have people tell me I have a chip on my shoulder or I'm sensitive if someone barks at me. I could see how girls were pushed around, socked and stuff. But I was good in sports, I came to be the best swimmer, basketball, and I was looked up to. So I could afford to be on my own and left alone. They were allowing us to go out and get jobs. When you get out, you're not worth nothing."

She worked for several months at a hospital "which was really a dump. It was mostly black and low-income whites, though there were a number of patients from middle-income high rises nearby. I really couldn't understand it, after Holy Family. I thought that was a typical hospital—it was spotless. When I saw this one, it was filthy, with bugs on the food cart, I thought, 'Oh God.' I only stayed there for two months.

"I used to have to be forced to get out of bed in the morning and go there. I'd rarely work a weekend when I was supposed to. (Laughs.) Which isn't me. That's why I said I gotta get outa here, because it was getting to me, and that's goofy. They never had any sheets. They never had anything the patient needs. Like they were paying so much money for a room. I'm not lying, don't think I'm nuts. There wasn't a morning when we had linen before ten, eleven o'clock. The patients, they're awakened at seven. We never had adequate help and the other aides, they didn't really fulfill the patient's needs. I was about the only white aide in the hospital and they were wondering what I was doing there."

I have a hard time dealing with black patients, because they're really sensitive. You're gonna think I'm rotten, but when I go into a room I don't have a great attitude. I'm not blah, but if I don't feel like talking, I don't talk. I'll give 'em a bath, but I'm not making up a bunch of conversation just to make them feel good.

It happened just last week. I was in a room with a black patient and she had her hair set in rollers, and she looked like about twenty something. I couldn't see her hair, whether it was graying. She happened to be forty-one. I asked her what she was in for and she said arthritis. I said, "God, you look like about twenty-something." She felt great. She said, "Gee, thanks." I said, "I really can't tell a black's age, they always seem so much younger." If you call 'em colored they have a fit. If you call 'em black, they'll have a fit. So you don't call 'em. So she got so upset. "Why are blacks so different? You mean you can't tell a white person's age?" They just don't show it, not as much, in my opinion. Oh, she started yellin'. I was patient with her.

I think blacks demand more attention—like little piddley stuff she could reach for, she wanted me to get her. I mean, they're going to take advantage of being waited on like whites. Because she's black, she'll get white service, too.

I'm not prejudiced really, but they all put their money under their pillows, while the whites put it in a drawer. I was making her bed, so I turned her on the side and I put her purse on the window. I walked out of her room and I heard her saying, "That white bitch stole my purse!" She was really yelling. I looked on the window and it was right in front of her. And then she said, "Well, stay here, you probably stole something out of it anyway." I was going to walk out of the room and she said, "Hey, white girl, can you come back and fix the blankets up a little neater?" They were really perfect. By that time, you felt like kickin' her right in the mouth. Rarely do I put up with it. I just say, "Do you want your bed made? Get somebody else."

Like I was going to give a black person a bath and I was too lazy to walk and get some soap way down in the utility room, so I got the soap that was in the bathroom. So she said to me, "What do you think I am, a dog? That I'm going to use that soap that white hands have washed their hands on." So I told her it was a fairly new bar and I said, "What does color got to do with the bar of soap?" She went on and on, so I told her I wasn't going to give her a bath, because sometimes you can't do anything right for 'em.

White patients are just as bad. But the blacks always bring up their color. The whites are just a pain in the neck too. Blacks are more offensive, but whites nag you more about the stuff they don't get.

When I first started at Holy Family, I really couldn't stand it, 'cause I really didn't want the job. I was just doing it to get out of Maryville for a couple of hours. When I got on the floor, I didn't know beans. I was dumb. You may think I'm nuts, but I really feel myself capable in whatever I do. So I learned what was up fast, and went out of my way to do extra stuff, to take care of blood pressures and bandages and stuff, so

I'd be left alone so I could do my work. I wouldn't have anybody on my back checking me. If they wanted something done, they could get it done, you know?

You always get a nurse, you wonder what she's doing there. They're blah, bad news, crabby, they try to push you around—which is how I'm afraid I'm going to turn out. Most nurses, they sit at the desk. They chart and take care of the medications. As far as patient contact, they don't get any at all. It's the aides, you know? The nurses don't do anything except give a shot. The head nurse is at the desk constantly, with the doctor's orders, so the aides get all the contact. That's why I figure if I'm going into nursing, I won't have any contact with the patients anyway.

I'd go nuts. I'm just doing it because it's a good job and if times ever become like the Depression, they always need nurses. I'd still like to get a master's, go into law school or something. Everybody thinks I'm nuts: "What are you going to nursing school for if you hate it?" Because I can do my work well and I can put up with it, even if it drives me nuts.

You either get patients who don't want a bath at all and then report you for not giving them a bath, or patients who fake near bath time that they have chest pains so you'll give them a bath, and the next minute you see them walking around the hall and they're visiting.

With orthopedics, with the geriatric, it's really discouraging. The nursing homes have given them terrible care and they have sores you wouldn't believe—bones, tendons, everything showing. I change the dressings and soak them and try to position them where they're not on a sore. But anywhere you put them they're aching.

Lots of times they get bladder infections. You'll just make a bed and they'll urinate right on the clean side. You'll have to, okay, man, start again. You turn them over on the clean side and then they'll have a BM. Sometimes this goes on four or five times. You have to make a patient's bed at least three or four times a day to do good work. It takes about four hours to get all the patients really clean. By the time you're done, you feel so good. But a nurse comes up and says, "So-and-so needs their bed changed, they crapped all over." It really gets discouraging. Each time you go in that room you want to kill them.

I get done at three-thirty. But lots of times it's three-thirty and someone falls out of bed or pulls out their IV's or you know . . . Well, I'll stay. But a lot of kids cut out at even a quarter to three. I usually punch them out, 'cause they're good about it in the morning.

She straightens out a cushion behind me. "Uh . . . do you want to lean back, so you can get more comfortable?" "You're talking like a nurse's aide interested in the patient." "I forgot what we were talking about."

If you ever hear someone crying out in pain . . . ?

I could care less. If the nurse gets there right away or next year, I don't care. That's a rotten attitude, it really is. God, I'd go nuts if I was in the hospital and someone treated me that way. What gets me so mad is: if I'm ever in the hospital, I'd be a typical patient. I'll probably be worse than all of them. And yet I can't stand them.

But I don't know, you get to like some of them. There was this old man, he died recently. He came in terrible from nursing homes and we got him really good care. He was bad news. Like he'd never eat because he thought he'd have to pay for it and he didn't have the money. He was just stubborn. He'd do everything to get you. But you knew he was confused and senile. He went back to the nursing home and I saw him and he was all shriveled up, and you wouldn't believe the sores on his body. I was so mad. I was going to write a note to the nursing home and really do something about it.

I think what am I going to do when I get about seventy and depend on somebody. And what am I going to do if I'm laying in bed—a lot of times they aren't conscious—you wonder, God, what am I going to do? I say, hey, when I reach seventy, here I go—I'm committing suicide. But I'm too chicken to commit suicide, no matter what treatment I get.

I'm not the same as if they were conscious and I really couldn't get away with it. I don't treat a patient as well as if they were with it. We had an elderly patient, she was eighty—she claimed she had a Ph.D.—and she was deaf. Aw, she was terrible, taking everything and throwing it at the wall, hitting me in the head with her spoon, as I was feeding her. I wasn't as nice as I should have been. I was kinda having fun, which was pretty terrible. I knew I had to feed her and she'd spit it out. So I had fun. She was getting so mad I was getting a kick out of putting the food in her mouth. I remember thinking that night, God, that was pretty rotten. I never hit a patient, even though I got slugged a couple of times. But I could have been more gentle with her. Oh, I was terrible. The nurses see me as something different, as somebody really good with patients, when in fact I'm not. I put up a front. But they wouldn't believe. Patients are always reporting me for my attitude, but the nurses don't see that side of me.

I do good work. A couple of times when I've been reported, it's not for the care I've given, it's what I say to them. And that's not really nice.

You're supposed to be sympathetic. My attitude, it's rotten. I stop and wonder why I don't really care about people. I want to be accepted and them to think I'm okay, you know? It's funny. Yet I don't give anyone else the time of the day.

I think it's something about Maryville. There was this rigid discipline. We had this one nun, but oh, I couldn't stand her. If you cried, you were really bad news. She literally made everybody cry. She was always yelling and never paid attention to who she was hitting. I remember walking out the door with this girl and hearing her tell this nun to go to hell. The nun called me back and said, "What'd she say?" Oh, I'm not gonna tell her. So she made me work for her from eight thirty in the morning until ten o'clock at night. I had to wash all the stairs, scrub 'em. I was done about four o'clock, I did it pretty fast. I had a system of sweeping. I thought I showed her, hmm, only four o'clock and I'm through. She made me do it all over again.

She had to teach, take care of our dorm, keep the library, and be dean of our high school. You're going to think this is strange, she was so tough, so brutal, I sort of admired her because she was good at her many jobs. ·

Has she been your model . . . ?

I know! Don't mention! (Laughs.) She had me when I was three. I could never get rid of her. Every time I moved up, she was there. Where we ate and where our dorms was was quite a distance. When we were not even five years old, we had to go from where we slept to where we ate in single file and freezing weather and not say a word. Not touch the snow. You couldn't drop your mitten. I remember a night where I was feeling around in the snow, so she punished everybody for it. She kept you in line. If somebody got out of line, she punished everybody. She had this big paddle and she had a strap in the other hand and, boy, that was bad news. She'd spank kids and hit 'em and they'd go to bed and everybody was crying. (Giggles.)

Someone dared me get out of line and go sneak to my bed. I was the one why everybody was getting punished. I faked I was asleep, so she said, "Cathleen Moran, get over here!" And boy, do I remember! She beat me and I had to kneel and say the rosary a couple of hours. So everybody had this fear of her, always punching. She used to say she had these five brothers and every time you got out of line, you got punched. Her fist—her knuckles, they're each her brother. Oh, she was a terror.

As I got into high school I didn't see her as much. I'd be studying late and she'd come up. She'd be depressed. I never noticed that side of her.

She started telling me things—how she'd hit someone and didn't want to. She was like really a sensitive person. She really cared. And that's—I remember understanding her more, but not liking her any more. I thought she was weak and I couldn't understand it.

Before, even though you feared her and she beat you . . . ?

She was great. She was good in everything she does. It gave me the creeps to listen to her now. It's like weak patients complaining and stuff like that. That's how she was. I can't put up with that and she wouldn't put up with that with me. I know I'm just as weak as everybody else and I don't like that. Some of the nurses are nice and care about patients, and I don't really want to be bothered.

I don't know any nurse's aide who likes it. You say, "Boy, isn't that rewarding that you're doing something for humanity?" I say, "Don't give me that, it's a bunch of baloney." I feel nothin'. I like it because I can watch the ball games in the afternoon.

That's why if I'm a nurse, I'd go into administrative work and I'd work in surgery. The only thing you have to deal with in surgery is who you work with. You don't have to deal with the patient—like sympathize with them and say, "Gee, we couldn't get all the cancer out," and stuff like that. I like working in ICU [Intensive Care Unit] because they're all half-dead, and you can give a patient good care and not have to deal with them. I'd enjoy that. It's terrible.

You're always saying it's terrible.

You feel kinda rotten when you see somebody else dealing with them . . .

Your conscience bothers you?

Um . . . rarely. After I leave the hospital I forget all about it. What gets me the most is that if I was in the hospital, I'd be a pain in the neck. I know I'm very weak and that's why I don't get involved with patients, because I'm just like them. A lot of nurses say, "God, it's great that you're not able to get involved and do your work well. It's good that you're not sympathetic, that you could care less."

There are a lot of good nurses who do feel something towards the patient. When someone dies they feel kinda: "Oh, so-and-so died." So I say, "I'll take them to the morgue." I'll get 'em wrapped up, because it doesn't bother me. Usually when they die they crack all over and you have to get them cleaned up and tie their hands up and their feet and put a white sheet over their head, put them on a cart and take them to the morgue.

That really gets me, though—the morgue. It's down in the basement, isolated from everything. It's a long hall. They got little dark lights and it's a funny sound from the boiler room—mmmmmm (humming). That sometimes get me. It doesn't make me afraid of death, though I am. It doesn't give me the creeps. You open the freezer and see all dead bodies and everything seems meaningless. Couple years and I'll be there and someone's gonna take me down . . .

Couple years . . . ?

Well, you never know. God, when it's my turn . . . Usually orderlies do it, because it's tough getting them into this little box. When I go down, rarely do I think I'm putting a human being, someone with a life, into this freezer. They have jars of eyes and stuff and I find it interesting, and everybody's screaming and running out. For kicks, someone locked the door on me. But that doesn't bother me, because I don't get involved. There's no fear if you're never involved in something. I go in and look at the autopsies and stuff. Everybody's saying, "Oh, God, I think if I was laying on that table, what if I—." Then, boy, I got problems, because I start to think and it bugs me. I'm a very sensitive person, and if I start to think of myself as a patient, forget it. I don't want no part of it.

Do you ever get the feeling you're like a machine?

I never thought of myself in terms of a machine—though that's what I am. I don't have no feelings. I do, but somehow I don't have them any more. I can't explain. It's kinda goofy. My brother just went into the service. I got along well with him. He was really good to me. He filled out forms for me. My mother said, "Aren't you gonna miss him?" Well, I'll miss him 'cause I'll have to fill out all the forms myself. And because he was a good companion. But I never let myself think about a real feeling for him.

If I daydream about him or anything, I find it a sign of weakness. Sometimes I think of the good times I had at Maryville. Sometimes I can't even remember making a bed. I'll know I've done something, but I can't really think of when I done it.

When I'm through at three-thirty, I'm usually watching the ball game. And then I'll ride my bike for hours, along the lake, or anyplace that you haven't got a million people in the way. I'll read for a couple of hours, then I'll ride back. I do a lot of reading. I like philosophy. It's sort of like a struggle, what I'm going through. I love Jean-Paul Sartre. I read all his books. I try to find out about myself and relate it to the world around me. I know I can't, because I don't relate. I always get a negative attitude about myself. But I do feel quite capable of anything I do. I was going to go into physical education. But she said, "That's for dummies."

Who said?

The nun. But that's dealing with people, too. You know what? I had no patience for someone who didn't get it like this (snaps fingers), because I got it. That's why I knew I couldn't be a teacher. No matter what I'd do, I'd have the same attitude. And I'm trying to get rid of the attitude.

I had to coach a team a couple of months ago. To me, when you're going to do something, it's not for fun. Nothing's ever for fun. They wanted to have a good time and play. I said, "Have a good time and play when you're practicing on your own, but when you're in a tournament, it's not for fun. You're working." You have to strive and be the best. Number one. But I don't care if you lost, if you played a good game. If they have a rotten attitude and won, I tell 'em they've lost.

Nurses tell me to go into sports because it's something I enjoy. But it's the same thing no matter what I do. I'd be detached. I've won trophies. I would walk up there and get the trophy and it was no big thing. Everybody's saying, "Boy, you act like you're mad about getting it." I can't stand when someone shows emotion, if someone's excited. If I'm excited about something, I'll keep it to myself, I repress it.

One night, Christmas Eve, I was working and a patient had a colostomy and couldn't accept surgery. He's fighting off the drugs. He's such a strong guy. We heard a loud crash and this guy had taken out his IV's, thrown it against the wall, taken the TV, thrown that against the wall, threw his tables outside the window. It was all a mess. And he had been tied down, leather restraints. Everybody was panicking. They called the police, and all the patients were crying. I thought I could deal with him and I wasn't afraid of what he was up to. But I couldn't deal with the patients crying. The nurse told me to quiet them down. I said, "I can't be bothered." Everybody was nervous and I just wasn't.

He wasn't weak, he was fighting. He doesn't know that he's got strength then. I didn't care that he was having problems. It didn't bother me. It was a difficult task to get him settled and to straighten him out. And that I enjoyed. Because he wasn't laying in bed, he was fighting.

I love to work with 99's, emergencies, when patients are kicking the bucket and they're trying to save 'em. You don't have to deal with the patient, you deal with the work. You're trying to save his life. Though I don't think of it as a life, I think of it as a job.

Do you care whether he lives or dies?

No, I really don't. It's not that I won't give him my care. My attitude doesn't affect my work. If someone's almost dead, I'll spend hours putting the tube through their nose, suctioning out the stuff, so they'll live. But I don't care. But yet I know that's not right. I'm just trying to figure it out . . .

CRADLE TO THE GRAVE

ROSE HOFFMAN, PUBLIC SCHOOL TEACHER

I'm a teacher. It's a profession I loved and still love. It's been my ambition since I was eight years old. I have been teaching since 1937. Dedication was the thing in my day. I adored teaching. I used to think that teachers had golden toilets. (Laughs.) They didn't do anything we common people did.

She teaches third grade at a school in a changing neighborhood. It is her second school in thirty-three years. She has been at this one for twenty years. "I have a self-contained group. You keep them all day."

Oh, I have seen a great change since January 6, 1937. (Laughs.) It was the Depression, and there was something so wonderful about these dedicated people. The teachers, the children, we were all in the same position. We worked our way out of it, worked hard. I was called a Jewish Polack. (Laughs.) My husband tells me I wash floors on my knees like a Polack. (Laughs.) I was assigned to a fourth grade class. The students were Polish primarily. We had two colored families, but they were sweet. We had a smattering of ethnic groups in those times—people who worked themselves out of the Depression by hard work.

I was the teacher and they were my students. They weren't my equal. I loved them. There isn't one child that had me that can't say they didn't respect me. But I wasn't on an intimate basis. I don't want to know what's happened in the family, if there's a divorce, a broken home. I don't look at the record and find out how many divorces in the family. I'm not a doctor. I don't believe you should study the family's background. I'm not interested in the gory details. I don't care if their father had twenty wives, if their mother is sleeping around. It's none of my business.

A little girl in my class tells me, "My mom's getting married. She's marrying a hippie. I don't like him." I don't want to hear it. It is not my nature to pry. Even a child deserves a certain type of privacy in their personal life. I don't see where that has anything to do with what a child studies. I came from a broken home. My mother died, I was eight years old. Isn't that a broken home? I did all right.

I have eight-year-olds. Thirty-one in the class and there's about twenty-three Spanish. I have maybe two Appalachians. The twenty-three Puerto Ricans are getting some type of help. The two little Applachians, they never have the special attention these other children get. Their names aren't Spanish. My heart breaks for them.

They have these Spanish workers that are supposed to help the Puerto Rican children in their TESL program [Teaching English as a Second Language]. I'm shocked that English is the second language. When my parents came over I didn't learn Jewish as a first language at the taxpayers' expense. The Polish didn't learn Polish as a first language But now they've got these Spanish-speaking children learning that at our expense. To me, this is a sin. As long as they're in this country, English should be the first language. This is my pet peeve. One of these teachers had this thick Spanish accent. So they picked up this accent too. He pronounces dog "dock." That's horrid.

The language! I could never use some of the words I hear. Up to five years ago I could never spell a four-letter word. Now I can say them without any embarrassment. The kids come right out and say it: "Teacher, he said a bad word." I said, "What's the word?" He said, "Jagoff." I said, that's not a bad word. And they all started to laugh. I said, "Jagoff means get out of here." They laughed. I came home and asked my husband, "What's jagoff?" So he explained the gory details to me. I didn't know it before. These children know everything. It's shocking to me because I think that anyone that uses that language doesn't know any better. They don't have command of any language. (Sighs.) But maybe I'm wrong, because brilliant people use it nowadays, too. I must be square.

There's a saying: Spanish people don't look you straight in the eye because of their religious background. It isn't respectful. I don't believe that. These children, they look you straight in the eye when they use those words. I have never learned how to use these four-letter words until

I came into contact with them. I never could even swear. Now I'm brazen. I had a fight with my husband one day. You know what I said to him? "Fuck you." (Laughs.) And I never talked that way. (Laughs.) I hear it all the time from the students. They use it the way we use "eat" and "talk." They don't say "pennies," they say, "f-pennies." Every word. It's a very descriptive adjective.

They knew the words in the old days, I'm sure. But they knew there was a time and place for it. I have never had this happen to me, but I was told by some teachers that the children swear at them. A child has never done that to me.

I loved the Polish people. They were hard-working. If they didn't have money, they helped out by doing housework, baby-sitting for ten cents an hour. No work was beneath them. But here, these people—the parents—came to school in the morning. This is a social outpost for them. They watch their kids eat free breakfasts and lunches. There isn't any shame, there isn't any pride. These Polish people I knew, there was pride. You didn't dare do anything like that. You wouldn't think of it.

I see these parents here all the time. A father brings his kids to school and he hangs around in the hall. I think it's dangerous to have all these adults in the school. You get all these characters. I'm afraid to stay in my room unless I lock the door.

We see them at recess. They're there at lunch time. These people, they have a resentment that everything is coming to them. Whereas the Polish people worked their way out of the Depression. They loved property. They loved houses. My father loved his little house and if anyone would step on the grass, he would kill them. (Laughs.) He'd say, "Get out of here! This is mine!" (Softly.) There was a great pride. These people, they have no pride in anything, they destroy. Really, I don't understand them.

They take the shades. They take the poles. Steal everything. Every window is broken in our shcool. Years ago, no one would ever break windows. These kids, if they're angry with you, they'll do terrible things. (Sighs.) Yes, the neighborhood is changing and the type of child has been changing, too. They're even spoiling a nice little Jewish boy who's there.

There were middle- and upper-class people and their children were wonderful. There was an honor system. You'd say. "I'm going to the office for a moment. You may whisper." And they would obey. I was really thrilled. I don't dare do that now. I don't even go to the toilet. (Laughs.) I'm a strong teacher, but I'm afraid to leave them.

In the old days, kids would sit in their seats. If I had to leave the room for a few minutes, I'd say, "Will you please be good?" And they were. These kids today will swear, "We'll be good, we'll be good." I don't know what it is, their training or their ethnic background—or maybe it goes back to history. The poor Spanish were so taken they had to lie and steal to survive. I tell them, "You don't have to lie and cheat here. Everyone is equal." But their background . . .

The first contingent of Puerto Ricans that came in were delightful. They were really lovely kids. I adore some of them. I don't care what ethnic group you belong to, if you're a low-down person, I don't like you.

Today they have these multiple chairs instead of the pedestals, seats that were attached. The kids slide all over the room. Anything to make life more difficult. (Laughs.) If I didn't laugh at these things, I couldn't last. Whereas it was a pleasure to teach a motivated child, how do you motivate *these* children? By food? By bringing cookies to school? Believe me, these children aren't lacking in anything. If I ask for change for a dollar, I can get it. They have more money . . . We have seventeen that get free lunches, and they all have this money for goodies.

I've always been a strong disciplinarian, but I don't give these kids assignments over their head. They know exactly what they do. Habit. This is very boring, very monotonous, but habit is a great thing for these children. I don't tell them the reason for things. I give them the rote method, how to do it. After that, reasoning comes. Each one has to go to the board and show me that they really know. Because I don't trust the papers. They cheat and copy. I don't know how they do it. I walk up and down and watch them. I tell you, it's a way of life. (Laughs.)

At nine o'clock, as soon as the children come in, we have a salute to the flag. I'm watching them. We sing "My Country 'Tis of Thee." And then we sing a parody I found of "My Country 'Tis of Thee."

> To serve my country is to banish selfishness
> And bring world peace
> I love every girl and boy
> New friendships I'll enjoy
> The Golden Ruly employ
> Till wars shall cease.

And then we sing "The Star-Spangled Banner." I watch them. It's a dignified exercise. These children love the idea of habit. Something schmaltzy, something wonderful.

I start with arithmetic. I have tables-fun on the board—multiplication. Everything has to be fun, fun, fun, play, play, play. You don't say tables, you say tables-fun. Everything to motivate. See how fast they can do it. It's a catchy thing. When they're doing it, I mark the papers. I'm very fast. God has been good to me. While I'm doing that, I take attendance. That is a must. All this happens before nine fifteen, nine twenty.

The next thing I do is get milk money. That's four cents. I have change. I'm very fast. Buy the milk for recess and we have cookies that I bring. To motivate them, to bribe them. (Laughs.) I also buy Kleenex for them, because they'll wipe their nose . . . (Laughs.) By nine forty, which is the next period, I try to finish the marking. Two of the children go to a TESL program. (Sighs.)

Then I have a penmanship lesson on the board. There it is in my beautiful handwriting. I had a Palmer Method diploma. On Mondays I write beautifully, "If we go to an assembly, we do not whistle or talk, because good manners are important. If our manners are good, you'll be very happy and make everyone happy, too." On Friday we give them a test. They adore it. Habit, they love habit.

They drink their milk. I have to take them to toilet recess. I have to watch them. No one goes unless they're supervised. We watch them outside. If there's too much monkey business, I have to go in and stop them. When they raise their hands in class, I let them go, even if they're lying. I tell them, "If you're lying and get in trouble, you won't be able to go again." So I hope they tell me the truth every once in a while.

About eleven o'clock, I give them an English workbook. I pass the free lunch tickets out about a quarter to twelve. Sometime during the day I give them stretching exercises. Sideways, then up and down, and we put our hands on our hips and heads up and so on. I'm good at it. I'm better than the kids.

I have reading groups. One is advanced, one is the middle, and one is the lowest. At quarter to two we have our spelling—two words a day. Six words a week, really. If I did any more, it's lost. I tried other ways, they did everything wrong. I didn't scold them. I researched my soul. What am I doing wrong? I found out two words a day is just right. Spelling is a big deal. We break the words. We give them sentences. I try to make it last till two o'clock. Fifteen, twenty minutes, that's their attention span. Some days it's great. Some days I can't get them to do anything.

I take them to the toilet again because they're getting restless. Again you watch them. From quarter after to about two thirty we read together. I give them music, too. That's up to me, up to my throat. They love music. I have it two, three times a week. At two thirty, if they're good, I give them art. I make beautiful Valentines. We show them how to decorate it. And that's the day. If they're not good—if they scream and yell and run around—I don't give them art. I give them work. If they're not nice to me, I'm not going to be nice to them. I'm not going to reward them.

Three fifteen, they go home. I'm never tired. I go shopping. I give every store on my way home a break. At twelve o'clock I go shopping, too. I have to get away from the other teachers. They're always talking shop.

I don't take any work home with me. With these children, you show them their mistakes immediately. Otherwise they forget. When I'm home, I forget about school, absolutely, absolutely, absolutely. I have never thought of being a principal. I have fulfilled my goal.

As for retirement, yes and no. I'm not sixty-five yet. (Laughs.) I'm not tired. It's no effort for me. My day goes fast, especially when I go out the night before and have a wonderful time. I'm the original La Dolce Vita. If I have a good time, I can do anything. I can even come home at two, three in the morning and get up and go to work. I must have something on the outside to stimulate me.

There are some children I love. Some have looks and brains and personality. I try not to play favorites. I give each one a chance to be monitor. I tell them I'm their school mother. When I scold them, it doesn't mean I hate them. I love them, that's why I scold them. I say to them, "Doesn't your mother scold you?"

These children baffle me. With the type of students we had before, college was a necessary thing, a must. They automatically went because their parents went. The worship of learning was a great thing. But these children, I don't know . . . I tell them, "Mrs. Hoffman is here, everybody works." Mr. Hoffman teases me: "Ah, ah, here comes Mrs. Hoffman, everybody works." Working is a blessing. The greatest punishment I can give these children is not to do anything. If they're bad, you just sit there and we fold our hands. I watch them. They don't want a teacher, they want a watcher. I say, "Mrs. Hoffman is too dumb to do teaching and watching. If you want me to be a teacher, I'll be glad to be a teacher. If you want me to be a watcher, I'll have to watch you."

The younger teachers have a more—what is their word?—relaxed attitude. It's noisy and it's freedom, where they walk around and do everything. I never learned to teach under conditions like that. The first rule of education for me was discipline. Discipline is the keynote to learning. Discipline has been the great factor in my life. I discipline myself to do everything—getting up in the morning, walking, dancing, exercise. If you won't have discipline, you won't have a nation. We can't have permissiveness. When someone comes in and says, "Oh, your room is so quiet," I know I've been successful.

There is one little girl who stands out in my mind in all the years I've been teaching. She has become tall and lovely. Pam. She was not too bright, but she was sweet. She was never any trouble. She was special. I see her every once in a while. She's a checker at Treasure Island. She gives no trouble today, either. She has the same smile for everyone.

CARMELITA LESTER, PRACTICAL NURSE, OLD PEOPLE'S HOME

She arrived from the West Indies in 1962. She has been a practical nurse for the past five years. "You study everything about humanity, the human body, all the way through. How to give the patient care, how to make comfortable . . . Most of the time I work seven days."

We're in a private room at a nursing home for the elderly. "Most of them are upper, above middle class. I only work for private patients. Some may have a stroke, some are maybe confused. Some patients have nothing wrong with them, but relatives just bring.them and leave them here."

As she knits, she glances tenderly at the old, old woman lying in the bed. "My baby here has cerebral thrombosis. She is ninety-three years old."

I get in this morning about eight-thirty. I shake her, make sure that she was okay. I took her tray, wipe her face, and give her cereal and a cup of orange juice and an egg. She's unable to chew hard foods. You have to give her liquids through a syringe. She's supposed to get two thousand cc per day. If not, it would get dry and she would get a small rash and things like those.

The first thing in the morning, after breakfast, I sponge her and I give her a back rub. And I keep her clean. She's supposed to be turned every two hours. If we don't turn her every two hours, she will have sores. Even though she's asleep, she's got to be turned.

I give her lunch. The trays come up at twelve thirty. I feed her just the same as what I feed her in the morning. In the evening I go to the kitchen and pick up her tray at four o'clock and I do the same thing again. About five thirty I leave here and go home. She stays here from five thirty until eleven at night as floor care, until the night nurse come.

You have to be very, very used to her to detect it that she's having an attack. I go notify that she's having a convulsion, so the nurse come and give her two grains of sodium amytal in her hips. When she gets the needle it will bring down her blood pressure. Because she has these convulsions, her breathing stops, trying to choke. If there's nobody around, she would stifle.

Some days she's awake. Some days she just sleeps. When she's awake she's very alert. Some people believe she isn't, but she knows what's going on. You will hear her voice say something very simple. Other than that, she doesn't say a word. Not since she had that last heavy stroke last year. Before that, she would converse. Now she doesn't converse any more. Oh, she knows what's going on. She's aware, she knows people by the voices. If a man comes in this room, once she hears that voice, I just cannot undress her. (Laughs.)

She knows when I'm not here. If I'm away too long, she gets worried, sick. But she got used to it that I have to go out sometimes. She knows I'll be back, so she's more relaxed now. Oh, sometimes I sit here and get drowsy. I think of the past and the future. Sometime I think when I was a little girl in Cuba and the things I used to do.

If I'm not doing nothing after I get through with her, it's a drag day. I laugh and I keep myself busy doing something. I may make pillows. I sell 'em. Sometimes I'll be writing up my bills. That's my only time I have, here. If I don't feel like doing that, well, I'll make sure she's okay, I'll go down into the street and take a walk.

The work don't leave my mind. I have been so long with her that it became part of me. In my mind it's always working: "How's she getting along?" I worry what happened to her between those hours before the night nurse report. If I go off on a trip, I'll be talking about her. I'll say, "I wonder what happened to my baby." My girl friend will say, "Which baby are you talking about?" I'll say, "My patient." (Laughs.) I went to Las Vegas. I spent a week there. Every night I called. Because if she has these convulsions . . .

My baby, is not everyone can take of her through this illness. Anybody will be sittin' here and she will begin to talk and you don't know it. So you have to be a person that can detect this thing coming along. I called every night to find out how she was doin'. My bill was seventy-eight dollars. (Laughs.) If she's sick, I have to fly back. She stays on my mind, but I don't know why. (Laughs.)

She works through a nurses' registry. "You go where they send you. Maybe you get a little baby." She had worked at a general hospital before. "I used to float around, I worked with geriatric, I worked with pediatric, I worked with teen-agers, I worked with them all. Medical-surgical. I've been with her two years. As long as she's still going." (Laughs.)

In America, people doesn't keep their old people at home. At a certain age they put them away in America. In my country, the old people stay in the home until they die. But here, not like that. It's surprising to me. They put them away. The first thing they think of is a nursing home. Some of these people don't need a nursing home. If they have their own bedroom at home, look at television or listen to the radio or they have themselves busy knitting . . . We all, us foreigners, think about it.

Right now there's a lady here, nothing wrong with her, but they put her away. They don't come to see her. The only time they see her is when she say, "I can't breathe." She wants some attention. And that way she's just aging. When I come here, she was a beautiful woman. She was looking very nice. Now she is going down. If they would come and take her out sometimes . . .

We had one lady here about two years ago, she has two sons. She fell and had a broken hip. They called the eldest son. He said, "Why call on me? Call the little one. She gave all the money to that little one." That was bad. I was right there.

All these people here are not helpless. But just the family get rid of them. There is a lady here, her children took her for a ride one day and push her out of the car. Let her walk and wander. She couldn't find her way home. They come and brought her here. And they try to take away all that she has. They're tryin' to make her sign papers and things like those. There's nothing wrong with her. She can dress herself, comb her hair, take a walk . . . They sign her in here, made the lawyers sign her in. They're just in for the money. She will tell you, "There's nothin' wrong with me."

Things that go on here. I've seen many of these patients, they need help, but they don't have enough help. Sometimes they eat and sometimes they don't. Sometimes there's eight hours' wait. Those that can have private nurse, fine. Those that can't suffer. And this is a high-class place. Where *poor* old people . . . (She shakes her head.)

The reason I got so interested in this kind of work, I got sick. One evening my strength just went. My legs and everything couldn't hold. For one year I couldn't walk. I had twelve doctors. They couldn't find out what was wrong. I have doctors from all over the United States come to see. Even a professor from Germany. A doctor from South Carolina came, he put it in a book. My main doctor said, "You have to live with your condition 'cause there's nothing we can do." I said to him, "Before I live this way, I'd rather die." 'Cause I couldn't feed myself, I couldn't do nothin'. This life is not for me.

They took me home. I started prayin' and prayin' to God and things like those and this. Oral Roberts, I wrote to him several letters. Wrote from my heart. Still I was crippled. Couldn't put a glass of water to my mouth. The strength had been taken away. I prayed hard.

One night I was in bed and deeply down in my sleep. I heard electricity. Like when you take an electric wire and touch it. It shot through both my legs. Ooohhh, it shocked so hard that I woke up. When I woke up, I felt it three times. The next morning I could raise this leg up. I was surprised.

The next night I felt the same thing. The third night I felt the same thing. So I got up and went to the bathroom. I went back to the doctor and he said, "That's surprising." Ooohhh. I can't believe it. There is a miracle. This is very shocking.

What do you think cured you?

God.

Did Oral Roberts help?

Yes.

How?

By prayin' sincere from his heart.

I was a nurse before, but I wasn't devoted. I saw how they treated people when I was there. Oh, it was pitiful. I couldn't stand it. And from that, I have tender feelings. That changed me. That's when I decided to devote myself.

I feel sorry for everybody who cannot help themselves. For that reason I never rest. As soon as I'm off one case I am on another. I have to sometimes say, "Don't call me for a week." I am so tired. Sometimes I have to leave the house and hide away. They keep me busy, busy, busy all the time. People that I take care of years ago are callin' back and askin' for me.

Plenty of nurses don't care. If they get the money, forget it. They talk like that all the time. They say to me, "You still here?" I say, "Yes." "Oh, you still worry about that old woman." I say, "That's why she pays me, to worry about her." Most of the nurses have feelings.

If I had power in this country, first thing I'd do in nursing homes, I would hire someone that pretended to be sick. 'Cause that's the only way you know what's goin' on. I would have government nursing homes. Free care for everybody. Those hospitals that charge too much money and you don't have insurance and they don't accept you, I would change that—overnight.

Things so bad for old people today—if I could afford to buy a few buildings, I would have that to fall on. You got to be independent. So you don't have to run there and there and there in your old age. They don't have enough income. I don't want to be like that.

An elderly person is a return back to babyhood. It give you a feeling how when you were a teen-ager, you're adult, you think you're strong and gay, and you return back to babyhood. The person doesn't know what's happening. But you take care of the person, you can see the difference. It makes you sad, because if you live long enough, you figure you will be the same.

POSTSCRIPT: *A few months after this conversation, her "baby" died.*

THE QUIZ KID AND THE CARPENTER

BRUCE FLETCHER, TREE NURSERY ATTENDANT

Nobody likes to grow old, but I'm afraid I grew old at a very early age. The years went by quickly when I was very young, and all too quickly in the years when I should have been having fun. I became a concerned old man at a very early age. I began to grow gray when I was twenty-one . . .

He was one of the original Quiz Kids—first program, June, 1940. He was the youngest. "I was seven, going on eight." He participated in the network program for three years, 1940 to 1943. He is thirty-nine years old.

My specialty was Greek mythology and natural history. These two subjects were what they asked me about on the show. At home I'd sit on the floor and go through the book and recite off the names of the birds. My Aunt Louise thought this was very great and very wonderful. So she called in the neighbors to have me perform. One of the neighbors called the newspapers and they came and photographed me and reported on me. I was considered a child prodigy.

After three years as one of the Quiz Kids, I was eleven and pretty obnoxious, I'm afraid. When you're seven years old, these things are tolerable. When you're eleven and becoming an adolescent, these things become intolerable. It was considered wise that I retire earlier than age fifteen, which was considered the graduation age for the Quiz Kids. I wondered what happened. From then on, I was just plain Bruce Fletcher.

My big ambition was to go to New York and Columbia University. When a Midwestern hick arrives in New York, you start at the bottom—and I did. I worked in a factory and was amused by the way it was run. Eight o'clock the bell rang, all the machines started, and you started working like little machines yourself.

I found a job at a very exclusive men's club for the social register only. What amused me was something that existed far beyond its time: servants were treated as servants. I cleared twenty-nine dollars a week plus two meals. They were slip-cowish, and this hateful chef sought to give it to the employees. Things became so desperate that one of the servants went up to a club member with some sausage that you wouldn't feed a puppy that was starving, and he said, "Here, you eat this."

I liked the factory much better, aside from the money. I was glad to be a cog in the wheel. At least it wasn't humiliating. I felt that I could just go through the day's work, make enough money, oh, that I could go to the Met three times a week or Carnegie Hall, and I could more or less live my life properly when my time was my own.

I was a young Columbia man while I worked in a cafeteria from 6:30 A.M. to 3:00 P.M. I was much respected by the management, even though I drove the people that I worked with insane, because I had standards they couldn't cope with. I cannot stand laziness and neglect when I'm breaking my neck and somebody else is holding up the wall. I would scream bloody murder and carry on like a demon and a tyrant.

Through Columbia, I got a job as a proofreader at one of the biggest law firms in New York. Whatever the case, the law firm brought me back to the fact that I was not just somebody's scullery maid. The people either liked me very much or hated me with a purple passion. But I was respected. I've been respected on every job I ever had.

It wore out my eyes, just like you had them grated on a grindstone. You have to read small print all day long and keep your eyes glued to it. Also, we had handwritten documents that the lawyers would send in. Some of their handwriting was like Egyptian hieroglyphics. We ran into ridiculous situations. If something went wrong, we would be blamed and heads would roll like cabbage stalks.

I left under circumstances of considerable honor. I was given a farewell luncheon by half the staff of the law firm, meaning the lawyers themselves. I was asked to make a speech and I was much applauded.

The most I made was seventy-five dollars a week. I consider making good money in this life where you can walk into a supermarket and you can fill up the grocery cart with everything you choose without having to add the prices of every item. This should have gone out in the thirties, when there was never enough money to go around. Ha ha. I did in New York what I do now. I add up the prices when I put things in the grocery cart to make sure that the purse matches the fancy.

During the years 1960 to 1968, he was on the west coast and in Texas. He worked as an announcer for three different radio stations, favoring classical music. With his collection of ten thousand phonograph records, he made tapes for broadcasts. One job "consumed me day and night for a year and a half. Those were the happiest times of my life."

"Since coming back to Chicago in 1968, I have considered myself in retirement. At thirty-six I was no longer young. People hire people at age twenty. They don't hire people age thirty-six. Oh, I've felt old since my twenties."

I now work in a greenhouse, where we grow nothing but roses. You walk in there and the peace and quiet engulfs you. Privacy is such that you don't even see the people you work with for hours on end. It is not always pretty. Roses have to have manure put around their roots. So I get my rubber gloves and there I go. Some of the work is rather heavy.

The money isn't good. The heat in the summer almost kills me. Because there you are under a glass roof where everything is magnified. There's almost no ventilation, and I am literally drenching with perspiration by the time the day is over and done with. But at least I don't have somebody sneak up behind you and scream in your ear abuse. I had enough of that.

The reason I like this job is because my mind is at ease all day long, without any tensions or pressures. Physically it keeps me on my toes. I'm a little bit harder and tougher than I was. I'm on my feet all day. I have an employer who's the best one I ever had in my life. There has never been the slightest disagreement, which is a miracle. Everyone says, "Bruce is hard to get along with." Bruce is not difficult to get along with if I had intelligent people to work with, where people are not after me or picking on me for that and that and another thing.

I tend to concentrate so much on what I'm doing. That's why I scare very easily. If anyone comes up behind me and speaks to me very suddenly when I'm at work, I'm concentrating so thoroughly I nearly jump through the roof.

I start at seven fifteen in the morning, and the first thing I do is cut roses. They have to be cut early in the morning. The important thing is to cut them so that they're rather tightly closed. Bees and butterflies don't last very long because there's no nectar and pollen. We cut the roses when they're so tightly closed that they can't get at them. If they're kept in refrigeration and in water with the stems trimmed properly, they'll be fresh a week later.

Of course, there's always the telephone. That is a big problem. The greenhouses extend what seem to be miles from the telephone, but you can always hear it, even at a distance. It means a great big long run to get it, and pray that they won't hang up before you can answer it. That usually means orders to be taken. Sometimes the day gets too much and I feel I want to die on the spot.

When the day is over I go to the library. If it's a night of operas or concerts, I time myself accordingly. I always do as I did in New York. Unless I had to go stand in the standing room line at the Met, which meant getting there right after work, I'd go home, take a nap, so that I won't fall asleep at the performance. And then come back and get as much sleep as I possibly can. The day isn't complete unless I fall asleep with the reading light on and a book in my hand.

I don't know what's going to happen to me. It would be much more convenient if I had cancer and passed away and say, "Oh, how tragic," and I could have the peace of the grave. I don't know. I'd love to be back in radio, in the classical music business. I blossomed forth like the roses in the greenhouse . . . I was in my own kind of work.

Peace and quiet and privacy have meant a great deal to me in the years since I made my escape. I didn't feel free as one of the Quiz Kids. Reporters and photographers poking you and knocking you around and asking ridiculous questions. As a child you can't cope with these things. I was exploited. I can't forgive those who exploited me.

I would have preferred to grow up in my own particular fashion. Had I grown up as others did, I would have come out a much better person. In school, if I would fail to answer a question, the teacher would lean forward and say in front of the class, "All right! Just because you were one of the Quiz Kids doesn't mean that you're a smart pupil in my class." I wish it had never happened.

(Softly) But we were unique at the time. The Depression was over. America was the haven and all good things were here. And I was the youngest of the Quiz Kids. Of course, I'm a has-been. The Quiz Kids itself has been a has-been. But it brought forth something that was not a has-been. It achieved history, and that is where I'm proud to have been a part of it. (Laughs.) Ah, the time of retirement has come and I'm in it! I'm in it!

NICK LINDSAY, CARPENTER/POET

*T*hough *he lives in Goshen, Indiana, he considers his birthplace "home"—Eddystone Island, off the coast of South Carolina. At forty-four, he is the father of ten children; the eldest, a girl twenty-six, and the youngest, a boy one and a half years old.*

He is a carpenter as well as a poet, who reads and chants his works on college campuses and at coffeehouses. "This is one of the few times in my life I had made a living at anything but carpentry. Lindsays have been carpenters from right on back to 1755. Every once in a while, one of 'em'll shoot off and be a doctor or a preacher or something. [His father, Vachel Lindsay, was a doctor as well as a celebrated poet.] Generally they've been carpenter-preachers, carpenter-farmers, carpenter-storekeepers, carpenters right on. A man, if he describes himself, will use a verb. What you do, that's what you are. I would say I'm a carpenter.

"I started workin' steady at it when I was thirteen. I picked up a hammer and went to drive in nails. One man I learned a lot from was a janitor, who didn't risk the ebb and flow of the carpentry trade. You can learn a lot from books about things like this—how nails work, different kinds of wood."

He dropped out of high school. "It's a good way to go. Take what you can stand and don't take any more than that. It's what God put the tongue in your mouth for. If it don't taste right, you spit it out."

Let me tell you where the grief bites you so much. Who are you working for? If you're going to eat, you are working for the man who pays you some kind of wage. That won't be a poor man. The man who's got a big family and who's needing a house, you're not building a house for him. The only man you're working for is the man who could get along without it. You're putting a roof on the man who's got enough to pay your wage.

You see over yonder, shack need a roof. Over here you're building a sixty-thousand-dollar house for a man who maybe doesn't have any children. He's not hurting and it doesn't mean much. It's a prestige house. He's gonna up-man, he's gonna be one-up on his neighbor, having something fancier. It's kind of into that machine. It's a real pleasure to work on it, don't get me wrong. Using your hand is just a delight in the paneling, in the good woods. It smells good and they shape well with the plane. Those woods are filled with the whole creative mystery of things. Each wood has its own spirit. Driving nails, yeah, your spirit will break against that.

What's gonna happen to what you made? You work like you were kneeling down. You go into Riverside Church in New York and there's no space between the pews to kneel. (Laughs.) If you try to kneel down in that church, you break your nose on the pew in front. A bunch of churches are like that. Who kneels down in that church? I'll tell you who kneels. The man kneels who's settin' the toilets in the restrooms. He's got to kneel, that's part of his work. The man who nails the pews on the floor, he had to kneel down. The man who put the receptacles in the walls that turn that I-don't-know-how-many horsepower organ they got in that Riverside Church—that thing'll blow you halfway to heaven right away, pow!—the man who was putting the wire in that thing, he kneeled down. Any work, you kneel down—it's a kind of worship. It's part of the holiness of things, work, yes. Just like drawing breath is. It's necessary. If you don't breathe, you're dead. It's kind of a sacrament, too.

One nice thing about the crafts. You work two hours at a time. There's a ritual to it. It's break time. Then two hours more and it's dinner time. All those are very good times. Ten minutes is a pretty short time, but it's good not to push too hard. All of a sudden it comes up break time, just like a friend knocking at the door that's unexpected. It's a time of swapping tales. What you're really doing is setting the stage for your work.

A craftsman's life is nothin' but compromise. Look at your tile here. That's craftsman's work, not art work. Craftsmanship demands that you work repeating a pattern to very close tolerances. You're laying this tile here within a sixteenth. It ought to be within a sixty-fourth of a true ninety degree angle. Theoretically it should be perfect. It shouldn't be any sixty-fourth, it should be ∞ tolerance. Just altogether straight on, see? Do we ever do it? No. look at that parquet stuff you got around here. It's pretty, but those corners. The man has compromised. He said that'll have to do.

They just kind of hustle you a little bit. The compromise with the material that's going on all the time. That makes for a lot of headache and grief. Like lately, we finished a house. Well, it's not yet done. Cedar siding, that's material that's got knots in it. That's part of the charm. But it's a real headache if the knots falls out. You hit one of those boards with your hammer sometime and it turns into a piece of Swiss cheese. So you're gonna drill those knots, a million knots, back in. (Laughs.) It's sweet smelling wood. You've got a six-foot piece of a ten-foot board. Throwing away four feet of that fancy wood? Watcha gonna do with that four feet? A splice, scuff it, try to make an invisible joint, and use it? Yes or no? You compromise with the material. Save it? Burn it? It's in your mind all the time. Oh sure, the wood is sacred. It took a long time to grow that. It's like a blood sacrifice. It's consummation. That wood is not going to go anywhere else after that.

When I started in, it was like European carpentering. But now, all that's pretty well on the run. You make your joints simply, you get pre-hung doors, you have machine-fitted cabinet work, and you build your house to fit these factory-produced units. The change has been toward quickness. An ordinary American can buy himself some kind of a house because we can build it cheap. So again, your heart is torn. It's good and not so good.

Sometimes it has to do with how much wage he's getting. The more wage he's getting, the more skill he can exercise. You're gonna hire me? I'm gonna hang your door. Suppose you pay me five dollars an hour. I'm gonna have to hang that door fast. 'Cause if I don't hang that door fast, you're gonna run out of money before I get it hung. No man can hurry and hang it right.

I don't think there's less pride in craftsmanship. I don't know about pride. Do you take pride in embracing a woman? You don't take pride in that. You take delight in it. There may be less delight. If you can build a house cheap and really get it to a man that needs it, that's kind of a social satisfaction for you. At the same time, you wish you could have done a fancier job, a more unique kind of a job.

But every once in a while there's stuff that comes in on you. All of a sudden something falls into place. Suppose you're driving an eight-penny galvanized finishing nail into this siding. Your whole universe is rolled onto the head of that nail. Each lick is sufficient to justify your life. You say, "Okay, I'm not trying to get this nail out of the way so I can get onto something important. There's nothing more important. It's right there." And it goes—pow! It's not getting that nail in that's in your mind. It's hitting it—hitting it square, hitting it straight. Getting it now.

If you see a carpenter that's alive to his work, you'll notice that about the way he hits a nail. He's not going (imitates machine gun rat-tat-tat-tat)—trying to get the nail down and out of the way so he can hurry up and get another one. Although he may be working fast, each lick is like a separate person that he's hitting with his hammer. It's like as though there's a separate friend of his that one moment. And when he gets out of it, here comes another one. Unique, all by itself. Pow! But you gotta stop before you get that nail in, you know? That's fine work. Hold the hammer back, and just that last lick, don't hit it with your hammer, hit it with a punch so you won't leave a hammer mark. Rhythm.

I worked at an H-bomb plant in South Carolina. My work was building forms. I don't think the end product bothered me so much, 'cause Judgment Day is not a thing . . . It doesn't hang heavy on my heart. It might be that I should be persuaded it was inappropriate . . .

They got that big old reactor works with the heavy water and all that. This heavy equipment runs there day and night, just one right after another, going forty miles an hour, digging that big old hole.

Now you're gonna have to build you a building, concrete and steel. You ship in a ready-mixed plant just for that building. A pump on the hill. It starts pumping concrete into the hole. It's near about time for the carpenters. We're building forms for the first floor of that thing. I was the twenty-four-hundredth-and-some-odd carpenter hired at the beginning. That's how big it was. There was three thousand laborers. Each time we built one of these reactors there would be a whole town to support it. We built a dozen or so towns in this one county.

We all understood we were making H-bombs and tried to get it done before the Russians built theirs, see? That's what everybody thought. It was one of those great secret jobs where you had guards at the gates, barbed wire around the place, spies, and all that kind of foolishness.

Some people call it the hard lard belt, some call it the Bible belt. Mostly just farmers who stepped from behind the plow, who had tenants or were tenants themselves. It was a living wage in that part of the country for the first time since the boll weevil had been through. And boy, you can't downrate that. It seems like the vast comedy of things when a Yankee come and got us to build their H-bomb, part of the fine comedy that she should come and give us the first living wage since the War of Northern Aggression—for this.

In Bloomington, Indiana, I saw a lot of women make their living making bombs. They had a grand picnic when they built the millionth bomb. Bombs they're dropping on people. And the students came to demonstrate against the bombs. Maybe these women see no sense in what they're doing, but they see their wages in what they're doing . . .

Some people will say, "I'm a poet. I'm better than you. I'm different. I'm a separate kind of species." It doesn't seem to me poetry is that way. It seems to me like mockin'birds sing and there's hardly ever a mockingbird that doesn't sing. It's the same way with poetry. It just comes natural to 'em, part of what we're made for. It's the natural utterance of living language. I say my calling is to be a carpenter and a poet. No contradiction.

(Chants.) Work's quite a territory. Real work and fake work. There's fake work, which is the prostitution. There is the magic of payday, though. You'll say, "Well, if you get paid for your work, is that prostitution?" No indeed. But how are you gonna prove it's not? A real struggle there. Real work, fake work, and prostitution. The magic of payday. The groceries now heaped on the table and the new-crop wine and store-bought shirts. That's what it says, yes.

IN SEARCH OF A CALLING

NORA WATSON, EDITOR

Jobs are not big enough for people. It's not just the assembly line worker whose job is too small for his spirit, you know? A job like mine, if you really put your spirit into it, you would sabotage immediately. You don't dare. So you absent your spirit from it. My mind has been so divorced from my job, except as a source of income, it's really absurd.

As I work in the business world, I am more and more shocked. You throw yourself into things because you feel that important questions— self-discipline, goals, a meaning of your life—are carried out in your *work*. You invest a job with a lot of values that the society doesn't allow you to put into a job. You find yourself like a pacemaker that's gone crazy or something. You want it to be a million things that it's not and you want to give it a million parts of yourself that nobody else wants there. So you end up wrecking the curve or else settling down and conforming. I'm really in a funny place right now. I'm so calm about what I'm doing and what's coming . . .

She is twenty-eight. She is a staff writer for an institution publishing health care literature. *Previously she had worked as an editor for a corporation publishing national magazines.*

She came from a small mountain town in western Pennsylvania. "My father was a preacher. I didn't like what he was doing, but it was his vocation. That was the good part of it. It wasn't just: go to work in the morning and punch a time clock. It was a profession of himself. I expected work to be like that. All my life, I planned to be a teacher. It wasn't until late in college, my senior year, that I realized what the public school system was like. A little town in the mountains is one thing . . .

"My father, to my mind, is a weird person, but whatever he is, he is. Being a preacher was so important to him he would call it the Call of the Lord. He was willing to make his family live in very poor conditions. He was willing to strain his relationship to my mother, not to mention his children. He put us through an awful lot of things, including just bare survival, in order to stay being a preacher. His evenings, his weekends, and his days, he was out calling on people. Going out with healing oil and anointing the sick, listening to their troubles. The fact that he didn't do the same for his family is another thing. But he saw himself as the core resource in the community—at a great price to himself. He really believed that was what he was supposed to be doing. It was his life.

Most of the night he wouldn't go to bed. He'd pull out sermons by Wesley or Spurgeon or somebody, and he'd sit down until he fell asleep, maybe at three o'clock in the morning. Reading sermons. He just never stopped. (Laughs.)

I paper the walls of my office with posters and bring in flowers, bring in an FM radio, bring down my favorite ceramic lamp. I'm the only person in the whole damn building with a desk facing the window instead of the door. I just turn myself around from all that I can. I ration my time so that I'll spend two hours working for the Institution and the rest of the time I'll browse. (Laughs.)

I function better if they leave me alone more. My boss will come in and say, "I know you're overloaded, but would you mind getting this done, it's urgent. I need it in three weeks." I can do it in two hours. So I put it on the back burner and produce it on time. When I first went there, I came in early and stayed late. I read everything I could on the subject at hand. I would work a project to the wall and get it really done right, and then ask for more. I found out I was wrecking the curve, I was out of line.

The people, just as capable as I and just as ready to produce, had realized it was pointless, and had cut back. Everyone, consciously or unconsciously, was rationing his time. Playing cards at lunch time for three hours, going sun bathing, or less obvious ways of blowing it. I realized: Okay, the road to ruin is doing a good job. The amazing, absurd thing was that once I decided to stop doing a good job, people recognized a kind of authority in me. Now I'm just moving ahead like blazes.

I have my own office. I have a secretary. If I want a book case, I get a book case. If I want a file, I get a file. If I want to stay home, I stay home. If I want to go shopping, I go shopping. This is the first comfortable job I've ever had in my life and it is absolutely despicable.

I've been a waitress and done secretarial work. I knew, in those cases, I wasn't going to work at near capacity. It's one thing to work to your limits as a waitress because you end up with a bad back. It's another thing to work to your limits doing writing and editing because you end up with a sharper mind. It's a joy. Here, of all places, where I had expected to put the energy and enthusiasm and the gifts that I may have to work—it isn't happening. They expect less than you can offer. Token labor. What writing you do is writing to order. When I go for a job interview—I must leave this place!—I say, "Sure, I can bring you samples, but the ones I'm proud of are the ones the Institution never published."

It's so demeaning to be there and not be challenged. It's humiliation, because I feel I'm being forced into doing something I would never do of my own free will—which is simply waste itself. It's really not a Puritan hang-up. It's not that I want to be persecuted. It's simply that I know I'm vegetating and being paid to do exactly that. It's possible for me to sit here and read my books. But then you walk out with no sense of satisfaction, with no sense of legitimacy! I'm being had. Somebody has bought the right to you for eight hours a day. The manner in which they use you is completely at their discretion. You know what I mean?

I feel like I'm being pimped for and it's not my style. The level of bitterness in this department is stunning. They take days off quite a bit. They don't show up. They don't even call in. They've adjusted a lot better than I have. They see the Institution as a free ride as long as it lasts. I don't want to be party to it, so I've gone my own way. It's like being on welfare. Not that that's a shameful thing. It's the surprise of this enforced idleness. It makes you feel not at home with yourself. I'm furious. It's a feeling that I will not be humiliated. I will not be dis-used.

For all that was bad about my father's vocation, he showed me it was possible to fuse your life to your work. His home was also his work. A parish is no different from an office, because it's the whole countryside.

There's nothing I would enjoy more than a job that was so meaningful to me that I brought it home.

The people I work with are not buffoons. I think they're part of a culture, like me, who've been sold on a dum-dum idea of human nature. It's frightening. I've made the best compromise available. If I were free, economically free, I would go back to school. It galls me that in our culture we have to pay for the privilege of learning.

A guy was in the office next to mine. He's sixty-two and he's done. He came to the Institution in the forties. He saw the scene and said, "Yes, I'll play drone to you. I'll do all the piddley things you want. I won't upset the apple cart by suggesting anything else." With a change of regimes in our department, somebody came across him and said, "Gee, he hasn't contributed anything here. His mind is set in old attitudes. So we'll throw him out." They fired him unceremoniously, with no pension, no severance pay, no nothing. Just out on your ear, sixty-two. He gets back zero from having invested so many years playing the game.

The drone has his nose to the content of the job. The politicker has his nose to the style. And the politicker is what I think our society values. The politicker, when it's apparent he's a winner, is helped. Everyone who has a stake in being on the side of the winner gives him a boost. The minute I finally realized the way to exist at the Institution—for the short time I'll be here—was not to break my back but to use it for my own ends, I was a winner.

Granted, there were choices this guy could have made initially. He might have decided on a more independent way of life. But there were all sorts of forces keeping him from that decision. The Depression, for one thing. You took the job, whatever the terms were. It was a straight negotiation. The drone would get his dole. The Institution broke the contract. He was fired for being dull, which is what he was hired to be.

I resist strongly the mystique of youth that says these kids are gonna come up with the answers. One good thing a lot of the kids are doing, though, is not getting themselves tied up to artificial responsibilities. That includes marriage, which some may or may not call an artificial responsibility. I have chosen to stay unmarried, to not get encumbered with husband and children. But the guy with three kids and a mortgage doesn't have many choices. He wouldn't be able to work two days a week instead of five.

I'm coming to a less moralistic attitude toward work. I know very few people who feel secure with their right just to be—or comfortable. Just you being you and me being me with my mini-talents may be enough.

Maybe just making a career of being and finding out what that's about is enough. I don't think I have a calling—at this moment—except to be me. But nobody pays you for being you, so I'm at the Institution . . .

When you ask most people who they are, they define themselves by their jobs. "I'm a doctor." "I'm a radio announcer." "I'm a carpenter." If somebody asks me, I say, "I'm Nora Watson." At certain points in time I do things for a living. Right now I'm working for the Institution. But not for long. I'd be lying to you if I told you I wasn't scared.

I have a few options. Given the market, I'm going to take the best job I can find. I really tried to play the game by the rules, and I think it's a hundred percent unadulterated bullshit. So I'm not likely to go back downtown and say, "Here I am. I'm very good, hire me."

You recognize yourself as a marginal person. As a person who can give only minimal assent to anything that is going on in this society: "I'm glad the electricity works." That's about it. What you have to find is your own niche that will allow you to keep feeding and clothing and sheltering yourself without getting downtown. (Laughs.) Because that's death. That's really where death is.

SECOND CHANCE

MARIO ANICHINI, STONE CUTTER

In the yard outside the shop are statues in marble and stone of saints, angels, and fountains. The spirit of Look Homeward, Angel *and W. O. Gant hovers tempestuously. Yet, M. Anichini, artisan, has never been more relaxed. His son and colleague, Bob, interjects a contemporary note: "We also work in foam, fiberglass, polyurethanes . . ."*

In Italy I was working in marble a little bit. I was a young kid. In Lucca, a young kid do this, do that. Little by little I learned. When I was about twenty I came to this country here. I couldn't do anything like that, because of here we had a Depression. From '27 to '55 I was a butcher. For twenty-eight years . . .

I started to get a little ulcer in my stomach. I had sciatica. So I hadda quit. So I stay for one year, I don't do nothing. But after, I feel I could do something. The plaster business, the tomb business. As soon as I started it, I started to feel better.

BOB: *He was about fifty-five years old when he started this business again. My mother thought he was losing his mind. But he insisted. Everybody from the area where he came from in Tuscany has a relative or somebody in the art business. You have Florence . . .*

There's change a lot. We use rubber to make a mold now. We used to use some kind of glue. It was only good for about ten pieces. Now with a rubber mold we can make three hundred, four hundred pieces. In Italy you gotta go to school one year to make a mold. Before, I used to make one piece, stone or marble. Maybe you a millionaire and you want to make it your bust. Okay, how much you pay? Now nobody want to spend that much money. Over here I don't see so much good stone to work with.

BOB: *We used to sell statuary and fountains: a nymph holding a jug, pouring water. All of a sudden, with the ecology bit, people want to hear water running. In the city they want to be close to the country. So there's a combination of art and nature. When we started, I was quite against it. Who's going to buy a fountain? We put 'em indoors now as humidifiers. People are putting statues in their yards. There is such a demand for it we built a factory.*

I remember when I quit the butcher business, I was sick. When I started this business, I became better and better and I feel good and enjoy myself.

BOB: *For grave sites people in the old days wanted a certain statue, St. Anthony or St. Anne or something like that. We don't have much call for saints these days, especially now with the Church . . .*

People will laugh. Every time they see me, they see me better and better. I used to work in the basement. They say, "You eat too much dust down there, and you getting better and better. Before you work in the butcher shop, very nice, very airy, everything, you used to be sick. How come?"

BOB: *My dad had another man that didn't feel too well at what he was doing. He worked with my father in this—what he did as a kid, too—and he got healthy and fat and stuff like that. (Laughs.) My dad was an old man fifteen, twenty years ago. Today he's a young man.*